W9-DCY-726

INTERNATIONAL HANDBOOK OF
CROSS-CULTURAL COUNSELING

INTERNATIONAL HANDBOOK OF
CROSS-CULTURAL COUNSELING

Cultural Assumptions and Practices Worldwide

LAWRENCE H. GERSTEIN
Ball State University

P. PAUL HEPPNER
University of Missouri, Columbia

STEFANÍA ÆGISDÓTTIR
Ball State University

SEUNG-MING ALVIN LEUNG
The Chinese University of Hong Kong

KATHRYN L. NORSWORTHY
Rollins College

Los Angeles | London | New Delhi
Singapore | Washington DC

For information:

SAGE Publications, Inc.
2455 Teller Road
Thousand Oaks, California 91320
E-mail: order@sagepub.com

SAGE Publications Ltd.
1 Oliver's Yard
55 City Road
London EC1Y 1SP
United Kingdom

SAGE Publications India Pvt. Ltd.
B 1/I 1 Mohan Cooperative Industrial Area
Mathura Road, New Delhi 110 044
India

SAGE Publications Asia-Pacific Pte. Ltd.
33 Pekin Street #02-01
Far East Square
Singapore 048763

Printed in the United States of America

Library of Congress Cataloging-in-Publication Data

International handbook of cross-cultural counseling : cultural assumptions and practices worldwide / editors, Lawrence H. Gerstein . . .[et al.].
　　p. cm.
Includes bibliographical references and index.
ISBN 978-1-4129-5955-1 (cloth)
ISBN 978-1-4129-5956-8 (pbk.)
　1.　Cross-cultural counseling.　I. Gerstein, Lawrence H.
BF636.7.C76I566 2009
361′.06—dc22　　　　　　　　　　　　　2009017311

This book is printed on acid-free paper.

09　10　11　12　13　10　9　8　7　6　5　4　3　2　1

Acquisitions Editor:	Kassie Graves
Editorial Assistant:	Veronica K. Novak
Production Editor:	Carla Freeman
Copy Editor:	QuADS Prepress (P) Ltd.
Typesetter:	C&M Digitals (P) Ltd.
Proofreaders:	Annette R.Van Deusen, Victoria Reed-Castro
Indexer:	Jeanne Busemeyer
Cover Designer:	Gail Buschman
Marketing Manager:	Carmel Schrire

Contents

PART II. THE COUNSELING PROFESSION AROUND THE WORLD

Foreword

Within the last few decades, the disciplines of counseling and counseling psychology have enjoyed a significant increase in their numbers and impact on the science and professions of counseling and psychology. Their goal of servicing populations in need through professional skills and talents that are sensitive to individual and collective differences has appealed widely to those seeking to improve the human condition through human contact. With a defining commitment to care, compassion, empathy, and connection, counseling psychology and the entire counseling profession has uniquely positioned itself as a major resource for meeting the many pressing challenges of our global era. Indeed, I believe no other specialty in psychology has been as unrelenting and constant in reminding the field of psychology of its obligations, responsibilities, and duties to promote diversity, to respond to injustice, and to advance the human condition. This conclusion is especially apparent in the entire counseling profession's teaching, research, services, and advocacy regarding ethnic, racial, and cultural minorities. Clearly, counseling psychology has emerged as psychology's conscience.

And now, with the publication of the *International Handbook of Cross-Cultural Counseling,* the entire counseling profession is addressing the many challenges of our global era by examining counseling psychology's assumptions and practices throughout the world, with special attention to the importance of shaping and accommodating its purposes, roles, and functions to cultural and international differences. In my opinion, the current *International Handbook* provides a substantive foundation for resisting the pressures of hegemonic globalization to impose a uniform and homogenized Western-based culture across the world. The handbook achieves this purpose by reminding counselors, psychologists, and others that the basic assumptions that guide our theories and practices are cultural constructions, and as such, subject to ethnocentric abuse when considered universally applicable and relevant.

The current handbook also challenges counseling psychology, the counseling profession, and the field of psychology in general to address the difficult global challenges the world is facing, including globalization, rapid sociotechnical change, violence, war, poverty, racism, climate change, and population growth and migration. These challenges are exacting a heavy toll at individual and collective levels. There is widespread confusion and uncertainty regarding personal, societal, and national identities along with disabling levels of fear, anxiety, despair, and anger. In the face of this social upheaval, societies and nations are fractionating, collapsing, and disintegrating and in the process, giving rise to fundamentalism, fanaticism, hate, xenophobia, and governmental oppression.

In discussing the current status of counseling psychology and the counseling profession across numerous countries and cultures, the editors and contributors of the current handbook have created the definitive text on international foundations, issues, and directions for the entire field of counseling. This is the case because the handbook is an unduplicated resource preparing students, teachers, and professionals with the knowledge and professional tools necessary to serve international populations in international settings with appropriate psychologies.

In my opinion, the volume is essential reading for counseling psychologists, counselors, and for related professionals. In each chapter there is the story of counseling's growth and current status in different nations written by authoritative national sources. There is also the story of how unique historical, cultural, and national events and forces serve to shape a discipline's identity and implications. Perhaps this was not a major intent of the volume, but in so many ways—if read from this perspective—this handbook provides a rich commentary on the sociology of a profession or science's development. The reader—whether student, teacher, scholar, or healer— is in for a rare intellectual treat and ultimately a new awareness of the counseling profession's potential and responsibilities for meeting the global challenges of our times.

Anthony J. Marsella
Atlanta, Georgia, 2009

Acknowledgments

We want to thank our spouses and partners (Annie, Dawa Lhamo, Deena, Dennis, Mary), children (Guðný Helgadóttir, Arnbergur Smárason, Lilja Björk Dennisdóttir, Ellen Björk Dennisdóttir, Eric Lee, Erica, Timothy, and Grace), grandchildren (Tenzin Choedon, Mikael, Haidyn, and Kane), other family members, colleagues, and students for the unconditional support and understanding we received throughout the process of thinking about this book and actually putting our ideas to paper. Your input and encouragement helped make a very complex and challenging project much easier.

Without the involvement of the authors who wrote chapters about counseling in their own countries, this handbook could not have happened. The rich perspectives you shared have educated us about many topics not the least of which is a better understanding of psychology and counseling worldwide. Furthermore, through our contact with each of you we have been greatly stimulated and we have reflected in new ways about culture, context, human behavior, language, and culturally sensitive and affirming approaches to interacting with individuals from cultures other than our own. The benefits we acquired through collaborating with you will forever influence how we act in the world and will definitely enrich us as teachers, researchers, trainers, practitioners, and global citizens.

We also deeply appreciate the unwavering support, encouragement, and excitement we always received from our Acquisitions Editor, Kassie Graves, at Sage Publications. You provided us with the necessary resources, feedback, and inspiration to both begin and complete this project. Your careful and wise stewardship helped deepen the content of this book and expand our vision of cross-cultural counseling.

Additionally, we want to thank the production, editorial, and graphic design staff of Sage Publications who converted our manuscript from a series of papers to an integrated tangible book. In particular, we are grateful to Veronica Novak who spent countless hours working on the mechanics of the entire project and numerous other tasks, Carla Freeman who served as our production editor, Shankaran Srinivasan who managed the intricate process of copyediting the entire text performed by his talented team of professionals (Kumaran Sathasivam, Krishan Pradeep Joghee, Rajasree Ghosh, and Amy Ayers), and Gail Buschman who designed the cover of the book.

Finally, we want to express our appreciation to the scholars who reviewed the proposal for this handbook: Diane McDermott (University of Kansas), Paula T. Tanemura Morelli (University of Hawaii), Walter Lonner (Western Washington University), Lucila Ramos-Sánchez (Santa Clara University), David L. Blustein (Boston College), John Romano (University of Minnesota), and Ellen Hawley McWhirter (University of Oregon). Your helpful comments contributed to strengthening this handbook and crystallizing the content.

PART I

Issues, Challenges, and Opportunities for the Counseling Profession Worldwide

1

Cross-Cultural Counseling

History, Challenges, and Rationale

LAWRENCE H. GERSTEIN,
P. PAUL HEPPNER, STEFANÍA ÆGISDÓTTIR,
SEUNG-MING ALVIN LEUNG, AND KATHRYN L. NORSWORTHY

Global economics, foreign and domestic policies, and technological advances have contributed to the emergence of a worldwide system of countries and cultures all mutually affecting one another. Larger, more powerful nations have significant influence on the daily lives of citizens of smaller ones (Friedman, 2000), while smaller, less powerful nations have the potential to make a global influence through advanced communication and computer technologies (Friedman, 2005). From another perspective, modern physics has demonstrated that we are all interconnected (Bohm, 1980), leading some scholars to suggest that this perspective is even relevant to counseling (Bozarth, 1985; Gerstein & Bennett, 1999; Lucas, 1985). When electrons move in one area of space, others change position, even though the links are not readily visible. Furthermore, events happening in one location can simultaneously occur in another location.

While the world gets smaller and we become more aware of our interconnectedness, the global population continues to exponentially increase. Issues such as poverty, substandard living conditions, malnutrition, human rights abuse, illiteracy, and environmental pollution have risen dramatically (United Nations Population Division, 2007). Human migration and immigration connected to political oppression, economics, and poverty, and the need for employment brings challenges for everyone involved. Obviously, ethnopolitical conflict, war, natural and human disasters, and situations of mass trauma, such as the 9/11 attacks on the United States, the 2005 tsunami in Southeast Asia, the recent terrorist attacks in Mumbai (India) in December 2008, and the 2008 Myanmar (Burma) cyclone reverberate globally and require responses beyond the borders of the countries in which the events took place. The same can be said for the global economic crisis that began in 2008 affecting all nations around the world.

Counseling and counseling psychology are embedded in this worldwide system of interconnectedness, with the United States having taken the historical lead in the development of the counseling profession, which is now expanding rapidly to other parts of the globe (Heppner, Leong, & Gerstein, 2008; Leong & Ponterotto, 2003; Pedersen & Leong, 1997). It is rather apparent, therefore, that U.S.-based models of psychology and counseling have greatly influenced both positively and negatively the science and practice of the mental health professions worldwide. The entire counseling field, however, needs to be responsive to 21st-century human, environmental, and technological concerns, with particular awareness and sensitivity of, and respect for, the cultural contexts from which they arise. With an ethic of care, compassion, responsibility, and nonharm at the heart of the counseling profession, there is a strong foundation relying on culturally appropriate and effective strategies to help guide our efforts to meet such challenges.

As will become apparent in this and the following chapters, while there is a growing worldwide recognition of interconnectedness in the counseling professions and a strong interest in expanding the scope of counseling to include international issues, currently there is no book and very few published journal articles on these topics. This handbook, therefore, is the first of its kind. It is structured to provide a comprehensive resource with a strong theoretical, research, and practical focus. The book also provides an in-depth discussion about the status and current developments of the counseling profession in numerous countries around the world. Additionally, the cultural assumptions tied to mental health help seeking, the nature and structure of counseling in the various countries, and indigenous approaches to assisting persons with psychological concerns are addressed as well.

This particular chapter focuses on the importance of the counseling professions embracing an interconnected philosophy of understanding the human experience, the history of the U.S. counseling profession and international issues, and the international work of non-U.S. professionals. It also provides definitions of important concepts and terms found throughout the book

and an overview of the rationale and vision for the book.

INTERCONNECTEDNESS, THE GLOBAL ENVIRONMENT, AND NEED FOR PSYCHOLOGICAL ASSISTANCE

Martin Luther King Jr. (U.S. civil rights leader), Paulo Freire (Brazilian liberation activist), Thich Nhat Hanh (Vietnamese Monk and peace worker), His Holiness The Dalai Lama (Tibetan Monk, leader of the Tibetan people, and Nobel Peace Prize Laureate), Aung San Suu Kyi (Myanmar [Burma] Nobel Peace Prize Laureate and prodemocracy leader under house arrest), and many other revered world leaders have all pointed out that our humanity, liberation, and futures are inextricably woven together. In other words, when individuals or groups of people suffer, experience oppression, discrimination, or exploitation, or are thwarted in their growth and development, we all suffer and are harmed. Our humanity is damaged. Stated another way, the well-being and freedom of others supports and contributes to our own well-being and vice versa.

One of the historic strengths of counseling and counseling psychology is its emphasis on human growth and development, an ethic of care, compassion, and more recently, its focus on firmly centering context and culture in understanding human functioning, and conceptualizing and implementing intervention and research strategies. The professional care ethic grounding counseling professionals' work requires knowledge of individuals' psychological concerns or problems as well as an understanding of their cultural, ethnic, racial, and national identities, and their social locations, group associations, and places of residence. The more we as counseling professionals know about people around the world, the greater empathy, warmth, respect, and connection we feel toward those who were previously not known. When one has direct knowledge and contact with individuals who have experienced human suffering, the more compelled one may become to take action to support people in reaching their potential and to change or eliminate any conditions that create and maintain such suffering.

Thus, an increased awareness and knowledge of others and their circumstances beyond the confines of one's own communities, cultural groups, and countries sets the stage for our becoming responsible and action-oriented global citizens and mental health helping professionals who are actively engaged in contributing to a world that supports human potential, freedom, and liberation. Pawlik (1992) offered a similar observation when speaking of some functions of the internationality of psychology. He reported that one function is facilitating cross-national understanding and goodwill among individuals. In part, the International Council of Psychologists (ICP) was established in 1941 to achieve this goal (Pawlik & d'Ydewalle, 1996) in addition to advancing the science and practice of psychology worldwide.

Due to the rapid process of globalization, where cultures and countries influence one another, with the most profound effects coming from larger global economies such as the United States, there is a disturbing trend toward cultural homogenization (Bochner, 1999). Before discussing the implications of this trend, it is important to define the term *globalization* as it has been applied in many different ways in the literature, including the counseling literature. For Chapters 1 through 8 (Part I), globalization refers to increased contact between countries affecting, for instance, economic, social, cultural, and political features of life. Interdependence among nations is thought to be an essential component of globalization (see Figure 1.1).

Rapid globalization and the attendant pressures toward cultural homogenization can disrupt cultures

Term	Definition	Usage
Internationalization of counseling	An ongoing process of integrating knowledge from research and practice derived from different cultures and employing this knowledge to solve problems in local and global communities. Involves collaboration and equal partnerships where cultural sensitivity and respect are necessary for success. Efforts to indigenize the field of counseling in various regions in order that theories, practice, and systems are established and anchored in the local culture (Leung et al., Chapter 6).	Inconsistent
Globalization	Varies with the context of analysis. In general, means an increasing interaction across national boundaries that influence many aspects of life (e.g., economic, social, cultural, and political). For instance, globalization frequently refers to the growing economic interdependence of nations worldwide (United Nations Economic and Social Survey of Asia and the Pacific [UNESSAP], 1999).	Inconsistent
Psychologist	In the United States, persons with a doctoral degree in psychology from an organized, sequential program in a regionally accredited university or professional school (see http://www.apa.org/about).	Inconsistent
Counseling	A focus on using a broad array of psychological strategies and activities aimed at the process of helping others to reach individual, group, organizational, and systems goals.	Inconsistent
Counseling psychology	In the United States, a psychological specialty that integrates theory, research, and practice with a sensitivity to cultural and diversity issues to facilitate through a variety of strategies (e.g., individual, family, group, community, systems, organizational) personal and interpersonal functioning across the life span with a focus on emotional, social, vocational, educational, health-related, developmental, and organizational concerns (see http://www.div17.org/students_defining.html).	Inconsistent

(Continued)

Term	Definition	Usage
Culture	A socially transmitted phenomenon learned through enculturation and socialization that is passed on from one generation to the next and one individual to another. Information sharing of knowledge allows people to behave in ways found to be acceptable, understandable, and meaningful to one another in that culture. As such, there is a shared collective experience of a specific group of people. That is, the individuals recognize themselves and their cultural traditions as unique as compared with other people and other cultural traditions. Variability and complexity in behavior is expected, but there are also regularities or common patterns in behavior (Gerstein et al., 2007; Peoples & Bailey, 1994; Schultz & Lavenda, 2001).	Inconsistent
Cultural psychology (*Volkerpsychologie*)	Enhancing the understanding of people in a historical and sociocultural context using concepts meaningful within that culture (Adamopoulos & Lonner, 2001).	Inconsistent
Indigenous psychology	Psychological knowledge that is native, not transported from another location, and constructed for its people (Kim, 1990) by scholars from the culture under consideration (Adamopoulos & Lonner, 2001).	Consistent
Transcultural psychology	The entire discipline of psychology focused on ensuring that theories and findings have transcultural application, and not the naive transference of one culture to another without the recognition of the specific context (Hiles, 1996).	Inconsistent
Multicultural counseling	Both a helping role and process employing strategies and goals congruent with individuals' experiences and cultural values. Recognizes persons' identities in individual, group, and universal dimensions. Advocates using universal and culture-specific techniques and roles in the healing process (Sue & Torino, 1994).	Inconsistent
Multicultural psychology	Investigates the effect of race, racism, ethnic culture, and/or xenophobia on psychological constructs such as attitudes, cognitions, psychological processes, and behaviors (APA, 2003).	Inconsistent
Cross-cultural counseling	The pursuit and application of universal and indigenous theories, strategies (e.g., direct service, consultation, training, education, prevention), and research paradigms of counseling and mental health help seeking grounded in an in-depth examination, understanding, and appreciation of the cultural and epistemological underpinnings of countries located worldwide.	New definition (Inconsistent in the literature)
Cross-cultural psychology	A discipline of psychology primarily focused on how culture affects behavior with an aim of developing an inclusive universal psychology (Adamopoulos & Lonner, 2001) and research that is frequently comparative in nature.	Inconsistent
Cross-national counseling	Collaborative professional activities (e.g., program development and implementation, training, teaching, consultation) jointly pursued by mental health professionals residing in at least two countries.	New definition
Transnational	Focus on the worldwide intersections of nationhood, race, gender, sexuality, and economic status, in the context of an emergent global capitalism that reinforces colonialism and oppression. In transnational discourses, there is an emphasis on the elimination of global north/south hierarchies by embracing and valuing the multiplicity of cultures, languages, experiences, voices, and so on (Mohanty, 2003).	Consistent

Figure 1.1   Key Terms and Definitions

and identities in smaller, more vulnerable countries (Arnett, 2002), including the "globalization" of the counseling profession. Counselors and counseling psychologists in the West, particularly in the United States, are members of professions that have significant influence on the development of similar fields outside the West (Heppner, Leong, & Chiao, 2008; Leong & Blustein, 2000; Leung, 2003). In fact, the U.S. counseling profession is currently engaged in a systematic internationalization process. Thus, it is highly probable that the counseling and counseling psychology professions originating in the United States and grounded in U.S. worldviews, values, principles, and practices are greatly impacting the evolution of counseling in other countries. The chapters on the counseling profession around the world in Part II of this handbook confirm this assumption. Yet, as is also evidenced in Part II, numerous efforts are also under way by professionals outside the United States to "indigenize" the counseling profession in their home countries based on the specific cultural contexts (Leung, 2003; Tanaka-Matsumi, 2004). Moreover, the work of professionals in countries other than the United States is also broadening the thinking and worldviews of individuals in the entire counseling profession (e.g., see Chapters 7 and 8).

As reported in many chapters in Part II of this handbook, individuals throughout the world, particularly those who live in rural areas or have little income, continue to seek the assistance of indigenous healers when experiencing a host of problems, including ones of a psychological nature. These chapters have the potential to even further expand the thinking and worldviews of counseling professionals regardless of where they might reside. For example, in Argentina (see Chapter 29), Puerto Rico (see Chapter 31), and Ecuador (see Chapter 30), many people still visit a *curandero* (i.e., healer) or *chaman* when they experience emotional, mental, or psychological problems. Visiting indigenous healers for such problems is also popular among individuals in Kyrgyzstan (see Chapter 17), Nigeria (see Chapter 33), and the rural people of South Africa (see Chapter 32). In Iceland (see Chapter 21), an overwhelming number of individuals seek out a fortune-teller, and in India (see Chapter 16), some individuals will visit an astrologer to help them with their psychological concerns.

In Pakistan (see Chapter 15), Islamic teachings and practices are heavily embedded in models and strategies of counseling, while in Malaysia (see Chapter 14), Buddhist, Hindu, and Islamic principles and practices have been infused with different paradigms of counseling. Buddhist ideology and practices have been integrated into models of counseling in Singapore (see Chapter 13) as well. The cultural context in Japan also has been embedded in unique models of counseling. As reported in Chapter 9, Morita therapy is an indigenous Japanese form of psychotherapy. The goal of this approach is to help the client dissolve the self by accepting his or her own feelings and problems, and those of significant others, just as they are. Naikan therapy is another approach that is indigenous to Japan derived from a sect of Japanese Buddhism. This approach also helps clients focus away from and dissolve the self by assisting them with understanding what others feel and think, and accepting significant others as they are (Sato, 1998).

The cultural context not only affects cultural norms but also the type of stressful problems clients experience, clinical assessment, and the type of counseling interventions developed and employed (see Cheung, 2000). As stated earlier, the chapters in this handbook, particularly those in Part II, clearly illustrate how the cultural context differentially affects the manner in which people seek help for difficult life problems, the nature of clients' presenting problems, and the development of effective counseling interventions and appropriate counseling protocols.

Obviously, indigenous approaches to counseling throughout the world based on unique cultural contexts have the potential to greatly enrich the entire counseling profession. In fact, this impact is already occurring as the internationalization of the profession continues to evolve and affect the activities of mental health professionals worldwide.

It should be noted that the term *internationalization* is often either not defined or inconsistently defined in the literature, resulting in confusion and an inability to clearly and accurately discuss pertinent issues and challenges. For the purpose of consistency in this chapter and in Chapters 2 to 8, therefore, it is important to highlight that we have generated a definition of internationalization that is relevant to counseling within a global context. As shown in Figure 1.1, our definition stresses a collaborative process of acquiring information through counseling research and practice from various cultures in a sensitive manner and using the results to solve issues at home and abroad. Furthermore, our definition focuses on the indigenization of counseling in different countries whereby the profession itself and all its features are tied to the local culture (see also Chapter 7).

Depending on how the field of counseling in the United States further develops, it can either support the unique circumstances of mental health professionals in other countries or it can become a part of the larger process of global homogenization, thereby disrupting cultures, identities, and ways of life (Arnett, 2002; Marsella, 1998; Pedersen, 2003). Therefore, in the internationalization process, it is crucial to avoid the colonizing effect of the unconscious exportation of Western U.S.-based counseling models and their implicit worldviews, values, and counseling and research strategies. Mental health professionals worldwide who are engaged in the internationalization of counseling must be keenly aware of the importance of critically examining and evaluating the validity and applicability of Western models of counseling and psychology, particularly ones derived in the United States, as they are transported to countries outside the West. Embracing such a perspective can enhance the probability that when models and strategies are constructed and employed from culture to culture, or country to country, they indeed support the development and well-being of the members of the communities to be served. It is also essential to understand that colleagues "across the world have developed tremendous knowledge bases through their research and practice spanning hundreds and thousands of years" (Heppner, Leong, & Chiao, 2008, p. 79). Stated another way, counseling and counseling psychology must be reconstituted and indigenized country by country, and culture by culture, to affirm and effectively respond to local needs and concerns

(Pedersen, 2003). This can only be done successfully through meaningful engagement, collaboration, and learning among colleagues globally.

Related to the importance of establishing and maintaining worldwide professional relationships is the fact that the process of evolution has demonstrated that, contrary to the popular belief in Darwin's "survival of the fittest," diversity is the key to the survival, enhancement, and prosperity of all living organisms and systems (Wheatley, 2006). Creativity, complexity, and reinvention based on local context and changing circumstances all contribute to organisms, including human beings, surviving and reaching their full potential as they face new challenges. This concept is quite applicable not only for humans but also for the profession of counseling itself. In rising to the occasion of making counseling and counseling psychology relevant and applicable within a wide range of contexts and cultures, a broader range of knowledge and skills will emerge. By sharing these diverse ways of responding to the needs and concerns of local people, our repertoire as a global profession for healing, helping, and problem solving increases and becomes more complex, both in the contexts of our own cultures and countries and also when we cross cultural and national borders to work, teach, practice, or conduct research in settings other than our own. In the end, culturally related knowledge from around the world will bring tremendous advantages to help conceptualize intervention strategies to address old problems with new solutions (Heppner, Leong, & Chiao, 2008).

We also view counseling as peace work (Norsworthy & Gerstein, 2003). In the face of escalating global violence, conflict, and misunderstanding, the knowledge and skills brought to the table by counselors and counseling psychologists has never had more relevance. At the end of the day, counseling professionals graduate from training programs that equip them to do much more than work in individual offices. As counseling professionals, we have specialized knowledge and skills in advocacy, social justice, nonviolent communication, conflict resolution, problem solving, negotiation, and other elements of peace building and social change.

Furthermore, we learn to understand group process, to facilitate group dialogue, and to design and implement group interventions aimed at supporting and fostering deeper respect, appreciation, and understanding of self and others. The old adage, "with knowledge comes responsibility," calls on all of us to use our knowledge and skills to engage in what is called in the Jewish tradition *Tikkun olam,* repairing or changing the world (Brown, 1997). Given the magnitude of the current global problems we are all facing, never has the need been greater to reach beyond our own borders for understanding and to join hands with our global brothers and sisters, particularly those in our counseling profession, to create a more peaceful, just, compassionate, and loving world.

HISTORY OF U.S. PSYCHOLOGY PROFESSION AND INTERNATIONAL ISSUES

The first International Congress of Psychology took place in 1889 in Paris, France (Evans & Scott, 1978). According to Brehm (2008), from the very inception of the field of psychology in the 19th century, there was a tie between professionals in the United States and Europe. At this time, psychology was a collaborative project pursued by William James in Massachusetts, Ivan Pavlov in St. Petersburg, and Wilhelm Wundt in Leipzig. The first International Congress of Psychology to be held in the United States was scheduled to occur in 1913, but it failed to transpire because of a power struggle among the U.S. psychologists (Evans & Scott, 1978). Eventually, the Congress was convened in 1929 at Yale University with J. McKeen Cattell serving as the president (Evans & Scott, 1978).

At the time of World War I and for years to follow, however, U.S. psychologists were focused on the United States (Sexton & Misiak, 1984), and they tended "to ignore or neglect psychology abroad" (Rosenzweig, 1984, p. 877). Interestingly though, psychology in the United States flourished because European psychologists fleeing fascism rooted in Germany immigrated to North America.

The European influence on U.S. psychology is truly remarkable (as well as psychology from other countries such as China). For example, common strategies such as gestalt psychology, psychoanalysis, psychological statistics, the Rorschach test, Pavlovian classical conditioning, and intelligence testing emanate from Europe (Sexton & Misiak, 1984).

In the early 1940s, the American Psychological Association (APA) formed the Committee on International Planning (CIP). An early goal of this group was to communicate with psychologists abroad and determine their needs. One conclusion from this effort was the assumption that non-U.S. psychologists needed "American literature from 1940 on" (Hunter, Miles, Yerkes, & Langfeld, 1946, p. 123). Another was the need to develop a list of psychologists living abroad.

In 1944, the Committee on International Relations in Psychology (CIRP) replaced the CIP. The main mission of CIRP continues to be developing contact between psychologists in the United States and psychologists living elsewhere. In 1996, the CIRP introduced an important new feature in the APA journal the *American Psychologist*—a special section on international psychology. It should be mentioned that 20 years earlier, in 1977, a special issue of the *American Psychologist* was published featuring research and conceptual articles written by psychologists living outside the United States, including Israel, Iran, Costa Rica, the former Soviet Union, Mexico, India, and Japan (Cole, 1977). The APA International Affairs Committee generated the idea for this special issue.

In 1979, the APA Office of International Affairs (OIA) was established and a full-time staff person was hired (S. Leverty, personal communication, March 4, 2009). OIA serves as APA's central clearinghouse for international information, activities, and initiatives within APA's central offices and across the association. This office also leads outreach and interaction with APA's international members and affiliates, coordinates APA's participation and representation in international venues, and facilitates exchange with national psychology associations and global policy bodies (http://www.apa.org/international/contactus.html).

APA also has a separate Division (52) of International Psychology whose members are U.S.

psychologists and psychologists from other countries. As stated on the Division 52 Web site, the Division "represents the interest of all psychologists who foster international connections among psychologists, engage in multicultural research or practice, apply psychological principles to the development of public policy, or are otherwise concerned with individual and group consequences of global events" (see http://www.internationalpsychology.net/about).

As of February 2009, there were about 3,500 international affiliate members of APA. These psychologists are also members of their own national psychology associations. There are also around 3,000 APA members and student affiliates living outside the United States (http://www.apa.org/international/faq-apaint.html). As Fleishman (1999) remarked, "Psychology is now a global discipline" (p. 1009).

Clearly, the discipline of psychology in the United States has a long history of engaging in international activities. As reported by Kelman and Hollander (1964) in the early 1960s, the most common international activity pursued by U.S. psychologists was collaborative research. Later on in this chapter and in the remainder of this handbook, it will become apparent that U.S. psychologists are now engaged in many more diverse and rich international activities. Perhaps, this is because in the 1980s, U.S. psychologists became more interested in psychology elsewhere (Rosenzweig, 1984; Sexton & Misiak, 1984).

While U.S. psychologists may have become more interested in international work in the 1980s and the years to follow, it appears that, in general, they were not fully equipped to employ culturally appropriate and effective theories, methods, and strategies. Some scholars believed that U.S. psychologists had very limited information about the international literature (Kennedy, Scheirer, & Rogers, 1984; Rosenzweig, 1999; Sexton & Misiak, 1984), especially if it was not published in English (Ardila, 1993; Brandt, 1970; David, 1960; Rosenzweig, 1984) or by leading figures in psychology outside the United States (Denmark, 1998). These observations and more current observations have led many scholars to claim that U.S. psychology is ethnocentric (Berry,

Poortinga, Segall, & Dasen, 1992; Leung, 2003; Marsella, 1998; Pedersen & Leong, 1997; Takooshian, 2003), U.S.-centric (Leong & Ponterotto, 2003), or Anglocentric (Cheung, 2000; Trimble, 2001). Indeed, in a recent analysis of a sample of psychology journals, Arnett (2008) argued that American psychology has focused on 5% of the world's population and neglected the other 95%. Within this context, many scholars have claimed that one of the biggest challenges facing U.S. psychologists is now overcoming their ethnocentrism (e.g., Gerstein, 2006; Heppner, 2006; Heppner, Leong, & Chiao, 2008; Leong & Blustein, 2000; Marsella, 1998).

Interestingly, some authors have argued that the U.S. psychology literature is read by persons around the world (Ardila, 1982; Rosenzweig, 1984), while individuals in the psychology and counseling professions in the United States rarely read publications in other languages (Leung, 2003; Ægisdóttir, Gerstein, & Çinarbaş, 2008). English also has been viewed as the language of psychology (Russell, 1984), with the U.S. journals the most preferred outlet for publication (David & Swartley, 1961). While some have concluded that psychologists publishing in non-English-language journals are isolated (Ardila, 1982) because their publications are not read by English-reading professionals, others have argued just the opposite. For instance, Smith (1983) stated that the professional who reads only English is isolated. Psychologists in non-English-language countries usually "have access to a wide literature because of the common multilingualism" (p. 123). Smith went on to claim that to increase English language professionals' knowledge base, it is important for doctoral programs in these countries to reinstate the foreign language requirement. In the early 1960s, there was an effort led by the Council of Editors of the APA to include a greater number of non-English-language abstracts in *Psychological Abstracts* and *Contemporary Psychology* (David & Swartley, 1961). This practice, however, has been discontinued. *Psychological Abstracts* no longer covers publications not written in the English language (Draguns, 2001).

Offering a somewhat different analysis about the influence of U.S. psychology on other countries, Ardila (1982) claimed that psychologists tend to know the research and issues of their own countries best and that "the implicit *Weltanschauung* (worldview) of psychology today is the worldview of a specific culture in a specific moment of history" (p. 328). Consistent with this perspective, Moghaddam (1987) argued that there are three worlds of research and practice in psychology. The first is knowledge and application tied solely to the United States, while the second is psychological knowledge and application established by other industrialized nations. Finally, the third world of psychology has evolved from developing countries. Commenting on the impact of American psychology from around 1893 to 1968, Berlyne (1968) indicated, "American psychologists have earned the abundant gratitude of the rest of the world. But like all parents of ambitious children . . . they had better not expect much in the way of thanks" (p. 452). Of course, this is a paternalistic perspective that infantilizes professionals outside the West and renders invisible the colonial elements of the internationalization process.

Psychology grew dramatically around the globe following World War II (Brehm, 2008) and in the past few decades of the 20th century (Draguns, 2001). As of 2008, there were national psychological associations in more than 90 countries. Seventy-one of these associations were members of the International Union of Psychological Science (IUPsyS) representing countries in every continent. The IUPsyS consists of no more than one national member association per country. The IUPsyS also accepts affiliated organizations. In 2008, there were approximately 12 of these groups. This organization was founded in Stockholm in 1951 with 11 charter organizations. The Assembly of the Union last met in Berlin in July of 2008 in conjunction with the XXIX International Congress of Psychology (Ritchie, 2008). Three years earlier, the union president, Bruce Overmier stated that "the Union remains focused on fulfilling its mission to advance psychology as an applied and basic science by serving as the voice for psychology on an international level" (Ritchie, 2008, p. 930). The International Congress of Psychology will hold its XXX conference in Cape Town, South Africa, in 2012.

HISTORY OF U.S. COUNSELING PROFESSION AND INTERNATIONAL ISSUES

The history of the counseling professions' involvement in international activities also dates back many years beginning in the 1940s (for details on developments from 1940 to 1969, see Heppner, Leong, & Chiao, 2008; Savickas, 2007; Chapter 2, this volume). For this chapter, we will begin with a discussion of internationalization efforts that began in the 1980s. During this time, U.S. counseling psychologists and counselor educators began to secure Fulbright positions. Since then, 112 individuals have secured awards in 45 countries, such as the former Soviet Union, Turkey, England, Sweden, Iran, Norway, Australia, Iceland, Peru, Malaysia, and Zambia (McWhirter & McWhirter, 2009).

Another major development in the internationalization of the U.S. counseling psychology profession also occurred in the 1980s (Heppner, Leong, & Chiao, 2008). In 1988, Bruce Fretz, the incoming editor of *The Counseling Psychologist* (*TCP*)—the flagship journal of APA Division 17 (Society of Counseling Psychology), launched the *International Forum* (*IF*). Fretz (1999) claimed that this forum "was as much a hope for something to develop as it was a reflection of a body of knowledge ready to be disseminated" (p. 40). The mission of *IF* was (and still is) to offer "a venue where psychologists learn to cross borders, whether physical or psychological, to be enriched and to enrich others" (Kwan & Gerstein, 2008, p. 182). At first, however, this section of *TCP* featured articles almost entirely written by U.S. counseling professionals who shared their international experiences. This trend began to change when P. Paul Heppner became the editor of *TCP* in 1997. As a result of some modifications in how *TCP* functioned (e.g., appointment of leaders in the international movement in counseling psychology as *IF* coeditors, instituting a more culturally sensitive review process, and selecting the first international scholar, S. A. Leung from Hong Kong, to serve as associate editor), a greater number of international counseling professionals began to publish in *TCP* (Heppner, Leong, & Chiao, 2008). In short, through the efforts of the former (Paul Pedersen, Frederick Leong, Joseph Ponterotto, and David Blustein) and current (Kwong-Leim Karl Kwan and Lawrence H. Gerstein) *IF* editors, and especially since 2000, an even greater number of international scholars have published their works in *TCP*. The authors of *IF* articles have been professionals residing in many countries (e.g., Turkey, the People's Republic of China, Spain, Norway, Taiwan, Japan, South Africa, Korea, India, Israel, and West Samoa/American Samoa), oftentimes writing about features of counseling in their home country.

Two other developments connected to *TCP* are important to mention. First, in 2007, to increase the likelihood that editorial board members were both competent in evaluating articles of an international nature and appreciative of the importance of publishing articles written by non-U.S. scholars, *TCP* added four persons to the board who had cross-cultural expertise and were born outside the United States. These individuals had ties with Asia, Europe, and the Middle East. Three of these scholars lived outside the United States (Kwan & Gerstein, 2008).

The second new development connected to *TCP* is the fact that in 2008, a page in the beginning of each journal issue was devoted to displaying the journal's title, *The Counseling Psychologist*, in 24 different languages. This modification was implemented in an attempt to present *TCP* as a more inclusive, affirming, and welcoming periodical to counseling professionals residing throughout the world (Kwan & Gerstein, 2008).

One other important development that occurred in the 1980s must be highlighted. The Minnesota International Counseling Institute was launched in 1989 by the counseling psychology faculty (i.e., Thomas Skovholt, Sunny Hansen, John Romano, and Kay Thomas) affiliated with the University of Minnesota. International practitioners and scholars have attended this biennial Institute designed to address the science and practice of cross-cultural counseling.

In 1991, Paul Pedersen published a seminal article where he argued that culture is central to all counseling (Pedersen, 1991). Since that time, Pedersen has been considered one of the key leaders of the cross-cultural counseling movement. While Pedersen's 1991 publication had an impact on the counseling profession at the time, by the middle of the 1990s, it was clear that few accepted or understood an international focus for the field (Heppner & Gerstein, 2008).

This situation changed dramatically in the U.S. counseling psychology profession in the first decade of the 21st century (Heppner, Leong, & Chiao, 2008). During this time, greater systematic organizational efforts were put in place to embrace international issues, foster collaboration between United States and international counseling scholars, and share knowledge relevant to counseling psychology in the United States and abroad. In this regard, five of the six presidents of the APA Society of Counseling Psychology from 2003 to 2009 selected an international theme for their presidency. In 2003–2004, as president of this society, Louise Douce helped reenergize the counseling psychology profession's interest in international issues. Douce introduced a forum at the APA convention where counseling professionals interested in international topics could meet and discuss their interests and vision for the field. She also chose globalization of counseling psychology as her presidential theme (Douce, 2004). Douce claimed, "Counseling psychology can enhance the human condition in many ways by expanding from local and regional realities, not national politics. I envision a movement that transcends nationalism—including our own—and truly fosters a global village" (p. 145).

P. Paul Heppner, as the next president of the society in 2004–2005, focused on the internationalization of counseling psychology and the importance of becoming cross-culturally competent (Heppner, 2006). Consistent with this focus, he expanded the international scholar's breakfast and reception at the APA convention, first introduced by Douce during her presidency to encourage, in part, strengthening collaborative relationships between professionals living in different countries; an important need that was identified in a survey conducted on Division 17 members living outside the United States (Watkins, Lopez, Campbell, & Lew, 1986). Furthermore, Heppner in collaboration with Lawrence H. Gerstein, in 2005, launched the "International Section" within the society (http://www.international counselingpsychology.org). Basically, the mission of this section is to encourage, promote, and facilitate a scientist-professional model of counseling psychology in international contexts in the United States and around the globe through research, service, teaching, training, policy development and implementation, and networking. Not surprisingly, in his presidential address, Heppner (2006) reported that "greater cross-cultural competence will promote a deeper realization that counseling occurs in a cultural context and will increase not only counseling effectiveness but also the profession's ability to address diverse mental health needs across different populations around the globe" (p. 148).

The next president of the society in 2005–2006, Roberta Nutt (2007), also embraced globalization as one of her themes. In fact, her presidential speech was titled "Implications of Globalization for Training in Counseling Psychology."

The second major initiative of Linda Forrest during her presidency of the society in 2007–2008 was the planning and implementation of the society's first ever "International Conference of Counseling Psychology," held in Chicago, Illinois, in March 2008. The theme of this highly successful conference was "Creating the Future: Counseling Psychologists in a Changing World." There were more than 1,400 attendees, including 109 international scholars from more than 40 countries. The number of attendees did not reflect, however, the many international students and scholars residing in the United States who attended the conference. Forrest (2008) reported that the "conference laid down a solid and healthy foundation for an international future for the Society of Counseling Psychology" (p. 8). It should be mentioned that in the planning of the 2001 Houston Counseling Psychology Conference, an international committee was also established to network with counseling psychologists from outside the United States and to encourage them to present and attend the conference (Fouad et al., 2004). While 1,052 individuals attended this conference, our impression was that the proportion of persons from countries other than the United States was rather small.

The more recent upsurge in the U.S. counseling and counseling psychology professions' activity connected to international pursuits is intimately tied to the rapid development and evolution of the U.S. multicultural counseling movement (for more details, see Heppner, Leong, & Chiao, 2008; Heppner, Leong, & Gerstein, 2008; Chapter 2, this volume). As the focus of this movement expanded in the late 1980s to incorporate meeting the needs and concerns of diverse populations, including all people of color, individuals of different ethnic origins and socioeconomic status, persons of various sexual orientations, and individuals with different physical abilities, so it embraced serving international populations both in and outside the United States. Multicultural counseling scholars also developed and introduced unique research paradigms and methodologies to study these populations. Furthermore, these scholars launched creative and dynamic training models designed to educate U.S. graduate students in counseling about culturally sensitive conceptual and intervention approaches that could be used to understand and effectively and appropriately assist such populations.

Since 2000, there has been a dramatic increase in the international activities of U.S. counselors and counseling psychologists (e.g., Gerstein, 2006; Gerstein & Ægisdóttir, 2005a, 2005b, 2005c; Heppner, 2006; Heppner & Gerstein, 2008; Heppner, Leong, & Chiao, 2008; Heppner, Leong, & Gerstein, 2008; Kwan & Gerstein, 2008; Leong & Blustein, 2000; Leong & Ponterotto, 2003; Leung, 2003; McWhirter, 1988a, 1988b, 1988c; Norsworthy & Gerstein, 2003; Pedersen & Leong, 1997; Ægisdóttir & Gerstein, 2005). A growing number of U.S. counselors and counseling psychologists have traveled abroad to experience and investigate different cultures, enrich themselves, and provide a host of educational (e.g., lectures, courses, workshops), research, and applied (e.g., counseling, consulting) services (see Heppner, Leong, & Chiao, 2008). As a result of this increase in travel outside the United States, counselors and counseling psychologists have developed and shared with others a much greater desire to pursue international issues. That is, they have shown more interest in collaborating with scholars, educators, researchers, practitioners, administrators, and government officials outside the United States. A sizable number of educators in U.S. counseling graduate programs have also turned their attention to training students to effectively serve international clientele, including preparing students to teach and consult overseas. Additionally, U.S. counseling scholars have disseminated information on how to conduct appropriate and valid cross-cultural research (Ægisdóttir et al., 2008), and they have published literature (Cheung, 2000; Gerstein & Ægisdóttir, 2005a, 2005b, 2005c, 2007; Leong & Ponterotto, 2003; Leung, 2003; Pedersen, 2003; Pedersen & Leong, 1997; Ægisdóttir & Gerstein, 2005) on the importance of counselors and counseling psychologists developing and demonstrating an appreciation, respect, and understanding of international cultures and models of psychology and counseling.

Without a doubt, the developments associated with the rising interest in international topics among U.S. counseling professionals can be traced to the enhanced ease of contact and communication (e.g., e-mail, Skype) between people residing in all four corners of the globe, and the knowledge, information, and cultural understanding resulting from such interactions (see Heppner, 1997; Heppner, Casas, Carter, & Stone, 2000; Heppner, Leong, & Chiao, 2008; Heppner, Leong, & Gerstein, 2008). These developments also emanate from the consequences of globalization and the rapidly growing population of international scholars and students associated with U.S. educational institutions. The rich interpersonal exchanges occurring in U.S. counseling training programs between international and U.S.-based individuals have contributed to the latter group acquiring a deeper appreciation and curiosity about cultures worldwide, a recognition to some extent about the function and status of the counseling professions outside the United States and to a lesser extent the role of psychological help seeking around the world. These interactions also have recently contributed to international scholars and students exploring and evaluating the cross-cultural relevance and validity of U.S.-derived counseling theories, methods, and strategies in their home countries. In fact, many counseling professionals around the world, including persons located in the United States, have voiced strong reservations about adopting U.S. counseling paradigms and interventions in other countries (Gerstein & Ægisdóttir, 2005a, 2005c, 2007; Heppner, 2006; Heppner, Leong, & Chiao, 2008; Leong & Ponterotto, 2003; Leung, 2003; Leong & Blustein, 2000; Pedersen, 2003; Pedersen & Leong, 1997). A growing number of serious concerns and questions have been raised about the cross-cultural validity and applicability of employing U.S. models with non-U.S. populations (Gerstein & Ægisdóttir, 2005a, 2005c, 2007; Leong & Blustein, 2000; Leong & Ponterotto, 2003; Leung, 2003; Marsella, 1998; Pedersen, 2003; Pedersen & Leong, 1997) and the ethnocentric nature of counseling psychology (Cheung, 2000; Heppner, 2006; Heppner, Leong, & Chiao, 2008; Heppner, Leong, & Gerstein, 2008; Leung, 2003; Leong & Leach, 2007; McWhirter, 2000; Norsworthy, 2006).

INTERNATIONAL WORK OF NON-U.S. PROFESSIONALS: AN OVERVIEW

The pursuit of international work has not only been the purview of U.S. psychologists and counseling professionals. Globalization has greatly enhanced opportunities for cross-national collaboration among counseling professionals worldwide. While we are unaware of an organized effort to internationalize the counseling profession outside the United States, counseling professionals throughout the world have engaged in a variety of international activities, as counseling becomes an established field within and across national borders. Perhaps in Europe, there has been no need to launch a formal organized effort to internationalize the counseling profession because the borders of the European countries are so fluid. Europeans, including mental health professionals, often travel from country to country for pleasure and work, and they frequently speak multiple languages found in Europe. Given this reality, we suspect that European mental health professionals have a very different mind-set about internationalization as compared with their U.S. colleagues. That is, they have no need to formally internationalize the counseling profession since interacting with professionals from different European countries has been part and parcel of their existence for a very long time. Furthermore, European mental health professionals, as compared with U.S. professionals, have been engaged in the pursuit of cross-cultural research for many years. Therefore, there does not seem to be a systematic awakening among European mental health professionals to internationalize the counseling profession. In fact, the European professionals have naturally embraced an international focus for a much longer period of time than U.S. counseling professionals who have more recently systematically organized an international agenda.

As stated earlier, U.S. counseling professionals have increasingly been engaged in collaborative international activities, including conducting research and scholarly work, providing training and service, and engaging in consultation (e.g., Gerstein, 2006; Heppner, 2006; Heppner, Leong, & Chiao, 2008; Norsworthy, 2006). Counseling professionals in other countries also frequently participate and collaborate. In fact, many local leaders have served as the "architects" of cross-border and cross-national activities. Furthermore, non-U.S. counseling professionals have performed numerous cross-cultural research studies and cross-national applied projects outside their own countries.

There are a multitude of channels through which non-U.S. counseling professionals have engaged actively in international work. First, there has been a great deal of academic activity for years in the Asian region involving counseling scholars from multiple countries. The Asian-Pacific Counseling and Guidance Association and the Chinese Association of Psychological Testing have been active for a long time and have routinely held conferences drawing scholars from several countries. Taiwanese counseling scholars have been particularly active in collaborating with their colleagues in other Asian countries.

For instance, in 1997, Ping-Hwa Chen was invited to Hong Kong, China, and Singapore to discuss with their scholars how the Taiwan school guidance system was developed (Chen, 1999). In 2008, the inaugural Asia Pacific Rim International Counseling Conference was held in Hong Kong, and the conference was co-organized by professional counseling associations in Hong Kong and Australia (Leung, 2008).

In Europe, counseling scholars from Italy have actively collaborated with researchers from other countries as well, particularly other European countries. In many ways, their level of cross-national collaboration has been far-reaching, such as the Bologna Project to promote international education at the undergraduate level. With the founding of the Laboratory for Research and Intervention in Vocational Guidance (LaRIOS) at the University of Padua more than 15 years ago, Italian counseling professionals began to conduct research studies on vocational psychology with scholars worldwide. For example, LaRIOS investigators performed research with Leon Mann of the University of Melbourne on decision making, self-efficacy beliefs, and coping strategies; with Sunny Hansen through the Minnesota International Counseling Institute on how to design supportive counseling services for students at the University of Padua; with John Krumboltz of Stanford University on career choice; with Scott Solberg and Kimberly Howard of the University of Wisconsin–Milwaukee on perceived support, self-efficacy beliefs, and school-career indecision; and with Robert Lent (University of Maryland) and Steven Brown (Loyola University) on the relationships between self-efficacy beliefs and job satisfaction. LaRIOS scholars have also conducted collaborative research on the relationships between self-regulation abilities, study abilities, school achievement, and levels of school-career indecision among middle and high school adolescents with Barry Zimmerman of the City University of New York; relationships between assertiveness, self-efficacy beliefs, and quality of life with Willem Arrindell of the University of Groningen (the Netherlands); problem-solving abilities with Puncky Heppner and Mary Heppner of the University of

Missouri; the concept of work, study, and leisure time with David Blustein of Boston College and Hanoch Flum of Ben Gurion University (Israel); and coping strategies in young and old adolescents with Erica Frydenberg of Melbourne University (Australia).

Non-U.S. counseling scholars have also traveled to different countries to train and teach students and professionals. Professionals affiliated with LaRIOS, for instance, have trained psychologists, career service providers, and teachers in the Republic of Guinea-Bissau, Malta, and Singapore. Anthony Naidoo from Stellenbosch University in South Africa has been involved in the development and training of community psychologists in Mexico, Eritrea, and Norway as well. Moreover, with his colleagues, he took part in community and adolescent and male development programs in Mexico, Puerto Rico, Norway, the United Kingdom, and Turkey. Furthermore, Naidoo has engaged in community service learning projects with international partners in the Congo DRC and the United States, and eco-therapy interventions with partners in the United States and Norway.

Finally, it is important to mention that there is an international group of scholars collaborating on research and other projects through the Life Design International Research Group. The members of this group are Salvatore Soresi (LaRIOS, Italy), Laura Nota (LaRIOS, Italy), Jean Guichard (Institut National d'Etude du Travail et d'Orientation Professionnelle—Conservatoire National des Arts et Métiers, Paris, France), Jean-Pierre Dauwalder (University of Lausanne, Switzerland), Raoul Van Esbroeck (Vrije Universiteit Brussel, Belgium), Jérôme Rossier (Institute of Psychology, University of Lausanne, Switzerland), and Mark Savickas (Behavioral Sciences Department, Northeastern Ohio University College of Medicine, the United States).

Counseling professionals from outside the United States have been heavily involved in the activities of international professional organizations as members, presenters, and leaders. For example, non-U.S. counseling professionals were instrumental in the effort to form the Counseling Psychology Division (Division 16) of the International Association of Applied Psychology (IAAP), and they also have served on the executive board of IAAP since its inception as the International Association of Psychotechnology in 1920, where its first Congress met in Geneva, Switzerland. Likewise, international counseling professionals have been actively involved in the International Association for Counselling, an organization that holds regular academic conferences (e.g., International Roundtable for the Advancement of Counselling) as well as publishing an international journal titled *International Journal for the Advancement of Counselling* (Harper, 2000; Lee, 1997). As of February 2009, the editorial board of this journal included counseling professionals from 21 countries. Moreover, international counseling professionals have been intimately associated with the Society of Vocational Psychology Section and the International Section of the Society of Counseling Psychology of the APA. Non-U.S. professionals can be members and leaders of the International Section. In fact, the bylaws of this group specify that the executive committee must include non-U.S.-based members in the elected role of section cochair and membership cochair.

International counseling professionals also have regularly presented at numerous conferences outside their home country. For example, they have shared their work at the convention meetings of the International Union of Psychological Sciences Congress, International Association for Cross-Cultural Psychology (founded in 1972), International Association for Educational and Vocational Guidance, APA, American Counseling Association, National Career Development Association, IAAP, International Conference on Psychology, Interamerican Congress of Psychology, European Congress of Psychology, World Congress for Psychotherapy, Asian American Psychological Association, and Society of Vocational Psychology.

A third prominent way that non-U.S. counseling professionals have engaged in scholarly activities around the world involves editorial responsibilities. International professionals have served as editors, associate editors, and members of editorial boards of many major counseling and psychology journals with an international focus. As a result, international counseling professionals have made important contributions to the development of the international counseling literature and the advancement of a scientific foundation for the entire profession (Skovholt, Hansen, Goh, Romano, & Thomas, 2005).

Another way that non-U.S. (and U.S.) counseling professionals have participated in international activities is through relief work. Non-U.S. professionals have been actively involved in response efforts to natural disasters of a global magnitude, including providing mental health services, for instance, to victims and survivors of the 2004 (December 26) Tsunami in Southeast Asia (Chatterjee, 2005; Miller, 2005). Additionally, many mental health professionals, including psychiatrists, social workers, psychologists, and counselors have participated in a range of projects connected to the World Health Organization (WHO) and other nongovernment organizations (NGOs). International counseling professionals also provided psychosocial and psychological support to victims of the 2008 (May 12) Sichuan Earthquake in China via global-level organizations such as the United Nations Children's Fund (UNICEF, 2008) and the International Federation of Red Cross (2008).

Through the international relief efforts just mentioned and others, mental health professionals offered their expertise by developing culture-based, train-the-trainer programs aimed at strengthening local capacity to address posttrauma mental health concerns thought to become a heavy burden to the affected nations in the years to come (Miller, 2005). In an age where nations are no longer separated by geographic distance because of advances in communication technologies, counseling professionals have demonstrated through these efforts that they can effectively collaborate to assist and provide relief to persons who have experienced a natural and/or human disaster.

Collaboration among scholars from different corners of the world is not only important to provide effective relief in response to disasters, but such collaboration and increased opportunities for travel, learning, and disseminating information are extremely critical for the advancement of the science and practice of counseling and psychology. The results of effective collaboration have the potential to enhance the development of both universals (etics) in psychology and counseling and also the potential to stimulate the development of particulars (emics) or culture-specific information in psychology and counseling.

Unfortunately, though, it can be argued that the results of such collaboration and international projects designed to advance the science and practice of counseling are disseminated unilaterally. That is, these outcomes are more often than not published in the English language scholarly literature. Furthermore, when published in the non-English literature, these outcomes tend to go unnoticed in English-speaking countries such as the United States, and consequently, this work is often not read in many parts of the world. Stated more specifically, there is much more information available in the United States and English language literature about U.S. counseling professionals' work than there is about non-U.S. or non-English-speaking scholars' efforts in non-English-speaking countries. Taken together, these biases hinder the internationalization of counseling and psychological science (Draguns, 2001).

Despite these biases, a perusal of programs at various conventions and congresses in psychology around the world (e.g., Interamerican Congress of Psychology, European Congress of Psychology, Southeast Asia Psychology Conference, South African Psychology Congress) suggests that international collaboration and the sharing of knowledge are blooming. For instance, at the 2009 European Congress of Psychology (n.d.), there were numerous programs and keynote speeches focused on the dissemination of country-specific knowledge and reports of collaborative efforts among scholars from different countries in Europe. Furthermore, one aim of the European Federation of Psychologists' Associations (EFPA) founded in Germany in 1981 and that currently includes 34 member associations representing around 200,000 psychologists in Europe (EFPA, 2007) is to promote communication and cooperation between member associations in Europe. Another aim is to facilitate contacts with international bodies of psychology and related disciplines and to be an important source of advice to European institutions, government, political, social, and consumer organizations. Yet another aim is to disseminate psychological knowledge and professional skills to effectively assist European citizens (EFPA, 2007). Consistent with these aims, with the development of the European certificate in psychology (EuroPsy), opportunities for European psychologists to work and participate in other European countries have been greatly enhanced.

One aim of the Asian Psychological Association (APsyA), which was founded at the First Convention of the Asian Council of Psychologists in Jakarta, Indonesia, in 2005, is also to encourage the development of psychology within Asian countries and to promote collaboration among Asian psychologists living in Asia. By recognizing the difference between the psychology of Western, more individualistic nations, and Eastern, more collectivistic nations, APsyA's goal is to encourage collaboration among interdisciplinary, cross-cultural, and interethnic individual psychologists to develop an Asian psychological paradigm designed to better comprehend and serve the unique needs of Asian people (Jaafar, n.d.).

KEY CONCEPTS AND TERMS: DEFINITIONS AND CHALLENGES

Before concluding this chapter with a discussion about the rationale, vision, and purpose of this handbook, it is essential to present operational definitions of concepts and terms found throughout this handbook. We also believe that it is critical to briefly highlight some of the challenges associated with these definitions. Additionally, we think that it is important to note that there is inconsistency in how many of these concepts and terms are both defined and used in this handbook with the exception of Chapters 1 through 8, where they are defined in a consistent fashion. In fact, in the counseling and psychology literatures worldwide, these concepts and terms are inconsistently defined.

Mental Health Provider Titles and Functions

Throughout the world, there are major inconsistencies in the definition and use of the title *counselor* (Heppner & Gerstein, 2008), *psychologist* (Rosenzweig, 1982), and *counseling psychologist*. Professional counselors in the United States must hold a master's degree or higher in counselor education. Yet counseling as it is known in the United States also does not exist in all parts of the world (Heppner, Leong, & Gerstein, 2008; Savickas, 2007). In the United States, according to the National Board of Certified Counselors (NBCC), counseling may be described as follows:

> A process whereby specially trained individuals provide (a) academic, career or vocational guidance; (b) problem-solving support and expertise; (c) support and/or expertise specific to certain biological threats; or (d) support and expertise to individuals, families, and communities as they strive towards optimum wellness. (see http://www.nbccinternational .org/home/about-professional-counseling)

In other parts of the world (e.g., India), the term *counseling* is used to denote the activities of many different diverse professionals (e.g., lawyers, bankers, financial advisors, physicians, nurses, indigenous healers, mental health practitioners). Furthermore, professional counselors are quite often located in school settings, and the standard professional training may be at the bachelor's or master's level. In this handbook, the use of the term *counselor* may refer to professionals who are trained in counselor education programs, or a counselor may refer to professionals or community members not part of the "counseling profession" as defined by NBCC who use counseling knowledge and skills in their work.

In many countries, there is no term for psychology or psychologist, and if there are, these terms do not mean the same as they do in Western nations (Abi-Hashem, 1997). The training and educational requirements to become a psychologist (Russell, 1984), counselor, or counseling psychologist vary greatly from country to country as well. In the United States, a person must have a doctoral degree to become a psychologist (see Figure 1.1). In South, Latin, and Central America, in contrast, an individual needs the equivalent of a bachelor's degree, while in Europe and many parts of Asia (e.g., Taiwan, China, Korea, and Japan), a master's degree or an equivalent diploma is required. In the early 1990s, Rosenzweig (1992) indicated that a master's degree was the modal credential for psychologists worldwide. This observation continues to be accurate in 2009.

While it is highly likely that a mental health provider and client in the United States understand the meaning of the term *counseling* and share similar assumptions about this meaning, in other countries, it cannot be assumed that both parties perceive this function the same way (Cheung, 2000). As a result, Cheung (2000) has argued, "Counseling must be deconstructed in the context of the culture in which it is offered" (p. 124).

Keeping in mind Cheung's (2000) warning about the importance of deconstruction, the definition of counseling we embrace and the one guiding the chapters in Part I is very broad and general (see Figure 1.1). We believe that this definition can capture the practice of counseling in many countries featured in this handbook. Basically, counseling involves the use of diverse psychological interventions to assist individuals, groups, organizations, and systems with the achievement of their goals.

The discipline of counseling psychology, and the title *counseling psychologist*, also does not exist in many parts of the world (e.g., France, Argentina, India, Israel, Japan, Peru, the Netherlands, Iceland, El Salvador). Furthermore, where the terms do exist, they are very different and loosely defined (Heppner, Leong, & Gerstein, 2008; Savickas, 2007). The definition of counseling psychology adopted in the United States appears in Figure 1.1. This definition is quite specific, and it stresses an integration of science and practice guided by the importance of embracing culture, diversity, and human development to assist individuals and groups with a host of issues. This is the definition guiding the content in the chapters in Part I of this handbook, but it is not necessarily the one employed by authors of the chapters appearing in Part II of the book.

A very clear definition of counseling psychology can also be found in Hong Kong. According to Leung, Chan, and Leahy (2007), the Counseling Psychology Division of the Hong Kong Psychological Society has defined counseling psychology "as the application of psychological knowledge, psychotherapeutic skills and professional judgment to facilitate enhanced human functioning and quality of life" (p. 53). In China, in contrast, there is no highly specific definition of counseling psychology. It is simply viewed as psychological helping (Chang, Tong, Shi, & Zeng, 2005).

A precise and descriptive definition of counseling psychology, however, can be found in Canada. Citing the Colleges of Psychologists of Ontario, which is the body that licenses psychologists in Canada, Young and Nicol (2007) reported that counseling psychology "is the fostering and improving of normal human functioning by helping people solve problems, make decisions, and cope with stresses of everyday life" (p. 21). In South Africa, in comparison, the definition is not very specific (Savickas, 2007). Watson and Fouche (2007) claimed that counseling psychology has a positive and solution focus with an emphasis on health and well-being. The definition of counseling psychology in Australia is also broadly construed. Counseling psychology in this country involves helping persons and groups with acute, developmental, and normal challenges across the life span (Pryor & Bright, 2007).

As Savickas (2007) observed and we concur, regardless of the definition of counseling psychology or counseling psychologist employed throughout the world, it appears that most definitions appear to "share the root conception that counseling psychology concentrates on the daily life adjustment issues faced by reasonably well-adjusted people, particularly as they cope with career transitions and personal development" (pp. 183–184).

Defining Culture

There has been an even longer and more extensive debate in anthropology and cross-cultural psychology about the definition of *culture*. In anthropology, most scholars have been influenced, however, by Tyler's definition introduced in 1871. Tyler stated that culture is a "complex whole which includes knowledge, belief, art, morals, law, custom, and any other capabilities and habits acquired by man as a member of society" (Moore, 1997, p. 17). Therefore, culture is seen as a set of learned behaviors and ideas human beings acquire as members of a society or a specific group. Such behaviors and ideas, however, do not result from nature (biology) but from the socialization or enculturation process (Gerstein, Rountree, & Ordonez, 2007). Most anthropologists also claim that there are four basic components of a culture: (1) it is socially transmitted through enculturation; (2) knowledge (people share enough knowledge that they can behave in ways that are acceptable and meaningful to others, so that they do not constantly misunderstand one another); (3) there are shared behavioral regularities or patterns; and (4) there are shared collective experiences of a specific group (Gerstein et al., 2007).

Ho (1995) also discussed a definition of culture from an anthropological perspective. He indicated that culture can be conceptualized externally or internally. Ho argued that for counseling psychologists, the internalized culture acquired through enculturation is more relevant to practice. He defined internalized culture "as the cultural influences operating within the individual that shape (not determine) personality formation and various aspects of psychological functioning" (p. 5). Examples of internalized culture are gender, psychological maturity, and identification with a class. Furthermore, Ho reported that subjective culture as conceptualized by Triandis (1972) can be considered internalized culture with examples being worldview, cognitive map, and life space.

Cross-cultural psychologists have also introduced definitions of culture. Segall, Lonner, and Berry (1998), for example, claimed that historically, culture was conceptualized as something external to the individual, a shared approach to life by individuals interacting in a common group and through the processes of enculturation and socialization transmitted from generation to generation. Additionally, Segall et al. reported that in the late 1990s because

of the cognitive approaches, individuals were no longer seen as "pawns or victims of their cultures but as cognizers, appraisers, and interpreters of them" (p. 1104). Instead, culture was thought to emerge from transactions between persons and their environment.

In the counseling professions, a number of scholars have offered definitions of culture. For instance, Pedersen (1993) presented a broad definition of culture that is very different from the ones mentioned above. He stated that culture includes demographic (e.g., age, gender), status (e.g., social, economic), and ethnographic (e.g., ethnicity, nationality) variables along with affiliations (formal and informal). In contrast, Sue and Sue (2003) defined culture as "all those things that people have learned in their history to do, believe, value, and enjoy. It is the totality of ideals, beliefs, skills, tools, customs, and institutions into which each member of society is born" (p. 106). Finally, Ponterotto, Casas, Suzuki, and Alexander (1995) concluded that for most counseling scholars, culture is a learned system of meaning and behavior passed from one generation to the next.

Given the diversity in how culture has been defined by anthropologists, cross-cultural psychologists, and counseling professionals in the United States, there are many obvious conceptual, methodological, and applied challenges inherent to the practice and science of counseling within and outside the U.S. borders. These challenges can become even more magnified when engaging in cross-cultural counseling. For the purposes of Chapters 1 to 8, therefore, the definition of culture we subscribe to and the one guiding Chapters 2 through 8 can be found in Figure 1.1. This definition is drawn from the anthropology literature discussed at the beginning of this section. As such, it is based on the work of Tyler.

Defining Cultural Psychology

In general, though there is some inconsistency in the definition of *cultural psychology*, it can be defined as a field dedicated to enhancing an understanding of individuals within their cultural context by employing concepts that are meaningful within the particular culture of interest (Adamopoulos & Lonner, 2001). For the purposes of Chapters 1 to 8, we employ this definition (see Figure 1.1). Triandis (2000) claimed that cultural psychologists frequently investigate cultures other than their own, often relying on ethnographic methods tied to cultural anthropology. Studying the meaning of constructs (emic) in a culture is of greatest interest to cultural psychologists, and they refute the notion that culture and cultural variables are independent of the individual. Instead, they view culture as an integral, critical, and inseparable part of the human mind (Adamopoulos & Lonner, 2001). For further detailed discussion about cultural psychology, including methodological strategies employed, see Chapter 5.

Defining Indigenous Psychology

According to Kim (1990), *indigenous psychology* is psychological knowledge that emerges from the target culture rather than knowledge that comes directly or indirectly from another location. Although admittedly today, there are many ways that most cultures are affected by outside influences, the focus of indigenous psychology is on developing a knowledge base that evolves from this process constructed for the individuals in the specific culture (Kim, 1990); that is, "behavior as seen from people's own viewpoint" (Brislin, 1990, p. 28). This knowledge is acquired by scholars from the target culture (Adamopoulos & Lonner, 2001). The definition just mentioned is used consistently in the psychology literature and will be employed (see Figure 1.1) in the chapters in Part I. (For a more detailed discussion of indigenous psychology, see Chapter 5.) The main purpose of indigenous psychology is to establish a knowledge base that has meaning within a specific culture (e.g., Kim, Park, & Park, 2000). This approach embraces "insiders" (emic) as well as "outsiders" (etic) viewpoints, and it also advocates the use of both qualitative and quantitative methodologies (Kim, Yang, & Hwang, 2006).

There has been a dramatic increase in indigenous psychology worldwide (Allwood & Berry, 2006). In part, psychology can be considered quite new in

some parts of the world and reinvented (Pedersen, 2003; Yang, 1997; Yang, Hwang, Pedersen, & Daibo, 2003) or reinvigorated in other locations. Furthermore, in a number of regions of the world, the issue of the relevance of constructs and strategies to the culture is driving the development of indigenous forms of psychology (Sinha & Holtzman, 1984). Therefore, it is not surprising that indigenous psychology is developing mostly in non-Western countries (Allwood & Berry, 2006). According to Pedersen (2003), "Indigenous psychology is not a universal psychology but rather reminds us that psychological principles cannot be assumed to be universally similar" (p. 401).

Indigenous practices and models of counseling are critical, therefore, to the development of the counseling and counseling psychology professions worldwide (Leung, 2003), if in fact unique models and strategies that are culturally appropriate and effective are to be established and employed. As stated earlier, some authors (e.g., Leung, 2003) have claimed that theories and strategies of counseling psychology in the United States are indigenous to the U.S. cultures. Therefore, serious questions can be raised about the suitability of these theories and strategies to other cultures and countries. An indigenous paradigm of counseling, in contrast, would be much better suited to reflect and capture the unique cultural values, norms, and behaviors of each culture or country.

Defining Transcultural Psychology

Another term that is sometimes found in the psychology literature but more often found in the psychiatry and nursing literature is *transcultural psychology*. According to Hiles (1996), transcultural psychology is interested in making certain that psychological results and theories derived in one culture are applicable in other cultures rather than the naive transference of one culture to another without recognition of the specific context (see Figure 1.1). Transcultural application involves critically determining when to apply psychological concepts, findings, and practices across cultures.

Defining Multicultural Counseling

As will become clear in Chapter 2, the line between cross-cultural counseling and multicultural counseling has been and continues to be ambiguous. Some authors have used the two terms interchangeably as if they are equivalent. In fact, early on in the multicultural counseling literature, authors (e.g., LaFromboise & Foster, 1992; Sue, 1981; Vontress, 1979) used the term *cross-cultural counseling* and not multicultural counseling to describe the work of a mental health professional serving a client from a different culture, ethnicity, and/or country. Originally, even the multicultural counseling competencies were called *cross-cultural competencies* (see Sue, Arredono, & McDavis, 1992).

In this chapter, we will stress the point that multicultural counseling and cross-cultural counseling have many shared values and goals, yet they also differ in their foci and applications. Nonetheless, the two approaches complement each other and provide invaluable perspectives in counseling that serve to delineate culture-related issues within and beyond geographic and national boundaries.

In the 1970s and early 1980s, when the impact of culture and issues related to cultural bias were being discussed in the counseling literature, the term *cross-cultural counseling* was often used. Yet when the term *multicultural counseling* and *multiculturalism* started to gain attention, cross-cultural counseling was used less frequently. Indeed, into the 1990s, multicultural counseling had become the preferred term among many scholars. As suggested by Sue et al. (1998),

> Originally called "cross-cultural counseling/therapy," this usage has become progressively less popular and has been superseded by the term MCT (Multicultural Counseling and Therapy). Because it is inclusive, MCT may mean different things to different people (racial/ethnic minorities emphasis, sexual orientation emphasis, gender emphasis, and so on); thus it is very important for us to specify the particular populations we are referring. (p. 13)

The history of multicultural counseling is closely connected to the social and political development in the United States, such as the civil rights movement. The multicultural movement in counseling began in the 1960s and 1970s and challenged the cultural bias behind the Eurocentric counseling theories and practice. It also called attention to forces of racism, discrimination, and prejudice that had caused much injustice in the U.S. mental health delivery system as well as in the larger social and cultural system.

There are many definitions of multicultural counseling that, for the most part, share more similarities than differences. Jackson (1995) defined multicultural counseling as "counseling that takes place between or among individuals from different cultural backgrounds" (p. 3). Smith (2004) offered a broader definition and suggested that "multicultural counseling and psychology refers not merely to working with diverse populations, but to an approach that accounts for the influences of culture and power in any therapeutic relationship" (p. 4). The definition we embrace and the one guiding the chapters in Part I can be found in Figure 1.1. Basically, this definition takes into consideration the unique cultural background of mental health professionals and their clientele and the universality of their experiences and culture so that professionals can provide culturally effective, appropriate, and sensitive services. Recent formulations of multicultural competencies have underscored the importance of an advocacy and social justice perspective (Enns & Sinacore, 2005; Goodman et al., 2004; Toporek, Gerstein, Fouad, Roysircar-Sodowsky, & Israel, 2005; Vera & Speight, 2003). Accordingly, it has been suggested that multicultural counseling should include in its repertoire of interventions advocacy actions and personal empowerment that engage clients as coparticipants to confront oppressive forces in their environments and systems, including racism, discrimination, prejudice, and social injustice. Thus, in many ways, even the content of multicultural counseling is indigenous to the U.S. cultural context. Regardless of the definition, multicultural counseling is fully anchored on the ideals of multiculturalism that emphasizes the value of diversity and the moral obligation to treat individuals from diverse cultural groups with respect and dignity (e.g., Fowers & Richardson, 1996; Sue et al., 1998).

Multicultural counseling in an international context could take many forms and also address culture-specific issues. The literature on multicultural counseling has served as an important starting point for international scholars to expand or build new frameworks to focus on multicultural issues salient to their particular geographic areas. Multicultural counseling could also be synthesized with a cross-cultural perspective, where the concept of culture is studied more globally across national borders.

Defining Multicultural Psychology

In the *Encyclopedia of Multicultural Psychology* (Jackson, 2006), the term *multicultural psychology* appears to be defined as an umbrella field that encompasses a diverse group of subdisciplines (e.g., cross-cultural psychology, multicultural counseling, and race psychology) in psychology. Members of this field use research methodologies and training strategies to understand the role of culture in human behavior and to generate results to accomplish this task. Many different populations in and outside the United States are the focal point of investigation. According to Jackson, the main assumption of multicultural psychology is that to understand differences between people, it is best to study culture and not race.

The APA (2003) multicultural guidelines offer a very different perspective on multicultural psychology. These guidelines indicate that multicultural psychology focuses primarily on the influence of race, racism, ethnic culture, and/or xenophobia on psychological constructs (e.g., attitudes, psychological processes, behaviors). For the purpose of Chapters 1 to 8, we embrace (see Figure 1.1) the definition of multicultural psychology found in the APA guidelines.

Defining Cross-Cultural Psychology

A distinctive feature of cross-cultural counseling is its close alignment with the field of cross-cultural psychology. Cross-cultural psychology was defined by Berry, Poortinga, Segall, and Dasen (1992) as "the study of similarities and differences in individual psychological functioning in various cultural and ethnic groups; of the relationships between psychological variables and sociocultural, ecological, and biological variables; and of current changes in these variables" (p. 2). There are many definitions of cross-cultural psychology in the literature. In general, these definitions are inconsistent and tend to focus on different features. Lonner and Adamopoulos (1997) reviewed various definitions of cross-cultural psychology and identified the following themes: (a) It (cross-cultural psychology) is interested in understanding the nature and reasons behind human diversity and universals at the level of the individual; (b) it uses research methodologies that allow researchers to study in the widest range of cultural contexts and settings where human behavior occurs; (c) it assumes that culture is one of the critical factors contributing to individual differences in behavior; (d) it involves comparisons of behavior occurring in two or more cultural settings; and (e) its ultimate goal is the development of psychology that would become increasingly "universal" in its scope and application. Throughout Part I, we rely on a definition of cross-cultural psychology (see Figure 1.1) based on the writing of Adamopoulos and Lonner (2001). This definition takes into account the influence of culture on behavior toward the goal of establishing an inclusive universal psychology. Our definition also stresses comparative research rather than research performed in one country or with one culture.

Defining Cross-Cultural Counseling

The themes often linked with cross-cultural psychology have also become salient features of cross-cultural counseling. In fact, cross-cultural counseling derived its knowledge base from the rich research literature of cultural and cross-cultural psychology (Leung & Chen, in press; Leung & Hoshmand, 2007). Draguns (2007) argued that cross-cultural counseling is concerned with accurately understanding the culture-specific and universal aspects of human problems as well as the process of helping. Furthermore, Pedersen (2000) reported that in cross-cultural counseling, all behavior should be understood from the context of one's culture. Sue et al. (1992) and Lonner (1985) even claimed that all counseling is cross-cultural. What is inherent in this description is that mental health professionals need to cross the boundaries of culture or disentangle culture to reach the person or client.

Some writers (e.g., Pedersen, 1995) have indicated that cross-cultural counseling is concerned with cross-border cultural transitions, culture- and reverse-culture shocks, the process of acculturation, along with comparisons of individuals across national borders to facilitate accurate cultural understanding in counseling encounters. Another common description of cross-cultural counseling that can be extrapolated from the literature is that it is the science and practice (e.g., direct service, consultation, training, education, prevention) of counseling devoted to investigating and establishing the common and unique features of the culture-behavior interaction of persons residing in at least two different countries. Yet another description we extrapolated from the literature is that cross-cultural counseling is the investigation of the relevance and validity of specific theories, strategies, and research paradigms of counseling employed in a similar fashion in two or more countries through an in-depth examination of the cultural and epistemological underpinnings of each country. Cross-cultural counseling also aims at the development of a counseling profession that is relevant internationally (Leung, 2003; Savickas, 2007). In general, the phrase *cross-cultural counseling* has frequently been employed to capture the international and national application of counseling strategies across cultures (Pedersen, 2004; Pedersen, Draguns, Lonner, & Trimble, 2002).

Given the historic inconsistent use and definition of the term *cross-cultural counseling*, we offer a new definition of this phrase (see Figure 1.1) that frames the discussion found in the chapters in Part I. Our definition indicates that cross-cultural counseling incorporates universal and indigenous theories, strategies, and research paradigms of counseling and help seeking based on the cultural and epistemological assumptions of countries around the world.

Defining Cross-National Counseling

The term *cross-national counseling* has been used in the counseling literature by a few authors. At times, scholars have used the term to discuss collaboration between professionals across borders. Others have discussed conducting research on two or more nationalities as cross-national counseling. Until now, however, this term has not been defined. No doubt, the lack of an operational definition for cross-national counseling and the apparent use of this term to refer to various activities has contributed to potential confusion and misunderstanding among counseling professionals. To facilitate a clearer understanding of the use of this term in the chapters in Part I, we introduce a specific definition for cross-national counseling (see Figure 1.1). This definition assumes that cross-national counseling involves mental health professionals from at least two countries collaborating on some professional activity such as consultation or program development.

Defining Transnational

Finally, at times, the term *transnational* will be used in this handbook. This term originates in the feminist literature. We have offered a definition of transnational in Figure 1.1. In general, this term has been defined as the worldwide intersections of nationhood, race, ethnicity, gender, sexuality, and economic status with an emphasis on the elimination of global north/south hierarchies by embracing and valuing the multiplicity of cultures, languages, experiences, and voices (Mohanty, 2003).

OVERVIEW, RATIONALE, AND VISION OF BOOK

We have structured this handbook to provide a tool for understanding and potentially functioning effectively cross-culturally, cross-nationally, and in international settings. This handbook discusses a wide repertoire of research, theoretical, and professional issues and a broader perspective regarding the appropriate roles and activities of mental health professionals around the world. It also addresses numerous issues affecting diverse populations and the relevant place that counseling and psychology has globally. In many chapters, our authors critically discuss the relevance and validity of adopting U.S. counseling theories and approaches in other countries. As such, the appropriateness of cultural assumptions and strategies derived in the United States are analyzed, critiqued, and questioned. Ultimately, we hope that this handbook will contribute, in part, to helping counselors, psychologists, and other mental health professionals throughout the world become more effective when performing international, cross-national, and cross-cultural work.

There are three sections of this handbook. Part I includes eight chapters, each with a different focus and each coauthored by at least one of the book coeditors and other scholars. These chapters are quite unique in that they provide a systematic and comprehensive discussion and analyses about various conceptual, methodological, professional, and practice issues connected to the pursuit of international activities. Topics covered in this section are, for instance, the similarities and differences of multicultural and cross-cultural psychology and counseling; the status of the counseling profession in and outside the United States; U.S. counseling models exported worldwide; methodological issues when studying culture; the internationalization of the counseling profession; and benefits, challenges, and outcomes of collaboration among counseling professionals across borders.

The chapters in Part II of this handbook describe some aspect of counseling across nine regions of the world, including East Asia (Japan, Taiwan, South Korea, and China), Southeast Asia (Singapore and Malaysia), South Asia (Pakistan and India), Central Asia (Kyrgyzstan), Europe (Italy, Great Britain, Ireland, Iceland, Sweden, France, the former USSR, and Greece), the Middle East (Israel, United Arab Emirates, and Turkey), the Americas and the Caribbean (Canada, Colombia, Venezuela, Argentina, Ecuador, and Puerto Rico), South and West Africa (South Africa and Nigeria), and Oceania (Australia). Mental health scholars from around the globe were invited to

contribute chapters to this section. They were selected because each of them was considered an expert and familiar with the counseling/psychology profession in his or her region.

These experts were given a number of possible topics (e.g., background about the country, relevant cultural assumptions, use of counseling services, indigenous models of psychology and counseling, use of Western models of counseling and psychology) to focus their chapter. We expected these authors to discuss the cultural and epistemological assumptions framing the counseling profession and how help seeking was perceived and practiced in their country regardless of how they chose to organize their chapter. As the coeditors, we were each responsible for working closely with contributors from various regions of the world to provide feedback and to enhance continuity in the subject matter addressed throughout the book.

As will become evident when reading this handbook, these chapters do differ greatly in their coverage of the topics provided to the contributors. The chapters are consistent, however, in providing a cultural context for understanding the counseling profession in each country and to a large extent the nature and function of mental health help seeking. Furthermore, many of these chapters explore the epistemological assumptions that frame the counseling professions in the targeted culture and/or country. As such, these chapters discuss the salient norms, values, attitudes, and behaviors underlying a particular culture and/or country, and in specific, how these constructs are related to various aspects of counseling, including help seeking. More specifically, to varying degrees, these chapters highlight the role of religion, spirituality, the family, ethnicity, sexual mores, political philosophy and structure, economics, employment, and linguistics in this regard. As the role of culture within counseling in various countries around the globe is underscored in each chapter of this section of the book, we believe readers will become more aware and knowledgeable about a broad array of unique international issues in counseling. They will also develop a stronger motivation and skill set to engage in international work.

Part III of the book contains a conclusion chapter. In this chapter, the editors of the book discuss a number of topics, including themes throughout the book; ethical issues tied to international work; implications of the content presented in this handbook for the counseling profession in the United States and elsewhere; future directions for international work (e.g., theory, research, training, and practice); recommendations concerning cross-cultural counseling competencies; how to integrate international issues into the counseling training program; and strengths, challenges, and opportunities of international collaboration.

We are hopeful that this handbook will make a very unique contribution to the scholarly literature in psychology and counseling. This handbook is intended for counseling graduate programs, students, practitioners, educators, researchers, program planners, policymakers, trainers, consultants, and administrators worldwide. We believe that this handbook could be used as a core resource for graduate students, purchased at the beginning of their program and used throughout their graduate training. This handbook also may be used as a supplementary text for graduate-level courses, such as multicultural counseling, diversity counseling, introduction to counseling, research design, professional issues seminars, practica, and cross-cultural psychology. In programs that do have an international or cross-cultural counseling class, this handbook could serve as the primary text.

In addition, we think that this handbook may be used as a resource and inspiration for counselors, psychologists, and other mental health professionals around the world who are interested in various aspects of international, cross-national, and cross-cultural work. For instance, professionals and educators in fields related to counseling, such as cross-cultural psychology, social work, clinical psychology, education, psychiatry, psychological anthropology, and psychiatric nursing, may find this handbook to be an important resource as well.

CONCLUSION

There is a great need to recognize and embrace the different forms of counseling around the world.

Through this handbook, we hope that readers will acquire a deeper understanding and respect for the cultural assumptions guiding counseling and help-seeking behaviors in a host of countries. We also trust that readers will develop an appreciation and admiration for indigenous models and intervention strategies employed in many different countries.

Examining the cultural values and practices of persons in diverse countries can lead to not only a better understanding of such countries but also a richer perspective about one's own culture and various approaches to counseling not often reported in the scholarly literature (e.g., Cheung, 2000; Pedersen & Leong, 1997). This in turn can lead to a further development and refinement of counseling models and strategies in the United States and elsewhere. It can also contribute to a comprehensive base of psychological knowledge about human behavior that is critical to effectively engage in counseling around the globe (Heppner, 2006; Heppner, Leong, & Chiao, 2008; Heppner, Leong, & Gerstein, 2008). More important, through exposure to the indigenous and shared models of counseling reported in this handbook, there is the potential of successfully confronting the challenge of cultural encapsulation (Wrenn, 1962), since increased awareness can result in the identification of our own biases and the discovery of new frameworks (Pedersen & Leong, 1997), worldviews, and approaches toward others.

As stated early on in this chapter, the European countries dominated psychology in the late 19th century with U.S. psychology following suit in the post–World War II years. It appears, however, that there is a major shift occurring in psychology with a more equally balanced arsenal of power shared by the psychology professions throughout the world (Cole, 2006). For U.S. psychologists, as they learn about psychology elsewhere, they will be more equipped to comprehend the limits of the science, practice, and professional development attributes of psychology in the States, and in so doing, they will be better prepared to assist persons in the United States (Mays, Rubin, Sabourin, & Walker, 1996) and in other countries.

Though we appear to be in a renaissance period of counseling around the world with counseling professionals outside the United States closely scrutinizing their practices and theories, and U.S. professionals questioning the cross-cultural validity and applicability of their strategies and methodologies, it remains to be seen if a strong and truly indigenous global counseling movement can be maintained and strengthened. The chapters in this handbook attest to the importance of becoming much more cognizant and supportive of this movement and the strength, creativity, talents, and determination of counseling professionals worldwide to make certain that the movement is successful. Ultimately, the success of a dynamic indigenous, cross-cultural, and cross-national counseling movement can greatly enhance our conceptual understanding of common and unique aspects of behavior and enrich the strategies we employ in our counseling, research, and training. At the same time, such a movement will affirm some of the core principles and philosophies of counseling endorsed throughout the world: that is, understanding, respecting, and embracing cultural values, norms, and behaviors regardless of person, ethnicity, nationality, or country. The science and practice of counseling worldwide can only benefit from such an outcome, as can the citizens of this planet.

REFERENCES

Abi-Hashem, N. (1997). Reflections on international perspectives in psychology. *American Psychologist, 52,* 569–573.

Adamopoulos, J., & Lonner, W. J. (2001). Culture and psychology at a crossroad: Historical perspective and theoretical analysis. In D. Matsumoto (Ed.), *Handbook of culture and psychology* (pp. 11–34). New York: Oxford University Press.

Allwood, C. M., & Berry, J. W. (2006). Origins and development of indigenous psychologies: An international analysis. *International Journal of Psychology, 41,* 243–268.

American Psychological Association. (2003). Guidelines on multicultural education, training, research, practice, and organizational change for psychologists. *American Psychologist, 58,* 377–402.

Ardila, R. (1982). International psychology. *American Psychologist, 37,* 323–329.

Ardila, R. (1993). Latin American psychology and world psychology: Is integration possible? In U. Kim & J. Berry (Eds.), *Indigenous psychologies: Research and experience in cultural context* (pp. 170–176). Newbury Park, CA: Sage.

Arnett, J. J. (2002). The psychology of globalization. *American Psychologist, 57,* 774–783.

Arnett, J. J. (2008). The neglected 95%: Why American psychology needs to become less American. *American Psychologist, 63,* 602–614.

Berlyne, D. E. (1968). American and European psychology. *American Psychologist, 23,* 447–452.

Berry, J. W., Poortinga, Y. H., Segall, M. H., & Dasen, E. R. (1992). *Cross-cultural psychology: Research and applications.* Cambridge, UK: Cambridge University Press.

Bochner, S. (1999). Cultural diversity within and between societies: Implications for multicultural social systems. In P. B. Pedersen (Ed.), *Multiculturalism as a fourth force* (pp. 19–60). Washington, DC: Taylor & Francis.

Bohm, D. (1980). *Wholeness and the implicate order.* London: Routledge.

Bozarth, J. D. (1985). Quantum theory and the person-centered approach. *Journal of Counseling and Development, 64,* 179–182.

Brandt, L. (1970). American psychology. *American Psychologist, 25,* 1091–1093.

Brehm, S. S. (2008). Looking ahead: The future of psychology and APA. *American Psychologist, 63,* 337–344.

Brislin, R. W. (1990). Applied cross-cultural psychology: An introduction. In R. W. Bristin (Ed.), *Applied cross-cultural psychology* (pp. 9–33). Newbury Park, CA: Sage.

Brown, L. S. (1997). The private practice of subversion: Psychology as tikkun olam. *American Psychologist, 52,* 449–462.

Chang, D. F., Tong, H., Shi, Q., & Zeng, Q. (2005). Letting a hundred flowers bloom: Counseling and psychotherapy in the People's Republic of China. *Journal of Mental Health Counseling, 27,* 104–116.

Chatterjee, P. (2005). Mental health care for India's tsunami survivors. *Lancet, 365,* 833–834.

Chen, P. H. (1999). Towards professionalism: The development of counseling in Taiwan. *Asian Journal of Counseling, 6,* 21–48.

Cheung, F. M. (2000). Deconstructing counseling in a cultural context. *The Counseling Psychologist, 28,* 123–132.

Cole, M. (1977). About this special issue. *American Psychologist, 32,* 903–904.

Cole, M. (2006). Internationalism in psychology: We need it now more than ever. *American Psychologist, 61,* 904–917.

David, H. P. (1960). Reciprocal influences in international psychology: A summary report of the 1959 APA Symposium. *American Psychologist, 15,* 313–315.

David, H. P., & Swartley, W. M. (1961). Toward more effective international communication in psychology. *American Psychologist, 16,* 696–698.

Denmark, F. L. (1998). Women and psychology: An international perspective. *American Psychologist, 53,* 465–473.

Douce, L. A. (2004). Globalization of counseling psychology. *The Counseling Psychologist, 32,* 142–152.

Draguns, J. G. (2001). Toward a truly international psychology: Beyond English only. *American Psychologist, 56,* 1019–1030.

Draguns, J. G. (2007). Universal and cultural threads in counseling individuals. In P. B. Pedersen, J. G. Draguns, W. J. Lonner, & J. E. Trimble (Eds.), *Counseling across cultures* (6th ed, pp. 21–36). Thousand Oaks, CA: Sage.

Enns, C. Z., & Sinacore, A. L. (Eds.). (2005). *Teaching and social justice: Integrating multicultural and feminist theories in the classroom.* Washington, DC: American Psychological Association.

European Congress of Psychology. (n.d.). *The 11th European Congress of Psychology.* Retrieved February 19, 2009, from http://www.ecp2009.no/

European Federation of Psychologists' Associations. (2007). *Activity plan 2007–2009 of the executive council of EFPA to the general assembly.* Prague, Czech Republic: Author.

Evans, R. B., & Scott, F. J. D. (1978). The 1913 International Congress of Psychology: The American Congress that wasn't. *American Psychologist, 33,* 711–723.

Fleishman, E. A. (1999). Applied psychology: An international journey. *American Psychologist, 54,* 1008–1016.

Forrest, L. (2008). *Reflections on the international counseling psychology conference.* American Psychological Association Society of Counseling Psychology Newsletter, *Spring,* 1, 7, 8.

Fouad, N. A., McPherson, R. H., Gerstein, L., Blustein, D. L., Elman, N., Helledy, K. I., et al. (2004). Houston, 2001: Context and legacy. *The Counseling Psychologist, 32,* 15–77.

Fowers, B. J., & Richardson, F. C. (1996). Why is multiculturalism good? *American Psychologist, 51,* 609–621.

Fretz, B. R. (1999). Polishing a pearl and a diamond. *The Counseling Psychologist, 27,* 32–46.

Friedman, T. L. (2000). *The Lexus and the olive tree: Understanding globalization.* New York: Anchor.

Friedman, T. L. (2005). *The world is flat: A brief history of the twenty-first century.* New York: Farrar, Straus & Giroux.

Gerstein, L. H. (2006). Counseling psychologists as international social architects. In R. L. Toporek, L. H. Gerstein, N. A. Fouad, G. Roysircar-Sodowsky, & T. Israel (Eds.), *Handbook for social justice in counseling psychology: Leadership, vision, and action* (pp. 377–387). Thousand Oaks, CA: Sage.

Gerstein, L. H., & Bennett, M. (1999). Quantum physics and mental health counseling: The time is . . . ! *Journal of Mental Health Counseling, 21,* 255–269.

Gerstein, L. H., Rountree, C., & Ordonez, M. A. (2007). An anthropological perspective on multicultural counselling. *Counselling Psychology Quarterly, 20,* 375–400.

Gerstein, L. H., & Ægisdóttir, S. (Guest Eds.). (2005a). Counseling around the world [Special issue]. *Journal of Mental Health Counseling, 27,* 95–184.

Gerstein, L. H., & Ægisdóttir, S. (Guest Eds.). (2005b). Counseling outside of the United States: Looking in and reaching out [Special section]. *Journal of Mental Health Counseling, 27,* 221–281.

Gerstein, L. H., & Ægisdóttir, S. (2005c). A trip around the world: A counseling travelogue! *Journal of Mental Health Counseling, 27,* 95–103.

Gerstein, L. H., & Ægisdóttir, S. (2007). Training international social change agents: Transcending a U.S. counseling paradigm. *Counselor Education and Supervision, 47,* 123–139.

Goodman, L. A., Liang, B., Helms, J. E., Latta, R. E., Sparks, E., & Weintraub, S. R. (2004). Training counseling psychologists as social justice agents: Feminist and multicultural principles in action. *The Counseling Psychologist, 32,* 793–837.

Harper, F. D. (2000). Challenges to counseling professionals for the new Millennium [Editorial]. *International Journal for the Advancement of Counselling, 22,* 1–7.

Heppner, P. P. (1997). Building on Strengths as we move into the next millennium. *The Counseling Psychologist, 25,* 5–14.

Heppner, P. P. (2006). The benefits and challenges of becoming cross-culturally competent counseling psychologists: Presidential address. *The Counseling Psychologist, 34,* 147–172.

Heppner, P. P., Casas, J. M., Carter, J., & Stone, G. L. (2000). The maturation of counseling psychology: Multifaceted perspectives from 1978–1998. In S. D. Brown & R. W. Lent (Eds.), *Handbook of counseling psychology* (3rd ed., pp. 3–49). New York: Wiley.

Heppner, P. P., & Gerstein, L. H. (2008). International developments in counseling psychology. In E. Altmaier & B. D. Johnson (Eds.), *Encyclopedia of counseling: Changes and challenges for counseling in the 21st century* (Vol. 1, pp. 260–266). Thousand Oaks, CA: Sage.

Heppner, P. P., Leong, F. T. L., & Chiao, H. (2008). A growing internationalization of counseling psychology. In S. D. Brown & R. W. Lent (Eds.), *Handbook of counseling psychology* (4th ed., pp. 68–85). Hoboken, NJ: Wiley.

Heppner, P. P., Leong, F. T. L., & Gerstein, L. H. (2008). Counseling within a changing world: Meeting the psychological needs of societies and the world. In W. B. Walsh (Ed.), *Biennial review in counseling psychology* (pp. 231–258). Thousand Oaks, CA: Sage.

Hiles, D. (1996). *Cultural psychology and the centre-ground of psychology.* Paper presented at the XXVI International Congress of Psychology, August 16–21, Montreal, Quebec, Canada.

Ho, D. Y. F. (1995). Internalized culture, culturocentrism, and transcendence. *The Counseling Psychologist, 23,* 4–24.

Hunter, W. S., Miles, W. R., Yerkes, R. M., & Langfeld, H. S. (1946). Committee on international planning. *American Psychologist, 1,* 123–124.

International Federation of Red Cross and Red Crescent Societies. (2008, June). *China: Sichuan earthquake.* Retrieved February 25, 2009, from http://www.ifrc .org/docs/appeals/08/MDRCN00309.pdf

Jaafar, J. L. S. (n.d.). *The second convention of the Asian Psychological Association: A message from the president elect of the 2nd convention.* Retrieved February 19, 2009, from http://umweb.um.edu.my/apsya/

Jackson, M. L. (1995). Multicultural counseling: Historical perspectives. In J. G. Ponterotto, J. M. Casas, L. A. Suzuki, & C. M. Alexander (Eds.), *Handbook of multicultural counseling* (pp. 3–16). Thousand Oaks, CA: Sage.

Jackson, Y. (Ed.). (2006). *Encyclopedia of multicultural psychology.* Thousand Oaks, CA: Sage.

Kelman, H. C., & Hollander, E. P. (1964). International cooperation in psychological research. *American Psychologist, 19,* 779–782.

Kennedy, S., Scheirer, J., & Rogers, A. (1984). The price of success: Our monocultural science. *American Psychologist, 39,* 996–997.

Kim, U. (1990). Indigenous psychology: Science and applications. In R. W. Bristin (Ed.), *Applied cross-cultural psychology* (pp. 142–160). Thousand Oaks, CA: Sage.

Kim, U., Park, Y. S., & Park, D. H. (2000). The challenge of cross-cultural psychology: The role of indigenous psychologies. *Journal of Cross-Cultural Psychology, 31,* 63–75.

Kim, U., Yang, K. S., & Hwang, K. K. (2006). *Indigenous and cultural psychology: Understanding people in context.* New York: Springer.

Kwan, K. L. K., & Gerstein, L. H. (2008). Envisioning a counseling psychology of the world: The mission of the international forum. *The Counseling Psychologist, 36,* 182–187.

LaFromboise, T. D., & Foster, S. L. (1992). Cross-cultural training: Scientist-practitioner model and methods. *The Counseling Psychologist, 20,* 472–489.

Lee, C. C. (1997). The global future of professional counseling: Collaboration for social change. *International Journal of Intercultural Relations, 21,* 279–285.

Leong, F. T. L., & Blustein, D. L. (2000). Toward a global vision of counseling psychology. *The Counseling Psychologist, 28,* 5–9.

Leong, F. T. L., & Leach, M. M. (2007). Internalizing counseling psychology in the United States: A SWOT analysis. *Applied Psychology: An International Review, 56,* 165–181.

Leong, F. T. L., & Ponterotto, J. G. (2003). A proposal for internationalizing counseling psychology in the United States: Rationale, recommendations and challenges. *The Counseling Psychologist, 31,* 381–395.

Leung, S. A. (2003). A journey worth traveling: Globalization of counseling psychology. *The Counseling Psychologist, 31,* 412–419.

Leung, S. A. (2008, July). *Indigenization and internationalization in counseling: Contradiction or complementation.* Keynote address delivered at the Inaugural Asia Pacific Rim International Counseling Conference, Hong Kong.

Leung, S. A., Chan, C. C., & Leahy, T. (2007). Counseling psychology in Hong Kong: A germinating discipline. *Applied Psychology: An International Review, 56*(1), 51–68.

Leung, S. A., & Chen, P.-W. (in press). Developing counseling psychology in Chinese communities in Asia: Indigenous, multicultural, and cross-cultural considerations. *The Counseling Psychologist.*

Leung, S. A., & Hoshmand, L. T. (2007). Internationalization and international publishing: Broadening the impact of scholarly work in counseling. *Asian Journal of Counselling, 14,* 141–154.

Lonner, W. J. (1985). Issues in testing and assessment in cross-cultural counseling. *The Counseling Psychologist, 13,* 599–614.

Lonner, W. J., & Adamopoulos, J. (1997). Culture as antecedent to behavior. In J. W. Berry, Y. H. Poortinga, & J. Pandey (Eds.), *Handbook of cross-cultural psychology: Theory and method* (Vol. 1, pp. 43–83). Boston: Allyn & Bacon.

Lucas, C. (1985). Out at the edge: Notes on a paradigm shift. *Journal of Counseling and Development, 64,* 165–172.

Marsella, A. J. (1998). Toward a "global-community psychology": Meeting the needs of a changing world. *American Psychologist, 53,* 1282–1291.

Mays, V. M., Rubin, J., Sabourin, M., & Walker, L. (1996). Moving toward a global psychology: Changing theories and practice to meet the needs of a changing world. *American Psychologist, 51,* 485–487.

McWhirter, J. J. (1988a). Counseling psychology and the Fulbright Program: The Australian connection. *The Counseling Psychologist, 16,* 303–306.

McWhirter, J. J. (1988b). The Fulbright Program in counseling psychology. *The Counseling Psychologist, 16,* 279–281.

McWhirter, J. J. (1988c). Implications of the Fulbright Senior Scholar Program for counseling psychology. *The Counseling Psychologist, 16,* 307–310.

McWhirter, J. J. (2000). And now, up go the walls: Constructing an international room for counseling psychology. *The Counseling Psychologist, 28,* 117–122.

McWhirter, P. T., & McWhirter, J. J. (2009). *Historical antecedents: Counseling psychology and the Fulbright Program.* Unpublished manuscript.

Miller, G. (2005). The tsunami's psychological aftermath. *Science, 309,* 1030–1033.

Moghaddam, F. M. (1987). Psychology in the three worlds: As reflected by the crisis in social psychology and the move toward indigenous third-world psychology. *American Psychologist, 42,* 912–920.

Mohanty, C. T. (2003). *Feminism without borders: Decolonizing theory, practicing solidarity.* Durham, NC: Duke University Press.

Moore, J. D. (1997). *Visions of culture.* Thousand Oaks, CA: Sage.

Norsworthy, K. L. (2006). Bringing social justice to international practices of counseling psychology. In R. L. Toporek, L. H. Gerstein, N. A. Fouad, G. Roysircar-Sodowsky, & T. Israel (Eds.), *Handbook for social justice in counseling psychology: Leadership, vision, and action* (pp. 421–441). Thousand Oaks, CA: Sage.

Norsworthy, K. L., & Gerstein, L. (2003). Counseling and building communities of peace: The interconnections. *International Journal for the Advancement of Counseling, 25*(4), 197–203.

Nutt, R. L. (2007). Implications of globalization for training in counseling psychology: Presidential address. *The Counseling Psychologist, 35,* 157–171.

Pawlik, K. (1992). Psychologie international: Aufgaben und Chancen [International psychology: Tasks and chances]. *Psychologie in Osterreich, 12,* 84–87.

Pawlik, K., & d'Ydewalle, G. (1996). Psychology and the global commons: Perspectives of international psychology. *American Psychologist, 51,* 488–495.

Pedersen, P. (1993). The multicultural dilemma of white cross-cultural researchers. *The Counseling Psychologist, 21,* 229–232.

Pedersen, P. (1995). *The five stages of culture shock: Critical incidents around the world.* Westport, CT: Greenwood Press.

Pedersen, P., Draguns, J., Lonner, W., & Trimble, J. (2002). *Counseling across cultures* (5th ed.). Thousand Oaks, CA: Sage.

Pedersen, P. B. (1991). Multiculturalism as a generic approach to counseling. *Journal of Counseling and Development, 70,* 6–12.

Pedersen, P. B. (2000). Cross-cultural counseling. In A. E. Kazdin (Ed.), *Encyclopedia of psychology* (Vol. 2, pp. 359–361). Washington, DC: American Psychological Association.

Pedersen, P. B. (2003). Culturally biased assumptions in counseling psychology. *The Counseling Psychologist, 31,* 396–403.

Pedersen, P. B. (2004). Cross-cultural counseling. In W. E. Craighead & C. B. Nemeroff (Eds.), *The concise Corsini encyclopedia of psychology and behavioral science* (3rd ed., pp. 236–237). Hoboken, NJ: Wiley.

Pedersen, P. B., & Leong, F. (1997). Counseling in an international context. *The Counseling Psychologist, 25,* 117–122.

Peoples, J., & Bailey, G. (1994). *Humanity: An introduction to cultural anthropology* (3rd ed.). Minneapolis, MN: West.

Ponterotto, J. G., Casas, J. M., Suzuki L. A., & Alexander C. M. (Eds.). (1995). *Handbook of multicultural counseling.* Thousand Oaks, CA: Sage.

Pryor, R. G. L., & Bright, J. E. H. (2007). The current state and future direction of counseling psychology in Australia. *Applied Psychology: An International Review, 56*(1), 7–19.

Ritchie, P. L. J. (2008). Annual report of the International Union of Psychological Science (IUPsyS). *International Journal of Psychology, 43,* 929–935.

Rosenzweig, M. R. (1982). Trends in development and status of psychology: An international perspective. *International Journal of Psychology, 17,* 117–140.

Rosenzweig, M. R. (1984). U.S. psychology and world psychology. *American Psychologist, 39,* 877–884.

Rosenzweig, M. R. (1992). Psychological science around the world. *American Psychologist, 47,* 718–722.

Rosenzweig, M. R. (1999). Continuity and change in the development of psychology around the world. *American Psychologist, 54,* 252–259.

Russell, R. W. (1984). Psychology in its world context. *American Psychologist, 39,* 1017–1025.

Sato, T. (1998). Agency and communion: The relationship between therapy and culture. *Cultural Diversity and Mental Health, 4,* 278–290.

Savickas, M. L. (2007). Internationalisation of counseling psychology: Constructing cross-national consensus and collaboration. *Applied Psychology: An International Review, 56*(1), 182–188.

Schultz, E. A., & Lavenda, R. H. (2001). *Cultural anthropology: A perspective on the human condition.* London: Mayfield.

Segall, M. H., Lonner, W. J., & Berry, J. W. (1998). Cross-cultural psychology as a scholarly discipline: On a flowering of culture in behavioral research. *American Psychologist, 53,* 1101–1110.

Sexton, V. S., & Misiak, H. (1984). American psychologists and psychology abroad. *American Psychologist, 39,* 1026–1031.

Sinha, D., & Holtzman, W. H. (Eds.). (1984). The impact of psychology on Third World development [Special issue]. *International Journal of Psychology, 19,* 3–192.

Skovholt, T., Hansen, S., Goh, M., Romano, J., & Thomas, K. (2005). The Minnesota International Counseling Institute (MICI) 1989–Present: History, joyful moments, and lessons learned. *International Journal for the Advancement of Counselling, 27,* 17–33.

Smith, R. J. (1983). On Ardila's "International Psychology." *American Psychologist, 38,* 122–123.

Smith, T. B. (2004). *Practicing multiculturalism: Affirming diversity in counseling and psychology.* Boston: Allyn & Bacon.

Sue, D. W. (1981). Critical incidents in cross-cultural counseling. In D. W. Sue (Ed.), *Counseling the culturally different* (pp. 259–291). New York: Wiley.

Sue, D. W., Arredono, P., & McDavis, R. J. (1992). Multicultural counseling competencies and standards: A call to the profession. *Journal of Multicultural Counseling and Development, 20,* 64–89.

Sue, D. W., Carter, R. T., Casas, J. M., Fouad, N. A., Ivey, A. E., Jensen, M., et al. (1998). *Multicultural counseling competencies: Individual and organizational development.* Thousand Oaks, CA: Sage.

Sue, D. W., & Sue, D. (2003). *Counseling the culturally diverse: Theory and practice.* New York: Wiley.

Sue, D. W., & Torino, G. C. (1994). Racial-cultural competence: Awareness, knowledge, and skills. In R. T. Carter (Ed.), *Handbook of racial-cultural psychology and counseling: Vol. 2. Training and practice* (pp. 3–18), New York: Wiley.

Takooshian, H. (2003). Counseling psychology's wide new horizons. *The Counseling Psychologist, 31,* 420–426.

Tanaka-Matsumi, J. (2004). Japanese forms of psychotherapy: Naikan therapy and Morita therapy. In U. P. Gielen, J. M. Fish, & J. G. Draguns (Eds.), *Handbook of culture, therapy, and healing* (pp. 277–292). Mahwah, NJ: Lawrence Erlbaum.

Toporek, R. L., Gerstein, L. H., Fouad, N. A., Roysircar-Sodowsky, G., & Israel, T. (Eds.). (2006). *Handbook for social justice in counseling psychology: Leadership, vision, and action.* Thousand Oaks, CA: Sage.

Triandis, H. C. (1972). *The analysis of subjective culture.* New York: Wiley.

Triandis, H. C. (2000). Dialectics between cultural and cross-cultural psychology. *Asian Journal of Social Psychology, 3,* 185–195.

Trimble, J. E. (2001). A quest for discovering ethno-cultural themes in psychology. In J. G. Ponterotto, J. M. Casas, L. A. Suzuki, & C. M. Alexander (Eds.), *Handbook of multicultural counseling* (2nd ed., pp. 3–13). Thousand Oaks, CA: Sage.

United Nations Children's Fund. (2008, November). *Six month report: China earthquake emergency.* Retrieved February 25, 2009, from http://www.unicef.org.hk/sichuan/6monthsrpt_e.pdf

United Nations Economic and Social Survey of Asia and the Pacific. (1999). *Part two: Asia and the Pacific into the twenty-first century.* Bangkok, Thailand: Poverty and Development Division.

United Nations Population Division. (2007). *World population prospects: The 2006 revision.* New York: United Nations.

Vera, E. M., & Speight, S. L. (2003). Multicultural competence, social justice, and counseling psychology: Expanding our roles. *The Counseling Psychologist, 31,* 253–272.

Vontress, C. E. (1979). Cross-cultural counseling: An existential approach. *Personnel and Guidance Journal, 58,* 117–122.

Watkins, C. E., Jr., Lopez, F. G., Campbell, V. L., & Lew, D. E. (1986). Facilitating the involvement of Division 17 members living outside the United States. *The Counseling Psychologist, 14,* 592–593.

Watson, M. B., & Fouche, P. (2007). Transforming a past into a future: Counseling psychology in South Africa.

Applied Psychology: An International Review, 56(1), 152–164.

Wheatley, M. J. (2006). *Leadership and the new science: Discovering order in a chaotic world* (3rd ed.). San Francisco: Berrett Koehler.

Wrenn, C. G. (1962). The culturally encapsulated counselor. *Harvard Educational Review, 32,* 111–119.

Yang, K. S. (1997). Indigenising Westernized Chinese psychology. In M. H. Bond (Ed.), *Working at the interface of cultures: Eighteen lies in social science* (pp. 62–76). New York: Routledge.

Yang, K. S., Hwang, K. K., Pedersen, P. B., & Daibo, I. (Eds.). (2003). *Progress in Asian social psychology: Conceptual and empirical contributions.* Westport, CT: Praeger.

Young, R. A., & Nicol, J. J. (2007). Counselling psychology in Canada: Advancing psychology for all. *Applied Psychology: An International Review, 56*(1), 20–32.

Ægisdóttir, S., & Gerstein, L. H. (2005). Reaching out: Mental health delivery outside the box. *Journal of Mental Health Counseling, 27,* 221–224.

Ægisdóttir, S., & Gerstein, L. H. (in press). International counseling competencies: A new frontier in multicultural training. In J. C. Ponterotto, J. M. Casas, L. A. Suzuki, & C. A. Alexander (Eds.), *Handbook of multicultural counseling* (3rd ed.). Thousand Oaks, CA: Sage.

Ægisdóttir, S., Gerstein, L. H., & Çinarbaş, D. C. (2008). Methodological issues in cross-cultural counseling research: Equivalence, bias, and translations. *The Counseling Psychologist, 36,* 188–219.

2

The Intersection of Multicultural and Cross-National Movements in the United States

A Complementary Role to Promote Culturally Sensitive Research, Training, and Practice

P. PAUL HEPPNER, STEFANÍA ÆGISDÓTTIR,
SEUNG-MING ALVIN LEUNG,
CHANGMING DUAN, JANET E. HELMS,
LAWRENCE H. GERSTEIN, AND PAUL B. PEDERSEN

This chapter focuses on the multicultural movement as well as the cross-national movement in the U.S. counseling profession. As will become clearer in the pages to follow, the term *cross-national movement*, as compared with *cross-cultural movement*, in our opinion, more accurately characterizes the internationalization of the counseling profession in the United States. It is not uncommon for graduate students and professionals in counseling and counseling psychology to be confused about the similarities and differences between "multicultural," "cross-cultural," and "cross-national" issues. Are they one and the same? Or do they coexist side by side? Are they rivals? As discussed in Chapter 1 (this volume), these are often confusing questions, in part because of the changing definitions as well as the introduction of new terms over time.

Unfortunately, the multicultural and cross-national movements in counseling, and the larger discipline of psychology, have not enjoyed a consensus of the meaning of its labels (Olson, Evans, & Shoenberg, 2007).

The purpose of this chapter is threefold. First, the chapter aims to promote greater understanding of the differences and similarities of the U.S. multicultural and cross-national movements. The history and evolution of these movements will be very briefly sketched, including associated foci, goals, and competencies. Briefly, the U.S. multicultural movement refers to the evolution of thought related to understanding the cultural context within all aspects of the U.S. counseling profession (research, practice, and training). The cross-national movement in the U.S. counseling profession refers to the evolution of thought about culturally sensitive collaboration about all aspects of the counseling profession among counseling professionals across countries. Although we present these movements separately, it is important to understand that they are not in reality separate movements but rather that the lines are blurred and a Venn diagram of scholars associated with each movement would overlap significantly. Second, the chapter will discuss the historical and current uneasy tensions that sometimes exist between the U.S. multicultural and cross-national movements in the U.S. counseling profession. These tensions are a function of many events, including the histories of these movements, the motivations of scholars for joining these movements, shifting resources, the shrinking of time and space, especially in the last decade, and the ever-changing evolution of terms and worldviews of leaders involved in these movements. It is very important to address these tensions and to be clear that in our view it is neither desirable nor possible for one movement to replace the other.

The third purpose of this chapter is to propose a complementary role between the multicultural and cross-national foci in promoting culturally sensitive research and applied interventions in the U.S. counseling professions. We suggest that each movement has the same long-term goal of increasing cultural awareness and sensitivity to create more applicable research and promote more effective counseling practices in the counseling profession around the world.

THE U.S. MULTICULTURAL MOVEMENT IN COUNSELING

The past few decades have witnessed a multicultural movement in the United States that has, in many ways, revolutionized the entire specialty of counseling in the country. From being literally nonexistent some 40 years ago, multicultural counseling and psychology has become an established specialty (Ponterotto, 2008) and has been viewed as "the fourth force in counseling" (Pedersen, 1999b). Today, one can hardly find a text book or an issue of any professional journal in the field of counseling

and counseling psychology that does not include chapters or articles that directly address multicultural issues or have chapters or articles on any topic without integrating multicultural issues. In this section, we provide a very brief overview of the history of the U.S. multicultural movement in the counseling profession. In this chapter, the *U.S. multicultural movement in counseling* refers to the evolution of thought (in research, practice, and training) related to the conceptualization of the unique cultural context of both the helping professional and his or her clientele to more accurately assess, understand, develop, and implement helpful interventions (see Ponterotto, 2008).

The multicultural movement, however, did not occur easily or quickly (see, e.g., Casas, 1984; Heppner, Casas, Carter, & Stone, 2000; Jackson, 1995; Ponterotto, Casas, Suzuki, & Alexander, 2001); instead, it has been a journey, a no-return journey. Ponterotto (2008) outlined the growth of multicultural counseling and psychology as being born in the 1960s, experiencing its establishment as a specialty in the 1980s, maturing and expanding in the 1990s, and growing beyond borders and disciplines in the most recent decade. Although in many ways the process was nonlinear, with many "bumps and curves in the road," this chronological view highlights a developmental process of the multicultural movement in counseling and psychology. The advancement of this movement is not only reflected in its developmental maturity but also in its diversification and growth of younger branches so as to now encompass not only U.S. racial ethnic minorities but a very broad range of marginalized groups (e.g., women, persons of different sexual orientations, older adults, individuals with physical challenges), in resonance with the societal pulses, and in its organizational and systemic contexts.

Prior to 1960, only a few counseling articles addressed racial issues, and when they did, it was primarily in relation to African Americans (Jackson, 1995). Additionally, in the 1940s and 1950s, minorities, including African Americans, were not actively involved in what was then known as the personnel and guidance movement (Jackson, 1995), which was connected to the American Personnel and Guidance Association (APGA), now called the American Counseling Association (ACA). The birth of a multicultural movement in the United States was greatly affected by the civil rights movement in the 1960s (Neville & Carter, 2005). The nationwide racial upheavals led to substantial debate regarding the "counseling needs of culturally different clients, as well as the efficacy of services available to certain populations" (Robinson & Morris, 2000, p. 239). The discussion at the time mainly focused on racial issues, particularly African-American-related issues, recognizing that racism had led to the "covert and overt racist practices for several decades" (Robinson & Morris, 2000, p. 239) by the counseling profession, psychological organizations, and mental health systems. Also at that time, Wrenn (1962) warned of the dangers of a "culturally encapsulated counselor" who was unaware and insensitive to the cultural worldview of clients. Although his words were very clear, his message was neither widely understood nor followed.

During the 1960s, there was a dramatic increase in the racial and cultural diversity of counselors, resulting in greater attention being paid to diverse populations of clients (Aubrey, 1977). In fact, in 1966, the APGA adopted a policy urging counselors to serve culturally disadvantaged individuals (Hoyt, 1967), and in 1968, the Association of Black Psychologists was formed. Furthermore, William Banks led a campaign in 1969 at the APGA Conference to establish an Office of Non-White Concerns in the Association (Jackson, 1995). Later, in 1972, this office was transformed into a division of the APGA called the Association for Non-White Concerns. This organization changed its name in 1985 to the Association for Multicultural Counseling and Development (AMCD). Not surprisingly, this association embraced all counselors of color and focused on helping all persons of color (Jackson, 1995). In the 1970s, the AMCD launched the first counseling journal devoted to multicultural issues, the *Journal of Non-White Concerns* (now called the *Journal of Multicultural Counseling and Development* [*JMCD*]). Three special issues in the 1970s of

APGA's flagship journal, *Personnel and Guidance Journal*, also focused on multicultural issues and for the first time were guest edited by Paul Smith and Derald Wing Sue, counseling professionals of color (Jackson, 1995).

Formal attempts were also begun for the first time in the 1960s within the American Psychological Association (APA) to raise awareness of the needs of U.S. racial and ethnic minorities. For instance, in the late 1960s, African American psychologists called for attention to racial issues, the elimination of racist themes in APA journals, and the establishment of programs for addressing racial concerns (Guthrie, 1998). To respond to such calls, the APA created the Ad Hoc Committee on Equality of Opportunity in Psychology in 1963 and the Commission on Accelerating Black Participation in Psychology in 1968. The APA also held the Vail Conference (in 1973), where the organization took steps to encourage the psychology profession to prepare students to function in a multiracial society (Korman, 1974)—affirmative action programs and diverse training programs became associated with basic ethical obligations. These were examples of structural changes that preceded the formation of APA Division 45, Society for the Psychological Study of Ethnic Minority Issues, in the late 1970s.

Interest in multicultural counseling, or what was then sometimes also called cross-cultural counseling, increased substantially in the 1970s. During the 1970s, the academy in psychology (which had been largely responsible for the popular racial inferiority theories for a sizable portion of the last century) started to pay more attention to the "culturally different" or "minorities" (Jackson, 1995) and their psychological needs (Sue, 1977). Research on cross-racial and multicultural issues in counseling emerged on university campuses, and the dialogue about the role of race in the counseling process started to appear in counseling journals (e.g., Vontress, 1971). Multicultural researchers and theorists openly recognized that the mainstream counseling models and theories had failed not only to meet the needs of African Americans but also all racial/ethnic minority clients (Sue, 1977; Vontress, 1971). Moreover, a significant amount of empirical evidence became available that racial minorities were extremely underrepresented among both the mental health providers and mental health service recipients (Atkinson & Thompson, 1992).

There had been a growing awareness of inequalities and discrimination around gender, sexual orientation, and people with disabilities, as well as children, adolescents, and older adults in the United States (see Heppner et al., 2000). For example, events with the second wave of the feminist movement that dealt with both legal and cultural inequality, as well as the gay rights movement in the 1960s through the 1980s (especially the monumental event of homosexuality being removed from their list of mental disorders by the American Psychiatric Association in 1973; Rothblum, 2000), all contributed significantly to the broadening of the scope of equality and the multicultural movement. Thus, the notion of multicultural counseling was also strengthened and mutually complemented by voices of other social groups who shared similar experiences of discrimination and prejudice. In aggregate, these voices challenged the counseling profession to examine its core values and to reformulate its conceptualization and practice to accommodate diversities in the population, including culture, gender, sexual orientation, and physical challenges (see Jackson 1995, for more details). By the turn of the 20th century, multicultural counseling had evolved to favor a broad definition of culture, to include demographic (e.g., gender), status (e.g., economic), and ethnographic (e.g., nationality) variables (e.g., Pedersen, 1999a; Sue et al., 1998), based on the rationale that "the broad definition of culture is particularly important in preparing counselors to deal with the complex differences among clients from every cultural group" (Pedersen, 1999a, p. 5). However, it is fair to say there has been considerable disagreement about the theoretical relation between counseling and culture (Pedersen, 2003).

Moreover, during the 1980s and 1990s, multicultural issues were centrally reflected in the priorities and activities of professional organizations. For example, in the late 1990s, multicultural counseling competency requirements were written into the practice and training standards of the AMCD (American Association for Counseling and Development, now known as the ACA), APA Divisions 17 (Society of Counseling Psychology) and 45 (Society for the Psychological Study of Ethnic Minority Issues; Ridley & Kleiner, 2003), and the APA (e.g., APA, 1993). Driven by the quest for knowledge to serve the culturally and racially different, theorists and researchers achieved significant and unprecedented progress in multicultural issues in the 1980s and 1990s. The term *multicultural counseling* began to appear in the counseling literature more frequently; the literature also grew extensively during this period, including numerous journal articles, handbooks (e.g., Ponterotto, Casas, Suzuki, & Alexander, 1995), and scholarly journals devoted to publishing empirical and conceptual articles on multicultural counseling (e.g., *Journal of Multicultural Counseling and Development*). Numerous theories were developed in the areas of racial identity, acculturation, worldviews, and values (Ponterotto, 2008). These theories provided tools for understanding not only between-group differences among different races/cultures but also within-group differences. Additionally, these theories enabled the examination of complex intrapersonal and interpersonal processes (i.e., multicultural competencies) through which counselors can engage in culturally sensitive counseling (Constantine, Miville, & Kindaichi, 2008).

With these advancements in multicultural studies, the multicultural competence movement emerged; for example, Sue, Arredondo, and McDavis (1992) presented the first tripartite model of multicultural competence, which emphasized the role of awareness, knowledge, and skills in multicultural competence. This model was first published in the *JMCD* and the competencies identified by these authors were drawn, in part, from a position paper, "Cross-cultural Counseling Competencies," produced by APA Division 17 (Sue et al., 1982), and the *APA Guidelines for Providers of Psychological Services to Ethnic, Linguistic, and Culturally Diverse Populations* (APA, 1991).

Research addressing the counseling needs of women, men, and individuals of different sexual orientations have burgeoned since the 1980s (Betz & Fitzgerald, 1993), and age and disability have also started gaining attention from the multicultural research community. With the recognition that the U.S. society has been oppressive to many individuals, a most recent expansion of the multicultural movement has emerged: social justice counseling (Warren & Constantine, 2007). More recently, social class has also been recognized as an individual identity that leads to unearned privileges or disadvantages and deserves professional attention (see Liu & Ali, 2008). In 2008, social justice was depicted as "the overarching umbrella that guides our profession (Sue & Sue, 2008, p. 292).

In the 2000s, multicultural counseling has become a major area of scholarly inquiry as well as a major force in counseling (Pedersen, 1999c). Multiculturalism has become a mainstream value in professional organizations such as the ACA and APA (Heppner et al., 2000). Clearly, the multicultural movement has traveled a long way and become a diversified and inclusive area of counseling and counseling psychology. Its advancement has also reflected the political and cultural climate of the society. Although many would agree there has been an increased awareness and commitment to diversity issues over the last 40 years, many would also say there has "often been tension and many of the changes have not come easily" (Heppner et al., 2000, pp. 30–31), and clearly there is still a long way to go (see, e.g., Heppner et al., 2000; Jackson, 1995; Ponterotto, 2008; Ponterotto et al., 1995, 2001; Sue & Sue, 2008).

THE GROWING CROSS-NATIONAL MOVEMENT IN THE U.S. COUNSELING PROFESSION

In this section, we provide a very brief overview of the history of the growing cross-national movement of counseling psychology in the United States (see Heppner, Leong, & Chiao, 2008, for more details). The *cross-national movement in the U.S. counseling profession* refers to the evolution of thought related to culturally sensitive collaboration among counseling professionals across countries, including sharing knowledge related to research, practice, and service. In essence, although the inclusion of international perspectives began in the 1940s (Savickas, 2007), there has been a relatively slow growth in U.S. counseling psychology until the beginning of the 21st century (Heppner, Leong, & Chiao, 2008). Since 2000, however, there has been quite an accelerated interest in cross-national initiatives. For example, there is an increasingly supportive infrastructure within several U.S. professional counseling psychology associations (e.g., the International Section was established in 2005 within the Society of Counseling Psychology), a rising number of scholarly publications on international topics as well as international samples in the professional journals, growing interest in training international students and promoting cross-cultural competencies in all students, and greater cross-national communication and collaboration (see Heppner, Leong, & Chiao, 2008). The level of change in all the developments just mentioned, however, has been relatively small and in many ways still in its infancy compared with the U.S. multicultural counseling movement. The change in the internationalization of the counseling profession has been a function of the synergy of a number of factors, such as (a) social, economic, political, and environmental events and forces; (b) the advances in the U.S. multicultural movement; (c) pioneering leaders and scholars who conceptualized the utility of internationalizing counseling psychology; (d) a critical mass of voices articulating the profound role of culture in the work of counseling professionals in the United States and around the globe; and (e) structural changes within professional organizations that promote cultural perspectives (see Heppner, Leong, & Chiao, 2008).

Some of the earliest cross-national efforts occurred in the 1950s and 1960s as U.S. counseling psychologists were asked to consult with leaders in other countries to help international colleges develop a similar counseling profession. For example, after World War II, a number of U.S. counseling leaders (e.g., W. Lloyd, E. G. Williamson, D. Super, H. Borow, and L. Brammer) served as consultants to the Japanese government. Similarly, in the 1960s, counseling psychology leaders (e.g., C. G. Wrenn, F. Robinson) provided consultation to establish the counseling profession in England. In the 1960s, Donald Super and his colleagues also began to engage in international research on work values connected to career choice. Beginning in the early1980s, the second wave of counseling psychologists going abroad were most often Fulbright scholars who taught and/or conducted research for 3 to 12 months in other countries (see Hedlund, 1988; Heppner, 1988; McWhirter, 1988; Nugent 1988; Skovholt, 1988).

Other early efforts to increase cross-cultural communication within the counseling profession began in the mid-1960s with the creation of a new journal, the *International Journal for the Advancement of Counseling (IJAC)*. This journal has provided a major arena for scholarly exchanges on issues of guidance and counseling from international perspectives. Similarly, then-editor Fretz began the International Forum in *The Counseling Psychologist (TCP)* to promote communication about international topics. Although Fretz's call was clear, the message was not widely received, with the vast majority of the articles being written by U.S. scholars describing their experiences as Fulbrighters or visiting scholars.

During these early years, it was not uncommon for counseling psychologists to question the value of such international experiences. For example, McWhirter (2000) wrote that "my professional colleagues were supportive and happy for me, but many could not understand why a counseling psychologist would want to take his family to Turkey for anything other than a brief tourist trip, and some even questioned that" (p. 117). The motivations of counseling psychologists interested in international issues were also often questioned; McWhirter (2000) described an incident where a colleague presumed the motivation for such international work to be "only looking for an excuse for foreign travel" (p. 118). Such attitudes and beliefs undoubtedly affected the development of the international movement in the counseling profession. Clearly ahead of the times, also in the 1980s, the Minnesota

International Counseling Institute was created by counseling psychology faculty at the University of Minnesota (e.g., T. Skovholt, S. Hansen, J. Romano, K. Thomas). This institute provided (and continues to offer) a biennial gathering of international psychological and educational professionals that promoted scholarly exchanges among counseling professionals from around the world.

Although there was an increased focus on multicultural issues within the counseling profession during the 1990s (see Casas, 1984; Heppner et al., 2000; Jackson, 1995; Ponterotto, 2008; Watkins, 1994), an increased focus on international topics was less evident within U.S. counseling psychology (see Heppner, Leong, & Chiao, 2008). Also at the this time, the cross-cultural movement in psychology, which emphasized comparative research across cultures, was very active, but relatively few U.S. counseling psychologists seemed to be actively involved in this specialty.

Paul Pedersen published a landmark article in 1991 (more fully articulated in 1999) in which he proposed that culture, defined broadly, is generic to all counseling; his conceptualization of culturally focused counseling emphasized the centrality of the cultural context within all dimensions of the counseling profession, including both multicultural counseling and cross-cultural counseling across two countries. Nonetheless, the discipline of U.S. psychology, including the counseling profession, continued to be characterized as a white middle-class enterprise "conceived in English, thought about in English, written about in English, and taking into account problems relevant to Anglo-Saxton culture" (Ardila, 1993, pp. 170–171).

It is important to note, however, that during the 1990s, a number of individuals in the U.S. counseling profession who would later become vocal proponents of the cross-national movement were being affected greatly by the growing U.S. multicultural counseling movement. More specifically, the worldview of many of these individuals was becoming more culture-centered (see Pedersen, 1999a) and, in essence, gaining multicultural competencies that would later be extended to cross-national contexts and thus serve as the foundation of a culture-centered cross-national movement in U.S. counseling psychology. In this way, the U.S. multicultural movement was very important in promoting cultural sensitivities in the work of some members of the counseling profession that would later serve as the foundation to examine the utility of the cultural context cross-nationally.

At the dawn of the 21st century, advances in communication, transportation, manufacturing, and technology began to alter the world greatly, most notably the Internet, which dramatically changed the flow of information and resources and modified radically our relationships, our recreation, and the way we work and play. With the shrinking of space-time, the world has not only become increasingly interconnected but interdependent along numerous dimensions (e.g., economically, environmentally; Friedman, 2005). Moreover, the cross-cultural understanding of values and customs of different societies became a key to survival and success (Friedman, 2005). During this time, many university leaders worldwide began to articulate the need for universities to prepare students who would have relevant cultural skills to contribute to the societal needs around the globe (Heppner, Leong, & Chiao, 2008). In short, counseling faculty at many U.S. universities were reinforced to extend their work into international contexts, and communication within the counseling profession began to greatly increase worldwide.

In the late 20th and early 21st centuries, more authors who were also actively involved in the U.S. multicultural movement articulated the failure of U.S. counseling psychology to incorporate cross-cultural perspectives in their work (e.g., Cheung, 2000; Gerstein & Ægisdóttir, 2005a; Heppner, 2006; Leong & Ponterotto, 2003; Leong & Blustein, 2000; Leung, 2003; Marsella, 1998; Pedersen & Leong, 1997). For example, Cheung (2000) wrote aptly,

> The meaning of counseling may seem obvious to American psychologists. The understanding of its meaning by American clients is assumed. In another cultural context, however, counseling may imply a different nature of relationship to both the provider and the recipient. Counseling needs to be deconstructed in the context of the culture in which it is offered. (p. 124)

Similarly, but more recently, Arnett (2008) argued that American psychology has focused on 5% of the world's population and neglected the other 95%.

In 1997, the incoming editor of *TCP*, P. Paul Heppner, observed that the increased internationalization of the world not only suggested the need for change in the education and training of the next generation of U.S. counseling psychologists but also a shift from viewing the counseling profession in the United States as an insular enterprise to a part of a larger global movement (Heppner, Leong, & Chiao, 2008). After some policy and structural changes (e.g., forum editors and reviewers with cross-cultural sensitivities and well versed in international issues), a number of articles appeared in *TCP* in the next 6 years that more fully articulated a strong rationale for internationalizing U.S. counseling psychology, the pervasiveness of cultural influences across all dimensions of the counseling profession (particularly culturally encapsulated assumptions within the prevailing counseling theories and practices), descriptions and examples of the state of counseling professions in other countries, obstacles and challenges prohibiting change in the profession, and recommendations for internationalizing U.S. counseling psychology (e.g., Cheung, 2000; Heppner, 2006; Leong & Blustein, 2000; Leong & Ponterotto, 2003; McWhirter, 2000; Pedersen & Leong, 1997).

By the first part of the 21st century, therefore, numerous scholars had articulated the need to attend to the cultural context in U.S. counseling psychology and abroad and to be mindful of simply transporting empirical findings and theories from the United States to other countries with a different cultural context (e.g., Cheung, 2000; Leong & Ponterotto, 2003; Heppner, 2006; Leung, 2003; Marsella, 1998; Segal, Lonner, & Berry, 1998). Moreover, the emphasis on the cultural context reiterated and built on similar messages from within the multicultural movement in the United States (Heppner, Leong, & Chiao, 2008). The previous conceptualization of internationalization as "helping" our international colleagues had begun to fade, and a host of scholars were developing qualitatively different cross-national collaborative relations (e.g., Lent, Brown, Nota, & Soresi, 2003; also see Chapters 7 and 8, this volume). A number of training programs launched curriculums aimed at enhancing cross-cultural competencies that were built on the established U.S. multicultural counseling competencies (e.g., Alexander, Kruczek, & Ponterotto, 2005; Friedlander, Carranza, & Guzman, 2002; Heppner & Wang, 2008). These efforts were significant in that not only did they represent some of the earliest formal international education immersion programs but even signified inclusion of cross-cultural competencies into the cultural education of future counseling professionals.

In addition, it is only in the last decade that there has been some increase in the number of publications, including international topics and samples of counseling outside the United States (e.g., Gerstein & Ægisdóttir, 2005a, 2005b, 2007; Heppner, 2006; Heppner, Leong, & Gerstein, 2008; Kwan & Gerstein, 2008; Leong & Blustein, 2000; Leong & Ponterotto, 2003; Leong & Savickas, 2007; Pedersen, Draguns, Lonner, & Trimble, 2008; Ægisdóttir & Gerstein, 2005). Even though the counseling field has seen an increased interest in international topics, publications on international samples in contemporary journals appear at an alarmingly low rate. For instance, Gerstein and Ægisdóttir (2007) found that international topics only accounted for about 6% of publications between the years 2000 and 2004 in four U.S. counseling journals.

The 21st century also witnessed an increasing number of counseling psychologists with different types of cross-national experiences. For instance, 112 counseling psychologists received 127 Fulbright Senior Scholar grants across 77 universities in 45 countries (McWhirter & McWhirter, 2009), more counseling psychologists had work-related experiences abroad, and the number of international students receiving graduate degrees in counseling from U.S. training programs also began to increase (see Heppner, 2006). Additionally, by 2005, 152 international counseling and student development specialties from 40 countries had participated in the Minnesota International Counseling Institute (Skovholt, Hansen, Goh, Romano, & Thomas, 2005).

In 2002 in Singapore, F. Leong, M. Savickas, P. Pedersen, I. Gati, and R. Young spearheaded the beginning of Division 16 (Counseling Psychology) in the International Association of Applied Psychology, marking the advent of a global counseling psychology organization within applied psychology. Furthermore, in 2003, L. Douce, as president of the APA Society of Counseling Psychology, chose globalization as her presidential theme. In 2 of the next 3 years, the succeeding presidents of the Society (P. Heppner and R. Nutt) also had a significant focus on international issues (see Heppner, Leong, & Chiao, 2008). In 2008, President L. Forrest organized the first International Conference on Counseling Psychology, which was held in Chicago, Illinois. This conference underscored the importance of understanding the role of culture, having respect for the international professional community, and promoting international collaboration as key processes of internationalization.

Other organizations also hosted international conferences for the first time. For example, in 2003, the Society of Vocational Psychology, a section within APA Division 17, held its first international conference in Coimbra, Portugal, followed by another in Canada 2 years later. Additionally, the Association for University and College Counseling Center Directors (AUCCCD) started to internationalize its work in counseling centers (see Heppner, Leong, & Chiao, 2008). Moreover, in 2004, the APA approved the Resolution on Culture and Gender Awareness in International Psychology, which was similar to the APA multicultural guidelines (APA, 2003) but different in that it focused on international aspects of psychology. This resolution called for the development of a multicultural mind-set and the need to increase cross-cultural competencies in international psychology. In short, at the beginning of the 21st century, major counseling psychology professional organizations and the APA began to internationalize their focus and establish structures in their organizations to promote greater international collaboration.

At the same time, the counseling profession was growing rapidly around the globe. Subsequently, numerous descriptions of the history and current status of counseling professions in a wide array of countries were published, such as Gerstein and Ægisdóttir (2005a, 2005b), Leong and Savickas (2007), and Heppner, Leong, and Gerstein (2008). These and additional international articles published in *TCP* and other U.S. journals significantly increased the amount of information available about the state of the counseling profession around the world (Heppner, Leong, & Gerstein, 2008). In brief, the counseling profession was vigorously growing worldwide at the beginning of the 21st century, with different identities, various training, accreditation, and credentialing standards, and a wide array of professional service delivery models to address a broad range of societal needs across diverse cultures. In essence, not only was the counseling profession active worldwide, there were also systematic efforts to promote collaboration among counseling professionals across countries (Heppner, Leong, & Chiao, 2008; Heppner, Leong, & Gerstein, 2008).

UNEASY TENSIONS BETWEEN THE MULTICULTURAL AND CROSS-NATIONAL MOVEMENTS

Although there are many commonalities in the U.S. multicultural and cross-national movements, there have been points of divergence and tensions between these two approaches that are important to discuss. To some extent, the tensions are not only mired in definitional issues of the terms tied to these movements but also complicated by definitions that have changed over time (see Chapter 1, this volume). In this section, we will refer to the broader multicultural movements in education as well as the larger profession of psychology. In addition, we will also refer to the smaller multicultural counseling movement as well as the cross-national movement in counseling; the former has undoubtedly contributed to the establishment of the foundation and greatly affected the conceptualization of the cultural framework of the latter in the United States. Moreover, both the multicultural and cross-national movements in the U.S. counseling profession have been influenced by the larger multicultural movements in education and psychology.

Historically, the broad U.S. multicultural education movement emerged from the civil rights movement of the 1960s and 1970s, and it was motivated by social justice and equality (Banks, 2004; Olson et al., 2007). Similarly, although the larger multicultural psychology movement (as well as the multicultural counseling movement) has expanded to include a variety of sociodemographic populations, it also began as a movement to incorporate principles of race, racism, and ethnic culture into the psychological literature (including the counseling literature). It was primarily a movement instigated by people of color (Helms, Henze, Mascher, & Satiani, 2005; Miville, 2008). Moreover, multicultural psychology and counseling focused on what the U.S. scholars were not doing well and critiqued the existing monocultural theories and counseling frameworks and in a way was operating from a position of lower power.

Conversely, the U.S. cross-national movement in counseling initially focused on transporting U.S. counseling psychology to other countries in the 1950s and 1960s (e.g., establishing U.S.-based counseling models in Japan). Thus, the movement started with what Western psychologists did well and could offer to other countries; thus, the early cross-national counseling psychologists operated from positions of power, which is often the case today (see Chapters 7 and 8 of this volume for additional discussions on this issue). Isolated concerns were expressed over the homogeneous exportation of this knowledge and values to other countries with varying degrees of cultural dissimilarity (see Wrenn, 1962, and Chapter 1 of this volume). At this time, there was little connection with and little influence from the larger cross-cultural psychology movement. In the last two decades, the cross-national movement has been influenced by the need to address the growing interrelatedness across the globe (Olson et al., 2007), and been motivated primarily by the need to learn more about different cultures around the world. More recently, grounded in part in the U.S. multicultural counseling movement, the cross-national movement has also focused on the quest to promote the development of culturally contextual knowledge bases in the counseling profession. Initially, the majority of the scholars in the U.S. cross-national movement in counseling had been white, but this is increasingly less so. Pedersen (2003) observed that the motivation for studying cultural similarities and differences has over time evolved from a defense of colonization to a demonstration of political activism, to the development of affirmative action and/or the justification of elitism, toward a more interdependent global perspective.

Historically, there has been a tendency to view the larger U.S. multicultural psychology and cross-cultural psychology as separate approaches with little overlap. The historical backgrounds, motivations, and often differing worldviews of these approaches have played a role in some of the tension between these two movements. Conversely, at this time, the U.S. multicultural counseling movement and the cross-national movement in the counseling profession share more commonalities, particularly a similar focus on examining the cultural context, and an emphasis on cultural complexities within counseling. Yet some of the old tensions between these movements still remain. We focus briefly on three areas of tension: (1) omissions and ambiguities related to the lack of integration of multicultural counseling into the cross-national movement in counseling, (2) applications of methodologies within U.S. psychology to nondominant racial and cultural groups, and (3) implications arising from resource limitations.

Omissions and Ambiguities

One source of tension has been the lack of recognition and integration of the larger multicultural psychology movement with the cross-cultural psychology movement and to a lesser extent the movements within the U.S. multicultural counseling with cross-national approaches in counseling. Previously, when psychologists (mostly nonminority) discussed internationalizing psychology or had been rewarded for their efforts to internationalize psychology, one rarely found references to the growing body of literature that has given race and ethnic culture a place in U.S. American psychology (e.g., Kaslow, 2000).

Multicultural psychology, as discussed in the APA multicultural guidelines (APA, 2003), pertains primarily to the effects of race, racism, ethnic culture, and/or xenophobia on psychological constructs (e.g., attitudes, psychological processes, behaviors). Additional aspects of human diversity, including gender, social class, and sexual orientation, are covered in other APA guidelines or position papers. The effects of race and ethnic culture have been studied, discovered, and used as the basis of interventions in primarily U.S. American minority psychology. Helms and Richardson (1997), for instance, contended that the term *multiculturalism* shifts psychologists' focus from the power dynamics associated with the sociopolitical constructs of race and racism to less emotionally laden sociodemographic categories, such as socioeconomic status. There is also the concern that the power dynamics of racism may become even more problematic as psychologists attempt to internationalize psychology because it may be wrongly assumed that oppression of ethnic minorities and/or immigrant groups is not racism.

In addition, prior to the diversification of U.S. psychology, the tendency was to study white (i.e., dominant group) people's reactions to people of color and/or to use white Americans as the normalcy standard against which the minority-status groups were compared as a means of quantifying the minorities' levels of abnormality. Thus, research that focused primarily on anti-black racism reflected this first tendency, and the "deficit model," reflected in concepts such as the "achievement gap," reflected the other. The parallel, especially in cross-cultural psychology, is evident in the study of dominant or host groups' biases toward immigrant groups and the use of host cultures to define appropriate behavioral standards for the so-called immigrant groups.

Although it is the case that U.S. psychology has not incorporated multicultural principles as fully as it should, there are now enough multicultural scholars to make it harder to ignore the effects of racial/cultural discrimination and biases on victims as well as beneficiaries of these societal dynamics. However, a concern is that as psychologists engaged in the

U.S. exportation of psychology to other countries, they will not have the skills to also export the fairness principles of multicultural psychology if they have not been adequately trained in the discipline (Giorgis & Helms, 1978). In short, the concern is that as the concept of multiculturalism has an ambiguous meaning in some quarters of the internationalization efforts, there is a greater danger of imposing dominant cultures onto members of subordinated cultures (see Chapter 4 of this volume for further discussions of concerns about exportation).

Using Methodologies to Impose Cultures

One legacy of cross-cultural psychology is the knowledge regarding the mechanics of translating assessment tools for use across cultures and countries. The concept of cultural equivalence or ensuring that instruments are measuring the same phenomena across countries emanates from cross-cultural psychologists and is an acknowledgment of the importance of addressing cultural factors in research designs (see Chapter 5, this volume). In the past, though, *cultural equivalence* was narrowly defined by U.S. psychologists as being synonymous with linguistic equivalence (American Educational Research Association [AERA], APA, National Council on Measurement in Education, 1999, Chapter 9; Peña, 2007). Therefore, it is the perception of many U.S. minority scholars that this narrow focus on just linguistic equivalence or meaning of constructs, using sophisticated statistical techniques, has resulted in negligence of issues such as bias related to using traditional U.S. methodologies in assessing nondominant racial and cultural groups within the United States (e.g., Heppner, 2006; Heppner, Leong, & Chiao, 2008; Quintana, Troyano, & Taylor, 2001; Ægisdóttir, Gerstein, & Çinarbaş, 2008). Multicultural theorists in the United States have also been strong advocates for requiring researchers and practitioners to recognize and change the racial/cultural power dynamics in the counseling and psychology research and treatment processes (Helms et al., 2005). Therefore, some multicultural counseling scholars in the United

States are concerned that U.S. cross-cultural psychologists will erroneously equate methodological or statistical sophistication with attention to racial/cultural factors and, as a result, wrongly conclude that the latter do not matter. In essence, there has been a history of not recognizing the extent to which U.S. scholars have inappropriately imposed their own racial and cultural socialization perspectives on research participants and not adequately considered the socialization experiences and worldviews of their research participants and clients (also see discussion in Chapter 5, this volume).

Shifting Resources

Historically, calls for inclusion of race in psychology have resulted in emotionally laden reactions, which U.S. psychologists have managed by making race invisible. Helms et al. (2005) reported that most psychology training programs, professional associations, and journals have predominantly white memberships who either have been reluctant to focus on racial matters or do not know how to do so in ways that are respectful of the interracial and/or intercultural dynamics of research participants and those who study them. Mak, Law, Alvidrez, and Perez-Stable (2007) reviewed 379 NIMH-funded clinical trials that were published between 1995 and 2004 and found that racial/ethnic and/or gender analyses could not be conducted in more than half of them. That is, very few financial resources had been allotted to focus on examining the mental health concerns of African American, Latino/Latina American, Asian American, and Asian American/Pacific Islander (ALANA) populations.

Some U.S. scholars within the larger multicultural psychology and multicultural counseling movements are concerned that the burgeoning focus on international populations threatens to remove even these limited resources from native U.S. minority-status populations. Such diminished resources might not only be limited to financial resources but may also include access to psychological education as well. It is already the case that students born in other countries outnumber their ALANA counterparts in U.S.

colleges and universities. As the focus of educational systems shifts to active recruitment of international students, and affirmative action programs in the United States disappear, so may a multicultural psychology that is relevant to the life circumstances of native-born ALANA populations. In short, some scholars are concerned that the limited resources available for enriching multicultural psychology and multicultural counseling in the United States are rapidly being shifted to internationalizing initiatives in psychology and counseling in a manner that denies the existence of race and culture as important aspects of how people function worldwide.

In sum, the tensions and concerns between scholars in both the U.S. multicultural psychology and cross-cultural psychology movements, as well as between U.S. scholars in the multicultural and cross-national counseling movements, deserve examination and discussion. It is important to address these concerns and to disentangle the foci of different psychology groups involved in cross-national activities (e.g., cross-cultural psychology, cultural psychology, and the U.S. cross-national movement in the counseling profession). Much more examination and understanding of the tensions is needed to move the profession toward a more integrated culture-centered approach within the profession. In the next section, we identify many commonalities between the multicultural and cross-national movements in counseling and the larger discipline of psychology and suggest complementary roles of these two schools of thought.

A COMPLEMENTARY ROLE TO PROMOTE CULTURALLY SENSITIVE RESEARCH, TRAINING, AND PRACTICE

Although there may be different perspectives about the definitions, foci, and constructs associated with multicultural psychology, multicultural counseling, cross-cultural psychology, and the more recent cross-national movement in counseling, there also are many important areas of convergence. What follows is a discussion of the complementary roles of the U.S. multicultural and cross-national movements within the

counseling profession (see Heppner, Leong, & Chiao, 2008) and of how such integration may enhance culturally sensitive research, practice, and training in the counseling field.

Both the U.S. multicultural and cross-national schools of thought in counseling focus on understanding human behavior in the cultural context and strive to make the important role of culture more visible and transparent across a wide range of behaviors. These range from help seeking, counseling theory and the counseling process, to issues related to language, power, and privilege. Thus, both movements focus on behaviors and psychological processes within a larger environmental context. Moreover, the importance of a person's worldview is emphasized and, relatedly, one's ability to understand others from different cultures. Therefore, both movements are concerned with issues of cultural bias and ethnocentrism (e.g., Cheung, 2000; Leong & Blustein, 2000; Norsworthy, 2006). For example, many U.S. multicultural scholars have discussed cultural biases in the counseling process (e.g., ethnocentric counseling theories) and in testing (Sue & Sue, 2008). Scholars in both movements strive to reduce bigotry and stereotyping in counseling theory, research, and practice, and promote a core value of appreciating differences, and the assumption that being different does not imply being "less than" or "inferior" but simply being different. In fact, differences are not only to be tolerated but valued and celebrated.

Also shared by the multicultural and cross-national movements is a developmental perspective in conceptualizing behavior and psychological processes, such that starting at an early age, one learns to view his or her world in a socially constructed manner. For instance, it is understood that individuals can learn and internalize a racist or sexist worldview; moreover, biases, stereotypes, and prejudices can be unlearned over time. Thus, both schools promote the value of intercultural learning (see Olson et al., 2007). Specifically, both movements have emphasized the necessity of increasing one's awareness and knowledge of one's own values, cultural socialization processes, and worldview, as well as greater knowledge of others who have different worldviews and experiences.

Moreover, both movements have emphasized the utility of a host of culturally sensitive skills, particularly interpersonal skills, to enhance and improve intergroup communication and the ability to interact appropriately, comfortably, and effectively with individuals from different cultural groups. Both schools of thought, therefore, insist that cultural competencies be articulated and synthesized into U.S. counseling training programs and the respective ethical codes (e.g., Heppner, Leong, & Chiao, 2008; Heppner, Leong, & Gerstein, 2008; Marsella & Pedersen, 2004; Pedersen, 2007; Ægisdóttir & Gerstein, in press).

In essence, there seems to be a great deal of commonality between the foci of the U.S. multicultural and cross-national movements within the counseling profession. Because of the growing appreciation in the United States of cultural contexts in shaping individuals' behavior and psychological processes, there is an immense possibility for these two areas of inquiry, or schools of thought, to inform each other. We will briefly discuss how the common goals of U.S. multicultural movement and cross-national movement in counseling cannot only complement each other but also have a bidirectional influence on each other in theory, research, practice, and training.

Training

There are very significant needs to train the next generation of counseling professionals to be culturally competent not only with diverse U.S. populations (including international populations) but also with populations around the world (see Ponterotto et al., 1995, 2001; Sue & Sue, 2008). Moreover, there is a growing need to train culturally competent scholars to cross boundaries and collaborate with colleagues from other countries. In essence, the common training focus on behavior as an act-in-context not only suggests an opportunity to collaborate across these two schools of thought but also potentially to enhance cultural training outcomes by exposing counseling students to both multicultural and cross-cultural training strategies (see Heppner, Leong, & Chiao, 2008).

Although great strides have been made in multicultural training, Constantine et al. (2008) indicated

that there remain a number of questions about the effectiveness of multicultural training. The challenge is not only how to define and assess multicultural competencies (see Constantine et al., 2008) but also how to promote it in the next generations of counselors. Based on some of the literature on multicultural and cross-cultural training experiences, there seems to be a synergistic effect on trainee cultural competencies when students receive training aimed at both multicultural and cross-cultural competencies. For example, there is some evidence within the multicultural training literature that exposure may be an important activity to reduce ethnocentric worldviews (Kiselica, 1998). Similarly, research on study abroad and immersion programs, even less than 4 weeks in duration, has suggested that such programs can have powerful effects on students, most notably leading to further engagement in cross-cultural experiences (see Fischer, 2009). Other data indicate that brief but intense cross-cultural immersion programs deepen cultural awareness and enhance cultural sensitivities, as well as broaden participants' worldviews (Chien et al., 2008; Huang, et al., 2008). Two- to four-week immersion programs, for instance, with multiple contacts of extended duration each day may provide students with an opportunity to explore more deeply a new cultural context, especially within cross-cultural interpersonal relationships. Furthermore, such intense immersions may deepen students' sensitivity to the cultural context in new or different ways compared with studying various multicultural issues while in their home culture. And, more important, it is highly possible that the previous multicultural competencies and mind-set of students allow them to benefit maximally from such cross-cultural immersion. To further explore the effect of such cultural immersion experiences, qualitative methodologies and single-subject methodologies may be useful. Such research strategies may not only provide a richer understanding of the impact of different types of cultural training but may also provide information about the additive and cumulative effects of different training activities over time. Marsella and Pedersen (2004) and Ægisdóttir and Gerstein (in press) suggested a wide array of international education activities that could be examined and compared with the various multicultural training approaches currently in use in U.S. counseling training programs.

Research

There is no doubt that counseling research programs conducted on U.S. multicultural populations and populations in other countries may inform one another. For example, a legacy that multicultural counseling theorists, researchers, and practitioners have contributed to psychology is the alternative paradigms for conceptualizing racial and cultural factors (Pedersen, Crethar, & Carlson, 2008). In particular, the focus on replacing sociodemographic categories (e.g., race) with psychological racial (e.g., racial identity) and ethnic cultural (e.g., cultural values) constructs and related variables has been a major contribution of multicultural psychology and multicultural counseling. Such contributions have many implications for how minority-status groups are studied in other cultural contexts by international colleagues or cross-national researchers in the counseling profession. Conversely, the research on nationalists (non-U.S.) living in other countries where they are not socially oppressed based on race may provide additional insight into how culture can shape nonracist behavior, as well as how social oppression operates in harming its victims.

Another example pertains to two closely related topics, applied problem solving and coping (e.g., Folkman & Moskowitz, 2004; Heppner, Witty, & Dixon, 2004; Somerfield & McCrae, 2000). Overall, U.S. scholars have added greatly to this line of research over the years. However, Heppner (2008) maintained that U.S. scholars have tended to approach coping and applied problem solving in a culture-blind manner, overlooking or ignoring the cultural context in most of the research studies in this area. This omission is serious because the cultural context affects all aspects of applied problem solving and coping (see Heppner, 2008). As a result, the existing body of literature on this topic does not tell the whole story but rather has greatly oversimplified

the many complexities and nuances within coping across different U.S. cultural groups. When a coping inventory was developed based on Asian values and theories, very different factors emerged that were not included in U.S. coping inventories (see Heppner et al., 2006). These Asian-based findings might provide useful information for future investigations aimed at understanding Asian American coping strategies. For example, the unique cultural strategies found in Taiwan will provide a more valid information about coping among other U.S. cultural groups that adhere to collectivistic values and customs. Similarly, research findings on the racial stress of African Americans (Utsey & Ponterotto, 1996) might be applicable to other cultural groups in countries outside the United States. Moreover, conducting culturally sensitive research not only in the United States but in many cultures and countries will greatly expand the depth and richness of the counseling and psychology knowledge base and may further stimulate the development of theoretical models that more accurately depict how people respond to stressful life events around the world (Heppner, 2008).

In short, U.S.-based multicultural research and cross-national research that examines human behavior across different cultural contexts has the potential to expand our conceptualizations of psychological processes and their interaction with culture (e.g., ethnic identity, racial identity, self-construal, applied problem solving and coping). Therefore, integrating research findings found in the United States and abroad has a great potential to broaden our current understanding of how culture affects individuals' behavior and psychological processes. Moreover, as researchers across the globe become aware of each others' research interests and activities, more cross-national collaboration may occur. This will greatly enhance counseling research around the world.

Practice

There are also many ways in which the intersection of the U.S. multicultural movement and cross-national movements in counseling can enhance counseling practice. For example, the aim of the APA multicultural guidelines has been to promote culturally sensitive practice (as well as education, training, and research) in counseling minority populations in the United States (APA, 2003; Arredondo et al., 1996; Sue, Arredondo, & McDavis, 1992). The underlying principles included (a) studying and valuing the socialization processes of people in their cultural contexts, (b) examining the adverse effects of minority status on individuals (i.e., power dynamics), and (c) recognizing that studying and providing services to people belonging to minority cultural groups requires an understanding of the counseling professional's own racial and cultural dynamics. These principles are the foundation of an array of multicultural counseling competency guidelines. These guidelines for culturally sensitive counseling services (and research) in the United States may also be useful in counseling a cross-national clientele. An asset of multicultural counseling is that if psychologists learn how to apply its principles properly, multicultural counseling can potentially diversify counseling worldwide and thereby reveal unacknowledged strengths of disenfranchised populations while alleviating the psychological damage caused by racism and xenophobia. In essence, because all behaviors are learned and displayed in a cultural context (e.g., African Americans or international students studying within the United States, a Hakka woman in Taiwan), it is essential that all those in the counseling professions accurately understand the cultural context with which they are engaged.

Moreover, "If practitioners are to understand traditional African Americans, Chinese Americans, Japanese Americans, and Mexican Americans, they must first understand traditional Africans, Chinese, Japanese, and Mexican cultures" (Henderson, Spigner-Littles, & Milhouse, 2006, p. vii). For instance, research on Asians' experiences in Asia may enhance the understanding of the cultural adjustment of Asians in the United States; their behaviors can be understood in relation to cultural socialization in both cultures. Such inquiry may help researchers understand the processes of cultural preservation and acculturation of ethnic minorities in the United States. It may also provide information about the existence and consequences of cultural value shifts among Asians in Asia, which have been occurring in recent years in many Asian countries as the result of exposure to Western cultures. Similarly, if practitioners in South Korea are to understand U.S. expatriates, they must also understand the U.S. cultural contexts from where their expat clients were socialized.

In sum, there is a great deal of potential for the U.S. multicultural and cross-national movements in counseling to enrich one another. These two schools of thought have many common goals. A concerted collaboration between these two movements can enhance the sophistication of counseling research worldwide, expand the complexities of current knowledge and theoretical models, increase the range of counseling interventions, and, in essence, enhance counseling effectiveness across a range of populations in the United States and beyond.

Despite the benefits just mentioned, there are also some limitations in the cross-fertilization of U.S. multicultural and cross-national movements in counseling. Leung and Chen (in press) identified three limitations in applying U.S. multicultural counseling internationally. They argued that, first, U.S. multicultural counseling is founded on the ideals, principles, and philosophical beliefs behind the U.S. political and social system. These include the definitions of social justice, equality, cultural democracy, and human rights, which are often highly culturally laden. Multiculturalism in the United States has been associated with many politically charged terms such as *affirmative action*, *quotas*, *civil rights*, *discrimination*, *reverse discrimination*, *racism*, *sexism*, and *political correctness* (Smith, 2004; Sue et al., 1998). These are unique terms with meanings and implications derived from racial relationships in the United States and the history of its social and political system. Leung and Chen (in press) maintained that the U.S.-based multicultural counseling literature should not be "exported" to other countries without modification and contextual adaptation. The principles (e.g., equality, justice) behind multicultural counseling might be universal, yet the meaning, operational definitions, and timing and pace of implementation of these principles may vary across cultures and contexts. Leung and Chen (in press) suggested that, second, multicultural counseling in the United States explored populations and issues that are specific to the U.S. contexts. It focused mostly on ethnic and cultural groups in the United States, such as African Americans, Hispanics, Asian Americans, and Native American Indians, and on the cultural and political dynamics triggered by majority-minority relationships. As such, multicultural counseling does not address issues that are salient to ethnic groups and cultural minorities in regions around the world who might have a different majority-minority relationship history. Leung and Chen (in press) observed that, moreover, research studies on multicultural counseling have focused mostly on samples in the United States and very few research studies published in U.S. journals employed international samples (Arnett, 2008; Ægisdóttir et al., 2008). Hence, findings and conceptualization derived from these studies have limited generalization to different ethnic and cultural groups around the world. Finally, studies on U.S. samples (minority and majority groups), the research questions examined, the theories tested and developed, and the methods used are highly grounded in the U.S. cultural context and worldview. Similarly, the social and political reality in other countries needs to be considered in understanding psychological processes.

CONCLUSION

Multicultural and cross-national foci in the counseling profession have similar core values, and there is substantial overlap between the two areas of inquiry in both theory and practice—most notably understanding behavior within cultural contexts. Not surprisingly, many scholars in the counseling profession have participated in both movements. As Pedersen observed, "Each of us is guided by our own 1,000 cultural teachers, some domestic and some from other countries" (personal communication, February 26, 2009). Therefore, scholars have called for "culturally informed counseling" (Pedersen,

2008). The focus tying these two perspectives together is not only an increased understanding of cultural differences but also valuing cultural differences and diversity. Moreover, both approaches emphasize the need for intercultural learning and the necessity of cultural competencies of counseling researchers, trainers, and practitioners. We contend that the differences that exist between the two perspectives should be viewed as mutually enriching and complementary rather than evidence of rivalry. It is neither desirable nor possible for one movement to replace the other. Yet it is important to not ignore the tensions between these two movements but rather continue this dialogue to promote greater integration and extension of the many important views and conceptualizations emerging from these two perspectives about how culture affects individual functioning around the world.

A significant challenge with integrating the U.S. multicultural and cross-national movements in the counseling profession involves changing definitions of what we do and the introduction of new terms over time as well as a broad array of differing perspectives on culture and its influence (see Pedersen, 2003). Pedersen (2008) suggested that ultimately, counseling and psychology theories require an understanding of every behavior in the cultural context in which that behavior was learned and displayed. Thus, the ultimate objective of culture-centered counseling is accuracy. This includes not only an accurate assessment, meaningful understanding, and appropriate interventions for our clients but also an acknowledgment of the culturally learned assumptions of oneself as a counselor and the assumptions on which counseling is based (Pedersen, 2008). Both the U.S. multicultural counseling movement and a culture-focused cross-national movement can promote progress toward this end. Together, the counseling profession has a much better chance of being successful.

REFERENCES

Alexander, C. M., Kruczek, T., & Ponterotto, J. G. (2005). Building multicultural competencies in school counselor trainees: An immersion experience. *Counselor Education and Supervision, 44*, 255–266.

American Educational Research Association, American Psychological Association, National Council on Measurement. (1999). *Standards for educational and psychological testing.* Washington, DC: American Educational Research Association.

American Psychological Association. (1991). *Guidelines for providers of psychological services to ethnic, linguistic, and culturally diverse populations.* Washington, DC: Author.

American Psychological Association. (1993). Guidelines for providers of psychological services to ethnic, linguistic, and culturally diverse populations. *American Psychologists, 48,* 45–48.

American Psychological Association. (2003). Guidelines on multicultural education, training, research, practice, and organizational change for psychologists. *American Psychologist, 58,* 377–402.

Ardila, R. (1993). Latin American psychology and world psychology. In U. Kim & J. Berry (Eds.), *Indigenous psychologies* (pp. 170–176). Newbury Park, CA: Sage.

Arnett, J. J. (2008). The neglected 95%: Why American psychology needs to become less American. *American Psychologist, 63,* 602–614.

Arredondo, P., Toprek, R., Brown, S. P., Jones, J., Locke, D. C., Sanchez, J., et al. (1996). Operationalization of the multicultural counseling competencies. *Journal of Multicultural Counseling and Development, 24,* 42–78.

Atkinson, D. R., & Thompson, C. E. (1992). Racial, ethnic and cultural variables in counseling. In S. D. Brown & R. W. Lent (Eds.), *Handbook of counseling psychology* (pp. 349–382). New York: Wiley.

Aubrey, R. F. (1977). Historical development of guidance and counseling and implications for the future. *Personnel and Guidance Journal, 55,* 288–295.

Banks, J. A. (2004). Multicultural education: Historical development, dimensions, and practice. In J. A. Banks & C. A. McGee Banks (Eds.), *Handbook of research on multicultural education* (pp. 3–29). San Francisco: Jossey-Bass.

Betz, N., & Fitzgerald, L. F. (1993). Individuality and diversity: Theory and research in counseling psychology. *Annual Review of Psychology, 44,* 343–381.

Casas, J. M. (1984). Policy, training, and research in counseling psychology: The racial/ethnic minority perspective. In S. D. Brown & R. W. Lent (Eds.), *Handbook of counseling psychology* (pp. 785–831). New York: Wiley.

Cheung, F. M. (2000). Deconstructing counseling in a cultural context. *The Counseling Psychologist, 28,* 123–132.

Chien, W.-Y., Chou, L.-C., Lai, P.-H., Lee, Y.-H., Chen, C.-L., Ting, S.-H., et al. (2008, August). The benefits and challenges of being the BCCIP visitors. In P. P. Heppner & L.-F. Wang (Cochairs), *Multiple benefits of a bidirectional cross-cultural immersion program.* Symposium presented at the annual meeting of the American Psychological Association, Boston, MA.

Constantine, M. G., Miville, M. L., & Kindaichi, M. M. (2008). Multicultural competence in counseling psychology practice and training. In S. D. Brown & R. W. Lent (Eds.), *Handbook of counseling psychology* (pp. 141–158). Hoboken, NJ: Wiley.

Fischer, K. (2009, March 6). Study Abroad directors adjust programs in response to recession. *Chronicle of Higher Education,* pp. 25–26.

Folkman, S., & Moskowitz, J. T. (2004). Coping: Pitfalls and promise. *Annual Review of Psychology, 55,* 745–774.

Friedlander, M. L., Carranza, V. E., & Guzman, M. (2002). International exchanges in family therapy: Training, research, and practice in Spain and United States. *The Counseling Psychologist, 30,* 314–329.

Friedman, T. L. (2005). *The world is flat: A brief history of the twenty-first century.* New York: Farrar, Straust, & Giroux.

Gerstein, L. H., & Ægisdóttir, S. (Guest Eds.) (2005a). Counseling around the world [Special issue]. *Journal of the Mental Health Counseling, 27,* 95–184.

Gerstein, L. H., & Ægisdóttir, S. (2005b). Counseling outside of the United States: Looking in and reaching out. *Journal of Mental Health Counseling, 27,* 221–281.

Gerstein, L. H., & Ægisdóttir, S. (2007). Training international social change agents: Transcending a U.S. counseling paradigm. *Counselor Education and Supervision, 47,* 123–139.

Giorgis, T. W., & Helms, J. E. (1978). Training international students from developing nations as psychologists: A challenge for American psychology. *American Psychologist, 33,* 945–951.

Guthrie, R. V. (1998). *Evan the rat was white: A historical view of psychology.* Needham Heights, MA: Allyn & Bacon.

Hedlund, D. E. (1988). Counseling psychology and the Zambian Fulbright program. *The Counseling Psychologist, 16,* 288–292.

Helms, J. E., Henze, K. T., Mascher, J., & Satiani, A. (2005). Ethical issues when white researchers study ALANA and immigrant people and communities. In J. E. Trimble & C. Fisher (Eds.), *Handbook of ethical research with ethno-cultural populations and communities* (pp. 299–324). Thousand Oaks, CA: Sage.

Helms, J. E., & Richardson, T. Q. (1997). How multiculturalism obscures race and culture as differential aspects of counseling competency. In H. Coleman & D. Pope-Davis (Eds.), *Multicultural counseling competencies* (pp. 60–79). Thousand Oaks, CA: Sage.

Henderson, G., Spigner-Littles, D., & Milhouse, V. H. (2006). *A practitioner's guide to understanding indigenous and foreign cultures.* Springfield, IL: Charles C Thomas.

Heppner, P. P. (1988). Cross-cultural outcomes of a research Fulbright in Sweden. *The Counseling Psychologist, 16,* 297–302.

Heppner, P. P. (1997). Building on strengths as we move into the next millennium. *The Counseling Psychologist, 25,* 5–14.

Heppner, P. P. (2006). The benefits and challenges of becoming cross-culturally competent counseling psychologists. *The Counseling Psychologist, 34,* 147–172.

Heppner, P. P. (2008). Expanding the conceptualization and measurement of applied problem solving and coping: From stages to dimensions to the almost forgotten cultural context. *American Psychologist, 63,* 803–816.

Heppner, P. P., Casas, J. M., Carter, J., & Stone, G. L. (2000). The maturation of counseling psychology: Multifaceted perspectives, 1978–1998. In S. D. Brown & R. W. Lent (Eds.), *Handbook of counseling psychology* (pp. 3–49). New York: Wiley.

Heppner, P. P., Heppner, M. J., Lee, D.-G., Wang, Y.-W., Park, H.-J., & Wang, L.-F. (2006). Development and validation of a collectivistic coping styles inventory. *Journal of Counseling Psychology, 53,* 107–125.

Heppner, P. P., Leong, F. T. L., & Chiao, H. (2008). The growing internationalization of counseling psychology. In S. D. Brown & R. W. Lent (Eds.), *Handbook of counseling psychology* (pp. 68–85). New York: Wiley.

Heppner, P. P., Leong, F. T. L., & Gerstein, L. H. (2008). Counseling within a changing world: Meeting the psychological needs of societies and the world. In W. B. Walsh (Eds.), *Biennial review in counseling psychology* (pp. 231–258). Thousand Oaks, CA: Sage.

Heppner, P. P., & Wang, L.-F. (2008, March). *The multiple benefits of a bidirectional cross-cultural immersion program.* Invited pre-conference presentation at the International Counseling Psychology Conference, "Creating the Future: Counseling Psychologists in a Changing World," Chicago, IL.

Heppner, P. P., Witty, T. E., & Dixon, W. A. (2004). Problem-solving appraisal and human adjustment: A review of 20 years of research utilizing the Problem Solving Inventory. *The Counseling Psychologist, 32,* 344–428.

Hoyt, K. B. (1967). Attaining the promise of guidance for all. *Personnel and Guidance Journal, 45,* 624–630.

Huang, P.-C., Chao, J.-C., Chou, Y.-C., Chang, Y.-P., Chu, S.-Y., & Wang, L.-F. (2008, August). Cross-cultural competence development of the BCCIP. In P. P. Heppner & L.-F. Wang (Cochairs), *Multiple benefits of a bidirectional cross-cultural immersion program.* Symposium presented at the annual meeting of the American Psychological Association, Boston, MA.

Jackson, M. L. (1995). Multicultural counseling: Historical perspectives. In J. G. Ponterotto, J. M. Casas, L. A. Suzuki, & C. M. Alexander (Eds.), *Handbook of multicultural counseling* (pp. 3–16). Thousand Oaks, CA: Sage.

Kaslow, F. W. (2000). Establishing linkages through international psychology: Dealing with universalities and uniquenesses. *American Psychologist, 55,* 1377–1388.

Kiselica, M. S. (1998). Preparing Anglos for the challenges and joys of multiculturalism. *The Counseling Psychologist, 26,* 5–21.

Korman, M. (1974). National conference on levels and patterns of professional training in psychology: The major themes. *American Psychologist, 29,* 441–449.

Kwan, K. L. K., & Gerstein, L. H. (2008). Envisioning a counseling psychology of the world: The mission of the International Forum. *The Counseling Psychologist, 36,* 182–187.

Lent, R. W., Brown, S. D., Nota, L., & Soresi, S. (2003). Testing social cognitive interest and choice hypotheses across Holland types in Italian high school students. *Journal of Vocational Behavior, 62,* 101–118.

Leong, F. T. L., & Blustein, D. L. (2000). Toward a global vision of counseling psychology. *The Counseling Psychologist, 28,* 5–9.

Leong, F. T. L., & Ponterotto, J. G. (2003). A proposal for internationalizing counseling psychology in the United States: Rationale, recommendations, and challenges. *The Counseling Psychologist, 31,* 381–395.

Leong, F. T. L., & Savickas, M. L. (2007). Introduction to special issue on international perspectives on counseling psychology. *Applied Psychology: An International Review, 56,* 1–6.

Leung, S. A. (2003). A journal worth traveling: Globalization of counseling psychology. *The Counseling Psychologist, 31,* 412–419.

Leung, S. A., & Chen, P.-W. (in press). Developing counseling psychology in Chinese communities in Asia: Indigenous, multicultural, and cross-cultural considerations. *The Counseling Psychologist.*

Liu, R. M., & Ali, S. R. (2008). Social class and classism: Understanding the psychological impact of poverty and inequality. In S. D. Brown & R. W. Lent (Eds.), *Handbook of counseling psychology* (pp. 159–175). Hoboken, NJ: Wiley.

Mak, W. W. S., Law, R. W., Alvidrez, J., & Perez-Stable, E. J. (2007). Gender and ethnic diversity in NIMH-funded clinical trials: Review of a decade of published research. *Administration and Policy in Mental Health and Mental Health Services Research, 34,* 497–503.

Marsella, A. J. (1998). Toward a "global-community psychology": Meeting the needs of a changing world. *American Psychologist, 53,* 1282–1291.

Marsella, A. J., & Pedersen, P. B. (2004). Internationalizing the counseling psychology curriculum: Toward new values, competencies, and directions. *Counseling Psychology Quarterly, 17,* 413–423.

McWhirter, J. J. (1988). The Fulbright program in counseling psychology. *The Counseling Psychologist, 16,* 279–281.

McWhirter, J. J. (2000). And now, up go the walls: Constructing an international room for counseling psychology. *The Counseling Psychologist, 28,* 117–122.

McWhirter, P. T., & McWhirter, J. J. (2009). *Historical antecedents: Counseling Psychology and the Fulbright Program.* Unpublished manuscript.

Miville, M. (2008). Race and ethnicity in school counseling. In H. L. K. Coleman & C. Yeh (Eds.), *Handbook of school counseling* (pp. 177–194). New York: Routledge.

Neville, H. A., & Carter, R. T. (2005). Race and racism in counseling psychology research, training, and practice: A critical review, current trends, and future directions. *Counseling Psychologist, 33,* 413–418.

Norsworthy, K. L. (2006). Bringing social justice to international practices of counseling psychology. In R. L. Toporek, L. H. Gerstein, N. A. Fouad, G. Roysircar-Sodowsky, & T. Israel (Eds.), *Handbook for social justice in counseling psychology: Leadership, vision, and action* (pp. 421–441). Thousand Oaks, CA: Sage.

Nugent, F. A. (1988). Counseling psychology and the West German Fulbright program. *The Counseling Psychologist, 16,* 293–296.

Olson, C. L., Evans, R., & Shoenberg, R. F. (2007). *At home in the world: Bridging the gap between internationalization and multicultural education.* Dupont Circle, Washington, DC: American Council on Education.

Pedersen, P., & Leong, F. (1997). Counseling in an international context. *The Counseling Psychologist, 25,* 117–122.

Pedersen, P. B. (1991). Multiculturalism as a generic approach to counseling. *Journal of Counseling & Development, 70,* 6–12.

Pedersen, P. B. (1999a). *Culture-centered counseling interventions: Striving for accuracy.* Thousand Oaks, CA: Sage Publications.

Pedersen, P. B. (Ed.). (1999b). *Multiculturalism as a fourth force.* Philadelphia: Taylor & Francis.

Pedersen, P. B. (Ed.). (1999c). *Multicultural counseling as a fourth force.* Philadelphia: Taylor & Francis.

Pedersen, P. B. (2003). The multicultural context of mental health. In T. B. Smith & P. S. Richards (Eds.), *Practicing multiculturalism* (pp. 17–32). Boston, MA: Allyn & Bacon.

Pedersen, P. B. (2007). Ethics, competence, and professional issues in cross-cultural counseling. In P. B. Pedersen, J. G. Draguns, W. J. Lonner, & J. E. Trimble (Eds.), *Counseling across cultures* (pp. 5–20). Thousand Oaks, CA: Sage.

Pedersen, P. B. (2008). Ethics, competence, and professional issues in cross-cultural counseling. In P. B. Pedersen, J. G. Draguns, W. J. Lonner, & J. E. Trimble (Eds.), *Counseling across cultures* (pp. 5–20). Thousand Oaks, CA: Sage.

Pedersen, P. B., Crethar, H. C., & Carlson, J. (2008). *Inclusive cultural empathy: Making relationships central in counseling and psychotherapy.* Washington, DC: American Psychological Association.

Pedersen, P. B., Draguns, J. G., Lonner, W. L., & Trimble, J. E. (Eds.). (2008). *Counseling across cultures* (6th ed.). Thousand Oaks, CA: Sage.

Peña, E. D. (2007). Lost in translation: Methodological considerations in cross-cultural research. *Child Development, 78,* 1255–1264.

Ponterotto, J. G. (2008). Theoretical and empirical advances in multicultural counseling and psychology.

In S. D. Brown & R. W. Lent (Eds.), *Handbook of counseling psychology* (pp. 121–140). Hoboken, NJ: Wiley.

Ponterotto, J. G., Casas, J. M., Suzuki, L. A., & Alexander, C. M. (Eds.). (1995). *Handbook of multicultural counseling*. Thousand Oaks, CA: Sage.

Ponterotto, J. G., Casas, J. M., Suzuki, L. A., & Alexander, C. M. (Eds.). (2001). *Handbook of multicultural counseling*. Thousand Oaks, CA: Sage.

Quintana, S. M., Troyano, N., & Taylor, G. (2001). Cultural validity and inherent challenges in quantitative methods for multicultural research. In J. G. Ponterotto, J. M. Casas, L. A. Suzuki, & C. M. Alexander (Eds.), *Handbook of multicultural counseling* (pp. 604–630). Thousand Oaks, CA: Sage.

Ridley, C. R., & Kleiner, A. J. (2003). Multicultural competence: History, themes, and issues. In D. B. Pope-Davis, H. L. K. Coleman, W. Ming, & R. L. Toporek (Eds.), *Handbook of multicultural competencies in counseling and psychology* (pp. 3–20). Thousand Oaks, CA: Sage.

Robinson, D. T., & Morris, J. R. (2000). Multicultural counseling: Historical context and current training considerations. *Western Journal of Black Studies, 24,* 239–253.

Rothblum, E. D. (2000). Somewhere in Des Moines or San Antonio: Historical perspectives on lesbian, gay, and bisexual health. In R. M. Perez, K. A. DeBord, & K. J. Bieschke (Eds.), *Handbook of counseling and psychotherapy with lesbian, gay, and bisexual clients* (pp. 57–80). Washington, DC: American Psychological Association.

Savickas, M. L. (2007). Internationalization of counseling psychology: Constructing cross-national consensus and collaboration. *Applied Psychology: An International Review, 56,* 182–188.

Segall, M. H., Lonner, W. J., & Berry, J. W. (1998). Cross-cultural psychology as a scholarly discipline: On a flowering of culture in behavioral research. *American Psychologist, 53,* 1101–1110.

Skovholt, T., Hansen, S., Goh, M., Romano, J., & Thomas, K. (2005). The Minnesota International Counseling Institute (MICI) 1989-present: History, joyful moments, and lessons learned. *International Journal for the Advancement of Counseling, 27,* 17–33.

Skovholt, T. M. (1988). Searching for reality. *The Counseling Psychologist, 16,* 282–287.

Smith, T. B. (2004). *Practicing multiculturalism: Affirming diversity in counseling and psychology.* Boston: Allyn & Bacon.

Somerfield, M. R., & McCrae, R. R. (2000). Stress and coping research: Methodological challenges, theoretical advances, and clinical applications. *American Psychologist, 55,* 620–625.

Sue, D. W., Arredondo, P., & McDavis, R. J. (1992). Multicultural counseling competencies and standards: A call to the profession. *Journal of Multicultural Counseling and Development, 20,* 64–88.

Sue, D. W., Bernier, Y., Durran, A., Feinberg, L., Pedersen, P. B., Smith, E. J., et al. (1982). Position paper: Cross-cultural counseling competencies. *The Counseling Psychologist, 10,* 45–52.

Sue, D. W., Carter, R. T., Casas, J. M., Fouad, N. A., Ivey, A. E., Jensen, M., et al. (1998). *Multicultural counseling competencies: Individual and organizational development.* Thousand Oaks, CA: Sage.

Sue, D. W., & Sue, D. (2008). *Counseling the culturally diverse: Theory and practice.* Hoboken, NJ: Wiley.

Sue, S. (1977). Community mental health services to minority groups: Some optimism, some pessimism. *American Psychologist, 32,* 616–624.

Utsey, S. O., & Ponterotto, J. G. (1996). Development and validation of the Index of Race-Related Stress. *Journal of Counseling Psychology, 43,* 490–501.

Vontress, C. E. (1971). Racial differences: Implication to rapport. *Journal of Counseling Psychology, 18,* 7–13.

Warren, A. K., & Constantine, M. G. (2007). Social justice issues. In M. G. Constantine (Ed.), *Clinical practice with people of color* (pp. 231–242). New York: Teachers College Press.

Watkins, C. E., Jr. (1994). On hope, promise, and possibility in counseling psychology or some simple, but meaningful observations about our specialty. *The Counseling Psychologist, 22,* 315–334.

Wrenn, C. G. (1962). The culturally encapsulated counselor. *Harvard Educational Review, 32,* 111–119.

Ægisdóttir, S., & Gerstein, L. H. (2005). Reaching out: Mental health delivery outside the box. *Journal of Mental Health Counseling, 27,* 221–224.

Ægisdóttir, S., & Gerstein, L. H. (in press). International counseling competencies: A new frontier in multicultural training. In J. C. Ponterotto, J. M. Casas, L. A. Suzuki, & C. A. Alexander (Eds.), *Handbook of multicultural counseling.* Thousand Oaks, CA: Sage.

Ægisdóttir, S., Gerstein, L. H., & Çinarbaş, D. C. (2008). Methodological issues in cross-cultural counseling research: Equivalence, bias, and translations. *The Counseling Psychologist, 36,* 188–219.

3

The Counseling Profession In- and Outside the United States

LAWRENCE H. GERSTEIN,
P. PAUL HEPPNER, REX STOCKTON,
FREDERICK T. L. LEONG, AND STEFANÍA ÆGISDÓTTIR

As will become apparent from this chapter and practically every other chapter in this handbook, the counseling profession is much larger than any one country (Heppner, 2006). And, contrary to the belief of some, the profession outside the United States is thriving, making important discoveries about human behavior and the science and practice of counseling, and effectively meeting the needs of the clients being served. Furthermore, the counseling profession outside the United States has much to offer professionals in the United States, and it is incumbent on U.S. counselors and counseling psychologists, and for counseling professionals worldwide for that matter, to actively acquire knowledge about the field as it is practiced elsewhere (Heppner, Leong, & Gerstein, 2008).

This chapter begins by discussing the counseling movement in the United States and how it has evolved to embrace an international focus and agenda. Following this, it is argued that the counseling profession is quite vibrant and active in more than one specific country, that is, the United States. Next, the chapter addresses the importance of counselors and counseling psychologists developing a strong cross-cultural sensitivity to effectively perform in diverse cultures and in different countries. The current status of the internationalization of the counseling profession is then discussed. Challenges revolving around defining various important terms and concepts in the field of counseling are covered next. The chapter ends with a presentation of various trends and challenges for counseling professionals worldwide and some recommendations for addressing these challenges.

THE COUNSELING PROFESSION EXISTS BEYOND ONE COUNTRY

In the sense of human beings listening to and assisting one another, counseling has been practiced in some form or another throughout history. It could be associated with a hypothesized genetic predisposition toward altruism. Some writers (e.g., Torrey, 1972) have drawn comparisons between witchdoctors and psychiatrists or psychotherapists. Torrey in his classic book, *The Mind Game: Witchdoctors and Psychiatrists,* argued that these individuals rely on similar philosophies and strategies to help people. That is, these helpers are effective when the persons they assist are instilled with hope, have faith in their provider's talents, believe in the treatment, expect positive outcomes, share the same worldview, and experience a similarity in how the helper cognitively and perceptually approaches the world. While it is true that people from the same culture are more likely to embrace a similar worldview, and cognitive and perceptual style, these factors and the others mentioned by Torrey are all critical in his view to the outcome of a healing relationship, be it with a witchdoctor or a psychiatrist.

Counseling as a formal discipline, however, is now just a hundred years old with the launching of the vocational guidance movement, whereas natural healers or witchdoctors as Torrey called them have been around since ancient times. Beginning in the United States, counseling spread to Great Britain and Europe, and then expanded throughout the world (Stockton, Garbelman, Kaladow, & Terry, 2007). The process of international expansion has been greatly aided through the efforts of national and international organizations dedicated to the helping profession.

Perhaps more than any other individual, Hans Hoxter was responsible for the development of counseling worldwide (Ivey, 2003). He was personally responsible for helping found two international organizations, the International Association of Educational and Vocational Guidance (IAEVG) in 1950 and the International Roundtable for the Advancement of Counselling (IRTAC) in 1966. In 1997, IRTAC was renamed as the International Association for Counselling (IAC).

Hoxter was a remarkable man, one of the truly great figures in the counseling movement. He was a contemporary of other luminaries in counseling and psychology such as Jean Piaget, Leona Tyler, and Gilbert Wrenn (Ivey, 2003). His special talent was to bring people and organizations together. For example,

he worked to gain consultative status with organizations such as the United Nations, UNESCO, and many other international organizations of this caliber (Borgen, 2003). IAC continues to bring together professionals from around the world in their annual meetings that are held in various countries each year. In addition, IAC members can be part of a "working group" that interacts throughout the year, reporting on their activities at the annual meeting. These meetings provide a venue that facilitates exchange between individuals around the world. Another effective mechanism for the exchange of ideas, practices, and research is through the *International Journal for the Advancement of Counselling* published by the IAC. This is a valuable resource for articles from professionals worldwide. Among its other accomplishments, the founding of counseling organizations nationally, in several countries, has been a direct result of the influence of IAC.

National organizations, particularly in the West, have begun to develop an international focus. Examples of this include the National Board of Certified Counselors (NBCC), which is a national certification organization. NBCC, however, operates with a broad counseling mission (see Chapter 7 this volume). This organization established NBCC International (NBCC-I) in 2003 "to strengthen counseling and highlight counseling needs throughout the world" (NBCC, 2009). Not long after its founding, the Southeast Asia tsunami of 2004 occurred, and NBCC-I became active in collaboration with other groups, including the World Health Organization (WHO), in providing support to mental health professionals who offered counseling services to those affected by the tsunami. Currently, through a series of international conferences, NBCC-I brings together counselors and other helping professionals throughout the world.

The American Counseling Association (ACA) that serves as an umbrella structure for counselors in the United States through both its divisions and individual members has had a major influence on the development of counseling internationally. Particularly after World War II, influential U.S. counselors who were ACA members, primarily university faculty, began to travel to other countries and to serve as a resource for those interested in counseling.

Various divisions of ACA such as the Association for Multicultural Counseling and Development (AMCD), National Career Development Association (NCDA), and other divisions that became active in international outreach also encouraged these individual efforts. In some ACA divisions, there is a formal committee structure for international activities. Also, the ACA publication, the *Journal of Counseling and Development,* at times, features articles with an international focus. The annual ACA conference brings together many international counselors who interact with colleagues from the United States and other countries throughout the world. In addition to the informal connections that are made at receptions for international visitors, various convention programs also provide a venue for international speakers who both contribute to the knowledge base and stay current with the professional developments of their Western counterparts (e.g., U.S. counselors).

The American Psychological Association (APA) has a long-standing interest and involvement in international activities as well. There is an Office of International Affairs in the national headquarters, an International Division (52), and substantial international activity in many of the other divisions, including Division 17, the Society of Counseling Psychology (see Chapter 1, this volume).

Counseling psychology in the United States has a long and distinguished history (see reviews by Blocher, 2000; Borgen, 1984; Heppner, 1990; Heppner, Casas, Carter, & Stone, 2000; Meara & Myers, 1999; Scott, 1980; Whiteley, 1980, 1984). In 1946, Division 17 (then called Personnel and Guidance Psychology) of the APA was founded. The historic establishment of Division 17 was in many ways the cumulative confluence of the vocational guidance, mental hygiene, and psychometric movements, all of which began in the early 1900s. Just 7 years later, in 1953, the division name was changed to Counseling Psychology; in 2002, the name was changed once again to the Society of Counseling Psychology. The division has maintained its position within the larger APA for now more than 60 years, at one point having more than 3,000 members within the division and

another 11,000 counseling psychologists in other divisions of the APA. "Although Division 17 formally represents organized counseling psychology [in the U.S.], the profession has now evolved beyond any one organization" (Heppner et al., 2000, p. 37) and currently includes very important collaborative relations with several other organizations such as the Council of Counseling Psychology Training Programs (which has today considerable strength within U.S. professional psychology) as well as the Association of Counseling Center Training Agencies (which also has evolved into a strong force within organized psychology). The combined efforts of these and other professional groups represent a very strong voice for counseling psychology in the United States (Heppner et al., 2000). In 2005, an International Section of Division 17 was formed by more than 150 international and U.S.-based counseling professionals to provide a voice for individuals specifically interested in international issues. The overall mission of this section continues to be encouraging, promoting, and facilitating a scientist-professional model of counseling psychology in international contexts in the United States and worldwide through research, service, teaching, training, policy development and implementation, and networking. The members of the section interact through a newsletter, listserv, and Web site (http://www.internationalcounselingpsychology.org).

Major national conferences followed the founding of the Counseling Psychology Division initially in 1951 with the Northwestern Conference and later with conferences such as the Greystone Conference (1964), Georgia Conference (1987), Houston Conference (2001), and Chicago Conference (2008); the latter of which was the historic first International Counseling Psychology Conference held in the United States. In addition, doctoral training in counseling psychology has received a great deal of attention over the years, with initial accreditation of doctoral training programs more than 50 years ago (1952); as of this writing, there are more than 70 APA-accredited doctoral programs in counseling psychology in the United States. Moreover, in the 1980s, a standardized credentialing or licensing system was begun in every state in the United States. Counseling psychologists have also maintained an active program of empirical research for more than 50 years with increasing "methodological sophistication and rigor, and providing important new knowledge that is furthering the development of theories and practice relevant to counseling psychology" (Heppner et al., 2000, p. 37). The combination of long-standing strong professional organizations within U.S. counseling psychology, an active and growing sophistication of evidence-based knowledge, a wide array of accredited training programs, and a respectable and standardized credentialing system had led to the perception that "counseling psychology [in the U.S.] is strong, vibrant, politically active, and expanding" (Heppner et al., 2000, p. 37).

In fact, in 2005, Heppner, then president of the Society of Counseling Psychology of the APA proclaimed, "It is a great time to be a counseling psychologist. We have strong knowledge bases and practice skills, and we have strong professional organizations" (Heppner, 2006, p. 170). In essence, the counseling psychology profession in the United States has evolved from the late-19th-century vocational guidance movement to a strong, mature, vibrant, politically correct, active, and expanding profession (Heppner et al., 2000). For many years, it seemed that the heart of counseling psychology was Division 17 (Society of Counseling Psychology) of the APA. As was stated earlier, Division 17 was established in 1946, and for quite a long time it represented organized counseling psychology. The U.S. counseling psychology profession, however, has now evolved beyond any one organization, and it includes viable, active, and politically strong groups such as the Council of Counseling Psychology Training Programs, the Association of Counseling Center Training Agencies, the Academy of Counseling of Psychology, the Council of the Specialty of Counseling Psychology, and other organizations (see Heppner et al., 2000). Although there is considerable overlap in the membership of the Society of Counseling Psychology and some of the other counseling organizations mentioned earlier (e.g., ACA, ICA), there has not been a great deal of direct organizational coordination and collaboration. Given the great needs for consultation, training, and on-the-ground service, it is hoped that more official contact between various counseling organizations throughout the world will be forthcoming in the near future.

Perhaps for a variety of reasons, it may seem to some people that counseling psychology is a U.S. discipline (Heppner, Leong, & Chiao, 2008; Leung, 2003; McWhirter, 1988). It must be stressed, however, that while counseling psychology as a specialized formally recognized discipline or a professional label is not common outside the United States, the services provided by counseling psychologists in the United States certainly are offered by individuals (e.g., general psychologists, guidance counselors, clergy, nurses, social workers, physicians, fortune-tellers) living in other countries. Moreover, as Pedersen (2005) so eloquently stated, "The functions of counseling have been practiced for thousands of years and are not merely an invention of the last century or two" (p. xi). Similarly, sometimes erroneously U.S.-based counseling psychologists assume that counseling psychology in the United States is the most advanced or most well-developed specialty across the globe (Heppner, Leong, & Chiao, 2008). In fact, for the most part, many U.S. counseling psychologists have not received much exposure to the counseling professions in other countries. We are so encapsulated in the United States, we lack awareness of the implications, and our international colleagues sometimes get annoyed with our ignorance combined with our individualistic perspectives (Heppner, 2007). Our sense, as well, is that frequently U.S. counseling psychologists are oblivious to the counseling professions in other countries and know very few, if any, international counseling scholars. This lack of exposure and knowledge, however, is understandable for many reasons. In general, U.S. training programs do not offer much information about counseling and counseling psychology outside the United States. There is lack of information about the functions of organized counseling outside the United States that is published in U.S. counseling journals (especially, prior to 2005). Furthermore, U.S. libraries typically do not subscribe to foreign counseling and psychology journals. The lack of exposure to and perhaps the lack of ability of U.S. scholars to read publications not written in the English language also contribute to U.S. counseling professionals being oblivious to the profession in other countries. Also, in the United States, prior to 2000, there was a general lack of international focus in counseling and counseling psychology beyond the U.S. borders. In fact, many international scholars, especially before the year 2005, experienced difficulties when trying to publish or present at professional conferences on issues relevant to populations outside the United States (e.g., Leung, 2003; Ægisdóttir & Gerstein, in press).

Nonetheless, the lack of exposure in the United States to counseling professions around the world is quite unfortunate because it represents a tremendous loss to U.S. counseling psychologists and counselors. The many chapters in this book from numerous countries indicate the development of a broad range of knowledge acquired from around the world. Not only has such knowledge been unavailable to U.S. counseling professionals until now with the publication of this book, a lack of information about counseling and psychology worldwide also means less awareness and comprehension about different cultural contexts and what they mean for counseling (see Chapter 9, Japan; Chapter 10, South Korea; Chapter 35, United Arab Emirates, this volume). These limitations not only restrict U.S. counseling psychologists' knowledge base but also their worldview and understanding of humanity around the globe.

The current economic recession in the United States, beginning in the year 2008, that has expanded worldwide, reminds us about how interconnected countries are in modern times. With economic globalization and increased technology, many countries and cultures have experienced greater pressure toward cultural change than ever before. Such change can be perceived as positive and negative. Oftentimes, societies are resistant to economic, social, and political changes and hang on to cultural traditions sometimes beyond their original intent. Berry (1997), for instance, describing the power of culture stated that "individuals generally act in ways

that correspond to cultural influences and expectations" (p. 6). It is also true that even the most ancient of societies is not static in their beliefs and practices. Sometimes very slowly, but in other places quite rapidly, change occurs, be it positive or negative. For instance, current technology, such as cell phones and the Internet, makes instant communication between individuals who are geographically separated possible. This can enhance the sharing of ideas, worldviews, and ways of living.

Migration to cities and tourism are additional factors that expose cultures to change. Sadly, the forced migration as a result of wars also brings about rapid change and social disruption. We suspect that when societies go through rapid change, the climate for counseling develops. Then, counseling services, formal or informal, provide solace and guidance that are often interrupted and even destroyed.

It is difficult to keep up with the exponential expansion of counseling worldwide. Counseling is a natural progression as countries develop a resource base and begin to react to profound demographic changes. "When a nation lacks the financial and organizational capital to reinvest in the country, mental health and other services tend to remain underdeveloped—despite the need for these services that is often present in such times of crisis" (Stockton et al., 2007, p. 80). Fortunately, though, this lack of resources is sometimes mitigated by the contributions of nongovernmental organizations (NGOs) or foreign government assistance that provides assistance for counseling services. Thus, from an early-20th-century beginning by either internal development or external aid, counseling has become a worldwide phenomenon, and U.S. counseling professionals must accept this reality and actively develop a much broader and richer understanding of the diverse cultures and countries around the globe.

THE IMPORTANCE OF CROSS-CULTURAL SENSITIVITY

Almost 50 years ago, Gilbert Wrenn (1962) raised concerns about counselors' cross-cultural insensitivities in a landmark book, *The Counselor in a Changing*

World. Wrenn was particularly concerned about counselors' inability to understand others from a different culture, and in essence, he warned of the dangers of cultural encapsulation. "Although Wrenn's message was clear about the importance of counselors' understanding of their own worldviews and how these may affect their work with clients from different cultures, it was not widely received" (Heppner, Leong, & Chiao, 2008, p. 69). This notion of being insensitive to other's worldviews, or ethnocentrism, has been suggested as perhaps "the biggest impediment" (Marsella & Pedersen, 2004, p. 414) to the internationalization of the counseling profession. In fact, many scholars have identified ethnocentrism as a major challenge (e.g., Cheung, 2000; Gerstein, 2006; Heppner, 2006; Heppner, Leong, & Chiao, 2008; Kwan & Gerstein, 2008; Leong & Blustein, 2000; Leong & Leach, 2007; Leong & Ponterotto, 2003; Leung, 2003; Marsella, 1998; McWhirter, 2000; Norsworthy, 2006; Pedersen & Leong, 1997; Segall, Lonner, & Berry, 1998).

Ethnocentrism is particularly problematic because "when we are unaware of cultural issues, it is difficult to know what we do not know" (Heppner, Leong, & Chiao, 2008, p. 77). And, when counseling professionals are unaware of the cultural context in their interactions with international colleagues, their lack of awareness significantly affects their understanding, sensitivity, and appropriate responses (Heppner, Leong, & Chiao, 2008). Sometimes, the lack of cross-cultural awareness of U.S. counseling psychologists and counselors is overlooked, and our international colleagues simply dismiss our responses as innocent and uninformed behavior coming from outsiders or foreigners who just lack cultural knowledge. In addition, sometimes the emphasis on individualism within the dominant Eurocentric culture in the United States can also result in a more self-centered orientation in contrast to more collectivistic cultures. And sometimes, the combination of perceived cultural insensitivity and individualism will result in serious negative perceptions of U.S. scholars, ranging from annoyance to frustration to anger. As Heppner (2006) noted, "It is all too easy to offend our international colleagues" (p. 169). Because cross-cultural insensitivities, slights, and disrespectful behavior often occur without the U.S. counseling professionals' awareness, they often

continue their insensitive actions and may never get corrected. Such ongoing negative consequences can inhibit or even curtail cross-cultural and cross-national collaboration.

As a greater number of U.S. counseling psychologists and counselors perform work beyond their geographical borders, though, their awareness of their limited knowledge about the world's cultures and its implications for counseling may increase. A very strong statement about the information available about cultures worldwide was voiced by Arnett (2008). He persuasively argued that psychological research published in six premier APA journals focused primarily on Americans who make up less than 5% of the world's population. Therefore, the currently published research in the premier U.S. journals has ignored the remaining 95% of the world's population. The same can be said about research in counseling and counseling psychology. Gerstein and Ægisdóttir (2007) found that counseling journals included few studies on international populations and topics. Based on his review, Arnett concluded that the "mainstream of American Psychology has so far been largely oblivious to international contributions and remains largely an insular enterprise" (p. 603). And, unfortunately, this conclusion also applies to the U.S. counseling and counseling psychology professions. Leung (2003) even stated that it is possible for U.S. counseling psychology students to obtain a PhD without ever reading an international article!

CURRENT STATUS OF INTERNATIONALIZATION OF THE COUNSELING PROFESSION

Recently, a number of scholars have reported on the breadth and depth of the counseling profession across the globe (e.g., Gerstein & Ægisdóttir, 2005a, 2005b; Heppner & Gerstein, 2008; Heppner, Leong, & Gerstein, 2008; Leong & Savickas, 2007; Stockton et al., 2007). In essence, the counseling profession is growing rapidly worldwide, not only in size but stature. The counseling profession is developing at different rates in non-Western countries, and while it is a very specialized field in the United States, in other countries, where psychology is poorly established, many types of professionals and paraprofessionals who have received little to no training are offering counseling services (Cheung, 2000).

Although there are many cross-national similarities and differences in the identity and credentials of counselors and counseling psychologists and in the breadth and function of their professional associations (Heppner & Gerstein, 2008; Heppner, Leong, & Gerstein, 2008), the cumulative impact of our international colleagues and their professional groups worldwide is revealing, informative, exciting, and inspiring. Moreover, the recent development of an International Division of Counseling Psychology (Division 16) in the International Association of Applied Psychology, the oldest applied psychology association in the world, is very exciting and indicates the growing internationalization of the counseling profession.

Furthermore, as this first *International Handbook of Cross-Cultural Counseling* attests to, there is much to learn from counseling professionals around the world. This includes learning about shared and indigenous perspectives in counseling and psychology worldwide, current research findings and conceptual models, and unique strategies of psychology and counseling practice around the globe. In fact, it is our opinion that an opportunity to learn from our international colleagues is one of the most exciting new developments within the counseling specialty. We also anticipate that increased international collaboration will have the potential to change the entire face of counseling and counseling psychology forever. As Heppner (2006) claimed, international contact and collaboration will "enhance the sophistication of our research, expand our knowledge bases, increase the range of counseling interventions, and in essence, increase counseling effectiveness across a wide range of populations" (p. 169). Clearly, U.S. counseling professionals can benefit greatly from an understanding of counseling in other countries and cultures.

DEFINITIONAL CHALLENGES FOR THE COUNSELING PROFESSION

As reported in Chapter 1 of this volume, the definitions for *counseling, counselor,* and *counseling psychologist* are not consistent throughout the world. Neither is there consistency in current uses of these terms nor the required credentials to use one of these professional titles. In the United States and in Canada, a doctoral degree is required to be eligible to obtain the title of "counseling psychologist." In other parts of the world, counseling psychology is a master's- or bachelor's-level profession, or such a professional title may not even exist. Moreover, what is considered professional counseling in the United States and Canada does not necessarily reflect how professional counseling is practiced elsewhere. For example, in Great Britain, an attorney or a legal representative is also a counselor. In the United States, there are financial counselors, genetic counselors, nutritional counselors, home improvement counselors, and executive coaches/counselors. Therefore, it is critical to differentiate professional counseling and counselors from other types of services and providers. Stated differently, it is essential to clarify and stipulate what professional counseling is and what it is not.

Regardless of how counseling is defined around the world, individuals in every country and culture still have to cope with emotional and physical suffering. Such suffering can come in different forms and can be experienced quite differently from culture to culture and from country to country. As Frank and Frank (1993) reported in their classic book *Persuasion and Healing: A Comparative Study of Psychotherapy,* from a Western perspective, many individuals are struggling with feelings of demoralization. However, as Tyler, Brome, and Williams (1991) so eloquently stated, there are many ways to be human. They proposed that their ethnic validity model of psychotherapy is predicated on the assumption "that there are a variety of ways of being human and these ways are not directly translatable into one another" (p. 25). Similarly, extrapolating from Tyler et al.'s model, there are also many forms of healing in the world, including professional counseling, to match these multiple ways of being human.

In the United States and many other Western countries, there is a strong Cartesian (Descartes) dualistic philosophy and methodology of intervention, be it psychological or otherwise. For instance, if a person in the United States is clinically depressed, he or she will tend to seek help from a mental health professional (e.g., counselor, counseling psychologist, psychiatrist). If on the other hand, an individual in the United States is having a heart problem, he or she will visit a cardiologist. In general then, persons in the United States prefer to see a medical doctor for problems with their bodies and a mental health professional for concerns about their minds.

In many other cultures or countries, a person in need will seek out a "helper" who offers services to treat a broad range of problems. Such helpers conceptualize individuals in terms of their whole body, mind, and spirit. They embrace a holistic approach to caring for others integrating intervention strategies such as communication, rituals, herbs, touch, and prayer. In general, it would appear that in many Western countries, especially the United States, mental health professionals gravitate to a dualistic, analytic approach (treat the mind not the body; treat the body and not the mind), while in the East (Asia) and parts of South, Latin, and Central America, they embrace a holistic, integrated approach (treat both the mind and the body). It is important to note also that persons' help-seeking behavior is greatly influenced by the health service system of each country regardless of its grounding in a dualistic or holistic philosophy.

There are also some important distinctions that can be stated about differences in the way mental health professionals in the West think about and approach counseling. U.S. counseling professionals, in general, are very practical and pragmatic. Many believe that all the problems experienced by clients are solvable. Furthermore, being pragmatic, U.S. counseling professionals are not as interested in philosophical issues and challenges. They approach their work as problem solvers frequently using functional approaches such as cognitive-behavioral therapy, dialectic therapy, and solution-focused therapy. In contrast, mental health professionals in Europe, in general, are much more interested in philosophical issues and challenges, and as such, they value discussions with their clients about meaning and purpose. They also believe that not all problems are solvable. European counselors and psychologists are also baffled by the extensive use in the United States

of educational and other tests in counseling. Counseling in Europe, therefore, is often about phenomenological exploration and finding meaning. Therefore, existential therapy based on the writings of Rollo May and Victor Frankl often guides the work of European mental health professionals.

Not surprisingly, the educational training programs for mental health professionals in the United States and Europe stress different bodies of knowledge and skills. In the United States, there is a heavy emphasis on the acquisition and enactment of various skills. In Europe, in contrast, there is an extensive focus on philosophy and the establishment of a rich conceptual framework and ability to think and express thoughts. In fact, it is not uncommon to be just trained in one or very few theoretical frameworks. Moreover, in European counseling training programs, students sit for essay examinations not multiple choice tests. Additionally, in Europe, graduate students rarely take classes. Instead, there is an apprenticeship model of learning, where the student has individual meetings with a professor and/or participates in informal discussions with other students at locations apart from campus. In Great Britain, for example, a graduate student in counseling receives a highly personalized and individualized education.

While generalizations often lead to misunderstandings and conflicts, sometimes they help capture the essence of situations. Given this caveat, European mental health professionals frequently perceive U.S. mental health professionals as technicians and mechanical, while professionals in the United States often view their European counterparts as philosophers. If these stereotypes are even somewhat accurate, then it follows that individuals who earn a PhD in counseling/counseling psychology in Europe have obtained a Doctorate of Philosophy, whereas persons earning a similar degree in the United States have obtained a Doctorate of Pragmatism!

Given the observations stated above, at the most basic level, counseling professionals around the world, particularly U.S. counseling professionals, must acquire information on the unique and common function of counseling and the shared and specific roles of mental health professionals in different countries. Speaking at an IAC conference, Hoxter (1998) defined counseling as follows:

> A method of relating and responding to others with the aim of providing them with opportunities to explore, clarify, and work towards living in a more personally satisfying and resourceful way . . . and may be used in widely different contexts and settings. (p. 29)

There are a variety of other definitions promulgated by professional organizations, including the APA Society of Counseling Psychology, Division 17, as well as professional societies in various other countries. The central theme of each definition though is *the counselor as a helping professional.*

Since professional counseling as we think of it today began in the United States, and has grown rapidly throughout the world, there is sometimes an assumption, as stated earlier, that a Western or U.S. model of counseling has to be the most desired one. A Western or U.S. style of counseling, however, may clash with local or national cultural traditions that are highly significant to the populace. Emavardhana (2005) noted that the Western concept of counseling, for example, often emphasizes the importance of the individual, which can run counter to the more traditional beliefs in community prevalent in many developing world societies. The role of the family, including extended family, clan, and tribe cannot be overemphasized. T. Dodson, who has worked extensively in Latin America, concurs and comments on the common bonds of cultural values regarding family that exist within Latin America: "A counselor would be wise to consider the family impact of the change process that an individual is going through while going through a counseling experience" (personal communication, January 24, 2009).

This emphasis on the communal is exemplified in a story related by L. Levers (personal communication, January 19, 2009), who was asked to counsel an influential African male who had been kidnapped and then later rescued. She agreed to meet the individual at his home, which was in effect a compound. She was surprised that not only was the client present for the meeting but many members of his extended family and friends were also in attendance. Rather than a 1-hour session, the counseling lasted throughout the day, and meals were even served. Levers reported that despite her initial surprise, the event went well and the client felt relief.

As Bradley (2000) has noted, cultural misunderstandings can occur through nonverbal ways, as well. This became very apparent early in the career of one of the coauthors of this chapter, Rex Stockton, when he was on sabbatical leave in Spain and also attending a conference in Holland. Stockton's Spanish colleagues would place themselves physically very close to him and his Dutch colleagues, equally friendly, expressed friendship by shaking hands while keeping an arm's length distance. This is also true of eye contact; in some cultures, avoidance of eye contact is a mark of showing respect rather than being regarded as evasive.

Stockton's thinking about counseling also has been informed by contact with a Ghanaian psychologist trained in Western theories and procedures. This psychologist spent several years working in an African mental hospital and talks about the importance of ancestors in some counseling settings. As S. Atindanbila (personal communication, February 15, 2006) related, when counselors in certain settings believe that progress is being made in the course of therapy, they have to understand that unless the client thinks that his or her ancestors will approve of their altered, presumably more therapeutic behavior, they will not change. Thus, it is incumbent on counselors and counseling psychologists to understand the local culture as well as counseling theory.

Levers (2006) who has conducted research with African traditional healers, underscores the importance of acknowledging local customs and indigenous practices when working in areas devastated by illness such as the treatment of HIV/AIDS. She noted that "at least 80% of all Africans throughout sub-Saharan Africa continue to seek health care services from traditional healers" (L. Levers, personal communication, January 19, 2009). The most enlightened Western programs have responded by providing information and training to the traditional healers.

Western counselors and counseling psychologists are sometimes surprised by the central role of religion in the lives of many other clients. When Stockton was first asked to provide training in Africa (Botswana) for human services personnel who worked with individuals who had HIV/AIDS, he made it a point to spend considerable time reading about African history and culture in general and Botswana in particular. Nevertheless, he was surprised when after beginning the training, a participant raised her hand and said, "Prof, don't you think we should begin with a prayer?" Although surprised, Stockton was able to say, "I need all the help I can get," and another participant then led a prayer. After this, a weeklong workshop proceeded with a prayer at the beginning of each day. Integration of prayer into the workshop content was appreciated by the participants and probably contributed to their positive response.

Wherever they work, counselors and counseling psychologists have to figure out how to conduct their activities in ways such as to reduce stigma. This is not only true with dreaded diseases such as HIV/AIDS, but even in more innocuous settings, this can be a major problem. A counselor from Mauritius who was trained in the United States related that she had to change her "mental health counselor" title to "counselor" once she started her private practice in her country so as to minimize stigma. This stigma is not restricted to Mauritius, but in either personal work or contacts with others, it seems to be a worldwide phenomenon (J. d'Argent, personal communication, January 21, 2009).

Some more traditional cultures place importance on storytelling and singing and dancing more so than is typical of the U.S. tradition. For example, in several African countries, when Stockton has provided training or consultation, participants who were either human service professionals or clients had almost always honored the occasion with a ceremonial dance and song. The meaning and intrinsic purpose of the ceremony can be very life affirming and may provide some solace in lives that, too often, are affected by poverty and disease.

Counseling in its broadest form, therefore, has been and is increasingly prevalent worldwide.

However, beyond some fundamental values and common themes, it is expressed in ways that accommodate to various cultures and traditions. Above all else, it remains a means to formally provide help to those in need across a broad spectrum from vocational to mental health counseling services.

TRENDS AND CHALLENGES FOR COUNSELING PROFESSIONALS WORLDWIDE

Counseling principles may be enduring, but they are shaped by the needs of society, and we can expect that as the world is evolving, changes in both the profession of counseling and the provision of counseling services will also take place. People worldwide will continue, however, to be challenged by traditional counseling issues such as family and relationship problems, career choice, and finding employment, as well as stress, mood, anxiety, and other emotional concerns. With that being said, while it is obviously difficult to predict the future of counseling around the world, some developments can be anticipated with reasonable certainty. For example, we believe that the dire, potentially explosive nature of the world's urban slums will likely intensify. Additionally, there is also mounting evidence of the dramatic rise in addiction to the Internet, especially in Asian countries.

The number of individuals displaced and negatively affected by climate change will probably multiply as well. Individuals will continue to be traumatized by conflicts, civil wars, ethnopolitical conflicts, migration and immigration, and natural disasters. As long as the field of counseling remains supple, respectful of other cultures, research based, innovative, cooperative with other disciplines, and true to its core values, it should be in a position to play an important role in ameliorating some small fraction of our world's very significant ills.

As stated earlier and throughout this book, technology has made it possible for people to communicate in ways incomprehensible in prior generations. This technology and the emerging new technologies have great potential for training, practice, supervision, and networking in the field of counseling regardless where professionals are located. We do not know what will evolve or how technology will evolve (who would have predicted YouTube or FaceBook a generation ago?), but for certain, this rich and dynamic resource will produce momentous changes that will provide for challenges as well as opportunities.

The trend toward various national counseling organizations expanding their view to have a more international focus is likely to continue. It is hoped that this will be coupled with the increasing advancement of national and regional counseling organizations in countries where counseling is not as fully developed as is possible. While we cannot know with certainty the shape or disposition of counseling in the future, we can be sure that the need for this service and the need for counselors and counseling psychologists will only increase.

The need for other types of healers around the world will also be important in the years to come. It is critical, therefore, that counseling professionals either develop a respect for such individuals or remain appreciative of their work. However, there must be a clear recognition of what professional counseling is and who is qualified to provide such services. Perhaps, a concept often used in conducting research might help readers to better understand this challenge. Gelso (1979) introduced the *bubble hypothesis* as a way to think about balancing the importance of external and internal validity when formulating a research study. On one hand, it is essential to control the variables in a study (internal validity) in order to rule out confounding variables and competing hypotheses. On the other hand, it is important to capture the "real" environment connected to the variables of interest (external validity) in order to increase the likelihood of studying the rich context of interest and the "behavior" of interest in the natural environment. Achieving an acceptable balance between internal and external validity is frequently the best scenario to expect. In the context of the current discussion about the great diversity in how counseling is defined, how counseling is practiced, and who offers the service, a balance is also desirable. If the concepts of counseling, counselor,

and counseling psychologist are broadened to include all forms of healing and all types of healers worldwide, the external validity of these concepts would be greatly increased. If this were the case, it would be challenging to identify a profession of counseling or a professional using the title counselor or counseling psychologist. Counseling professionals are not genetic counselors or financial counselors.

In contrast, if there was a much more specific and concrete definition of counseling, and greater quality control monitoring the practice of professional counseling and the use of the title counselor or counseling psychologist worldwide, the internal validity of these concepts would be greatly increased. As a result though, few people around the world would be able to practice counseling or use the title of counselor or counseling psychologist. Striking a balance between internal and external validity in the context just described is quite challenging given the diversity in the counseling profession and the diverse cultural context throughout the world. At the very least, it is important to establish an agreed on set of competencies and base of knowledge. Then, it would be possible to consider counseling as a profession in different countries instead of thinking that anyone who is involved in healing or helping is a counselor or a member of such a profession.

There is also a need for a very basic universal declaration of ethical principles in counseling and some common training paradigm to prepare counselors and counseling psychologists. While ethics are culture bound, it would seem possible for counseling professionals regardless of where they reside to agree on basic principles such as do no harm, provide competent services, act responsibly, and demonstrate respect to clients. Having a shared basic ethical framework throughout the world could instill greater hope in potential clients; serve to network counseling professionals around a common goal; and offer the profession a shared language for dialogue, discussion, and possible important competencies. Accomplishing these tasks will not be easy. The many professional associations discussed earlier in this chapter are key to the success of such an endeavor as they are often the gatekeepers and policymakers linked with the counseling fields around the world.

Another major challenge touched on very early in this chapter is the tension between the hegemony of the U.S. model of counseling and psychology and the indigenization of counseling and psychology elsewhere, especially in Asia (e.g., Japan, Taiwan, China) (see Leong, 2002). At this point, as stated earlier, there is a greater flow and exportation of U.S. models of counseling to other countries. One might say that there is a "McDonaldization" of counseling and psychology infiltrating countries worldwide. U.S. counseling professionals must seriously think about the consequences of continuing to uncritically export their models or accept the request of non-U.S. counseling professionals to import such models. U.S. counseling professionals must also contemplate this issue alongside the importance of respecting and embracing indigenous approaches to counseling found in other countries.

One other challenge must be mentioned, though it is discussed in much greater detail in Chapter 2 in this volume. There is a tension in the United States between counseling professionals who focus on domestic cultural issues and those who attend to international cultural topics. The reality of limited available resources to address the needs of both domestic and international populations is valid and critical to both meeting the needs of diverse clientele and securing the viability and prosperity of the counseling profession. At a recent meeting of the APA Educational Leadership Conference, one of the authors of this chapter observed that a majority of the participants informally surveyed through the use of DataMite software during a large group discussion indicated that international work would take away needed resources from the domestic U.S. population. Respondents also reported that focusing on international work would place limits on other coursework. Additionally, some respondents considered shifting the focus to international work another form of racism, where we treat "international work" as exotic and glamorous and yet ignore the same populations when they are in our own backyard (e.g., working in Mexico is positively viewed, while working with Mexican Americans is shunned).

There have been some anecdotal reports in the U.S. counseling profession of racial ethnic minorities not approving of the field's interest in international activities. From another perspective, some cross-cultural researchers outside the United States have commented that the U.S. multicultural counseling movement is about advocacy and justice, not scientific inquiry. Furthermore, some of these cross-cultural psychologists have stated that U.S. multicultural counseling professionals are preoccupied with race and ethnicity and more interested in social change than pursuing research for the sake of science.

It would seem, therefore, that the multicultural counseling movement and the cross-cultural and cross-national counseling movements might be on a collision course. As outlined in Chapter 2, however, all the movements can learn from each other, all can be enriched through respectful collaboration, and ultimately the science and practice of psychology and counseling will benefit from cross-fertilization. Some solutions focused on bringing the multicultural, cross-cultural, and cross-national counseling movements closer together are also discussed in Chapter 2. Regardless of the specific solution, what is required is the ability to think and act outside the self-serving box of each movement. In fact, the paradigms to resolve the conflicts between the movements are inside the box. It is fruitless and dangerous to believe that the counseling profession in the United States or elsewhere must choose between a domestic or international focus. Both foci are essential for the continued successful evolution of a vibrant and culturally rich and effective profession of counseling. Throughout the world, what is needed in the field of counseling is a new paradigm and a new way of thinking and acting. For as Heppner (2006) predicted, "In the future, the parameters of counseling psychology will cross many countries and many cultures" (p. 170). More specifically, the accumulative knowledge bases of the counseling profession will be grounded in the scientific and applied discoveries of counseling professionals from all corners of the world. As Leong and Blustein (2000) stated, "We need a global perspective that recognizes and is open to other cultures in other countries, whether on this continent or across the oceans, on the other side of the world" (p. 5).

CONCLUSION

It is rather apparent that the counseling profession is blossoming worldwide. This is good news as the rising number of psychological and other concerns experienced by people around the globe speaks of the importance of a highly effective profession that can function appropriately and successfully across borders and between cultures. There is increasing evidence that counseling professionals everywhere are waking up to the reality that they must embrace and enact both an insider or emic (culture specific) and outsider or etic (transcending culture) view about human behavior, culture, and a host of counseling theories, strategies, and methodologies. The available communication tools (e.g., e-mail, Skype) to many counseling professionals, including those located in remote regions of the world, have made it possible for a very large number of persons to actively and immediately connect and network with each other. The future success of a global integrated and collaborative counseling profession depends, in part, on maximizing the use of such tools. More important, it requires suspending biases, embracing differences and commonalities, and valuing and respecting multiple and diverse paradigms of conceptualizing human behavior, and also strategies to promote well-being and address problematic behaviors and situations. Additionally, it requires an extensive understanding of the philosophy and mechanics of cross-cultural validity to pursue valid, reliable, and useful indigenous and cross-cultural theories, strategies, and research methodologies (Ægisdóttir, Gerstein, & Çinarbaş, 2008).

We firmly believe that the counseling profession in the United States and elsewhere is at crossroads, and there is no turning back. Instead, we fully expect to witness an exponential shift in how members of the counseling profession throughout the world interact with each other and work together to serve the needs of diverse populations. As was stated earlier in this chapter, international collaboration has a great deal of potential to strengthen the science and practice of the counseling profession, as well as greatly enhance our knowledge of the cultural context (see Heppner, 2008; Heppner, Leong, & Chiao, 2008; Leong & Blustein, 2000). Over time, such collaborative efforts will result in a tapestry of knowledge that will "put the puzzle together as an extraordinary picture of a worldwide psychology" (Heppner, Leong, & Chiao, 2008, p. 82) and counseling profession. Until that time, counseling professionals especially those in the United States must be diligent in their actions and clearly recognize that "as counseling psychology is transported to other cultures, we need to address the fundamental issues of counseling by whom, counseling for whom, and counseling for what" (Cheung, 2000, p. 130).

REFERENCES

Arnett, J. J. (2008). The neglected 95%: Why American psychology needs to become less American. *American Psychologist, 63*, 602–614.

Berry, J. W. (1997). Lead article: Immigration, acculturation, and adaptation. *Applied Psychology: An International Review, 46*(1), 5–68.

Blocher, D. H. (2000). *The evolution of counseling psychology.* New York: Springer.

Borgen, F. H. (1984). Counseling psychology. *Annual Review of Psychology, 35*, 579–604.

Borgen, W. A. (2003). Remembering Hans: His ongoing legacy for guidance and counselling. *International Journal for the Advancement of Counselling, 25*(2/3), 83–88.

Bradley, G. (2000). Responding effectively to the mental health needs of international students. *Higher Education, 39*, 417–433.

Cheung, F. M. (2000). Deconstructing counseling in a cultural context. *The Counseling Psychologist, 28*, 123–132.

Emavardhana, T. (2005, December). *Counseling across borders: How to counsel within the Thai culture.* Keynote presentation at the 11th International Counseling Conference, Bangkok, Thailand.

Frank, J. D., & Frank, J. B. (1993). *Persuasion and healing: A comparative study of psychotherapy* (3rd ed.). Baltimore: Johns Hopkins University Press.

Gelso, C. J. (1979). Research in counseling: Methodological and professional issues. *The Counseling Psychologist, 8,* 7–35.

Gerstein, L. H. (2006). Counseling psychologists as international social architects. In R. L. Toporek, L. H. Gerstein, N. A. Fouad, G. Roysircar-Sodowsky, & T. Israel (Eds.), *Handbook for social justice in counseling psychology: Leadership, vision, and action* (pp. 377–387). Thousand Oaks, CA: Sage.

Gerstein, L. H., & Ægisdóttir, S. (Guest Eds.). (2005a). Counseling around the world [Special issue]. *Journal of Mental Health Counseling, 27,* 95–184.

Gerstein, L. H., & Ægisdóttir, S. (Guest Eds.). (2005b). Counseling outside of the United States: Looking in and reaching out! [Special section]. *Journal of Mental Health Counseling, 27,* 221–281.

Gerstein, L. H., & Ægisdóttir, S. (2007). Training international social change agents: Transcending a U.S. counseling paradigm. *Counselor Education and Supervision, 47,* 123–139.

Heppner, P. P. (Ed.). (1990). *Pioneers in counseling and human development: Personal and professional perspectives.* Washington, DC: American Association of Counseling and Development.

Heppner, P. P. (2006). The benefits and challenges of becoming cross-culturally competent counseling psychologists. *The Counseling Psychologist, 34,* 147–172.

Heppner, P. P. (2007, September). *The role of culture in applied problem solving and coping: Overlooked and almost forgotten.* Keynote address presented at the IAEVG International Guidance Conference General Assembly, Padua, Italy.

Heppner, P. P. (2008). Expanding the conceptualization and measurement of applied problem solving and coping: From stages to dimensions to the almost forgotten cultural context. *American Psychologist, 63,* 803–816.

Heppner, P. H., Casas, J. M., Carter, J., & Stone, G. L. (2000). The maturation of counseling psychology: Multifaceted perspectives, 1978–1998. In S. D. Brown & R. W. Lent (Eds.), *Handbook of counseling psychology* (3rd ed., pp. 3–49). New York: Wiley.

Heppner, P. P., & Gerstein, L. H. (2008). International developments in counseling psychology. In F. T. L. Leong, E. M. Altmaier, & B. D. Johnson (Eds.), *The encyclopedia of counseling psychology: Changes and challenges for counseling in the 21st century* (Vol. 1, pp. 263–265). Thousand Oaks, CA: Sage.

Heppner, P. P., Leong, F. T. L., & Chiao, H. (2008). The growing internationalization of counseling psychology. In S. D. Brown & R. W. Lent (Eds.), *Handbook of counseling psychology* (4th ed., pp. 68–85). New York: Wiley.

Heppner, P. P., Leong, F. T. L., & Gerstein, L. H. (2008). Counseling within a changing world: Meeting the psychological needs of societies and the world. In W. B. Walsh (Ed.), *Biennial review in counseling psychology* (pp. 231–258). Thousand Oaks, CA: Sage.

Hoxter, H. (1998, August). *Counselling as a profession.* Paper presented at the meeting for the International Association for Counselling, Paris, France.

Ivey, A. E. (2003). Hans Zacharias Hoxter: Building counseling internationally. *International Journal for the Advancement of Counselling, 25*(2/3), 95–108.

Kwan, K. L. K., & Gerstein, L. H. (2008). Envisioning a counseling psychology of the world: The mission of the international forum. *The Counseling Psychologist, 36,* 182–187.

Leong, F. T. L. (2002). Challenges for career counseling in Asia: Variations in cultural accommodation [Special issue]. *Career Development Quarterly, 50,* 277–284.

Leong, F. T. L., & Blustein, D. L. (2000). Toward a global vision of counseling psychology. *The Counseling Psychologist, 28,* 5–9.

Leong, F. T. L., & Leach, M. M. (2007). Internalizing counseling psychology in the United States: ASWOT analysis. *Applied Psychology: An International Review, 56,* 165–181.

Leong, F. T. L., & Ponterotto, J. G. (2003). A proposal for internationalizing counseling psychology in the United States: Rationale, recommendations, and challenges. *The Counseling Psychologist, 31,* 381–395.

Leong, F. T. L., & Savickas, M. L. (2007). Introduction to special issue on international perspectives on counseling psychology. *Applied Psychology: An International Review, 56,* 1–6.

Leung, S. A. (2003). A journal worth traveling: Globalization of counseling psychology. *The Counseling Psychologist, 31,* 412–419.

Levers, L. L. (2006). Identifying psychoeducational HIV/AIDS interventions in Botswana: Focus groups and related rapid assessment methods. In C. Fischer (Ed.), *Qualitative research methods for the psychological professions* (pp. 377–410). New York: Elsevier Press.

Marsella, A. J. (1998). Toward a global-community psychology: Meeting the needs of a changing world. *American Psychologist, 53,* 1282–1291.

Marsella, A. J., & Pedersen, P. B. (2004). Internationalizing the counseling psychology curriculum: Toward new values, competencies, and directions. *Counseling Psychology Quarterly, 17,* 413–423.

McWhirter, J. J. (1988). The Fulbright program in counseling psychology. *The Counseling Psychologist, 16,* 279–281.

McWhirter, J. J. (2000). And now, up go the walls: Constructing an international room for counseling psychology. *The Counseling Psychologist, 28,* 117–122.

Meara, N. M., & Myers, R. A. (1999). A history of Division 17 (Counseling Psychology): Establishing stability amid change. In D. A. Dewsbury (Ed.), *Unification through division: Histories of divisions of the American Psychological Association* (Vol. 3, pp. 9–41). Washington, DC: American Psychological Association.

National Board of Certified Counselors. (2009). *NBCC international history.* Retrieved March 30, 2009, from http://www.nbccinternational.org/home/about-nbcc-i/about-history

Norsworthy, K. L. (2006). Bringing social justice to international practices of counseling psychology. In R. L. Toporek, L. R. Gerstein, N. A. Fouad, G. Roysircar-Sodowsky, & T. Israel (Eds.), *Handbook for social justice in counseling psychology: Leadership, vision, and action* (pp. 421–441). Thousand Oaks, CA: Sage.

Pedersen, P. (2005). Series editor's foreword. In R. Moodley & W. West (Eds.), *Integrating traditional healing practices into counseling and psychotherapy* (pp. xi–xii). Thousand Oaks, CA: Sage.

Pedersen, P., & Leong, F. (1997). Counseling in an international context. *The Counseling Psychologist, 25,* 117–122.

Scott, C. W. (1980). History of the division of counseling psychology: 1945–1963. In J. M. Whiteley (Ed.), *The history of counseling psychology* (pp. 25–40). Monterey, CA: Brooks/Cole.

Segall, M. H., Lonner, W. J., & Berry, J. W. (1998). Cross-cultural psychology as a scholarly discipline: On a flowering of culture in behavioral research. *American Psychologist, 53,* 1101–1110.

Stockton, R., Garbelman, J., Kaladow, J., & Terry, L. (2007). The international development of counseling as a profession. In W. K. Schweiger, D. A. Henderson, T. W. Clawson, D. R. Collins, & M. W. Nucholls (Ed.), *Counselor preparation: Programs, faculty, trends* (12th ed., pp. 75–97). New York: Taylor & Francis Group and National Board for Certified Counselors.

Torrey, E. F. (1972). *The mind game: Witchdoctors and psychiatrists.* New York: Emerson Hall.

Tyler, F. B., Brome, D. R., & Williams, J. E. (1991). *Ethnic validity, ecology, and psychotherapy: A psychosocial competence model.* New York: Plenum Press.

Whiteley, J. M. (1980). *Counseling psychology: A historical perspective.* Schenectady, NY: Character Research Press.

Whiteley, J. M. (1984). A historical perspective on the development of counseling psychology as a profession. In S. D. Brown & R. W. Lent (Eds.), *Handbook of counseling psychology* (pp. 3–55). New York: Wiley.

Wrenn, C. G. (1962). *The counselor in a changing world.* Alexandria, VA: American Personnel and Guidance Association.

Ægisdóttir, S., & Gerstein, L. H. (in press). International counseling competencies: A new frontier in multicultural training. In J. C. Ponterotto, J. M. Casas, L. A. Suzuki, & C. A. Alexander (Eds.), *Handbook of multicultural counseling.* Thousand Oaks, CA: Sage.

Ægisdóttir, S., Gerstein, L. H., & Çinarbaş, D. C. (2008). Methodological issues in cross-cultural counseling research: Equivalence, bias, and translations. *The Counseling Psychologist, 36,* 188–219.

4

Exportation of U.S.-Based Models of Counseling and Counseling Psychology

A Critical Analysis

KATHRYN L. NORSWORTHY,
P. PAUL HEPPNER, STEFANÍA ÆGISDÓTTIR,
LAWRENCE H. GERSTEIN, AND PAUL B. PEDERSEN

Collaboration and partnerships across cultures are increasingly important in this age of global connection. What happens in one part of the world now affects people, economies, and governments on the other side of the globe. How a problem is solved in one culture or region can be a valuable source of learning for people facing a similar challenge in another part of the world. Counseling and counseling psychology are certainly part of this interconnected process, as evidenced by the increasing numbers of professionals traveling to other parts of the world to teach, research, and consult, and by the thousands of international students enrolled in Western university counseling and psychology training programs. Yet, we are faced with the sobering reality that Western, and particularly U.S., corporations, governments, and even organized counseling and psychology exert tremendous influence and power globally. Fortunately, conversations are emerging in our professions regarding

how to internationalize in ways that support indigenous development of the professions within each country or culture rather than fostering uncritical exportation of Western models (Leung, 2003; Norsworthy, 2006; Pedersen, 2003; Yang, Hwang, Pedersen, & Daibo, 2003).

Several scholars have indicated that U.S. counselors and psychologists within the American Counseling Association and the American Psychological Association (APA) are becoming more aware of the importance of cultivating cross-cultural and international partnerships of mutuality rather than operating from a hegemonic, potentially colonizing, stance in the global arena (Chung, 2005; Gerstein, 2006; Pedersen, 2003; Rice & Ballou, 2002). As we acknowledge that we all have much to learn from one another, noting the importance of bi- and multidirectional learning, we move closer to a more relevant global counseling profession, one that truly centers culture, context, and identities in the theory, practice, and research of counseling. Cross-national collaboration and partnering that supports the interests and understanding of all people is increasingly critical in this age of globalization and the attendant pressures toward global "homogenization" and "assimilation" (Bochner, 1999).

This chapter explores the issues associated with the transportation of Western counseling models to cultures and countries outside the West. Inherent in this discussion is an examination of the efforts of U.S.-based counseling and psychology researchers in conducting research aimed at informing multicultural, cross-cultural, and transnational work. To this end, we begin this chapter by exploring efforts in the counseling field to understand the role of culture in the counseling profession and in the often blurred distinction between cross-cultural and cultural counseling and psychologies, their research methodologies, their assumptions, and their goals. Attention is given to how to bring this understanding to cross-cultural counseling. With this foundation, we move to an exploration of the context and variables setting the stage for the uncritical transportation of counseling knowledge and skills, particularly from the United States to other countries and regions of the world. Conceptualizing this process as potentially colonizing, we offer an explanation of psychological colonization and imperialism, the dynamics and effects of this process, and how these global power arrangements contextualize the inherent problems connected to the uncritical exportation of U.S. counseling models. We close the chapter with a call for decolonizing and support for indigenizing counseling and counseling psychology around the globe, setting the stage for upcoming chapters that offer more detailed explorations of these topics.

As Paul Pedersen (2003) pointed out regarding U.S. counseling psychology, "We have been all too ready to 'teach' and to 'lead' other countries but perhaps not nearly ready enough to 'learn' and to 'follow'" (p. 397). He goes on to remark, "Counseling psychology does not 'belong' to any single cultural, national, or social group," (p. 398) and wisely acknowledges that the goal is not so much the internationalization of counseling psychology "but more properly about the reinvention of counseling psychology as a profession in a global context" (p. 402).

CROSS-CULTURAL AND CULTURAL COUNSELING AND PSYCHOLOGY: UNDERSTANDING THE BACKGROUND

With the increased interest in culture as an important fourth force in counseling (e.g., Pedersen, 1999), one logically assumes that U.S. counseling professionals working with culturally diverse clientele across one or more countries would possess awareness and knowledge about cultural influences on behavior and psychological processes and about the limitations of uncritically applying U.S. theories outside their cultural context. Counseling professionals need to demonstrate cultural competence and be tentative in their approaches. This points to the importance of understanding the centrality of culture in how humans grow, develop, and manifest distress and psychological problems and disorders. As the world gets smaller, counseling and psychology are in greater need of research and theoretical frameworks for understanding and counseling clients across the spectrum of lived human experience. This section offers a discussion of the contributions and conundrums of cultural and cross-cultural research and psychology in our somewhat fledgling attempts at research and practice within and across cultures.

An interest in studying and understanding contextual influences on behavior is not new. In fact, this interest can be traced all the way back to Wilhelm Wundt's extensive writings on *Volkerpsychologie* in 1900 (Adamopoulos & Lonner, 2001). In particular, during the past 40 years we have witnessed more systematic and increasingly methodologically sophisticated (van de Vijver, 2001) cross-cultural and cultural research in psychology (especially social psychology). Attention to issues of cross-cultural international research and practice has a shorter history in counseling and counseling psychology. It is only in the past decade that there has been an increase in the number of publications including international topics and samples of counseling outside the Unites States (e.g., Gerstein & Ægisdóttir, 2005a, 2005b, 2005c, 2007; Heppner, 2006; Heppner & Gerstein, 2008; Heppner, Leong, & Gerstein, 2008; Kwan & Gerstein, 2008; Leong & Blustein, 2000; Leong & Ponterotto, 2003; Leong & Savickas, 2007; Pedersen, Draguns, Lonner, & Trimble, 2008; Ægisdóttir & Gerstein, 2005). Even though the counseling field has seen an increased interest in international topics, publications in contemporary journals appear at an alarmingly low rate. For instance, Gerstein and Ægisdóttir (2007) found that international topics only accounted for about 6% of publications between the years 2000 and 2004 in four U.S. counseling journals.

Most scholars within Western psychology and counseling treat culture as an important factor influencing persons' thoughts, feelings, and behaviors (e.g., feminist, multicultural, cross-cultural, and cultural movements within counseling and counseling psychology) rather than as a confounding or nuisance variable. Pike (1966) first introduced the emic/etic framework (from linguistics), positing that both aspects were the same single and unified reality seen from two different vantage points. A dualistic perspective has emerged regarding etic (universal) and emic (relativistic) approaches in studying culture. Indeed, the interpretation that divides emic and etic into polarized alternatives may indicate one of the most obvious cultural biases in Western psychology, a point argued convincingly by Pedersen, Crethar, and Carlson (2008) in their discussion of cultural empathy and the Western categorization into a quantitative framework. This is perhaps a clear illustration that, indeed, we can learn from the more holistic, nondualistic contributions of indigenous psychology, where there is more credit given to qualitative interpretations in a balance of quality and quantity rather than a one-sided approach.

Currently, the status of culture in psychological theory and the methods used to study culture remain under debate as does the definition of culture (Gerstein, Rountree, & Ordonez, 2007), and it is useful to understand the current debate in Western psychology. Those approaching culture emphasizing an emic or relativistic stance aim to achieve the best possible description of psychological processes in a culture, employing concepts used in that particular culture. In contrast, within the etic approach, psychological phenomena are conceptualized and investigated using universal concepts (Triandis, 2000). Thus, *emic* represents the insider view, whereas the *etic* approach is the outsider view, using concepts that are considered common across cultures. By employing concepts common across cultures (etic), cross-cultural/national comparisons are possible (Lonner, 1999; Triandis, 2000; Ægisdóttir, Gerstein, & Çinarbaş, 2008).

The contrasting emphases of cultural and cross-cultural psychology are somewhat in line with the emic/etic debate. Cross-cultural psychology is a section of psychology mainly focused on how culture affects behavior, and the aim is to develop an inclusive universal psychology (Adamopoulos & Lonner, 2001). Most of the research is comparative, whereby culture or cultural variables are treated as independent variables affecting individuals' behaviors and psychological processes. Culture is treated as independent of the person's psychological makeup, as either moderating or mediating behavior. Scholars identifying with cross-cultural psychology employ varied types of methodologies, and their main challenges are resolving issues of equivalence of constructs, methods, and bias (Adamopoulos & Lonner, 2001; Brislin, 1986; Brislin, Lonner, & Thorndike, 1973; van de Vijver & Leung, 1997; Ægisdóttir et al., 2008). A major challenge within cross-cultural psychology is the lack of causative and explanatory power of cultural variables and culture as a construct (independent variable), which limits theory building. Most often, etic, or derived etic (Berry, 1999), approaches are employed within cross-cultural psychology and counseling research.

The basic purpose of cultural psychology is enhancing the understanding of people in a historical and sociocultural context (Adamopoulos & Lonner, 2001). Studies within cultural psychology see culture as central to the understanding of human processes and behavior. With this approach, the culture and the person or psyche are seen as inseparable

(Miller, 1997); thus, culture cannot be treated as an independent variable, and cross-cultural comparisons are seen as inappropriate. Rather, individuals are understood in their cultural contexts—a relative, ontological stance best suited for qualitative means of inquiry. With this approach, the primary challenge is translating subjectively defined phenomena into a theoretical context within the constraints of relativism (Adamopoulos & Lonner, 2001). Those advocating for indigenous psychology (e.g., Kim, 2001) seem to share this conceptualization with cultural psychologists.

In short, there has been a debate and controversy between cross-cultural psychologists and universalists on the one hand and cultural psychologists and relativists on the other. Both approaches to investigating and conceptualizing culture have their merits and challenges and can potentially provide the proverbial "two sides to the coin" for a more complete, holistic picture. This debate is akin to the ideographic versus nomothetic controversy in personality psychology (e.g., Lonner, 1999) as well as the objective-subjective (statistical-clinical) debate in clinical psychology (e.g., Meehl, 1954; Ægisdóttir et al., 2006). The main questions revolve around how one can use group data and empirical results in understanding a unique individual. Many counseling professionals are aware of the value of both nomothetic (e.g., use of standardized test data) and idiographic (clinical interview) data, and they are able to operate from a more holistic framework by integrating these sources of information to be of assistance to an individual client, a family, a couple, a group, or a community. Similarly, scholars studying cultural influences on behavior often bridge emic and etic approaches by using both quantitative and qualitative types of inquiry to obtain a better understanding of cultural influences of behavior and psychological processes. The issue of where to place culture in psychological theory (outside of or as an integral part of the human mind) remains unresolved, though U.S. multicultural counseling scholars emphasize the importance of viewing cultures and identities as central in understanding human functioning (Sue & Sue, 2008). Other counseling

professionals have suggested that we should look to anthropology when attempting to examine the relationship between culture and human behavior (Gerstein et al., 2007).

How do the issues connected with the concepts of etic/emic and cross-cultural/cultural psychology perspectives translate into counseling practice? And what are the implications of exporting theories developed in one country or culture to another? Kim (2001), a supporter of indigenous psychology, argued that mainstream psychological theories are emic and culture-bound; in essence, they are deeply rooted in Euro-American values of rationalism, freedom, and individualism. Thus, many, if not most, counseling and psychotherapy approaches are founded on an individualistic philosophy that emphasizes individual freedom, self-reliance, autonomy, and uniqueness. These values, however, are often inconsistent with collectivistic values that emphasize social responsibility and the preservation and well-being of the group (Lee & Sue, 2001). Thus, there are serious questions about whether dominant U.S. models of psychotherapy and counseling, especially individual approaches, and the attendant professional roles of the counselor or psychotherapist generalize to individuals from cultural backgrounds who do not share these values and worldviews. The role of the counseling professional as advisor, social change agent, or facilitator of indigenous support or healing systems might, for instance, be more fitting in some cultural contexts than in others (e.g., Atkinson, Thompson, & Grant, 1993).

By using a more holistic approach that values both perspectives as part of a broader perspective, we find that many psychological constructs are universal or etic (e.g., well-being, coping, dysphoria, anxiety). But their expressions may differ significantly across cultures (e.g., Heppner, 2008; Lee & Sue, 2001; Tanaka-Matsumi, 2001). For example, cross-cultural and cultural research on psychopathology has demonstrated that "culture has a major influence on identification, labeling, course, and outcome of maladaptive behavior" (Tanaka-Matsumi, 2001, p. 280). The effectiveness of various counseling approaches may vary by culture as well. However, studies testing the effectiveness of empirically supported treatments across cultures and nations are scarce (Draguns, 2004), but they are greatly needed to help discern cultural effects. Both the science and practice of the counseling profession would greatly benefit from research that focused on understanding indigenous healing approaches as well as their efficacy (e.g., Jaipal, 2004; Lei, Askeroth, Lee, 2004; Lei, Lee, Askeroth, Bursteyn, & Einhorn, & 2004; Tanaka-Matsumi, 2004). Furthermore, investigations exploring the possible integration of traditional U.S. Western counseling approaches with indigenous cultural healing systems are also long overdue.

One general criterion to evaluate the appropriateness of a theory to a new cultural context is the cultural distance between the culture/country in which a theory was developed versus applied (Triandis, 1994, 2001). The greater the distance, in terms of cultural values, language, politics, and so forth, the less congruence or applicability the theory might have. Cultural syndromes, or recognizable characteristics and patterns (Triandis, 1993, 1996, 2001), offer useful ways to assist in evaluating such applicability, as well as adapting and bridging counseling theories to other cultural contexts. Triandis (1993) noted that cultural syndromes can be identified when shared elements of subjective culture (e.g., attitudes, beliefs, norms) "(a) are organized around a theme, (b) there is evidence that the within-culture variance of these constructs is small relative to the between-cultures variance, and (c) there is a link between these patterns of subjective culture and geography" (p. 155). Triandis (2002, chap. 1) also suggested that cultural syndromes promote a focus on constructs that we can measure and get beyond the more general notions of "culture." Examples of cultural syndromes include collectivism-individualism, which can be either vertical (subordination to authority) or horizontal (equity orientation), tightness-looseness (many-few social norms/rules), and complexity-simplicity (information societies–hunters, gatherers). The belief is that the closer the target culture is to the culture in which the theory was developed, the more applicable the theory might

be to the new cultural context, in part or total or with modification.

A deeper look at the questions and issues in cross-cultural research and theory application must be accompanied by an analysis of the larger global context in which the professions of counseling and counseling psychology are emerging, particularly through the lens of power, privilege, and influence. Where we currently stand as a "profession in a global context" (Pedersen, 2003, p. 402) involves seeing as clearly as possible the global politics of counseling and psychology and identifying what it will take to reinvent the profession so that it is relevant for the 21st century and beyond.

EXPORTATION OF U.S. COUNSELING MODELS: ISSUES AND CHALLENGES

The U.S.-based counseling profession, as well as psychology in general, has had a dramatic influence on the practice and science of psychology and counseling outside the United States (Blowers, 1996; Cheung, 2000; Gergen, Gulerce, Lock, & Misra, 1996; Gerstein & Ægisdóttir, 2005b; Jing, 2000; Leong & Ponterotto, 2003; Leung, 2003). Professionals around the world have embraced many of the theories, methods, and strategies developed and employed in the United States. This trend began in the middle of the 20th century, accelerated toward the end of that century, and continues in this current century. Whereas there are no data to substantiate why this happened or how widespread this influence might be, it seems to us that there may be several reasons. First, professionals from outside the United States were drawn to the apparent "scientific" sophistication and merit of psychology and counseling in the United States. Second, many of these professionals were able to easily access the scholarly U.S. literature published. Psychologists in the United States have dominated this literature, with international colleagues having little or no success publishing in U.S. (and other Western) counseling and psychology journals (Gerstein & Ægisdóttir, 2005a, 2005b, 2005c). Third, a large number of international students have studied counseling and/or psychology in the United

States and later secured employment in their home country armed with U.S.-based knowledge bases. Finally, a sizable number of U.S. psychologists and counselor educators have traveled abroad (e.g., exchange programs, Fulbright, consultation) and have disseminated their knowledge and skills through service, teaching, and research.

Cross-national collaboration in the counseling profession goes back at least half a century or more. As discussed in Chapter 2 of this book, some of the earliest cross-national collaboration occurred in the 1950s and 1960s as U.S. counseling psychologists (W. Lloyd, E. G. Williamson, D. Super, H. Barrow, and L. Brammer) were asked to consult with the Japanese government to help establish a counseling profession similar to that in the United States (Heppner, Leong & Chiao, 2008). In the 1960s, again U.S. counseling psychologists (C. G. Wrenn, F. Robinson) provided international consultation to establish a counseling profession modeled on the U.S. system. In essence, the goal seemed to be to transport counseling models that were achieving some success in the United States to other countries. In doing so, however, it was not simply transporting a model of counseling but also the dominant U.S. cultural norms, practices, and values underlying the counseling model. As discussed earlier, the transportation of counseling models based on the U.S. cultural context can become problematic when the values of the recipient's culture differ substantially from those of the United States.

For example, when Heppner first visited Taiwan in 1989, several of the Taiwanese counseling faculty indicated they were experiencing difficulties in applying the well-known U.S.-based Rogerian counseling model with Taiwanese clients. In Taiwan, the word for counselor is synonymous with teacher, and students were accustomed to seeking help from elders, including teachers (and later counselors), to receive advice. But the Rogerian approach does not typically engage in advice-giving but rather provides therapeutic conditions through unconditional positive regard to facilitate the development of the person (Rogers, 1951). However, the counseling techniques related to reflection and unconditional positive regard did not provide the direct advice the Taiwanese clients expected, which created significant problems, such as premature client termination. In short, the uncritical exportation of the widely accepted U.S.-based Rogerian counseling theory and methods did not achieve the same level of success within the different Taiwanese cultural context, which emphasized filial piety, respect, and seeking advice from elders.

Unfortunately, the Taiwan example is not an isolated incident. Around the turn of the 21st century, several scholars articulated concerns about transporting U.S.-based counseling models to other countries. For example, Cheung (2000) aptly noted as follows:

> The meaning of counseling may seem obvious to American psychologists. The understanding of its meaning by American clients is assumed. In another cultural context, however, counseling may imply a different nature of relationship to both the provider and the recipient. Counseling needs to be deconstructed in the context of the culture in which it is offered. (p. 124)

Cheung indicated that culture defines what constitutes clients' problems, the cause of the problems (see Cheung, 1988), and the solutions and therapeutic interventions (see Sue & Sue, 1990). In essence, Cheung argued that it is problematic and thus inappropriate to simply transport a counseling theory and methods from one culture to another without examining the culturally encapsulated assumptions of the model's congruence with the recipient's cultural context.

Several scholars have discussed the need to examine the culturally encapsulated assumptions within prevailing U.S.-based counseling theories and research methods (e.g., Gerstein, 2006; Heppner, 2006; Heppner, Casas, Carter, & Stone, 2000; Heppner, Leong, & Gerstein, 2008; Heppner, Wampold, & Kivlighan, 2008; Leong & Blustein, 2000; Leong & Ponterotto, 2003; McWhirter, 2000; Norsworthy, 2006; Pedersen 2003; Pedersen & Leong, 1997). Cheung (2000) highlighted several of these assumptions in U. S. counseling psychology:

Counseling psychology has been encapsulated in ethnocentric assumptions that are taken to be universal. The theories, research, and practice of counseling psychology, as a specialized profession, originate in the United States but are assumed to be universally applicable. When transported to another culture where the field of psychology in general and counseling psychology in particular is fledging, it is simply transported. There has often been little regard as to the applicability of the theories and practices. (p. 123)

In short, the rather wholesale transportation of U.S.-based counseling theories and research models has not only resulted in inappropriate generalizations of U.S.-based models but also led to another instance of Western Eurocentric domination, or Western psychological hegemony. Such neocolonialism can not only deepen inequities but also be destructive of indigenous cultures.

As previously discussed, until quite recently, U.S. counseling and psychology have been imported and exported worldwide almost without restrictions, oversight, or careful attention to the consequences or implications. It would seem that, in general, U.S. professionals have uncritically transported, promoted, and shared U.S. models of counseling and psychology with persons in other countries. Concurrently, a number of U.S. scholars (Douce, 2004; Leung, 2003; Marsella, 1998; Pedersen, 2003) have noted that the U.S. counseling profession itself is still facing the challenge of ethnocentrism, isolation, cultural encapsulation, and hegemony. Very early in the history of the U.S. counseling profession, Wrenn (1962) also spoke of a similar challenge, characterizing U.S. counselors as culturally encapsulated. In part, he suggested that counselors protect themselves against the uncomfortable reality of change by maintaining an encapsulation within their subculture. Pedersen and Leong (1997) expanded on this observation by urging the counseling psychology profession to examine the culturally encapsulated assumptions of its theories, models, and practices.

Apparently, cultural encapsulation has not prevented U.S. mental health professionals from exporting their models and strategies around the world. Some writers have even suggested that Western experts in psychology and Western volunteers engaged in activities outside of the West were prone to practicing a form of psychological colonization, neocolonialism (Lugones & Spelmann, 1983) and cultural imperialism. Leong and Ponterotto (2003) further argued that "the belief that American psychology is in some ways more advanced or superior to other national psychologies is U.S.-centric and isolationist" (p. 383). Again, although no formal research has been conducted on this topic, there is substantial ethnographic, anecdotal, and case study evidence based on the experiences of both U.S. and non-U.S. professionals.

Typically, *colonialism* refers to nations exploring new areas, occupying the territory, controlling its inhabitants, and creating colonies ruled by the colonizing nation's government (Said, 1993). *Colonization* has been defined as "a system of domination characterized by social patterns or mechanisms of control which maintain oppression and which vary from context to context" (Moane, 1994, p. 252). Imperialism (Said, 1993), where a more powerful nation or society enforces its stance of superiority through domination and control, reinforces colonization through exertion of "dominant values, practices, and meanings within the colonized context." This renders the perspectives of the colonized invisible while simultaneously negatively stereotyping and 'othering' (objectifying) the colonized group" (Norsworthy, 2006, p. 424). From this perspective, a country or culture may undergo psychological colonization even if the colonizing nations have no significant physical presence. According to Norsworthy (2006),

Due to the overwhelming power differential and the exertion of control by the colonizers over the minds, bodies and spirits of those colonized, many colonized individuals internalize these negative qualities. . . . According to Memmi (1965) those who are colonized may develop attitudes of dependency and ambivalence toward the colonizers, including feelings of hate, fear, admiration, affection, and sometimes, identification. At the same time, the colonizers depend on the colonized for their status and identity, survival and comfort while simultaneously projecting their disowned aspects on to the colonized group. Thus, there is interdependency between the colonizers and the colonized that leads to ambivalence for each group with regard to the other. Enforced by the colonizers, a kind of social and psychological complementarity develops that can become deeply entrenched and difficult to change (Kenny, 1985). (pp. 424–425)

Thus, it is critical to understand the dynamics and intricacies of psychological colonization and imperialism, including how each of us has learned and internalized the attitudes and behaviors connected with positions of privilege and oppression. Our experience has been that the deeper the levels of understanding, the more we can avoid perpetuating domination-subordination dynamics. Furthermore, we are able to act differently and engage in collaboration, genuine power sharing (Cheung, 2000; Norsworthy, 2006; van Strien, 1997; Wang & Heppner, Chapter 8, this volume), and mutuality in our international collaborations and partnerships. The mutual respect and attitude of "learning from one another" also fosters a valuing and appreciation of the indigenous values, beliefs, and behaviors of diverse cultures and countries. Moreover, the collaboration and mutual respect promotes a deeper understanding that professionals around the world have the knowledge and skills to create indigenous counseling models that are relevant to their contexts. Our experience has been that authentic cross-national collaboration and power-sharing, along with ongoing reflection about the relationship dynamics among the members of the team, can lessen the potential for psychological colonization (Norsworthy, 2006). Such discussions and reflection are important because everyone has been enculturated into these systems, dynamics, and structures of power, privilege, domination, and subordination; subsequently, we often unconsciously enact our part in the dynamic when we have not done our own personal "decolonization" work of "conscientization" (Freire, 1972). Conscientization involves becoming aware of and understanding the dynamics of colonization, domination, and subordination

and one's own associated attitudes, thoughts, feelings, and behaviors. Furthermore, real conscientization demands taking action to change the oppressive conditions, including learning how to liberate ourselves from the colonized mentality and associated behaviors to engage in creative collaboration and partnership.

It is important to note that endorsing and implementing these principles cannot insure that U.S. mental health professionals will not continue to promote or maintain psychological colonization and cultural imperialism outside the United States or that colleagues outside the United States will not collude with this process. Nonetheless, such principles can serve as a framework to help guide our culturally sensitive professional work. As Pedersen (2003) so cogently stated,

> Given the difficulty of conducting psychological research, it is essential that the presence of cultural bias be acknowledged in a global context so that we do not confuse the discipline of psychology with the more narrowly defined boundaries of "American" psychology. (p. 403)

This same warning and recommendation can apply to various practices of the counseling profession. When practicing different forms of counselor interventions (e.g., individual or group counseling, consultation, prevention), mental health professionals can be aware of the cultural bias inherent in models developed in the United States and then proceed in developing indigenous counseling models in their own cultures and countries.

Applying counseling theories and research models from one culture to another requires considerable cross-cultural competencies to understand how and why they work in one cultural context, as well as how they may or may not work in another cultural context. Scholars have identified a wide array of obstacles and challenges confronting the U.S. counseling profession to becoming cross-culturally competent. Heppner, Leong, and Chiao (2008) summarized some of these obstacles as (a) short and superficial contacts with international colleagues; (b) a limited number of major U.S. institutions to support the internationalizing of the profession; (c) a tendency to believe one's own behaviors are typical of others; (d) feelings of superiority as a profession relative to other countries; (e) lack of exposure and knowledge to the work of international colleagues; (f) xenophobia; (g) difficulty in understanding and accepting others' worldviews; (h) inability to accept differences across cultures as simply differences; (i) an overemphasis on internal validity; and (j) psychological reactance, defensiveness and other personality styles that contribute to the obstacles above (e.g., Gerstein & Ægisdóttir, 2005a, 2005c; Heppner, 2006; Leong & Ponterotto, 2003; Leong & Santago-Riveria, 1999; Leung, 2003; Marsella, 1998; Segall, Lonner, & Berry, 1998).

Problems emerging from a lack of cross-cultural competence may be two-sided. On the one hand, U.S. scholars and practitioners in our counseling and psychology training programs can lack cultural sensitivity and hold encapsulated attitudes such as "U.S. professionals are the experts." U.S. scholars steeped in an individualistic, personal agency and assertiveness paradigm, coupled with the lack of cultural competencies, may be particularly prone to cultural insensitivity and be oblivious to differences and thus feel superior. The other side pertains to internalized racism and/or the colonized mentality of some international colleagues who have been led to believe that "even the moon is bigger in the United States" and that in some way one comes to believe their ideas are inferior or even that they are inferior beings. Internalized racism, coupled with a lack of cultural competence, may lead one to be prone to wholesale adoption of U.S.-based counseling theories and research methods. Moreover, as discussed earlier, sometimes, these two dynamics can promote a comfortable or ambivalent collusion. Another set of consequences may be the adoption of counseling theories and research models that are culturally inappropriate and most likely less effective for the recipient's culture. Such theories and models might also continue the colonizer-colonized cycle, and they could potentially be a waste of time in the therapeutic process.

Another dimension of the wholesale exportation of U.S.-based counseling theories pertains to graduate students from other countries studying counseling and counseling psychology in the United States. During the course of studying for a master's or doctoral degree, international students are typically taught almost exclusively about Western, U.S.-based counseling models. Even when students are warned about adopting these Western models uncritically, the Western-based assumptions frequently become instilled in the thinking processes of international students, often unknowingly. When this happens, these students are frequently unaware of assumptions, based on a Western cultural context; subsequently, when they return to their home country to practice, the Western-based assumptions can create obstacles in responding appropriately in their home cultures. For example, when one international graduate student returned to her home country from the United States to practice counseling for a few months, it took some time to recognize that some of her assumptions and ways of behaving, the norm in the United States, were incongruent with her home culture; a turning point was when she realized that even though both she and her supervisor were Taiwanese, their interaction was nonetheless cross-cultural. This realization then sparked additional reflection and awareness of the different cultural dynamics affecting her thinking and behavior.

In short, although there are many benefits to sharing information across cultures, there are also some challenges that require additional awareness, discussion, and examination. Understanding the dynamics of colonization and imperialism in relation to the transportation of counseling and psychology outside the United States and bringing a reflective stance to our international partnerships, counseling training, and cross-cultural/intracultural research will increase the likelihood of culturally sensitive and effective collaboration with our cross-national colleagues.

CONCLUSION

This chapter underscores the importance of understanding the major questions and conundrums in contemporary cultural and cross-cultural research as they relate to the cross-national movement in the counseling profession. The chapter also illustrates the need for an awareness of more emic, indigenous research to contribute to a complex counseling and psychology capable of responding to the myriad of challenging contemporary global mental health problems through "culture-centered perspectives on human behavior" (Pedersen, 2003, p. 402).

We have maintained that the exportation of U.S. psychology and counseling can become an instrument of psychological colonization, particularly in relation to the exportation of U.S. counseling models to non-Western contexts. Based on their research with groups from Southeast Asia (e.g., Thailand), Khuankaew and Norsworthy (2005) observed, "When we work with groups to analyze their suffering, globalization emerges as a root cause of the structural inequities encountered in the Global South" (p. 3). Furthermore, local activists and grassroots communities in Thailand (where Khuankaew and Norsworthy engage in collaborative projects focusing on issues of violence against women, HIV/AIDS, and other social problems) consistently express the view that "globalization, by definition, is a destructive force in the region" partially because "at the global level, countries of the Global North define the rules and standards regarding how globalization should work and who should benefit" (p. 3). The same themes emerge when discussing the impact of the unaware Western "expert" or researcher who enters their spaces to provide "help" or to study without a real understanding of the culture, context, desires, concerns, and priorities of local people.

In addition, it is important to highlight how international students deal with the cross-cultural challenges while studying in the United States and then on returning to their home countries, and how such challenges are also intertwined with U.S. values, worldviews, and models of counseling. Few programs include sufficient examination of these complex cultural issues in the curriculum (Heppner, Leong, & Chiao, 2008; Leong & Ponterotto, 2003), including the conscientization of students so that they do not internalize U.S. counseling models as universal and the standard of practice globally.

In 2004, the APA, noting the current issues related to exportation of U.S. psychology, passed a resolution focusing on bringing culture and gender awareness to international psychology in an effort to offer guidance in the internationalization movement (see Appendix, end of chapter). Steps such as these signal a recognition by organized U.S. psychology that it is time to seriously attend to how we interact at the global level and how psychology can contribute to the common good of all citizens of the world, not just those in the West.

The analysis presented in this chapter allows us to understand the problems and challenges associated with the cross-national movements in counseling and counseling psychology around the globe. From here, it is important to explore examples of decolonization, conscientization, partnership, and collaboration in cross-cultural, cross-national, and international research, training, and practice. In upcoming chapters, there is a focus on indigenization, whereby psychology and counseling are being invented and "reinvented in new and innovative ways" based on the premise that "psychological principles cannot be assumed to be similar" and "are based on ancient historical traditions in history, religion, and many other fields or disciplines not typically seen as relevant to psychology" (Pedersen, 2003, p. 401). These indigenous models in the chapters to follow include the voices and work of psychological providers who are noncounseling professionals or are involved in healing and helping in contexts where counseling is not established as a helping profession.

The forthcoming chapters also highlight the benefits of cross-national collaboration and partnerships in research and practice and feature the partnerships between counseling psychologists and grassroots community leaders, and nongovernmental and governmental groups involved in responding to social issues and challenges. Additionally, several international scholars and counseling professionals describe their experiences of completing their counseling training in the United States and their discoveries on returning to their home countries to work and practice. Through these narratives, models of creative collaboration emerge, and we can learn more about how to create an interconnected mosaic among mental health professionals around the globe.

REFERENCES

Adamopoulos, J., & Lonner, W. J. (2001). Culture and psychology at a crossroad: Historical perspective and theoretical analysis. In D. Matsumoto (Ed.), *Handbook of culture and psychology* (pp. 11–34). New York: Oxford University Press.

American Psychological Association. (2004). *Resolution on culture and gender awareness in international psychology.* Washington, DC: Author.

Atkinson, D. R., Thompson, C. E., & Grant, S. K. (1993). A three dimensional model for counseling racial/ethnic minorities. *The Counseling Psychologist, 21,* 257–277.

Berry, J. W. (1999). Emics and etics: A symbiotic conception. *Culture and Psychology, 5,* 165–171.

Blowers, G. H. (1996). The prospects for a Chinese psychology. In M. H. Bond (Ed.), *The handbook of Chinese psychology* (pp. 1–14). Hong Kong: Oxford University Press.

Bochner, S. (1999). Cultural diversity within and between societies: Implications for multicultural social systems. In P. B. Pedersen (Ed.), *Multiculturalism as a fourth force* (pp. 19–60). Washington, DC: Taylor & Francis.

Brislin, R. W. (1986). The wording and translation of research instruments. In W. J. Lonner & J. W. Berry (Eds.), *Field methods in cross-cultural research* (pp. 137–164). Beverly Hills, CA: Sage.

Brislin, R. W., Lonner, W. J., & Thorndike, R. M. (1973). *Cross-cultural research methods.* New York: Wiley.

Cheung, F. M. (1988). Surveys of community attitude toward mental health facilities: Reflections or provocations? *American Journal of Community Psychology, 16*(4), 877–882.

Cheung, F. M. (2000). Deconstructing counseling in a cultural context. *The Counseling Psychologist, 28,* 123–132.

Chung, R. C-Y. (2005). Women, human rights, and counseling: Crossing international boundaries. *Journal of Counseling and Development, 83*(3), 262–268.

Douce, L. A. (2004). Globalization of counseling psychology. *The Counseling Psychologist, 32,* 142–152.

Draguns, J. (2004). From speculation through description toward investigation: A prospective glimpse at cultural research in psychotherapy. In U. P. Gielen, J. M. Fish, & J. G. Draguns (Eds.), *Handbook of culture,*

therapy, and healing (pp. 369–387). Mahwah, NJ: Lawrence Erlbaum.

Freire, P. (1972). *Pedagogy of the oppressed.* New York: Herder & Herder.

Gergen, K. J., Gulerce, A., Lock, A., & Misra, G. (1996). Psychological science in cultural context. *American Psychologist, 51,* 496–503.

Gerstein, L. H. (2006). Counseling psychologists as international social architects. In R. L. Toporek, L. H. Gerstein, N. A. Fouad, G. Roysircar-Sodowsky, & T. Israel (Eds.), *Handbook for social justice in counseling psychology: Leadership, vision, and action* (pp. 377–387). Thousand Oaks, CA: Sage.

Gerstein, L. H., Rountree, C., & Ordonez, M. A. (2007). An anthropological perspective on multicultural counseling. *Counselling Psychology Quarterly, 20,* 375–400.

Gerstein, L. H., & Ægisdóttir, S. (2005a). Counseling around the world. *Journal of Mental Health Counseling, 27,* 95–184.

Gerstein, L. H., & Ægisdóttir, S. (Guest Eds.). (2005b). Counseling outside of the United States: Looking in and reaching out [Special issue]. *Journal of Mental Health Counseling, 27,* 221–281.

Gerstein, L. H., & Ægisdóttir, S. (2005c). A trip around the world: A counseling travelogue! *Journal of Mental Health Counseling, 27,* 95–103.

Gerstein, L. H., & Ægisdóttir, S. (2007). Training international social change agents: Transcending a U.S. counseling paradigm. *Counselor Education and Supervision, 47,* 123–139.

Heppner, P. P. (2006). The benefits and challenges of becoming cross-culturally competent counseling psychologists. *The Counseling Psychologist, 34,* 147–172.

Heppner, P. P. (2008). Expanding the conceptualization and measurement of applied problem solving and coping: From stages to dimensions to the almost forgotten cultural context. *American Psychologist, 63,* 803–816.

Heppner, P. P., Casas, J. M., Carter, J., & Stone, G. L. (2000). The maturation of counseling psychology: Multifaceted perspectives from 1978 to 1998. In S. D. Brown & R. W. Lent (Eds.), *Handbook of counseling psychology* (3rd ed., pp. 3–49). Thousand Oaks, CA: Sage.

Heppner, P. P., & Gerstein, L. H. (2008). International developments in counseling psychology. In E. Altmaier & B. D. Johnson (Eds.), *Encyclopedia of counseling: Changes and challenges for counseling in the 21st century* (Vol. 1, pp. 260–266). Thousand Oaks, CA: Sage.

Heppner, P. P., Leong, F. T. L., & Chiao, H. (2008). A growing internationalization of counseling psychology.

In S. D. Brown & R. W. Lent (Eds.), *Handbook of counseling psychology* (4th ed., pp. 68–85). Hoboken, NJ: Wiley.

Heppner, P. P., Leong, F. T. L., & Gerstein, L. H. (2008). Counseling within a changing world: Meeting the psychological needs of societies and the world. In W. B. Walsh (Ed.), *Biennial review of counseling psychology* (1st ed., pp. 231–258). New York: Taylor & Francis.

Heppner, P. P., Wampold, B. E., & Kivlighan, D. M. (2008). *Research design in counseling* (3rd ed.). Belmont, CA: Thompson Brooks/Cole.

Jaipal, R. (2004). Indian conceptions of mental health, healing and the individual. In U. P. Gielen, J. M. Fish, & J. G. Draguns (Eds.), *Handbook of culture, therapy, and healing* (pp. 293–308). Mahwah, NJ: Lawrence Erlbaum.

Jing, Q. (2000). International psychology. In K. Pawlik & M. R. Rosenzweig (Eds.), *International handbook of psychology* (pp. 570–584). London: Sage.

Kenny, V. (1985). The post-colonial personality. *The Crane Bag, 9,* 70–78.

Khuankaew, O., & Norsworthy, K. L. (2005). Crossing borders: Activist responses to globalization by women of the Global South. *Globalization Research Center, University of South Florida, Occasional Papers on Globalization, 2*(2), 1–12.

Kim, U. (2001). Culture, science, and indigenous psychology: An integrated analysis. In D. Matsumoto (Ed.), *The handbook of culture and psychology* (pp. 51–75). New York: Oxford University Press.

Kwan, K. L. K., & Gerstein, L. H. (2008). Envisioning a counseling psychology of the world: The mission of the international forum. *The Counseling Psychologist, 36,* 182–187.

Lee, J., & Sue, S. (2001). Clinical psychology and culture. In D. Matsumoto (Ed.), *The handbook of culture and psychology* (pp. 287–305). New York: Oxford University Press.

Lei, T., Askeroth, C., & Lee, C. (2004). Indigenous Chinese healing: Theories and methods. In U. P. Gielen, J. M. Fish, & J. G. Draguns (Eds.), *Handbook of culture, therapy, and healing* (pp. 191–212). Mahwah, NJ: Lawrence Erlbaum.

Lei, T., Lee, C., Askeroth, C., Bursteyn, D., & Einhorn, A. (2004). Indigenous Chinese healing: A criteria-based meta-analysis of outcomes research. In U. P. Gielen, J. M. Fish, & J. G. Draguns (Eds.), *Handbook of culture, therapy, and healing* (pp. 213–251). Mahwah, NJ: Lawrence Erlbaum.

Leong, F. T. L., & Blustein, D. L. (2000). Toward a global vision of counseling psychology. *The Counseling Psychologist, 28,* 5–9.

Leong, F. T. L., & Ponterotto, J. G. (2003). A proposal for internationalizing counseling psychology in the United States: Rationale, recommendations, and challenges. *The Counseling Psychologist, 31,* 381–395.

Leong, F. T. L., & Santago-Riveria, A. L. (1999). Climbing the multiculturalism summit: Challenges and pitfalls. In P. Pedersen (Ed.), *Multiculturalism as a fourth force* (pp. 61–74). Philadelphia: Brunner/Mazel.

Leong, F. T. L., & Savickas, M. (2007). Introduction to special issue on international perspectives on counseling psychology. *Applied Psychology: An International Review, 56,* 1–6.

Leung, S. A. (2003). A journey worth traveling: Globalization of counseling psychology. *The Counseling Psychologist, 31,* 412–419.

Lonner, W. J. (1999). Helfrich's "Principle of Triarchic Resonance": A commentary on yet another perspective on the ongoing and tenacious etic-emic debate. *Culture and Psychology, 5,* 173–181.

Lugones, M. C., & Spelmann, E. V. (1983). Have we got a theory for you! Feminist theory, cultural imperialism and the demand for "the woman's voice." *Women's Studies International Forum, 6,* 573–581.

Marsella, A. J. (1998). Toward a "global-community psychology": Meeting the needs of a changing world. *American Psychologist, 53,* 1282–1291.

McWhirter, J. J. (2000). And now, up go the walls: Constructing an international room for counseling psychology. *The Counseling Psychologist, 28,* 117–122.

Meehl, P. E. (1954). *Clinical versus statistical prediction.* Minneapolis: University of Minnesota Press.

Memmi, A. (1965). *The colonizer and the colonized.* Boston: Beacon Press.

Miller, J. G. (1997). Theoretical issues in cultural psychology. In J. W. Berry, Y. H. Poortinga, & J. Pandey (Eds.), *Handbook of cross-cultural psychology: Theory and method* (Vol. 1, 2nd ed., pp. 85–128). Boston: Allyn & Bacon.

Moane, G. (1994). A psychological analysis of colonialism in an Irish context. *The Irish Journal of Psychology, 15*(2/3), 250–265.

Norsworthy, K. L. (2006). Bringing social justice to international practices of counseling psychology. In R. L. Toporek, L. H. Gerstein, N. A. Fouad, G. Roysircar-Sodowsky, & T. Israel (Eds.), *Handbook for social justice in counseling psychology: Leadership,* vision, and action (pp. 421–441). Thousand Oaks, CA: Sage.

Pedersen, P. (1999). Culture-centered interventions as a fourth dimension in psychology. In P. Pedersen (Ed.), *Multiculturalism as a fourth force* (pp. 3–18). Philadelphia: Brunner/Mazel.

Pedersen, P. B. (2003). Culturally biased assumptions in counseling psychology. *The Counseling Psychologist, 31*, 396–403.

Pedersen, P. B., Crethar, H. C., & Carlson, J. (2008). *Inclusive cultural empathy: Making relationships central in counselling and psychotherapy.* Washington, DC: American Psychological Association.

Pedersen, P. B., Draguns, J. G., Lonner, W. J., & Trimble, J. E. (2008). *Counseling across cultures* (6th ed.). Thousand Oaks, CA: Sage.

Pedersen, P. B., & Leong, F. (1997). Counseling in an international context. *The Counseling Psychologist, 25*, 117–122.

Pike, K. L. (1966). *Language in relation to a unified theory of the structure of human behavior.* The Hague, the Netherlands: Mouton.

Rice, J., & Ballou, M. (2002). *Cultural and gender awareness in international psychology.* Washington, DC: American Psychological Association, Division 52, International Psychology, International Committee for Women.

Rogers, C. (1951). *Client-centered therapy.* Boston: Houghton Mifflin.

Said, E. W. (1993). *Culture and imperialism.* New York: Knopf.

Segall, M. H., Lonner, W. J., & Berry, J. W. (1998). Cross-cultural psychology as a scholarly discipline: On a flowering of culture in behavioral research. *American Psychologist, 53*, 1101–1110.

Sue, D. W., & Sue, D. (1990). *Counseling the culturally different: Theory and practice* (2nd ed.). New York: Wiley.

Sue, D. W., & Sue, D. (2008). *Counseling the culturally diverse: Theory and practice* (5th ed.). New York: Wiley.

Tanaka-Matsumi, J. (2001). Abnormal psychology and culture. In D. Matsumoto (Ed.), *The handbook of culture and psychology* (pp. 265–286). New York: Oxford University Press.

Tanaka-Matsumi, J. (2004). Japanese forms of psychotherapy: Naikan therapy and Morita therapy. In U. P. Gielen, J. M. Fish, & J. G. Draguns (Eds.), *Handbook of culture, therapy, and healing* (pp. 277–292). Mahwah, NJ: Lawrence Erlbaum.

Triandis, H. C. (1993). Collectivism and individualism as cultural syndromes. *Cross-Cultural Research, 27*, 155–180.

Triandis, H. C. (1994). *Culture and social behavior.* New York: McGraw-Hill.

Triandis, H. C. (1996). The psychological measurement of cultural syndromes. *American Psychologist, 51*, 407–415.

Triandis, H. C. (2000). Dialectics between cultural and cross-cultural psychology. *Asian Journal of Social Psychology, 3*, 185–195.

Triandis, H. C. (2001). Individualism and collectivism: Past, present, and future. In D. Matsumoto (Ed.), *The handbook of culture and psychology* (pp. 35–50). New York: Oxford University Press.

Triandis, H. C. (2002). Odysseus wandered for 10, I wondered for 50 years. In W. J. Lonner, D. L. Dinnel, S. A. Hayes, & D. N. Sattler (Eds.), *Online readings in psychology and culture* (Unit 2). Bellingham, WA: Center for Cross-Cultural Research, Western Washington University. Retrieved January 26, 2009, from http://www.ac.wwu.edu/~culture/triandis2.htm

van de Vijver, F. (2001). The evolution of cross-cultural research methods. In D. Matsumoto (Ed.), *The handbook of culture and psychology* (pp. 77–97). New York: Oxford University Press.

van de Vijver, F., & Leung, K. (1997). *Methods and data analysis for cross-cultural research.* Thousand Oaks, CA: Sage.

van Strien, P. J. (1997). The American "colonization" of northwest European social psychology after World War II. *Journal of the History of the Behavioral Sciences, 33*, 349–363.

Wrenn, C. G. (1962). The culturally encapsulated counselor. *Harvard Educational Review, 32*(4), 444–449.

Yang, K. S., Hwang, K. K., Pedersen, P. B., & Daibo, I. (Eds.). (2003). *Progress in Asian social psychology: Conceptual and empirical contributions.* Westport, CT: Praeger.

Ægisdóttir, S., & Gerstein, L. H. (2005). Reaching out: Mental health delivery outside the box. *Journal of Mental Health Counseling, 27*, 221–224.

Ægisdóttir, S., Gerstein, L. H., & Çinarbaş, D. C. (2008). Methodological issues in cross-cultural counseling research: Equivalence, bias, and translations. *The Counseling Psychologist, 36*, 188–219.

Ægisdóttir, S., White, M. J., Spengler, P. M., Maugherman, A. S., Anderson, L. A., Cook, R. S. et al. (2006). The meta-analysis of clinical judgment project: Fifty-six years of accumulated research on clinical versus statistical prediction. *The Counseling Psychologist, 34*, 341–382.

Appendix: APA Resolution on Culture and Gender Awareness in International Psychology

Adopted by the APA Council of Representatives July 28, 2004

WHEREAS an estimated 60 percent (or more) of the world's psychologists now live outside the US (Hogan, 1995);

WHEREAS psychologists outside of the US have generated perspectives, methods and practices that correspond to the needs of the people in their societies and data that are relevant to the development of a more complete psychology of people (Bhopal, 2001; Espin & Gaweleck, 1992; Martin-Baro, 1994; Weiss, Whelan & Gupta, 2000; Winslow, Honein, & Elzubeir, 2002);

WHEREAS US leadership in world psychology is sometimes perceived as disproportionately influential, partly because of access to research funds, an abundance of US publication outlets and the wide acceptance of the English language (Kagitcibasi in Sunar, 1996; Sloan 2000);

WHEREAS US psychology needs to more fully consider the ramifications of national and cultural perspectives and indigenous psychologies (Castillo, 2001; Frank & Frank, 1991; Sue & Zane 1987) in its research, practice and educational efforts (Best & Williams, 1997; Draguns, 2001; Segall, Lonner, & Berry, 1998);

WHEREAS US grounded, normed, and structured measures dominate US empirical psychology, while internationally based, qualitative methods such as community action research are less known or valued in the US (Denzin & Lincoln, 2001; Murray & Chamberlain, 1999; Robson, 1993);

WHEREAS US assessment procedures, tests and normative data have been used extensively in other countries, sometimes without consideration of cultural differences that affect reliability and validity (Dana, 2000);

WHEREAS people of other cultures have adopted US methods of clinical diagnosis and intervention and US psychology has also exported these methods based on US norms and values to other cultures (Foa, Keane, & Friedman, 2000; Mezzich, 2002; Nakane & Nakane, 2002; Thorne & Lambers, 1998);

WHEREAS there is a need to develop and disseminate materials that will facilitate the training of psychologists to conduct culturally-appropriate research and practice around the world as well as within the culturally diverse United States (diMauro, Gilbert, & Parker, 2003; Friedman, 1997; Hays, 2001);

WHEREAS universities and colleges have called upon faculty and departments to internationalize their courses and curriculum, given the increasing number of international students at North American institutions (Marsella & Pedersen, 2002; Woolf, Hulsizer, & McCarthy, 2002);

WHEREAS most individuals from the United States, including psychologists, do not speak a second language or read journals or books in another language other than English, and therefore are unlikely to be familiar with firsthand sources of international research in other countries other than English speaking countries;

WHEREAS research focused on immigration and discrimination against immigrants and undocumented immigrants is sparse (Esses, Dovidio, Jackson & Armstrong, 2001; Evans, 2002; Martin, 1994);

WHEREAS decades of psychological studies have demonstrated that scientifically sound practice requires taking into account issues of gender and culture at all stages of the research process (Bem, 1993; Brodsky & Hare-Mustin; 1980; Harding, 1987; Schmitz, Stakeman & Sisneros, 1996; Sherif, 1979; Spence, 1987; White, Russo & Travis, 2001);

WHEREAS psychologists have demonstrated how privilege and oppression affect the lives of women and men across sexual orientations, disabilities, social class, age, ethnic and religious memberships (APA Guidelines for Psychological Practice with Older Adults, 2003; Banks, 2003; Eberhardt & Fiske, 1998; Gershick, 2000; Sidanius, Levin, Federico & Pratto, 2001; Sidanius & Pratto, 1999);

WHEREAS women world wide experience discrimination in terms of resources and access to food, health care, inheritance, credit, education, vocational training, hiring, fair compensation for paid work, family and public rights, individual mobility and travel, and religious education and participation, and they also may face legal, societal, cultural and religious practices which justify and endorse this discrimination (Bianchi, Casper & Peltola, 1999; Goode, 1993; Hauchler & Kennedy, 1994; Smeeding & Ross, 1999; United Nations, 2000; United Nations Population Fund, 2000), and psychology could address these global problems internationally (United Nations, 2000; United Nations Population Fund, 2000);

WHEREAS, as a result of gender discrimination, women internationally constitute a majority of the poor, and female headed families are the lowest income groups in many countries around the world (Blossfield, 1995; Duncan & Edwards, 1997; Goldberg & Kremen, 1990; McLanahan & Kelly, 1998); moreover, educational achievements and opportunities and

literacy rates for women are significantly less than for men (United Nations Department of Public Information, 1995; UNESCO, 2002);

WHEREAS, as a result of gender discrimination, women experience violations of their body integrity, interpersonal violence and physical abuse (Center for Policy Alternatives, 1998; European Women's Lobby, 2000; Nylen & Heimer, 2000); and under repressive systems, in wars, and in postwar conditions, women are targeted for violence (Comas-Diaz & Jansen, 1995);

WHEREAS, as a result of gender discrimination individuals with differently gendered identity and gender expression experience violence and discrimination within many societies from both the populace and from those in authority (Dworkin & Yi, 2003);

WHEREAS psychologists strive to promote international peace and understanding and to decrease ethnic and gender violence;

WHEREAS, in contrast to the United States where professional practices and policies generally are in concert with and support governmental structures, in many other countries, psychologists must advocate for social justice and oppose unjust governmental structures and policies (Fox & Prilleltensky, 2001; Martin-Baro, 1994; Moane, 1999; Moler & Catley, 2000; Nandy, 1987);

WHEREAS knowledge management, production and dissemination of information are also affected by global politics and economics in ways that maintain social inequality (Capra, 1996; Fox & Prilleltensky, 2001; Giddens, 2000; Harding, 1993; Wallerstein, 1992);

WHEREAS the field of psychology could benefit significantly from the expansion of its knowledge base through international perspectives, conclusions and practices (Bronstein & Quina, 1988; Gielen & Pagan, 1993; Marsella, 1998; Nandy, 1983; Pareek, 1990);

WHEREAS the opportunity for mutual benefit and greater effectiveness in solving global problems is at hand in research partnerships across nations and cultures if psychologists proceed with critical awareness and a commitment to gender, cultural, social, economic and religious justice (Sloan, 1996);

WHEREAS psychologists have a responsibility to better understand the values, mores, history and social policies of other nations and cultures that affect generalizations and recommendations about best practices (Schmitz, Stakeman & Sisneros, 1996);

WHEREAS psychologists are committed to culture fair and gender fair competent unbiased practice (APA Guidelines on Cross Cultural Education and Training, Research, Organizational Change and Practice for Psychologists, 2002; APA Guidelines for Practice with Girls and Women (Draft), 2002; APA Guidelines for Psychotherapy with Lesbian, Gay and Bisexual Clients, 2000; American Psychological Association, A New Model of Disability, 2003);

WHEREAS psychologists are ethically guided to "recognize that fairness and justice entitle all persons to access to and benefit from the contributions of psychology" and to "respect the rights, dignity, and worth of all people" (American Psychological Association, Ethical Principles of Psychologists and Code of Conduct, 2002);

WHEREAS the International Committee for Women Task Force of Division 52, International Psychology, has developed an important position paper on "Cultural And Gender Awareness in International Psychology" that identifies critical areas of consideration for psychologists to consider in cross-cultural research (Rice & Ballou, 2002);

THEREFORE LET IT BE RESOLVED that the American Psychological Association will:

(1) advocate for more research on the role that cultural ideologies have in the experience of women and men across and within countries on the basis of sex, gender identity, gender expression, ethnicity, social class, age, disabilities, and religion.

(2) advocate for more collaborative research partnerships with colleagues from diverse cultures and countries leading to mutually beneficial dialogues and learning opportunities.

(3) advocate for critical research that analyzes how cultural, economic, and geopolitical perspectives may be embedded within US psychological research and practice.

(4) encourage more attention to a critical examination of international cultural, gender, gender identity, age, and disability perspectives in psychological theory, practice, and research at all levels of psychological education and training curricula.

(5) encourage psychologists to gain an understanding of the experiences of individuals in diverse cultures, and their points of view and to value pluralistic world views, ways of knowing, organizing, functioning, and standpoints.

(6) encourage psychologists to become aware of and understand how systems of power hierarchies may influence the privileges, advantages, and rewards that usually accrue by virtue of placement and power.

(7) encourage psychologists to understand how power hierarchies may influence the production and dissemination of knowledge in psychology internationally and to alter their practices according to the ethical insights that emerge from this understanding.

(8) encourage psychologists to appreciate the multiple dilemmas and contradictions inherent in valuing culture and actual cultural practices when they are oppressive to women, but congruent with the practices of diverse ethnic groups.

(9) advocate for cross national research that analyzes and supports the elimination of cultural, gender, gender identity, age, and disability discrimination in all arenas—economic, social, educational, and political.

(10) support public policy that supports global change toward egalitarian relationships and the elimination of practices and conditions oppressive to women.

BE IT FURTHER RESOLVED that the American Psychological Association (1) recommend that Boards and Committees consider the impact of the globalization of psychology and the incorporation of international perspectives into their activities, and (2) charge the Committee on International Relations in Psychology, in collaboration appropriate APA Boards and Committees, to implement any directives from the Council of Representatives that result from the adoption of the resolution.

REFERENCES

American Psychological Association (2000). *Guidelines for psychotherapy with lesbian, gay and bisexual clients.* Washington, DC: Author.

American Psychological Association. (2002). Ethical principles of psychologists and code of conduct. *American Psychologist, 57* (12).

American Psychological Association. (2002). *Guidelines for psychological practice with girls and women (Draft).* Joint Task Force of APA Divisions 17 and 35, American Psychological Association.

American Psychological Association. (2002). *Guidelines on cross cultural education and training, research, organizational change and practice for psychologists.* Washington, DC: Joint Task Force of APA Divisions 17 and 45.

American Psychological Association. (2003*). Guidelines for psychological practice with older adults.* Washington, DC: Division 12-Section II and Division 20 Interdivisional Force on Practice in Clinical Geropsychology.

American Psychological Association. (April, 2003). Special Issue. A new model of disability. *American Psychologist, 58,* 279–311.

Banks, M. E. (2003). Disability in the family: A life span perspective. *Cultural Diversity and Ethnic Minority Psychology, 9,* 367–384.

Bem, S. L. (1993). *The lenses of gender.* New Haven: Yale University Press.

Best, D., & Williams, J. (1997). Sex, gender, and culture. In J.W. Berry, M. H. Segall, & C. Kagitcibasi (Eds.), *Handbook of cross-cultural psychology: Social behavior and applications* (V.3, pp. 163–212). Needham Heights, MA: Allyn & Bacon.

Bhopal, K. (2001). Researching South Asian women: issues of sameness and difference in the research process. *Journal of Gender Studies, 10,* 279–286.

Bianchi, S. M., Casper, L. M., & Peltola, P. K. (1999). A cross-national look at married women's earnings dependency. *Gender Issues, 17(3),* Summer, 3–33.

Blossfield, H. P. (Ed.). (1995). *The new role of women, Family formation in modern societies.* Boulder, CO: Westview Press.

Brodsky, A., & Hare-Mustin, R. (1980). Part one: The influence of gender on research. In A. Brodsky & R. Hare-Mustin (Eds.), *Women and psychotherapy* (pp. 3—34). New York: Guilford Press.

Bronstein, P., & Quina, K. (Eds.). (1988). *Teaching a psychology of people.* Washington, DC: American Psychological Association.

Capra, F. (1996). *The web of life.* New York: Anchor Books.

Castillo, R. (2001) Lessons from folk healing practices. In W-SA. Tseng & J. Streltzer (Eds.) *Culture and psychotherapy: A guide to clinical practice* (pp. 81–101). Washington, DC: American Psychiatric Association.

Center for Policy Alternatives. (1988). *America's economic agenda: Women's voices for solutions. Health care and security.* Women's Economic Leadership Summit, Washington, DC, White House and Center for Policy Alternatives, April 3–5, 1997.

Comas-Diaz, L., & Jansen, M. A. (1995). Global conflict and violence against women. *Peace and Conflict: Journal of Peace Psychology, 1* (4), 315–331.

Dana, R. H. (2000). An assessment-intervention model for research and practice with multicultural populations. In R. H. Dana (Ed.), *Handbook of cross-cultural and multicultural personality assessment* (pp. 5–16). Mahwah, NJ: Lawrence Erlbaum.

Denzin, N., & Lincoln, Y. (Eds.) (2001). *Handbook of qualitative research.* Thousand Oaks, CA: Sage Publications, Inc.

di Mauro, D., Gilbert, H., & Parker, R. (Eds.) (2003). *Handbook of sexuality research training initiatives.* London: Carfax.

Draguns, J. G. (2001) Toward a truly international psychology: Beyond English only. *American Psychologist, 56,* 1019–1030.

Duncan, S., & Edwards, R. (Eds.) (1997). *Single mothers in an international context: Mothers or workers?* London: University College London Press.

Dworkin, S. H., & Yi, H. (2003). LGBT identity, violence and social justice: The psychological is political. *International Journal for the Advancement of Counseling, 25,* 269–279.

Eberhardt, J. L., & Fiske, S. T. (Eds.) (1998). *Confronting racism: The problem and the response.* Thousand Oaks, CA: Sage.

Espin, O., & Gaweleck, M. A. (1992). Women's diversity: Ethnicity, race, class and gender in theories of feminist psychology. In L. Brown and M. Ballou, *Personality and psychopathology, feminist reappraisals.* New York: Guilford Press.

Esses, V. M., Dovidio, J. F., Jackson, L. M., & Armstrong, T. L. (2001). The immigration dilemma: The role of perceived group competition, ethnic prejudice and national identity. *The Journal of Social Issues, 57(3)*, 389–412.

European Women's Lobby. (January, 2000). *Unveiling the hidden data on domestic violence in the European Union.* Brussels: European Women's Union Studies.

Evans, C. (2002). At war with diversity: U.S. language policy in an age of anxiety. *Bilingual Research Journal, 26(2)*, 485–491.

Fernando, S., Ndwgwa, D., Wilson, M. (Eds.) (1998). *Forensic psychiatry, race, and culture.* New York: Routledge.

Foa, E. B., Keane, T. M., & Friedman, M J. (Eds.) (2000). *Effective treatments for PTSD: Practice guidelines from the International Society for Traumatic Stress Studies.* New York: Guilford Press.

Fox, D., & Prilleltensky, I. (2001). *Critical psychology.* London: Sage Publications, Inc.

Frank, J. D., & Frank, J. B. (1991). *Persuasion and healing: A comparative study of psychotherapy.* Baltimore, MD: Johns Hopkins.

Friedman, S. (Ed.) (1997). *Cultural issues in the treatment of anxiety.* New York: Guilford.

Gershick, T. (2000). Towards a theory of disability and gender. *Signs, 24*, 1263–1269.

Giddens, A. (2000) *Runaway world: How globalization is reshaping our lives.* New York: Routledge.

Gielen, U. P., & Pagan, M. (1993). International psychology and American mainstream psychology. *The International Psychologist, 34(1)*, 16–19.

Goldberg, G.S., & Kremen, E. (1990). *The feminization of poverty: Only in America?* New York: Praeger.

Goode, W. J. (1993). *World changes in divorce patterns.* New Haven, CT: Yale University Press.

Harding, S., (Ed) (1987). *Feminism and methodology.* Bloomington: Indiana University Press.

Harding, S. (1993). *The radical economy of science toward a democratic future.* Bloomington, IN: Indiana University Press.

Hauchler, I., & Kennedy, P.M. (Eds.) (1994). *Global trends, The world almanac of development and peace.* New York: Continuum Publishing.

Hays, P. A. (2001). *Addressing cultural complexities in practice: A framework for clinicians and counselors.* Washington, DC: American Psychological Association Books.

Hogan, J. D. (1995) International psychology in the next century: Comment and speculation from a U.S. perspective. *World Psychology, 1*, 9–25.

Marsella, A. J. (1998). Toward a global psychology: Meeting the needs of a changing world. *American Psychologist, 53*, 1282–1291.

Marsella, A. J., & Pedersen, P.B. (2002). *Fifty ways to internationalize the curriculum of Western psychology.* APA Continuing Education Workshop. Chicago: American Psychological Association.

Martin, S. F. (1994). A policy perspective on the mental health and psychosocial needs of refugees. In A. J. Marsella, T. Bornermann, S. Ekblad, & J. Orley, *Amidst peril and pain: The mental health and well-being of the world's refugees* (pp. 69–80). Washington, DC: American Psychological Association.

Martin-Baro, I. (1994). *Writings for a liberation psychology.* Cambridge, MA: Harvard University Press.

McLanahan, S. S., & Kelly, E. L. (1998). *The feminization of poverty: Past and future.* Princeton, NJ: Office of Population Research.

Mezzich. J. E. (2002). International surveys on the use of ICD-10 and related diagnostic systems. *Psychopathology, 35(2–3)*, 72–75.

Moane, G. (1999). *Gender and colonialism: The psychological analysis of oppression and liberation.* New York: St. Martin's Press.

Moler, D., & Catley, B. (2000) *Global America: Imposing liberalism on a recalcitrant world.* Westport, CT: Praeger.

Murray, M., & Chamberlain, K. (Eds.). (1999). *Qualitative health psychology theories and methods.* London: Sage Publications Ltd.

Nakane, Y., & Nakane, H. (2002). Classification systems for psychiatric diseases currently used in Japan. *Psychopathology, 35(2–3)*, 191–194.

Nandy, A. (1983). Towards an alternative politics of psychology. *International Social Science Journal, 25 (2)*, 323–338.

Nandy, A. (1987). *Traditions, tyranny, and utopia.* Delhi: Oxford University Press.

Nylen, L., & Heimer, G. (April, 2000). *Sweden's response to domestic violence.* Stockholm: The Swedish Institute.

Pareek, U. (1990). Culture-relevant and culture-modifying action research for development. *Journal of Social Issues, 45*, 110–131.

Rice, J. K., & Ballou, M. (2002). *Cultural and gender awareness in international psychology.* Washington,

DC: American Psychological Association, Division 52, International Psychology, International Committee for Women.

Robson, C. (1993). *Real world research*. Oxford, UK: Blackwell.

Schmitz, C. L., Stakeman, C., & Sisneros, J. (1996). Educating professionals for practice in a multicultural society: Understanding oppression and valuing diversity. *Families in Society, 82 (6)*, 612–622.

Segal, M. H., Lonner, W. J., & Berry, J. W. (1998). Cross cultural psychology as a scholarly discipline: On the flowering of culture in behavioral research. *American Psychologist, 53*, 1101–1110.

Sherif, C. W. (1979). Bias in psychology. In J. A. Sherman & E. T. Beck (Eds.), *The prism of sex: Essays in the sociology of knowledge*. Madison, WI: The University of Wisconsin Press.

Sidanius, J., Levin, S., Federico, C. M., & Patto, F. (2001). Legitimizing ideologies: The social dominance approach. In J. T. Jost & B. Major (Eds.), *The psychology of legitimacy: Emerging perspectives on ideology, justice and intergroup relations*. New York: Cambridge University Press, pp. 307–331.

Sidanius, J., & Pratto, F. (1999). *Social dominance: An intergroup theory of social hierarchy and oppression*. New York: Cambridge University Press.

Sloan, T. S. (1996). Psychological research methods in developing countries. In S. Carr & J. Schumaker (Eds.), *Psychology in the developing world* (pp. 38–45). London: Praeger.

Sloan, T. (Ed) (2000). *Critical psychology: Voices for change*. Hampshire, England: Plagrave.

Smeeding, T. M., & Ross, K. (1999). *Social protection for the poor in the developed world: The evidence from LIS*. Washington, DC: Inter-American Development Bank.

Spence, J. (1987). Masculinity, femininity, and gender-related traits: A conceptual analysis and critique of current research. In B. A. Maher & W. B. Maher (Eds.), *Progress in experimental research in personality, (V. 13*, pp. 1–97). New York: Academic Press.

Sue S., & Zane, N. (1987). The role of culture and cultural techniques in psychotherapy: A critique and reformulation. *American Psychologist, 42*, 37–45

Sunar. D. (1998). An interview with Cigdem Kagitcibasi. *World Psychology, 2*, 139–152.

Thorne, B., & Lambers, E. (Eds.) (1998). *Person-centered therapy: A European perspective*. London: Sage Publications, Ltd.

United Nations Department of Public Information. (1995). *Beijing platform for action*. New York: United Nations.

UNESCO. (2002). *Literacy rates*. New York: United Nations Educational, Scientific and Cultural Organization.

United Nations. (2000). *The world's women 2000: Trends and statistics*. New York: Author.

United Nations Population Fund. (2000). *Lives together, worlds apart: Men and women in a time of change*. New York: Author.

Wallerstein, I. (1992). America and the world today, yesterday and tomorrow. *Theory and Society, 21*, 1–28.

Weiss, E. Whelan, D. Gupta, G. (2000). Gender, sexuality and HIV: Making a difference in the lives of young women in developing countries. *Sexual and Relationship Therapy, 15*, 234–245.

White, J. W., Russo, N. F., & Travis, C. B. (2001). Feminism and the decade of behavior. *Psychology of Women Quarterly, 25*, 267–279.

Winslow, W., Honein, G., Elzubeir, M. (2002). Seeking Emirati women's voices: The use of focus groups with an Arab population. *Qualitative Health Research, 12*, 566–576.

Woolf, L. M., Hulsizer, M. R., & McCarthy, T. (2002). *Internationalization of introductory psychology: Challenges, benefits, and resources*. Twenty-Fifth annual National Institute on the Teaching of Psychology, St. Petersburg Beach, FL, January 2–5, 2002.

5

Theoretical and Methodological Issues When Studying Culture

STEFANÍA ÆGISDÓTTIR,
LAWRENCE H. GERSTEIN, SEUNG-MING ALVIN LEUNG,
KWONG-LIEM KARL KWAN, AND WALTER J. LONNER

Most scholars today agree that engaging in and disseminating results from cross-cultural and cultural research is an important component of the advancement of the science and practice of counseling and counseling psychology. However, issues and debates surrounding the construct of culture are often complicated and controversial. The issues of the importance of emic (culture-specific) and etic (transcending culture) constructs in advancing knowledge in psychology and the value of universality (discovering universal laws; i.e., cross-cultural comparative studies, hypothetico-deductive positivistic or postpositivistic framework) versus cultural relativism (all "laws" are emic, constructivism) continue to plague those engaged in cross-cultural and cultural research. In this chapter, we examine the two often "opposing forces" of universalism and cultural relativism in the study of cultural influences on behavior and discuss methodological and conceptual challenges and issues facing each approach. The benefits of each approach for enhancing psychological and counseling

knowledge are discussed as well. Finally, we provide some examples from anthropology that may benefit counseling scholars interested in cross-cultural research and in bridging the gap between cultural relativism (emics) and universalism (etics) to further enhance the science of counseling and psychology.

WHY DO PHENOMENA HAVE TO BE EITHER *THIS* OR *THAT*? OR, DO THEY?

Throughout the history of psychology, there have been complications and debates similar and related to the debates about emics and etics, and cultural relativism and universalism. These debates can be traced to ontological concerns (the nature of being, existence, and reality: What exists?) and epistemological questions (the nature, scope, and limitations of knowledge: What is knowledge? How is it acquired?). Some examples include the validity of subjective as compared with objective realities; the nomothetic (e.g., psychological tests and other quantitative methods) versus idiosyncratic (e.g., interview and other qualitative techniques) debate in the assessment and understanding of an individual's functioning; and the statistical versus clinical controversy surrounding clinical judgment. All these debates and dilemmas can be tied to the same issues: What is an appropriate and valid source of knowledge? And what is the nature of existence and reality? Moreover, with these diverse points of view come different methods and approaches to seeking knowledge and gaining an understanding of human psychological functioning.

When exploring how these divergent views have been resolved, scholars have usually concluded that both debated polarities have something to offer and that one does not exclude the other. For instance, those involved in clinical assessment have concluded that both idiosyncratic and clinical (e.g., clinical interview) data and nomothetic and statistical (e.g., results from psychological tests, decision rules) data complement one another and can be combined to gain a more holistic and perhaps more accurate assessment of a person (e.g., Strohmer & Arm, 2006; Ægisdóttir et al., 2006). Furthermore, counseling professionals in the United States are trained to attend both to the subjective realities of their clients (e.g., asking clients about their phenomenological experiences with diagnostic labels such as depression) and to the objective, observable diagnostic signs clients may be displaying (e.g., comparing signs against a diagnostic rubric) and to consult the outcome literature on empirically supported interventions. Thus, ideally, counseling professionals consult two sources of knowledge and realities (the subjective and the objective) and bridge these two to be of the best help to their clients. In short, the complexity of human existence is acknowledged. This also involves abandoning philosophical purism and a polar opposite mentality for a functionalist view with the belief that it offers a more comprehensive understanding of the individual.

Whereas in counseling practice, this pragmatic functionalist philosophical stance of seeking knowledge from both idiographic and nomothetic sources is considered acceptable and, in fact, best practice, in counseling and psychology *research,* the issue becomes more complicated. This is because psychology and counseling are heavily influenced by the positivistic framework and the scientific method, which can be traced back to the time when psychology was branching off from philosophy and struggling to be considered a scientific discipline in line with the natural sciences. This struggle between the subjective world and the objective world becomes extremely salient in studies involving the construct of culture. The struggle is exemplified in the emic-etic debate, the controversy concerning universalism versus cultural relativism, and the issues revolving around the merits of quantitative and qualitative research methodologies.

It is not surprising, therefore, that scholars interested in culture and cultural influences on behavior conceptualize and approach their investigation from different frameworks and methodologies. For instance, one can group, compare, and contrast how different disciplines approach the study of culture (e.g., psychology and anthropology). One can further group scholars within these disciplines into subcategories based on their conceptualization of culture and their methods, aims, and goals. These subcategories span cross-cultural psychology, cultural psychology, indigenous psychology, cultural anthropology, social anthropology, and psychological anthropology (e.g., Adamopoulos & Lonner, 2001; Triandis, 2000). Furthermore, and to some degree regardless of the discipline (psychology, anthropology), one can categorize cultural studies based on ontological and epistemological schools of thought. Therefore, one can adhere to the thought of cultural relativism and take an emic epistemological stance in which one can understand individuals' psychological functioning only in the context of their culture, using culture-specific concepts that are meaningful and deemed appropriate by natives within that culture (e.g., Lett, 1996). This relativistic stance is constructivist in that meaning and knowledge is considered a human construction and therefore leads one to qualitative research. Or one can adhere to the universalistic school of thought.

Here, one operates from the assumption that there are core human characteristics shared across cultures (e.g., aggression; Bond & Tedeschi, 2001) that can be studied using scientific methods. Etic constructs (or derived etics, e.g., Berry, 1999) that are regarded meaningful and appropriate by the community of scientific observers are the main focus within this school of thought (Lett, 1996).

Lonner (in press), when speaking for the universalist position, identified seven levels of universals in terms of the feasibility and importance of each for psychological science. The levels range from simple universals (e.g., human sexuality) that are invariant across cultures to cocktail party universals (e.g., phenomenological experiences of psychological pain; meaning hermeneutics) that are difficult to categorize and compare. Universalists operate from the hypothetico-deductive framework of positivism. Absolutism has also been mentioned within this context. The absolutist view is that there is one absolute truth about human behavior that can be studied and understood using etic concepts and the scientific experiment (positivism). Within absolutism, culture and cultural influence on behavior are not considered of value but are considered to be masking and standing in the way for absolute laws to be identified (Adamopoulos & Lonner, 2001, Hwang, 2005). Within the absolutist view, theories and approaches should be equally effective and appropriate regardless of culture. Some say (e.g., Shweder, 1990) that absolutism and therefore ethnocentrism characterize mainstream scientific psychology (U.S. psychology)—a viewpoint shared by both cultural and cross-cultural psychologists, who place culture at the core of their inquiries, even though they approach the construct of culture differently.

STUDYING CULTURE

Although culture has been of some interest to psychology scholars and researchers in the United States since World War II or even earlier (Adamopoulos & Lonner, 2001; Marsella, Dubanoski, Hamada, & Morse, 2000; Segall, Lonner, & Berry, 1998), it was not until the mid- to late 1960s that systematic cross-cultural and cultural research began to emerge. Up to that time period or even later, an absolutist Eurocentric/ethnocentric framework mostly guided the research agenda, namely translating and indiscriminately testing U.S- (or Western-) developed psychological inventories (e.g., personality and intelligence tests) and theories in countries outside the United States. This was done without much consideration given to cultural bias in the constructs and theories being tested and the methodology employed (Adamopoulos & Lonner, 2001; Marsella et al., 2000). In the 1970s, however, more attention was paid to the conceptual challenges with this absolutist stance and the methodological problems in cross-cultural comparative research using Euro-American tools. During this time, for instance, the first book was published on psychology on methodological issues and problems in cross-cultural research: *Cross-Cultural Research Methods*, by Brislin, Lonner, and Thorndike (1973). Since that time, additional publications have followed (e.g., Lonner & Berry, 1986; van de Vijver & Leung, 1997a) introducing scholars to the unique challenges of cross-cultural and cultural research. Additionally, during this time the controversy between universalist and relativist, and emic versus etic approaches to understanding and studying cultural influences on behavior began to emerge.

In psychology, scholars have aligned with different schools of thought and methodologies when studying culture, depending on the fundamental goals of their efforts. These schools include indigenous psychology, cultural psychology, and cross-cultural psychology. According to Adamopoulos and Lonner (2001), in the indigenous approach, psychological phenomena are studied in their specific cultural context by scholars indigenous to that culture. The main goal is to develop an indigenous psychology that has meaning and that benefits people within a specific culture (e.g., Kim, Park, & Park, 2000). The indigenous approach advocates the perspectives of both "insiders" (emic) and "outsiders" (etic), which necessitates multiple methodologies (qualitative, quantitative) (Kim, Yang, & Hwang, 2006). The primary theoretical challenge for this approach is avoiding existing conceptualization of behavior and psychological processes and therefore determining what is indigenous (Adamopoulos & Lonner, 2001).

As with the indigenous approach, the basic purpose of the cultural approach is to advance the understanding of individuals in their cultural context. In contrast to the indigenous approach, however, those who identify as cultural psychologists often study cultures other than their own (Triandis, 2000), many times employing ethnographic methods originating in cultural anthropology. Quantitative methods are also sometimes applied. The meaning of constructs within a culture is of greatest interest (emic), and those adhering to this perspective refute treating culture and cultural variables as independent of the person. Instead, culture is viewed as an integral, important, and inseparable part of the human mind (Adamopoulos & Lonner, 2001). Cultural psychologists espouse a relativistic framework, and explicit comparison between cultural groups is not of interest and does not make sense to these professionals. Often, the epistemological framework guiding this type of approach is constructivist, in which meaning and knowledge is considered a construction of the mind. The main theoretical challenge for the relativistic stance is conceptualizing culture to fit the idea of it being an integral and inseparable part of the human mind. Thus, it appears that the theorization of culture could be so inclusive that it becomes useless. Additionally, Adamopoulos and Lonner noted inconsistencies in how cultural psychologists have conceptualized culture. Furthermore, they questioned if meaning can be a scientific object of explanation.

Those adhering to the cross-cultural approach generally obtain data from many cultures with the aim of studying their similarities and differences in psychological functioning. Constructs shared across cultures are investigated, and the primary purpose is the development of an inclusive universal psychology (etics/derived etics, e.g., Berry, 1999) and discerning how and why contextual factors affect the universal core of human functioning (Adamopoulos & Lonner, 2001; Triandis, 2000). In cross-cultural studies, culture and cultural variables are often treated as quasi-independent variables either moderating or mediating behavior. Therefore, cultural variables can be separated from the individual and approximated by tests and inventories (e.g., demographic variables, psychological variables, societal variables). A positivistic ontological stance is usually taken within this framework. The main methodological challenges of this comparative framework are issues of equivalence of constructs and observations, bias, and levels of analysis (Adamopoulos & Lonner; Smith, 2002, chap. 7). Theoretical challenges of the universalist comparative framework have to do with the status of culture within it as an intervening variable that has no explanatory or causative power. As Adamopoulos and Lonner (2001) stated, "This results in the degradation of the status of culture and makes it much easier to ignore in theory construction" (p. 24).

The approaches to studying culture just mentioned have different aims, challenges, and merits; yet they can also complement one another. In the following sections, we discuss in more detail the cross-cultural, cultural, and anthropological frameworks and approaches with connotation to the emic-etic and the relativist-universalist distinctions. Even though commonalities can be derived from cultural psychology and anthropology, we submit that counseling scholars interested in international counseling psychology performing cross-cultural and cultural research might draw some important lessons from anthropology in studying cultures.

METHODOLOGICAL ISSUES

Etics, Universalism, and the Cross-Cultural Approach

The term *etic* is derived from the word *phonetics*, which in linguistics refers to universal sounds used in human language regardless of their meaning in a particular language (Pike, 1967). In psychology and anthropology, therefore, the etic perspective relies on extrinsic concepts and categories that have meaning to scientific observers. Etic concepts transcend culture, and the etic approach relies on a descriptive system (taxonomy, categorization) that is equally valid for all cultures so that similarities and differences between cultures can be found (Helfrich, 1999). Etic perspectives to studying and understanding culture are closely linked to cross-cultural approaches, even though emic constructs may also be of interest to cross-cultural psychologists. *Cross-cultural psychology* and *cross-cultural strategies* refer to collecting data in two or more cultures. Within this comparative framework, the generalizability of psychological theories and approaches is examined to see how culture affects theories and approaches, and to offer suggestions about adaptations to a new cultural context (Helfrich, 1999). More specifically, *cross-cultural etic approaches* refer to the "study of similarities and difference in individual functioning in various cultural and ethnic groups; of the relationship between psychological variables and sociocultural, ecological, and biological variables; and of changes in these variables (Berry, Poortinga, Segall, & Dasen, 1992, p. 2). With cross-cultural and etic strategies to studying human functioning, therefore, concepts (e.g., counseling expectations) that exist in the cultures of interests are the subject of focus. With this approach, culture is "elevated" to the status of a quasi-independent variable that may either mediate or moderate behavior (Adamopoulos & Lonner, 2001). Since with this approach cultural groups are compared on a particular variable, teasing out measurement artifacts (e.g., different meaning attached to the constructs under study: counseling expectations) as potential explanations of cultural differences becomes the main challenge. These artifacts or confounds are issues of bias and equivalence.

Bias

In cross-cultural comparison, between-group differences found in test scores could be viewed as evidence of cultural differences on underlying traits or characteristics. However, cross-cultural scholars have identified a number of possible biases that could cause researchers to misattribute observed similarities and differences to culture. Unfortunately, many cross-cultural research studies have been published that did not pay

sufficient attention to bias (e.g., Berry, Poortinga, Segall, & Dasen, 2002; Ægisdóttir, Gerstein, & Çinarbaş, 2008). Furthermore, van de Vijver and Tanzer (2004) commented that "the history of psychology has shown various examples of sweeping generalizations about differences in abilities and traits of cultural populations which, upon close scrutiny, were based on psychometrically poor measures" (p. 264). Thus, one important consideration to increase the rigor in cross-cultural research is controlling for bias. According to van de Vijver and Leung (1997a), *bias* is "a generic term for all nuisance factors threatening the validity of cross-cultural comparison" (p. 10). They identified three main types of bias: construct bias, method bias, and item bias.

Construct bias occurs when the construct measured (e.g., coping) is not the same across cultural groups (van de Vijver & Leung, 1997a, 1997b). Construct bias is a concern in cross-cultural comparisons when (a) there is only partial overlap in the definition of the target construct across cultures (e.g., how coping is defined might be different across cultures), (b) the behaviors associated with a particular construct vary in appropriateness across culture (e.g., coping strategies prized in one culture might not be cherished in another), and (c) there is insufficient sampling of relevant behaviors associated with a construct (e.g., a measure of coping does not comprehensively include major coping strategies in the target cultures) (van de Vijver & Poortinga, 1997; van de Vijver & Tanzer, 2004). To minimize the impact of construct bias, researchers should examine if the definition and expression of a construct is the same across cultural groups in the instrument development or selection process. Van de Vijver and Tanzer (2004) identified two strategies that could effectively deal with construct bias. The first method is called *decentering*, where the measures used are developed or adapted simultaneously in the cultures in which they are to be administered. In this process, researchers eliminate and modify words, ideas, and concepts that are not shared across these cultural groups. The resulting instruments consist of items and samples of behavior that have more or less identical meaning and relevance to all participants. The second method to eliminate construct bias is the *convergence approach.* Here the researchers either develop or use culture-specific instruments relevant to each of the target cultures that are administered to participants from all the target cultures. Similarities of findings across instruments (e.g., same patterns of cross-cultural differences on all instruments) support the validity of the cross-cultural results, whereas discrepancies across measures suggest biases (van de Vijver & Leung, 1997a). Ægisdóttir et al. (2008) also suggested that if an instrument developed in only one of the cultures under study is to be used for cross-cultural comparison, new culture-specific emic items relevant to the construct could be constructed in the other culture and added to the instrument to decrease construct bias. While only identical items can be compared cross-culturally, the inclusion of culture-specific items may indicate cultural differences that the original instrument would not have detected. Instead of developing new items, researchers could also include open-ended response options on the measures prompting respondents for additional thoughts regarding the construct. These responses might indicate additional cross-cultural differences and similarities regarding the construct.

When construct bias is properly managed, observed cross-cultural differences might still be compounded by method bias. Method bias occurs when aspects or characteristics of an instrument or its administration elicit diverse responses from members of a different culture, resulting in "unwanted inter-group differences" (van de Vijver & Leung, 1997b). Van de Vijver and Tanzer (2004) identified three sources of method bias: (1) there is sample bias when the characteristics of the samples compared are different (e.g., education, age), (2) there is administration bias when the data collection procedures and processes vary across cultural groups (e.g., in-person versus Web-based methods of data collection, test administrators with different levels of expertise), and (3) there is instrument bias when differences in response styles exist among the cultural groups (e.g., social desirability, stimulus familiarity, extreme scoring).

To control for method bias, researchers should use designs (e.g., scales, interviews) that make sense to the cultures under study. They should also use samples that are equivalent in sociodemographic characteristics (e.g., age, gender, education, socioeconomic status). Furthermore, they should standardize data collection procedures through developing detailed protocols for test administration, scoring, and interpretation. Additionally, test administrators should receive training such that they have the necessary cultural sensitivity and technical knowledge required for cross-cultural data collection. Moreover, methodological procedures should be used (e.g., test-retest method, structural equation modeling) to assess and discern response styles that might jeopardize cross-cultural comparisons (e.g., Cheung & Rensvold, 2000).

The third kind of bias challenging valid cross-cultural comparisons is item bias, also referred to as *differential item functioning* (van de Vijver & Leung, 1997b). This is a bias at the item level of an instrument caused by erroneous or inaccurate item translation or the use of test items that are inappropriate or irrelevant (e.g., items describing experiences or activities that are unfamiliar) to some of the cultural groups under study. Item bias is present if participants who have the same standing on an underlying trait (e.g., have equal math ability and skill) do not have the same probability of getting a correct answer on a target item.

Item bias can be managed through the use of a range of item bias analysis techniques, including Item Response Theory (IRT), analysis of variance (ANOVA) procedures, structural equation methods (SEM), and logistic regression, to determine if the distribution of item scores for individuals who have equivalent standing on a latent trait is the same across cultural groups (van de Vijver & Leung, 1997b; Ægisdóttir et al., 2008). In addition to using psychometric strategies to detect possible item bias, researchers using multiple language versions of instruments should follow a rigorous language translation procedure to eliminate bias. Prior to translating an instrument, though, investigators should be careful when selecting and adapting an instrument so as to minimize construct, method, and item bias and to ensure that its content and structure are consistent with the cultural context where the instrument is to be administered. A number of authors have written about translation methods (e.g., Brislin, 1976, 1986; Hambleton & de Jong, 2003; Shiraev & Levy, 2006; van de Vijver & Hambleton, 1996; van de Vijver & Leung, 1997a; Ægisdóttir et al., 2008) that are reflected in the standards of the International Test Commission (ITC). In brief, the following procedures have been recommended: (a) Employ bilingual persons speaking the original and target languages to conduct the translation. They need to be familiar with test construction, the construct under study, and the cultures of interest. (b) Use a committee of persons rather than a single person at different stages of the translation process to reduce biases of an individual person. This is done by comparing the individual translations and developing a single translated version of the instrument based on consensus agreement among the translation committee. (c) Perform a back-translation using either a committee of persons or a single individual, where the translated version is converted back to its original-language version. (d) Compare the back-translated version of the measure to the original version and make corresponding modifications to increase equivalence. (e) Pretest the translated version by, for instance, administering both language versions of the instrument to bilingual individuals (in the two target languages) to determine language equivalence. (f) Assess the translated instruments' reliability and validity and potential bias, and compare this with psychometric properties of the original language version. (g) Document and report in published articles the translation procedures, the challenges involved, and the evidence of the translated versions' equivalence.

It is important to note that method bias and item bias might not be exhibited uniformly on different levels of scores (or scales) or an item of an instrument (van de Vijver & Leung, 1997a; Ægisdóttir et al., 2008). A bias is considered uniform when its effect is more or less the same across all levels of the scores. It is considered nonuniform if the effects of bias are not the same for all score levels.

In sum, bias is a major threat to validity in cross-cultural comparisons. The greater the cultural distance (e.g., language, social structure, political structure, climate, human development index) between the cultures under investigation, the greater the potential bias is (Triandis, 2001; Ægisdóttir et al., 2008). Counseling researchers need to identify the types of biases that are likely to exert an influence on their studies and make deliberate efforts to minimize their potential impact on their designs and findings. If at all possible and appropriate, structured tests administered in standardized conditions are less likely to be influenced by bias than are open-ended question formats (e.g., Ægisdóttir et al., 2008). While it is impossible to rule out bias entirely, the documentation of steps taken to reduce, rule out, and assess bias allows researchers to interpret cultural differences in psychological and counseling constructs more accurately.

Equivalence

Equivalence is closely related to bias such that the less the bias, the greater the equivalence. Direct cross-cultural comparisons are greatly challenged and cannot be accurately performed unless the equivalence of the measures that are used has been ensured. Equivalence has been conceptualized in at least two complementary ways. Lonner (1985) discussed four types: functional, conceptual, metric, and linguistic. Functional equivalence refers to the various functions tied to constructs across cultures. For instance, if different functions are connected to behaviors or activities across cultures, their parameters cannot be used for cross-cultural comparison. One example of a nonequivalent habit or phrase salient for the first author is the common U.S. greeting, "Hi, how are you?" While in the United States this greeting is basically met with a simple "Hello" response, in some other cultures this greeting may elicit long accounts of how the person receiving the greeting is actually doing and feeling at that time. Thus, in this example the greeting does not have functional equivalence. Another classic example is pet ownership. In the United States, dogs and cats are often treated as family members, whereas in other cultures they are annoyances and, at best, food. Issues of functional equivalence can often be resolved in the translation of measures.

Conceptual equivalence is closely related to *functional equivalence* and refers to the meaning associated with a concept. Psychological help seeking may, for instance, mean seeking help from a professional mental health provider in one culture, whereas it could mean seeking advice from a shaman or a family member in another. *Metric equivalence* according to Lonner (1985) refers to the psychometric properties (validity, reliability, item distribution) of the tools (e.g., scales) used in cross-cultural research, whereas *linguistic equivalence* refers to the form, structure, reading difficulty, and naturalness of the items used to elicit information about the construct under study (Lonner, 1985; van de Vijver & Leung, 1997a; Ægisdóttir et al., 2008).

A complementary conceptualization of equivalence was introduced by van de Vijver and Leung (1997a). They distinguished between four levels of equivalence that have a hierarchical order: construct nonequivalence, construct or structural equivalence, measurement unit equivalence, and scalar equivalence. At the lowest end, representing a total lack of equivalence, is *construct nonequivalence,* referring to constructs being so dissimilar or nonexistent across cultures (e.g., culture-bound syndromes) that they cannot be compared. This conceptualization incorporates Lonner's (1985) lack of functional equivalence. The second level of equivalence in van de Vijver and Leung's conceptualization is *construct or structural equivalence*. It refers to the meaning attached to a construct and the construct's nomological network (convergent and divergent validity) (e.g., Ægisdóttir et al., 2008). At this level, a construct might have the same definition and meaning (e.g., career interests) across cultures, yet the operational definitions may differ. For example, the meaning and conceptual structure of *career interests* might be the same across cultures and may predict similar outcomes, but the operational definitions could differ (i.e., activities to express the same interest type vary across cultures).

The third level of equivalence is *measurement unit equivalence* (van de Vijver, 2001; van de Vijver & Leung, 1997a). Here, the scales used to measure the concept are equivalent, but their origins are different across groups. In some instances, there is a known constant that can be applied to one measure to make the measures equivalent. The most commonly used example to illustrate measurement unit equivalence is the measurement of temperature using Kelvin and Celsius scales (e.g., van de Vijver & Leung, 1997a). Even though the both the scales are at the interval level of measurement, they cannot be directly compared because they have different origins. To make them comparable, a constant of 273 (their origins differ by 273) needs to be added to the Kelvin scale. Only then do the temperatures measured by these two scales have the same meaning. Counseling scholars are familiar with measurement unit equivalence in their practice. For instance, in some cases different cut-scores on psychological inventories are used to identify psychological characteristics (e.g., personality traits) of individuals from different groups (Ægisdóttir et al., 2008), and thus different scores on a measure represent the same quality (meaning) based on group memberships. Biases affecting the origins of scale scores render valid cross-cultural comparisons difficult.

The last and highest level of equivalence is scalar equivalence. *Scalar equivalence* refers to complete score comparability. It is achieved if the same instrument is employed as a measure across cultures, using an equivalent unit of measurement, and bias has been ruled out (van de Vijver & Leung, 1997a). When this level of equivalence has been reached, scale scores using mean score comparisons can be performed between cultural groups. Establishing scalar equivalence involves the use of psychometric procedures. van de Vijver and Leung (1997b) maintained that statistical techniques employed to demonstrate structural equivalence of instruments across cultures (e.g., correlation matrices and factor structures) are insufficient in assessing scalar equivalence—a similar factor structure of a construct does not assure scalar equivalence. Van de Vijver and Leung recommended the use of internal validation procedures such as intracultural techniques to examine if empirical data are consistent with theoretical expectations for each of the cultures that are compared (e.g., to examine if the order of item difficulty of an intelligence test is the same in different cultures). Differential item functioning techniques (e.g., IRT) could also be used to check for item bias and uniformity of item bias. Therefore, various techniques used to assess for bias (e.g., van de Vijver & Leung, 1997b; Ægisdóttir et al., 2008) should be applied before measures are compared across cultures.

Merits of the Etic, Universalistic, Cross-Cultural Approach

Despite the challenges involved in valid cross-cultural comparisons, the cross-cultural approach has informed psychological theory and practice in important ways. For instance, in personality psychology, extensive research worldwide has been performed on the NEO Personality Inventory (NEO-PI-R; McCrae & Costa, 1997). This research has measured the "Big Five" personality factors that have been found to be somewhat robust across cultures, even though their robustness does not preclude other culturally specific personality factors (e.g., Ho, 1996). We refer the reader to Church and Lonner (1998) and Smith, Bond, and Kagitçibasi, (2006), who provided comprehensive overviews of the cross-cultural research on personality. Likewise, extensive cross-cultural research has been performed on the "abnormal" personality (e.g., Tanaka-Matsumi, 2001; Tanaka-Matsumi & Draguns, 1997). This research has, for example, indicated that for schizophrenia, some universal core symptoms have been reported even though the prognosis and course of the symptoms vary by sociocultural context. Furthermore, extensive cross-cultural research has been performed on emotions and emotional display rules (e.g., Matsumoto, 2001, in press), human development (e.g., Kagitçibasi, 1996; Smith et al., 2006), values (Hofstede, 1980), and cultural syndromes and the self (Triandis, 2001) that have greatly influenced psychological theory, research, and practice.

In addition to the accumulation of knowledge regarding cultural similarities and differences in psychological variables across cultures, it cannot be denied that these and other efforts to examine and identify universals in psychology have made many scholars aware of the dangers of indiscriminately exporting theories developed within individualistic Anglo-American frameworks to cultures founded on different values and philosophies. Over the years, there has been increased sophistication in the research methodologies employed (attention to bias and equivalence) and more demands made on researchers to document the validity of their methodologies and findings (e.g., van de Vijver, 2001).

The crux of cross-cultural and etic approaches is comparative research using quasi-experimental methods, wherein culture and cultural variables are treated as independent variables either mediating or moderating behavior. What remains unresolved, though, is the status of culture and cultural variables in explaining observed differences among cultural groups. It stands to reason that culture (e.g., nationality) and cultural variables (individualism, collectivism) are never more than *descriptions* of observed differences. Designating them an explanatory power is highly suspect. Therefore, within the often positivistic hypothetico-deductive approach espoused within cross-cultural psychology, a serious limitation is placed on the type of theoretical development possible and the usefulness of the construct of culture (e.g., Adamopoulos & Lonner, 2001; Kim, 2001).

Emics, Cultural Relativism, and the Cultural Approach

Another school of thought within psychology focusing on cultural influences on behavior is cultural psychology. The main purpose of this framework is to increase the knowledge and understanding of the person in a cultural context (Adamopoulos & Lonner, 2001). As mentioned earlier, cross-cultural comparisons are not of interest within this approach but rather investigation of the meaning constructs have within a specific culture. This approach to cultural studies espouses emic constructs that are unique to a culture. *Emic* is extracted from the word *phonemics*, which is a linguistic concept that focuses on the meaning and context of words (Pike, 1967). In anthropological linguistics, regardless of variations, an emic unit of data or an emic construct remains the same entity and means the same thing for insiders of a culture (Pike, 1967). For example, a *strike* means "emically" one thing within the sports of U.S. baseball; yet, within the world of English speakers, a strike "etically" comprises many different types of events. Thus, an emic construct is derived and operationalized through the eyes of natives in a particular cultural system. It reflects the insiders' reported beliefs, thoughts, attitudes, and behavioral practices (Harris, 1968). For instance, in Chinese culture, filial piety is a normative familial concept that defines intergenerational relationships in terms of the reverence and obedience the junior generation (i.e., children) is morally obliged to reciprocate for the beneficence afforded by the senior generation (i.e., parents, grandparents) within a family. The moral mandate, in turn, prescribes normative behaviors the junior generations are expected to follow such that the senior generation and the family name are graced with honor and face (Kwan, 2000). When adult children defer their life decisions (e.g., career, mate selection) to the expectations of parents or live with parents and grandparents after marriage, for example, these behaviors follow certain rules and serve a functional purpose within the cultural context that may not be explicitly observable or understood by an (outside) investigator. An emic construct, therefore, points to a rule-system in a culture that needs to be teased out by the investigator through an intracultural analysis (Price-Williams, 1975). In this case, an understanding of filial piety cautions scholars not to label these filial behaviors as "dependent," "indecisive," or "immature" (Kwan, 2000), which may be the meaning attached to the values and behaviors in another culture such as in the United States.

In anthropology and within cultural psychology, an emic focus refers to studying a culture ipso facto (i.e., as it is). It is a locality-specific perspective from which descriptions (e.g., how a certain pattern of behaviors is labeled) and meanings (e.g., function or purpose of a certain pattern of behaviors) of observed phenomena are derived and understood in the context of the local culture rather than interpreted with reference to external criteria or a priori assumptions ascribed to or imposed by the investigators. Therefore, it is a relativistic framework in contrast to a universalistic one. The goal is to gain an insider's perspective of the phenomena of interest within a given culture and to adopt the local language or even create a new term to best capture and explain the observations (e.g., filial piety).

Methods

Cultural psychologists operating from the relativistic (constructivist) framework tend to rely on qualitative methods. They focus on raw data and seek to understand the constructs on the basis of the meanings and functions they serve within the cultural context. This is a discovery-oriented approach, in contrast to the positivistic cross-cultural approach, in which one tests or compares observed material against a priori assumptions or theory. In fact, the positivistic cross-cultural approach has been criticized by cultural researchers (relativists) for imposing a Euro-American structure, meaning, and values on other cultures and thus psychologically colonizing them (Kim, 1995, 2001; Kim & Berry, 1993). Therefore, along with immersing oneself (geographically or psychologically) in the unfamiliar culture to acquire or develop the "insider's" lens, the cultural researcher is to refrain from imposing an external set of cognitive or phenomenological references (e.g., an existing construct, a hypothesis) in the data-analytic, labeling, and explanatory process. Direct comparison across cultures is not of interest in this approach and may, in some cases, not make sense, given that emic constructs might not exist outside the cultures in which they were conceived. For this reason, some scholars have even voiced the concern that the cultural relativistic approach rejects the possibility of scientific knowledge and that the insights gained from this stance are no more than historical accounts (Helfrich,

1999; Hunt, 2007). Triandis (1976), however, indicated that indirect comparison of a given phenomenon between cultures is possible.

Bias

As with the cross-cultural approach, there are some methodological challenges that cultural (relativist) researchers focusing on emics need to confront and solve. One common critical question asked by positivists (universalists) relates to whose construction of reality is being reported in books and articles on results of cultural studies (e.g., Adamopoulos & Lonner, 2001; Helfrich, 1999). Is it the participants' construction, the observers,' or the readers'? This criticism points to the ontological and epistemological framework of the relativist, which is in contrast with the traditional scientific viewpoint of the positivists.

Regardless of the ontological and epistemological debate, though, engaging in qualitative research—the research methodology most often applied to understand how individuals construct meaning—has methodological challenges that need to be confronted and resolved. There are, for instance, various types of biases that may confound qualitative data collection, analyses, and interpretations. These can be grossly categorized into method bias and interpretive bias. In terms of method bias, one critical issue that needs to be attended to is the selection of participants in a study. To increase the validity of the information obtained about a cultural group, participants need to be representative of the cultural group to increase the generalizability of the conceptual analysis. Good representation is considered more important than the size of the sample (Bernard, 1995), and frequently purposive or dimensional sampling strategies are used (Miles & Huberman, 1994). That is, the sample is selected so as to best answer the research question (e.g., to ensure all viewpoints are represented).

Another type of method bias has to do with a study's internal validity. To enhance rigor of qualitative research, triangulation has been suggested (e.g., Devers, 1999; Kuzel, 1998). This technique refers to using multiple data sources (e.g., people, events), multiple investigators, and/or methods (e.g., interviews, observations). Triangulation, then, will elucidate different aspects of experiences and context and reduce bias tied with any one method, investigator, and data source. Furthermore, transparency in data collection and analysis (Fossey, Harvey, McDermott, & Davidson, 2002) is suggested so that consumers of the research can see if and how competing accounts and disconfirming evidence within the data were explored and interpreted, and how the researcher's own values and thinking process contributed to the analysis. Moreover, this also involves demonstrating the extent to which the participants' views and knowledge were honored (Fossey et al., 2002).

There is also potential for bias in interpretation. To reduce this type of bias, it is extremely important that the participants' views be presented in their own voices (e.g., verbatim quotes in reports) (Fossey et al., 2002). In addition, to decrease this type of bias, a validation process needs to be implemented in which the research participants themselves are involved in the data analysis and interpretation process such that they provide their view of the credibility of interpretations and findings. Moreover, investigators need to keep a reflective journal of notes on how their own personal characteristics, feelings, values, and biases may be influencing their work. This may help researchers manage and to some degree separate their own experiences and interpretations from their observations. In terms of the external validity of the study and to provide a richer interpretation and understanding of the data, it is extremely important that the investigator provide detailed descriptions of the cultural context in which the research takes place (Devers, 1999; Fossey et al., 2002).

In sum, the cultural relativistic approach to studying culture espouses the use of qualitative methods to best capture the phenomenological world of people in their cultural context. Meaningfulness in a specific cultural context at a specific point in time is a central focus. The main methodological challenge with this approach is making sure that the voices of participants are heard and that accurate recording and interpretations are offered. To ensure the accuracy of such studies while recognizing the subjectivity involved in them, qualitative researchers have incorporated in their methodology means to increase the rigor of their projects by confronting and resolving bias in their methods and interpretation. Lonner and Hayes (2007), in discussing the life and contributions of the cultural psychologist Ernest E. Boesch, give examples of how a cultural psychologist deals with the concept of "culture."

Merits of the Relativistic, Emic, Cultural Approach

The cultural relativistic approach to studying culture and the focus on emic constructs have informed psychology and counseling in important ways. An important development, for instance, is the attempt in the *DSM* diagnostic system (American Psychiatric Association [APA], 2000) to recognize culture-bound syndromes as valid and meaningful constructs. These culture-bound syndromes (emic constructs) refer to recurrent, locality-specific patterns of aberrant behavior and troubling experiences that are indigenously considered an illness, or an affliction. These syndromes represent "localized, folk, diagnostic categories that frame coherent meanings for repetitive or patterned sets of troubling experiences and observations" (APA, 2000, p. 898) that may or may not be linked to a particular *DSM* diagnostic category. A number of the culture-bound syndromes discussed in the *DSM-IV-TR* are actually formal psychiatric diagnoses in their culture of origin. For example, *qi gong psychotic reaction, shenjung-shuairuo,* and *koro* are diagnosable mental disorders in the Chinese Classification of Mental Disorders. These culture-bound syndromes are linked to common practice (e.g., *qi gong*) and etiological beliefs of diseases that are specific to the (Chinese) cultural context.

In addition to the discovery of culture bound syndromes, numerous studies have been performed on culture, context, and human development. We recommend Gardiner's (2001) and Gardiner, Mutter, and Kosmitzki's (1998) comprehensive reviews of

this topic. There are also many studies on justice and morality (e.g., Leung & Stephan, 2001) that examined these concepts from both a cultural relativistic point of view and a universalistic framework. Additionally, Berry (e.g., 1976) suggested an ecological framework in studying persons in their cultural context and highlighted how the ecological context constructs culture, which in turn affects one's cognitive style.

It is clear that the cultural approach has informed psychology. The most important contribution in our mind is its (as in the contemporary cross-cultural approach) emphasis on cultural context and the danger and limitations of imposed etics. The emphasis on cultural relativism as an opposing force to absolutism has resulted in scholars searching for emic variables to fully comprehend individuals in their cultural context. An example is the Chinese personality. Ho (1996), for instance suggested filial piety to be an important personality variable in Chinese culture. Similarly, in constructing the Chinese Personality Assessment Inventory (CPAI), which was developed using a combined emic-etic approach (Cheung et al., 1996), it was discovered that in addition to universal personality constructs also found in Western personality theories (e.g., Leadership, Optimism vs. Pessimism, Emotionality), indigenous personality constructs derived from the local context were needed to accurately depict the Chinese personality. These included filial piety, trust, persuasion tactics, and group communication styles (Cheung et al., 2001).

Despite the positive developments that have emerged as a result of the cultural relativistic stance, and despite the quality control strategies implemented in qualitative research geared toward enhancing internal and external validity, the issue of the value of meaning and interpretation as explanations still remains unresolved in the scientific community (Adampoulos & Lonner, 2001).

Lessons From Anthropology: Enhancing Cultural Validity in Counseling Research

Anthropology as a discipline is at the core of the cultural sciences (Adamapoulos & Lonner, 2001). Anthropology is the study of humans, their origins, and their variations. This discipline has been around for at least as long as psychology. There are a number of differences in how psychologists and anthropologists approach studying cultural influences on behavior. In general, anthropologists strive to understand phenomena such as culture by looking at shared patterns of thought and action among people within a culture (emics), whereas psychologists (especially those who identify as cross-cultural psychologists) may be more prone to focusing on behavior and psychological processes as universal features of all humans (etics) (Ross, 2004). Both these approaches are important as they can inform each other. This has not often been the case, though.

One important reason for this disconnect is the difference in the ontological and epistemological frameworks employed, as previously discussed. Few psychologists have built on the foundation of anthropology (perhaps considering their approach unscientific), and few anthropologists have pursued projects grounded in psychology (perhaps seeing their approach as too mechanical and lacking construct, functional, and conceptual validity). Ross (2004) even claimed that "it often seems as if psychologists are reinventing the wheel, rather than building on the foundation provided by some of anthropology's work" (p. 9). Similarly, Ross argued that there is limited research in anthropology that has employed clear methods, and fewer projects that considered the results generated in psychology. The two groups of professionals also differ in the formulation of a priori hypotheses when conducting research. Psychologists tend to stipulate hypotheses a priori to connect predictions to theory, establish and implement methodology, possibly reduce experimenter bias, and potentially increase the validity and generalizability of findings. Anthropologists, however, infrequently generate hypotheses a priori, believing that such predictions can bias the methodology, threaten researcher objectivity, and influence the results (Gerstein, Rountree, & Ordonez, 2007).

Many anthropologists question, as do cultural psychologists affiliated with the cultural relativist view presented earlier, the use of the construct of culture as a quasi-independent variable affecting behavior and whether members of a culture act and think in a similar way (Ross, 2004). Some have even argued that cultures should only be investigated "within their own unique framework" (Laungani, 2007, p. 33). It is our opinion, though, and this is also espoused by others (e.g., Adamopoulos & Lonner, 2001; Helfrich, 1999; Hunt, 2007), that such extreme views do nothing to enhance the science of psychology. Efforts are needed to bridge the two polar-opposite dichotomous viewpoints (i.e., etic-emic; universalism-cultural relativism; positivism-constructivism) (see also Helfrich, 1999) and to take a more pragmatic stance in conceptualizing and studying cultural influences on behavior and psychological processes. An anthropological view to cultural research might be a step in that direction in that it may enhance the methodological repertoire of counseling researchers.

In anthropology, as in psychology, theory is very important and closely connected to practice. In anthropology, theory informs ethnography (the practice of researching and writing about the culture of local communities) and the results of ethnography inform larger theories of culture (Barnard, 2000). There are four basic elements of theory in social anthropology (questions, assumptions, methods, & evidence) along with two other specific aspects of investigation:

> (a) observing a society as a whole, to see how each element of that society fits together with, or is meaningful in terms of, other such elements; [and] (b) examining each society in relation to others, to find similarities and differences and account for them. (Barnard, 2000, p. 6)

The first aspect of investigation, "observing society as a whole," involves understanding how variables are related, for example, how attitudes about help-seeking are linked to collectivism. The second aspect, "examining each society in relation to others," deals with gathering information on the similarities and differences, for instance, between the help-seeking behaviors of individuals from European and Asian societies. When engaged in such comparisons, it is essential that researchers have a deep understanding of each culture and a strong theoretical framework to guide the effort (Markus & Kitayama, 1991; Ross, 2004).

Anthropological theory can also help frame the research questions or topics of interest, the design methodology and data collection strategy, the analyses, the interpretation of the findings, and the feedback process to the stakeholders. Anthropologists often first immerse themselves in a culture to formulate research questions and topics for investigation. As participant observers, they may interact with a host of stakeholders and they may gather information, for instance, on human behavior (e.g., affect, cognition, behavior), the environment, and cultural, social, economic, and physical structures in targeted locations. Through the use of participatory mapping (an ethnographic technique), they can also collect additional information from key informants about these structures and the interactions of individuals connected to a specific locale. Basically, mapping involves touring an area with key informants and asking these individuals to share their observations and experiences about particular topics and/or life in general in this location (Agar, 1996; Bernard, 2002; Crane & Angrosino, 1984).

The data collected from participant observation and mapping help familiarize and educate the anthropologist about the unique and common norms, values, attitudes, expectations, behaviors, structures, and environment of the culture under investigation. Possessing this information contributes to the formulation of research questions, topics for investigation, and the appropriate methodology and analyses to be employed. Frequently, anthropologists engage relevant stakeholders in the entire research process from conceptualization to implementation to data analyses to interpretation of the findings. Selecting a research design is also "influenced by the social, political, technological conditions and particularly by the existing states of knowledge within the culture at a given period of time" (Laungani, 2007, p. 99).

Anthropology has much to offer counseling professionals interested in conducting research in a foreign culture (Gerstein et al., 2007). One anthropologist (Varenne, 2003) also reported that anthropological concepts could assist counseling professionals involved in applied international work. Anthropology has a long history of studying specific cultures (Geertz, 1973; Shweder & Sullivan, 1993) not only by comparing the similarities and differences within and between cultures but also by understanding them within a geographical, historical, and social context (Ross, 2004). Interestingly, very little has been written about the application of anthropological methods to the study of counseling in general and of multicultural counseling specifically (Gerstein et al., 2007). Even less has been written on integrating such methods when performing cross-cultural counseling research. Counseling professionals have adapted, however, a number of anthropological research methods without attributing these strategies to anthropology. Many of the qualitative methodologies employed within the counseling profession can be traced to anthropology, sociology, and linguistics. For instance, such strategies as in vivo observation, participant observation, interviewing, and ethnography have their roots in these disciplines.

Gerstein et al. (2007) contended it was an oversight of the U.S. multicultural counseling movement to not draw from anthropology in the development of multicultural theories, applied strategies, and training paradigms. We contend that the cross-cultural/ international counseling movement must not make this same mistake. The implications of doing this and also ignoring the literature accumulated by cultural, cross-cultural, and indigenous psychology can be quite serious and can result in conducting invalid and irrelevant studies, drawing erroneous and inappropriate conclusions from such research, providing poor and ineffective client services, violating cultural norms, attitudes, and behaviors, and even threatening the existence of a culture itself.

Not all cultures can be studied and assessed in terms of numbers. In some cultures, individuals cannot relate to numbers as a way to capture their thoughts, feelings, and/or experiences. Therefore, it might be inappropriate to use self-report instruments containing a reductionistic item response format (e.g., Likert-type scale) with individuals living in cultures that value storytelling and oral tradition (e.g., Gerstein et al., 2007; van de Vijver & Leung, 1997a; Ægisdóttir & Gerstein, in press; Ægisdóttir et al., 2008). Employing such a numeric instrument with this population may substantially decrease the richness, utility, validity, and heuristic value of the obtained data. For members of cultures that are not used to this type of self-presentation, a more effective method to collect information about them would be studying their use of symbols, artifacts, and storytelling or observing their behavior. When investigators employ methodologies that are more congruent with the targeted cultures, there is a greater probability that the acquired responses from participants will be much more descriptive, accurate, and revealing and richer. Obviously, there are tremendous challenges involved in conducting cross-culturally valid comparative studies of cultures where individuals differ in how they gather, process, and interpret information and experiences.

There are a number of anthropological methods that can be used to address such challenges effectively. Ethnography is a valuable methodological tool used to capture the unique and shared aspects of a particular culture. Ethnography is descriptive in nature, and it provides the interested party with a detailed understanding of cultural phenomena and nuances. Ethnography can target a couple of specific cultural variables or focus on a broader examination of general lifeways or daily traditions in a culture (Bernard, 1995; Gerstein et al., 2007). Most often, anthropologists employ qualitative methods when performing ethnography, but quantitative methods can be used as well, depending on the nature of the research (Bernard, 1995). Critical to the validity of the obtained results is the method of thick description. This strategy takes into consideration the behavior of interest, the context, and the interaction between the two. An effective thick description conveys to an outsider the meaning of the behavior(s) under investigation.

Not surprisingly, anthropologists acquire much more revealing and valid information through extended periods of time in the field. This is in sharp contrast to cross-cultural counseling researchers, who often spend a limited time in the field and instead rely on interviews and survey methodology to collect data. Anthropologists believe that to investigate and more fully comprehend diverse cultures, it is critical to understand the ways of living and collective cognitive schemas of the targeted population. This can be accomplished only by spending long periods of time in the culture. In lieu of this, it is imperative that those engaged in cross-cultural comparative research or international research collaborate and consult with natives about appropriate and culturally congruent methodologies.

Anthropologists rely heavily on participant observation to collect data during all phases of a study. This strategy is thought to decrease the potential of participant reactivity (Ross, 2004). The goal of this strategy is to live in a culture for an extended period of time to gather valid and rich "insider" information and to blend in with the population or become somewhat unnoticeable (Gerstein et al., 2007). Through this strategy, the investigator can develop a deep rapport with the population and, at times, the needed language skills (Ross, 2004). One must be cautious, however, about becoming enmeshed in the target culture or "going native," as this has the potential of decreasing an investigator's objectivity (DeLoria, 1969). Knowing the native language greatly enhances the validity and outcome of participant observation.

Information generated through participant observation can assist in shaping culturally relevant research questions and methodologies. The strategy is also helpful when quantitative methods might be inappropriate to investigate certain phenomena (Bernard, 1995). There are a number of participant observation strategies that anthropologists may employ, for example, field notes and interviewing. Sanjek (1990) reported that it is critical in participant observation research for the anthropological investigator to generate extensive, descriptive, and detailed field notes through the use of, for instance, a diary, a journal, a log, and/or jottings. Such notes allow the researcher to document biases and observations, and they represent one source of data to be analyzed in the later stages of a study. Qualitative strategies are frequently used to code the notes and to capture common themes to describe and evaluate the cultural variable of interest (Gerstein et al., 2007).

Interviewing is another important participant observation strategy employed by anthropologists. In fact, anthropologists rely heavily on this strategy to understand members of a culture, the context of the culture, and the environment connected to the culture (Gerstein et al., 2007). By listening to the voices of members of the targeted cultures, anthropologists obtain rich data and reduce the potential error of drawing inferences based on invalid methods and/or sources. Of course, this assumes selecting a sufficient number of appropriate informants. A sample is representative when all relevant persons and groups have an equal opportunity in the selection process.

Anthropologists prefer to conduct unstructured or semistructured interviews since interviewees have a greater chance to openly and freely share their responses through these formats as compared with structured interviews. Bernard (1995) claimed that anthropologists most often conduct unstructured interviews because this approach encourages a wide range of responses from the interviewees. Regardless of the interviewing strategy employed, the information that is gathered can be assessed through qualitative procedures, and the results can help increase the investigator's understanding of the targeted cultures (Gerstein et al., 2007).

Free listing is yet another method used by anthropologists to gather data. The goal of this strategy is to acquire "a list of culturally relevant items on which most of the informants agree" (Ross, 2004, p. 90). There are various techniques used to generate these lists, ranging from asking participants to simply name the elements to using computer-generated, weighted lists that are presented to the participants. The listing process can also range from being unrestricted and unconditioned (generate as many elements as possible related to a construct) to restricted (name a limited number of elements) and conditioned (e.g., generate all the causes leading to . . .). The results obtained can offer some understanding of the items that are most culturally salient and relevant to the targeted population.

While the aforementioned anthropological methods appear useful when studying the cultural influence on behavior and psychological processes, some (Ross, 2004) have suggested that anthropology lacks conceptual and methodological clarity and that, as a result, there are limitations to the obtained findings, theories, and the heuristic value of building a valid knowledge base. Ross furthered stated that for anthropology to possess sound predictions, it must have "fine-tuned methodologies that allow for formal comparisons of the individual results" (p. 23).

To increase cultural validity, generalizability, relevance, and the appropriateness of findings obtained from international and cross-cultural counseling research and to reduce the potential for bias, it is critical that counseling researchers employ mixed designs (e.g., quantitative and qualitative) drawn from both anthropology and psychology. As Whiting (1968) has argued, there are many different types of data that can be studied in cross-cultural comparisons. Predictive models based on empirical data are highly valued by anthropologists interested in sound cultural descriptions (Ross, 2004). These models may permit comparing data across tasks, methods, and theories.

There are also many different strategies that anthropologists use to analyze data. A few will be discussed here. Content or thematic analysis is often employed to examine patterns and themes generated by qualitative methods. Trained raters and/or computer programs are employed to assess and categorize the descriptive data. Frequently, the researcher is intimately involved in this process as well. The results generated by this type of analysis can offer a deep understanding of the cultural variables under investigation.

Another common analytic technique used by anthropologists is informant agreement/disagreement. Numeric data are well suited for this technique, though at times qualitative data can also be transformed into numbers. Analyzing agreement data first involves setting up an informant-by-response matrix and then assessing differences and similarities between the participants (Ross, 2004). There are a number of strategies that can be used to conduct this assessment, including a weighted and unweighted agreement calculation, and much more sophisticated approaches known as correlational agreement analysis and weighted similarity measures. Multidimensional scaling based on the informant's level of agreement is another sound technique to assess agreement/disagreement. Ultimately, the results of an agreement/disagreement analysis can crystallize "the underlying dynamics within a given domain in a given culture" (p. 22).

The cultural consensus model (Romney, Weller, & Batchelder, 1986) in anthropology addresses how many informants are needed to draw sound conclusions about a cultural domain and how to recognize culturally correct responses. This is critical to determining whether the obtained data and interpretations can represent a consensus among the informants and any identifiable deviations. The consensus model uses agreement/disagreement data in the analysis of participants' responses. Frequently, statistical procedures are employed to analyze the data. It should be mentioned that a cultural consensus model must be tied to a theory to choose the participants and to interpret the obtained data (Ross, 2004).

Clearly, cross-cultural and international counseling researchers can enhance their research methodologies by adopting some of the anthropological strategies that we have discussed. Our profession is in the very early stages of conducting international research, and employing these strategies can strengthen studies and bolster the validity of the results. Furthermore, we have very few cross-cultural findings reported in the counseling literature. There are cross-cultural studies on problem solving (e.g., Heppner, Witty, & Dixon, 2004), coping (e.g., Heppner, 2008), and psychological help-seeking and counseling expectations (e.g., Surgenor, 1985; Todd & Shapira, 1974; Ægisdóttir & Gerstein, 2000, 2004). Some questions can be raised, however, about the cross-cultural validity (e.g., construct equivalence and bias, measurement equivalence and bias) of these studies, questions that could be addressed by also employing anthropological methods. As a result of the shortcomings in the cross-cultural and international counseling literature, it would appear

that description and observation would represent a good first step when conducting research. The anthropological strategies discussed earlier are useful in this regard. Employing them can help capture the unique meaning and importance of various counseling constructs and intervention strategies relevant to diverse cultures and societies.

Emic data can be considered building blocks for cross-cultural counseling researchers to tease out what is truly (or entirely) indigenous and what aspects may be shared by other cultures toward the delineation of universal constructs or etic. Price-Williams (1975) noted that within a framework of the sociology of knowledge, all etic systems become emic. Descriptive methods adapted from anthropology enable and challenge researchers to examine the cultural lens through which observed data from a different culture are organized and interpreted (i.e., with reference to the local context or to an existing framework). Furthermore, Draguns (1996) cautioned that neither the emic perspective nor the etic one should be considered inherently superior or inferior. Moreover, Draguns offered the analogy that the etic approach "provides an unsurpassed panoramic view . . . of Paris from the top of the Eiffel Tower, but offers no substitute for the immersion into the hustle and bustle of street life, normal or disturbed, within a specific milieu" (p. 49).

CONCLUSION

Despite our call and that of others (see also Adamopoulos & Lonner, 2001; Ægisdóttir et al., 2008) for combined etic-emic approaches and methodologies when studying culture, the status of culture in psychological theory and the methods used to study culture remain under debate. The etic-emic debate continues to be dualistic even though Pike (1967) introduced the emic-etic framework such that both aspects were the same single and unified reality seen from two different points of view—the insider and the outsider views.

Today, most contemporary scholars would probably agree that the study of culture and the influence of culture on behavior and psychological processes could contribute tremendously to the science and practice of psychology and counseling. Whereas the field of counseling in the United States is in its infancy in appreciating the value of a more global knowledge base and studying cultural variations (within and between ethnic groups and nationalities) in psychological functioning, the history of this focus is much longer in anthropology and various disciplines in psychology (e.g., social psychology). It is our belief that counseling researchers have much to learn from these efforts. In this chapter, we described some of these efforts. Cultural context is and continues to be an important construct in describing and understanding human functioning. Despite the importance of this construct, how one conceptualizes and investigates culture and culture's role in theories remains an important challenge for the future of both counseling and psychology.

In this chapter, we outlined the conceptual and methodological challenges involving the construct of culture, which is characterized by a dualistic, either-or mentality. We also suggested that this dualistic framework be abandoned and replaced by a more holistic functionalistic framework. In particular, we recommended combining etic and emic approaches and methodologies and placing a greater importance on the centrality of culture in theory development and application. It would deeply enrich counseling scholars to know how culture influences behavior, to know how culture and personality interact, and to know how culture is constructed (e.g., Adamopoulos & Lonner, 2001). Acquiring this understanding would substantially contribute to our knowledge base in psychology and counseling. We urge counseling and psychology professionals to continue to tackle the challenge of conceptualizing and investigating culture. Such a sustained effort can only enhance our ability to be a profession concerned with the well-being of *all* human beings.

REFERENCES

Adamopoulos, J., & Lonner, W. J. (2001). Culture and psychology at a crossroad: Historical perspective and theoretical analysis. In D. Matsumoto (Ed.), *Handbook of culture and psychology* (pp. 11–34). New York: Oxford University Press.

Agar, M. H. (1996). *The professional stranger: An informal introduction to ethnography.* New York: Academic Press.

American Psychiatric Association. (2000). *Diagnostic and statistical manual of mental disorders* (4th ed., Text rev.). Washington, DC: Author.

Barnard, A. (2000). *History and theory in anthropology.* Cambridge, UK: University Press.

Bernard, H. R. (1995). *Research methods in anthropology.* New York: AltaMira Press.

Bernard, H. R. (2002). *Research methods in anthropology: Qualitative and quantitative methods* (3rd ed.). Walnut Creek, CA: AltaMira Press.

Berry, J. W. (1976). *Human ecology and cognitive style: Comparative studies in cultural and psychological adaptation.* New York: Wiley.

Berry, J. W. (1999). Emics and etics: A symbiotic conception. *Culture and Psychology, 5,* 165–171.

Berry, J. W., Poortinga, Y. H., Segall, M. H., & Dasen, P. R. (1992). *Cross-cultural psychology: Research and applications.* Cambridge, UK: Cambridge University Press.

Berry, J. W., Poortinga, Y. H., Segall, M. H., & Dasen, P. R. (2002). *Cross-cultural psychology: Research and applications* (2nd ed.). Cambridge, UK: Cambridge University Press.

Bond, M. H., & Tedeschi, J. T. (2001). Polishing the jade: A modest proposal for improving the study of social psychology across cultures. In D. Matsumoto (Ed.), *Handbook of culture and psychology* (pp. 309–324). New York: Oxford University Press.

Brislin, R.W. (1976). Comparative research methodology: Cross cultural studies. *International Journal of Psychology, 11,* 213–229.

Brislin, R. W. (1986). The wording and translation of research instruments. In W. J. Lonner & J. W. Berry (Eds.), *Field methods in cross-cultural research* (pp. 137–164). Beverly Hills, CA: Sage.

Brislin, R. W., Lonner, W. J., & Thorndike, R. M. (1973). *Cross-cultural research methods.* New York: Wiley.

Cheung, F. M., Leung, K., Fan, R., Song, W. Z., Zhang, J. X., & Zhang, J. P. (1996). Development of the Chinese Personality Assessment Inventory (CPAI). *Journal of Cross-Cultural Psychology, 27,* 181–199.

Cheung, F. M., Leung, K., Zhang, J. X., Sun, H. F., Gan, Y. G., Song, W. Z., et al. (2001). Indigenous Chinese personality constructs: Is the Five-Factor

Model complete? *Journal of Cross-Cultural Psychology, 32*, 407–433.

Cheung, G. W., & Rensvold, R. B. (2000). Assessing extreme and acquiescence response sets in cross-cultural research using structural equation modeling. *Journal of Cross-Cultural Psychology, 31*, 188–213.

Church, A. T., & Lonner, W. J. (1998). The cross-cultural perspective in the study of personality: Rationale and current research. *Journal of Cross-Cultural Psychology, 29*, 32–62.

Crane, J. G., & Angrosino, M. V. (1984). *Field projects in anthropology: A student handbook* (2nd ed.). Prospect Heights, IL: Waveland Press.

DeLoria, V. (1969). *Custer died for your sins: An Indian manifesto.* New York: MacMillan.

Devers, K. J. (1999). How will we know "good" qualitative research when we see it? Beginning the dialogue in health service research. *HRS: Health Service Research, 34*, 1153–1188.

Draguns, J. G. (1996). Multicultural and cross-cultural assessment: Dilemmas and decisions. In G. R. Sodowaky & J. C. Impara (Eds.), *Multicultural assessment in counseling and clinical psychology* (pp. 37–84). Lincoln, NE: Buros Institute of Mental Measurements.

Fossey, E., Harvey, C., McDermott, F., & Davidson, L. (2002). Understanding and evaluating qualitative research. *Australian and New Zealand Journal of Psychiatry, 36*, 717–732.

Gardiner, H. W. (2001). Culture, context, and development. In D. Matsumoto (Ed.), *Handbook of culture and psychology* (pp. 101–117). New York: Oxford University Press.

Gardiner, H. W., Mutter, J. D., & Kosmitzki, C. (1998). *Lives across cultures: Cross-cultural human development.* Boston: Allyn & Bacon.

Geertz, C. (1973). *The interpretation of cultures.* New York: Jossey Bass.

Gerstein, L. H., Rountree, C., & Ordonez, M. A. (2007). An anthropological perspective on multicultural counseling. *Counselling Psychology Quarterly, 20*, 375–400.

Hambleton, R. K., & de Jong, J. H. A. L. (2003). Advances in translating and adapting educational and psychological tests. *Language Testing, 20*, 127–134.

Harris, M. (1968). *The rise of anthropological theory: A history of theories of culture.* New York: Thomas Y. Crowell.

Helfrich, H. (1999). Beyond the dilemma of cross-cultural psychology: Resolving the tension between etic and emic approaches. *Culture and Psychology, 5*, 131–153.

Heppner, P. P. (2008). Award for distinguished contributions to the international advancement of psychology. *American Psychologist, 63*, 803–816.

Heppner, P. P., Witty, T. E., & Dixon, W. A. (2004). Problem-solving appraisal and human adjustment: A review of 20 years of research utilizing the Problem Solving Inventory. *The Counseling Psychologist, 32*, 344–428.

Ho, D. Y. F. (1996). Filial piety and its psychological consequences. In M. H. Bond (Ed.), *Handbook of Chinese psychology* (pp. 155–165). Hong Kong: Oxford University Press.

Hofstede, G. (1980). *Culture's consequences: International differences in work-related values.* Beverly Hills, CA: Sage.

Hunt, R. C. (2007). *Beyond relativism: Rethinking comparability in cultural anthropology.* New York: AltaMira Press.

Hwang, K.-K. (2005). From anticolonialism to postcolonialism: The emergence of Chinese indigenous psychology in Taiwan. *International Journal of Psychology, 40*, 228–238.

Kagitçibasi, C. (1996). *Family and human development across cultures.* Mahwah, NJ: Erlbaum.

Kim, U. (1995). Psychology, science, and culture: Cross-cultural analysis of national psychologies in developing countries. *International Journal of Psychology, 30*, 663–679.

Kim, U. (2001). Culture, science, and indigenous psychologies. In D. Matsumoto (Ed.), *Handbook of culture and psychology* (pp. 51–75). New York: Oxford University Press.

Kim, U., & Berry, J. W. (1993). *Indigenous psychologies: Research and experience in cultural context.* Thousand Oaks, CA: Sage.

Kim, U., Park, Y. S., & Park, D. H. (2000). The challenge of cross-cultural psychology: The role of indigenous psychologies. *Journal of Cross-Cultural Psychology, 31*, 63–75.

Kim, U., Yang, K. S., & Hwang, K. K. (2006). *Indigenous and cultural psychology: Understanding people in context.* New York: Springer.

Kuzel, A. J. (1998). Naturalistic inquiry: An appropriate model for family medicine. *Family Medicine, 18*, 369–374.

Kwan, K.-L., K. (2000). Counseling Chinese peoples: Perspectives of filial piety. *Asian Journal of Counselling, 7*, 23–42.

Laungani, P. D. (2007). *Understanding cross-cultural psychology.* Thousand Oaks, CA: Sage.

Lett, J. W. (1996). Emic/etic distinctions. In D. Levinson & M. Ember (Eds.), *Encyclopedia of cultural anthropology* (pp. 382–383). New York: Henry Holt.

Leung, K., & Stephan, W. G. (2001). Social justice from a cultural perspective. In D. Matsumoto (Ed.), *Handbook of culture and psychology* (pp. 375–410). New York: Oxford University Press.

Lonner, W. J. (1985). Issues in testing and assessment in cross-cultural counseling. *Counseling Psychologist, 13,* 599–614.

Lonner, W. J. (in press). The continuing challenge of discovering psychological "order" across cultures. In A. Chastiosis, S. Breugelmans, & F. van de Vijver (Eds.), *Fundamental questions in cross-cultural psychology.* Cambridge, UK: Cambridge University Press.

Lonner, W. J., & Berry, J. W. (Eds.). (1986). *Field methods in cross-cultural research.* Beverly Hills, CA: Sage.

Lonner, W. J., & Hayes, S. H. (2007). *Discovering cultural psychology: A profile and selected readings of Ernest E. Boesch.* Charlotte, NC: Information Age.

Markus, H. R., & Kitayama, S. (1991). Culture and the self: Implications for cognition, emotion, and motivation. *Psychological Review, 98,* 224–253.

Marsella, A. J., Dubanoski, J., Hamada, W. C., & Morse, H. (2000). The measurement of personality across cultures. Historical, conceptual, and methodological issues and considerations. *American Behavioral Scientist, 44,* 41–62.

Matsumoto, D. (2001). Culture and emotion. In D. Matsumoto (Ed.), *Handbook of culture and psychology* (pp. 171–194). New York: Oxford University Press.

Matsumoto, D. (in press). Culture and emotional expression. In C. Y. Chiu, Y. Y. Hong, S. Shavitt, & R. S. Wyer (Eds.), *Problems and solutions in cross-cultural theory, research, and application.* New York: Psychology Press.

McCrae, R. R., & Costa, P. T. (1997). Personality trait structure as a human universal. *American Psychologist, 52,* 509–516.

Miles, M. B., & Huberman, A. M. (1994). *Qualitative data analysis: An expanded sourcebook* (2nd ed.). Thousand Oaks, CA: Sage.

Pike, K. L. (1967). *Language in relation to a unified theory of structure of human behavior* (2nd ed.). The Hague, the Netherlands: Mouton.

Price-Williams, D. R. (1975). *Explorations in cross-cultural psychology.* San Francisco: Chandler & Sharp.

Romney, A. K., Weller, S. C., & Batchelder, W. H. (1986). Culture as consensus: A theory of culture and informant accuracy. *American Anthropologist, 88,* 313–338.

Ross, N. (2004). *Culture and cognition: Implications for theory and method.* Thousand Oaks, CA: Sage.

Sanjek, P. (1990). *Fieldnotes.* Ithaca, NY: Cornell University Press.

Segall, M. H., Lonner, W. J., & Berry, J. W. (1998). Cross-cultural psychology as a scholarly discipline: On the flowering of culture in behavioral research. *American Psychologist, 53,* 1101–1110.

Shiraev, E., & Levy, D. (2006). *Cross-cultural psychology: Critical thinking and contemporary applications* (3rd ed.). Boston: Allyn & Bacon.

Shweder, R. A. (1990). Cultural psychology: What is it? In J. W. Stigler, R. A. Shweder, & G. Herdt (Eds.), *Cultural psychology: Essays on human cognitive development* (pp. 1–43). New York: Cambridge University Press.

Shweder, R. A., & Sullivan, M. A. (1993). Cultural psychology: Who needs it? *Annual Review of Psychology, 44,* 497–523.

Smith, P. B. (2002). Levels of analysis in cross-cultural psychology. In W. J. Lonner, D. L. Dinnel, S. A. Hayes, & D. N. Sattler (Eds.), *Online readings in psychology and culture* (Unit 2). Bellingham, WA: Center for Cross-Cultural Research, Western Washington University. Retrieved March 28, 2009, from http://www.ac.wwu.edu/~culture

Smith, P. B., Bond, M. H., & Kagitçibasi, Ç. (2006). *Understanding social psychology across cultures: Living and working in a changing world.* Thousand Oaks, CA: Sage.

Strohmer, D. C., & Arm, J. R. (2006). The more things change, the more they stay the same. *The Counseling Psychologist, 34,* 383–390.

Surgenor, L. J. (1985). Attitudes toward seeking professional psychological help. *New Zealand Journal of Psychology, 14,* 27–33.

Tanaka-Matsumi, J. (2001). Abnormal psychology and culture. In D. Matsumoto (Ed.), *Handbook of culture and psychology* (pp. 265–286). New York: Oxford University Press.

Tanaka-Matsumi, J., & Draguns, J. G. (1997). Culture and psychopathology. In J. W. Berry, M. H. Segall, & C. Kagitçibasi (Eds.), *Handbook of cross-cultural psychology: Social behavior and applications* (Vol. 3, 2nd ed., pp. 449–492). Boston: Allyn & Bacon.

Todd, J. L., & Shapira, A. (1974). US and British self-disclosure, anxiety, empathy, and attitudes to psychotherapy. *Journal of Cross-Cultural Psychology, 5,* 364–369.

Triandis, H. C. (1976). Approaches toward minimizing translation. In R. Brislin (Ed.), *Translation: Applications and research* (pp. 229–243). New York: Wiley.

Triandis, H. C. (2000). Dialectics between cultural and cross-cultural psychology. *Asian Journal of Social Psychology, 3,* 185–195.

Triandis, H. C. (2001). Individualism and collectivism: Past, present, and future. In D. Matsumoto (Ed.), *Handbook of culture and psychology* (pp. 35–50). New York: Oxford University Press.

van de Vijver, F. J. R. (2001). The evolution of cross-cultural research methods. In D. Matsumoto (Ed.), *Handbook of culture and psychology* (pp. 77–97). New York: Oxford University Press.

van de Vijver, F. J. R., & Hambleton, R. K. (1996). Translating tests: Some practical guidelines. *European Psychologist, 1,* 89–99.

van de Vijver, F. J. R., & Leung, K. (1997a). *Methods and data analysis for cross-cultural research.* Thousand Oaks, CA: Sage.

van de Vijver, F. J. R., & Leung, K. (1997b). Methods and data analysis of comparative research. In J. W. Berry, Y. H. Poortinga, & J. Pandey (Eds.), *Handbook of cross-cultural psychology: Vol. 1: Theory and method* (pp. 257–300). Boston: Allyn & Bacon.

van de Vijver, F. J. R., & Poortinga, Y. H. (1997). Towards an integrated analysis of bias in cross-cultural assessment. *European Journal of Psychological Assessment, 13,* 29–37.

van de Vijver, F. J. R., & Tanzer, N. K. (2004). Bias and equivalence in cross-cultural assessment: An overview. *European Review of Applied Psychology, 47,* 263–279.

Varenne, H. (2003). On internationalizing counseling psychology: A view from cultural anthropology. *The Counseling Psychologist, 31,* 404–411.

Whiting, J. W. M. (1968). Methods and problems in cross-cultural research. In G. Lindzey & E. Arsonson (Eds.), *Handbook of social psychology* (Vol. 2, pp. 693–728). Cambridge, MA: Addison-Wesley.

Ægisdóttir, S., & Gerstein, L. H. (2000). Icelandic and American students' expectations about counseling. *Journal of Counseling and Development, 78,* 44–53.

Ægisdóttir, S., & Gerstein, L. H. (2004). Icelanders' and U.S. nationals' expectations about counseling: The role of nationality, sex, and Holland's Typology. *Journal of Cross-Cultural Psychology, 35,* 734–748.

Ægisdóttir, S., & Gerstein, L. H. (in press). International counseling competencies: A new frontier in multicultural training. In J. C. Ponterotto, J. M. Casas, L. A. Suzuki, & C. A. Alexander (Eds.), *Handbook of multicultural counseling* (3rd ed.). Thousand Oaks, CA: Sage.

Ægisdóttir, S., Gerstein, L. H., & Çinarbaş, D. C. (2008). Methodological issues in cross-cultural counseling research: Equivalence, bias, and translations. *The Counseling Psychologist, 36,* 188–219.

Ægisdóttir, S., White, M. J., Spengler, P. M., Maugherman, A. S., Anderson, L. A., Cook, R. S. et al. (2006). The meta-analysis of clinical judgment project: Fifty-six years of accumulated research on clinical versus statistical prediction. *The Counseling Psychologist, 34,* 341–382.

6

Internationalization of the Counseling Profession

An Indigenous Perspective

SEUNG-MING ALVIN LEUNG,
THOMAS CLAWSON, KATHRYN L. NORSWORTHY,
ANTONIO TENA, ANDREEA SZILAGYI, AND JENNIFER ROGERS

In ways and magnitude unseen in previous generations, the forces of globalization and internationalization have altered the spectrum and nature of economic, business, and financial activities and transformed the lives of individuals around the globe. Notable authors on the subject of economic globalization observed that globalization has substantially accelerated the flow of capital and human resources around the world, diminished national and geographic boundaries, and leveled the competitive playing field among nations varying in resources and status of development (e.g., Friedman, 2006; Greenwald & Kahn, 2009). The counseling profession, as a human service discipline, has also been involved in a movement of internationalization in the past decade. Internationalization is a movement initiated and led by scholars in the United States aiming to capture the immense possibilities for collaboration among counseling and psychological professionals worldwide, made possible by advances in technologies and communication tools that have greatly reduced the distance that has separated regions and countries (e.g., Douce, 2004; Gerstein & Ægisdóttir, 2005; Heppner, 2006; Leong & Blustein, 2000; Leong & Ponterotto, 2003; Savickas, 2007). Internationalization is also prompted by the awareness that counseling professionals can no longer afford to be ethnocentric and unilateral (Leong & Ponterotto, 2003), that a linear and monocultural perspective of psychology and counseling cannot adequately respond to mental health challenges, such as poverty, migration, natural disasters, overpopulation and urbanization, and international war and violence, which are global in size and impact (Marsella, 1998; Marsella & Pedersen, 2004). Outside the United States, internationalization is broadly seen as an important and positive move that will strengthen the counseling profession worldwide (Savickas, 2007).

We would like to accomplish several goals through this chapter. First, we explore the special meaning of internationalization to the counseling profession, and the role that internationalization can play in facilitating the development of the counseling profession. Second, we conceptualize indigenization as an important concurrent step to internationalization, drawing from the rich literature on indigenous psychology to identify broad strategies to indigenize the counseling profession. Third, we discuss the interface between internationalization and indigenization, and highlight initiatives from the U.S.-based National Board for Certified Counselors Inc. & Affiliates (NBCC) as examples of how internationalization efforts can enhance mental health delivery and capacity building at the local, indigenous level. We hope these examples illustrate how internationalization and indigenization can coexist and complement each other. In this chapter, we argue that "internationalization" and "indigenization" are not dichotomous processes with incompatible goals. Ideally, they are actually mutually informing processes that enhance the substance and relevance of the counseling profession in local settings and around the globe.

THE MEANING OF INTERNATIONALIZATION TO THE COUNSELING PROFESSION

At this point, the discipline has not reached a consensus on what constitutes "internationalization," yet a number of key themes can be extracted from the literature (also see Chapter 1, this volume). First, internationalization refers to the nurturance of a global perspective in counseling scholarship, through our teaching, research, and service. Coming from a U.S. counseling psychology perspective, Leong and Ponterotto (2003) proposed that internationalization should be carried out at multiple levels, including (a) methods of psychological science (e.g., through diversifying research design and methodology to accommodate research in diverse cultural contexts), (b) profession-based initiatives (e.g., facilitate international connection and cooperation at the level of corresponding psychological associations), (c) initiatives

from the Division of Counseling Psychology (e.g., formalizing international goals, objectives, and action plans into the counseling psychology agenda), and (d) counseling program-specific activities (e.g., enhancing students' exposure to international events and internship opportunities at the program training level to facilitate international perspectives and competence). Leung and Hoshmand (2007) suggested that an international perspective should be centrally reflected in the counseling literature. They asserted that internationalization requires counseling scholars and students to anchor their scholarly work on what has been done around the world by (a) integrating and synthesizing relevant studies from around the world into the review of literature and/or research conceptualization, (b) diversifying the cross-cultural composition of research samples, and (c) extrapolating research findings in light of the global literature and the counseling community.

Second, internationalization refers to the facilitation of collaboration among counseling professionals globally, in practice, research, and training (Gerstein & Ægisdóttir, 2007; Heppner, 2006). This mutual support and the aggregation of strengths could elevate the substance and standing of the counseling profession locally and internationally. As discussed in Chapter 4 of this volume, Heppner (2006) suggested that cross-cultural competence is a prerequisite to effective cross-border collaborations.

Some authors have cautioned against the assumption that internationalization and international collaboration should be led by U.S. professionals. Pedersen (2003) suggested that the United States might have a longer history and experience in the development of psychology (and counseling), yet internationalization "is not a contest or a competition to see who is superior or more advanced" (p. 397). Similarly, Leung (2003) maintained that the concept of equal partnerships is important to international collaboration, emphasizing that "collaboration should be structured as between equal partners, not from a perspective that certain paradigms or models are superior or inferior" (p. 416).

Third, internationalization refers to the indigenization of the counseling profession in local settings and discovering the culture-specific elements that are central to practice in one's own region. Savickas

(2007) identified indigenization as one of the main goals of the international counseling psychology community, suggesting that the profession should "formulate and implement strategies that facilitate development of indigenous psychological theory and research that are grounded in the specific cultural context where they are practiced" (p. 186). Indigenization stands in contrast to a "transfer of technology" approach, in which counseling is viewed as a system of theory, research, and practice that could be imported or transferred from one region to another (Leung, 2003; Pedersen, 2003).

Indeed, in regions around the world where counseling is starting to develop, it is all too easy for internationalization to follow the paths and leadership of regions where counseling is more developed (e.g., the United States) and to search for a universal system of theories, research, and standards of practice that could be applied worldwide. However, the "one-size-fits-all" approach will not meet the diverse mental health needs of individuals across cultures. It will also serve to disengage the counseling profession from the richness of cultural differences and diversities of those we serve. Referring to the limited cultural validity of U.S. psychology, Leong and Ponterotto (2003) pointed out that "with the increasing recognition for the need for cross-cultural and international research has come the realization that U.S. psychology is really an indigenous psychology" (p. 384). As such, internationalization should not be the "Americanization" or "Westernization" of counseling being wrapped around on the outside by a nice wrapping paper with an "international" label.

Contextualizing the Internationalization of the Counseling Profession

A number of trends and developments inside and outside the United States have facilitated the unintentional internationalization of the counseling profession from the United States to other parts of the world. Three distinguishable waves include (1) the need for counseling in post–World War and postconflict regions, (2) international students completing degrees in U.S. counseling programs bringing their training

back to their home countries, and (3) the growing international emphasis of counseling and psychology professional organizations in the United States.

First, the aftermath of U.S. engagement in two World Wars and subsequent regional interventions, such as in Korea, Vietnam, or the Balkans, led to the exportation of the idea and practice of counseling to affected regions. Furthermore, according to Yakushko (2005),

The fall of the Soviet Union created a unique situation for people who have lived behind the Iron Curtain . . . The change in the political and economic systems of the newly formed independent states resulted in unprecedented changes in the lives of millions of people. (p. 161)

Yakushko (2007) also emphasized that political changes have profound effects on career development and vocational paths of citizens of these countries. For example, career counseling, established in the United States in the early 20th century, spread into post-war Europe, where rebuilding economies gave rise to a logical request for this knowledge and expertise.

In the wake of political and societal restructuring, such as in former Soviet bloc countries, the need for services in the helping fields was also paramount (Watts, 1997). Nations looked to other nations for new models to help their societies, and the United States was willing to send "experts." Because of their interests and connections, these experts often worked in foreign venues without connections to U.S. policy. For example, Szilagyi and Paredes (in press) discussed Romania as an example of a country relying on U.S. experts and using the U.S. model as a framework for developing its own system of counseling:

A clearly defined scope of practice that integrates tasks identified in various government policies will help Romanian counselors better articulate their professional role . . . A professionalization strategy that borrows from the experiences of counseling practitioners in the United States [will focus upon] the simultaneous development of a counseling association, counselor training standards, credentialing mechanism, and expansion of the knowledge base. (p. 11)

Szilagyi and Paredes (in press) commented that the development of counseling as a practice and a profession in post–Communist Romania has been expedited by drawing on the history of counseling in the United States. The formalization of the profession started in 1995 (Peteanu, 1997), and the progress made in under 15 years has been quite remarkable. It is not merely a strategically good time for the growth of counseling; there is also a clear need for counseling skills to assist Romania and its people in assuming their new identities and new roles in the world. Even though Romania has drawn from the successes and failures of the professional models developed in the United States to accelerate her own formalization process, the counseling profession in Romania is still distinctly Romanian and seeks to serve the needs of its citizens at this critical juncture in the nation's history.

Education is another aspect of the unintentional internationalization of the counseling profession. The concept of school counselors, an outgrowth of the career development movement, aroused strong international interest (e.g., Canales & Blanco-Beledo, 1993; Gysbers & Henderson, 2006). This concept is currently championed by UNESCO in all its 192 member nations. Most countries have some form of "guidance" in the schools. As a result of funding by the National Defense Education Act of 1958 (NDEA) many guidance and counseling institutes and master's degree programs were established in the United States. These educational programs became accessible to hundreds, and now thousands, of foreign students. International students who study in the United States have provided valuable knowledge to their American classmates and have no doubt enriched the quality of training. The international perspectives developed through cross-cultural interactions inside and outside the classroom can prepare all students to face the global world. At the same time, as discussed in Chapter 4 (this volume), international students educated in U.S. settings can face significant challenges in navigating or influencing the distinctly American and "U.S-centric" counselor training programs, particularly when, as is usually the case, they are the only or one of a very few international students in a particular program.

Most U.S.-educated international counseling professionals return to their home countries to teach, research, and/or practice, bringing their knowledge of the U.S. profession with them. Clearly, after four decades of training international master's and doctoral students in counseling and counseling psychology, the U.S. model of counselor training and education has had a significant impact on the development of the counseling profession in many countries. Indeed, with the U.S. model in mind, professionals in many countries have influenced their home country policy and practice. Yet, while there was probably no intent on "exporting" the profession for any sort of imperialistic purpose, the values and worldviews connected to dominant U.S. counseling paradigms often accompanied the "uncritical" exportation process (see Chapter 4, this volume, for further discussions). To date, we note a paucity of discussion in the literature during the early years regarding how to deal with the cultural relevancy issues connected to bringing a distinctly U.S. counseling paradigm into countries outside the West. Of course, as Gilbert Wrenn noted, the U.S. counseling profession was and still is also dealing with cultural encapsulation issues within its own U.S.-generated counseling theories, models, and practices (Wrenn, 1962). We agreed with Gerstein and Ægisdóttir (2007) that students and teachers of counseling, including international students, should be encouraged to critically evaluate the applicability of theories (e.g., education, counseling, psychological theories) that originated in the United States or other parts of the Western world to their own cultures.

Finally, in the past decade, professional organizations in the United States (e.g., American Counseling Association [ACA], American Psychological Association [APA]) have expressed a strong interest in developing international linkages and collaborations (e.g., Douce, 2004; Gerstein & Ægisdóttir, 2007). International students who have returned home following study in the United States have heard much about these professional organizations during their professional training, and many have attended ACA or APA conferences. Publications by these professional organizations are widely read and cited in the international literature, and the annual conventions of these organizations often attract sizable international attendees. The positive collaborative liaisons being created by these professional organizations and individuals have laid the necessary groundwork for current and future efforts to develop the counseling profession internationally.

From here, internationalization of the counseling profession needs to proceed in ways that are different from the process of economic globalization (see Chapter 1, this volume). Unlike trading and manufacturing, there is very limited room for international outsourcing, offshoring, supply-chaining, or uploading of counseling or mental health services (Friedman, 2006). Counseling and mental health services usually require direct personal interactions with clients conducted by professionals with similar cultural and language backgrounds. Counseling services provided from someone at a distant site are unlikely to meet substantial local needs (Greenwald & Kahn, 2009). Furthermore, internationalization should not mirror the negatives of globalization, such as monopolizing of multinationals, importation/imposition of values from dominant economies, elimination of local, indigenous enterprises, and perpetuation of a unitary, homogenous system of practice (Stiglitz, 2003). Internationalization of the counseling profession should be a process to develop and enhance the mental health capacities of nations and cultures in ways that are consistent with local cultures and settings. This capacity-development function of internationalization is best illustrated by the following excerpt by economists Greenwald and Kahn (2009) from their book titled *Globalization: The Irrational Fear That Someone in China Will Take Your Job*:

> The clear implication of this extensive diversity among nations is that individual countries and their governments must establish their own policies, even in a supposedly global world. They best understand the possibilities and constraints by local conditions, and they have to live with those consequences. The principle of vesting decisions in those most familiar with the relevant conditions is reinforced by the complementary principle that better decisions are made by those who are subject to the cost and benefits of their choices. (pp. 50–51)

In summary, internationalization in counseling is a continuous process of synthesizing knowledge generated through research, scholarship, and practice from different cultures and using this knowledge to solve problems in local and global communities. Internationalization involves collaborations and equal partnerships in which cultural sensitivity and respect are required for success. Most important, internationalization should be accompanied by continuous efforts to indigenize the counseling profession in different regions so that counseling theories, practice, and systems are developed and anchored in the local culture. Counseling must first become relevant to local communities before it can make a difference across national borders. Hence, *internationalization* is the preferred term for this chapter, compared with *globalization*, because internationalization conveys a clearer message of collaboration under the conditions of equal partnership and the preservation of cultural diversity. With that in mind, in the following section, we examine the broad meaning of indigenization based on the literature on indigenous and cultural psychology and discuss how indigenization could be carried out in the counseling profession.

APPROACHES TO INDIGENIZE THE COUNSELING PROFESSION

Sinha (1997) suggested that the term *indigenous* bears two basic features. First, it refers to something that is native and not transplanted from the outside. Second, it refers to something that is of and designed for the natives. Similarly, Blowers (1996) defined *indigenous* as "the study of grass-roots thinking, the everyday, the commonplace, as ingrained among inhabitants of a community and a culture" (p. 2). *Indigenous* reflects "the sociocultural reality" of a given society, which might be different or similar to realities in other societies or cultures (Sinha, 1997). Accordingly, indigenous psychology was referred to by Ho (1998) as "the study of human behavior and mental processes within a cultural context that relies on values, concepts, belief systems, methodologies, and other resources indigenous to the specific cultural groups under investigation" (p. 94). Indigenous psychology is a tradition in psychology that is grounded in the assumption that human behavior should best be interpreted and understood from indigenous frames of reference and culturally derived categories, rather than from the standpoint of imported categories and foreign theories (Ho, 1998; Kim, Yang, & Hwang, 2006; Kunkel, Hector, Coronado, & Vales, 1989; Sinha, 1997). Indigenous psychology takes the position that Western theories of psychology are essentially indigenous models and that "only by recognizing the nature of mainstream theories as indigenous, can we arrive at true (vs. illusory) universals" (Greenfield, 2000, p. 232).

Indigenization is a continuous, ongoing process rather than a finished product (Sinha, 1997). Enriquez (1993) distinguished between two broad routes to indigenize psychology, which were called "indigenous from within" and "indigenous from without." "Indigenous from without" was similar to what Sinha (1997) called "indigenization of the exogenous." It refers to a process of transforming and adapting imported psychological theories, concepts, and methods to make them appropriate to and correspond with the local cultural context. Researchers should not assume that a particular theory or approach is valid universally unless it is proven to be the case. In contrast, in the "indigenous from within" approach, researchers rely on a process of "internal indigenization" (Sinha, 1997) and develop theories, categories, and constructs from within a culture, using indigenous information or informants as primary sources of knowledge. The purpose is to generate indigenous theories and models that fully reflect local cultural characteristics.

The indigenization of the counseling profession should be approached from without and from within (Leung & Chen, in press). "Indigenous from without" is most concerned with issues of contextual relevance and adaptability. Leung and Chen (in press) suggested that the cultural relevance of counseling theories could be enhanced by (a) adapting and

enriching counseling theories and concepts based on the knowledge of local researchers and practitioners about local cultural and contextual characteristics, (b) testing the adapted counseling theories using local samples and diverse research methodologies in the natural contexts of local participants, and (c) generating alternative models and frameworks where both the indigenous and universal elements are addressed and integrated. The "indigenous from without" approach allows counseling scholars to achieve one of the major goals of internationalization and indigenous psychology, which is to discover psychological universals in social, cultural, and ecological contexts (Kim & Berry, 1993; Kim et al., 2006).

However, many cross-cultural scholars perceive "indigenous from without" as an accommodative approach in which "new and different perspectives are simply added on to an existing paradigm (Kim, Park, & Park, 2000, p. 65). As such, the outcomes do not challenge the basic scientific paradigms that characterize Western counseling and psychology. "Indigenization from within" is regarded as the more "authentic" approach to indigenizing psychology. Yet it is an approach that will require time, as well as concerted efforts and resources from those within the target culture.

Blowers (1996), incorporating both the "from within" and "from without" approaches, posited that the indigenization of psychology could proceed via three different levels. The first is the *local* level, which is the study of what is on the mind of the ordinary person in a particular culture, such as the processes that shape personality, motivation, and behavior (e.g., culture-specific views on mental health). The second level is *national*, which is the development of psychology as a formal and institutionalized discipline anchored to the needs and characteristics of the local culture (e.g., training programs, certification systems). The third level is *practice*, referring to the study of psychological intervention and practices that have been developed and used effectively within a cultural context (e.g., use of various culture-based alternative counseling treatments; see Moodley & West, 2005). The levels of indigenization introduced by Blowers (1996) offered a useful taxonomy for counseling scholars to indigenize counseling from within their own cultural settings (Leung & Chen, in press) as well as to modify and adapt imported models and practices to indigenize from without.

Indigenization at the national or institutional level is extremely critical (Diaz-Loving, 2005; Sinha, 1997). First, a core group of counseling scholars (including practitioners) must articulate, define, and agree on an indigenous agenda relevant to the local context. Second, indigenous scholarship must be valued and supported by the institutions and organizations where they are conducted. Third, scholars have to develop a mechanism to disseminate indigenous theory and practice locally and internationally. Fourth, the institutionalized system has to maintain, renew, and expand its capabilities to deal with evolving national and cultural concerns. Indigenization in counseling can be viewed as a continual process of capacity development involving people, resources, and cultural insights.

A case of indigenization at the national level was described by Gabrenya, Kung, and Chen (2006), who studied the Taiwan Indigenous Psychology Movement (TIPM). Gabrenya et al. (2006) described the indigenization of psychology in Taiwan as "a social phenomenon occurring in a historical, political, and cultural context" (p. 598). The authors found that the TIPM has helped psychologists study issues that were more relevant to the concerns of Taiwan, to develop an indigenous intellectual identity, and to accumulate a volume of research in multiple domains within psychology that can inform practice.

"Indigenous from without" and "indigenous from within" are important pathways to indigenize the counseling profession in diverse cultural regions. The weaving together of cultural-universals and cultural-specifics will continue to be an important task for counselors and psychologists worldwide (Poortinga, 1999). Whereas sustainable, indigenous efforts generate rich and diverse local knowledge that is relevant and valid to local settings, the next important linkage to address is between indigenization and internationalization. That is, how can

indigenous knowledge and experience accumulated in a culture be transformed and become useful internationally (Poortinga, 2005)? In the following section, we feature the work of the NBCC in the United States to illustrate the interface between internationalization and indigenization. NBCC's forthcoming examples underscore the point that internationalization and indigenization in counseling are parallel, complementary, and mutually enhancing processes.

BUILDING INDIGENOUS COUNSELING CAPACITY THROUGH INTERNATIONAL EFFORTS: THE CASE OF NBCC

Developing the counseling profession globally is a long and complex process requiring partnerships, mutual interactions, formulation, planning, and careful implementation. This section explores an intentional effort on the part of the NBCC to collaborate and support the development and indigenization of the counseling profession in local contexts. *Counseling* in this context is the profession (i.e., institutional-structural level), which, of course, includes the practice. The history, agenda, and strategies of the NBCC have always reflected domestic and international priorities and have operated from a mutually influencing global and national perspective. For example, Clawson (2001) noted that "the inevitability of the global economy, the strides in communication technology, and the surge of international distance education changed the discussions [concerning the possibility of promoting a counseling profession worldwide] from 'whether' to 'how' can a strategy be developed" (p. 1).

Both the nature and mission of counseling lend themselves to internationalizing. Counseling as a body of knowledge is a flexible, evolving discipline that can be shared, transformed, and refined for application in cultures and countries around the world (Clawson, 1999). In addition, the mission of the counseling profession is to help those with needs through individually and culturally sensitive counseling interventions; thus, it is a mission compatible with, and facilitated by, internationalization. A counseling profession in a global context increases the number of people who are served and helped by counseling while magnifying the visibility and influence of the profession and its values. The NBCC assumes that much of the counseling work can be done by local experts, practitioners, allied professionals, and policymakers with no influence from the NBCC or the U.S. counseling community. Yet the NBCC could serve as an alliance to facilitate the development of an infrastructure or professional system where local counseling activities would take place.

In its efforts to support the provision of urgently needed counseling services and the professionalization of counseling, the NBCC engaged in a number of strategies in 2001, including (a) gaining recognition as a nongovernmental organization (NGO) through world bodies, (b) developing close contacts with five existing counselor certification boards in other countries (Australia, Britain, Canada, Ireland, and New Zealand), and (c) offering technical assistance to countries who were considering or were in the process of developing counselor credentials. To provide financial support for the global projects, the NBCC in the United States offered an initial financial investment, supported by international funding from organizations with whom the NBCC has formed alliances.

U.S. professionals need to take precautions to avoid actions and attitudes that could be perceived as imperialist by the nations and cultures involved in internationalizing efforts. However, "certainly no profession has more experience and tools in cultural sensitivity than counseling" (Clawson, 2001, p. 2). The U.S. Multicultural Counseling Competencies (Sue et al., 1998) promote awareness regarding the need to guard against an ethnocentric, U.S.-dominant, culture-based approach. Also, given that counseling in the United States is a profession that is well aware of the need for identity and autonomy due to its developmental history (e.g., Heppner, Casas, Carter, & Stone, 2000), practitioners are in a unique position to deeply empathize with countries facing challenges and concerns about professional identity. With a healthy balance of cultural sensitivity, understanding of quality practice, and awareness of

lessons we learned from our developmental journey as a profession, the NBCC felt that it could assist countries with their own emerging context-based professional counseling movements to define the basic tenets of their counseling professions, including counselor development, counselor education/training, supervised practice/experience, and ethical standards and guidelines (Clawson, 2001). The international efforts by the NBCC have been guided by what Gerstein and Ægisdóttir (2007) called an *anthropological model*, where the professional counseling movement is implemented with full involvement of the host community without disruption to its national integrity or identity.

Although some have been concerned that internationalization efforts may undermine domestic professional endeavors, the NBCC argued that the international development of the counseling profession benefits credentialed counselors and their clients in the United States, as stated by Clawson (2001):

> The point I think we've missed in the United States is that international recognition of counseling by world bodies and nations can only help the prestige of counseling here. Not only will recognition by organizations like the United Nations Educational, Scientific and Cultural Organization (UNESCO) or the World Health Organization (WHO) enhance our stature at home, but it will give future generations of National Certified Counselors (NCCs) far greater possibilities for global practice—whether via Internet or emigration. (p. 2)

In 2003, the NBCC developed an international division, NBCC International (NBCC-I) and successfully pursued recognition and collaboration with the World Health Organization (WHO) and United Nations Educational, Scientific and Cultural Organization (UNESCO). Currently, NBCC-I is engaged in major cooperative projects with WHO and is officially recognized by UNESCO as an NGO.

NBCC International and Mental Health Facilitator

In this section, we detail an example of an international effort taken up by the NBCC to internationalize and indigenize counseling to meet urgent local needs in various parts of the world: the Mental Health Facilitators (MHF) project. Over the past 8 years, the NBCC has established a process for helping interested countries develop local standards of practice and monitor quality practice through certification. The NBCC approach has been to support the development of indigenous mental health capacity while recognizing the problems with "uncritical exportation" of mental health delivery system based on U.S. assumptions about human behavior (Gerstein & Ægisdóttir, 2007). The MHF project is intended to be a unique, intentional, indigenous mental health model that enriches and advances the theories and techniques that are effective with diverse populations. It invites people living in diverse cultures to share their expertise with each other (Clawson, 2001).

Although more than 450 million people worldwide are faced with unmet mental health needs, 1 in 4 people meets criteria for a diagnosable mental health disorder (WHO, 2001). Thus, a great need has emerged for available and effective global mental health care. One major obstacle is the scarcity of competent mental health care providers worldwide. Low-income countries rank highest in the critical shortage of mental health resources (WHO, 2001). The need to proactively address this gap has been identified by WHO and various other national and international organizations.

At a 2003 meeting of leaders of the NBCC and its affiliates and WHO Director of Department of Mental Health and Substance Dependence, Dr. Benedetto Saraceno, the idea to develop a system to address urgent international mental health needs was deliberated. To respond to the concerns of underserved and never served populations around the world, NBCC proposed that its international division, NBCC-I, help with the development of a specific program of intervention. NBCC-I, comprising an international board of directors, collaborated with WHO's Department of Mental Health and Substance Dependence to develop the MHF project. MHF is a certificate program aiming to strengthen trainees' competence to meet mental health needs in diverse local communities. The MHF program has

the following unique features: (a) It is a flexible training program on mental health knowledge designed to be applied locally based on cultural context and needs, (b) it is aimed at recognizing and responding to people with mental health disorders who would otherwise remain unserved, and (c) it is exclusively designed to be delivered in a culturally specific way. Pedersen (2003) reminded us that in the internationalization and indigenization process, it is important to remember that countries and cultures rely on a range of "helpers and healers," many of whom are not professionals, in responding to local mental health needs. In accordance with this point, the MHF is not designed as a professional certification; thus, it does not imply mastery of the knowledge and skills at a level attained by mental health professionals. The MHF training program can be used to build capacity among service providers at various levels (e.g., Hinkle, Kutcher, & Chehil, 2006). For example, informal community care and services are offered by grassroots community members who have not received formal mental health education or training. This nonclinical level of mental health care emphasizes psychological support or advisement by community leaders, family groups, and local elders (including indigenous healers). At the primary health care level, general medical practitioners, nurses, and other health care personnel with higher health care skills can provide acute and long-term treatment to individuals with a variety of mental disorders. MHF training can be used to supplement the efforts of traditional health care providers. Furthermore, mental health facilitators can augment their knowledge and skills with advanced, specialized training, including a focus on functioning within a mental health care team to provide family support and education, follow-up monitoring, and targeted counseling.

The MHF training program has a number of strengths:

1. Since the MHF training is transdisciplinary, traditional professional helping disciplines are not reinforced, and competencies are linked to mental health needs of specific populations rather than to professional ideologies. Thus, individuals with

MHF training can effectively respond to community mental health needs, without being constrained by issues of professional identification.

2. Mental health facilitation also provides equitable access to quality first-contact interventions (including mental health promotion; advocacy; monitoring; referral and treatment) that respect dignity and human rights, meet population needs, and are based on current global, regional, or local sociocultural, economic, and political realities.

3. Context-specific competencies are identified and included in MHF training programs by local stakeholders. As a consequence, consumers and policymakers can assume that MHF training provides culturally relevant services to the local population. The MHF training curriculum is a dynamic document that is revised at regular intervals based on input from institutions and individuals who provide MHF training.

4. Individuals seeking MHF training, which may differ by vocation and location, represent a broad cross section of society. The diversity of trainee backgrounds, augmented by context-specific training content, increases the possibility that services can fill various gaps in mental health care. It provides added human resources for governments and NGOs to position mental health interventions where they are most needed. For example, priorities may focus on the development of community-based mental health responses to natural disasters or the development and delivery of suicide risk mitigation strategies. Other priorities may include identification, initial intervention, and long-term monitoring of individuals with mental disorders in collaboration with existing health care providers. This flexibility can help policymakers, service providers, communities, and NGOs meet local mental health needs without costly investments in infrastructure. The introduction of MHF training can also be expected to facilitate the continual development and delivery of therapeutic community-based care consistent with the WHO recommendations for addressing global mental health needs.

The MHF training model provides culturally relevant training to local personnel, who can offer valuable services in low- and middle-income countries. The program equips local mental health service providers with skills and culturally specific strategies to serve in their communities, and to bridge the gap between mental health needs and service availability. We believe that if operated continuously, this model will bring substantial gains in well-being to individuals and communities where they reside.

MHF programs are implemented in a variety of ways. NBCC-I has funded training in Mexico, Malawi, and Malaysia. Training in China, Bhutan, Botswana, and Bulgaria are also seriously being considered. Future training will be made available via local government funding, via joint funding by foundations and local NGOs, and through university teams assisting with culture-centered curriculum development. More information on the MHF initiative, NBCC-I, and other NBCC projects can be found on the National Board for Certified Counselors Web site at http://www.nbcc.org.

INTERNATIONALIZATION AND INDIGENIZATION AS PROFESSIONAL ATTITUDES AND VISIONS

In this chapter, we have examined the meaning and nature of internationalization. We also discussed the importance of developing counseling in indigenous cultural contexts and identified categories and levels of indigenization that could be carried out by counseling professionals to advance the cultural relevance of counseling theory and practice. Internationalization and indigenization are parallel, compatible, and complementary processes that could enhance the substance and standing of the counseling profession in one's own country as well as internationally. We have used initiatives taken by the NBCC as examples of international efforts to strengthen indigenous mental health service delivery.

Internationalization and indigenization both involve professional behaviors and actions, yet we would like to emphasize the importance of internationalization and indigenization as professional attitudes and visions. We want to identify three aspects of internationalization and indigenization as attitudes. First, internationalization and indigenization require counseling professionals to have a global mind-set, as well as awareness and understanding of the characteristics and needs of individuals in diverse cultural settings. Second, internationalization and indigenization require counseling professionals to respect counseling practice and scholarship developed around the world and to avoid an attitude of ethnocentrism, professional and cultural encapsulation, and/or cultural superiority (Heppner, 2006; Pedersen, 2003). Third, internationalization and indigenization require the counseling profession to value one's cultural practice and scholarship without underestimating or overestimating the potential contributions of these materials locally and internationally. Indigenization will not attain its desired outcomes if counseling professionals underestimate the value of their own indigenous content, as they will always look elsewhere to "import" theories and practice that might not be culturally relevant. Conversely, internationalization will become a unilateral process if counseling professionals in one region overestimate the universality of the indigenous content they have developed and seek to "export" it to other cultural regions.

Internationalization as a vision for the counseling profession, and the professional and scholarly benefits that could be derived from the process have been articulated by many leaders of the counseling profession in the past decade (e.g., Douce, 2004; Gerstein & Ægisdóttir, 2005; Heppner, 2006; Kwan & Gerstein, 2008; Leong & Blustein, 2000; Leong & Ponterotto, 2003; Savickas, 2007). Yet we would also like to emphasize the importance of seeing indigenization as a vision, particularly for counseling professionals in regions where counseling is developing. In some of these regions, there is a still strong tendency to regard the established counseling literature developed in the United States or Western countries as the dominant source of knowledge to inform research and practice (e.g., defining merit of academic publications in terms of whether they are published in venues in the Western world) and to see their professional systems as the blueprint to follow (e.g., Leung & Hoshmand, 2007). We hope that a vision of indigenization in counseling will slowly take root in these regions: (a) that counseling professionals will look more into their own cultural contexts, in research and practice, and value their own discovery; (b) that counseling professionals will nurture indigenous scholarship and publication venues, and influence their peers and institutions to give these venues the same level of respect that they have been giving to scholarly venues in the Western world; (c) that counseling professionals will develop and appreciate their indigenous and international identities; and (d) that there will be a stronger synthesis of indigenous literature to inform global research and practice.

CONCLUSION

Internationalization and indigenization are shaped by our attitudes and visions, and they are ongoing processes that have to be carried on by generations of counseling professionals. We presented some rationales and conceptual directions in this chapter and provided examples of implementation. It is our hope that internationalization and indigenization can be synthesized into the everyday work of counseling professionals and that through concerted efforts, the profession can make a bigger difference locally and globally.

REFERENCES

Blowers, G. H. (1996). The prospects for a Chinese psychology. In M. H. Bond (Ed.), *Handbook of Chinese psychology* (pp. 1–14). Hong Kong: Oxford University Press.

Canales, L., & Blanco-Beledo, R. (1993). Professions and educational counseling in Mexico and Latin America. *Journal of Career Development, 20,* 51–55.

Clawson, T. W. (1999, October). *Expanding professions globally: Seeing the United States as a place to bring professional interests.* Speech presented at Center for Quality Assurance and International Education (CQAIE) Conference, Washington, DC.

Clawson, T. W. (2001, April). *Globalization: Not a foreign concept.* Speech presented at Center for Quality Assurance and International Education (CQAIE) Conference, Montreal, Quebec, Canada.

Diaz-Loving, R. (2005). Emergence and contributions of a Latin American indigenous psychology. *International Journal of Psychology, 40,* 213–227.

Douce, L. A. (2004). Society of counseling psychology Division 17 of APA presidential address 2003: Globalization of counseling psychology. *The Counseling Psychologist, 32,* 142–152.

Enriquez, V. G. (1993). Developing a Filipino psychology. In U. Kim & J. W. Berry (Eds.), *Indigenous psychologies: Research and experience in cultural context* (pp. 152–169). Newbury Park, CA: Sage.

Friedman, T. L. (2006). *The world is flat: A brief history of the twenty-first century.* New York: Farrar, Straus & Giroux.

Gabrenya, W. K., Jr., Kung, M-C., & Chen, L-Y. (2006). Understanding the Taiwan Indigenous Psychology Movement: A sociology of science approach. *Journal of Cross-Cultural Psychology, 37,* 597–622.

Gerstein, L. H., & Ægisdóttir, S. (2005). A trip around the world: A counseling travelogue! *Journal of Mental Health Counseling, 27,* 95–103.

Gerstein, L. H., & Ægisdóttir, S. (2007). Training international Social Change Agents: Transcending a U.S. counseling paradigm. *Counselor Education and Supervision, 47,* 123–139.

Greenfield, P. M. (2000). Three approaches to the psychology of culture: Where do they come from? Where can they go? *Asian Journal of Social Psychology, 3,* 223–240.

Greenwald, B. C., & Kahn, J. (2009). *Globalization: The irrational fear that someone in China will take your job.* Hoboken, NJ: Wiley.

Gysbers, N. C., & Henderson, P. (2006). *Developing and managing your school guidance program* (4th ed.). Alexandria, VA: American Counseling Association.

Heppner, P. P. (2006). The benefits and challenges of becoming cross-culturally competent counseling psychologists: Presidential address. *The Counseling Psychologist, 34,* 147–172.

Heppner, P. H., Casas, J. M., Carter, J., & Stone, G. L. (2000). The maturation of counseling psychology: Multifaceted perspectives, 1978–1998. In S. D. Brown & R. W. Lent (Eds.), *Handbook of counseling psychology* (3rd ed., pp. 3–49). New York: Wiley.

Hinkle, J. S., Kutcher, S. P., & Chehil, S. (2006, October). *Mental health facilitator: Curriculum development.* Paper presented at the NBCC Global Mental Health Conference: Focus on the Never Served, New Delhi, India.

Ho, D. Y. F. (1998). Indigenous psychologies: Asian perspectives. *Journal of Cross-Cultural Psychology, 29,* 88–103.

Kim, U., & Berry, J. W. (Eds.). (1993). *Indigenous psychologies: Research and experience in cultural context.* Newbury Park, CA: Sage.

Kim, U., Park, Y.-S., & Park, D. (2000). The challenge of cross-cultural psychology: The role of indigenous psychologies. *Journal of Cross-Cultural Psychology, 31,* 63–75.

Kim, U., Yang, K-S., & Hwang, K. K. (2006). *Indigenous and cultural psychology.* New York: Springer.

Kunkel, M. A., Hector, M. A., Coronado, E. G., & Vales, V. C. (1989). Expectations about counseling in Yucatán, Mexico: Toward a "Mexican psychology." *Journal of Counseling Psychology, 36,* 322–330.

Kwan, K. K.-L., & Gerstein, L. H. (2008). Envisioning a counseling psychology of the world: The mission of the international forum. *The Counseling Psychologist, 36,* 182–187.

Leong, F. T. L., & Blustein, D. L. (2000). Toward a global vision of counseling psychology. *The Counseling Psychologist, 28,* 5–9.

Leong, R. T. L., & Ponterotto, J. G. (2003). A proposal for internationalizing counseling psychology in the United States: Rationales, recommendations, and challenges. *The Counseling Psychologist, 31,* 381–395.

Leung, S. A. (2003). A journal worth traveling: Globalization of counseling psychology. *The Counseling Psychologist, 31,* 412–419.

Leung, S. A., & Chen, P.-W. (in press). Developing counseling psychology in Chinese communities in Asia: Indigenous, multicultural, and cross-cultural considerations. *The Counseling Psychologist.*

Leung, S. A., & Hoshmand, L. T. (2007). Internationalization and international publishing: Broadening the impact of scholarly work in counseling. *Asian Journal of Counselling, 14,* 141–154.

Marsella, A. J. (1998). Toward a "global-community psychology": Meeting the needs of a changing world. *American Psychologist, 53,* 1282–1291.

Marsella, A. J., & Pedersen, P. B. (2004). Internationalizing the counseling psychology curriculum: Toward new values, competencies, and directions. *Counseling Psychology Quarterly, 17,* 413–423.

Moodley, R., & West, W. (2005). *Integrating traditional healing practices into counseling and psychotherapy.* Thousand Oaks, CA: Sage.

Pedersen, P. B. (2003). Culturally biased assumptions in counseling psychology. *The Counseling Psychologist, 31,* 396–403.

Peteanu, M. (1997). Educational and vocational guidance in Romania: Short history. *Revista de Pedagogie, 1*(12), 314–324.

Poortinga, Y. H. (1999). Do cross-cultural differences in behavior imply a need for different psychologies. *Applied Psychology: An International Review, 48,* 419–432.

Poortinga, Y. H. (2005). The globalization of indigenous psychologies. *Asian Journal of Social Psychology, 8,* 65–74.

Savickas, M. L. (2007). Internationalization of counseling psychology: Constructing cross-national consensus and collaboration. *Applied Psychology: An International Review, 56,* 182–188.

Sinha, D. (1997). Indigenous psychology. In J. W. Berry, Y. H. Poortinga, & J. Pandey (Eds.), *Handbook of cross-cultural psychology* (Vol. 1, pp. 129–170). Needham Heights, MA: Allyn & Bacon.

Stiglitz, J. E. (2003). *Globalization and its discontents.* New York: W. W. Norton.

Sue, D. W., Carter, R. T., Casas, J. M., Fouad, N. A., Ivey, A. E., Jensen, M., et al. (1998). *Multicultural counseling competencies: Individual and organizational development.* Thousand Oaks, CA: Sage.

Szilagyi, A. A., & Paredes, D. M. (in press). Professional counseling in Romania: An introduction. *Journal of Counseling and Development.*

Watts, A. G. (1997). The role of career guidance in societies in transition. *Revista de Pedagogie, 1*(12), 417–428.

World Health Organization. (2001). *The world health report 2001: Mental health, new understanding, new hope.* Geneva, Switzerland: Author.

Wrenn, C. G. (1962). The culturally encapsulated counselor. *Harvard Educational Review, 32,* 444–449.

Yakushko, O. (2005). Mental health counseling in Ukraine. *Journal of Mental Health Counseling, 27,* 161–167.

Yakushko, O. (2007). Career development issues in the former USSR. *Journal of Career Development, 33*(4), 299–315.

7

Crossing Borders in Collaboration

KATHRYN L. NORSWORTHY, SEUNG-MING ALVIN LEUNG,
P. PAUL HEPPNER, AND LI-FEI WANG

The internationalization of counseling and counseling psychology encourages cross-national contact among professionals around the world (Heppner, 2008; Leung, 2003; Pedersen & Leong, 1997). These "border crossings" can involve travel across regions for the purposes of work, research, study, and teaching, and inevitably bring challenges, learning, and potential growth.

In the midst of our efforts to internationalize, we are recognizing the significant influence and impact of U.S. psychology in defining the field globally. Meaningful internationalization acknowledges the importance of reinventing counseling and counseling psychology as professions "in a global context" (Pedersen, 2003, p. 402) and of indigenizing the discipline by professionals from countries and cultures outside the United States (Kim, Yang, & Hwang, 2006; Marsella & Pedersen, 2004). Yet Arnett (2008) concluded that most psychological research is conducted with individuals from the United States, or less than 5% of the global population, and is most often assumed to be universally applicable. Given the vastly different worldviews, cultures, and contexts of the remaining 95%, current psychological knowledge and skill sets are grossly incomplete and unrepresentative of most of the human population on this planet. Thus, cultural competency and ongoing efforts to cultivate a respectful, power-sharing approach to international work is a prerequisite for Western counselors and psychologists engaged in international research and practice. Additionally, international students educated in Western institutions face challenges in navigating the U.S. education system and society as well as in translating or transforming Western-based models into culturally grounded, indigenous counseling and counseling psychologies appropriate for people in their home countries.

Recognizing the need to offer guidance in the internationalization process, in 2004, the American Psychological Association (APA) passed the "Resolution on Culture and Gender Awareness in International Psychology" (see Appendix, Chapter 4, this volume). This document noted the significant influence of U.S. psychology globally, challenged Western psychologists to become aware of ethnocentric attitudes and practices in our international work, and suggested adding an international focus in our training programs. The resolution reminds psychologists to engage in efforts at unlearning colonizing and hegemonic attitudes as well as practices we may have internalized in our training. Rice and Ballou (2002), leaders in the development of the resolution, emphasized five principles to be centralized in our international work: (1) understanding experiences in diverse cultures and contexts, (2) respect for pluralism based on differences, (3) awareness and analysis of power, (4) critical analysis of Western perspectives, and (5) international and interdisciplinary social-cultural perspectives. In Chapter 4 (this volume), Norsworthy, Heppner, Ægisdóttir, Gerstein, and Pedersen discuss this topic in greater detail and emphasize the importance of cultivating and employing "decolonizing" methodologies in our international activities. The five principles explicated by Rice and Ballou point in the directions of mutuality, power sharing, and building a field that is truly relevant for the diversity of human experience around the world. Reflections by professionals from various countries and regions engaging in cross-cultural and cross-national professional activities or study regarding how they collaborate, learn, and negotiate their relationships, work, and educational experiences can offer invaluable insights about the internationalization process.

With these points in mind, we will discuss three kinds of "border crossings" in counseling and counseling psychology. Based on more than 20 years of conducting research with colleagues in Taiwan and other parts of the world, Puncky Heppner (United States) weaves together current literature and his own experiences with cross-cultural and cross-national research teams, particularly focusing on the benefits, challenges, and personal qualities of the researchers. Then, using auto-ethnographic narratives, Alvin Leung (Hong Kong) and Kathryn Norsworthy (United States) describe what they have learned through their experiences of crossing borders. Alvin offers a first-person account of his own experiences in traveling to the United States for graduate school, then returning to his home country to work and "indigenize" the largely Western knowledge base accompanying him. Kathryn describes her 12-year

process of collaborating in research, practice, and activism projects with Southeast Asian colleagues in grassroots, nongovernmental, and governmental venues, particularly highlighting the partnership with Thai colleague, Ouyporn Khuankaew. All three coauthors emphasize the importance of understanding the context of the country in which one works or studies and outline strategies for successful collaboration. We also review challenges to effective cross-cultural and cross-national partnerships and learning, offering suggestions about functioning effectively in these relationships and environments. Finally, we discuss critical events linked with our collaborative international relationships and the role of creating reciprocal and mutually beneficial relationships. Li-fei Wang (Taiwan) concludes the chapter by noting themes, observations, and recommendations for the ongoing internationalization of counseling and counseling psychology, with a particular focus on cross-national and cross-cultural partnerships as a valuable source of learning, growth, and influence on the professions of each partner's home country.

CROSSING BOUNDARIES: CROSS-CULTURAL AND CROSS-NATIONAL RESEARCH COLLABORATION

(PUNCKY HEPPNER)

Psychological research across all psychological specialties published in APA journals has focused "narrowly on Americans" and neglected the rest of the world's people (Arnett, 2008, p. 602). Consequently, the generalizability of the research conducted by most U.S.-based psychologists to populations outside the United States is not only questionable but also seriously restricts the utility or applicability of research by U.S. psychologists. Despite a growing internationalization of U.S. counseling and counseling psychology (Heppner, Leong, & Gerstein, 2008), the counseling profession in the United States is not an exception and is still an insular profession (see Cheung, 2000; Leung, 2003) with relatively little collaborative cross-national research.

Cross-cultural and cross-national research collaboration has been extremely rewarding in my career and has greatly affected me personally and professionally, in terms of my worldview as a research psychologist and the way I think about and conceptualize my research. In Chapter 8 (this volume), Li-fei Wang and I discuss our long-term personal and professional collaborative relationship within the context of our developmental cultural journey from a more personal and auto-ethnographic perspective. Based primarily on that relationship as well as other research with international graduate students, in this section I provide a brief overview of some of the benefits of crossing borders to establish cross-national and cross-cultural research collaboration.

In my view, research collaborations between U.S. counseling psychologists and colleagues in other countries, especially non-Western countries, have the potential to greatly enhance "the depth and richness of our knowledge bases and theoretical models" (Heppner, 2008, p. 814). I reached this conclusion after more than 20 years of conducting cross-cultural and cross-national collaborative research as well as analyzing the development of the coping and applied problem-solving research that I conducted in my career. I believe that my research maps very well onto the broader U.S. research bases on these topics (see Heppner, 2008). In essence, I believe that cross-national collaboration not only provides a much more complex and rich data base in psychology but also substantially broadens our psychological theories and greatly expands the cultural competencies and the worldviews we bring to our professional work and our personal lives.

How Can Cross-National and Cross-Cultural Collaboration Strengthen Research in Counseling Psychology?

There is a wide array of benefits from conducting cross-cultural research. I will briefly discuss five benefits: (1) examining the external validity or generalizability of research findings across different cultures; (2) creating knowledge pertaining to how different cultural contexts affect psychological processes;

(3) broadening one's perspective of particular psychological constructs; (4) enhancing the researchers' cultural awareness, knowledge, and skills, which in turn enhance their sensitivities in future cultural research; and (5) deepening personal and professional relationships among the investigators.

First, for some time scholars have maintained that cross-cultural research can be very useful to test the external validity of research findings in other cultures (Heine & Norenzayan, 2006; Quintana, Troyano, & Taylor, 2001; Ægisdóttir, Gerstein, & Çinarbaş, 2008). In short, there has been a tendency to assume that research findings, repeatedly yielded under tightly controlled experimental conditions, are universal and that they are applicable across cultures. Thus, over the years, scholars have issued cautions about the tendency to assume the universality of research findings, and they have specifically urged testing the generalizability of the findings in other cultures. This issue of external validity has been examined particularly with regard to the utilization of instruments developed in one cultural context (most often in the United States) and subsequently used in another culture. Previously, researchers had suggested that such inventories be carefully translated linguistically (in terms of form, meaning, and structure) to ensure equivalence or comparability across cultures (see Lonner, 1985). Lonner, however, also suggested other types of equivalence such as functional equivalence (referring to the function of the behavior being studied), conceptual equivalence (similarity in meaning), and metric equivalence (the manner in which constructs are quantified). In short, there are many measurement complexities in cross-cultural research. One basic purpose of cross-cultural research collaboration is to test the external validity or generalizability of research findings from one sample or culture to another culture.

Second, from my experience, cross-national collaboration among international colleagues can promote a greater understanding of psychological processes within different cultural contexts, particularly indigenous culture norms, values, and customs in cultures outside the United States. In so doing, we not only learn more about the nuances within particular cultural phenomena, but such research also offers possibilities for deepening our understanding of new or different psychological processes in another culture. For me, it is most exciting to deepen my scientific understanding of a coping process in another cultural context and to find coping processes not explored in the U.S.-based literature that may very well apply to various U.S. populations or other cultural groups in other countries (see Heppner, 2008). In this way, the counseling profession can greatly expand our knowledge bases of psychological processes related to psychological and vocational adjustment as well as physical health within different cultural contexts across the globe. Such knowledge bases are particularly beneficial because far too often, the cultural context has been ignored in U.S. psychology (Arnett, 2008; Heine & Norenzayan, 2006; Heppner, 2008). For example, I have learned very clearly from my research that coping constructs based on the dominant U.S. culture do not come close to telling the whole story about coping across U.S. cultural groups or cultures around the world (see Heppner, 2008). In short, cross-national collaborative research can promote the development of knowledge bases by specifically explicating how cultural dynamics affect psychological processes. In so doing, we participate in developing psychological knowledge that reflects the diverse cultures of the world. To me, it is a wonderful feeling after conducting research for more than 30 years on applied problem solving and coping to still look forward to contributing to a more complex and inclusive knowledge base of how people handle stressful events in their lives across diverse cultures.

In the past, there has been an overreliance on Western-based theories, which not only marginalizes non-Western cultures (Heine & Norenzayan, 2006) but also served to greatly limit our own knowledge bases and psychological theories. However, by studying constructs in more than one cultural context, different variables or complexities can be identified that not only "paint an increasingly detailed picture" (Heine & Norenzayan, 2006, p. 254) and a "much more complex mosaic" (Heppner, 2008, p. 806) of our constructs but also greatly expand our conceptualization of cultural similarities and differences. In this way, cross-cultural research can enhance the sophistication of our research, expand the depth and richness of our psychological knowledge, promote the development of more complex theoretical models (Heine & Norenzayan, 2006; Heppner, 2008; Quintana et al., 2001), and increase the range and effectiveness of our counseling interventions across a broad range of populations (Heppner, 2008).

Third, cross-cultural, and cross-national research teams in particular can provide many opportunities to broaden one's perspective of psychological phenomena and aid in understanding particular psychological constructs at a more complex level. For example, it is often difficult for scholars from very different cultures to learn from one another through professional publications that are in different languages or unfamiliar publications outlets. In essence, important knowledge bases are inaccessible across countries and continents. Cross-national partnerships can enhance the team members' cultural sensitivities as well as promote the flow of cultural information across countries and cultures. Thus, collaboration among international colleagues can expand our awareness of the nuances and complexities of psychological constructs that might not have been apparent from one's primary cultural perspective (Heine & Norenzayan, 2006; Heppner, 2006, 2008). One such example from my experience was the development of an East-Asian-based Collectivistic Coping Styles (CCS) inventory (Heppner et al., 2006), which was greatly influenced by the cultural worldviews of the Taiwanese and Korean members of our research team. Our research found that the CCS contained new coping factors not found in U.S.-based coping inventories (Heppner et al., 2006). These results have implications for coping not only in Taiwan and Korea but also quite likely for ethnic minority groups in the United States and for future theoretical development. In my view, we stand to learn tremendously by getting outside our ethnocentric worldviews and listening to others' perspectives based on cultures different from our own.

Fourth, cross-cultural and cross-national research collaboration can greatly enhance one's cultural awareness, knowledge, and skills (AKS; see multicultural guidelines by American Psychological Association, 2003; Sue, 2003). That is, my experience has been that both my international colleagues and I have greatly enhanced our cultural AKS not only from our research but also through talking and working as colleagues. The latter sometimes involves hours of discussion, cross-cultural observations, reflection, and even processing aspects of our relationship. Not surprisingly, the more we enhance our cultural AKS, the better or more sophisticated our research becomes.

Finally, successful cross-cultural and cross-national research collaboration has typically deepened our personal and professional relationships. For me, this has been a profoundly gratifying outcome or benefit. It is this spirit of not only collaborating but also reaching across cultural similarities and differences to connect both interpersonally as well as emotionally that helps achieve a research goal. And when it is all done, the relationships are most meaningful and celebratory, can last a lifetime, and also serve as the bases for additional cross-national collaborations, most often with increased cultural sensitivities.

A Few Factors That Can Enhance Cross-Cultural and Cross-National Research Collaboration

Depending on the magnitude of cultural differences among team members, it is generally insufficient for cross-national researchers to only have a wide array of research skills; successful cross-cultural and cross-national research collaboration often require cross-cultural competencies. In Chapter 8 (this volume), Li-fei and I discuss a number of factors that affected our cross-national collaborations. Based on our work, I will briefly highlight and elaborate on four factors that seem particularly relevant for research collaboration: (1) cross-cultural competencies, (2) reciprocal and mutually beneficial as well as respectful personal and professional relationships,

(3) active problem solving, and (4) having common content-specific expertise. It is important to note that all four of these factors synergistically add exponentially to cross-cultural and cross-national collaboration.

Cross-national teams are unique in that members often bring very different cultural perspectives, not only about the research topic but also about many other aspects of the research project. Partners may have differing expectations of how each will behave with each other as colleagues, how they might express agreement or disagreement, and the manner of dividing research tasks. From our experiences, a critical component of cross-national collaboration pertains to the cross-cultural competence that the team members bring to the team. The cultural AKS competencies involve a wide range of skills (see analyses by Worthington, Soth-McNett, & Moreno, 2007). In addition, in this context it has been important for me to remain cognizant that I am a white American male and of the sociopolitical dynamics that sometimes accompany that part of my identity. Moreover, since the focus of our research has been on cultural dynamics different from my own, I make special efforts to remember that I am a cultural outsider who is most often unaware of the many cultural complexities we are investigating. That is, the greater the members' cross-cultural competencies, the more skills they have to effectively deal with the myriad research decisions as well as their working alliance. This also requires the ability to focus on the research tasks while remaining cognizant of the cultural context.

Another very important factor in cross-national research pertains to the reciprocal and mutually beneficial and respectful personal and professional relationships among collaborators (see Singer, 2008). In our view, the relationship can be best conceptualized as a working alliance. An open, egalitarian, respectful, deep, trusting, and caring relationship can go a long way in promoting a successful cross-national research project. This type of relationship is often characterized by the mutuality of goals, bonds that develop through honest and genuine interpersonal reactions and disclosures, power sharing, reciprocity, and a reflexive examination of the personal and professional relationship.

Even with the best communication, there will be many obstacles, misperceptions, and problems to resolve. Thus, it is also essential for cross-national collaborators to have good problem-solving skills to resolve a wide array of methodological issues, content-specific decisions, statistical questions, and data collection procedures. Moreover, many times problem solving revolves around cultural issues. From our experience, it is extremely important for the collaborators to be aware that when they come from outside the cultural context of investigation, they need to be mindful that their understanding is most likely limited and incomplete. Thus, it can be helpful to "listen more than talk," to focus on acquiring a deeper understanding of the cultural context, and to ask questions to seek information or clarify. Conversely, we have learned that sometimes the "outsider" is also in a good position to offer different perspectives or share observations that might stimulate additional thinking or brainstorming in the team.

It is helpful for each cross-national research team member to have content-specific knowledge to contribute to the collaboration. In our view, the most successful cross-national research teams do not consist of one member "helping" the other but rather recognizing that each member has strengths that he or she brings to the team, whereby the combined strengths within the team support high-quality research.

In sum, there are many benefits to cross-national research collaboration, all of which can strengthen the counseling profession. We strongly encourage scholars to cross not only national boundaries to engage in cross-national research but also cultural boundaries to immerse themselves in other cultures to learn more about the multifaceted influences of culture on human behavior. In so doing, we become better cross-cultural researchers. In the end, "conducting culturally sensitive research in many cultures will greatly expand the depth and richness of our knowledge bases and theoretical models . . . which will make us better psychologists, better scholars, teachers, mentors, therapists, consultants—and better people" (Heppner, 2008, p. 814).

This section has elucidated the benefits and challenges of cross-national research partnerships. The ideas presented are also quite relevant to cross-national education and practice. In the following sections, Leung and Norsworthy take a narrative turn, giving more personal accounts of their "border crossings" and what can be learned in each case.

BORDER CROSSING TO AN UNFAMILIAR HOME TURF: COUNSELING PROFESSIONALS RETURNING HOME

(SEUNG-MING ALVIN LEUNG)

As the counseling profession develops and becomes more visible in countries around the world, international students have increasingly chosen to undertake advanced study in fields related to counseling, psychology, and mental health in the United States and in other countries where established programs are available. Many of these students eventually assume leadership positions in counseling research, training, and practice in the United States or back in their home countries. Wherever they choose to advance their careers, international graduates of counseling training programs are valuable "ambassadors" of the profession, as they bring unique perspectives to the field of counseling that are local and global, indigenous and international.

In this section, I would like to elaborate on the experience of international graduates who choose to return to their home cultures after an extensive period of study and involvement in the field of counseling in the United States. I explore the process of adjustment and adaptation that they might have to go through and examine the personal and professional benefits that could be derived from this journey. This section is conceptualized in reference to my personal experience and is therefore written from a first-person perspective.

Adaptation and Adjustment

After residing in the United States first as an international student, then as a counseling psychology faculty member at two different universities, I decided to return to Hong Kong, a place where I was born and raised, to take up a faculty position. The decision was made after a long period of deliberation, reflection, and struggle. It was the beginning of a tedious process of preparing for and making the move. It also involved saying goodbye to the social and professional networks that I and my family had become attached to over the years as we grew and progressed in our life stages. Beneath feelings of excitement and anticipation over the opportunities ahead, there were a host of negative feelings, including confusion, fear, sense of loss, and sadness.

Indeed, the journey to reenter my home culture was not an easy one. I found that the process of cultural adaptation was more complex and longer than I had expected, more painful and lonely than I had anticipated, yet more rewarding and fruitful than I had imagined. I would like to elaborate on three aspects of culture-related challenges requiring adaptation and adjustment, which were (1) social and cultural identity, (2) cultural limitations of scholarship I learned in the United States, and (3) professional isolation. I would also like to discuss strategies that I employed to cope with these challenges.

The first challenge is cultural identity. After years of residing in the United States, I have integrated facets of U.S. culture into my identity. At the beginning stage of my entrance back to my home culture, I experienced significant distress and confusion because I was not sure where my "home" was. I felt "homesick" and I missed being around my "home" in the United States, even though I was physically residing in the place that I was born and raised. The struggle with social and cultural identity was expressed in many other forms, including language, food, social space, and interpersonal relationships. The cognitive and emotional nature of the experience could be conceptualized as a case of reverse culture shock (Leung, 2007; Pedersen, 1995). I came to realize that I had to actively engage in a process of re-acculturation and re-adaptation to a once familiar home turf. In retrospect, I have learned three important lessons from my experience in making transitions across borders back to my home culture. First, I found out that re-acculturation and re-adaptation are ongoing processes, and after more than 12 years of reentering my home culture, I am still re-acculturating and re-adapting. Second, crossing borders often involves synthesizing multiple social and cultural identities (e.g., synthesizing my U.S.-acquired identity with my evolving Chinese identity), and the more the layers of identities one has accumulated, the harder it is to re-acculturate and re-adapt because the home culture is unlikely to provide the multiplicities of experiences required of the multicultural identities. Third, finding individuals who have similar cross-cultural transition and/or retransition experiences is instrumental in consolidating and sustaining the re-acculturation process. I have been able to find empathy, support, and encouragement from those with similar sojourning experiences as mine.

The second challenge is cultural limitation of scholarship I learned in the United States. International counseling psychologists often return home with a sense of mission, hoping to use and apply what they have learned in their own cultural context. They discover very soon that what they have learned has to be substantially adapted to be useful and meaningful in their home context. I would like to describe two experiences as illustrations. First, having been trained in the United States, I had become quite fluent in my English usage and my professional vocabulary was all in English. Initially, I had trouble teaching my classes in the Chinese language. Counseling is indeed a process based on the local language, and my lack of language fluency was a major barrier in teaching and in counseling supervision. I was quite embarrassed, as Chinese was supposed to be my first language. Fortunately, this was a problem that could be overcome through hard work. I started to develop detailed lecture notes and presentation outlines in Chinese, and through that I was able to conduct my classes more fluently. After several years of refining and upgrading my Chinese course materials, I was able to improve the impact of my teaching, and my student course evaluation ratings have also improved substantially. Second, with years of training and professional experience in counseling psychology, I was expected by students and professionals to be an "expert" in the field. I soon found out that my knowledge of counseling is actually knowledge of counseling in the United States and that I know very little about the counseling system in Hong Kong. I have to learn and relearn my context to make my knowledge and expertise applicable. An important aspect of counseling in Hong Kong is its application in educational settings, and I have to teach many counseling-related classes to teachers. To supplement my lack of knowledge about the local setting, I collaborated with experienced teachers, visited schools, and talked to my students who were teachers and used them as my "informants." In the span of a few years, I was able to contextualize my teaching and training materials substantially. I have used a similar process to contextualize other skills I learned in the United States, including setting up a counseling lab, editing a journal, and conducting career development workshops. Drawing from the above experiences, I think that it is important for counseling psychologists who crossed borders to return home to understand that a "transfer-of-technology" approach is not adequate (Pedersen, 2003). They should bear in mind that they need a significant period of time to refamiliarize with their home cultures and contexts and that much effort is needed to "indigenize" their teaching and scholarship.

The third challenge is professional isolation. There were few counseling psychologists in Hong Kong and fewer with the training experiences that I had. At times, I have to explain to others the nature of my training and professional credentials. There were times when I felt being misunderstood, unappreciated, and disappointed. The first few years of my reentry to Hong Kong were actually characterized by a strong sense of loneliness and isolation. I felt that I was all by myself in my journey to be "the one who would make a difference in my profession." In my effort to escape from my despair, I came to the realization that I had to be humble and should not think of myself as superior to others because of my past experience in the United States. Through this new perspective, I was able to regain my professional and personal energies and to reorient

myself toward the future. I was able to slowly establish a local professional support network and at the same time maintain my contacts with colleagues in the United States. I learned that to make a difference at home, I have to work with others and I have to abandon my sense of superiority/inferiority and think of myself as one of them, locally and internationally.

Maintaining and Broadening Impact

Slowly and surely, counseling professionals crossing borders to return home will adapt and adjust to the cultural and professional realities in their home turf. As they mature in their careers, their work will increasingly make an important impact to the counseling profession locally and internationally. Sustaining their impact, however, requires conscious efforts to take care of one's professional and physical well-being, as well as to locate the niche where they could make their best contribution.

First and foremost, counseling professionals who return to their home countries might find themselves overwhelmed by demands from all sides to share their expertise. As they become more established, as their scholarly work is adapted and grounded in local contexts, many opportunities would arise locally and internationally. Yet from my experience as a counseling psychologist who also specializes in career and life planning, I realize how important it is to prioritize my goals and activities and to avoid overstretching. To avoid going over my limits, I have learned to avoid "overestimating" my ability, to share opportunities, and to say "no" to requests and demands that are very tempting. Counseling psychologists who crossed borders are often driven by a sense of mission, yet to maintain their capacity to fulfill goals and objectives that are important, they need to be on guard against stress and burnout.

Second, to broaden their impact, counseling professionals returning to their home countries have to find ways to accommodate and balance between local and international professional objectives. Using myself as an example, I am fully aware of the need to indigenize, adapt, and document my scholarly work in Chinese so that I could share with professionals in my community. At the same time, there are also expectations from my institution to publish my scholarly work in leading journal venues in the Western world (often in English language) and to develop an international reputation in the field of counseling. The dual missions to make one's work relevant and known to people locally (e.g., indigenization) and to those in the international community are especially burdensome to counseling professionals who return to a home region where the counseling profession is at a beginning stage of development and where significant efforts are needed to adapt what they know about counseling to local people in local languages (Leung & Hoshmand, 2007). There is no magic solution to resolve this "dichotomy," yet I have the following experience to share.

First, one has to consider his or her personal mission. I have put significantly more time and efforts to "indigenize" because that was the major reason I returned to my home culture. Second, I have made significant efforts to be active in corresponding professional organizations at home and abroad. Through these professional activities, I was able to weave together indigenous and international professional goals and agendas. Third, I looked for opportunities to engage in scholarly projects that would facilitate indigenous and international objectives. For example, I have invited colleagues from various parts of the world to collaborate in seminars and workshops in Hong Kong and to serve as coinvestigators in research projects, the results of which could be published in local as well as international journal venues.

Finally, to maintain and broaden one's impact, counseling professionals returning to their home countries should seek ways to mentor future generations of counseling professionals who can carry on the tasks of indigenization and internationalization. Mentoring should not be limited to training of postgraduate students; returning counseling professionals can share their indigenous and international missions and visions with fellow counselors and scholars at home and in international settings. Meanwhile, they also serve as "role models" to students and peers through their active involvement in the local and international communities of counselors and psychologists.

In summary, international graduates in counseling who returned to their home cultures are unique assets to the counseling profession. Their multiple professional identities and affiliations are instrumental to cross-cultural and cross-national collaboration and the development of counseling internationally. Their understanding of multiple cultures and languages allows them to play the role as ambassadors of the counseling profession as well as to serve as "bridges" that connect cultures and nations so that counseling can become a truly international discipline.

CROSSING BORDERS IN PRACTICE AND SOLIDARITY WORK

(KATHRYN NORSWORTHY)

On the topic of internationalizing counseling psychology, Varenne (2003) remarked, "Recent scholars have also pointed out that once a dialogue has begun across what used to be boundaries, both sides will be involved in the constitution of a new field" (p. 397). This section chronicles some of the pivotal dialogues and experiences that have constituted my journey and contributed to my learning as a white, U.S. counseling psychologist working in South and Southeast Asia over the past 12 years. In the first section, I offer a brief auto-ethnography of how I came to work in the region and some highlights of the friendship and professional relationship between my Thai colleague, Ouyporn Khuankaew, and me that explain the evolution of several of my most important discoveries in connection to practicing outside the United States. In the latter part of this section, I reflect on our experiences of working together and with groups throughout Southeast and South Asia and articulate key learnings that may be useful for Western psychologists "crossing borders" to practice and do solidarity work outside their home countries and regions as well as back in our countries of origin.

The Beginning

My first trip to Asia was in 1985, awakening me to the teachings of Buddhism while in Ladakh, the Tibetan Buddhist state of northern India. A rich and diverse society, India penetrated into me, showing me how people holding a range of religions, worldviews, and cultures struggle to live under one flag. Of course, I come from a country of diversity, yet often we understand our own cultures through the reflections of someone else's. While pursuing Buddhist studies, I began to explore Thailand, finding a different expression of the same religion within a cultural context unique to this Southeast Asian country. During the next decade, I returned to this region many times, traveling, studying yoga and meditation, and spending hours talking with locals in the tea shops, markets, trains, and buses. Though I was aware that my understanding of the cultures of countries such as India and Thailand was quite limited, I do not think that I fully grasped just how complex, nuanced, and layered these societies actually are. I had not yet formed any close relationships with people from either country or spent extended time living, studying, or working there.

In 1996, during a Buddhist studies course in Barre, Massachusetts, I stumbled on a newsletter devoted to issues of international Buddhist women. Noting that the editor was a Thai professor of religion, Dr. Chatsumarn Kabilsingh, I resolved to pay her a visit on my next trip to Bangkok. Later that year, I found myself at Thammasat University sitting across the desk from Dr. Chat, discussing the recent and extraordinary gathering of more than 35,000 women just outside Beijing at the NGO Forum on Women. In exploring this and other topics, Dr. Chat determined that it would be beneficial for her feminist activist colleague, Ouyporn Khuankaew, and I to meet due to our common interests and commitments. Using the mailing address Dr. Chat provided during that meeting, I wrote to "Ms. Khuankaew," sharing my interests in Buddhism, various social issues such as violence against women, HIV/AIDS, and feminist counseling. Much to my delight, Ouyporn replied expressing interest in meeting and working together. We made a plan to offer a workshop focusing on counseling women survivors of violence in December 1997. I would "teach" the workshop and Ouyporn would translate.

In December 1997, my partner, Deena, and I traveled to Thailand, where we met Ouyporn for the first time. We all made our way to Kanchaniburi,

where Ouyporn and I would be facilitating the workshop with the staff of a local nongovernmental organization. As the workshop progressed, with me as the primary facilitator and Ouyporn translating, we increasingly began to turn to one another to discuss what to do next and to debrief the process. Ouyporn regularly and spontaneously added to my comments and very skillfully made the workshop more relevant and grounded in the Thai context. At the end of the 4 days, we shared with one another our experiences of working together on this project and quickly agreed that we were not satisfied with the arrangement of facilitator/translator. Because we both recognized that we each brought crucial and unique contributions to the table, we made an explicit commitment to shift to a cofacilitation, power-sharing approach. Furthermore, we pledged to regularly reflect on "the process" of our collaboration, both with one another, as well as with our local partners in future projects, to ensure that we stayed true to these values. We recognized that the dynamics of our own partnership would influence participants with whom we would be working. If they saw a Thai facilitator and a white U.S. facilitator sharing power, mutually respecting one another, and valuing one another's input and perspectives, we knew that this would influence the participants' own feelings of empowerment and agency.

Thus began our journey together. For the past 12 years, Ouyporn and I have worked with groups from Thailand, Cambodia, the refugee communities of Burma, as well as Asia regional groups and international groups, including participants from nearly every continent. While continuing to work with local partners on issues such as violence against women, HIV/AIDS, women's leadership, and feminist counseling, we now also collaborate with groups focusing on peace building, anti-oppression, social justice education, and capacity building through training of trainer experiences.

Over the span of our work, Ouyporn and I have spent considerable time engaging between ourselves and with local partners in a reflexive process focused on inventing, articulating, and refining the methodology we are using in our projects. We have deliberately noted the contributions from postcolonial theory; radical, critical, global, and transnational feminist theories; liberation theory; and participant action research (see Norsworthy & Khuankaew, 2004, 2006, 2008, for a full discussion of this evolving methodological framework). In keeping with the participant action principle of "passing the torch," we have supported and mentored a significant number of second- and third-generation practitioners into this liberatory model and now are proud to facilitate with many of them on projects around the region.

The years have also brought a deepening of the relationship between Ouyporn and me. In facing challenging and confusing critical workshop incidents, experiencing the joys and satisfaction of effective collaboration, through difficult dialogues in which we worked through misunderstandings and conflicts, we agree that our trust, respect, and appreciation for one another has exponentially deepened and increased. We recognize the multiple dimensions of our relationship to one another as mentors, teachers, friends, colleagues, and "sisters."

Reflections: What Is to Be Learned From These Experiences?

As a white, U.S. counseling and peace psychologist working and conducting research in South and Southeast Asia for more than a decade, I have learned much from and with Ouyporn and my other local collaborators, partners, and project participants, as well as from the experience of doing the work in so many parts of the region. However, it is clear to me that spending considerable time in India, Thailand, and other parts of Asia, studying indigenous spiritual practices, and absorbing and acclimating to the cultures were extremely important preparation for working in these countries. In cultivating a degree of comfort and appreciation of the cultures and the people as well as some basic skills in functioning in cultural contexts very different from my own, particularly during times of ambiguity and uncertainty, a "bonding" process began to take place that would serve as an important foundation for the challenges ahead. Still, I was quite naive initially and had only a superficial understanding of

the cultures and the people until I began to work in the region, developed personal relationships, studied the Thai language, and lived with people on a daily basis for more extended periods of time.

As is clear from my reflections about Ouyporn's and my initial experience with one another, consistent with my U.S. enculturation, I approached the situation as the "expert," assuming that Ouyporn would be the "support" person, and she did the same. Fortunately, for both of us, we each had strong feminist and social justice sensibilities that created dissonance about the initial power arrangements, and we were able to openly debrief and change the arrangements. Through Ouyporn's and my lived experiences and our respective educations, we were aware of the U.S. global dominance politically, economically, educationally, and militarily. We both knew that my country and disciplines, U.S. counseling and psychology, profoundly influence and affect the rest of the world, often through hegemonic systems defining "standards" by which others must or "should" operate (Leong & Ponterotto, 2003; Varenne, 2003). Over the years of work and dialogue with my Asian colleagues, this "concept" was brought to life. I frequently heard them express concerns. For example, one colleague from Burma living in exile in Thailand reported,

> We had a Western "expert" come in to consult with us about HIV/AIDS. He was a link to funding that could have really helped us set up crisis counseling services and train local personnel. But he thought we had to have "professionals" with master's degrees and Ph.D.'s to provide the services and this is not available at this time inside the country or in the refugee communities here in Thailand. Most of the universities in Burma have been closed down by the dictatorship. We escaped from the regime and do not have access to such education right now nor do most of us have legal documents so that we can attend Thai schools. So, he got frustrated and left. He did not want to work with us to see if we could come up with a more workable solution. (Tan, pseudonym to protect security; personal communication, July 17, 2004)

What comes to mind here is the justification statement for the 2004 APA Resolution on Culture and Gender Awareness in International Psychology, which encourages psychologists "to become aware of and act differently from the historical processes of global imperialism and colonialism by educating themselves about cultural and gender issues and systems of power, privilege, and domination in international psychology" (Rice & Ballou, 2002, p. 1).

Both Ouyporn and I have come to realize that we are likely to encounter the effects of colonization and imperialism in ourselves and in others (Comas-Diaz, 1994; Moane, 1994). My local partners, participants, and I were all enculturated into societies based on systems of hegemony, power, and oppression and, without awareness or conscientization, would likely enact internalizations of these dynamics. Thus, we were all challenged to "unlearn" these attitudes and behaviors and to develop a critical consciousness (Freire, 1972) in order to create collaborative partnerships among ourselves and with participants. As articulated in the multicultural competencies (Sue, Arredondo, & McDavis, 1992), this takes awareness, knowledge, and skills.

My local partners have also pointed out to me that their societies are hierarchical (Norsworthy & Khuankaew, 2006). If Westerners enter without an understanding of this, we run the risk of reinforcing already existing power dynamics that privilege particular groups and systematically exclude or silence other groups and their needs. This again points to the importance of getting to know the local context, including the social, political, cultural, and historical dimensions and, if possible, partnering with local colleagues who are committed to values of empowerment and justice, in preparation for doing research or practice projects.

Additionally, most work done outside the West is in English, so professionals traveling outside the West rarely have the opportunity to talk directly with people on the ground (unless the person speaks the language) (Norsworthy & Khuankaew, 2006). Therefore, it is important for Western counselors and psychologists to recognize the limits of their understanding of local psychologies, indigenous ways, contexts, issues, concerns, models of healing and "helping," and solutions. This makes a compelling case for arranging, when possible, to interact with local people holding a range of identities, social locations, levels of education, and diverse perspectives in preparation for and in the process of working, researching, and/or doing activism in countries outside our own.

Finally, theories, printed materials (e.g., books, tests, training manuals), research, and other professional literature that come from the West are constructed from a Western paradigm and worldview; thus, they may or may not be relevant, even with adaptation or redesign, for a context outside the West (Leung, 2003; Norsworthy & Khuankaew, 2006). This points to the importance of indigenization of counseling and psychology and suggests that the most useful role for the Western counselor or psychologist may be to offer to collaborate with local people in articulating and valuing their own knowledge, wisdom, and practices, then exploring in what ways (or not) Western perspectives can inform or map on in developing indigenous psychological and counseling paradigms, frameworks, and practices.

I have found that even when I have spent much time in a country or culture, learning the language, studying and reading, engaging in relationships and work, there is much I do not know. Acknowledging my outsider status (Lykes, 2001) and that I am always in learning mode allows me to be open to new information and feedback. Ouyporn and I count on one another to be truthful and frank in our reflections, and we encourage the same within our partnerships with local groups.

During the first few years, I found myself a bit immobilized by my efforts to be aware of the power arrangements and to "unlearn" the ways I had internalized Western privilege. Eventually, through ongoing reflection and conversation with Ouyporn and other local partners, I came to see that as an outsider (U.S. psychologist), I do have things to offer and can make valuable contributions to the work of the group precisely because of my "outsider" position.

For example, forging long-standing relationships with local partners is the key in developing the necessary mutual trust and honesty for engaging in authentic dialogue. These relationships, in combination with an explicit commitment to power sharing, lay the groundwork for ongoing, honest exchanges, where local partners and participants feel free to publicly accept or reject my ideas or input, and for me to publicly question or challenge their ideas. Ongoing reflection about the power dynamics also allows us to deepen our relationships by changing interactions that undermine mutuality and collaboration. Difficult dialogues, especially about power, can pave the way to effective and satisfying partnerships. Finally, when possible, engagement in similar reflexive processes between the groups with whom we work and ourselves can be very valuable in creating "decolonizing" processes, whereby group members take ownership for defining their own issues and concerns based on their cultural and community contexts and assert their ideas and perspectives in the process of developing solutions and action plans.

The learning and growth I have experienced through these border crossings also inform my work as a counselor educator and counseling psychologist back home in the United States. For example, in taking my practicum students to work in a local migrant community setting, we find that the issues for the migrant community greatly resemble those of the refugee community of Burma in Thailand. When students read Ouyporn's and my articles and chapters, they report that they feel more prepared to understand the challenges for people without legal documentation who are often on the receiving end of racism, xenophobia, and "psychological colonization," particularly in these social and political times in the United States. Furthermore, they comment on the importance of taking a power-sharing, collaborative stance, whereby they and their clients view one another as teachers and students in the therapeutic process, particularly since students and clients alike are in a conscientization process. As my colleague, Ouyporn Khuankaew, pointed out, "We all need to approach our cross-national work with a humble mind, acknowledging that we each stand to benefit and be most effective when we work in respectful, power sharing partnerships where everyone's input is valued and respected" (O. Khuankaew, personal communication, August 3, 2005).

REFLECTIONS AND CONCLUSIONS

(LI-FEI WANG)

Through the reflections of these authors on their border-crossing experiences, the limitations and impact of defining the field globally solely from U.S. psychology's point of view were highlighted. Furthermore, the authors emphasized the importance of revisiting the "global" understanding of counseling and counseling psychology as professions extending to countries and cultures worldwide. Throughout the chapter, the value and meaning of internationalization of counseling and counseling psychology were revealed.

The three coauthors who shared their personal "border-crossing" experiences pointed out how important it is to explore and understand the contexts and cultures of the country while developing transnational collaboration. Challenges, successful coping strategies, and suggestions for effective partnerships and collaboration were addressed. Critical factors and events demonstrating the value of creating reciprocal relationships based on mutuality and trust were described. Interestingly, all three authors reveal the ways in which their border-crossing experiences extended and enriched their own knowledge and practice of counseling psychology back in their home countries. Having local cultural informants with whom they had close relationships and regular communication, reflecting and redigesting their border-crossing experiences, and being open and flexible were major strategies for their learning, growth, and success.

In sum, the border-crossing adjustment and learning experience seems to be an ongoing spiral learning process that integrates "in-and-out" as well as "host-and-home" cultural learning processes. These experiences not only stimulate us to learn from the host country and culture but also propel us to redigest our home culture in a deeper way. Through self-reflection, communication, clarification, assimilation, and accommodation processes, we gradually develop our cross-cultural competencies and more deeply understand the importance of developing an interconnected international system of counseling and counseling psychology. Although there are more challenging, confusing, difficult, disappointing, lonely, and even misunderstanding experiences than we anticipate, our border-crossing experiences are more rewarding and fruitful than we could even imagine. We believe that learning from such border-crossing experiences not only increases our competencies in international collaboration but also enhances and deepens our understanding of our professions.

REFERENCES

American Psychological Association. (2003). Multicultural guidelines: Education, research, and practice. *American Psychologist, 58,* 377–402.

American Psychological Association. (2004). *Resolution on culture and gender awareness in international psychology.* Retrieved January 11, 2003, from www.apa.org/international/resolutiongender.html

Arnett, J. J. (2008). The neglected 95%: Why American psychology needs to become less American. *American Psychologist, 63,* 602–614.

Cheung, F. M. (2000). Deconstructing counseling in a cultural context. *The Counseling Psychologist, 28,* 123–132.

Comas-Diaz, L. (1994). An integrative approach. In L. Comas-Diaz & B. Greene (Eds.), *Women of color: Integrating ethnic and gender identities in psychotherapy* (pp. 287–318). New York: Guilford Press.

Freire, P. (1972). *Pedagogy of the oppressed.* New York: Herder & Herder.

Heine, S. J., & Norenzayan, A. (2006). Toward a psychological science for a cultural species. *Perspectives in Psychological Science, 1,* 251–269.

Heppner, P. P. (2006). The benefits and challenges of becoming cross-culturally competent counseling psychologists. *The Counseling Psychologist, 34,* 147–172.

Heppner, P. P. (2008). Expanding the conceptualization and measurement of applied problem solving and coping: From stages to dimensions to the almost forgotten cultural context. *American Psychologist, 63,* 803–816.

Heppner, P. P., Heppner, M. J., Lee, D.-G., Wang, Y.-W., Park, H.-J., & Wang, L.-F. (2006). Development and validation of a collectivistic coping styles inventory. *Journal of Counseling Psychology, 53,* 107–125.

Heppner, P. P., Leong, F. T. L., & Gerstein, L. H. (2008). Counseling within a changing world: Meeting the psychological needs of societies and the world. In W. B. Walsh (Ed.), *Biennial review in counseling psychology* (pp. 231–258). Thousand Oaks, CA: Sage.

Kim, U., Yang, K.-S., & Hwang, K. K. (2006). *Indigenous and cultural psychology.* New York: Springer.

Leong, F. T. L., & Ponterotto, J. G. (2003). A proposal for internationalizing counseling psychology in the United States: Rationale, recommendations, and challenges. *The Counseling Psychologist, 31,* 381–395.

Leung, S. A. (2003). A journey worth traveling: Globalization of counseling psychology. *The Counseling Psychologist, 31,* 412–419.

Leung, S. A. (2007). Returning home and issues related to "reverse culture shock." In H. D. Singaravelu & M. Pope (Eds.), *Handbook on counseling international students* (pp. 137–151). Alexandria, VA: American Counseling Association.

Leung, S. A., & Hoshmand, L. T. (2007). Internationalization and international publishing: Broadening the impact of scholarly work in counseling. *Asian Journal of Counselling, 14,* 141–154.

Lonner, W. J. (1985). Issues in testing and assessment in cross-cultural counseling. *The Counseling Psychologist, 13,* 599–614.

Lykes, M. B. (2001). Activist participatory research and the arts with rural Maya women: Interculturality and situated meaning making. In D. L. Tolman & M. Brydon-Miller (Eds.), *From subjects to subjectivities: A handbook of interpretive and participatory methods* (pp. 183–199). New York: New York University Press.

Marsella, A. J., & Pedersen, P. B. (2004). Internationalizing the counseling psychology curriculum: Toward new values, competencies, and directions. *Counseling Psychology Quarterly, 17,* 413–423.

Moane, G. (1994). A psychological analysis of colonialism in an Irish context. *Irish Journal of Psychology, 15*(2/3), 250–265.

Norsworthy, K. L., & Khuankaew, O. (2004). Women of Burma speak out: Workshops to deconstruct gender-based violence and build systems of peace and justice. *Journal for Specialists in Group Work, 29*(3), 259–283.

Norsworthy, K. L., & Khuankaew, O. (2006). Bringing social justice to international practices of counseling psychology. In R. I. Toporek, L. H. Gerstein, N. A. Fouad, G. Roysircar, & T. Israel (Eds.), *Handbook for social justice in counseling psychology* (pp. 421–441). Thousand Oaks, CA: Sage.

Norsworthy, K. L., & Khuankaew, O. (2008). A new view from women of Thailand on gender, sexuality, and HIV/AIDS. *Feminism and Psychology, 18*(4), 527–536.

Pedersen, P. (1995). *The five stages of culture shock: Critical incidents around the world.* Westport, CT: Greenwood Press.

Pedersen, P. (2003). Culturally biased assumptions in counseling psychology. *The Counseling Psychologist, 31*(4), 396–403.

Pedersen, P. B., & Leong, F. (1997). Counseling in an international context. *The Counseling Psychologist, 25,* 117–122.

Quintana, S. M., Troyano, N., & Taylor, G. (2001). Cultural validity and inherent challenges in quantitative methods for multicultural research. In J. Ponterotto, J. M. Casas, L. A. Suzuki, & C. M. Alexander (Eds.), *Handbook of multicultural counseling* (2nd ed., pp. 604–630). Thousand Oaks, CA: Sage.

Rice, J., & Ballou, M. (2002). *Cultural and gender awareness in international psychology.* Washington, DC: American Psychological Association.

Singer, J. A. (2008, December). The rich bounty of international collaboration. *Psychology International, 19*(5), 10–11.

Sue, D. W. (2003). *Overcoming our racism: The journey to liberation.* San Francisco: Jossey Bass.

Sue, D. W., Arredondo, P., & McDavis, R. (1992). Multicultural counseling competencies and standards: A call to the profession. *Journal of Counseling and Development, 70,* 477–484.

Varenne, H. (2003). On internationalizing counseling psychology: A view from cultural anthropology. *The Counseling Psychologist, 31*(4), 396–403.

Worthington, R. L., Soth-McNett, A. M., & Moreno, M. V. (2007). Multicultural counseling competencies research: A 20-year content analysis. *Journal of Counseling Psychology, 54,* 351–361.

Ægisdóttir, S., Gerstein, L. H., & Çinarbaş, D. C. (2008). Methodological issues in cross-cultural counseling research: Equivalence, bias and translation. *The Counseling Psychologist, 36,* 188–219.

8

Cross-Cultural Collaboration

Developing Cross-Cultural Competencies and Yuan-Fen

跨文化合作：發展跨文化能力與緣分

LI-FEI WANG AND P. PAUL HEPPNER

It was perhaps a serendipitous event in 1989 that began our relationship; but over the last 20 years, both of us have invested a great deal of effort to achieve a productive, meaningful, and exciting cross-cultural collaborative relationship. In many ways, our relationship reflects the Chinese notion of *yuan-fen,* which means that the relationship has been influenced by good deeds from a previous life and continues to have significant meanings and influence today.

Our relationship began when Puncky was invited to Taiwan as a visiting scholar for 2 weeks to present several workshops and lectures. During that trip, we had two primary professional interactions as well as several social interactions; 1 year later Li-fei became a counseling psychology doctoral advisee of Puncky. Subsequently, we worked together for 5 years in the United States. After that, for the next 15 years, we communicated intermittently via snail mail, e-mail, and Skype, as well as visiting each other's home

culture over 10 times collectively (from 2 weeks to 6 months). The frequency of communication has significantly increased over the years as the complexity of our collaboration and power sharing increased. We have collaborated across a full spectrum of professional and social activities, leading to outcomes such as (a) eight coauthored research publications; (b) numerous copresentations, at the American Psychological Association (APA) and other international conferences; (c) the creation and implementation of a 2-week Bidirectional Cross-Cultural Immersion Program (BCCIP) for students/faculty in both our departments; (d) the establishment of a dual-degree master's program for both departments; (e) the development of departmental and university memoranda of agreement to promote cross-national research, faculty and student exchanges, and graduate student training; (f) the linking of our major professional organizations; and (g) most important, a deep, meaningful, and close friendship.

141

The purpose of this chapter is to promote the development of knowledge, awareness, and skills related to cross-cultural collaboration within the counseling profession. We have found that the development of each of our cross-cultural competencies has played a critical role in our cross-cultural collaboration as well as the growth of the mutuality and power-sharing within our relationship. Without all of these elements, we could not have produced the type of collaborative outcomes as mentioned earlier. Therefore, it is our hope that by sharing our personal and professional development and cultural journeys (joys and challenges), as well as our problem-solving strategies, we might stimulate awareness of critical incidents, personal attributes and values, and important learning experiences that not only figured prominently in our cross-cultural journeys and development, but also occurred subsequently in our cross-cultural collaboration. Moreover, we hope that our sharing will be useful for other sojourners as well as help normalize the developmental process and challenges inherent in international collaboration. Finally, we hope that our sharing might give others the courage to take personal and professional risks within their cross-cultural journeys to enhance their cross-cultural sensitivity and even, ultimately, promote international collaboration among our colleagues.

Through our own self-reflection and intensive discussion, we will discuss four critical incidents that affected the growth of our collaborative relationship within each of our individual cross-cultural journeys: (1) positive initial contacts, (2) repeated exposure and significant cross-cultural immersions, (3) integration of the two cultural contexts over time, and (4) actively promoting the acquisition of cross-cultural competencies in others for navigating the two cultural contexts. Each of us will discuss a little about our development, specifically our joys, personal challenges, problem-solving strategies, and cross-cultural discoveries and growth within these critical events and, most important, the ways in which our personal characteristics (e.g., personality attributes, values, coping styles) moderated those experiences. Perhaps the most important factor underlying our productivity has been the development of an evolving and ever-deepening personal and professional cross-cultural relationship throughout our 20-year

friendship. Finally, in the last section of the chapter, we will draw some conclusions based on our experiences about developing meaningful and productive cross-cultural collaborative relationships.

In terms of my background, I (Li-fei Wang) am a Taiwanese middle-class, heterosexual, able-bodied woman from a cultural background with an intermix of Taiwanese, Hakanese, Chinese, Japanese, and native Taiwanese cultures. Obedience, filial piety, loyalty to family, hard work, emphasis on interpersonal harmony, and being calm and quiet are encouraged in my culture. In addition, education is highly valued in both my family and society, which gave me the courage to explore and a willingness to learn more about new cultures. Although I had traveled to 12 countries in my 20s, my understanding of other cultures was on a very surface and even "Taiwanese-ethnocentric" level.

In terms of my background, I (Puncky Heppner) am a white, heterosexual man of German-Russian descent with early socialization within a very predominantly American German and Scandinavian, low-income, rural cultural context in North Dakota and Minnesota. Common values within the intersection of these cultural perspectives included emotional restraint (especially in public), a strong work ethic (especially thoroughness, attention to detail, meeting responsibilities), a strong emphasis on education, love of land (and the family homestead), and a strong sense of fairness and social justice (see McGoldrick, Giordano, & Pearce, 1982). From a diversity perspective, my early life experiences led to a narrow worldview and very little exposure to other cultures; for example, as a high school senior, the only people I knew who had traveled abroad were my uncles who fought in World War II. However, beginning in the 1970s as a graduate student, and especially since the 1990s as a faculty member, many of my experiences within the U.S. multicultural movement led to the development of multicultural awareness, knowledge, and skills (see Sue & Sue, 2008); these multicultural competencies would later provide the foundation for the development of cross-cultural competencies, which further enhanced my multicultural competencies.

POSITIVE INITIAL CONTACTS

Regardless of what we heard about the other's culture, our initial positive contacts based on real interactions (as opposed to our mostly stereotypical impressions) provided us with important knowledge as well as the will to explore more about the other's culture. In retrospect, if our initial contacts at such an early phase of our cross-cultural journeys had been negative, we may likely have experienced too much anxiety in this particular cross-cultural journey, and we might not have even pursued a personal and professional relationship. For example, although I (Li-fei) had traveled to 12 countries, in retrospect, from a cross–cultural developmental perspective, I acted as a "tourist" and had very little knowledge about living in the United States and its people and cultures. For example, my first visit to the United States (1987) as a tourist provided me with very surface but important information. My first impression of Americans was that they were knowledgeable, friendly, respectful, and warmly welcoming of me. The various customs and rules seemed to be clear, simple, and easy to follow. My positive impression stimulated me to consider pursuing a PhD in the United States. When I met Puncky in Taiwan (1989), his kind, respectful, sincere attitudes and scholarly manner attracted me to pursue a PhD under his guidance. At this point, for me, the meaning of cross-cultural experiences was simply different, interesting, and curious.

Similarly, my (Puncky) strongest precontact association with Taiwan was a vague stereotypical sense of "Formosa" as an exotic, beautiful, tropical island. From a cross–cultural developmental perspective, I had lived and worked as a visiting professor in two European countries (Sweden and England) for about 8 months and had traveled as a tourist in another 7 to 8 European countries; these experiences had taught me some important things about the role of culture in affecting human behavior, and I mostly understood that cultural differences did not mean that one culture was inferior to another culture. I had witnessed several incidences of ethnocentric and arrogant American behavior in Europe (e.g., derogatory comments about cultural norms and customs) and felt very embarrassed by the cultural insensitivity. However, I had very few experiences outside of the United States and Europe.

My first real contact with Asian culture, and specifically Taiwanese culture, was a 2-week trip as a visiting scholar (1989), during which I had numerous memorable experiences with Taiwan's counseling professionals, food, customs, values, and numerous historic sites such as temples, monuments, and national parks; I experienced the Taiwanese people as friendly, kind, genuine, generous, inquisitive, respectful, and industrious. At the end of the 2 weeks, I remember feeling astonished with how much I had learned about Taiwan and its people. I felt that I had increased my cultural knowledge of Taiwan tremendously (e.g., 50-fold). In retrospect, starting with a base knowledge level near 0, a 50-fold increase still left me near the bottom of the "unaware" category, but I had no idea of how much of the Taiwanese cultural complexities I did not know, nor have much knowledge of the differences that existed across various Asian cultures.

In sum, both of us had positive initial impressions of the other's culture, and our first real contact in the other's culture was very positive; these positive experiences were major factors that not only encouraged but inspired us to learn more about the other's culture. In retrospect, our initial impressions were based mostly on surface-level knowledge and appreciation of the other's culture as well as the specific people we encountered. Our worldviews were very Eastern and Western, respectively. We were relatively early in our cross–cultural development journeys; our relative lack of accurate cultural information also led us to many incorrect assumptions and conclusions about the other's culture (e.g., assuming that collectivism meant that everyone worked together harmoniously solely for the common good; Americans are liberal and live in a gender-equal society). We were largely unaware of how additional cross-cultural experiences could affect both our personal and professional development.

Nonetheless, despite our relative lack of cultural and country knowledge, we both possessed some personal attributes and values that helped to propel us forward. We both embraced not just an interest and positive impression of the opposite culture but a strong sense of curiosity and willingness to learn about each other's culture; this powerful quest to discover and learn, coupled with our safe and enjoyable initial contacts, were important factors that led us to take additional steps and risks in our cross-cultural journey. We both were able to tolerate quite a bit of ambiguity or uncertainty within the other's culture and brought a sense of humility about being an outsider in the other's culture. We both displayed a functional sense of humor (e.g., making fun of our cultural challenges) that lowered our initial anxieties. We also approached our cultural encounters in terms of seeking mutually beneficial relationships, an egalitarian "give and take" attitude of mutuality as opposed to a one-down, one-up position. In addition, our relatively simple (undifferentiated) but respectful cross-cultural attitudes engendered positive responses from people in the other's culture that not only lowered our initial anxieties but also provided additional opportunities that deepened our understanding of the host culture as well as deepening our relationship. In essence, a number of personal attributes and values not only allowed us to approach the other's culture but also led to positive cultural experiences and to our acquiring more cultural knowledge so that we both wanted to pursue greater contact with the other and his/her culture.

REPEATED EXPOSURE AND SIGNIFICANT CROSS-CULTURAL IMMERSIONS

Immersion in another culture for a significant period of time provides a very different type of experience from the one typically obtained from a short personal or professional trip. I (Li-fei) was an international student in the United States for 5 years (1990–1995). I (Puncky) was a Fulbright Scholar in Taiwan for 6 months (2002). In addition, I had worked closely with and mentored a dozen or so East Asian graduate students across the previous 12 years, which provided additional opportunities to understand Asian cultures prior to the immersion experience. These intense educational and work experiences of varying lengths provided us with very powerful, cross-cultural immersion experiences that

greatly increased our discoveries and knowledge of each other's culture as well as the process of developing meaningful and productive power-sharing, cross-cultural collaborative relationships. These outcomes contributed greatly to our cross-cultural development journeys, but in different ways for each of us. However, initially, we were mostly unaware that along with the many wonderful cross-cultural experiences would come innumerable daily problems in living and relationships; cultural and identity confusion; ineffective and inefficient problem solving; additional time demands, stress, anxiety, frustration, and so on, all of which would take an emotional toll on both of us. These types of experiences have also been depicted in United States racial-identity theories (e.g., Sue & Sue, 2008; Thompson & Carter, 1997) as well as in cultural transition/adaptation models (e.g., Berry & Sam, 1997; Pedersen, 1995). But most important, within the myriad problems and ambiguities, we began to learn not only to solve problems across our different levels of adjustment and cross-cultural knowledge but to do so with a growing cultural sensitivity that deepened the mutuality of our personal relationship, which allowed our power-sharing and professional collaboration to grow.

More specifically, I (Li-fei) was not only an international student in the United States but also the first international student in the counseling psychology program (in the Psychology Department) at the University of Missouri (MU). My pioneering role not only provided me with a unique and special status but also presented a challenging environment that was less sensitive to cross-national and cross-cultural differences. In my 5 years at MU, I experienced a broad array of exciting and challenging cross-cultural experiences, including both positive and negative emotions. Cultural differences caused many ambiguities around cultural norms and thus a great deal of confusion. There were numerous things that needed to be clarified and explained and hunches that needed to be tested. Moreover, my approach and tendency to withdraw created countless challenges. Not knowing how to resolve the challenges (e.g., by asking pointed questions), coupled with language restrictions, created many self-doubts and feelings of inferiority, all of which were in stark contrast to my previous exceptionally successful life as a teacher and counselor in Taiwan. In addition, my advisor (Puncky) and classmates also served as my cultural consultants and informants and significantly helped my understanding of American culture and subcultures. Over time, I acquired a deeper understanding of being a minority and a cross-cultural explorer. Although I cognitively believed in the benefits of new personal and professional explorations, the constant trial and error combined with language restrictions left me feeling overwhelmed, frustrated, and sometimes even like I was emotionally drowning. I gradually recognized that taking risks and not treating every obstacle as a personal fault was a useful strategy.

By sharing my own experiences and listening to people from different cultural backgrounds, I gradually recognized that there was not a superior or inferior culture, but just different cultures, which stimulated my worldview to become broader and more flexible. In addition, by frequently failing to overcome my language restrictions, I was able to more clearly understand the inner psychodynamics of being physically and psychologically challenged, as well as experiencing failure. Most important, from these experiences, I gained an understanding of developing cross-cultural relationships, cross-cultural empathy, and some ideas as to how to resolve cross-cultural challenges.

I (Puncky) had my first significant cultural immersion in Taiwan on my third trip to Taiwan, this time as a Fulbright Fellow. In terms of my cultural-development journey, I had now lived and worked as a psychologist in Ireland and South Africa for a total of 10 months. In these settings, I had learned a great deal about the many faces and lives of oppression, racism, privilege, greed, and different worldviews in both countries as well as the United States.

Living in Taiwan came at an intermediate point in my cross-cultural development. Subsequently, the experience brought many memorable and touching moments through (a) developing and deepening interpersonal relationships with faculty, students, and community members and (b) learning and experiencing Taiwanese and Chinese art, history, philosophy, architecture, religion, geography, food, medicine,

and social customs. At the same time, I experienced, on an almost daily basis, ambiguity and confusion in this Asian culture. Understanding interpersonal dynamics within Taiwanese culture was perhaps the most significant challenge, in large part because of insufficient information about cultural values, norms, and customs and because of the critically important language barrier. Sometimes the language barrier would present major obstacles, for example, with some street vendors; but even when Taiwanese would speak English frequently, often there would be misunderstandings and belabored communication. My lack of knowledge, awareness, and skills inhibited the deepening of both my personal and professional relationships with acquaintances as well as others I interacted with frequently. At times, learning the many ways in which Asian values were operationalized in Taiwanese cultural customs seemed way too hard, and I would retreat physically and psychologically in confusion (e.g., reduce and/or avoid interactions with certain people). In addition, even though many Taiwanese spoke English, I encountered many challenges related to restrictions in my ability to communicate in Mandarin and Taiwanese. This limitation not only inhibited communication but also greatly slowed my discoveries and learning of the culture and interpersonal dynamics and was costly in terms of time and energy. Although these limitations were significant, I was determined to further my learning, and devoted time and energy to understand more of the cultural nuances. To cope with this challenge, I used strategies such as (a) acquiring essential language skills related to fiscal transactions, basic social interactions, and transportation; (b) asking questions of cultural informants; (c) regularly reading English sources of Taiwanese culture–related topics, including local newspapers; (d) regularly visiting local museums, talking to shop owners, and so on; and (e) allowing for additional time in my schedule.

Throughout the highs and lows, I became particularly appreciative of "cultural informants," people who taught me about the culture. Perhaps most important was developing problem-solving strategies such as (a) taking interpersonal risks to explore ambiguities and asking for clarification; (b) practicing cultural norms and customs; (c) being willing to follow Taiwanese interpersonal styles; (d) accepting and interacting within cultural norms rather than assuming Western customs, (e) disclosing my experiences; (f) being able to find humor within the many "trial and error" daily interactions; (g) reminding myself that this was a normal, time-consuming process in a new culture; (h) not taking myself too seriously; (i) being humble in the face of my lack of knowledge; and (j) feeling secure and even "normal" in my insecurity. All of these helped a great deal in helping me to deepen relationships in Taiwan and make meaningful, personal connections.

In sum, our repeated exposure and significant cultural immersions in the other's culture not only allowed us to acquire knowledge of the other's culture but also showed us how to engage in the host's cultural norms and practices. In essence, such knowledge allowed us to gain some cross-cultural competencies and enjoy the other's culture more, which we found deeply gratifying. It is important to highlight that to reach this point, it was very helpful that we both valued and appreciated what we were learning and thus were willing to spend the time and effort to enhance our relationship and process our cultural learning. For example, we engaged in a wide range of activities, such as participating in cultural and social festivals, cooking, spending time with each other's families in their homes, and so on. At the same time, acquiring skills to interact in the other's culture was often tiring and frustrating and sometimes painful. In retrospect, such challenges were more difficult at earlier points in our cross-cultural development. Most important, we each began to acquire more cultural awareness, knowledge, and skills along with enough self-efficacy to approach difficult cultural impasses (e.g., asking the other for specific cultural information, asking for interpersonal feedback, finding ways of supporting each other) and, in doing so, learned more about the other's cultural dynamics, deepened our personal and professional relationship, and acquired ways of successfully interacting in the other's culture. Throughout this part of our cultural journey, our awareness of cultural differences

became clearer; we began to be sensitive to our worldview and to accept that what we understood from our cultural backgrounds did not mean that our "perceived reality" was accurate, best, or right. In essence, we were acquiring cross-cultural competencies, which greatly augmented both our relationship and cross-cultural collaboration.

In retrospect, some problem-solving strategies that seemed most helpful revolved around developing interpersonal competencies in each other's culture. Specifically, this included taking risks to disclose our confusion with cultural ambiguities as well as in our relationship, inquiring about ambiguities we experienced within the other's culture, asking for clarification of our feelings and understanding of the other's culture, and, most important, learning how and why cultural values were related to people's behaviors. For example, although the construct of collectivism seemed clear, the many ways it might be operationalized were ambiguous (e.g., there are different social rules for interacting with strangers, acquaintances, and family members). We also learned to attend more closely to the other's verbal (e.g., when a question was a suggestion; for example, sometimes a polite way of making a suggestion in Taiwan is done by asking a question such as, "Are you hungry?") and nonverbal behaviors (e.g., too much direct eye contact from a white American man can be misinterpreted as challenging by some Taiwanese men) and to learn to interpret them more accurately within the other's cultural context. All of these activities helped us to learn the cultural dynamics that initially were unknown and led to so much confusion. We also both gradually acquired a deeper sense of the joys and challenges of being a racial/ethnic minority in the other's culture after being part of the dominant culture in our home countries for so long. Specifically, we both experienced racial prejudice and discrimination. These experiences provided a range of feelings, such as frustration, hurt, anger, and betrayal, and they raised questions about our identity and even sometimes our desire to continue our cross-cultural journey.

Over time, we also became more comfortable in asking the other to serve as cultural informant, which increased our trust and appreciation of the other as well as the other's culture. Sometimes, in examining similarities and differences about our cultures, we also learned more about our own culture. Through our genuine and respectful interaction, we have learned to treat each other as "real" persons rather than just "authority figures"/"advisors" and "students"/ "advisees." We value and also respect each other deeply. Moreover, the more we shared, the more cultural empathy we acquired, and the more culturally sensitive and appreciative we became. In essence, the more we shared, the more we learned from each other about sensitive topics such as race and privilege, national and international politics, as well as global power arrangements, and our personal and professional worlds. In addition, we also both grew and developed in becoming more sensitive hosts for each other, which deepened our relationship and trust of each other as well.

INTEGRATION OF THE TWO CULTURAL CONTEXTS OVER TIME

Both during and after the immersion experiences, we each began a deeper process of reflecting and synthesizing what we had learned from our cultural experiences, and seeing how that knowledge fit, or did not fit, the cultural context of our home culture. For example, I (Li-fei) quickly discovered that when I applied the West-based psychological knowledge I had learned in graduate school, I could not obtain the same outcome with Taiwanese clients and from my students. Similarly, the interpersonal interaction patterns and problem-solving skills I acquired in the United States did not result in the intended outcomes in Taiwan. Although I felt confident about my PhD training and was aware of many cross-cultural differences, the limited applicability to my home culture was disappointing. Subsequently, I began to re-immerse myself in my home culture and to explore my own cultural heritage in greater depth. The challenges I encountered in this transition back to my home culture surprised me and subsequently led me to new research and practice topics.

For example, through my research and practice in Taiwan, I recognized that the integration of Western

and Eastern counseling experiences could enhance the effectiveness of counseling psychology. For instance, by contrast with emotional regulation theory in the United States, my research suggested that children in Taiwan attended less to emotional awareness and expression; rather, emotion management was much more important to meet cultural expectations around interpersonal harmony. I also started to recognize the importance and power of my cultural roots in psychological healing and the problem-solving process. I found that I learned a great many things about the counseling process in Taiwan from my Taiwanese clients and local practitioners, none of which was discussed in my Western PhD training. I found that I could perform more effective counseling when I was able to smoothly integrate Western counseling philosophies and techniques with the values and customs of my indigenous culture. For instance, education is highly valued in my country. I found that parents would have higher motivation to collaborate with me when I explained the concept of "receiving counseling" as a way to increase their child's learning and academic performance in school. It was also more acceptable to view "receiving counseling" when it was described as a way of "going to class" rather than receiving a "treatment." I also acquired a deeper understanding of diversity within my country, which I previously viewed as a uniform cultural society. I gradually recognized that I was raised in a diverse culture that included Taiwanese, Hakanese, Chinese, Japanese, and native Taiwanese cultures; moreover, through much cultural exploration and reflection, I not only became even more proud of my cultural heritage, but I also became more aware that the diversity of my cultural background is much more complex than I had previously thought. In short, through my research, practice, and personal reflections, I gradually recognized the powerful role that culture plays in human behaviors in Taiwan and the United States and especially in counseling and psychotherapy. This was not taught in my previous training.

A major reflection and integration activity for me (Puncky) spanned 5 to 6 years after the immersion stage (and still continues). An important part of my learning was to share my cross-cultural understanding with Taiwanese faculty and East Asian students in order to seek greater understanding of East Asian culture in general, and particularly Taiwanese culture. These discussions also included asking specific questions to clarify the cultural nuances and what might seem like contradictions within the culture (e.g., after a particular team meeting that did not seem very collectivist, I asked for clarification of the interpersonal dynamics). During this process, I was fortunate to be working closely with several international students from East Asia who were willing to share their cultural knowledge, which greatly augmented my understanding of various aspects of East Asia, specifically Taiwanese and Chinese cultures. In addition, I was also seeking greater understanding of my identity as a white, American, heterosexual, able-bodied man professor on a developmental cross-cultural journey with growing understanding of Taiwanese culture and to a lesser extent a few other cultures in East Asia (e.g., China). Although improving somewhat, my language restrictions still inhibited my interactions and learning about the cultural nuances.

In essence, my reflective cultural activities involved a clearer understanding of the assumptions and values in my culture and Taiwanese culture as well as being able to treasure various aspects of both cultures and even seemingly incompatible cultural customs. With reflection and greater cultural sensitivity and understanding also came greater understanding and empathy for people not only in my current but in past cross-cultural journeys in Taiwan along with my host and primary Asian confidant (Li-fei) as well.

In sum, reflection on our immersion experiences raised awareness of our own personal cultural heritage as well as our professional worldview as counseling psychologists, especially as we returned to work and live in our home cultures. Moreover, in our case, additional exposure and learning of the other's culture allowed us to not only broaden our worldview but also integrate our learning with a clearer understanding of the assumptions and values of each other's culture (and how others may perceive

us in the other's culture) as well as our own. In essence, an important outcome was greater culture-specific knowledge, awareness, and skills in both cultures that then allowed us to be more culturally sensitive and empathetic in our personal and professional relationship with each other and to more successfully navigate across both cultures with different language and customs. The more we learned from our cross-cultural journey and our cross-cultural relationship, the more benefits we experienced and treasured (e.g., understanding the other more fully; deeper, more trusting, disclosing, mutual, power-sharing relationships; more direct and less stressful communications). We also realized that this was a very complicated but highly rewarding process and considerably more complicated than we had ever imagined before. In retrospect, a major outcome of our reflection and integration was the ability to not just establish a relationship but build a deeper and more complex relationship with knowledge about the cultural context of relationships in each culture. More important, our cross-cultural competencies increased within each of us at roughly the same time, which allowed us to deepen our personal relationship and working alliance.

GENERATIVITY: PROMOTING OTHERS' CROSS-CULTURAL COMPETENCIES

As we both engaged in the integration of Eastern and Western cultures, we began to feel a strong sense of generativity to promote cross-cultural awareness, knowledge, and skills in our students and the next generation. We also began to more clearly understand that our professional organizations could greatly benefit through international collaboration. In essence, we began to see beyond our relationship and our professional collaboration and to envision ways in which we could contribute to a larger cross-national movement to not simply promote cross-cultural collaboration, but, more important, to enhance cultural sensitivity and cross-cultural competencies as central and core elements in our profession. In essence, our growing cross-cultural competencies allowed us to see more possibilities to advance cross-national research, training, and practice.

Although we still collaborate on joint research projects and professional presentations, we have also focused on several systemic interventions to promote the development of each other's cross-cultural development, particularly that of the next generation in counseling and educational psychology. For example, in 2005, we created and implemented a 2-week, Bi-Directional Cross-Cultural Immersion Program (BCCIP) for students and faculty in each other's universities. This program provides a 2-week-long intensive opportunity for professional, cultural, and individual exploration for our graduate students and faculty in counseling and educational psychology. The first immersion was in 2005; 13 students and 1 faculty member from National Taiwan Normal University (NTNU) came to the University of Missouri (MU). In 2007, 11 students and 3 faculty members from MU went to NTNU for 2 weeks. In 2008, 19 students and 2 faculty members from NTNU came to MU for 2 weeks. Our evaluations revealed powerful cross-cultural learning for both the visiting and host students on both personal and professional outcomes, such as increasing awareness of self-identity and career exploration as well as cross-cultural competencies (Chiao, Allen, He, Kanagui, & Garriott, 2008; Chien et al., 2008; Huang, Chao, Chou, Chang, & Chu, 2008; Wang, 2008).

In the fall of 2007, we also began to implement a dual-degree master's program for both departments. This program allows master's students from one department to study at the other's department for 1 year and obtain master's degrees from both institutions in 3 years. Initial informal feedback from students suggests that this program also promotes greater cross-cultural understanding on both personal and professional levels. Likewise, other systemic interventions led to (a) the development of departmental and university memoranda of agreement to promote cross-national faculty research (b) a Summer Internship Program for doctoral students to practice psychotherapy in Taiwanese university counseling centers, (c) a coordinated bachelor's-master's degree program, as well as (d) formal linkage of communication through the Web sites of our major professional organizations (i.e., Division 17 of APA and Taiwan Guidance and Counseling Association). The outcomes from these new programs have been deeply rewarding, and the process has also served to further deepen our personal and professional relationships.

It is important to note that these programs, which aimed at enhancing students' cross-cultural competencies, challenged us pedagogically. For example, we learned that our lectures on cross-cultural issues were well received by students but also fell short of our learning goals (e.g., students did not seem to be able to understand how specific cultural values affected culturally appropriate actions). Conversely, experiential teaching methods, especially those that facilitated even short immersion experiences between Taiwanese and U.S. students resulted in not only greater cross-cultural awareness but the initial development of cross-cultural relationships. We also learned that student's cross-cultural experiences seemed to be enhanced by having regular opportunities to process their experiences, either by journal writing or small group discussions and reflections. Our experiences led us to conceptualize cross-cultural learning within a developmental framework, and thus students with varying levels of cross-cultural experiences would need different types of pedagogical experiences to promote different students' cross-cultural development.

In addition, developing cross-cultural learning experiences across two countries necessitated not only program-development skills but also change-agent and system-level skills within our respective training programs, departments, and universities: for example, developing relationships with administrators, identifying resources and allies, conceptualizing and writing formal binding agreements between our universities. Our experience has been that such system-level changes involve more people (e.g., upper-level university administrators such as presidents, provosts, and deans as well as department chairs, faculty, and students). Consequently, these types of projects require sustained commitment to achieve satisfactory agreement among the various stakeholders. In addition, these cross-national programs required additional cross-cultural competencies, such as cross-cultural communication skills with university administrators from two cultures (culture-bridging skills). In addition, we have found it essential to be aware of our differential roles and power as we have interacted with others in each university and country; for example, sometimes the guest can say delicate things to upper-level administrators in a way that the host can not say (e.g., ask very direct questions about delicate topics such as the university's priorities and commitments).

Other cross-cultural competencies pertain to a broad range of cross-cultural problem-solving skills (as specified earlier in this chapter) as a multicultural team to resolve conflicts or impasses. Sometimes successful efforts in these activities are best characterized by a great deal of personal and professional trust, the type of trust that comes only after many experiences of being on the same team together. It involves not only knowing the other person's skills but also their reliability to follow through and trusting their value of and commitment for cross-cultural collaboration. It also involves a mutual "give and take," professionally and personally. All of these dynamics within a cross-cultural context underscores the importance of direct communication between us (Li-fei and Puncky), within us, mutual comfort and trust with each other, deep levels of sharing, and knowing each other's personality well enough to be able to support each other when we encounter difficult problems. In essence, these problem-solving activities are reflected in our communication patterns, and as with any team, the communication within the team directly affects our ability to reach our goals.

CONCLUSION

When we reflect on the many steps in our 20 years of cross-cultural collaboration, we are surprised about how many wonderful memories and outcomes have changed our personal and professional lives. We are also struck with how many challenges we went through and how lucky that we could be a team to resolve these challenges. In essence, it seems

so long ago since we first met. There have been many twists and turns in the development both of our personal and professional relationship and cross-cultural competencies in general. We end this chapter with some observations and conclusions about cross-cultural collaboration that we have drawn from our many experiences over the last 20 years that might be helpful to others who choose to pursue similar goals.

1. *Positive Initial Contacts.* Our initial positive contacts with the other's culture were critically important in not only lowering our anxieties but also enhancing our desire to learn more about the other's culture, both of which positively influenced us to continue a deeper exploration of the other's culture. Several personal attributes (e.g., openness, respect) and positive cultural experiences (e.g., being well received in the host culture) also played major roles to propel us forward in our cross-cultural journey. We found that a willingness to respect and learn about the host culture is a crucial attitude that promotes positive initial contacts. Because we also had inaccurate information about the other's culture, our initial attitudes also played an important role to examine and challenge various stereotypes that we held. Developing a positive relationship in one's first contact can create possibilities for future learning and collaboration.

2. *Building a Trusting, Mutually Beneficial, and Appreciative Relationship (with good yuan-fen).* Perhaps the most important factor underlying our relationship and productivity is our trust in each other and our relationship, which has been an evolving and ever deepening, power-sharing personal and professional cross-cultural relationship. It is important to note that our relationship and subsequent collaboration would most likely have been different if we only had a professional or personal relationship. That is, having both a personal and professional relationship was cumulative and provided a stronger and more holistic working alliance in our cross-cultural collaboration. In essence, the multi-layered relationship resulted in a broader array of

interactions that deepened our relationship and promoted more effective interactions as well as enhanced the longevity of collaboration. Without the stability and support of both a strong personal and a strong professional relationship, we doubt whether we would have been able to develop our existing levels of cross-cultural competence or be as successful in our professional pursuits. Because cross-cultural collaboration is built on a team of two or more people, a very important element is identifying and finding a partner with whom you can develop a good cross-cultural relationship, both on a personal and on a professional level. It is not possible for us to identify ideal characteristics to look for in a partner; as in developing personal or professional relationships in one's own culture, the ideal partner characteristics will differ across individuals. Moreover, we found the mutual respect, appreciation, power-sharing, and investment in a long-term relationship (known as good yuan-fen in Chinese culture) to be an important interpersonal factor that contributed to the development of the relationship. More specifically, within Chinese culture, relationships with good yuan-fen are those that by luck contain a special bonding characteristic, kinship, or chemistry that promotes the development of a good relationship. In essence, we not only respect each other but also appreciate the gifts that each of us brings to the relationship and feel lucky to be a part of this relationship.

We want to emphasize that a personal and professional relationship in one's own culture will most likely be different from a personal and professional relationship across two cultures because of the inherent cultural differences in establishing and maintaining personal and professional relationships. In our relationship, we found that it was essential to trust and even treasure the other's cultural perspective. We have experienced three different types of trust: (a) trust that you can be a good partner, (b) trust that your partner can be relied on, and (c) trust that you can collaborate in a mutually beneficial relationship and resolve challenges as a team. It is important to recognize that trust is not a given but is built over time and across many different experiences. When problems arise, sharing your thoughts, feelings, and concerns can be risky but also very helpful in developing a functional collaborative relationship.

3. Increasing Both of Our Cultural Competencies. Our process of cross-cultural collaboration has been greatly influenced by our level of multicultural and cross-cultural competence (knowledge, awareness, and skills), specifically, our culture-specific competence within the other's culture and our ability to resolve a myriad of challenges as a team of equal partners. We found that increasing our cross-cultural competencies was a bidirectional process. For us, it was important to not only increase levels of cultural competence in the other's culture, but also in our own culture. The more we learned about the other's culture, we then often redigested and reexplored our own cultural heritage (which seems to us as establishing a deeper cultural identity), which also resulted in a deeper understanding of both cultures. We also found that the more we appreciated and accepted our own culture, the more comfortable and accepting we became with ourselves, and subsequently, the more we became open to experience and value the host's culture. More important, these experiences have later been part of important research topics in our cross-cultural collaboration.

4. Learning by Experiencing. In essence, acquiring cross-cultural competencies necessitates a proactive, planful approach, as well as an active, reflective, and integrative process. From our experience, significant and repeated exposure and immersions into the host culture for a significant period of time are necessary in acquiring cross-cultural competencies (as well as deepening multicultural competencies). Although traveling as a tourist was a useful learning process, we learned much more about the other's culture when we studied or worked in that cultural context. The normal tasks of living were excellent learning opportunities, as were the daily interactions with students and colleagues. However, just living in another culture in and of itself is not sufficient to enhance cross-cultural competence. We found that it was essential to reflect on the cultural context (e.g., values, norms) and continually seek to learn more of the complexities and nuances of the host culture. Being tolerant and open-minded instead of being judgmental and ethnocentric seem to be useful attitudes. In addition, we found that it was important to actively seek multiple-experiential cross-cultural experiences to learn and develop cross-cultural competencies. More experiential cultural experiences provided more learning opportunities to acquire cross-cultural competencies.

More important, we found that immersing in the host culture for a significant period of time was often very challenging and at times an overwhelming process. We would like to highlight that what may feel like an "up and down" process is a normal developmental process. There are so many things to learn about another culture, and it is typical and normal to make mistakes. It is similar to learning other complex tasks; there is always trial and error. Although such a process may be normative, it does not mean that it does not hurt to "fall down and scrape one's knees" during the learning process. Trust us, it does!

In short, it seems to us that acquiring cross-cultural competencies is a learning process that involves many ambiguities and many joyous moments as well as challenges and frustrations. Although this process is normal, it is sometimes not easy. Over time, we have found it most helpful to accept and learn from all aspects of this part of our cultural journey.

5. *Problem-Solving Attitudes and Approach*. A critical process that greatly affected our learning was how we coped with the ambiguities, stress, and challenges we encountered in our cross-cultural relationship and in the host's culture. Most important, we found that being willing to approach and clarify the ambiguities and challenges has been very important in our learning, but it also requires courage, risk taking, and energy. We found that it was helpful to consult with the other to more clearly understand the cultural context and nuances, as well as treating difficulties as problems that need to be discussed and hopefully resolved. Conversely, we found that a

common reaction was to withdraw or to be critical of either the host's or one's own culture; these reactions did not help us much in our cross-cultural development over time. Similarly, we found that blaming ourselves for the difficulties—as if they were caused by a personal fault—did not help. Although withdrawal and self- and/or other-blame are all normal reactions, we encourage others to be gentle with themselves and acknowledge the trial-and-error process as well as the positive things that they are doing.

6. *Multiple Benefits in Preparing the Next Generation*. From our experiences when we began to teach our students about cross-cultural competencies in the preparatory seminar as well as the BCCIP immersion itself, we ourselves also acquired additional cross-cultural competencies. For example, our experiences led us to conceptualize the process of cross-cultural learning more clearly within a developmental and cultural context, and thus we could then develop learning strategies based on students' developmental levels and cultural knowledge. In doing so, we became more clearly aware of the specific knowledge, awareness, and skills needed to navigate these two specific cultures, such as emphasizing the consequences of the cultural context in human behavior in that culture, the complexities within oneself and the other in cross-cultural communication, and knowledge about the cross-cultural journey process.

7. *Serving a Bridging Role as a Change Agent*. It has been necessary to serve as a bridge as we tried to contribute to a larger cross-national collaborative movement. Similarly, as we began to work with our colleagues in our universities and professional organizations, we also were challenged to extend our cross-cultural competencies related to being change agents in a broader system. In essence, we began to understand our roles as change agents in terms of bridging two cultures, not only negotiating differences between two universities situated in two cultures but also implementing the cultural context within our home institutions to facilitate the

development of appropriate cross-cultural actions in developing our partnerships.

8. Institutional Support. Without institutional support, we could not provide various cross-cultural collaborative training programs (e.g., BCCIP, dual-degree master's programs) for our students. We have learned that institutional vision, support, and encouragement have been essential to pursue and continue our cross-cultural journey. From our experience, working closely with university leaders with international experience and vision has been essential and foundational in creating systemic changes that we as faculty could not have done alone without their guidance and support. In addition, we have recognized that our differential roles (e.g., guest) can be incredibly powerful to obtain institution support as we have interacted with others in each university and country. Thus, we found that our collaboration is an integration of Western and Eastern cultures into one effective and efficacious working team.

In conclusion, there have been many benefits from our cross-cultural collaboration, from scholarly products (publications and presentations), the development of international educational programs for students and faculty, and the development of cross-cultural competencies (awareness, knowledge, and skills). Moreover, our personal and professional lives have been greatly enriched by our cross-cultural journey and cross-cultural collaboration. That is, our cross-cultural journey and collaboration have changed our worldview, specifically how we view ourselves, the other, and what our profession might become to prepare the next generation to work and live in a global society. Our cross-cultural journey has resulted in a much deeper understanding of the multifaceted role of culture. We also found that such experiences were relevant for the

development of a broader, global counseling psychology. Thus, we have worked together to build a conducive cross-cultural learning environment for the next generation of counseling psychologists.

At the heart of our journey have been our personal and professional relationship and the way our relationship has evolved and deepened in the context of our cultural dances in both countries, often being uncertain of everything going on around us, what the next steps might or would be, and where we might end up. The cultural dances have also involved a give-and-take, a mutual and reciprocal process of developing an equalitarian relationship across different cultures, one where we are on equal ground with mutual respect and appreciation for each other's culture and intuition. Perhaps it was a serendipitous event, or perhaps it was a good yuan-fen, the good luck by which people with the right chemistry are brought together for some reason. We hope that others will find something meaningful or educational in learning about our cross-cultural journey and collaboration. And we hope that good yuan-fen will be with others on their cross-cultural journey and collaboration and change both their personal and professional lives along the way.

REFERENCES

Berry, J. W., & Sam, D. (1997). Acculturation and adaptation. In J. W. Berry, M. H. Segall, & C. Kagitcibasi (Eds.), *Handbook of cross-cultural psychology: Vol. 3. Social behavior and applications* (pp. 291–326). Boston: Allyn & Bacon.

Chiao, H., Allen, G. E. K., He, Y., Kanagui, M., & Garriott, P. O. (2008, August). Benefits of the BCCIP to host students. In P. P. Heppner & L.-F. Wang (Chairs), *Multiple benefits of a bidirectional cross-cultural immersion program.* Symposium conducted at the 2008 annual American Psychological Association Convention, Boston.

Authors' Note: An earlier version of this chapter was presented in Wang, L. & Heppner, P. P. (2007, August), Reciprocity in Developing Productive and Meaningful Cross-Cultural Relationships. In S. A. Leung & P. Chen (Cochairs), *International Counseling Psychology: Collaboration in a Flat World.* Symposium conducted at the 2007 Annual Meeting of the American Psychological Association, San Francisco, CA. We sincerely thank Yi-Jiun Lin and Catherine Hsieh for their helpful comments on an earlier version of this chapter.

Chien, W., Chou, L., Lai, P., Lee, Y., Chen, C., Ting, S., et al. (2008, August). The benefits and challenges of being the BCCIP's visitors. In P. P. Heppner & L. Wang (Chair), *The multiple benefits of a bidirectional cross-cultural immersion program.* Symposium conducted at the 2008 meeting of the American Psychological Association, Boston, MA.

Huang, P., Chao, J., Chou, Y., Chang, Y., & Chu, S. (2008, August). The cross-cultural experience and competent development of the BCCIP. In P. P. Heppner & L. Wang (Chair), *The multiple benefits of a bidirectional cross-cultural immersion program.* Symposium conducted at the 2008 meeting of the American Psychological Association, Boston, MA.

McGoldrick, M., Giordano, J., & Pearce, J. K. (Eds.). (1982). *Ethnicity and family therapy.* New York: Guilford Press.

Pedersen, P. (1995). *The five stages of cultural shock: Critical incidents around the world.* Westport, CT: Greenwood Press.

Sue, D. W., & Sue, D. (2008). *Counseling the culturally diverse: Theory and practice* (5th ed.). Hoboken, NJ: Wiley.

Thompson, C. E., & Carter, R. T. (1997). *Racial identity theory: Applications to individual, group, and organizational interventions.* Mahwah, NJ: Lawrence Erlbaum.

Wang, L. (2008, March). The benefit and challenge of a Bidirectional Cross-Cultural Immersion Program: A Taiwan-USA example. In C. Duan & C. Juntunen, *Training implication of the internationalization movement in counseling psychology.* Symposium conducted at the 2008 International Counseling Psychology Conference, Chicago.

PART II

The Counseling Profession Around the World

EAST ASIA

9

The Role of Japanese Culture in Psychological Health

Implications for Counseling and Clinical Psychology

精神的健康に日本文化の果たす役割：カウンセリング・臨床心理学への影響

MAKIKO KASAI

Japan consists of four large islands (Hokkaido, Honshu, Shikoku, and Kyushu) and more than 1,000 lesser, adjacent islands. About 70% to 80% of the country is forested, mountainous, and unsuitable for agricultural, industrial, or residential use, which has resulted in a high population density in the habitable zones located mainly in coastal areas. Japan is one of the most densely populated countries in the world and has the world's 10th largest population with about 128 million people in 2008. The capital city of Tokyo and several surrounding prefectures represent the largest metropolitan area in the world with more than 30 million residents. For the most part, Japanese society is linguistically and culturally homogeneous with small populations of foreign workers. Japan's history has been characterized by openness to influences from the outside world followed by long periods of isolation. A major economic power, Japan has the world's second largest economy as assessed by nominal Gross

Domestic Product (GDP) (Central Intelligence Agency, 2007). It is also the world's fourth largest exporter and sixth largest importer and a world leader in technology and machinery.

This chapter begins with a discussion of important cultural beliefs that inform concepts of self in Japan. It is followed by a discussion of psychological problems in Japan, approaches to counseling in Japan, and a discussion of contemporary issues in clinical and counseling psychology.

THE CULTURAL BACKGROUND OF JAPAN

Religions and Beliefs

Estimates indicate that 84% to 96% of Japanese people identify themselves as Shintoist or Buddhist, with a large number of believers endorsing the syncretism of both religions (U.S. Department of State, 2006). Taoism and Confucianism from China have also influenced Japanese beliefs and customs.

Japan has traditionally been identified as a Buddhist country. Buddhism first arrived in Japan in the sixth century from the southern part of Korea. Buddhism has been influential vis-à-vis the thoughts, senses, and behaviors of the Japanese people. Buddhism looks to convert worldly desires to enlightenment by making one take note of causalities with respect to worldly desires.

Another dominant Japanese religious belief is Shinto, the native religion of Japan, which was once its state religion. It is polytheistic and involves the worship of *kami* (spiritual essence), which is sometimes translated *god,* though perhaps *soul* or *spirit* would be more accurate; an even better translation would actually be *the sacred* (Sugimoto, 2003). Some kami are local and can be regarded as the spiritual being/spirit or genius of a particular place, but others represent major natural objects and processes (e.g., Amaterasu, the Sun goddess, or Mount Fuji). Shinto is an animistic belief system. Shinto's kami are collectively called *yaoyorozu no kami,* an expression literally meaning *8 million kami* but interpreted as meaning *myriad.* After World War II, Shinto ceased to be Japan's state religion, although it is still considered the native religion of Japan.

Whereas liberalism and individualism became the dominant philosophies that delineate concepts related to the self and society in Western Europe and North America, Confucianism became the dominant moral-political philosophy of Japan (Kim, 1994). Confucianism promotes collective welfare and harmony as its ultimate goal. Individuals are thought to be embedded and situated in particular roles and positions and are encouraged to put other people's and the group's interests before their own. The distinction between liberalism and Confucianism can be seen in the differences between individualism and collectivism.

Collectivism

Japan is typically described as a collectivistic country. Collectivism is often seen in the undifferentiated boundaries between self and others, which are porous among in-group members and allow thoughts, ideas, and emotions to flow freely (Kim, 1994). Markus and Kitayama (1991) described this relationship as one in which there is a willingness and ability to think about and feel what others are thinking and feeling, to absorb this information without being told, and to help others satisfy their wishes and realize their goals. Collectivism's qualities have been discussed in relation to the concept of *amae* (dependence) in Japanese culture (Doi, 1973/1981), which is another common concept used to describe the Japanese character.

Apart from the predominance of collectivism at the cultural level, there are other dimensions that differentiate collectivistic cultures from each other. For example, Kashima et al. (1995) showed that the dimension that distinguishes Koreans from Japanese is *relatedness.* Although both Korean and Japanese self-construals may have been relational in the past, World War II may have served as a watershed in affecting subsequent cultural changes in the two countries. After the war, the Japanese abandoned the traditional values inherent in interpersonal obligations, as they were seen as being too closely linked to the ultranationalism of the prewar government (Doi, 1973/1981). Japanese people today, especially those of the younger generation, may have disavowed the relational self. At the same time, those in their 30s and 40s seem to evince this loss of relatedness through retrospective nostalgia, and the recent Korean cultural-boom phenomenon (e.g., Korean TV series and movies) might reflect the longing for these emotional bonds.

Although the influence of traditional Japanese values has declined with modernization, some researchers agree that two important features of the relationship patterns still persist in Japan: devotion and indulgence (Azuma, 1986; Kim, 1994). According to Azuma (1986), when a Japanese child is born, the mother remains close to the child to make the child feel secure, to minimize the boundary between herself and the child, and to meet all the child's needs, even if that means a tremendous sacrifice on her own part. Japanese caregivers often say, "We can understand you, without you even saying anything," and they encourage children to understand not their own but rather others' intentions, emotions, and motivations and to be aware of others' expectations of them (Lewis, 1995).

This type of socialization creates, as previously mentioned, the bond of amae. Children's strong dependency needs, both emotional and existential, are satisfied by their mothers' indulgent devotion. As a child grows, he or she senses that it is through the mother that one obtains gratification, security, and love. As the child matures, he or she is motivated to maintain a close relationship with the mother and does so by pleasing the mother and behaving according to her wishes. The fear of potential separation from the mother is sometimes used to discipline the child (Azuma, 1986), and psychological and physical distance is often used by mothers to shape or correct children's behavior. By comparison, in the United States the punishment for children is to be "grounded," restricting them from leaving their bedrooms or houses. In Japan, the punishment might involve locking children out of the home (Vogel & Vogel, 1961). This physical distancing symbolizes the psychological separation that is considered traumatic to Japanese children (Kim, 1994).

This close mother-child relationship has been intensified by the cultural idealization of motherhood, which Ohinata (2002) calls "the motherhood myth." Ohinata (2000) writes that Japanese society glorifies motherhood while simultaneously exploiting it. Ohinata (2002) also points out that the motherhood myth has led people to believe that maternal love is sublime and that only women possess the innate ability to nurture children. In addition, many people in Japan believe that a mother should raise her child by herself for at least the first 3 years of the child's life. This belief pressures women to put their careers "on hold" when their children are born, and mothers are often blamed when their children later present problematic behavior. This also discourages women from fulfilling their potential in domains other than child-rearing and domestic work. Ohinata suspects that the continuing social pressure for Japanese women to choose either family or

career (but not both) has been one of the factors that has enhanced the current trend of late marriage among women and a low birth rate. According to a survey conducted in 2007 by the Ministry of Internal Affairs and Communications, the proportion of people, both male and female, who disagree that "a wife should stay at home" exceeded 50% for the first time.

Ego Development

In the field of Japanese clinical psychology, Hayao Kawai theorized a model of Japanese ego development and relationships based on Japanese mythology and Jungian psychology. He proposed that mythology is a deep cultural entity that works to formulate the very foundation of a nation and the existential substructure of a people (Kawai, 1986). He concluded that Japanese society is based on matriarchal consciousness.

Based on his analysis of Western myths, the Jungian analyst Erich Neumann (1954) proposed that the European ego attains its independence by slaying its parents, and the ego regains a relation with the world through the mediation of a woman. By comparison with Western patriarchal consciousness, matriarchal consciousness is explained in terms of "inclusion": It wraps up and unifies everything, regardless of its goodness or badness, and assumes that everything has absolute equality (Kawai, 1976/1994). In Japan, Kannon, who accepts everything as it is, is the positive Great Mother. Japanese religious belief is matriarchal and views mother-child unification as its foundation. Matriarchal religion accepts and saves everything, and everything is unified: There is no distinction between the subject and the object, human and nature, or good and bad. Ethics based on matriarchal principles value absolute equality among the children on mothers' laps. Everything is equal in a matriarchal society, and maintaining this equality is of the utmost importance. In contrast, patriarchal principles place emphasis on people's abilities and potential—that is, on individual differences and individual needs, satisfaction, and growth.

Until Western democracy and egalitarianism were introduced to Japan, inequality was accepted in real life, and Japanese people resigned themselves to their own fate or understood it as an element of their social position. The social order in Japan consists of positions and statuses that are based on age, career years, and so on; these are called *seniority systems* (Nakane, 1967), and they cannot be changed by the individual. When Western principles came to Japan, Japanese culture struggled to integrate Western individualism into its matriarchal thinking, and this shift may have contributed to personal and social problems in Japan.

PSYCHOLOGICAL PROBLEMS IN JAPAN

In recent years, various psychological problems of Japanese children and adolescents have increased, including nonattendance at school (*futoukou*), social withdrawal (*hikikomori*), bullying (*ijime*), and interpersonal relationship problems. Depression among adults has also increased. A culturally distinctive phobia, *taijin kyofusho*, also exists and resembles in some ways the social phobia detailed in the American Psychiatric Association (APA), *Diagnostic and Statistical Manual of Mental Disorders*, fourth edition (*DSM-IV*; 1994). People with these psychological problems, as well as the parents of afflicted children, have increasingly asked psychologists and psychiatrists for help.

Nonattendance at School

Nonattendance at school refers to a pattern of behavior in which a child does not attend school and stays mainly at home, often with his or her parents' knowledge (Lang, 1982). At first, the term *school refusal* was used to describe this problem. The term was gradually replaced with *school phobia*, which implies an explanatory concept for the behavior; it is also distinguished from truancy, whereby the child also stays away from home when absent from school (Kameguchi & Murphy-Shigematsu, 2001). Although the problem of school refusal in Japan dates back to the 1950s, the number of children

who refuse to go to school in the absence of specific physical reasons has increased dramatically. More than 127,000 cases were reported in 1998 (Ministry of Education, Culture, Sports, Science and Technology–Japan, 2007), the year in which the Ministry of Education officially started to use the term *nonattendance at school* (futoukou) for this problem. Most children involved are described as "good children" who want to go to school but for some reason cannot, to the great dismay of both their parents and themselves. Many psychologists have blamed schools or the education system for contributing to problems related to conformity, extreme pressure, or exclusively exam-oriented curricula. In response, the education system has changed to become more flexible and contain fewer curricula. The problem of nonattendance, however, has not decreased. Earlier reports on school refusal focused on a student's desire to escape from a bad situation at school, such as bullying; later, that pressure seemed to be replaced by pressures related to more general human relations problems (Ishida & Takei, 1987). This trend toward bullying has resurged in recent years, and there have been severe bullying cases that resulted in suicide or murder. In 2006, 4,688 children cited bullying as their reason for nonattendance (Ministry of Education, Culture, Sports, Science and Technology-Japan, 2007).

Some psychologists blame family and societal perspectives (Kawai, 1976/1994), such as changes in the structure of the Japanese family. Companies have removed men from the emotional and instrumental activities of their homes and families by demanding men's extreme loyalty and dedication to the workplace (Sugimoto, 2003). Men's preoccupation with work and their concomitant absence from the home has given rise to what have been aptly described as "fatherless families" (Wagatsuma, 1977). The resulting separation and imbalance in the family dynamics has been referred to as a pathology of the maternal society of Japan (Kawai, 1976/1994). As Kameguchi and Murphy-Shigematsu (2001) mentioned, this "mother-centered family" has long been blamed by some psychologists as a major contributor to school nonattendance. According to

Doi (1973/1981, 1988), the contemporary mother-child relationship has changed in such a way that many mothers are not capable of supplying security to their children or adequately addressing the dependency needs of their children. These mothers have ambivalence concerning their roles as mothers. In some cases, anxiety, depression, feelings of inadequacy, and a lack of self-identity significantly impair the child-rearing abilities of mothers whose children will not attend school.

Reports of clinical cases of children with disorders such as separation anxiety (Imai, 1998; Kawanaka, 1998) suggest that such children are trapped between their desire to separate and a need to remain with their mothers. The mothers in such families are overprotective and overinvolved and interfere in their children's lives. These children do not progressively develop the ability to separate psychologically, and when they reach the age at which they should be more autonomous, they are unable to engage in age-appropriate identity tasks. As a result, children simultaneously wish to rebel against their mothers' overinvolvement, while wanting to be indulged by their mothers (amae). By refusing to go to school, children use their strongest weapon against all-powerful and controlling mothers whose identities are defined by their children's academic performance. As the children become stronger, their actions may escalate to more overtly aggressive behavior (Kawai, 1986) and can lead to domestic violence from children against their mothers (Kasai, 1998; Kawai, 1986).

Freeters, NEETs, and Hikikomori

The term *freeter* refers to an adolescent or young adult who only works part-time and switches jobs freely. In contrast, adolescents or young adults who are not in employment, education, or training (NEETs) are not participating in any of the typical activities of young adulthood. Conflicts about not wanting to grow up and be independent may contribute to the growing number of NEETs and freeters. The increase of NEETs and freeters may also be related to Japanese family dynamics. Fathers in matriarchal societies become "understanding fathers," which means that they cannot stand up to their children or offer their own judgments, or they leave these matters to others. Some Japanese fathers seem to have only a weak sense of their role as fathers. Adolescents who cannot reject their child-like bonds with their mothers are called "eternal boys," as it seems that they cannot become adults. They cannot adjust to adult society because they live in a fantasy world—they believe that they have unique potentials and it is not easy for them to find a perfect place. They also believe that their maladjustments are caused by the negative aspects of society, that they do not want to be a part of society, and that they are not at fault for their own problems. They do not want to have full-time jobs, nor do they want any kind of full-time commitment (Japanese Institute for Labor Policy and Training, 2008).

In more severe cases, individuals exhibit social withdrawal (hikikomori), shut themselves in their rooms, and do not have any contact with people other than family members for several years (Zielenziger, 2006). In 2001, the Ministry of Health, Labor and Welfare of Japan defined *hikikomori* as "socially withdrawn at home for more than 6 months without going to work or school, and have no close interpersonal relationship other than with their family members." There are no reliable statistics regarding hikikomori cases, but it is estimated that there are between a half million and 1 million afflicted individuals across Japan. Hikikomori has also been cited as contributing to several murders, so it has become one of the more urgent problems to solve.

The behavior of some freeters, NEETs, and hikikomori may be related to the changing values of society, especially the value of work. Ishii-Kuntz (1989) analyzed data collected from the Public Opinion Survey on Attitudes Toward Society, conducted by the prime minister's office in 1986, which found that younger males had the most individualistic attitudes of all males, while older males had substantially stronger collectivistic attitudes and values. The analysis of data collected annually since 1971 shows a consistent decrease in collectivistic values and an increase in individualistic values. Many Japanese youths question the reward system of the mainstream, collectivistic culture. As a result, Japanese work managers view many youths with disdain as the youths are often preoccupied with individual rewards without bearing the concomitant obligations of individual sacrifice and the work ethic, which characterized an earlier generation.

In keeping with this new, individualistic trend, many companies have adopted principles based on individual capacities and abolished the lifetime employment system, which was the typical system for many Japanese companies. As a result, many workers have the option of changing jobs, but they also face the risk of being laid off. Work values have changed, and some youth do not look for full-time work; rather, they choose to stay in easy, part-time jobs. People who have competencies are more likely to be promoted to higher positions, and people who stay in a permanent, part-time position won't earn enough money to support themselves. This causes a disparity in economic power, which is a dominant social problem in Japan today.

Taijin Kyofusho

Taijin kyofusho refers to a culturally distinctive phobia in Japan, and in some ways, it resembles social phobia in the *DSM-IV* (APA, 1994). This syndrome refers to an individual's intense fear that his or her body, its parts, or its functions will embarrass the owner and either displease or be offensive to other people in terms of appearance, odor, body language, facial expressions, or movement. This syndrome is included in the official Japanese diagnostic system for mental disorders, and it involves sensing others' thoughts and desires. If a person is afflicted and becomes very sensitive, he or she may not be able to behave or perform at all. Taijin kyofusho can be influenced by the "group-oriented principle." According to Neumann (1954), the ego of Western culture is established after cutting the bonds with the mother and father, but the Japanese ego establishment process follows a path in which an individual emphasizes the balance and stability of the field as a whole. People with taijin kyofusho have difficulty maintaining relationships with others

and experience the conflict of wanting to establish their own individuality in a society based on the group-oriented principle (Kawai, 1988/1992).

In Western countries, people's behaviors are controlled through verbal contact; in Japan, however, people's behaviors are often controlled through nonverbal feelings of shame, and shaming may be used by parents to control children's behavior. The symptoms of taijin kyofusho resemble overresponsive, nonverbal reactions to experiencing shame. Taijin kyofusho has traditionally been a problem experienced by adolescents because it is a problem associated with ego establishment. Since the numbers of freeters and NEETs have increased in Japan, there are now more number of hikikomori than before. Japanese people have typically been afraid of how others see and think about them, and so the expectations of others become their standard for behavior. Inasmuch as one does not have a confident and autonomous self-identity, one will be afraid of such judgments; this is especially true of adolescents and people who have interpersonal difficulties.

Ijime (School Bullying)

Many features of school bullying are, on the face of it, similar across different countries (Kanetsuna, Smith, & Morita, 2006). Major types of bullying include physical, verbal, shunning or social exclusion, and "indirect" forms (i.e., not face-to-face), such as sending nasty notes and rumor spreading. *Ijime* is the Japanese term most similar to bullying and has been the subject of a research tradition spanning 20 years (Morita, Soeda, Soeda, & Taki, 1999). Following a chain of suicides of pupils in the mid-1980s, ijime was identified as a prominent social problem (Morita, 1996). In 1996, the Ministry of Education, Science, and Culture assigned school counselors to 150 schools to help victims of ijime (Toda, 2001). The number of incidents of ijime decreased through 2006, but there were several ijime-related suicides in 2007, and ijime is still prevalent in Japanese schools. There is also a new type of ijime using the Internet, called *cyberbullying*; to date, there have been no effective means of mitigating this new type of ijime.

While similar to bullying, ijime is more weighted toward verbal and indirect aggression and is more frequently characterized by within-grade relationships rather than older pupils bullying younger ones (Morita et al., 1999). The most common methods of ijime in Japan are social exclusion and rumor spreading, and a national survey of ijime in Japan reveals that 22% of elementary school children report having been bullied once per week (Morita et al., 1999). The majority of victims were found to have done nothing about it, and many children were also found to have done nothing when they saw someone else being bullied (Morita, 2001). A national survey on ijime found that 43% of victims did not tell teachers, and about half of the victims' parents did not realize that their children had been victimized (Morita et al., 1999). Toda (1997) argued that Japanese pupils who experience ijime are reluctant to tell adults as they feel too much shame, or they blame themselves for the problem and feel that they should deal with it on their own. In any case, most victims believe that they must simply put up with it. The importance of face-saving in Japanese society might suggest that seeking help would be more difficult for Japanese pupils than students in Western countries; Kanetsuna and Smith (2002) found that the fear of being attacked or becoming a new target of bullying discouraged most bystanders from intervening during occurrences of bullying. The difference between Japanese and Western cultures vis-à-vis ego structure reflects their relationships with others and may inform how problems arising from bullying and other problems are typically treated.

Depression

There is considerable evidence that Japanese and North Americans differ in the extent to which they emphasize intrapsychic and interpersonal concerns and that North Americans report positive feelings more frequently than Japanese (Mesquita & Karasawa, 2002; Oishi, 2002). North Americans tend to focus more on the positive aspects of their feelings as these are more relevant to having a successful life. The experience of having positive feelings is more closely tied to subjective well-being for North Americans than for Japanese; for people from collectivistic cultures (such as Japan), the fulfillment of role expectations is more closely tied to well-being (Suh, Diener, Oishi, & Triandis, 1998).

Many studies have also found clear positive correlations between independence and positive self-views, regardless of culture or negative (i.e., weaker) correlations between interdependence and positive self-views (Heine, Lehman, Markus, & Kitayama, 1999; Oyserman, Coon, & Kemmelmeier, 2002). Focusing on what is good about oneself tends to be associated with subjective well-being and self-efficacy, and it is negatively associated with dysphoria and depression (Taylor & Armor, 1996).

Japanese individuals' greater emphasis on maintaining harmonious interpersonal relationships compared with North American individuals has been discussed in a variety of domains. These concerns about harmony are seen as leading to less confrontation and more compromise in negotiations, such as bargaining and mediation (Leung, 1987). They are also thought to lead to a preference for a seniority-based reward system over a meritocratic system (e.g., Nakane, 1970), as the former is associated with less competition among colleagues. Doing things collectively, in a group, is important for Japanese; individuals behave in ways that will allow them to fit in with others (e.g., Kim & Markus, 1999), and they adjust their behaviors to conform with the expectations of significant others (Morling, Kitayama, & Miyamoto, 2002). However, many Japanese companies have started to adopt the Western style of work values, which focuses on people's abilities. This shift in the work-value system is related to overwork, health problems, and depression.

In societies characterized by hierarchical interdependence, *saving face* is important in work settings. As an individual's performance on group-relevant tasks affects the group's success, it becomes critical for individuals to be perceived as doing their best toward what are, in many cases, the shared goals of the group. Performance in working toward these group goals is viewed as being closely tied to effort, which means that how hard one works becomes a matter of moral significance. One's face will be maintained to the extent that one is seen as making an effort to do one's best and contributing to the group's welfare. Some evidence for this moralization of effort can be seen in the Japanese language. Effort (*doryoku*) and persistence (*gambaru*) have been rated as the first and second most frequently used words in Japanese, respectively. The extent of the value placed on hard work for the common good is also evident in certain cultural practices in the Japanese workplace, such as remarkably high rates of voluntary overtime (e.g., Kumazawa, 1996), the tendency of many to refuse to take paid holidays, and occasional instances of death by overwork (*karoshi*) (Nishiyama & Johnson, 1997). These situations tend to increase the incidence of depression among Japanese company workers; however, even when they are diagnosed with depression, they feel that they must continue working as much as they can, and this overwork can lead to suicide, especially among individuals in their 40s and 50s (Heine, 2005).

COUNSELING APPROACHES IN JAPAN

Indigenous Approaches

As would be expected then, positive or desirable feelings—and thus the goal of psychotherapies—differ between Japan and Western cultures. In Japan, the goal is to unite the self with the environment and lead the self into a natural, unselfconscious flow with the environment. The goal is not personal gratification but an actual merging or uniting with one's surroundings. Merging with the environment and dissolving the concept of the self as a separate entity—by focusing away from the self and forming a strong emotional connection with the environment—is the end in itself (Sato, 1998).

The first psychotherapy-related book was published in 1905 by Inoue, who integrated Buddhism with Eastern and Western psychology; it was titled *Psychotherapy* and revealed many of the parallels between Buddhism and psychotherapy processes.

Two indigenous psychotherapies, Morita therapy and Naikan therapy, originated in Eastern philosophy (Buddhism) and integrated Western psychotherapy into their methods.

Morita therapy, as established by Shoma Morita, is a uniquely Japanese form of psychotherapy established in the early 1920s (Kondo, 1974). The goal of Morita therapy is to help the client dissolve the self by accepting his or her own feelings and problems, and those of significant others, just as they are. Clients are taught not to worry, even if they cannot experience control over their feelings (Reynolds, 1980). The client learns that the key to recovery and a good life is to work, fit in, and become a constructive member of society by behaving in a correct manner (Reynolds, 1981).

A second form of psychotherapy to originate in Japan, Naikan therapy, has been practiced since the 1940s, and its method was derived from a common sect of Japanese Buddhism (Jodo-Shinshu) (Murase, 1974). The Naikan therapist focuses on helping a client focus away from and dissolve the self by helping him or her understand what others feel and think and accept significant others as they are (Sato, 1998).

In Japan, people maintain a sense of well-being by fitting in, merging with the social environment, dissolving the self, and preserving harmony with significant others (Markus & Kitayama, 1991, 1994). The most important features of the self are external and public—namely, status, roles, and relationships. Intersubjectivity results from interdependence and connection, and this intersubjectivity gives way to a heightened sense of the other and of the nature of one's relationship to the other, as well as the expectation of some mutuality. The goal is not to achieve individual awareness, experience, and expression but rather some attunement or alignment of one's reactions and actions with those of another; and intersubjective experiences result from these efforts and in turn foster these efforts. Thus in Japan, the positive or desirable emotional states or feelings are those of friendliness, affiliation, calmness, smoothness, and connectedness. The emotional state of anger experienced in an in-group setting is very troubling and considered extremely negative.

Approaches Adapted
From Western Psychotherapies

Many theories and interventions vis-à-vis counseling and various psychotherapies have been introduced in Japan. Their compatibility with collectivistic cultural values, interdependence, and matriarchal consciousness has affected the degree to which these theories have been adopted. For example, the maternal principle, which values empathy, acceptance, and support, is consistent with humanistic theories. Following the American psychologist Carl Rogers's visit to Japan in the 1950s, his theory spread rapidly across Japan, and many Japanese people still believe that counseling is nondirective, empathic, and accepting. Psychoanalysis was also introduced to Japan in the 1910s and taught in many universities. In addition, Kosawa (1954) developed his concept of the "Ajase-complex," which was a complex the child had with his or her mother. Okonogi (1978) explains this complex from the vantage of the Japanese matriarchal principle and finds its patriarchal counterpart in the Oedipus complex.

Kawai (1976/1994) studied Jungian psychology and introduced *hakoniwa,* or sandplay therapy, to Japan as a formal therapeutic medium. Kawai was a past president of the Japanese Clinical Psychology Association and the president of the Office of Culture. He has been a powerful and influential person not only in clinical and counseling psychology in Japan but also in Japanese society and culture, domestically and internationally. He integrated sandplay therapy principles with Japanese cultural practices (Enns & Kasai, 2003). The literal English translation of the Japanese word *hakoniwa* is box garden or miniature garden, and hakoniwa is embedded in values that focus on nonverbal communication, an action orientation rather than the expression of abstract emotional constructs, and an emphasis on holism that is nonlinear and views the integration of physical and mental well-being as necessary for growth.

Culturally Related
Techniques and Interventions

In most Western contexts, the characteristics of the psychotherapy contract are to verbalize as much

as one can. However the Japanese people have, in their long history, considered sensing and feeling others' thoughts nonverbally to be a virtue, as is acting on those sensations before saying a single word. These behaviors presume an unconscious sense of unification: If a Japanese person talks to another person and receives counseling about his or her private life, he or she wants to feel close to that person, as if they are mutual members of an in-group. He or she values the relationship with the therapist more than the therapeutic techniques or effectiveness offered therein and typically wants to give gifts and thank the therapist for his or her favors. It is a relatively new concept for Japanese individuals to pay for counseling or psychotherapy. If clients pay for counseling, they tend to feel distant from the therapist; it feels like a financial transaction and is therefore lacking in intimacy. For this reason, it is sometimes difficult for Japanese clients to have relationships that are at once professional and trusting.

The collectivists' emphasis on harmony within the in-group is also associated with saving the face of the other, avoiding conflict, and "smoothing out" interactions with others (Gudykunst & Nishida, 1994). It is easier for Japanese to display anger and fear toward members of out-groups than those of their own in-group (Matsumoto, 1990). Therefore, if a therapist confronts or presents ideas different from those of the client, the client will tend to agree with the therapist to save the therapist's face and maintain the relationship.

Finally, changing one's surrounding environment for one's own sake is difficult and in conflict with the prevailing value system that emphasizes acceptance. Therefore, clients tend to think that there is nothing they can do to change the problematic situations they are in and may feel helpless. The only thing they can do is endure those problems, and such endurance is a virtue in Japanese culture. It is common for clients to go to therapy or counseling as a last resort, when their problems have become severe.

Consistent with the close parent-child relationships established in Japan, parent-child side-by-side counseling sessions are common (Kawai, 1986). Typically, the mother takes her son or daughter to the session. Sometimes the child, the identified client, never comes to sessions, and sometimes the sons and daughters are in their 20s and 30s. The content of the counseling sessions with the mother depends on the therapist's theoretical orientation or the characteristics of the problem discussed. Together, they discuss parental guidance; the children's specific problems; the mothers' problems, if any; the mothers' personalities; family dynamics; and so on. It is often easier for Japanese mothers to come to counseling for their children's sake than for their own. From a counseling perspective, it is very important for the therapist to have clear goals for the therapy, and it is equally important to acknowledge that for Japanese people, presenting these goals too clearly makes clients anxious and defensive. Since parent-child side-by-side counseling sessions are very common, issues related to this practice have been well discussed and published in the Japanese psychotherapy literature (Yoshida, 2005).

COUNSELING AND CLINICAL PSYCHOLOGY IN JAPAN

A variety of professional associations related to counseling and clinical psychology have developed along separate tracks. One of the reasons for this situation is that counseling has developed in the practical and community fields, whereas psychotherapy has developed in the medical and university fields. All psychology fields, including counseling and clinical psychology, were divided into small associations. To increase the prosperity and wider understanding of psychology, however, the Japan Union of Psychological Associations (JUPA) was organized in 1999 and brought together 30 psychology-related associations. By the end of 2005, the number of associations in JUPA had increased to 41.

According to JUPA, in 2007 16 different qualifications, certifications, or licenses were issued by the various independent associations, although none are national licenses approved by government legislatures. For example, the Japanese Psychological Association, which was established in 1927 and has more than 7,000 members, has issued the *certified*

psychologist designation since 1990. This certification is reserved typically for those with psychology backgrounds. The Japanese Association of Counseling Science, which was established in 1967 and has more than 5,000 members, has issued the *certified counselor* designation since 1986. In 1982, some of the members of the Japanese Psychological Association diverged and established the Association of Japanese Clinical Psychology and proposed a *clinical psychology* licensure in cooperation with several other psychological associations. This group started to designate graduate schools for accreditation in 1988. As of 2007, there were 147 accredited graduate schools and 4 professional schools that train clinical psychologists (Otsuka, 2007), and there are more than 16,000 certified clinical psychologists in Japan.

Among many different associations and qualifications, the Association of Japanese Clinical Psychology and its license are considered the most prestigious and influential. One of the reasons for the recent growth in the number of clinical psychologists can be traced to the Ministry of Education's 1995 decision to send counselors into schools (especially, junior high schools) in response to the increasing number of problems, such as bullying and nonattendance at school. Since there is no licensing procedure with regard to counseling training for school counselors in Japan, the majority of school counselors in Japan are clinical psychologists.

For several years, national qualifications for clinical psychologists have been the most-discussed issue in this field. In 2006, a member of the Japanese government proposed national qualifications. Since that time, however, the prime minister has changed, and as of 2007, a bill for national qualifications for clinical psychologists had not yet cleared the Japanese Diet. Discussions about the future continue (Hiraki, 2006) and include (a) collaboration within the world of professional psychology; (b) the organization of professional licensing for different workplaces under different ministries; (c) the integration of the different statuses related to professional psychology; and (d) the limitations and jurisdictions of the license, as well as the educational and training levels required for the qualification. The Association of Japanese Clinical Psychology organized an international symposium in 2006 and conducted research (Tatara, Natori, & Kume, 2005) involving global comparisons of psychology professions, the present state of education and training systems for Japanese clinical psychologists, and the effects of psychotherapy and the abilities of clinical psychologists. These kinds of projects concerning the national-qualification process are ongoing.

CONCLUSION

Japan is an island country, and due to a long history of national isolation, it was a monoculture country. After the Meiji Period and World War II, Japan was internationalized rapidly, and family and value systems have changed. Historically, Japanese people coped with problems by applying traditional cultural methods. During the past 50 years, these traditional methods have been augmented with counseling and psychotherapy options. It is just in the past 20 years, however, that knowledge of counseling and psychotherapy has permeated the general population in Japan. The definition of and licensure issues for counseling and psychotherapy in Japan need to be discussed and resolved in culture-specific ways in the near future. We, the Japanese people, need to define our own identity in terms of this field, and not only advance it within our society, but offer it to the world.

REFERENCES

American Psychiatric Association. (1994). *Diagnostic and statistical manual of mental disorders, fourth edition. Washington* DC: American Psychiatric Association.

Azuma, H. (1986). Why study child development in Japan? In H. Stevenson, H. Azuma, & K. Hakuta (Eds.), *Child development and education in Japan* (pp. 3–12). New York: W. H. Freeman.

Central Intelligence Agency. (2007). *World fact book: Japan.* Retrieved March 27, 2007, from https://www .cia.gov/library/publications/the-world-factbook/ geos/ja.html

Doi, T. (1973/1981). *The anatomy of dependence.* Tokyo: Kodansha International.

Doi, T. (1988). *The anatomy of self.* Tokyo: Kodansha International.

Enns, C. Z., & Kasai, M. (2003). Hakoniwa: Japanese sandplay therapy. *The Counseling Psychologist, 31,* 93–112.

Gudykunst, W. B., & Nishida, T. (1994). *Bridging Japanese/North American differences.* Thousand Oaks, CA: Sage.

Heine, S. J. (2005). Constructing good selves in Japan and North America. In R. M. Sorrentino, D. Cohen, J. M. Olson, & M. P. Zanna (Eds.), *Cultural and social behavior: The Ontario Symposium* (Vol. 10, pp. 95–116). Mahwah, NJ: Lawrence Erlbaum.

Heine, S. J., Lehman, D. R., Markus, H. R., & Kitayama, S. (1999). Is there a universal need for positive self-regard? *Psychological Review, 106,* 766–794.

Hiraki, N. (2006, October). Recent operations of Japanese psychological world. In M. Tatara. (Ed.), *Handout of International Symposium on Psychological Professions* (pp. 29–33). Tokyo: The Association of Japanese Clinical Psychology.

Imai, A. (1998). Sanninn no tokokyohiji o motsu hahaoya e no shinriteki enjo [Psychological support of a mother with three school refusal children]. *Sonoda Gakuen Joshi Daigaku Sonbunshu, 33*(2), 37–48.

Inoue, E. (1905). *Psychotherapy.* Tokyo: Nankodo Shoten.

Ishida, K., & Takei, M. (1987). *Ushinawareta kodomo kukan* [The lost space for children]. Tokyo: Shinyosha.

Ishii-Kuntz, M. (1989). Collectivism or individualism? Changing patterns of Japanese attitudes. *Social Science Research, 73,* 174–179.

Japanese Institute for Labor Policy and Training. (2008). Tokushu wakamono no jiritsu shien [Support for independence of young adult]. *Business Labor Trend, 4,* 2–61.

Kameguchi, K., & Murphy-Shigematsu, S. (2001). Family psychology and family therapy in Japan. *American Psychologist, 56,* 65–70.

Kanetsuna, T., & Smith, P. (2002). Pupil insights into bullying, and coping with bullying: A bi-national study in Japan and England. *Journal of School Violence, 1*(3), 5–29.

Kanetsuna, T., Smith, P. K., & Morita, Y. (2006). Coping with bullying at school: Children's recommended strategies and attitudes to school-based interventions in England and Japan. *Aggressive Behavior, 32,* 570–580.

Kasai, M. (1998). Battered parents: Comparison between American and Japanese case studies. *Research*

Bulletin of Educational Sciences Naruto University of Teacher Education, 13, 47–54.

Kashima, Y., Yamaguchi, S., Kim, U., Choi, S., Gelfand, M. J., & Yuki, M. (1995). Culture, gender, and self: A perspective from individualism-collectivism research. *Journal of Personality and Social Psychology, 69,* 925–937.

Kawai, H. (1976/1994). *Bosei shakai nihon no byori* [The pathology of the mother-principled society of Japan]. Tokyo: Chuo Koronsha.

Kawai, H. (1986). Violence in the home: Conflict between two principles: Maternal and paternal. In T. S. Lebra & W. P. Lebra (Eds.), *Japanese culture and behavior: Selected readings* (pp. 297–306). Honolulu: University of Hawaii Press.

Kawai, H. (1988/1992). *The Japanese psyche: Major motifs in the fairy tales of Japan.* Putnam, CT: Spring.

Kawanaka, J. (1998). Tokokyohiji no sonogo to hahaoya no shinri katei tono kanren ni tuite [The relation between the development of school refusal children and their mothers' state of mind]. *Japanese Journal of Family Psychology, 12*(2), 89–107.

Kim, H., & Markus, H. R. (1999). Deviance or uniqueness, harmony or conformity? A cultural analysis. *Journal of Personality and Social Psychology, 77,* 785–800.

Kim, U. (1994). Individualism and collectivism: Conceptual clarification and elaboration. In U. Kim, H. C. Triandis, C. Kagitcibasi, S. Choi, & G. Yoon (Eds.), *Individualism and collectivism: Theory, method, and applications* (pp. 19–40). Thousand Oaks, CA: Sage.

Kondo, K. (1974). The origin of Morita therapy. In T. Lebra & W. Lebra (Eds.), *Japanese culture and behavior: Selected readings* (pp. 250–258). Honolulu: University of Hawaii Press.

Kosawa, H. (1954). Zaiaku ishiki no nishu: Ajase-complex [Two styles of guilty conscience: Ajase-complex]. *Japanese Journal of Psycho-analysis, 1,* 5–9.

Kumazawa, M. (1996). *Portraits of the Japanese workplace.* Boulder, CO: Westview Press.

Lang, M. (1982). School refusal: An empirical study and system analysis. *Australian Journal of Family Therapy, 3,* 93–107.

Leung, K. (1987). Some determinants of reactions to procedural models for conflict resolution: A cross-national study. *Journal of Personality and Social Psychology, 53,* 898–908.

Lewis, C. C. (1995). *Educating hearts and minds: Reflections on Japanese preschool and elementary school.* New York: Cambridge University Press.

Markus, H. R., & Kitayama, S. (1991). Culture and the self: Implications for cognition, emotion, and motivation. *Psychological Review, 98,* 224–253.

Markus, H. R., & Kitayama, S. (1994). The cultural construction of self and emotion: Implications for social behavior: A conceptual framework. In S. Kitayama & H. R. Markus (Eds.), *Emotion and culture* (pp. 89–130). Washington, DC: American Psychological Association.

Matsumoto, D. (1990). Cultural similarities and differences in display rules. *Motivation and Emotion, 14,* 195–214.

Mesquita, B., & Karasawa, M. (2002). Different emotional lives. *Cognition and Emotion, 16,* 127–141.

Ministry of Education, Culture, Sports, Science and Technology–Japan. (2007). *FY2006 white paper on education, culture, sports, science and technology.* Tokyo: Author. Retrieved April 13, 2009, from http://www.mext.go.jp/b_menu/hakusho/html/hpaa200601/index.htm

Morita, Y. (1996). Bullying as a contemporary behavior problem in the context of increasing "social privatisation" in Japan. *International Bureau Education, 26,* 311–329.

Morita, Y. (2001). *Ijime no kokusai hikaku kenkyu* [Cross-national comparative study of bullying]. Tokyo: Kaneko Shobo.

Morita, Y., Soeda, H., Soeda, K., & Taki, M. (1999). Japan. In P. K. Smith, Y. Morita, J. Junger-Tas, D. Olweus, R. Catalano, & P. Slee (Eds.), *The nature of school bullying: A cross-national perspective* (pp. 309–323). New York: Routledge.

Morling, B., Kitayama, S., & Miyamoto, Y. (2002). Cultural practices emphasize influence in the United States and adjustment in Japan. *Personality and Social Psychology Bulletin, 28,* 311–323.

Murase, T. (1974). Naikan therapy. In T. Lebra & W. Lebra (Eds.), *Japanese culture and behavior: Selected readings* (pp. 259–269). Honolulu: University of Hawaii Press.

Nakane, C. (1967). *Tate shakai no ningen kankei* [Seniority relationships]. Tokyo: Kodansha International.

Nakane, C. (1970). *Japanese society.* Los Angeles: University of California Press.

Neumann, E. (1954). *The origins and history of consciousness.* New York: Pantheon Books.

Nishiyama, K., & Johnson, J. V. (1997). Karoshi: Death from overwork: Occupational health consequences of Japanese production management. *International Journal of Health Services, 27,* 625–641.

Ohinata, M. (2000). Hito wa ikani sansaiji shinwa ni torawarete iruka [How people are caught in three-year-old myth]. *Boseiai Ishiki no Wana. [Trap of maternal love myth].* Tokyo: Nihon Hyoron sha.

Ohinata, M. (2002). Bosei ai shinwa karano Kaihou [Liberation from myth of maternal love]. *Journal of Pediatric Dermatology, 21,* 119.

Oishi, S. (2002). Experiencing and remembering of well-being: A cross-cultural analysis. *Personality and Social Psychology Bulletin, 28,* 1398–1406.

Okonogi, K. (1978). Nihon jin no Ajase complex [Ajase complex of Japanese people]. *Chuo Koron, 93*(6), 90–123.

Otsuka, Y. (2007). Rinshoshinrishi no shokatsudo [Activities by licensed clinical psychologist]. *Bulletin of Foundation of the Japanese Certification Board for Clinical Psychologists, 18,* 3–12.

Oyserman, D., Coon, H. M., & Kemmelmeir, M. (2002). Rethinking individualism and collectivism: Evaluation of theoretical assumptions and meta-analysis. *Psychological Bulletin, 128,* 3–72.

Reynolds, D. K. (1980). *The quiet therapies.* Honolulu: University of Hawaii Press.

Reynolds, D. K. (1981). Morita psychotherapy. In R. J. Corsini (Ed.), *Handbook of innovative psychotherapies* (pp. 489–501). New York: Wiley.

Sato, T. (1998). Agency and communion: The relationship between therapy and culture. *Cultural Diversity and Mental Health, 4,* 278–290.

Sugimoto, Y. (2003). *An introduction to Japanese society* (2nd ed.). New York: Cambridge University Press.

Suh, E., Diener, E., Oishi, S., & Triandis, H. C. (1998). The shifting basis of life satisfaction judgments across cultures: Emotions versus norms. *Journal of Personality and Social Psychology, 74,* 482–493.

Tatara, M., Natori, T., & Kume, T. (2005). News: Basic data for national qualification of clinical psychologists. *Journal of Japanese Clinical Psychology, 23,* 612–639.

Taylor, S. E., & Armor, D. A. (1996). Positive illusions and coping with adversity. *Journal of Personality, 64,* 873–898.

Toda, Y. (1997). Kyouiku gakubusei no ijime/ijimerare kenken to ijime ni taisuru ishiki [Bullying/bullied experiences and attitudes to bullying behavior among students in faculty of education]. *Tottori University Journal of the Faculty of Education and Regional Sciences, 6,* 19–28.

Toda, Y. (2001). Gakko ni okeru pia sapoto jissen no tenkai to kadai [Peer support: Its development in Japanese schools and some issues to be concerned]. *Tottori University Journal of the Faculty of Education and Regional Sciences, 2,* 59–75.

U.S. Department of State. Bureau of Democracy, Human Rights and Labor. (2006). *International religious freedom report 2006.* Retrieved April 12, 2007, from http://www.state.gov/g/drl/rls/irf/2006

Vogel, S. H., & Vogel, E. F. (1961). Family security, personal immaturity, and emotional health in a Japanese sample. *Marriage and Family Planning, 23,* 161–166.

Wagatsuma, H. (1977). Some aspects of the changing family in contemporary Japan: Once Confucian, now fatherless. *Daedulus, 106,* 181–210.

Yoshida, H. (2005). The contributions from psychoanalysis to the paralleled mother counseling in child psychotherapy and the problems involved in that therapeutic setting. *Japanese Journal of Clinical Psychology, 5,* 628–635.

Zielenziger, M. (2006). *Shutting out the sun: How Japan created its own lost generation.* New York: Random House.

10

Professional Accomplishments and Current Cultural Challenges of Counseling Psychology in South Korea

한국상담의 발전과 문화적 도전

CHANGDAI KIM, DONG MIN KIM,
YOUNG SEOK SEO, AND KAY HYON KIM

Counseling psychology has not had a long history in South Korea, as it has been practiced for at least 20 years and at most 50 years. However, counseling psychology has developed very rapidly during that time. This chapter first provides an overview of the historical development of the counseling profession in Korea, focusing on major initiatives in the areas of school counseling, mental health, youth counseling, and career counseling. The chapter then highlights essential cultural assumptions and values that have influenced Korean society and discusses culturally responsive counseling approaches.

HISTORICAL DEVELOPMENT AND MAJOR INITIATIVES OF THE COUNSELING PROFESSION

School Counseling

Counseling psychology was first introduced as a form of school counseling and guidance. With Korea's independence from Japanese colonial rule in 1945, the ideology of democracy and a child-focused educational paradigm replaced the previous approach of rote memorization and dictation; in essence, a new educational paradigm—called the "New Education Movement"—began. Wonshik

Chung, the second president of the Korean Counselors' Association, was the first to introduce counseling and guidance to Korean society. As one form of the New Education Movement, in 1957, for the first time, the Seoul Metropolitan Board of Education (SMBE) conducted counseling education for 40 teachers. This program ultimately trained about 400 teachers for school counseling at the SMBE and other government educational boards (Kim et al., 2000). In 1963, some scholars and middle and high school teachers who were interested in school counseling and guidance established the Korean Counselors' Association. The role and function of teachers who were trained in counseling later developed further with several changes to their title. In 1964, the licensure regulation for guidance teachers started, and this license changed the name of the discipline to "career school counselor" in 1990 and, thereafter, to "professional school counselor" in 1999.

Recent developments have been made in the school systems that appear to favor counselors. Korean society has witnessed a recent upsurge in school violence at all school levels. Furthermore, violence has become more heinous, and students committing violent acts against their peers are getting younger. According to a nationwide survey, 17.8% of elementary school students and 16.8% of middle school students were victimized by school violence in the previous year (Foundation for Preventing Youth Violence, 2006).

As a way of responding to and combating school violence, the National Assembly passed a bill, presented by the Department of Education in 2007, which features employing counselors at elementary- and secondary-education settings. This marks the first time that the Korean government has officially acknowledged the need for the presence of qualified counselors in school settings to help students with emotional and behavioral problems. Over the past decades, mental health professionals, including counselors, have made substantial efforts to enter the school systems, exploring ways to create positions in elementary, middle, and high schools. However, due to resistance among schoolteachers to accepting those whose primary role is not teaching, mental health professionals have had to provide their services primarily on a voluntary basis. Therefore, the passage of the bill and the corresponding employment of professional counselors signify that counselors have been recognized as vital members of the education team in the school setting and that school counseling has become a new specialty area for Korean counselors. However, the Korean counseling profession still needs to determine how to empower these new professionals with relevant knowledge, skills, and resources.

Mental Health Services: University Counseling Centers and Private Practices

University counseling has played a pivotal role in establishing counseling psychology in Korea as a mainstream mental health domain as well as a major psychological discipline. The practice of college and university counseling developed independently from school counseling and guidance with the establishment of a student counseling center at Seoul National University in 1962. Since that time, various counseling-related services, such as counseling, research, and information services, have been actively provided, as well as internship programs for counselor training (Kim et al., 2000). In short, counseling centers provided the foundational basis for counseling within Korean educational and psychological approaches, apart from the mental health medical approach.

Currently, there are approximately 350 counseling centers in colleges and universities around the country. University counseling centers deliver a wide range of services, including crisis intervention and outreach services as well as psychological testing and individual and group counseling. In addition, university counseling centers have played a vital role in training counselors and counseling psychologists. It cannot be overstated that until the year 2000, university counseling centers had been the only places where graduate students of counseling and other interested individuals were able to have access to systematically supervised clinical-training opportunities. More recently, other counseling institutions (e.g., youth counseling centers) provide similar experiences, but university counseling centers still provide the majority of opportunities for counselor training.

The increasing number of counselors in private practice is one of the biggest recent changes in the counseling profession in Korea. This change reflects positive changes in the public's perception of and attitude toward counseling services. Private practitioners start their own counseling agencies after receiving a master's or doctoral degree as well as related counseling certificates. Even as recently as 10 years ago, the number of counselors in private practice was very limited. However, the number is increasing rapidly.

Youth Counseling

Youth counseling has also been a major contributing factor in expanding the field of counseling in Korea. In 1999, the Korea Youth Counseling Institute (KYCI) was established pursuant to the Youth Foundational Law that was enacted in 1991. Sungsoo Park took an essential and major role in enacting this law and founded the KYCI based on this law. Since then, a nationwide network has been established for youth counseling. At the present time, this national system comprises 16 youth counseling support centers in each city and province and 141 local youth centers in each county and district. This network makes the youth counseling system a major nationwide network of the counseling profession. In addition, national licensure regulation for professional youth counselors was enacted in 2003, making the youth counseling profession a distinguished professional discipline in Korea.

In 2005, KYCI and local centers were challenged by the National Youth Commission (NYC), which is in charge of national-level youth politics. NYC wanted KYCI to invest more efforts in "youth at risk." Although the term *youth at risk* does not identify the inclusive criteria, implicitly it meant more serious cases that might involve more social costs without proper interventions. It also implied the need for services more than counseling and psychotherapy in the traditional sense.

Accordingly, a new service system, Community Youth Safety Net (CYS-Net), was developed at the end of 2005 (Koo et. al., 2005). This system was characterized by three components: (1) case management, (2) community-based intervention, and (3) comprehensive and tangible services. Clients within this system typically have multiple problems (e.g., poverty, divorced parents, delinquent peers, poor adjustment in school). The case manager, called a *youth companion* (YC), plans all the necessary services and coordinates the responsibilities of all participating agencies for a particular client. The YC also has the responsibility to ensure that services are delivered as planned. To provide the necessary services, local centers and individual YCs create a network among the potential service providers in the community. Within this network, services provided for a client include not only counseling and psychotherapy-based services but also tangible services, such as arranging part-time job opportunities, paying tuition for vocational training, legal consultation, housing, and so forth.

The CYS-Net is definitely different from the past service system in that more intensive and comprehensive interventions are provided to a more focused target population. However, in reality several problems emerged in the process of implementing this system. Among them, the most prominent was role conflict among counselors. Because most of the counselors have been trained with psychotherapy models, it was difficult for them to take on the roles established by the CYS-Net—that is, mostly conducting outreach and advocate services—as their primary ones. Indeed, some counselors would argue that the role of providing outreach and advocate services belongs primarily to social workers in public hearings and forums. This problem seems to be still an issue among the majority of counselors.

At present, the youth counseling system is considered one of the most well-established counseling services systems in Korea. However, there is a need to develop more specific counseling models for this youth population, particularly so that the function of a counselor will include the roles of teacher, direct supporter, and advocate.

Career Counseling

The economic "exchange currency" crisis of 1997 and 1998 had a great impact on many aspects in Korea, especially the behaviors, thoughts, and cultures related to jobs. Many Koreans experienced unexpected layoffs from their jobs, which they had regarded as lifelong jobs. Career transitions and the increase of "body value" (i.e., salary) became accepted as the new trend and focus for younger and competent workers.

In Korea, career counselors work in various sites. The Korean government (Department of Labor) opened employment support centers in every city and county and recruited 1,900 career counselors to help with the layoffs during 1997 and 2000. Of these, 1,500 counselors are still in their positions. Many private companies have been founded to provide headhunting services, job transition support, and recruitment support. In addition, every university must fund a career center to help students develop the knowledge and skills related to employment.

The younger generation of Korean professional counselors will have more opportunities to work as career counselors, headhunters, and recruitment specialists within university, government, corporate, and self-employed settings. In addition, several Internet companies also have opened recruitment and employment online counseling programs.

Recently, there has been a growing number of private counseling agencies and counseling centers of various sizes in nonprofit organizations. Korean society has become more familiar with counseling services. Considering the increasing numbers of counseling-related bodies, it is expected that the counseling profession will continue to develop in Korean society for the next several decades.

Who Are Counseling Psychologists?

At present, counseling professionals in Korea have various academic backgrounds, such as in education, psychology, child study, social work, nursing, and theology, among others. In addition, counseling professionals practice counseling in different work settings. Given their varying backgrounds and work settings, they do not typically identify themselves as psychologists. Rather, they prefer being called *counselors* or *counselor teachers*. It is probably more appropriate to call them *professional counselors,* which encompasses their different academic backgrounds. Therefore, we can define a professional counselor as a professional who provides counseling services.

In a broad sense, professional counselors are considered to be those who majored in a counseling-related field—such as education, psychology, child study, social work, or theology—at the master's or doctoral level. In a more concrete sense, only counselors certified by the government or counseling-related professional associations are considered professional counselors. However, this certificate only confirms the completion of required courses and training. This is different from a licensing regime, which grants exclusive authority to practice to those who hold a license. Nonetheless, the certificate issued by the government and related counseling associations is the only standard for the counseling profession that exists at this time.

PROFESSIONAL STRUCTURES OF COUNSELING

Professional Organizations

Today, the two major counseling-related professional bodies in Korea are the Korea Counseling Psychology Association (KCPA) and the Korea Counseling Association (KCA). The KCPA was founded as a separate entity within the Korea Psychology Association (KPA) in 1987, and it affirmed the academic independence of the counseling profession. Now, KCPA has more than 6,000 members and has issued certifications to counseling psychologists and publishes quarterly professional journals, such as the *Journal of Counseling and Psychotherapy.*

Since 1987, various counseling-related associations and academic bodies have been established. In the late 1990s, there were more than 20 counseling-related associations and academic bodies. Several scholars realized that one of the problems with this large number of related associations was that their operations were so sporadic and decentralized that they failed to effectively protect the interests of the counseling profession. Subsequently, they made an effort to rally five to six representative professional associations and started the KCA in 2000. KCA has more than 5,000 members, and it also has issued certifications to counselors and publishes a quarterly professional journal, the *Journal of Counseling Research*.

In addition to these two major organizations, there have been many counseling-related professional bodies of various sizes. One important challenge is for these various professional bodies to work together in a cooperative manner and administer uniform and proper ethical standards.

Licensure Regulation

The counseling-related licensing bodies in Korea are divided into governmental and professional organizations. National licensure in the counseling profession includes three licenses: professional youth counselor, professional occupational counselor, and professional counseling teacher. The other licenses are more appropriately viewed as certificates, and the major issuing bodies for these certificates are the KCPA and the KCA. The KCPA issues two levels of certificates and the KCA issues three levels of certificates. Other counseling-related associations also issue various certificates; however, these certificates are not generally recognized by the public.

One of the problems of regulations governing licensure is that no consensus exists on the standards of licensure. This remains one of the challenges for future development in the counseling profession in Korea. There is a need to establish a consistent certificate system that integrates the various certificates issued by the different professional organizations. This procedure would also include establishing a new standard for the certificates, monitoring the qualities of the certificates, and finally transforming this certificate into a national certificate.

Training for Professional Counselors in Korea

One of the important challenges in the Korean counseling profession is to establish an effective counselor education system. At present, many counselors have been trained in various undergraduate and graduate schools. However, there has not been a standardized educational program: Therefore, quality control of the counselor education training system has been lacking. Recently, several universities started counselor education programs at the undergraduate level. Although the increased interest in counseling is a positive sign, it could cause another problem: These undergraduate counseling programs are not differentiated from graduate programs. There is a need to systematize the counselor education programs in both graduate and undergraduate schools to ensure a graduated and continuous link between each course. To solve these problems, it is necessary to establish a standardized training curriculum. An accreditation system is also needed to monitor the quality of counselor training programs in Korea.

CULTURAL CONTEXT AND COUNSELING APPROACH

Although the history of the Korean counseling profession has not been long, there have been continuous suggestions that counseling services for Koreans should be different from those for people in Western cultures and that theories and techniques should be applied to Koreans within the Korean cultural context. Kim (1994b) maintained that the development of indigenous counseling theories suitable for Koreans must go beyond revising counseling techniques developed in Western cultures and that it is essential to explain the unique psychosocial dynamics within the Korean cultural context.

On the topic of cultural differences, many people tend to group the Asian countries, such as China, Japan, and Korea, into the same cultural group rather than considering the differences among specific ethnic subgroups. Therefore, cultural similarities have been emphasized, and those similarities have been generally assumed to be relevant to all or most subgroups regardless of ethnic backgrounds (Kim, Bean, & Harper, 2004). In this chapter, we discuss the most essential cultural assumptions and contexts that have influenced Korean values and the cultural relevance of different counseling approaches.

Religious Beliefs and Values: Confucianism

In Korean society, the percentages of those who adhere to Confucianism, Buddhism, and Christianity are generally equivalent. However, Confucianism can be considered the value system that has most fundamentally influenced Korean traditional values. Historically, Confucianism flourished during Korea's *Chosun* dynasty. Although Confucianism influenced East Asian cultures, such as those of China and Japan, Confucianism's influence in Korean culture was much greater than its influence on other ethnic groups (Cho, 2003). With respect to China, one possible reason for this is that the long period of communist rule could have suppressed some of the traditional values of Confucianism, such as strongly hierarchical social interactions, that are inconsistent with the beliefs of communism. With respect to Japan, after World War II they also abandoned some traditional values that had been dominant in the prewar government (Doi, 1981). With respect to Korea, the long history of invasion and rule by the Japanese could have promoted Korean adherence to their traditional Confucian value systems.

Since Confucianism was brought from China during Korea's Chosun dynasty, Confucianism has been a fundamental part of that belief system in Korean society, and the Korean people have practiced in their daily lives the philosophy of Confucius and his disciples for an extended period of time. Although modernization has rapidly taken place in Korean society over the past 50 years, these value systems are still pervasive.

The central tenet of Confucianism that influenced Korean society involves "relatedness with others in harmony." This emphasis on interpersonal relationships is often illustrated through collectivism in Asian ethnic groups (Goldstein, 1988). The nature

of collectivism in Korean society has emphasized well-defined hierarchical social roles and expectations. Collectivistic values in Korea are rooted in the virtue called *in*, which is one of the most essential principles in Confucianism. This principle has served as a basic guide to determine Koreans' social behaviors and can be found in the emphasis placed on conformity to familial and social norms, hierarchical family structure, self-control and restraint of emotional expression, respect for authority and elders, and prescribed gender role relationships (Kim, 1994b).

For Koreans, the primary dimension of social relationships is "we-ness" (Choi, 2000). Korean people have pursued oneness, which is based on the Korean cultural concept of *cheong*, which means a tight emotional bond, and valued interdependence of relationships rather than independence. Korean people often suppress their individual needs for the sake of harmonious relationships, and they have considered this behavior an important virtue, in contrast to the Western cultural value of individuality.

In consideration of these traditional values, counselors need to be aware of the importance of hierarchical collectivism when they work with Korean people. It is especially important to understand the difficulties and conflicts Korean people might experience due to the modernization that has rapidly taken place. Choi (2000) also argued that the counselor needs to cultivate cheong and we-ness when counseling Koreans.

Given the emphasis on harmony in human relations in Korean society, Koreans have developed *nun-chi*, which means sensitivity to others' needs. It is literally translated as "sensing the eyes." In other words, it is an interpersonal ability to read others' feelings and opinions by observing their nonverbal cues. Since Koreans consider withholding direct emotional expression and self-control important virtues, having nun-chi can smooth out human relations and maintain harmony and, therefore, is important in communication.

This cultural concept has implications for the counseling process and therapeutic relationship when working with Korean people. Due to their reluctance to express their feelings, counselors need to be careful not to pressure them to express their feelings in the initial sessions. Kim, Kwon, Sohn, and Hahn (2008) also maintained that for providing effective empathy with Korean clients, the counselor's ability to validate the client's experience is more important than the ability to explore the client's inner feelings. In addition, Korean clients found counseling services helpful when counselors were sensitive enough to understand their unexpressed feelings and even to differentiate implicit, unexpressed feelings from explicit expressions.

Another cultural concept that influences Korean people's social behaviors is *chae-myun,* which means "saving face." Chae-myun influences Koreans' psychosocial dynamics and works as one of the problem-solving methods among Koreans (Kim, 1994a). Due to the need to save face, Koreans tend to be less assertive and thus employ less confrontation in communication. This cultural value also influences Koreans' help-seeking behaviors. Korean people may seek help from their in-groups, such as families and close friends, rather than out-groups, such as counseling professionals. Although Korean people's perceptions of counseling and psychotherapy have changed recently, mental illness is still generally stigmatized in Korean society, and Koreans may feel embarrassed by the fact that they are seeing counselors or psychotherapists.

Given this cultural context, Kim (1994b) suggested the following guiding principles for counseling Koreans: (a) providing information about counseling, (b) providing thorough structures for counseling, (c) building trust, (d) providing short-term counseling objectives and problem-solving experiences, (e) providing future-oriented explorations and questions rather than focusing on past causes, (f) explaining the reasons for exploring past experiences, and (g) providing special consideration to the issue of shame when gathering information.

In addition, when working with Korean families it is important to respect people's dignity and their proper roles in the family, for example, with positive reframing and compliments, and to take advantage of these means to build a trustful therapeutic relationship (Berg & Jaya, 1993; Ho, 1987). Counselors also need to minimize the possibilities that authority figures (i.e., parents) might lose face and respect the hierarchical nature of the Korean family structure.

Family Values

Korean culture has a strong emphasis on the family. Historically, Korean family values were deeply based on the virtue of *hyo,* which means respecting parents and elders. The relations in Korean families are characterized by the hierarchy-defining relations between father and son and between husband and wife (Rohner & Pettengill, 1985). The expected roles within the family are strictly defined according to gender and age. These hierarchical family structures have also been extended to other parts of Korean society as the basis of general human relations and have, thereby, created interdependent social networks in Korean society (Shon & Ja, 1982).

The most essential cultural context related to family values is a strong emphasis on interdependence among family members. Korean parents, especially fathers, are often expected to support their children financially throughout the school years, and the children are expected to practice subordination and obedience. It is not uncommon to sacrifice individuals' needs to maintain harmonious relations within the family (Kim & Choi, 1994). For example, eldest sons and their wives are often expected to meet the daily living needs of the sons' parents. Therefore, the nature of interdependence in Korean families is an important cultural value to consider when discussing the psychological separation-individuation process that Western psychology considers a prerequisite for mental health. Koreans value interdependence, see fulfilling obligations in the family as a healthy way of life, and have emphasized family ties and conformity (Choi, 2000).

Given the cultural values related to family, Kim and his colleagues (2008) identified Korean therapeutic common factors and found that taking a parent-like counseling role was one of the important factors that influenced outcomes of counseling.

Chang (2000) also suggested a counseling approach that identifies an effective role for counselors for Korean people. In this approach, counselors need to assume the attitude of elders, especially parents. She suggested that the ideal role for counselors was similar to the characteristics of *umbujamo*, which means a stern father and an affectionate mother and has been considered an ideal image of parents in Korean society.

In addition, due to Koreans' emphasis on hierarchical social order, it is crucial to establish credibility and respect in the initial session (Lee, 1996). When counseling Korean adults, it is not uncommon for clients to ask personal questions, such as age and educational background, to verify the counselor's expertise since Koreans may ascribe credibility on the basis of their traditional measures of professional stature (i.e., gender, age, education level). In terms of effective counseling approaches, counselors need to anticipate the client's reliance on the counselors and need to take an active and direct role in the counseling process, especially in the initial sessions.

As discussed above, there are several cultural values that have shaped Korean society. It is important to understand the cultural context and to develop culturally sensitive new theories and techniques with modification of Western theories. These new models should reflect the cultural values of the Koreans as well as the desirable images of human nature in Korean society. In addition, these models will need to be validated through research in this area.

MULTICULTURAL CHALLENGES

The recent changes in the demographic picture of Korean society are an opportunity for Korean counselors to expand their roles and also take initiative. One of those changes has been triggered by the steady influx of North Korean defectors. Many of the defectors, who fled from their home country for economic and political reasons, are reported to experience mental health problems such as anxiety and depression (Keum, Joo, Kim, Kim, & Lee, 2005). Some counselors have already taken initiatives in helping them with their initial adjustment as

well as mental health issues. As the number of North Korean defectors is expected to increase in the upcoming years, it is very likely that more counseling psychologists will be called on to serve this population.

In addition, since the early 1990s, Korea has seen an unprecedented increase in foreign nationals and racially mixed Koreans. According to the Korea National Statistical Office (2007), it is estimated that more than 1 million foreign nationals live in Korea, with 7 out of 10 working illegally. The majority of foreign nationals are laborers from third-world countries and work at so-called 3D (dirty, difficult, and dangerous) jobs. In addition, interracial or interethnic marriages have exceeded 10% of the marriages in Korea, the rate climbing to 50% in certain rural areas. It can be said that Korea is rapidly becoming a multiethnic and multicultural society but without being prepared for accepting those with different race and ethnicity as members of the society.

Historically, foreign nationals and mixed-blood Koreans have been part of the Korean community due to its active cultural and commercial exchanges with other countries, as well as frequent invasions by foreign forces. Ironically, however, Koreans have held a deep-rooted monocultural and monoethnic ideology, which means that they look down on and even discriminate against racial minorities, especially those with dark skin. Therefore, the recent upsurge of foreign nationals and mixed-blood Koreans raises concerns regarding their psychological problems as well as their basic human rights. For instance, in addition to the problems caused by their illegal status (e.g., lack of health care, job insecurity, financial problems), foreign workers are likely to experience both overt and subtle discrimination due to their physical appearance and poor language skills. Children of internationals and mixed-bloods are in a much more difficult situation. In particular, children whose parents have poor language skills tend to be slow in language acquisition and subsequently low in academic achievement compared with their Korean peers. It is, therefore, not surprising that many of these children are sometimes misdiagnosed as having a learning disability.

In addition, international women who are married to Koreans, mostly residing in rural areas, have to learn a wide range of culturally defined and typically unfamiliar roles in a short time under conditions of considerable stress.

Helping cultural and social minorities can be an opportunity but simultaneously a challenge for Korean counselors. On one hand, by helping these individuals cope with vocational and personal concerns, Korean counselors will be able to achieve a visible presence in Korean society as a profession, which contributes to ameliorating the societal tension incurred by the hardship of these populations and their corresponding complaints against Korean society. In so doing, Korean counselors can enhance their recognition in society and also expand their areas of specialty. On the other hand, however, helping social minorities may be a challenge for many Korean counselors who have been and are still affected by the unique Korean societal milieu. In other words, the counselors may themselves have implicit and explicit biases against foreign nationals and racial minorities that have not been previously challenged. Korean counselors will be able to implement culturally appropriate and effective counseling programs that are designed to make a difference in the life of these emerging populations.

CONCLUSION

Despite the short history of the counseling profession in Korea, there has been rapid growth. This growth is attributed to many professionals' efforts and the cultural changes in Korean society. The counseling profession in Korea will need to continue its development. For further growth, it is essential to develop culturally sensitive counseling models and establish a standardized licensure system as well as an accreditation system for educational programs. Counseling professionals in Korea also need to recognize the increasing need for multicultural counseling perspectives given the growing population of defectors from North Korea as well as emigrant workers. Cooperation among counseling professionals and scholars across countries is important, as well as international exchanges in the counseling profession.

REFERENCES

Berg, I. K., & Jaya, A. (1993). Different and same: Family therapy with Asian American families. *Journal of Marital and Family Therapy, 19,* 31–38.

Chang, S. S. (2000). Reality dynamic counseling model: The approach of counseling for the Korean. *Korean Journal of Counseling and Psychotherapy, 12*(3), 17–32.

Cho, G. H. (2003). *Reading Koreans culturally: A psychological approach.* Seoul, South Korea: Nanam.

Choi, S. J. (2000). *Psychology of the Korean.* Seoul, South Korea: Joongang University Press.

Doi, T. (1981). *The anatomy of dependence.* Tokyo: Kodansha International.

Foundation for Preventing Youth Violence. (2006). *Status of school violence.* Retrieved January 13, 2008, from http://www.jikim.net

Ho, M. K. (1987). *Family therapy with ethnic minorities.* Newbury Park, CA: Sage.

Keum, M. J., Joo, Y. A., Kim, S. S., Kim, T. S., & Lee, J. Y. (2005). *Program development for North Korean refugee adolescents.* Seoul, South Korea: Korea Youth Counseling Institute.

Kim, C. D. (1994a). *The coping process of Koreans as compared to white Americans: The influence of culture.* Unpublished doctoral dissertation, Teachers College, Columbia University, New York.

Kim, C. D. (1994b). Cultural context of counseling science. *Korea Journal of Youth Counseling, 2*(2), 19–42.

Kim, C. D., Kwon, K. I., Sohn, N. H., & Hahn, Y. J. (2008). Counselors' factor facilitating effective change in counseling for Korean clients. *Korea Journal of Counseling, 9,* 961–986.

Kim, E. Y., Bean, R. A., Harper, J. M. (2004). Do general treatment guidelines for Asian American families have applications to specific ethnic groups? The case of culturally-competent therapy with Korean Americans. *Journal of Marital and Family Therapy, 30,* 359–372.

Kim, K. H., Kim, D. I., Kim, B. H., Kim, C. D., Kim, H. S., Nam, S. I., et al. (2000). *School counseling and guidance.* Seoul, South Korea: Hakjisa.

Kim, U., & Choi, S. H. (1994). Individualism, collectivism, and child development: A Korean perspective. In P. M. Greenfield & R. R. Cocking (Eds.),

Cross-cultural roots of minority child development (pp. 227–257). Hillsdale, NJ: Lawrence Erlbaum.

Koo, B. Y., Keum, M. J., Kim, D. I., Kim, D. M., Nam, S. I., Ahn, H. E., et al. (2005). *A study on the development of supporting system for youths at risk.* Seoul, South Korea: Government Youth Commission.

The Korea National Statistical Office. (2007). *Foreign residents.* Retrieved February 25, 2008, from http://www.nso.go.kr

Lee, C. H., & Kim, J. H. (1989). A study on the oriental model for counseling and guidance. *Korean Journal of Counseling and Psychotherapy, 2*(1), 5–15.

Lee, E. (1996). Asian Americans: An overview. In M. McGoldrick, J. Giorando., & J. K. Pearce (Eds.), *Ethnicity and family therapy* (pp. 227–248). New York: Guilford Press.

Rohner, R. P., & Pettengill, S. M. (1985). Perceived parental acceptance-rejection and parental control among Korean adolescents. *Child Development, 56,* 524–528.

Shon, S., & Ja, D. (1982). Asian families. In M. McGoldrick, J. Pearce, & J. Giordano (Eds.), *Ethnicity and family therapy* (pp. 208–229). New York: Guilford Press.

11

Counseling in China

Fast Moving, but What Is the Destination?

心理咨询在中国：发展迅速，但去向何方？

ZHI-JIN HOU, SEUNG-MING ALVIN LEUNG, AND CHANGMING DUAN

China is trying very intensely to catch up with the developed world, and she is accelerating her engine of economic and social development at a very rapid speed. The economic reforms and the subsequent open-door policy that have been ongoing for the past 30 years have unleashed immense growth energies from the vast population, which surpassed 1.3 billion in 2005 (National Bureau of Statistics of China, 2007). China has aspired to become a major world player, economically and politically. Economically, China is now one of the biggest economies in the world, and she has maintained positive economic growth for the past two decades. China has also sought to play a leading role in world affairs, and recently she was honored with the opportunity to host the 2008 Olympics in Beijing.

The process of social and economic modernization in China is also accompanied by the awareness that beneath the surface of an improving economic living standard, there are many human and psychological needs. Hou and Zhang (2007) pointed out that psychological problems among Chinese have become more prevalent and severe in recent years. They cited several trends in mental and psychological health from their review of the Chinese literature: (a) the incidence of various forms of mental illness is increasing (e.g., it was estimated that 26 million Chinese are suffering from depression alone); (b) suicide has become a major mental health concern, and it is the number one cause of death among individuals between 20 and 35; and (c) there is a huge disparity between the severity of problems presented by clients and the training and experience of the counselors who provide services.

To meet the massive mental health demands, counseling and psychotherapy in China is a discipline that is moving at a pace that matches the pace of economic and social change. Increasingly, counselors and mental health professionals are placed in schools, universities, and community agencies to provide services to the needy. Natural disasters, such as the recent earthquake (May 12, 2008) in Sichuan, have shown that psychological and mental health expertise is required and indispensable to a nation that is increasingly concerned with issues of human suffering and well-being. Indeed, since the turn of the 21st century, a number of major initiatives have been introduced that are intended to legitimize and professionalize psychological counseling in China and to aggregate a sizable group of interested individuals who could quickly acquire the know-how and be "sent" to the frontline to fill the mental health services gap. For example, the Chinese government has implemented a system licensing psychological counselors through the Chinese Ministry of Labor and Social Security Affairs (Zhong, Qian, Yao, & Xu, 2008). The Chinese Psychological Society (CPS) has also recently proposed and implemented a system of registering counseling and clinical psychologists (CPS, 2007a) and published the first edition of *Code of Ethics for Counseling and Clinical Practice* (CPS, 2007b). At the same time, academic programs in counseling and clinical psychology are also developing and expanding, aiming to produce master's- and doctoral-level trainees who would become the foundation of these specialties in China.

The purpose of this chapter is to document some of the major changes and initiatives that have taken place in the past decade and to identify areas of development that might be at risk of going "off-track" due to the pace of change and development. We would like to make the point that a discipline with academic vigor could not be built in a short span of time, and there are no short-cuts to developing a counseling profession that is based on a scholarly and scientific foundation and is synthesized with the cultural and social fabric of China. Simply importing a system of theories, research, and professional standards from the West could put together a profession with face validity yet without a firm foundation. Accordingly, as we discuss the

various initiatives and emerging trends, we would also like to share our views on what should be the priority for development and identify possible goals or destinations that the profession might aim toward, to maintain the long-term healthy development of a counseling profession that is still in the early formative stages (Hou & Zhang, 2007).

We would like to examine the following trends and developments in China: (a) the existing and emerging systems of credentialing counseling professionals, including those initiated by the government and by professional organizations; (b) the first code of ethics for counseling and clinical practice published by the CPS; (c) the status of research in counseling as reflected by recent content analyses of selected scholarly journals in China; and (d) the status of training programs in counseling in China as illustrated by selected exemplary university programs. In addition to sharing our views on strategic priorities and destinations, we would like to highlight the importance of strengthening the connection between counseling professionals in China and their counterparts in the international community and address what they can learn from each other to broaden the cross-cultural and multicultural foundation of the profession, so as to advance the profession worldwide.

RECENT DEVELOPMENTS IN LICENSURE AND CREDENTIALING OF COUNSELING PROFESSIONALS

China's First Credentialing System for Counselors

In the past decade, China has been experimenting with systems for credentialing counseling professionals despite the short history of the profession and a lack of academic programs that could provide adequate training in counseling. In 2001, the Chinese Ministry of Labor and Social Security Affairs (CMLSS), which is the national agency in charge of issuing and monitoring occupational licenses, established a licensure system for psychological counselors (Chinese Ministry of Health Affairs, 2002), which was updated in 2007 (National Committee on the Qualification and Credentialing of Psychological Counseling, 2007). Individuals with a minimum educational qualification of a junior college degree in any major (equivalent to 2 to 3 years of postgraduate education) could enroll in a government-sanctioned, 200-hour, continuing training course and on completion take a licensing examination. However, the actual number of required contact hours was only 80 hours, with the rest of the 200-hour requirement fulfilled by a variety of activities, including self-study and supervised practice. These training courses could be organized either by a university or by local groups or consortia that claimed to have qualified trainers. A person who passed the examination was granted a license to practice counseling as an "assistant psychological counselor." After completing additional experiences in relevant settings, counselors could also enroll in additional courses and take advanced examinations to qualify as "psychological counselors" and "senior psychological counselors" (National Committee on the Qualification and Credentialing of Psychological Counseling, 2007). In 2003, the Chinese Mental Health Association (CMHA), the agency in charge of monitoring the qualifications of mental health professionals in hospitals and health care agencies, also established a similar examination-based system of licensing psychotherapists for medical professionals (e.g., doctors or nurses) who were seeking involvement in the treatment of individuals with psychological concerns in medical settings (Zhong et al., 2008).

The licensure system established by the CMLSS and the CMHA was widely seen as a loosely monitored system with low entrance requirements. Individuals given the license to practice counseling might not have adequate academic training in core areas of counseling, such as psychology and education, and they are unlikely to have the needed expertise to work with clients with complex psychological and mental health concerns. Such a system also risked portraying counseling as a pseudo-profession that one could practice with only minimal and short-term training. The system is not comparable with the established credentialing systems in Western

countries in which the minimum educational qualification for entrance into the counseling profession is usually set at the master's degree level. However, given the massive demands for mental health services in China, one could also argue that a system with low entrance requirements has merits because it opens the door for many interested individuals to join the profession and to fill some of the service gaps, even though the overall quality of services provided by these individuals might be limited.

Although psychological counselor training courses and licensing procedures are currently in operation, licensed psychological counselors have yet to receive sufficient social recognition of their professional competence; subsequently, career and employment opportunities are quite limited at this time. There is the concern and perception that those who are licensed to practice might not have adequate skills and competence. As a result, places that employ psychological counselors (e.g., university counseling services) tend to rely more on the academic training and practice experience of applicants than on whether they have received the psychological counselor license.

The CPS Credentialing and Licensure System

In an effort to establish a more sustainable, rigorous, and university-degree-based system of training and credentialing of psychologists and mental health professionals, the CPS decided to offer its own version of registering clinical and counseling psychologists. Accordingly, the first edition of "Registration Criteria for Professional Organizations and Individual Practitioners in Clinical and Counseling Psychology" (hereafter, the "registration document") was published (CPS, 2007a). The registration document aimed to set explicit standards for training and credentialing in counseling and clinical psychology that are closely linked to university-based training. Specifically, the registration document defined the criteria to become (a) a recognized training program in clinical and counseling psychology, both at the master's and doctoral levels; (b) a registered clinical or counseling psychologist (at the master's and doctoral levels);

(c) a registered counseling/clinical supervisor; and (d) an approved internship site for training programs in counseling/clinical psychology. We would like to discuss three important indigenous features of the registration document.

First, the registration document views the clinical and counseling psychologist designations as almost synonymous, or to put it another way, the document did not seem to want to make a statement on what differentiates these two psychological specialties. It stated that "the specific definition of the clinical psychologist or counseling psychologist depends on how the academic degree program the candidate attended defines itself" (CPS, 2007a, p. 942). It defines clinical psychology as follows:

> One of the branches of psychology. It provides both knowledge of psychology and means of utilizing the knowledge to understand and promote mental health, physical health and social adaptation of individuals and groups. Clinical psychology has its emphasis on research about psychological problems of individuals and groups, in addition to treatment of severe mental disorders. (p. 945)

The definition of counseling psychology follows:

> One of the branches of psychology. It utilizes the knowledge of psychology to understand and promote mental health, physical health and social adaptation of individuals and groups. Counseling psychology has its emphasis on individual's general complaints in his/her daily lives in addition to promoting individual's good adaptation and coping. (p. 945)

There are many similarities between the two definitions (e.g., rooted in psychology, promote adaptation and mental health). In terms of differences, the key terms for clinical psychology seem to be *psychological problems, research,* and *severe mental health,* whereas for counseling psychology, the key tems are *general complaints* and *good adaptation and coping.*

We can only speculate on the implications of these definitions. By not entering into a debate on the difference between clinical and counseling psychology, the CPS might be trying either to simplify the system by viewing the two specialties as one group or to allow the differences to slowly emerge as training programs develop diverse emphases. The key word *research* was not included in the counseling psychology definition, and it is our hope that the omission is not intended to identify counseling psychologists as less competent from a scientific and research perspective.

Second, the document allowed for registration at the master's and doctoral levels. The registration document specified the academic, administrative, and organization features of accredited training programs. It outlined the foundation courses in psychology that students have to take at the master's degree level, including courses in ethics, psychometrics, biological bases, cognitive-affective bases, social bases, personality and human development, and psychopathology. It also required students to take specific practice courses that are typical of clinical and counseling psychology training around the world, such as theories of counseling and psychotherapy, assessment, laboratory experience and skills training, career development, counseling/clinical intervention, and practicum/internship. The practicum/internship (master's degree level) should consist of not less than 100 hours of supervised practice and 100 hours of individual and group supervision.

Doctoral-level programs require entering students to have completed the equivalent of the master's degree program described in the above paragraph. The registration document specified that doctoral programs also should include advanced courses in clinical or counseling psychology in the areas of ethics, diagnosis, research methods, statistics, and specific therapeutic techniques. It also required students to complete 150 hours of doctoral supervised practice as a practicum/internship and 100 hours of individual and group supervision.

It seems that the accreditation standards for counseling and clinical psychology programs set by the CPS were modeled after those of the American Psychological Association (APA), except that the former allows master's-level psychologists to enter the professional field to deliver the practice side of the training. Given the huge demand for counseling and psychotherapeutic services in China, this is indeed a strategy that could generate human resources in mental health efficiently. Master's-level psychologists who aspire for advanced training could enter doctoral programs to develop and refine their practice skills, as well as strengthen their competence in research. It is hoped that, in the longer term, these doctoral-level programs will produce a new generation of psychologists in China who could further advance the service, training, and scientific missions of the discipline.

Third, the registration document placed a high value on clinical/counseling supervision. Supervised practice is required in both master's- and doctoral-level training. The category of "registered supervisor" is someone who has attained registration (at the master's or doctoral level) as a counseling/clinical psychologist, and who has accumulated at least 800 postregistration psychotherapy hours and 80 supervision-practicum hours. It is not clear how many individuals would qualify to become registered supervisors given that this system of accreditation is at the very beginning stage. However, without a large group of qualified supervisors, the quality of training at the practice level could be significantly hampered (i.e., there would not be enough qualified supervisors to supervise master's- and doctoral-level trainees).

It is important to note that some progress has been made since the publication of the registration document. In 2007, the first group of 109 supervisors was granted registration. The registered supervisors were also granted reciprocal recognition by the International Federation for Psychotherapy (IFP) starting the same year. In 2008, 101 psychologists (clinical or counseling) passed the registration criteria and received formal registration. However, no training programs or internship sites were approved. The CPS also still has to reckon with the regulations of the National Education Bureau, which is the government agency responsible for approving, monitoring, and setting guidelines for all postgraduate-level programs in the country. It is still unclear if the bureau would allow CPS to define the content of postgraduate degree programs in counseling and clinical psychology.

The registration document aspired to set high standards for training and continuing education within clinical and counseling psychology in China. However, there are many challenges to its implementation. To set up accredited master's and doctoral training programs in counseling psychology, there has to be a sufficient number of teachers with adequate academic qualifications and practice experience. To establish accredited internship sites, qualified and experienced supervisors are needed to work with trainees. The small number of supervisors and psychologists who have been awarded registration status in so far can hardly meet the demand for trainers in universities and service centers. There are also challenges in generating public and government support for the registration standards. In China, academic initiatives (e.g., special course work and internship requirements for the training of counseling psychologists and clinical psychologists) without the support and sanction of the government are unlikely to survive and prosper. Consequently, CPS has to work with major universities that are interested in meeting its accreditation standards as well as with the government agencies who currently exercise control over postgraduate training resources and standards.

Summary of Recent Development in Licensure and Credentialing

In the past decade, China has implemented systems for credentialing psychological counselors, counseling psychologists, and clinical psychologists. In the case of credentialing psychological counselors (i.e., the psychological counselor licensure systems established by the Minister of Labor and Minister of Health Affairs), the set qualification is quite low (e.g., not even an undergraduate degree in psychology is required), and consequently, many interested individuals could become licensed by taking the licensure examination without enrolling in a substantive, university-based, academic training program. In the case of the registration system for counseling/clinical psychologists proposed by the CPS, the set qualification is quite high (e.g., extensive course work and practicum requirements), and as a result, very few individuals could meet the requirements and become registered (e.g., as of 2008, only 101 applicants were registered). Consequently, neither system appears to be satisfactory.

In his review of the development of school counseling in China, Jiang (2005) pointed out that China has to struggle with two perspectives of training and credentialing counseling professionals: *professionalism* and *crowd movement*. Professionalism requires trained professionals to conduct counseling intervention, and the logical path is the one that is already in place in the Western world, such as in the United States. Such a system is characterized by vigorous programs of counselor training and legislated registration systems that are closely monitored. Crowd movement refers to the mobilization of individuals who are volunteers and who are committed to becoming pioneers in the counseling profession even though they have not received training comparable with recognized professional standards. From this perspective, Jiang believed that professionalism is clearly the preferred route, if the required human and academic resources are available. However, Jiang conceded that both professionalism and crowd movement have to coexist given the tremendous demand for services, and professionals have to share the arena with those who are motivated but not properly or adequately trained. The latter could still produce positive outcomes, if given tasks that are less challenging, and the risk of causing harm could be minimized through ongoing training and supervision.

Even though Jiang (2005) was addressing school counseling personnel in his article, his thoughts on the dilemma between professionalism and crowd movement deserve much consideration. One can take the view that China needs a loose credentialing system (e.g., licensed professional counselors) as an interim measure so that partially trained counselors (with ongoing supervision and continuous training) could fill the mental health service gap. Yet starting from now and into the distant future, professionalism characterized by rigorous training/credentialing programs meeting international professional and academic standards should be the ultimate destination for the counseling profession.

ESTABLISHMENT OF THE FIRST *CODE OF ETHICS* FOR COUNSELING AND CLINICAL PRACTICE

The first edition of the *Code of Ethics for Counseling and Clinical Practice* (CPS, 2007b; hereafter referred to as *Code of Ethics*) was released by the CPS to guide the practice of psychologists in counseling/clinical service and training. The purposes of the *Code of Ethics* were to "allow the general public to achieve a better understanding of the core ideas of the professional ethics as well as the professional responsibilities in the field of psychotherapy and counseling practice" (CPS, 2007b, p. 947). The *Code of Ethics* provides guiding principles to handle complaints initiated against those who are registered as clinical and counseling psychologist in CPS.

The *Code of Ethics* is modeled after the *Ethical Principles of Psychologists and Code of Conduct* of the APA (2002). Five general principles are listed in the forefront as cardinal principles behind the code: (1) beneficence, (2) responsibility, (3) integrity, (4) justice, and (5) respect. These principles are very similar to those of the APA ethical principles, which identified beneficence and nonmalfeasance, fidelity and responsibility, integrity, justice, and respect for people's rights and dignity as the general principles (APA, 2002, pp. 3–4).

The *Code of Ethics* identifies seven clusters of ethical standards, namely, (1) professional relationship; (2) privacy and confidentiality; (3) professional responsibility; (4) assessment and evaluation; (5) teaching, training, and supervision; (6) research and publication; and (7) resolving ethical issues. A close examination of the specific code or standard suggests that the content is highly similar to those of the APA ethical code (APA, 2002). We will use two examples to illustrate the similarities. First, under point 1.9 in the *Code of Ethics,* it was stated that "clinical and counseling psychologists are prohibited to develop any sexual or romantic intimate relationship with those who once sought professional service from them for a period of 3 years following the last professional contact" (CPS, 2007b, p. 947). The stipulation is very similar to the APA ethical principles, which stated that "psychologists do not engage in sexual intimacies with clients/patients for at least two years after cessation after the termination of therapy" and "psychologists do not engage in sexual intimacies with former clients/patients even after a two-year interval except in the most unusual circumstances" (APA, 2002, p. 14). Second, the *Code of Ethics* stated that exceptions to confidentiality in counseling are (a) when a client is in danger of self-harm or harm to others, (b) when a client is found to have a transmittable life-threatening disease that would cause harm to others, (c) when abuses are involved, and (d) when disclosure is demanded by law. These exceptions are similar to the standards listed in the privacy and confidentiality section of APA ethical principles (APA, 2002, p. 7) as well as other international guidelines.

The publication of the *Code of Ethics* is indeed a very positive step forward. However, it should be noted that China is a large country, and it will take time for the ethical values and principles to be transmitted from the major cities and more developed regions to locations and settings in more remote regions. Moreover, the establishment of an ethical code does not guarantee ethical practice among professionals; a professional-society-based ethical code, if not backed by corresponding legislative codes or other forms of organizational or professional sanctioning, could become a "tiger without teeth," and individuals could still continue their unethical counseling practices once they stop being a member of the professional group. We hope that the CPS will form a system to ensure that the principles identified in the *Code of Ethics* are smoothly enforced, including a mechanism to monitor noncompliance, as well as resources devoted to setting up a fair and just procedural system where complaints are received, heard, and handled. It is through the implementation of a transparent and fair ethics monitoring system that future progress will be measured.

The Chinese *Code of Ethics* is heavily influenced by existing ethical codes in the Western world. We

hope that, in the years ahead, counseling and clinical psychologists in China could examine, modify, and expand the *Code of Ethics* to make the guidelines consistent with experiences, values, and beliefs of the Chinese cultural context. It is also imperative that the *Code of Ethics* be broadened to include the general field of psychology, instead of just targeting counseling and clinical professionals. As psychology becomes a prominent and mainstream discipline in China, psychologists in diverse subfields are likely to encounter ethical concerns and dilemmas, and the *Code of Ethics* should be applicable to all psychologists.

RESEARCH IN COUNSELING

Research is critical to the healthy development of counseling in China. According to Zhong (quoted in Li, Duan, Ding, Yue, & Beitman, 1994, p. 280), there were very few published articles in counseling and psychotherapy in China in the 1980s and early 1990s; and moreover, only 159 articles were identified between 1979 and 1992 in several key mental health and psychology journals. Li et al. (1994) observed that most of these 159 studies were case reports and records of the process of psychotherapeutic interaction. There were a few empirical studies, but "the quality of the studies is not advanced or well developed because true scientific psychotherapy is just beginning in China and aspects of major theories are not sufficiently understood" (p. 279).

Even though some authors are still concerned about the status of counseling research in China (e.g., Hou & Zhang, 2007; Leung, Guo, & Lam, 2000), now more than a decade later significant progress has been made at least in the number of published articles in counseling and the scope covered by these articles. We will summarize two recent journal content analyses conducted by Hou, Bai, Li, and Li (2008) and Hou, Gong, Yu, and Chang (2008) on key journals related to counseling.

The first content analysis (Hou, Bai, et al., 2008) involved the *Chinese Mental Health Journal* (*CMHJ*), a journal sponsored by the CMHA that has been published since 1987. The *CMHJ* is a national-level journal in China and covers diverse areas of mental health and psychology, including clinical psychology, psychiatry, psychosomatic medicine, educational psychology, and social psychology. The journal is now abstracted in scholarly databases both in China and overseas, including the ULRICH'S Index of International Journals and PsycINFO.

Hou, Bai, et al. (2008) identified a number of typical topics covered by counseling-related journals in the United States, including counseling intervention outcomes, counseling interventions in association with other treatments (e.g., medication), ethical issues, counseling techniques and applications, counseling processes, counselor qualification and professional development, and surveys on the status of counseling. Of the 2,536 articles published in *CMHJ* between 1997 and 2006 (excluding non-scholarly articles such as news and minutes of meetings), 400 articles (15.8% of total articles) were classified as within the above categories (the rest of the articles were articles with a medical emphasis or were in general psychology that were not judged to be within the turf of the counseling discipline). Several observations were made by Hou, Bai, et al. First, a majority of the 400 articles ($n = 261$ or 65.25% of total) were related to counseling intervention outcomes, including outcome studies with clients suffering from mental disorders ($n = 90$) and from physical disorders ($n = 60$), studies aiming to elevate the subjective well-being of normal individuals ($n = 83$), and case studies ($n = 28$) that described details of intervention and outcomes. Second, the next most frequent category was counseling techniques and applications ($n = 54$, 13.5% of total), involving articles that described concepts and techniques and their applications with specific concerns and issues. This category of articles included a small number of articles with indigenous content, including the adaptation of Western techniques and methods (e.g., the introduction of different methods of treating panic disorders) and integration with culture-based beliefs into conceptualization and treatment. For example, Zhang and Yang (1998) developed the Taoist cognitive psychotherapy to treat anxiety-related problems. The Taoist principles—of seeking gains without causing harm, being content with

what is available, countering stress or tough barriers through noncompetitive attitudes and tender strategies, and accepting the realities of life and being at peace with nature—are used to offer "doctrinal direction" in the process of exploring beliefs and cognitive restructuring. Third, research related to the process of counseling, an important aspect of counseling research in the United States, was underrepresented ($n = 28$, 7% of total articles). It is perhaps due to the methodological sophistication and time involved in studying the counseling process that many researchers were reluctant to investigate this area of research.

A similar content analysis was conducted on the *Journal of Chinese Clinical Psychology* (*JCCP*) by Hou, Gong, et al. (2008). *JCCP* is a national-level journal that has been published by the CMHA since 1993. *JCCP* is the flagship clinical psychology journal in China, aiming to cover the diverse aspects of clinical psychology, including psychological and educational assessment, theories and practice of psychotherapy and counseling, psychological characteristics of different client groups, and current mental health issues and development. Articles published in *JCCP* are abstracted in major databases in China as well as overseas, including PsycINFO, and Medline.

Hou, Gong, et al. (2008) analyzed the content of *JCCP* from 1993 to 2007. Using scholarly categories similar to those used in Hou, Bai, et al. (2008), they identified only 204 of a total of 1,832 articles (11.14% of total) falling within the general area of counseling. A majority of the 204 articles addressed counseling intervention outcome (85 of 204 articles, 41.7% of total), including psychological interventions as concurrent treatment to medical problems (e.g., use of biofeedback), interventions for different mental health disorders, mental health promotion, and case studies. The next most popular category was counseling theories and techniques (48 of 204 articles, or 23.6% of total). Even though the integration of counseling with Chinese culture was regarded as important by some articles in this category, Hou, Gong, et al. (2008) found very little evidence of indigenization. They found that articles were mostly concerned with how to use primarily Western established counseling concepts and strategies in the treatment of Chinese individuals instead of seeking a synthesis of Chinese culture into the conceptualization and treatment process. Meanwhile, Hou, Gong, et al. (2008) also noted a gradual increase in articles that studied "normal" individuals, from none in 1993 to about 24% of the articles in 2006. It reflected a growing awareness that counseling and psychotherapy are not just applicable to individuals with mental health concerns but also to others who might encounter situational and developmental transitions. In a clinical psychology journal, this is a noteworthy finding.

The content analyses conducted by Hou, Bai, et al. (2008) and Hou, Gong, et al. (2008) conveyed only a partial view of the status of research in China. The content analyses were restricted to two journals with a clinical mental health focus, and the identified content areas did not reveal the full spectrum of themes covered by the journals. For example, articles on general mental health and psychological adjustment, which is a common theme addressed in U.S. counseling journals, are not clearly reflected in the pre-identified content themes. Also, the number of journal articles does not convey the quality of the research and scholarship. Yet the increase in journal articles focusing on areas that are central to the counseling profession (e.g., counseling outcome, theories, and techniques) around the world is still a significant step forward. We expect that the number of counseling-related articles will increase further as research and development continues to progress within the Chinese scientific and scholarly community and as the profession of counseling becomes firmly rooted in Chinese soil both in career opportunities and government recognition. Synthesizing with the international literature is an important future direction. Even though abstracts of both of the journals examined in the above content analyses are now included in databases, such as PsycINFO, where scholars from around the world can access them, only researchers with Chinese language competence could comprehend the articles, which are in Chinese. In the future, it would be desirable if authors with bilingual competence could conduct topical reviews of these articles in other languages (e.g., English) so that key findings and theoretical advances could be introduced to and synthesized with the international literature.

Overall, it is important for the counseling profession in China to strengthen the quality of its research and scholarship. Improvements in scholarship should be reflected in future issues of academic journals, both in the quality of the articles published and the breadth of their coverage. We hope that these journals could be the final destinations for some of the best scholarly work on counseling in China and internationally.

RECENT DEVELOPMENTS IN TRAINING PROGRAMS

Training is perhaps one of the most urgent needs in the development of the counseling profession in China. Indeed, China has moved rapidly toward developing postgraduate training programs in various subspecialties in psychology, including those with an emphasis on counseling and clinical psychology (please note that the accreditation standards set by CPS described in the previous section of this chapter are not yet implemented). This section will describe, review, and analyze several counseling or counseling psychology training programs in China. We would like to (a) promote readers' understanding of the content of these programs, (b) identify unique indigenous themes and those that could be perceived as strengths, and (c) suggest ways that these training programs can be improved. We would like to note that our intention is not to use Western standards (e.g., APA training standards) to evaluate these programs. Instead, we want to discuss the goals and needs of training programs, resources considerations, and barriers to development that are specific to the Chinese cultural context. We believe that international readers would benefit from having a better understanding of these training programs so that they can help generate ideas and critiques useful to improving training in counseling in China and elsewhere.

First of all, we should note that in China counseling and counseling psychology programs are often not distinguished from those in clinical or school psychology (as illustrated by the discussion in the previous section on the definitions of clinical and counseling psychology given in the CPS registration document). Most of the training programs are housed in psychology departments, and a sizable number of these psychology departments are located within normal universities (i.e., comprehensive universities but with a substantial amount of resources devoted to training teachers and educational professionals). There are three subdisciplines of psychology that are usually identifiable: general psychology, educational and developmental psychology, and applied psychology. Counseling and counseling psychology are positioned as components of applied psychology or educational and developmental psychology, along with clinical and school psychology. As a result, most training programs do not differentiate the training for clinical, counseling, or school psychology students. One major reason is the lack of faculty trainers in each specialty area. Students in and graduates from those programs declare their emphasis area based first on their major advisor's primary interest and expertise (e.g., if a student's major advisor is not in counseling psychology, the student could not declare his or her primary expertise to be counseling psychology), and second, on the available types of practicum/internship experiences (e.g., the student might not have adequate practicum/internship experiences) as well as the student's research areas (e.g., dissertation study might not have addressed areas typical to counseling psychology). In recent years, however, some programs in top-tier universities (e.g., Beijing Normal University)—where there are faculty who themselves were trained as counseling psychologists—have started using counseling and counseling psychology to title their training programs and provide students with practice and research experiences that allow them to claim legitimacy as counseling psychologists.

China witnessed great efforts in clinical and professional training as the applied psychology disciplines became recognized in China in the early 1990s (Li et al., 1994). Initially, many training programs were mostly short-term in length (or longer term based on scattered, periodic workshops and seminars) and were Western theory-based, non-degree-awarding, and conducted by scholars from the West in collaboration with Chinese psychologists or psychiatrists (Hou & Zhang, 2007). In recent years, however, great efforts have been devoted to establishing graduate training programs, which has been on the priority list of the CMHA. As a result, psychology training programs (in general, educational/developmental, or applied psychology) both at the master's and doctoral levels have been established in many top-tier comprehensive and liberal arts universities throughout the country. At an amazing speed, some of the programs have produced a significant number of graduates and achieved feasible training structures and resources in terms of recruiting faculty, articulating training philosophies, specifying admission criteria, establishing degree requirements and standards, offering students relevant courses and experiences, and so forth. In the following section, we synthesize our observations of several well-known programs, including the PhD and MA training programs from Peking University, Beijing Normal University, and Central China Normal University. We hope that the common features observed from these programs could shed light on their strengths and limitations.

In all the above universities, the master's degree in counseling or clinical psychology is a post–BA degree program (which can be in psychology, medicine, or other disciplines), and applicants are screened for (a) completion of a BA degree, (b) required psychology courses, and (c) possessing sound personality and interpersonal skills suitable for working in helping professions. In addition, applicants seeking entrance into master's degree programs have to take a national entrance examination in psychology, unless they are exempted due to strong undergraduate academic achievements (e.g., psychology graduates with high GPAs in top universities). Those seeking entrance into doctoral programs have to take an entrance examination set by individual universities (as opposed to taking a national-level examination). These entrance examinations are designed to provide data for selection even though their validity is yet to be established. Once applicants are admitted into a master's degree program, the study period is typically 2 to 3 years; taking longer than 4 years to complete it is not generally allowed. Students are required to take courses in four areas: (1) required general courses, such as English, natural dialectical methods, and scientific socialism; (2) basic degree courses, such as statistics, research methods, counseling theories, psychological assessment theories and methods, psychopathology, and so forth; (3) specific degree courses, such as helping skills, group counseling, and ethical and legal issues; and (4) elective specialized courses, such as crisis intervention, school counseling, career development and planning, psychology of love and marriage, psychological health of the elderly, family therapy, play and sandbox therapy, and counselor personal development.

In counseling practice training, students are required to complete a specified number of hours in clinical shadowing, direct client contact, supervision, and personal growth/development via individual or group counseling. The training in the science of counseling psychology can be fulfilled by a required thesis and involvement in various research and scholarly activities offered by the university. The thesis completion needs to be under the direct supervision of a faculty advisor and approved by a thesis committee.

The PhD programs are typically 3 years beyond a master's degree. The admission requirements usually include (a) a master's degree in counseling or mental health related fields, such as psychiatry, medical psychology, and clinical psychology; (b) completion of all the required courses of the master's degree program in counseling; (c) completion of specified practicum and supervision hours; (d) English proficiency; and (e) at least one journal publication in the major journals in the field. In addition, applicants also need to demonstrate ability and skills in communication, interpersonal interactions, self-reflection, group or team collaboration, and social judgment.

The course work for PhD students also covers four areas: (1) required general courses, (2) basic degree courses, (3) specific degree courses, and (4) elective, specialized courses. The training in clinical skills is similar to that designed for master's

degree programs, only the number of hours required is higher. In the area of scientific research, students are to publish one to two articles of either theoretical or empirical work in one of the major journals in the field, in addition to a dissertation that has to include one or more empirical studies.

Overall, the programs offered by the institutions we reviewed are quite similar in their (a) training objective, (b) training model (scientist-practitioner), and (c) degree requirements. All these programs aspire to set high standards in both science and practice. Both master's and doctoral students are required and expected to publish in national top-tier journals in addition to their thesis and dissertation research. We can see at least two unique features embedded in the Chinese programs relative to most other countries: (1) dual emphasis on developing the knowledge and character of students and (2) requiring second-language proficiency.

"Comprehensive development" is a basic educational philosophy rooted in the Chinese culture—the belief that without good character and mental and physical health, knowledge and skills are useless, or useful for the wrong courses. Conversely, without knowledge and skills, having a good character and being healthy would not be adequate either. Accordingly, all graduate training programs in applied psychology are expected to produce graduates who show excellence in morality and integrity, intelligence and knowledge, and physical and mental health. For instance, in the training programs of the three universities reviewed in this section, the primary training objectives include the following elements: establishing a scientific worldview, namely, (a) pursuing the truth and deriving truth from facts and (b) loving the country, abiding by the law and regulations, having a good moral character, and actively contributing to the modernization of the country and serving the people. These "character" objectives are also clearly articulated by the Committee of Counseling and Psychotherapy of CMHA, a national-level professional body that sets mental health training priorities.

All postgraduate students are required to learn a second language (most students choose English) to be able to acquire subject knowledge from literature sources in other countries. Learning a third language is strongly encouraged. This requirement reflects the openness of training programs in embracing Western knowledge and skills. It is a requirement that helps prepare world citizens and international scholars for the global community. It also prepares applied psychologists who are motivated to make international connections and contribute to the internationalization of the counseling profession, as well as to the advancement and renewal of the Western approaches to counseling and psychology.

More and better seem to be the directions of counseling and counseling psychology training in the near future in China. More and more programs will be established and the quality of training will continue to rise—due to the attention of and support from national professional bodies such as the CMHA and CPS, and governmental entities such as the Ministry of Education. It is undeniable that applied psychology training programs in major Chinese universities are committed to excellence (as least from their program descriptions), but there are still substantial concerns, which include (a) the lack of professors who have sufficient academic preparation and qualification to instruct students and direct dissertations, and a mediocre salary structure that discourages potential trainees from pursuing academic careers at universities; (b) embracing Western theory and practice without sufficient attention paid to engaging students in learning and pursuing indigenous scholarly work; and (c) insufficient resources, including "hardware" resources that are important in counseling skill training (e.g., counseling labs) and human resources (e.g., practicum/internship supervisors and sites). Many questions about the future of counseling training remain unanswered, including (a) how to monitor the quality of training, (b) what are the substantive differences between clinical and counseling psychology training, (c) how to prepare students to meet the mental health needs of the mass population, and (d) how to incorporate and sequence layers of scientist-practitioner training into programs that also have to meet other uniform national requirements and standards (e.g., character and social

education, second language skills) within the typical time span allowable for postgraduate training.

THE ROADS AHEAD: SOME THOUGHTS ON FUTURE DESTINATIONS

It is abundantly clear from this review that China is moving at full speed toward professionalizing the counseling profession and legitimizing counseling as a mainstream academic discipline. We are excited about the progress that has been made in the past decade, yet we are also concerned that the profession might have set its focus on "moving quickly" without clarifying the destinations.

First, the counseling profession in China could be substantially strengthened by developing theories and practices that are consistent with the Chinese cultural context (Leung & Chen, in press; Savickas, 2007; Zhang, Hu, & Pope, 2002). The development of indigenous counseling in Chinese communities might include research that examines the utility of adapting Western theories and methods for local Chinese contexts, as well as discovering the idiosyncratic features of (a) diverse client populations in Chinese communities, (b) training and credentialing of counseling professionals, and (c) interventions that incorporate indigenous practices into treatment (Blowers, 1996). (Please refer to Chapter 6 of this volume for a detailed analysis on the nature of indigenization.) The promotion and development of indigenous research and practice should be synthesized into research, practice, journal publication, and postgraduate student training. It might be useful for scholars and practitioners in different Chinese communities in Asia and around the world (which at times are divided by geographic, social, and political boundaries) to develop a mechanism of collaboration such that the outcomes of indigenization could be used and tested in these communities.

Second, it would be useful for China to continue to revise its systems of credentialing counseling professionals so that a credible system of certifying/qualifying could be identified and implemented. Such systems should be (a) sustainable, with a continual supply of applicants who are graduates of comprehensive training programs offered by academic institutions; (b) recognized and endorsed by the government so that those certified to practice would have clear, visible, and attainable career paths; (c) trusted by the public so that the services provided by certified professionals would be perceived as competent, responsible, and ethical; and (d) supported by a workable system of monitoring that is transparent, just, and fair. We agree with Jiang's (2005) and Hou and Zhang's (2007) observation that the massive need for mental health services in educational and social service settings at the present moment might require the participation of paraprofessionals who have only received partial training in counseling practice. However, as time progresses and as training programs mature, there should be distinctions made between those who are professionally trained and those who might have received training at the paraprofessional level, and both types of individuals should have an important role to play in providing services now and into the distant future.

Third, we strongly suggest that the counseling profession in China aspire to use its skills and competence to meet diverse Chinese societal needs, including needs emerging in various social sectors (e.g., the unemployed, the economically disadvantaged living in remote regions) and from various social emergencies and disasters (e.g., earthquakes, snowstorms). In addition to offering treatments to clients in typical therapeutic contexts (e.g., one-to-one counseling, group counseling), counseling professionals should also pay attention to their potential roles as advocates for their clients, empower their clients to confront challenges and adversities in their environments, and contribute to changes in various social and cultural systems and subsystems to sustain the well-being of clients (Blustein, Elman, & Gerstein, 2001; Toporek, Gerstein, Fouad, Roysircar-Sodowsky, & Israel, 2005). Advocacy initiatives in China are still relatively new, and counseling professionals have to

proceed cautiously so that their actions are synchronized with those provided by various stakeholders within the social and political system (Leung & Chen, in press).

Fourth, it seems especially important for the counseling profession in China to maintain a strong tie with the counseling community internationally. Whereas internationalization has been promoted by the U.S. counseling profession after the discipline has become relatively mature, in contrast, internationalization has occurred in the Chinese counseling profession at the beginning stage of its development. To the present time, counseling professionals in China have been on the receiving end of various international contacts and collaborations, and they have benefited from training courses and events offered by their counterparts around the world (Hou & Zhang, 2007). As the counseling profession in China progresses and matures, it would be helpful for professionals to play a more active role in various forms of collaboration, as they should enrich the global counseling community through synthesizing Eastern and Western cultural values into their research and practice work (Leung, 2003).

REFERENCES

American Psychological Association. (2002). *Ethical principles of psychologists and code of conduct.* Washington, DC: Author.

Blowers, G. H. (1996). The prospects for a Chinese psychology. In M. H. Bond (Ed.), *Handbook of Chinese psychology* (pp. 1–14). Hong Kong, SAR, China: Oxford University Press.

Blustein, D., Elman, N., & Gerstein, L. (2001, August). *Executive report: Social action groups national counseling psychology conference.* Houston, TX: Author.

Chinese Ministry of Health Affairs. (2002). *State professional criteria of counselors.* Beijing, People's Republic of China: Central Broadcast and Television University Press.

Authors' Note: All three authors contributed equally to this chapter. We would like to thank Li Xixi for commenting on an earlier draft of this manuscript.

Chinese Psychological Society. (2007a). Registration criteria for professional organizations and individual practitioners in clinical and counseling psychology. *Acta Psychologica Sinica, 39*, 942–946. (In Chinese)

Chinese Psychological Society. (2007b). Code of ethics for counseling and clinical practice (first ed.). *Acta Psychologica Sinica, 39*, 947–950. (In Chinese)

Hou, Z-J., Bai, R., Li, X., & Li, W. X. (2008). A ten-year content analysis of articles on counseling and psychotherapy published in the *Chinese Mental Health Journal*. Unpublished manuscript, Beijing Normal University, People's Republic of China.

Hou, Z-J., Gong, J. H., Yu, S. J., & Chang, X. L. (2008). A content analysis of articles on counseling and psychotherapy published in *Journal of Chinese Clinical Psychology*. *Journal of Chinese Clinical Psychology, 16*, 557–560.

Hou, Z-J., & Zhang, N. (2007). Counseling psychology in China. *Applied Psychology: An International Review, 56*, 33–50.

Jiang, G. R. (2005). The development of school counseling in the Chinese mainland: A review. *Journal of Basic Education, 14*, 65–82.

Leung, S. A. (2003). A journal worth traveling: Globalization of counseling psychology. *The Counseling Psychologist, 31*, 412–419.

Leung, S. A., & Chen, P-W. (in press). Developing counseling psychology in Chinese communities in Asia: Indigenous, multicultural, and cross-cultural considerations. *The Counseling Psychologist*.

Leung, S. A., Guo, L., & Lam, M. P. (2000). Counseling psychology in higher educational institutions in China. *The Counseling Psychologist, 28*, 81–99.

Li, M-G., Duan, C., Ding, B-K, Yue, D-M., & Beitman, B. D. (1994). Psychotherapy integration in modern China. *Journal of Psychotherapy Practice and Research, 3*, 277–283.

Ministry of Labor and Social Security of the People's Republic of China. (2001). *Counseling psychologist: National vocation criterion*. Beijing, People's Republic of China: Central Radio & TV University Press.

National Bureau of Statistics of China (2007). *China statistical year*. Retrieved April 13, 2009, from http://www.stats.gov.cn/tjsj/ndsj/2007/indexeh.htm

National Committee on the Qualification and Credentialing of Psychological Counseling. (2007). *Occupational qualification for psychological counseling: An examination and assessment framework*. Beijing, People's Republic of China: Author.

Savickas, M. L. (2007). Internationalization of counseling psychology: Constructing cross-national consensus and collaboration. *Applied Psychology: An International Review, 56*, 182–188.

Toporek, R. L., Gerstein, L. H., Fouad, N. A., Roysircar-Sodowsky, G., & Israel, T. (Eds.). (2005). *Handbook of social justice in counseling psychology: Leadership, vision, and action*. Thousand Oaks, CA: Sage.

Zhang, W., Hu, X., & Pope, M. (2002). The evolution of career guidance and counseling in the People's Republic of China. *Career Development Quarterly, 50*, 226–245.

Zhang, Y.-L., & Yang, D.-S. (1998). The development of cognitive psychotherapy according to Taoism. *Chinese Mental Health Journal, 12*, 188–190.

Zhong, J., Qian, M., Yao, P., & Xu, K. (2008). Accountability in professional psychology: The improvement in Mainland China. In J. E. Hall & E. M. Altmaier (Eds.), *Global promise: Quality assurance and accountability in professional psychology* (pp. 190–198). Cary, NC: Oxford University Press.

12

A Shifting Professional Development and Identity in Taiwan

Integrating Western Counseling Psychology With the Spirit and Worldview of Taiwanese Culture

台灣諮商心理學專業發展與認同之移轉：
西方諮商心理學與台灣文化精神及世界觀的整合

LI-FEI WANG, HUNG CHIAO, AND P. PAUL HEPPNER

The counseling psychology profession in Taiwan (officially known as the Republic of China) has developed over the past 50 years. It was first imported from the United States as school guidance and later developed as the Division of Counseling Psychology (DCP) in the Taiwan Guidance and Counseling Association. Now, it has grown as a new and independent association, named the Taiwan Counseling Psychology Association in 2008. The development of the counseling psychology profession has been heavily influenced by (a) Taiwanese government policies, (b) economic growth and education, (c) Western counseling psychology, (d) significant societal events, and (e) the indigenous cultural

reflections of Taiwanese values among Taiwanese psychology researchers and practitioners (e.g., importance of interpersonal harmony, collectivistic and holistic perspectives, filial piety). The Taiwanese counseling psychology profession has been dramatically shaped by the Taiwan Psychologist Statute of 2001. This was the first national counseling psychology licensure system among all Asian countries. The counseling psychology profession in Taiwan is developing its own identity and uniqueness as a helping profession. It integrates an inheritance of Western counseling psychology with the spirit and worldview of the Taiwanese culture. The journey of finding their own identity as Taiwanese counseling psychologists has just begun, and the authors truly hope that this chapter can serve as a platform to share the development of the Taiwanese counseling psychology profession with their international colleagues.

This chapter first provides an analysis of the three major influences on the Taiwanese counseling psychology profession: (a) the school systems within the Taiwanese cultural context, (b) a synthesis of Western counseling psychology and indigenous cultural factors, and (c) the Taiwan Psychologist Statute of 2001. The last section of this chapter presents challenges and opportunities that Taiwanese counseling psychologists are encountering when developing an indigenous profession. Due to the limitation of space and their own biases, the authors cannot document all the people, organizations, and critical social events that have affected the development of the Taiwanese counseling psychology profession. However, they would like to acknowledge the synergetic group efforts of innumerable individuals in the counseling psychology profession in Taiwan: Taiwanese counseling psychologists (both researchers and practitioners), helping professionals across various disciplines (e.g., school educators, government officials, and lawmakers), and international institutions and faculty that have trained numerous Taiwanese counselors and counseling psychologists.

ROOTS IN THE SCHOOL SYSTEMS AND TAIWANESE CULTURAL CONTEXT

Although counseling psychology in Taiwan seems to be a relatively new profession, school guidance and counseling were first introduced in the 1950s from the United States (e.g., Chen, 1999). The Taiwanese Ministry of Education sent groups of university faculty members and school administrators to receive special training in school guidance from 1951 to 1962 (Zhang & Wu, 1999). The first guidance institute in 1960 was implemented at the National Overseas Chinese High School and Taipei Municipal Zhong Shan Girls High School (Zhang & Wu, 1999). Subsequently, guidance and counseling services were gradually implemented in all school systems. Since

1960, the development of counseling and counseling psychology have been intertwined and profoundly influenced by educational policies and school cultures. For example, when the national government developed the Six-Year National Development Plan in 1991, the school guidance and counseling projects were designed as the first and the most important part of the plan in national education policies (Chen, 1999).

An educational focus is preferred in Taiwan because (a) Taiwanese highly value education and wish to provide a better learning environment (physical and psychological) to their next generation; (b) counseling and/or psychotherapy is frequently associated with, or even stigmatized as, a psychological treatment for mental illness, whereas education is a very positive concept for people who actively seek personal growth and advancement; (c) the concept of "counseling" is similar to *jae-huo* (meaning "resolving the puzzles"), which is one of the teacher's critical responsibilities in Confucius's philosophy; and, (d) counselors have been employed in the guidance offices of elementary, middle, and high schools as well as universities since 1960 (Chen, 1999). Today, more than 78% of counseling psychologists are employed in school settings and university counseling centers (Lin, Hsieh, & Sun, 2008). Although counseling psychologists in Taiwan provide counseling services similar to those of U.S. psychologists, some of these professionals still call themselves counseling teachers rather than psychologists. Similarly, clients view themselves as "receiving counseling" in a manner of "going to class." This means they receive "education" rather than "treatment" in counseling.

In addition, throughout the development of the counseling psychology field in Taiwan, the profession has been associated with and has received resources from the educational system. For instance, after the licensure system was established, Taiwanese counseling psychologists found that there were very few employment opportunities for them in the marketplace. When they sought collaboration with administrators within education, medicine, and social welfare to create employment opportunities, their initial success in 2004 was in the creation of part-time employment positions in the elementary schools (Chao, Wang, & Yang, 2006).

However, these new opportunities in education also created new challenges for the counseling psychology profession in Taiwan. For example, when counseling psychologists provided services within elementary schools, they found their role and function was not simply to offer individual counseling to the children; they were also expected to play multiple roles, such as those of a counselor, consultant, educator, and collaborator for school counselors, teachers as well as parents. Because of the magnitude of collaboration between counseling psychologists and teachers, and the multiple roles of counseling psychologists within this unique cultural context, parameters of confidentiality were established to match the larger collectivistic culture. Sometimes these parameters conflicted with the Western perspective of ethical principles (Wang, Tu, & Chao, 2008). In sum, the professional development of Taiwanese counseling psychology has been shaped by the cultural norms and value of education (especially in the early years). Later, the profession was closely intertwined with school counseling and was consistently supported by the educational initiatives and policies of the government.

INFLUENCE OF WESTERN KNOWLEDGE OF COUNSELING PSYCHOLOGY AND INDIGENOUS CULTURAL VALUES

The Taiwanese counseling psychology profession has also been influenced by counseling psychology in the United States. Because many Taiwanese counseling psychology pioneers and leaders received their doctoral training in the United States, they adopted the U.S. training models, curricula, textbooks, and counseling theories and techniques when they first established counseling psychology training programs in Taiwan (Wang, 2008). For example, most of the graduate-level counseling psychology training programs still follow the accreditation models of the American Psychological Association and/or American Counseling Association (Chen, 1994). In addition,

school counselor training includes educational, developmental, cognitive, and counseling psychology at the bachelor level. However, the U.S. format of therapy and an emphasis on the clients' best interests did not quite match the cultural values of the Taiwanese people. As a result, counseling psychology has been viewed by the general public as a "Western import" (Jin, 1999).

An indigenous movement within Taiwanese psychology started in the late 1980s. Both scientific advancements and the practice of counseling have subsequently stimulated Taiwanese counseling psychologists to reevaluate Western imported counseling theories as well as their responsiveness to the indigenous culture and societal needs (Jin, 1999). Consequently, Taiwanese scholars have developed empirically supported indigenous counseling theories and models (e.g., Chen, 2005; Jin, 1997; Wang et al., 2008), and they are establishing a unique Taiwanese professional identity.

Lin (2008) analyzed the empirical studies published during 1993–2007 in the *Chinese Journal of Guidance and Counseling* (*CJGC*; formerly *Chinese Annual Report of Guidance and Counseling*). She found that 36% of the published studies used qualitative methodologies and 64% employed quantitative designs. The use of qualitative methodologies in counseling psychology, however, has rapidly increased. Fifty-four percent of the studies published in the *CJGC* from 2002 to 2006 used qualitative methodologies; family and relationships, counselor training and supervision, and psychological interventions were the most frequent research topics. Wang, Lin, Kao, Gian, and Lee (2004) found that a total of 45% of the counseling and psychotherapy qualitative research in Taiwan examined topics with children and adolescent populations. In addition, the majority of qualitative counseling studies not only identified the characteristics and inner worlds of clients but also examined the therapeutic factors and intervention strategies employed in counseling and psychotherapy (both individual and group treatment). These findings were different from the findings of counseling and psychotherapy qualitative research in North America and Germany (see Frommer,

Langenbach, & Streeck, 2004; Rennie, 2004), which emphasized the central role of the collectivistic cultural context within the family as well as the need for a broader ecological perspective for a wide range of professionals (e.g., school counselors, teachers, parents, counseling psychologists) to provide successful treatment for children.

These results have led some Taiwanese counseling psychologists to question the appropriateness of applying Western counseling theories and practices to Taiwanese clients with an Eastern cultural context. Subsequently, Taiwanese scholars have begun to establish indigenous models of counseling and psychotherapy (Wang et al., 2004). For example, studies have examined culturally specific elements of counseling, such as therapeutic factors tied to group work (e.g., Lin & Wang, 1998), individual counseling theories (e.g., Chen, 2005; Jin, 1997; Yee, 2005), school counseling (e.g., Wang, 2008), and group counseling (e.g., Wu, 2005). Drawing from these qualitative studies, scholars have begun to establish an indigenous knowledge base for the development of Taiwanese models of counseling and psychotherapy (Wang, 2008; Wang et al., 2004). For instance, following Lin and Wang's (1998) study on group therapeutic factors, the Group Therapeutic Factor Inventory (Wang & Lin, 2000) and Group Anti-Therapeutic Factor Inventory (Lin & Wang, 1999) were developed and applied to group studies in Taiwan (e.g., Chen, 2008; Sheu, 2004).

In general, there are now two types of indigenous models of counseling and psychotherapy in Taiwan: (1) integrative models of indigenous constructs and existing Western models and (2) indigenous models based solely on traditional Taiwanese culture. An example of the first integrative model is Jin's (1997) Chinese career model. He integrated the Buddhist Four Noble Truths (the nature of suffering, origin of suffering, cessation of suffering, way leading to the cessation of suffering) and the Buddhist four levels of awareness exploration (to open up the truth, indicate its meaning, gain more insights, and enter or become) with Western theories of career development and decision making. Jin indicated that the first step to approach career-related suffering is to

define what the burning question is, the suffering itself. Then people should research and unfold the resources of the suffering. The third step is to confirm that the problem is solvable. Finally, people should take planned actions to solve the problem. He also believed that the career counseling process can be structured using the Buddhist four levels of awareness exploration: initial opening stage, assessment and interpretation, insight, and decision making. Additionally, he used the Zi Wei Birth Chart, which is one of the most popular and the oldest Chinese fortune-telling methods, to illustrate the 12 significant sociocultural environment factors (parents, personal characteristics, siblings, spouse, children, wealth, illness and accidents, relocation/travel, friendship, occupation, real estate, life style and attitudes) that influence the career development of Chinese people. The Zi Wei Birth Chart nicely illustrates how Chinese people think about careers from a collectivistic perspective (i.e., a career is shaped by all 12 factors, not simply by individual efforts). In sum, Jin's work not only encourages Taiwanese career counselors to use indigenous tools to help Taiwanese people but also inspires career counseling psychologists to develop more culturally sensitive career theories and tools to best meet people's career needs in Taiwan.

In sum, the profession of counseling psychology in Taiwan is a unique blend of Western and Eastern knowledge tied to an Eastern cultural context. During the past 50 years, the Taiwanese counseling psychology profession has developed into a field that gradually integrates indigenous perspectives into both research and practice.

A PROFESSION MOLDED BY THE PSYCHOLOGIST STATUTE OF 2001

The third major influence on the development of the counseling psychology profession in Taiwan is the Psychologist Statute, which was passed in 2001 (for more details see Wang & Huang, 2006). In the late 1990s, a series of disastrous events and social problems stimulated an awareness of the necessity for qualified mental health services. Between 1999 and 2001, there was a significant increase in earthquake survivor suicides from 10.4% to 12.6%. This increase alerted the government to the need for mental health services and a national statute to regulate the professional practice of psychologists (Chang, 1998; Chen & Chen, 2000; Lin, 1998).

In 2001, the first national counseling psychology licensure system in Asia was passed by the Legislative Yuan of the Republic of China (Taiwan). It was named the Psychologist Statute. This statute quickly started to shape the professional identity of Taiwanese counseling psychologists. For example, the basic requirements of a qualified counseling psychologist candidate were established and included a master's degree in counseling psychology and a 1-year, full-time internship in a university counseling center, hospital, or community/school counseling center pre-certified by the DCP. In addition, counseling psychologists must pass a national examination covering the following subjects: human behavior and development; theories of counseling and psychotherapy; clinical application of counseling and psychotherapy (including professional ethics); group counseling and psychotherapy; psychological measurement, testing, and assessment; and mental health (including abnormal psychology). Once a person passes the national examination, he or she must join a local professional association to practice legally. In addition, he or she is required in the first 2 years to receive advanced training at qualified hospitals and also required to accrue 180 continuing education credits every 6 years to renew a license. Licensure has had a very significant impact on the profession. It has not only influenced the training and examination structure, it has also shaped the credibility and professional recognition of counseling psychology in the eyes of the general public. The existence of licensure has also helped expand the client population served by counseling psychologists from school systems to communities and even hospitals (Wang & Huang, 2006).

The Psychologist Statute has had a huge impact on the training and practice of the counseling profession in Taiwan; it has also changed how Taiwanese people perceive counseling as a profession. Traditionally, Taiwanese people would seek help from a respected elder within an extended family group, teachers,

Taoist priests, Buddhist nuns and monks, and fortune-tellers. As mentioned in the previous section about the roots of Taiwanese counseling psychology in education, one of the prevalent Taiwanese cultural values is to respect education, and thus those who have been professionally trained are given great respect. In Taiwan, many professional titles end with the key word *teacher* (e.g., accountant, lawyer, and physician). The Psychologist Statute sets up the professional standards and responsibilities for Taiwanese counseling psychologists; it also awards the name of "counseling teacher" to Taiwanese counseling psychologists. Since receiving services and/or education from a professional has no stigma attached to it, but is rather perceived as positive and forward moving, there is a wide array of counseling opportunities and mental health workshops provided by counseling psychologists for the general public. For example, in 2007 the most common mental health and help-seeking issues in Taiwan were family concerns (e.g., parent-child conflicts, couple conflicts), self-growth and identity issues, and interpersonal relationship issues (Teacher Chang Foundation Annual, 2007). School guidance offices, university counseling centers, and community counseling centers constantly deliver outreach prevention programs to meet people's needs for psychological education and market their therapy programs in a user-friendly manner. Before 2001, most of the general public was not familiar with the counseling profession and tended to see it as a foreign import. After the establishment of the Psychologist Statute, however, people not only learned about mental health prevention and interventions but also associated what they learned with counseling psychologists who receive their credentials from the government. At this point, more people tend to accept seeking professional mental health services. In sum, counseling psychologists in Taiwan have gradually promoted the awareness of mental health services by incorporating the cultural values of education, including respect for teachers and professionals.

Given the predominant psychopathology orientation in the Psychologist Statute, however, the traditional normal developmental emphasis of counseling psychology was threatened. There has also been a perception among students that hospitals are more preferable as internship sites because their experiences in these institutions with severe psychopathology may increase their marketability after graduation. Because of these developments, the training practice of counseling psychology in Taiwan now conceptualizes a psychopathology orientation as complementary and does not obviate the growth and developmental approach in actual practice (Wang & Huang, 2006).

After the Psychologist Statute was passed, Taiwanese counseling psychologists found that they needed a broader knowledge base than the one they had acquired from their previous Western training in counseling psychology. In addition, during the process of developing the Psychologist Statute, counseling psychologists became aware of the need to keep abreast of societal events and political opportunities that may have a significant influence on the stability of their profession. As a result, when counseling psychologists learned that the Mental Health Act was being revised by the Ministry of Health, they became active in the political process to assert their eligibility to qualify as mental health professionals. Consequently, counseling psychologists were included when the revised Mental Health Act was developed and passed in 2006. It is important to note, however, that this was the first time that counseling psychologists were included in the development of a Taiwanese national mental health policy. To effectively address future challenges, as well as promote its own identity, in 2008 the DCP became an independent new association named the Taiwan Counseling Psychology Association.

Although establishing a counseling psychology licensure system was challenging, maintaining and strengthening the profession has brought even more challenges. After the Psychologist Statute was passed in 2001, counseling psychologists were hard-pressed to create more employment positions for licensed counseling psychologists. Moreover, they also needed to build connections with the medical profession because the Psychologist Statute was based on the psychopathological model. To resolve the seeming contradiction between the developmental and psychopathology models and to create new positions for

counseling psychologists, the Executive Board members of the DCP proactively communicated and negotiated with the Ministry of Health and received support to create new counseling positions in hospitals. These experiences have reinforced the profession's collective vision to stay involved in the political arena to further enhance the recognition and status of counseling psychology in Taiwan.

CHALLENGES AND OPPORTUNITIES

The counseling psychology profession has gradually gained recognition from the Taiwanese Government, health providers, and general public. The quantity and quality of training programs, as well as the trainers and trainees, are improving to meet a broad array of societal needs in Taiwan. Moreover, the Psychologist Statute promoted the establishment of a professional identity for counseling psychologists in Taiwan. However, challenges and opportunities continue to appear. Five major challenges are discussed in the following sections.

Challenge 1: Strengthening the Existing Training and Internship Programs

As of 2008, the number of counseling psychology graduate programs in Taiwan has grown, from 8, when the Psychologist Statute was passed in 2001, to 28. Although the curricula of all the programs seem to meet the minimum requirement of the Psychology Statute for counseling psychologists, establishing a consensus for curricula and internship training is challenging, especially in a cultural context where people highly value harmonious relationships and are less likely to show disagreement with each other. The DCP has established ethical codes for counseling practice and selection criteria (e.g., numbers of individual and group supervision hours provided by licensed counseling psychologists, the ratio of supervisees to supervisors, types of services provided by interns) for internship sites. However, there is no legal power to regulate training by a professional organization or any other legislative body. Thus, a major challenge is to form consensuses and develop regulatory power through professional organizations (such as the American Psychological Association and the Association of Psychology Postdoctoral and Internship Centers in the United States) to create and maintain professional training standards. In 2008, the DCP received governmental support to regulate its internship guidelines, and now more and more training programs and internship sites are following the guidelines for interns (Wang & Huang, 2006). This is the first step to promote and maintain quality training in counseling psychology.

Another training challenge is to prepare future Taiwanese counseling psychologists to work effectively with their clients within a Taiwanese cultural context. Since research in Taiwanese counseling psychology is still in the process of developing its own unique focus and investigators are working to create culturally sensitive knowledge bases, many of the training programs continue to prepare their students based on Western theories and training models. The challenge is how to integrate knowledge from Western and indigenous models of counseling psychology into a training paradigm that will provide the best services to the Taiwanese people.

Challenge 2: Maintaining Professional Identity While Promoting Interdisciplinary Collaboration

Mental health providers in Taiwan have grown vigorously with the establishment of licensure for mental health professionals. For instance, a full-size mental health care team in Taiwan includes psychiatrists, social workers, counseling psychologists, clinical psychologists, and psychiatric nurses. Depending on the setting, schoolteachers, special education teachers, school administrators, and school counselors are also involved in school mental health teams. Some of the professionals just mentioned provide similar services as counseling psychologists. This creates confusion about the boundaries among the professionals across different disciplines and confusion for the general public. For example, clinical psychologists, social workers, and school counselors

all receive similar training in counseling techniques during their professional training. Therefore, the unique service contribution provided by counseling psychologists and other mental health professionals needs to be clearly articulated to the general public. Moreover, according to the internship regulations for counseling psychologists, counseling psychology students can be supervised by psychiatrists and licensed clinical psychologists. There is concern, however, whether counseling psychologists can maintain their professional identity if they are trained by other mental health providers. These questions depict some of the current struggles encountered by the Taiwanese counseling psychology profession and the ongoing negotiation process in the field itself and with other mental health colleagues.

Challenge 3: Creating More Employment Opportunities for Counseling Psychologists in Diverse Settings

It takes many years for any young profession to establish its role with the public. Because Taiwanese counseling psychology was initially rooted in the school systems, most counseling psychologists are employed in educational settings. However, in recent years, the number of licensed counseling psychologists has increased rapidly, and more than half of them do not work in a mental health–related career (Section of Research and Development, 2008). To face such a challenge, counseling psychologists have been actively seeking employment opportunities in schools, community settings, industry, and hospitals. A key issue is how counseling psychologists can successfully expand into these new employment settings and market their unique skills without threatening either the existing mental health professionals in these settings or their own professional identity.

Challenge 4: Building Indigenous Counseling Psychology Models

A fundamental challenge is to build indigenous counseling psychology models based on local

Taiwanese counseling practices and experiences. Promoting dialogue and collaboration between researchers and practitioners can greatly advance indigenous research and practice. Continuing to conduct both qualitative and quantitative studies through collaboration between researchers and practitioners can greatly facilitate indigenous models of counseling psychology and best practices (Chao et al., 2006; Wang et al., 2008).

We envision that the next step in developing an indigenous counseling psychology in Taiwan is for Taiwanese counseling psychology scholars and practitioners in the coming 20 years to publish their own theory and practice textbooks. Books consisting of Taiwanese indigenous theories, best cultural therapeutic experiences (best practices), and other international theories and practices have the potential to strengthen teaching and clinical training. The authors hope that these books can be translated into many other languages so that the Taiwanese counseling psychology profession can contribute to the broader international counseling psychology community.

Challenge 5: Internationalization and Addressing Local Societal Needs

Heppner, Leong, and Chiao (2008) identified the development of cross-national research collaboration as one of the challenges of internationalizing counseling psychology. Taiwanese counseling psychology researchers can choose to submit their manuscripts to international journals in English to promote internationalizing counseling psychology; however, such publications will be less likely to be read by Taiwanese Mandarin-speaking practitioners. If Taiwanese counseling psychologists choose to publish their work in the Chinese language in Taiwanese or Asian journals to fulfill local societal needs, international readers not fluent in Chinese will rarely be able to read these publications. Therefore, trying to find a balance between internationalization and meeting local societal needs is a serious challenge not only to many Taiwanese researchers but also other scholars around the world.

One attempt to overcome such language barriers and to promote a more effective and efficient information exchange is by integrating different international databases and encouraging researchers to write abstracts in at least one widely used international language (i.e., English). Although English readers will not be able to read an entire paper in Chinese, they will at least receive an overview of the study, and they can contact the authors for more information or, if they wish, to collaborate. For instance, although most of the articles in the *CJGC* and the *Bulletin of Educational Psychology,* two of the most popular counseling empirical research journals in Taiwan, are published in Chinese, since October 2007 international scholars can find English abstracts of the articles in the PsyINFO database.

CONCLUSION

With a growing recognition of more severe mental health and societal problems in Taiwan has come a corresponding growing need for counseling psychologists. Counseling psychologists now not only work in schools but also in communities, industry, and hospitals. Taiwanese counseling theories and models are in the process of transformation from a Western perspective to more integrated indigenous models that are culturally sensitive to adequately meet the needs of Taiwanese people. The passage of the Psychologist Statute has challenged counseling psychologists in Taiwan to engage in professional self-reflection. Yet, this challenge has provided counseling psychologists with a clearer vision of what their profession is and how they can further develop its future. The unwavering efforts of counseling psychologists in Taiwan have shaped the current status of the profession. Moreover, through the historical relationship between counseling psychology and school counseling as well as the profession's indigenous scholarship and role, the field has been gradually recognized for its unique function and place in Taiwan. It is hoped that these exciting developments in Taiwan will contribute to the evolution and effectiveness of the internationalization of the counseling psychology profession in the future.

REFERENCES

Chang, P. (1998). 催生臨床心理師法 [Expedite the statute of clinical psychologist]. *Health, Welfare & Environmental Magazine, 5,* 23–25.

Chao, H., Wang, L., & Yang, K. (2006). 諮商心理師國小校園服務方案之實施評估 [The program evaluation of counseling psychology services in elementary schools]. *Bulletin of Educational Psychology, 37*(4), 345–365.

Chen, G. (2008). *團體與個人層次變項對於團體治療性因素的影響：多層次縱貫研究分析* [The effects of the group-level and individual-level variables on group therapeutic factors: A longitudinal study of multilevel analysis]. Unpublished dissertation, National Taiwan Normal University, Taiwan, Republic of China.

Chen, P. H. (1994). *我國各級學校輔導諮商教育課程之分析及規劃* [The analysis and planning of the guidance and counseling curriculums in Taiwan]. Paper presented at the 1994 Symposium of the Six-Year Guidance Plan, Ministry of Education, Taipei, Taiwan, Republic of China.

Chen, P. H. (1999). Towards professionalism: The development of counseling in Taiwan. *Asian Journal of Counseling, 6,* 21–48.

Chen, P. H. (2005). *The self-relation in situation coordination counseling model for clients with interpersonal conflicts in Chinese communities.* Paper presented at the Annual Conference of the American Psychological Association, Washington, DC.

Chen, W., & Chen, Y. (2000). 尋找助人的春天—從心理助人專業立法談起 [Seeking the blossoming of the counseling services: A discussion of the needs and concerns of the Psychologist Statute]. *Journal of Medical Hope, 32,* 16–18.

Frommer, J., Langenbach, M., & Streeck, U. (2004). Qualitative psychotherapy research in German-speaking countries. *Psychotherapy Research, 14*(1), 57–75.

Heppner, P. P., Leong, F. T. L., & Chiao, H. (2008). The growing internationalization of counseling psychology. In S. D. Brown & R. W. Lent (Eds.), *Handbook of counseling psychology* (4th ed., pp. 68–85). New York: Wiley.

Jin, S. (1997). *生涯諮商與輔導* [Career counseling and guidance]. Taipei, Taiwan, Republic of China: Donghwa.

Jin, S. (1999). 諮商心理學之回顧與展望 [Reflections on and future visions of counseling psychology]. In Chinese Guidance Association (Ed.), *The major trends of guidance and counseling* (pp. 53–72). Taipei, Taiwan, Republic of China: Psychological.

Lin, C. H., Hsieh, Y. J., & Sun, C. T. (2008). 諮商心理師職業現況調查研究 [Practice survey of counseling psychologists in Taiwan]. *Chinese Journal of Guidance and Counseling, 23,* 117–145.

Lin, J. (1998). 結伴攜手推動心理師法 [A joint effort to promote a statute for psychologists]. *Guidance Quarterly, 34,* 1–3.

Lin, M. (2008, March). Toward the advance of professionalism, diversity, and international perspective of the *Chinese Journal of Guidance and Counseling*. In K. K. Kwan (Chair), *Chinese Journals and the Internationalization of Counseling Psychology*. Symposium conducted at the International Counseling Psychology Conference, Chicago.

Lin, M., & Wang, L. (1998). 團體治療性與反治療性重要事件之分析 [Therapeutic and anti-therapeutic important events in groups]. *Chinese Annual Report of Guidance and Counseling, 6,* 35–59.

Lin, M., & Wang, L. (1999). 團體反治療性因素量表之發展與編製 [Development of a scale of anti-therapeutic factors]. *Journal of Chinese Group Psychotherapy, 5*(2), 4–41.

Rennie, D. L. (2004). Anglo-North American qualitative counseling and psychotherapy research. *Psychotherapy Research, 14*(1), 37–55.

Section of Research and Development. (2008). 諮商心理師考訓用調查結果報告 [Survey of training, examination, and employment for licensed counseling psychologists]. Annual report presented at the 2008 annual meeting of the Division of Counseling Psychology, Taiwan Guidance and Counseling Association., Changhua, Taiwan, Republic of China.

Sheu, Y. (2004). *團體心理治療應用在精神科門診病患之成效* [The outcome study of group psychotherapy for psychiatric outpatients]. Unpublished doctoral dissertation, Chinese Medicine University, Taichung, Taiwan, Republic of China.

Teacher Chang Foundation. (2007). *張老師基金會2007年報* [Teacher Chang Foundation Annual in 2007]. Taipei, Taiwan, Republic of China: Teacher Chang Foundation.

Wang, L. (2008, October). *當諮商心理學者遇見國小輔導：研究與實務交織的學習歷程* [When a counseling psychologist meets elementary school counseling: A woven process of research and practice]. Keynote address presented at the 2008 annual conference of the Taiwan Guidance and Counseling Association, Changhua, Taiwan, Republic of China.

Wang, L., & Huang, S. (2006, August). Counseling psychology licensure in Taiwan: Professional identity and employment issues. In P. P. Heppner & L. Wang (Cochairs), *Current licensure issues in three countries: Commonalities and challenges.* Symposium conducted at the 2006 meeting of the American Psychological Association, New Orleans, LA.

Wang, L., & Lin, M. (2000). 團體治療性因素量表之發展與編製 [Development and validation of the Group Therapeutic Factor Inventory]. *Chinese Annual Report of Guidance and Counseling, 9,* 1–24.

Wang, L., Lin, S., Kao, M., Gian, W, & Lee, H. (2004, November). 國內諮商與心理治療質性研究 之研究方法回顧性分析 [Taiwan qualitative counseling and psychotherapy research: The methodology review]. Paper presented at the 2004 annual meeting of Chinese Guidance Association, Taipei, Taiwan, Republic of China.

Wang, L., Tu, S., & Chao, H. (2008). 國小駐校諮商心理師有效諮商策略之探索性研究 [An exploratory investigation of effective counseling frameworks for counseling psychologists working in elementary schools]. *Bulletin of Educational Psychology, 3,* 413–434.

Wu, S. (2005). 諮商團體領導原理的建構：螺旋式領導方法 [Constructing a model for leading counseling groups: A spiral model]. *Chinese Annual Report of Guidance and Counseling, 17,* 1–32.

Yee, D. (2005). 華人心性與倫理的複和式療法—華人文化心理治療的探原 [Ethical intervention and spiritual well-being as cultural therapeutics: Compound psychological healing in culturally Chinese societies]. *Indigenous Psychological Research in Chinese Societies, 24,* 7–48.

Zhang, Z., & Wu, Z. (1999). 中國輔導學會早期的功能與貢獻—兼論八十年來我國的輔導運動 [The early function and contribution of Chinese Guidance Association: The guidance movement in Taiwan for the last eighty years]. In Chinese Guidance Association (Ed.), *The major trends of guidance and counseling* (pp. 3–23). Taipei, Taiwan, Republic of China: Psychological Press.

SOUTHEAST ASIA

13

Counselling in a Multicultural Context

The Singapore Perspective

多元文化背景中的心理咨询: 新加坡观点

ESTHER TAN

This chapter traces the development of counselling in Singapore from its humble beginnings in the 1960s to attaining professional status in the 1980s. While sharing research findings that have helped inform and improve practice, the chapter will pay special attention to the efforts of practitioners and counsellor educators in recent years to adapt and indigenize Western counselling practices in an Asian, multicultural context.

The Republic of Singapore is an island state with a total land area of 267 square miles and a population of 4.8 million, making it one of the world's most densely populated countries. Singapore is a multiracial, multicultural, and multireligious society. Its population constitutes 75% Chinese, 14% Malay, 9% Indian, and 2% of other races. In terms of religion, Buddhists make up 43% of the population, Muslims 15%, Taoists 9%, Hindus 4%, and Christians 15%. Singapore is also very much a cosmopolitan city. Official statistics released by the government revealed that more than 25% of its population are foreigners from different ethnic backgrounds—Chinese from China, Hong Kong, and Malaysia; Indians from India; Koreans; Japanese; Indonesians; Filipinos; as well as individuals from North American and European countries (Singapore Department of Statistics, 2009).

This rich tapestry of ethnic and religious diversity in Singapore can be a real challenge to professional counsellors who have to work with clients from cultural backgrounds different from their own. To begin with, they must be sensitive to the between-culture differences of their clients. For example, Soong (1997) investigated adolescent students' preferences of counselling approaches and found that Hindu students from Indian-languages-speaking homes showed the greatest penchant for a client-centred approach, Chinese students from English-speaking homes preferred a cognitive approach, while Muslim students from Malay-speaking homes favoured a behavioural approach.

Preference for counselling approach is but one example of between-culture differences. Clients from different ethnic backgrounds also observe different traditions and cultural practices. For instance, while the Muslims refrain from eating between sunrise and sunset for a whole month during Ramadan (Malay word for the fasting month), many Chinese who are staunch Buddhists refrain from eating meat on the 1st and 15th day of the lunar month. In the social institution of marriage, matchmaking is widely practiced among the Indians, accepted even by well-educated professionals. Among the Chinese, however, mainly working class males turn to matchmaking agencies to bring in foreign brides from countries such as Vietnam, Cambodia, and China when they have difficulty finding a local bride. On the other hand, interethnic marriage has been on the increase in recent years among professionals of all races. Unfortunately, divorce rates are also the highest among interethnic marriages (Singapore Department of Statistics, 2007). All these cultural differences have implications for counselling in Singapore, especially in family and marriage counselling.

Besides understanding the cultural norms of the different ethnic groups, being sensitive to within-culture differences is just as important. A counsellor working with two clients from the same ethnic group cannot assume that they share common beliefs and traditions. The religious dimension, in addition to ethnic background, also must be taken into consideration. A Christian Tamil and a Christian Chinese may have more in common than a Christian Tamil and a Hindu Tamil. Education also plays a part. Local research has shown that among the Chinese in Singapore, those from lower-income families and those holding lower educational qualifications preferred traditional healers to seeking professional counselling (Lee & Bishop, 2001; Ow, 1998).

There is a dichotomy between Asian traditional beliefs and the values underpinning modern counselling that are perceived by some as "Western" and "foreign." Although professional counselling is gaining acceptance and recognition in Singapore,

many Chinese are still under the influence of Confucian ethics. To them, the values in counselling such as self-determination, independence, and self-expression are in direct conflict with traditional Chinese values of obedience to parents, respect for elders, exercise of control, and emotional restraint. Even the national shared values promoted by the government since 1989 reflect a preference for collectivism above individualism (Chew, 1990).

First conceived in 1988, the five national shared values incorporate elements of Singapore's cultural heritage—attitudes and beliefs—that have helped it survive as a nation. Top on the list is the value "nation before community and society above self." This is followed by the emphasis on "the family as the basic unit of society." The well-being of the individual ranks third as reflected in the shared value of "community support and respect for the individual." The last two shared values focus on the importance of consensus, harmony in community living, and nation building—"consensus, not conflict" and "racial and religious harmony" (ExpatSingapore, 2008).

As one can surmise from the ranking of the values, welfare of the community comes before that of the family, and the family is considered more important than the individual. Such values are in contradiction with the underlying values of Western counselling theories. As pointed out by Sue and Sue (1990), the assumptions on which modern counselling theories are based reflect democratic ideals of the white American cultural context that revolves around the uniqueness and dignity of the individual, the freedom to explore one's potential toward self-determined goals for the promise of a better life. This contradiction in values may be one reason why many Singaporeans, especially the Chinese educated, are reluctant to seek professional counselling. Working with Chinese mental patients, Ow (1998) found that their help-seeking behaviours included first self-help, then seeking help from relatives, friends, or traditional healers, and last, from mental health professionals. Self-help strategies included staying at home, taking tonic drink, purging medicines, or going on special diets. Traditional healing practices that were sought included acupuncture, aromatherapy, foot reflexology, fortune-telling, geomancy, herbal medicine, hypnosis, massage therapy, meditation, shamanism, and consultation with traditional healers, such as *bomohs* (Malay term for spiritual doctor) and temple liturgists.

While some clients wavered between traditional healings and modern therapy, others sought the help of traditional healers while undergoing therapy (Tan, Chee, & Long, 1980). Even in modern-day Singapore, it is not uncommon for a Chinese client, after a session with the therapist, to go to the temple to pray and make a donation to "bring harmony and luck to the family." A Hindu client may consult an astrologer and a counsellor at the same time. It has also been observed by school counsellors that some traditional Malay parents may insist on consulting the bomoh when their children appear emotionally disturbed instead of referring them for psychological assessment.

Samion (1999) interviewed individuals who had engaged the services of both professional counsellors and traditional healers. The findings indicated that the element of spirituality was a crucial aspect in the counselee/traditional healer relationship, but this element was lacking in the formal counselling context. The aspect of spirituality was one that counselees appreciated as helpful in enhancing their strength for problem solving. The study also found that the strength of the therapeutic relationship was closely linked to similarities in worldviews. Thus, working in a multiracial, multicultural, and multireligious context, professional counsellors in Singapore must be cognizant of the worldviews of their clients, their cultural backgrounds, and religious practices in order to build rapport and demonstrate empathy. Counsellors must keep in mind that most of the counselling approaches practiced today have their roots in American-European philosophical traditions, and they would need to adapt these approaches to the local cultural context.

THE DEVELOPMENT OF PROFESSIONAL COUNSELLING

Humble Beginnings

In Singapore, the development of professional counselling has a history of about five decades.

Before the 1960s, there was not a single counselling agency in the country. While social and personal problems of individuals were handled by social workers, mental health needs were taken care of by a few foreign-trained psychiatrists in the country's one and only public mental hospital. Patients who needed help with their emotional and psychological problems but whose conditions were not serious enough to warrant psychiatric treatment had nowhere to turn. Sometimes, their family members sought traditional approaches of cure by praying at the Chinese temple to "appease the spirits" or through consulting the bomoh (Sim, 1999; Tan, 1996).

The seed of professional counselling was sowed in 1961 when a few concerned individuals, including church pastors, missionaries, and medical doctors got together to set up the Churches Counselling Service to provide counselling services to the local community. Initially staffed by expatriates trained overseas, the centre was renamed Counselling and Care Centre in 1975. By then, all the expatriate staff had been replaced by local professional counsellors (Yeo, 1993b). Around the same time, addiction counselling began with the Singapore Anti-Narcotics Association (SANA), established in 1972. A few years later, the Singapore Armed Forces (SAF) set up its own counselling centre in 1977 to provide counselling services to national servicemen and their families (Sim, 1999).

Since then, there has been a steady growth and development of counselling centres initiated by religious bodies, voluntary welfare organizations, and the government. The most noteworthy has been the mushrooming of family service centres (FSCs) scattered all over the island state, a movement started in the 1980s and gathering momentum in the 1990s. These FSCs were one-stop social service agencies staffed by professionally trained counsellors, psychologists, and social workers. They were usually set up within or near the vicinity of public housing estates to provide a whole range of services such as casework management, group counselling, and family and marital counselling to members of the public (Tan, 2002). The cradle of school counselling was the National Institute of Education, the country's sole teacher training institute. It set up a guidance clinic on campus in 1974 to introduce counselling to schools and to provide counsellor education for teachers (Tan, 1990a, 1994b, 2004). As a result of intensive and extensive training programs conducted at the Institute, the government was able to post at least one professionally trained school counsellor in each of the 400 plus schools in the Republic by 2007 to provide educational guidance, personal counselling, and career counselling to students (Ministry of Education, 2007). Counselling as a helping profession has finally come of age.

Attainment of Professional Status

In the author's opinion, four indicators signify the professional status of a discipline—the establishment of a professional association, registration or licensing of practitioners in the field, accredited training for the profession, and research and publication specific to the profession. The first three "indicators" are addressed in this section, and research and publications are addressed in the next section.

In 1982, the Singapore Association for Counselling (SAC) was established to provide a common professional base for the advancement of counselling in Singapore. This event signified a national attempt to identify counselling as a profession. The SAC also published a code of ethics for professional practice to ensure that counsellors in Singapore maintain appropriate professional conduct.

To advance the professional status of trained counsellors, the SAC started a register for professionally trained counsellors in 2004 as well as an accreditation process to ensure the standard and quality of training programs in the country. This was another significant step toward professionalism in counselling (SAC, 2007).

As the pioneer agency in providing professional counselling in Singapore, Counselling and Care Centre was the first organization to spearhead training in counselling by initiating short-term certificate courses in basic counselling skills in the 1980s. Currently, the centre also runs a postgraduate diploma course in family and marital therapy conducted in conjunction with the Institute of Family Therapy in London.

Among the four local universities, the National Institute of Education was the first to introduce formalized counsellor education. In addition to postgraduate diploma courses in school counselling for teachers, the institute launched the MA in applied psychology program in 1997 to equip educational psychologists for the schools and counselling psychologists for the field (Tan, 2004). In January 2007, SIM University (UniSIM) launched a bachelor degree in counselling program leading to a postgraduate diploma in counselling, which is fully accredited by SAC. Responding to the growing demand for counsellor education, the National Institute of Education introduced an MA in counselling program in July 2008. In the meantime, UniSIM is planning to launch a master's program in counselling in July 2010.

Research and Publication

In any discipline, one important indicator of professionalism is the depth and breadth of research and development work carried out within its field. Since the introduction of formal counsellor education programs in the 1990s, a research culture has been inculcated amongst counsellor educators, counselling students, and practitioners in the field, resulting in the publication of books and research articles. The author has taken the liberty to categorize the research into three groups, including exploratory, validation, and evaluation studies.

The first group is exploratory studies to understand the help-seeking behaviours and characteristics of client groups. Ang and Yeo (2004) investigated the help-seeking behaviours of adolescent students and found that although 84.3% of the 488 students in the sample were aware of the availability of counselling services in their school, only 6.7% had approached a counsellor for help. A majority of the students reported turning to their friends (57.4%) or their parents (40.2%) for help when they were troubled. Most of the female students preferred same-sex counsellors, while the male students preferred opposite-sex counsellors.

Lim and Ang (2006) examined the relationship between control beliefs and help-seeking attitudes of university students and found that undergraduates who believed in changing oneself to adapt to reality (secondary control) showed more positive attitudes toward seeking professional help than those who believed in influencing existing realities as a means of coping (primary control). Gender differences in attitudes toward help seeking were reported by Ang, Lim, Tan, and Yau (2004) who found that female young adults were more positive toward seeking professional help than their male counterparts. Meanwhile, Ng and Lim (2006) examined the help-seeking behaviours of clients of an FSC ($N = 86$) and found that the main barriers to help seeking for clients from low-income families were low self-esteem, feelings of alienation from society, perceiving family as sufficient help, and worries that confidentiality would not be kept.

The second group of research studies seeks to examine the validity of Western career development theories and measures in the local context. Super (1983; Super, Savickas, & Super, 1996) postulated that the career maturity of adolescents increased with age alongside the development of cognitive development. To validate Super's theory, Tan (1989) surveyed adolescent students ($N = 1,380$) aged 12 to 18 years using the Australian version of Super's Career Development Inventory (CDI). The results showed a steady increase in the mean scores of all four aspects of career development—that is, career exploration, career planning, career knowledge, and career decision making, and there were significant age differences as well. These findings lent support to Super's theory that career maturity increases with age.

Tan (1990b) examined the validity of Holland's theory of career interest among Singapore secondary students ($N = 1,500$). Holland (1985, 1997) postulated that people can be categorised as predominantly one of six vocational personality types, which are realistic (R), investigative (I), artistic (A), social (S), enterprising (E), and conventional (C) To test the validity of Holland's theory in the Singapore context, his Self-Directed Search (SDS) was administered to a sample of 1,500 secondary students across the island. Item-subscale correlation of the SDS showed that most of the items contributed to the respective subscale. Also factor analysis of the items showed distinctively six factors corresponding to the six personality types. These findings provided sufficient evidence to support Holland's theory.

Research often leads to the development of indigenous counselling inventories and publications. In this respect, ongoing efforts among professionals and academics have led to the development of interest inventories and diagnostic checklists. One example is OSCAR (Orientation System for CAReers), a comprehensive computer-assisted career guidance program developed at the National Institute of Education (Tan, 1994a, 1995), which has been widely used in Singapore schools. There have also been efforts among professionals to publish books and resource materials in counselling, some of which have become basic reference and text books for local counsellor education programs in areas such as individual counselling (Tan, 1984; Yeo, 1981, 1993a), school counselling (Lui & Wong, 2006; Tan, 2004), and gerontological counselling (Metha & Ko, 2003; Ko, Metha, & Ko, 2007).

The third group of studies investigates current counselling practices in terms of client and counsellor preferences. Soong (1997) investigated preference for counselling approaches among secondary students ($N = 970$) from different ethnic origins and religious backgrounds. The cognitive approach was found to be the most preferred approach (49.7%), followed by the client-centred approach (34.5%), and the behavioural approach (15.8%). In the same study, Soong surveyed counsellors of Chinese (82), Malay (8), and Indian (10) ethnic origin ($N = 100$) and conducted in-depth interviews with 30 of these participants. The findings revealed that regardless of ethnicity, the majority of the counsellors preferred the client-centred approach when working with adult clients and cognitive approaches when working with students. Those working in FSCs often found themselves using the family systems approach. Many teacher counsellors in the sample found reality therapy to be effective when working with students referred for behavioural problems. As time was of essence in an achievement-oriented, highly competitive school system, the structured, solution-focused cognitive approach was also favoured (Soong, 1994, 1997).

ADAPTATION AND INDIGENIZATION OF COUNSELLING THEORIES AND PRACTICES

One major concern of professional counsellors in Singapore is to develop multicultural competence in counselling. Multicultural competence is generally defined as the extent to which counsellors possess appropriate levels of self-awareness, knowledge, and skills in working with individuals from diverse cultural backgrounds (Constantine, Hage, Kindaichi, & Bryant, 2007). Awareness competencies include sensitivity to one's cultural heritage, respecting differences, appreciating how one's own values may affect the counselee, and being comfortable with differences and sensitivity to circumstances. Knowledge competencies involve an understanding of the sociopolitical system, specific information about the particular group with whom the counsellor is working, and awareness of institutional barriers. In the area of skills competencies, the counsellor must be able to send and receive verbal and nonverbal responses accurately in each cultural context and apply intervention strategies that are appropriate to the counselee's cultural context (Sue, Arredondo, & McDavis, 1992). Axelson (1993) summed up multicultural competencies in counselling as counsellor awareness in four areas: (1) cultural total awareness (developments taking place in society, and specific cultural contexts), (2) self-awareness (strengths, values, assumptions, biases, stereotypes), (3) counselee awareness (worldviews, values, biases, assumptions), and (4) counselling procedure awareness (appropriate help-giving practices, intervention strategies).

Laungani (2004) noted that although Western models of therapy continue to be used among the Westernized clientele in large Asian metropolitan cities, therapists in Eastern cultures have reinvented their ancient traditional practices to develop indigenous approaches that are often based on a value system that is different from Western thinking. This section presents some of the cultural adaptations and integrations that have taken place in Singapore.

Influenced by the work of Jay Haley (1987), Yeo (1993a), a veteran and pioneer in the field of professional counselling, proposed a four-step problem-solving approach to counselling called PADI. *Padi* is the Malay word for paddy field, a term that is easily understood in Southeast Asia where rice fields are a common sight in the countryside. PADI stands for (1) Problem definition, (2) Attempted solutions, (3) Desired changes, and (4) Intervention plan. According to Yeo (1993a), PADI uses a person-centred approach in counselling. The focus of the therapy is to help clients develop insight into their problems or concerns by guiding them to explore their relationships with significant others (e.g., family members and colleagues), life events (e.g., marriage, birth of child, promotion at work), and environments (e.g., home and workplace). Yeo emphasizes that to be effective, the counsellor must also combine this person-centred approach with a family orientation. At first glance, the concept of having a family orientation in personal counselling appears to be contradictory. Such a notion, however, is acceptable in Singapore where the family has strong influences in the life and decision making of the individual. Thus, when a client presents a problem, the counsellor should be acquainted with his family relationships and assess how the family is affected or involved with his or her problem.

With the proliferation of literature on counselling and the diversity of counselling approaches, there is a need for integration as no single theory or approach is sufficient to address the intricacy of human issues. Lazarus (1989, 1992) observed that when counsellors adhere to one theoretical orientation, they tend to adopt identical interpersonal styles for all clients. Believing that clients have diverse needs that call for a wide range of interpersonal styles from their counsellors, Lazarus proposed a multimodal approach to counselling in which the counsellor's interpersonal style varies from one client to another. This flexible approach in multimodal therapy (MMT) is particularly relevant to the multicultural setting of Singapore, where clients from different cultural backgrounds may have different expectations of counsellor behaviour and the counselling relationship.

Lee and Wong (2004) took into consideration the importance of the interpersonal dimension in the Singapore context, adapted Lazarus's MMT, and proposed an ecological multimodal approach to counselling. They argued that although MMT takes into account the interpersonal aspect of personality function, this dimension has not been given sufficient attention as compared with the intraindividual dimensions such as behaviour, affect, imagery, and cognition. To make MMT more culturally relevant in Singapore, where there is a structured, elaborate social hierarchy and extensive interpersonal network, Lee and Wong recommended extending the interpersonal dimension within an ecological framework. Accordingly, ecological multimodal therapy (EMT) adopts a holistic view in which people and their environments constantly interact and influence each other. Conceptually, this dynamic relationship can be depicted in an ecological profile consisting of the following six systems:

1. The natural-ecological system, for example, weather and physical environment
2. The macrosocial system, for example, cultural values and political system
3. The microsocial system, for example, peers, neighbours, and friends
4. The extended family, for example, grandparents, uncles, aunts, and cousins
5. The immediate family, for example, parents and siblings
6. The person system, for example, cognition, affect, behaviour, biology, and imagery

There are two key concepts in EMT, structure and functionality. *Structure* refers to the properties that make up the six systems, for example, the physical environment in the natural-ecological system and values in the macrosocial system. *Functionality* refers to the roles and purposes of the properties and their interaction. Changes and disturbances in one system or between the properties within a system will lead to corresponding changes and disturbances in other systems. Lee and Wong (2004) claimed that the concept of the natural-ecological system is central to the Asian worldview that perceives the person as an indivisible part of nature. The ecological

profile can be used to understand and assess the client's interpersonal relationships as well as the strengths and weaknesses of the social support network. The following guiding questions are suggested by EMT to assess the client's ecological profile (Lee & Wong, 2004):

1. How has the problem/concern affected the client's thinking, behaviours, and feelings? (The person system)
2. To whom (e.g., family members, relatives, friends, professionals, and spiritual healers) will the client turn for help in times of crisis? (The immediate family, extended family, and microsocial system)
3. How does the client's presenting problem relate to other people and social institutions, for example, school, workplace, etc.? (The macrosocial system)
4. How is the client's presenting problem affected by his physical environment (e.g., housing condition, climate change, geographical location, etc.)? (The natural-ecological system)

In another attempt to adapt Western counselling approaches to the local context, Wong (2002a) proposed a multidimensional clinical interviewing (MCI) model to meet the diverse needs of the client and the interviewers. The MCI model could be used to guide an intake interview but could also be used at other stages of the counselling process, including assessment and intervention. Wong's model has eight dimensions:

1. *Level:* It refers to a comprehensive understanding of a client from the biological, psychological, and sociological level.
2. *Modality:* It integrates the approaches suggested by Lazarus (1989) and Satir, Banmen, Gerber, and Gomori (1991), Wong (2002a) suggested assessing modalities such as behavioural, sensory, and affective at the intrapersonal level and modalities such as parents, siblings, and peers at the interpersonal level.
3. *Domain:* It involves assessing the prevalence and pervasiveness of a client's problems in the various domains such as home, school, workplace, and neighbourhood.
4. *Method:* It refers to various assessment methods such as observation, psychological testing, and so on.

5. *Variable:* It refers to the collection of information concerning other important psychological constructs that are not covered by the other dimensions such as locus of control, coping style, and so on.

6. *Development level and issues of client:* It refers to the collection of information about developmental changes and developmental challenges facing the client.

7. *Time:* It highlights the importance of the counsellor to be time sensitive, collecting only relevant information about the past and present of the client.

8. *Culture:* It involves collecting information of various cultural influences (ethnicity, religion and spiritual orientation, generational influences, developmental and acquired disabilities, socioeconomic status and national origin, etc.).

Wong (2002a) also proposed eight stages in the assessment process: (1) planning (deciding on the level of assessment based on reason for referral), (2) preinterview (preparing for the interview), (3) beginning (rapport building), (4) working (information gathering), (5) closing (closure of interview session), (6) processing data, (7) conceptualizing and analyzing data, and (8) developing intervention goals. Wong recommended the MCI model as a generic approach to help counsellors conduct clinical interviews in a systematic manner regardless of their theoretical orientation.

Sensitivity toward religious practices of one's clients is another challenge for professional counsellors working in a multicultural context. Among the main religious groups in Singapore (Catholics, Protestants, Muslims, Buddhists, Taoists, and Hindus), Buddhists make up the biggest group, and the number is on the rise, having increased from 27% in 1980 to 43% in 2007 (Singapore Department of Statistics, 2007). To facilitate counselling practices with Buddhists clients, Wong (2002b) proposed the use of transformation therapy, which is an integrative approach to psychotherapy based on the Buddhist teaching of the "Four Noble Truths". The key idea in transformation therapy is that for suffering to cease before it arises, or to cease after it has arisen, it must be transformed into positive energy rather than existing in its negative form.

The Four Noble Truths describe the difficulties we face in life and how we can transcend these difficulties to become fulfilled, liberated, and free. The First Noble Truth states that suffering in this world is inevitable. The Second Noble Truth attributes the causes of sufferings to sensual cravings, worldly desires, and negative thoughts. The Third Noble Truth maintains that suffering will not last forever and that its cessation, which leads to well-being, is possible. The Fourth Noble Truth teaches the noble eightfold path leading to cessation of suffering and attainment of well-being.

The ultimate goal of transformation therapy is to help clients end their suffering to achieve a state of well-being. This can be done through the eight main therapeutic strategies of (1) transforming perception, (2) transforming thought, (3) transforming sensation and emotion, (4) transforming language and speech, (5) transforming behaviour, (6) transforming work, (7) transforming mind and body, and (8) transforming self or person. Wong (2002b) claimed that these therapeutic techniques arise from the amalgamation and integration of techniques used in Buddhist practices and modern psychology.

Convinced that indigenous therapies can coexist with, or even be integrated into, modern counselling practices, Lee (2006) proposed using explanatory models (EMs) in the counselling process. EMs refer to the ways in which life issues and events are interpreted and understood by clients, healers (counsellors, medical practitioners, and indigenous therapists), and significant others (e.g., family members, teachers, and peers) in a local social network (Kleinman, 1980). For the counsellors, their EMs are influenced by their theoretical orientation. A psychodynamic counsellor may identify the client's experience as anxiety and attribute it to some unresolved intrapsychic conflict carried over from a past relationship. To manage the anxiety, the counsellor helps the client be aware of unconscious materials through free association, dream analysis, or the analysis of transference. Similarly, a cognitive-behavioural counsellor may associate the anxiety with dysfunctional thoughts and use cognitive techniques to modify such thoughts. The question does not lie in which model is true but which model is more meaningful to the client. Clients and counsellors may hold similar or different EMs. A mismatch of EMs may affect the counselling relationship and hamper the treatment process. On the other hand, similarity between the client's EMs and the treatment approaches offered by the counsellor will result in a stronger therapeutic alliance and enhance the client's motivation for change. The therapeutic significance of the client-counsellor match on EMs has received some empirical support. Kim, Ng, and Ahn (2005) showed that a match on the client's and counsellor's causal attribution of problems led to higher ratings on client-counsellor alliance and counsellor empathy in comparison with those alliances in which there was a mismatch on causal attributions.

Lee (2006) advocated that "by understanding the client's EMs, a common ground can be established for negotiating a course of actions acceptable to both counsellor and client" (p. 60). Lee presented two case illustrations to show how this is done. In the first case, a young couple sought professional counselling as they were troubled by strained family relationships. Both sets of parents had objected to their marriage plans due to some superstitious beliefs, and they were torn between pleasing their parents and following their own hearts. While undergoing premarital counselling, the couple also secured the help of a fortune-teller who presented Chinese astrological concepts to convince the parents that it was a good match after all. After the parents had been won over, the wedding proceeded as planned. In the second case, a Chinese man who had harboured guilt feelings toward his late mother obtained release of his guilt through an indigenous practice. According to traditional Chinese belief, the spirits of the dead will return to earth to seek peace and attend to "unfinished business" during the seventh month of the lunar calendar, also known as the "ghost festival." To "appease" the dead, Buddhists and Taoists would offer burnt offerings such as paper "gold nuggets" and "bank notes" together with food and fruits. By burning his letter of apology together with incense papers for his late mother, the client felt a sense of relief, believing that he had finally "made peace" with his mother. In both cases, actions grounded in the client's culture were taken with the full knowledge and moral support of the therapist, who was open to the idea of integrating modern counselling with indigenous practices (Lee, 2002).

CONCLUSION

Singapore is unique in that it has a relatively short history of nation building (44 years of independence) yet very old cultural and religious practices dating back to ancient days. Its citizens have inherited five major traditions, including Hinduism, Buddhism, Confucianism, Christianity, and Islam, all of which have thousands of years of history. Singapore is also both an Eastern and a Western nation. The country's bilingual education system ensures that its citizens are fluent in English and in tune with the happenings of the Western world but at the same time also rooted in their own cultures. These unique features pose challenges for the development and practice of counselling in the country. To face up to these challenges, counsellors in Singapore have made modest but earnest efforts to develop multicultural competences and use research and experimentation to enhance counselling practices.

What have we learned in Singapore that we can share with fellow professionals in other parts of the world? First, we have learned that despite the availability of professional counselling services, some of our citizens are still reluctant to seek help, especially individuals from low-income families and those steeped in cultural traditions (Ang & Yeo, 2004; Ng & Lim, 2006). Since changing mind-sets is a long process, the best time to start is in childhood. By introducing counselling services in all the schools, the perceived "stigma" associated with counselling can be removed early on. In her capacity as clinical supervisor of school counsellors, the author has visited many schools to sit in live counselling sessions. It is both encouraging and gratifying to observe the ease and openness of the many children and youth who have come forward for counselling. It is hoped that these future citizens of Singapore will retain the same receptive attitude to counselling as they reach adulthood and enter the world of work. Only when a receptive attitude prevails among adults in the society can a paradigm shift be achieved.

Second, we have learned that counselling theories and techniques that have originated from the West are not necessarily incompatible with Asian value systems and Eastern cultural practices. In fact, research has yielded empirical evidence that some of these "Western" theories and "foreign" instruments used as tools in counselling are both valid and applicable in our Asian context (Tan, 1989, 1990b, 1994a, 1995). So rather than discarding these theories and practices as "irrelevant" and "inappropriate," we should "adopt," "adjust," "and adapt."

Third, experimentation of practitioners and counsellor educators in Singapore has shown that modern counselling practices can coexist with traditional cultural practices (Lee, 2002; Samion, 1999; Tan et al., 1980). There have also been fruitful efforts at adapting and indigenizing Western counselling theories and techniques as documented in this chapter (Ko et al., 2007; Lee, 2006; Lee & Wong, 2004; Wong, 2002a, 2002b; Yeo, 1993a).

Fourth, research and practice have confirmed the usefulness of using the multimodal approach in a multicultural context (Lee & Wong, 2004; Soong, 1997). Clients from different cultural backgrounds may differ in their personal beliefs and help-seeking behaviours. They may also have different expectations of the counsellor and the counselling process. To be effective, counsellors working in multicultural contexts must be knowledgeable of different models of counselling and flexible in their counselling approach.

Last, we have learned that it does not matter if the counsellor and the counselee come from different ethnic or cultural backgrounds. What matters is that they share similar worldviews or EMs. Counsellor's self-awareness and counselee awareness and matching the worldviews of both are the keys to establishing rapport and facilitating the counselling process (Lee, 2002; Samion, 1999; Soong, 1997).

Promoting and advancing counselling is a long, challenging journey for counsellors and educators alike. Much can be learned through mutual sharing

and exchange of ideas at the national or international level. While practitioners and counsellor educators in Singapore continue our efforts in adapting Western counselling practices and developing indigenous therapies, it is our hope that sharing our experiences with fellow professionals in other parts of the world can lead to further learning and mutual benefits.

REFERENCES

Ang, R. P., Lim, K. M., Tan, A. G., & Yau, T. Y. (2004). Effects of gender and sex role orientation on help-seeking attitudes. *Current Psychology, 23,* 203–214.

Ang, R. P., & Yeo, L. S. (2004). Asian secondary school students' help-seeking behaviour and preference for counselor characteristics. *Pastoral Care in Education, 22*(4), 40–48.

Axelson, J. B. (1993). *Counseling and development in a multicultural society.* Pacific Grove, CA: Brooks/Cole.

Chew, S. K. (1990). Nation-building in Singapore: A historical perspective. In J. Quah (Ed.), *In search of Singapore's national values* (pp. 36–45). Singapore: Times Academic Press.

Constantine, M. G., Hage, S. M., Kindaichi, M. M., & Bryant, R. M. (2007). Social justice and multicultural issues: Implications for the practice and training of counselors and counseling psychologists. *Journal of Counseling & Development, 85*(Winter), 24–29.

ExpatSingapore. (2008). *Information about Singapore: National Pledge of Allegiance of Singapore and the five shared values.* Retrieved May 17, 2008, from http:///www. expaptsingapore.com

Haley, J. (1987). *Problem solving therapy* (2nd ed.). San Francisco: Jossey-Bass.

Holland, J. L. (1985). *Making vocational choices: A theory of vocational personalities and work environment.* Englewood Cliffs, NJ: Prentice Hall.

Holland, J. L. (1997). *Making vocational choices* (3rd ed.). Englewood Cliffs, NJ: Prentice Hall.

Kim, B. S. K., Ng, G. F., & Ahn, A. J. (2005). Effects of client expectation for counseling success, client-counselor worldview match, and client adherence to Asian and European American cultural values on counseling process with Asian Americans. *Journal of Counseling Psychology, 52,* 67–76.

Kleinman, A. (1980). *Patients and healers in the context of culture.* Berkeley: University of California Press.

Ko, H., Metha, K., & Ko, S. M. (2007). *Understanding and counselling older persons: A handbook.* Singapore: SAGE Counselling Centre.

Laungani, P. (2004). Counseling and therapy in a multicultural setting. *Counselling Psychology Quarterly, 17,* 195–207.

Lazarus, A. A. (1989). *The practice of multimodal therapy: Systematic, comprehensive, and effective psychotherapy.* Baltimore: Johns Hopkins University Press.

Lazarus, A. A. (1992). Multimodal therapy: Technical eclecticism with minimal integration. In J. C. Norcross & M. R. Goldfried (Eds.), *Handbook of psychotherapy integration* (pp. 231–263). New York: Basic Books.

Lee, B. O. (2002). Chinese indigenous psychotherapies in Singapore. *Counseling and Psychotherapy & Research, 2,* 2–10.

Lee, B. O. (2006). Clients as co-healer. In H. W. Lui & S. S. Wong (Eds.), *Reflections on counseling: Developing practice in schools* (pp. 56–74). Singapore: Prentice Hall.

Lee, B. O., & Bishop, G. D. (2001). Chinese clients' belief systems about psychological problems in Singapore. *Counseling Psychology Quarterly, 14,* 219–240.

Lee, B. O., & Wong, S. S. (2004). An ecological multimodal approach to counseling. In E. Tan (Ed.), *Counseling in schools: Theories, processes, and techniques* (pp. 187–214). Singapore: McGraw-Hill.

Lim, K. M., & Ang, R. P. (2006). Relationship of primary versus secondary control beliefs to attitudes toward seeking help. *North American Journal of Psychology, 8,* 557–566.

Lui, H. W., & Wong, S. S. (2006). *Reflections on counseling: Developing practice in schools.* Singapore: Prentice Hall.

Metha, K., & Ko, H. (2003). *Gerontological counselling: An introductory handbook.* Singapore: SAGE Counselling Centre.

Ministry of Education. (2007). *Counselling services in schools.* Retrieved September 21, 2007, from http://www.moe.gov.sg

Ng, B. H., & Lim, K. M. (2006). Help-seeking behaviour of low income families in a family service centre setting. *Social Service Journal, 18,* 13–14.

Ow, R. (1998). Mental health care: The Singapore context. *Asia Pacific Journal of Social Work, 8*(1), 120–130.

Samion, S. (1999). *Counsellee's perceptions of their therapeutic alliance with traditional healers.* Unpublished master's thesis, Nanyang Technological University, Singapore.

Satir, V., Banmen, J., Gerber, J., & Gomori, M. (1991). *The Satir model: Family therapy and beyond.* Palo Alto, CA: Science and Behavior Books.

Sim, T. (1999). Development of counselling services in Singapore. *Asian Journal of Counselling, 6,* 49–76.

Singapore Association for Counselling. (2007). *Home page.* Retrieved September 21, 2007, from http://www.sac-counsel.org.sg

Singapore Department of Statistics. (2007). *Demographic indicators.* Retrieved September 21, 2007, from http://www.singstat.gov.sg

Singapore Department of Statistics. (2009). *Latest statistical news.* Retrieved April 10, 2009, from http:/www.singstat.gov.sg

Soong, C. (1994). Adapting Western counselling methods to the local context. *ASCD Review, 4*(2), 59–62.

Soong, C. (1997). *Adaptation of Western counselling approaches to an Asian multicultural context.* Unpublished doctoral dissertation, Nanyang Technological University, Singapore.

Sue, D. W., & Sue, D. (1990). *Counseling the culturally different.* New York: Wiley.

Sue, D. W., Arrendondo, P., & McDavis, R. J. (1992). Multicultural counseling competencies and standards: A call to the profession. *Journal of Counseling and Development, 70,* 477–486.

Super, D. E. (1983). A life-span, life-space approach to career development. *Journal of Vocational Behaviour, 16,* 282–298.

Super, D. E., Savickas, M. L., & Super, C. M. (1996). The life-span, life-space approach to careers. In D. Brown, L. Brooks, & Associates. *Career choice and development* (3rd ed., pp. 121–178). San Francisco: Jossey-Bass.

Tan, C. T., Chee, K. T., & Long, F. Y. (1980). Psychiatric patients who seek traditional healers in Singapore. *Singapore Medical Journal, 21,* 643–647.

Tan, E. (1989). The career maturity of Singaporean adolescents—where do we stand and what can be done? *Singapore Journal of Education, 10*(2), 40–45.

Tan, E. (1990a). Preparing teachers for pastoral care in Singapore schools. *Singapore Journal of Education, 11*(1), 57–64.

Tan, E. (1990b, December). *The validity of Holland's personality typology theory in an Asian culture.* Paper presented at the Fourth International Conference on Counseling, Sydney, New South Wales, Australia.

Tan, E. (1994a). Developing an indigenous computer-assisted career guidance programme for use in

Singapore schools. *Australian Journal of Career Development, 3*(3), 25–27.

Tan, E. (1994b). Teacher training in pastoral care: The Singapore perspective. In P. Lang, R. Best, & A. Lichtenberg (Eds.), *Caring for children: International perspectives on pastoral care and PSE* (pp. 196–206). London: Cassell.

Tan, E. (1995). The development of a computer-assisted career guidance programme for Singapore schools. *Singapore Journal of Education, 15*(2), 81–86.

Tan, E. (1996). Counselling in Singapore: Trends, issues and future directions. In W. Evraiff (Ed.), *Counseling in Pacific Rim countries* (pp. 109–122). San Mateo, CA: Lake Press.

Tan, E. (2002). Counselling psychology in Singapore: Development, issues and challenges. In A. G. Tan & M. Goh (Eds.), *Psychology in Singapore: Issues of an emerging discipline* (pp. 83–101). Singapore: McGraw-Hill.

Tan, E. (Ed.). (2004). *Counselling in schools: Theories, processes and techniques.* Singapore: McGraw-Hill.

Tan, N. T. (1984). *Handbook on counseling.* Singapore: Counselling and Care Centre.

Wong, S. S. (2002a). Multidimensional clinical interviewing (MCI): An integrative approach. In A. G. Tan & L. C. Law (Eds.), *Psychology in context: A perspective from the South East Asian societies* (pp. 232–249). Singapore: Linzi Media.

Wong, S. S. (2002b). Transformation therapy: An integrative approach to psychotherapy based on the Four Noble Truths. In A. G. Tan & L. C. Law (Eds.), *Psychology in context: A perspective from the South East Asian societies* (pp. 250–266). Singapore: Linzi Media.

Yeo, A. (1981). *A helping hand.* Singapore: Times Books International.

Yeo, A. (1993a). *Counselling: A problem-solving approach.* Singapore: Amour.

Yeo, A. (1993b). Counselling in Singapore: Development and trends. In A. H. Othman & A. Awang (Eds.), *Counselling in the Asia-Pacific region* (pp. 25–30). Westport, CT: Greenwood Press.

14

Multicultural Approaches to Healing and Counseling in Malaysia

Pendekatan Multi-Budaya Pemulihan Dan Kaunseling Di Malaysia

SEE CHING MEY, ABDUL HALIM OTHMAN,
SURADI SALIM, AND MD. SHUAIB BIN CHE DIN

Malaysia has been exposed to Western counseling and psychology since the 1950s, but practice remains relatively young. Contemporary Malaysian approaches to counseling and psychology reflect the revision of basic Western models, incorporating philosophical traditions, cultural history, and indigenous caregiving practices of a rapidly modernizing society. First associated with the medical field, counseling and psychology have spread widely to schools, the governmental sector, nongovernmental organizations (NGOs), business, and industry. This process has been challenging in Malaysia as counseling evolves from its Euro-American roots.

In this chapter, the educational, cultural, and practical aspects of the development of counseling and psychology in Malaysia are reviewed along with recent innovations in training and practice. Ethnic and professional issues as well as indigenous practices are given special focus.

THE MALAYSIAN CONTEXT

Malaysia is ethnically diverse, and its population professes a multitude of faiths. Malaysia is located in Southeast Asia and consists of two distinct parts. West Malaysia (or Peninsular Malaysia) lies between Thailand and the island nation of Singapore. East Malaysia comprises the states of Sabah and Sarawak on the island of Borneo (Kalimantan) and shares a common border with Indonesia.

The Federation of Malaya became independent from the United Kingdom on August 31, 1957. The federation was enlarged on September 16, 1963, by the accession of the British colonies of Singapore,

Sabah (then British North Borneo), and Sarawak. The name "Malaysia" was adopted on that date. Singapore left the federation on August 9, 1965 (Malaysia Ministry of Foreign Affairs, 2007).

Malaysia is now a federation of 13 states and three federal territories. Nine states in Western Malaysia have hereditary rulers (Sultans), and four others have titular governors. The three federal territories come directly under the central federal government.

Malaysia's land area is approximately 328,550 square kilometers, with a 2007 population of 27.17 million. Approximately, 32.2% of the population in 2007 was under the age of 15; 63.4% was between the ages of 15 and 64; and 4.4% was above age 65 (Department of Statistics Malaysia, 2007). Malaysia is considered one of Asia's most culturally diverse nations, with its multiethnic and multicultural population comprising Malays, Chinese, Indians, and other indigenous ethnic groups.

The Malays are Muslims. The Chinese are mostly Buddhists, Taoists, or Christians. The Indians are mainly Tamils from Southern India, and they are Hindus or Christians. There is also a sizable Sikh community. Eurasians and indigenous tribes make up the remaining population.

The constitution defines a Malay as being one who "professes the religion of Islam, habitually speaks the Malay language, conforms to Malay customs, and is the child of at least one parent who was born within the Federation of Malaysia before independence on the 31st of August, 1957." In the exercise of affirmative action to correct historical imbalances in economic and other fields, Malays and other defined communities are guaranteed special rights in the constitution (International Work Group for Indigenous Affairs [IWGIA], 2008).

Although *Bahasa Melayu* (Malay language) is the official language, English is a compulsory subject in all schools and is widely used and spoken. The official religion in Malaysia is *Islam*, but freedom of worship is practiced. As a result, it is common to see temples, mosques, and churches near each other.

The Federation of Malaysia is a constitutional monarchy, nominally headed by the Yang di-Pertuan Agong, commonly referred to as the King. The system of government is closely modeled after the British parliamentary system. In practice, however, much of the power is vested in the executive branch of the government, led by the Prime Minister and administered by the Cabinet. The Malaysian constitution stipulates that the Prime Minister must be a member of the *Dewan Rakyat*, the lower house of the parliament.

Malaysia maintains two sets of laws for its citizens. The national constitution forms the basis for civil law. The second set of laws is *syariah* (Islamic law), which applies only to Muslims. The federal government has little input into the administration of syariah since religion is a state's prerogative (along with land matters and administration). Thus, states can choose to administer syariah for their Muslim population, but interpretations obviously vary from state to state.

The cultural landscape of Malaysia remains diverse and vibrant, with festivals celebrated by its diverse populations, including *Hari Raya Puasa*, *Hari Raya Haji*, Christmas, Chinese New Year, *Deepavali* (the Hindu festival of lights), *Wesak*, and *Thaipusam*.

DEVELOPMENT OF COUNSELING

Guidance and counseling in Malaysia derive from the work and leadership of the counseling profession in the United States (Lloyd, 1987). The Malaysian Ministry of Education first accepted the importance of school guidance in its schools in 1963 and prepared a policy statement "which stipulated that all schools, especially secondary schools, should have their own guidance teachers" (Amir & Mohd Ali, 1984). Since then, guidance has been integrated into school education and has been aimed at promoting independent decision making. However, due to the lack of financial and human resources, initial guidance plans were not successfully implemented.

When drug involvement among the student population became worrisome in the 1980s, these plans were revived as the Ministry of Education reaffirmed the need for guidance and counseling teachers in the schools. Secondary schools reorganized themselves to include guidance and counseling activities. Guidance and counseling teachers received a reduced teaching load to allow them to perform their new duties. These teacher-counselors operated until 1996, when the Ministry of Education established the position of full-time school counselor. Since 2000, every secondary school has at least one full-time guidance and counseling officer.

Government-sponsored in-service training for drug counseling began in the 1980s, but these trainees came from the Ministry of Social Welfare, the Ministry of Home Affairs, and the Department of Prisons. Drug counseling was provided to inmates in government drug rehabilitation and aftercare programs. Such programs were also offered by a variety of voluntary agencies, mostly faith based.

The development of counseling in Malaysia reached its first professional milestone when a group of school counselors, counselor educators, and welfare officers interested in counseling came together to form the Malaysian Counsellor Association (now known as the Malaysian Counselling Association or PERKAMA) in January 1982. An association of more than 500 members, PERKAMA (*Persatuan Kaunseling Malaysia*) is the only national professional association for counseling.

In 1996, the Ministry of Education defined specific guidelines outlining the duties and functions of a school counselor in the school system. By then, counseling services had expanded into other government departments, industry and business corporations, religious institutions, rehabilitation centers, NGOs, and the community at large. Three decades after its formal introduction into schools, counseling has acquired prominence and is accepted as a crucial element in community development. A vital milestone was reached in 1998 with the enactment of the Counsellors Act (Act 580) to regulate the practice of professional counseling. The act provides for the establishment of a Board of Counselors, whose functions are to oversee counseling services, regulate the training and registration of counselors, and make recommendations to the government in relation to the standards of counseling services.

Every secondary school has a full-time guidance and counseling officer, and they are given a list of 25 tasks to carry out in their own way. Ideally, the Ministry of Education aims to achieve a ratio of one counselor to 500 secondary students, but this has not materialized. No official post exists for primary school counselors. Instead, the principal appoints a guidance and counseling teacher. Generally, their roles and functions pivot around academic counseling, career counseling, and psychosocial counseling.

Though the Ministry of Education has a list of more than 7,000 school counselors, only a small number of them have registered with the Board of Counselors. Many school counselors may not feel the need to register with the board because it is not a service requirement and there is no mechanism for them to obtain reimbursements for the fees and costs involved in registration. Some may lack the minimum training requirements or qualifications.

The Counsellors Act 1998 (Act 580) states that outside of the schools in Malaysia,

> [N]o person shall practice as a counselor, or use the title "registered counselor," or use or display any form of device representing that he is a registered counselor unless he is registered under the Counsellors Act 1998 (Act 580) (Subsection 22[1]). No person shall practice as a counselor unless he holds a valid practising certificate issued under this Act (Subsection 23[1]). Any person who contravenes this rule shall be guilty of an offence and shall on conviction be liable to a fine not exceeding thirty thousand ringgit or to imprisonment for a term not exceeding three years or both. (Subsection 22[2])

However, no prosecution has yet been taken to date.

Five factors have contributed to the need for counseling services in Malaysia. These are (1) rapid technological changes and industrial development; (2) the institution of democracy; (3) development and expansion of educational programs; (4) improved socioeconomic status (SES); and (5) changes in moral, belief, and social norms (Othman, 1971).

Rapid technological changes and industrialization have created many new occupations. With this vastly expanded job market, a need arises to seek matches between an individual's potential and ability and the advertised position. When counselors assist in this matching, productivity for the employer and job satisfaction for the employee are assured.

Democracy creates equal opportunities for the population to benefit from achieving higher levels of education and vocation. Counselors help students select courses or programs that suit their interests and vocational abilities.

Rapid urbanization and social changes affect traditional moral values, beliefs, and social norms. People have become more materialistic and individualistic. Traditional family institutions are threatened when both parents have to work and children are left to take care of themselves in the home or outside. Such unsupervised children and adolescents (the so-called latchkey kids in the United States) may easily become involved in antisocial activities that lead to juvenile crimes. Trained counselors are needed to rebuild affected families and to help parents use effective strategies to manage their delinquent children.

Feit and Lloyd (1990) argue that counseling is recognized as a profession in Malaysia because of three important ingredients that define a profession: ethical standards, licensure, and accreditation. They further add that a recognized counseling profession has specialized training and a strong identity. Johari (2001) agrees and lists additional criteria, including professional bodies. The provisions of the Counsellors Act 1998 (Act 580) confirms that counseling in Malaysia has indeed reached professional status.

Community Counseling and Private Practice

Community counseling services began in Malaysia through a variety of faith-based nonprofits and NGOs such as the Befrienders, Agape Counseling Center, Emmaus Counseling Center, Life-Line Counseling Center, Buddhist Gem Fellowship, PT Foundation (previously known as Pink Triangle), *Talian Sahabat Selangor,* and Islamic Religious Council (*Negeri Sembilan*). Most of these organizations initially offered telephone counseling services, and some now have licensed counselors providing face-to-face counseling services.

The current foci of these community agencies are child and adult mental health, wellness, and social skills training; thus, there is a demand for educational psychologists, child psychologists, play therapists, and music therapists to act as counselors. Children are often brought in for behavioral problems, learning disabilities, academic failure, and separation/adjustment problems. Youth and adolescents present personality disorders, relationship issues, truancy, behavioral problems, sexual victimization, academic failure, and career questions. Adults come in largely for marriage and family problems, adjustment issues, grief and bereavement, stress, and mental disorders (See, 2007). There is an increasing need for family, couple, marital, industrial, health, and addiction counseling, but counselor preparation has not kept up with the demand (Ng & Steven, 2001; Othman, 2000).

Counseling service providers in the country will definitely continue to increase as the rising number of training programs leads to more licensed practitioners entering the service. Private practice opportunities will also be created by heightened awareness of the role of counseling in the general population and by the promotion of employee assistance programs in forward-looking companies. However, private practice may remain an uncertain enterprise for counselors in Malaysia due to a lack of professional and legal guidelines. So far, no counseling program in Malaysia has offered training on making an enterprise out of private counseling. Despite increasing awareness, counseling remains an unclear service to many Malaysians, who are accustomed to the instant cure provided by a pill or two from a doctor and the nonmedical therapies such as herbal treatment, meditation, massage therapy, acupuncture, and exercise (e.g. tai chi and yoga).

Currently, most counseling practitioners and agencies are located in major cities in the country. In these settings, counselors, psychologists, and other mental health workers collaborate for the benefit of clients. Access to counseling services in small towns and rural areas is very limited. The authors speculate that online counseling or e-counseling may increase to meet this need.

In recent years, recognition of professional counseling by the public has increased as a result of the heightened visibility of professional counselors, improved standard of service delivery, and increased level of professionalism among counselors. However, the increased demand for counseling has led to an increase in the number of practitioners claiming to be therapists after undergoing training that falls below the minimum standards set by the board of counselors. While these individuals cannot use the title, "licensed counselor," there is nothing to prevent them from using the title, "therapist."

Ng and Steven (2001) view the future of counseling in Malaysia as very uncertain but challenging and the implications as varied. In our opinion, the counseling profession is now more certain of its direction, though the challenges remain.

PSYCHOLOGY IN MALAYSIA

Even though psychology originated in the second half of the 19th century, it was not until the 1960s that this discipline began to take root in Malaysia. Nevertheless, with national development, this discipline was accorded its rightful place, and the number of trained psychologists is beginning to increase steadily.

In Malaysia, psychologists generally conduct psychological testing and work with people with mental illness. The first proper attempt at community-based rehabilitation of people with mental illness occurred in Ipoh, where a mental health association and day care center were opened in 1967 and 1969, respectively.

In 1998, the National Mental Health Policy (NMHP) was approved by the Ministry of Health. *Mental wellness* is defined in this policy as follows:

> The capacity of the individual, the group, and the environment to interact with one another to promote subjective well-being and optimal functioning, and the use of cognitive, affective and relational abilities, towards the achievement of individual and collective goals consistent with justice. (SAMHSA National Mental Health Information Center, 2007)

The Malaysian Psychological Association (PSIMA) was founded in 1985 to provide a platform for its members to meet and interact while encouraging them to practice psychology in accordance with ethical guidelines and a professional code of ethics. Most of the 150 full or associate members are psychology educators from public and private universities around the country, graduates in psychology, and those practicing in various subdisciplines of psychology in the government, NGOs, and industry sectors. Currently, no process for the registration of psychologists in Malaysia exists, and psychologists are not yet governed by any acts of parliament.

In reality, the number of people with mental illness is increasing drastically. Daily tensions, problems, and frustrations contribute to anxiety and depression. Psychologists are not being sought after in Malaysia as they are in foreign countries, first of all because of a lack of public awareness of the role of psychologists. Second, people who are aware of the role of a psychologist may hesitate to consult one because of the social stigma that they are mad. Third, people tend to believe that mental illness can be solved by the family and traditional or religious healers.

At the same time, psychology in Malaysia is on far firmer footing today, though there is still a shortage of psychiatrists and clinical psychologists to meet the ratio set by the World Health Organization (WHO). As of 2006, Malaysia had only 165 psychiatrists and 33 clinical psychologists, but 719 psychiatrists and 364 clinical psychologists are needed to meet WHO's psychiatrist and population ratio (Kok, 2007).

THE STATUS OF COUNSELING AND PSYCHOLOGY TRAINING PROGRAMS

Because of speculation that the demand for professionally trained counselors would rapidly increase as the economy continued to grow and prosper during the 1980s, the training of counselors in the universities accelerated to meet the demand (Othman & Aboo Bakar, 1993). In 1976, the Universiti Malaya (UM) offered the first guidance and counseling major as part of the master of education program. Initially, the program was primarily research-based; however, it underwent some changes by including coursework.

The National University of Malaysia (*Universiti Kebangsaan Malaysia* [UKM]) Department of

Psychology introduced its counselor education program in November 1980. Other universities offering counseling programs include Putra University, Malaysia (*Universiti Putra Malaysia* [UPM]); Technological University of Malaysia (*Universiti Teknologi Malaysia* [UTM]); International Islamic University, Malaysia (*Universiti Islam Antarabangsa Malaysia* [UIAM]); University of Science, Malaysia (*Universiti Sains Malaysia* [USM]); University of Malaysia, Sarawak (*Universiti Malaysia Sarawak* [UNIMAS]), and University of Malaysia, Sabah (*Universiti Malaysia Sabah* [UMS]).

All the programs offered at the universities must follow the Standard and Qualification of Counselor in Training (2003) guidelines, where the minimum total credits offered by undergraduate programs must not be less than 120 credits and the minimum total credits offered by graduate programs must not be less than 48 credits.

The need for systematic quality training in counseling continues to exist despite the strides made thus far (Lloyd, 1987; Ng, 2003; Ng & Steven, 2001). With the increased number of counseling programs in the local universities and foreign offshore programs, we expect to see a drive toward increased quality and quantity of training programs due to competition; market demand because of increased awareness of counseling and related services in the society; and clarification and tightening of licensure requirements.

The number of training programs will continue to grow in the country as more local private universities and foreign universities develop counseling and related programs in response to social needs and students' demands for master's- and doctoral-level training. Thus, there may be more opportunities for foreign counselor-educators to teach specific approaches in counseling and supervision. This will provide greater opportunity for cross-fertilization of teaching and practice of counseling and supervision and further enhance the internationalization of the counseling profession.

With the increased number of master's- and doctoral-level graduates trained locally, we expect to see an increased number of Malaysian students going overseas for doctoral or postdoctoral training.

COUNSELING AND PSYCHOLOGY RESEARCH PARADIGMS IN MALAYSIA

Little research has been conducted in the fields of counseling and psychology in Malaysia as compared with Western countries. Generally, counseling and psychology research are conducted by master's and doctoral students fulfilling their degree requirements. Research is required to help Malaysian counseling professionals define and refine their purpose and direction, theory and practice, and training framework. Empirical findings are needed to guide improvements in the professionalization of counseling, allowing counselors and researchers to better shape the future of counseling through their own efforts rather than relying on the government. We expect an increase in research and publications in the counseling literature authored by Malaysian counseling professionals and foreign investigators who are interested in conducting studies in Malaysia.

INDIGENOUS MODELS OF HEALING AND COUNSELING

Traditional healing models, grounded in ethnic values and practices of Malays, Chinese, Indians, and other indigenous groups, including *bumiputeras* of Sabah and Sarawak, are holistic approaches that address the physical, spiritual, and psychological needs of clients. These healing models vary from one ethnic group to another. The cultures of different racial and ethnic groups influence many aspects of mental health problems and illnesses, including how clients communicate and manifest their symptoms, their styles of coping, their family and community supports, and their willingness to seek treatment. For example, the Chinese believe in the concept of *Yin* and *Yang*, the Indians use Ayurvedic medicine, the Kadazan believe in the powers of the *Bobohizan* (medicine women), and Malays subscribe to *semangat* (survival instinct).

Traditional Islamic Approaches to Healing

The following description refers only to the Malays, the dominant ethnic group of Malaysia, and should not be generalized to other groups, though the indigenous people, or bumiputras, in West Malaysia have some common healing concepts with the bumiputras of East Malaysia (*Kadazan, Dusun, Muruts, Iranun, Bajaus, Bugis,* and others).

Currently, the Malays are undergoing a tremendous transformation in their psychosocial makeup that affects their patronage of healing methods. As Muslims, their religious consciousness has a bearing on their choices of counseling methods and whom to patronize when in distress. Malays tend to subscribe to one or more of three approaches to healing: a traditional approach, a Western approach, and an Islamic approach.

Many Malays believe that mental illness is due to supernatural factors (fate, evil spirits, lightning, genie/spirits that cross the person's path), charms, spells, separation (as in the case of postpartum depression or *gila meroyan*), and food consumption (certain fruits make you feel cold or have *angin* [wind] in the body). Massage therapy is often practiced to reduce or eliminate the angin.

Traditional approaches also hold that evil spirits or fright causing the loss of semangat (survival instinct) may lead to illness. Semangat is a vital force present in a person. Healing practices aim to directly or indirectly bring back a person's semangat to his or her physical body through *menurun* (trance state and soul transfer), *jampi* (incantation), *mandi bunga* (special flower bath), and use of *orang halus* (help of a gentle spirit). Symptoms of this illness may be assessed through the changes of color in a chicken egg or kerosene lamp soot placed on thumbnails or beetle nuts.

The three main types of healing processes used in the traditional approach are (1) medicine, (2) spells, and (3) rituals (Stavovy, 1996). The medicines used include a range of herbal plant parts such as leaves, stems, roots, flowers, and seeds; animal sacrifices are also used as remedies for illness. A refrain of words repeatedly chanted during the healing process represents the spell. The ritual involves a traditional specialist using medicine and the words of the spell as a whole healing process or act. These healing practices are also used for protection against sorcery, spirits, and supernatural agents that cause physical and mental illness.

The Islamic approach subscribes to the idea of developmental dynamism, whereby humans are viewed from a positive point of view. Though a human's fate is already predetermined in *Loh Mahfuz* (the origin of the soul), he or she is able to change it. The Islamic models stress the healer's use of certain Quranic verses read over *air jampi,* or drinking water. Healing techniques can also include the reading of certain prescribed Quranic verses by the clients, incessant supplication (*doa*), abstaining from certain behavior, and upgrading one's religious consciousness.

Religious centers are thought to provide curative and restorative benefits (Raguram, Venkateswaran, Ramakrishna, & Weiss, 2002). In Malaysia, many Muslims troubled by emotional distress go to the *masjid* (mosque). The healing power in masjid resides in the site itself rather than in the religious leader or any medicines. Muslims believe that residing in or near a masjid has its healing potency and can play a part in reducing the mental and emotional symptoms.

Both traditional and Islamic approaches stress faith in the healer, and *se tiap penyakit ada ubatnya* (every illness has its panacea) is widely quoted. Illness is believed to be from *Allah* (God), and He decides whether or not a person is healed. Thus, the healer's duty is to ask for healing, but it is Allah's prerogative to heal.

A folk medicine practitioner in Malaysia is called a *bomoh, dukun,* or *pawang,* according to the period a student spends studying. The studies undertaken, which equip practitioners to prescribe proper medication to clients, cover the philosophy of life; therapeutic usages of herbs, metals, and animal parts; and effects of human behavior and living. Folk medicine practitioners, especially the elders, or *touks,* are treated with great respect, particularly in the rural community.

Folk medicine is inspired and guided by Islamic teachings. *Bomohs,* as well as their clients, believe in the comprehensiveness of these teachings and in the cure and protection from disease and harm described by the Quran and the *Sunnah* (the practice and sayings of the prophet). Using therapeutic means that are *halal* (lawful) and *tahir* (pure) is essential to maintaining good health; therefore, bomohs must not expose their clients to any unlawful or impure remedies.

Payment is minimal for traditional and Islamic healing methods. In many cases, the service is given free if the client cannot afford to pay.

It is difficult to gauge the successes and failures of traditional and Islamic approaches. One could say that they are as effective as Western models, especially if the illnesses are caused by nonbiological and affective factors, and they rely on the power of belief or faith.

Simultaneous use of traditional Islamic and Western approaches to treatment is emerging in the suburban areas, but the rural population would normally choose to go for traditional and Islamic approaches. One example, the group of clinics known as *Darus Shifa*, headed by Dato' Dr. Haron Din, are becoming very popular. Quranic verses and reference to various Islamic elements are used in this method. Dr. Din conducts classes using this approach around Malaysia, and he has many student followers. Because of the present worldwide movement toward a greater appreciation of Islamic teachings and practice, Darus Shifa's methods are becoming more appealing to Western-educated intellectuals. This traditional method has evolved over the years from its purely animistic origin to an integrated form of treatment, omitting elements incompatible with Islam (Darussyifa Online, 2008).

On the other hand, people in urban settings generally seek help from counselors and psychologists in hospitals where Western approaches are generally used. While Western approaches to therapy tend to be successful, they might be less effective for spiritual and existential issues. When medications are needed as a treatment for mental illness, Western models are often the primary choice.

In recent years, Islamic counseling has been much promoted. Islamic counseling emphasizes spiritual solutions, based on love and fear of Allah, to help individuals fulfill their responsibilities as servants of Allah. The principles of Islamic counseling also include confidentiality, trust, respect, recognizing the difference between arbitration and counseling, loving what is good for other people, making peace between people, concern about Muslim affairs, good listening habits, understanding others' cultures, the partnership between *Imams* (religious leaders) and professionals, awareness of the law of the land, and the ultimate goal of connecting people with Allah and offering spiritual solutions to them (Magid, 2007).

Nonetheless, Islamic counseling is a discipline that is vaguely defined and lacking a sound theoretical basis for developing models of intervention. Given that Islamic counseling is not yet in a form where its actual implementation can be monitored, guidelines need to be developed and integrated into a theoretical framework.

Taoist and Buddhist Approaches to Healing

The Chinese community in Malaysia often seeks Taoist and Buddhist approaches when an individual has physical or mental illness.

The purpose of Taoism is to immortalize the present physical body through techniques that promote a longer, healthier, happier, and wiser life. Taoism can be summarized by the principles of Yin and Yang and the evolution of these principles into the 64 hexagrams. The entire universe is an oscillation of the forces of Yin and Yang. Yang is the causative, active, creative principle of life and Yin is the resultant passive, destructive principle of death.

By contrast with Western concepts of mental health such as social attainment, self-development, progressive endeavor, and personal interpretation, Taoism advocates self-transcendence, integration with the law of nature, inaction, and an infinite frame of reference. In Taoism, various rituals, exercises, and substances are said to have positive effects on one's physical and mental health and are used to align one's self spiritually with cosmic forces or to enable ecstatic spiritual journeys. Internal alchemy and various spiritual practices are used by some Taoists to extend life even to the point of immortality.

Taoist healing practices include *Qi Gong, Tai Chi,* and *Tui Na* (massage therapy). *Qi* (Chi) means "energy," *Gong* (Kung) means "skill," so Qi Gong means "the skill of attracting vital energy." It refers to a wide variety of traditional "cultivation" practices that involve movement and/or regulated breathing designed to be therapeutic. Qi Gong, practiced for health maintenance purposes and therapeutic intervention, also teaches diaphragmatic breathing, an important component of the relaxation response in stress reduction.

Tai Chi, a mind-body practice that originated in China as a martial art, involves moving the body slowly and gently while breathing deeply. Tai Chi is sometimes called "moving meditation." Many people practice this exercise for various health purposes, such as to reduce stress, increase flexibility, improve muscle strength and definition, increase energy, stamina, and agility, and increase feelings of well-being.

Tui Na is another practice that originated in China. The word *Tui* means "pushing away abnormality." The word *Na* means the "taking out abnormality." Together these words represent manual or implemental manipulation of human meridian points to encourage, adjust, and balance the natural functions of the three folds of the body.

The Buddhist understanding of good health is similar, with its emphasis on the balanced interaction between the mind and body as well as between life and the environment. Illnesses tend to arise when the delicate equilibrium is upset, and Buddhist theory and practice aim to restore and strengthen this balance.

The Buddhist worldview is holistic and is primarily based on a belief in the interdependence of all phenomena and a correlation between mutually conditioning causes and effects. This belief is formulated by the principle of dependent origination, or law of conditionality, the causal nexus that operates in all phenomena—physical, psychological, and moral. In the physical realm, for example, all things in the universe are intimately interrelated as causes and effects without beginning and end, and the world is organically structured whereby all of its parts are interdependent. Similarly, in human society, every component is interrelated. The same is also found in the psychophysical sphere, where the mind and the body are interdependent parts of the overall human system.

Buddhism cites *karma* (deeds) as an important contributing factor to health and disease. From a Buddhist perspective, good health is the correlated effect of good karma in the past and present. This interpretation of health and illness in terms of karma emphasizes that there is a relationship between morality and health. The belief in karma can enable a person to cope with the painful aspects of life with tranquility rather than fruitless struggle or negative and depressing mental states because the acceptance helps a person to overcome despair and endure the condition.

Finally, traditional Chinese medicine, or herbalism, is also an important approach to healing. The herbs may be used whole or powdered, taken in capsules, or, more often, infused in water and drunk as tea. These herbs are often used to supplement a regular diet to prevent disease and mental illness.

While practicing the traditional healing system, the Chinese community in Malaysia has started to recognize the importance of Western mental health approaches in healing the mind and body. The educated Chinese community will explore Western approaches such as seeking a psychiatrist, psychologist, or counselor to combat mental illness. Nowadays, more and more Chinese traditional practitioners seek continuous education in learning concepts and principles of Western psychology.

Hindu Approaches to Healing

The Hindu community explains illness in specific ways. One must first understand that Hindu philosophy is intrinsically animistic. The physical world, which includes the body, is visible, but the spiritual world is invisible. *Wellness* is defined as harmony in body, mind, and spirit, and *unwellness* is disharmony. Many traditional Hindu healing systems for mental illness are based on supernatural and spiritual beliefs.

Many Indians in Malaysia seek help from a medium who acts as a vehicle for a deity's mind and voice. The medium possessed by a deity may identify the cause of the person's symptoms of physical and mental illness and prescribe ritual actions designed to transform the spirit from a source of affliction to a benevolent or neutral power, or to send the spirit away.

Ayurveda, a traditional Hindu science of healing, is also widely used. The term *Ayurveda,* combines *dyus,* meaning "life, vitality, health, longevity," and *veda,* meaning "science or knowledge (Crawford, 1989, p. 3). Ayurveda practitioners promote food and lifestyle as two main areas that affect our health and wellness. Yoga is an exercise of purification that helps individuals become morally strong, which is a prerequisite for spiritual discipline. Ayurveda adds elements of healing that are not found in Western medicine. According to Crawford (1989), there are three implications to the core of Ayurveda healing: (1) The body cannot be cured without considering the relationship of the body and mind; (2) spirituality can never be separated from personal development; and (3) the spiritual well-being of individuals promotes physical well-being.

In recent years, the knowledge and concepts of Western mental health have been integrated with Hindu traditional healing systems for the development of healing and preventive mental health problems in the Hindu community. The growing interest in Western mental health practice among Hindu traditional practitioners attests to a substantial interest in regaining humanistic mental health perspectives, and they stress that traditional healing and Western mental health practices are complementary to ensure a state of well-being.

CHALLENGES AND RECOMMENDATIONS TO FACILITATE INTERNATIONAL COUNSELING PROFESSIONAL COLLABORATIONS

Based on the discussion above, there are five challenges faced by the Malaysian counseling profession: (1) unavailability of a common model for counseling programs for the purpose of professional identity, (2) no uniformity in practical training practicum (internship and supervision) in counselor education programs, (3) cultural adjustment and relevance to counseling, (4) lack of research, particularly follow-up, experimental, and outcome research, and (5) competition from the traditional and indigenous forms of healing.

Institutions offering counseling programs use their own models and methods. One way to resolve this issue is for counseling to establish its own identity, that is, to be recognized as a distinct profession with emphasis on specializations such as AIDS counseling, marriage and family counseling, mental health counseling, addiction counseling, and school counseling.

In Western countries such as the United States, variations in counselor education programs are no longer a pressing issue because the Council for Accreditation of Counseling and Related Educational Programs (CACREP) handles matters pertaining to accreditation of counseling programs. However, in Malaysia, the Board of Counselors has yet to expand its role to include accreditation.

Another related issue involves practical training (practicum, internship, and supervision), where various levels of competency are required in different settings. To date, there is no uniformity across institutions in the practical training of counselors. Some practitioners argue that counselor trainees do not need lengthy academic preparation before they can be considered competent to do counseling. They believe that short courses cum practicum training outside the universities are sufficient to carry out counseling duties. However, some academicians disagree and argue that in order for counselors to be skilled and professional, they need longer academic preparation. The academic preparation program must include sufficient knowledge and skills, research foundations, practicum training, and internships to ensure counselor competence.

Many Malaysian counselor educators question whether the counseling processes and techniques learned abroad need to be modified to handle the cultural and religious issues of Malaysian clients. Because of the religious and racial diversity in Malaysia, the development of a "Malaysian" counseling approach will not be easy. However, most experts believe that counselors trained in a foreign country must learn to apply their skills and techniques to their own social and cultural milieu. Thus, it is necessary to set up local training institutions with a multicultural and diversity focus.

A coherent and indigenous theoretical counseling framework for the multiracial population is indicated. For counseling in Malaysia to continue to grow, counselors need to incorporate techniques from various therapeutic approaches.

The role of psychological testing and assessment needs further clarification and delineation in order for counselors to effectively incorporate them into their professional work. All these tests are imported from the West, and consideration needs to be given to language and cultural bias.

Malaysian society is culturally diverse, but multicultural counseling competence training in the counseling training programs is still lacking or not given due attention. Furthermore, counselors-in-training are increasingly presenting more severe and complex issues, for example, incest, abuse, teenager pregnancy, addictions, and mental illness. Therefore, counselors and counselor educators must establish culturally relevant, responsive, and effective theoretical and treatment competencies along with a coherent framework of counseling that is contextualized and empirically based for the different races in Malaysia.

Last, but not least, few studies in counseling employ quasi-experimental methodology or focus on counseling outcome evaluation. Thus, more research is needed to ensure the effectiveness of counselor education programs, training models, and treatment outcomes.

Salim (2004) added the additional challenge of the acceptance of counseling by various target groups. A variety of counseling services are needed in school settings (Hashim, 1994; Hussin, 1999) due to ever increasing social problems among school students such as drug addiction, smoking, gangsterism, robbery, and rape. These studies have urged the government, educators, and society to place counseling services as their best approach in handling these cases. However, studies also show that counseling services in schools have not been fully used or properly implemented. Currently, the services merely exist but do not benefit students for four main reasons: (1) Students are reluctant to seek help from school counselors, even though they know the services are available (Usha, 2000); (2) there is a misconception

of counselor's role as problem solver; (3) there is ineffective implementation of counseling services due the counselor's lack of skills and experience; and (4) role definitions of counselors may not emphasize counseling and psychological assessment.

There is a future for counseling in Malaysia. The Malaysian government, especially the Ministry of Education and Public Service Department, provides continuous support and encouragement for the development of counseling services in schools, institutions of higher learning, government agencies, and the private sector. Thus, counselors have to actively promote their services and at the same time educate the society to understand the importance of counseling services in promoting wellness in the community.

CONCLUSION

This chapter outlines a general background of counseling and psychology in Malaysia, beginning with how counseling was able to gain acceptance in society, leading to the establishment of an act to register counselors and supervise their activities. The training programs offered at the graduate and postgraduate levels are somewhat behind, and the universities will have to collaborate with overseas counterparts in order to share experiences and improve the training.

The counseling profession in Malaysia has many challenges ahead. There is an urgent need to explore the multicultural emphasis in the practice of counseling to provide more effective services to the overall population. Competent counselors need to be knowledgeable about perspectives and counseling approaches, embracing client populations of diverse racial, ethnic, religious, sexual, cultural, national, and socioeconomic backgrounds. There is a need for psychometric development and continued development of multicultural counseling competency in counseling training programs.

Promotion of closer professional collaboration among psychologists, physicians, psychiatrists, counselors, social workers, and other mental health professionals is also important. In any setting, they must coordinate their work on a particular case, sharing all necessary information to help the clients to restore health, establish clarity of mind, and develop life skills. The team approach promotes coordination and communication and can offer the client a one-stop effort, as opposed to many separate evaluations, interpretations, and plans. This approach provides better care than past individualized plans.

Fostering connections with regional and international associations through conferences, workshops, publications, and research is much needed. International collaboration is important to monitor trends in counseling through international cooperation, sharing resources and knowledge to address mental health problems.

REFERENCES

Amir, A., & Mohd Ali, A. L. (1984). Guidance and counseling in Malaysian schools: A review and critique. In *Third Asian workshop on child and adolescent development* (Vol. 2, pp. 1–18). Kuala Lumpur, Malaysia: Faculty of Education, University of Malaya.

Counsellors Act 1998 (Act 580). Malaysia Board of Counselors.

Crawford, C. (1989). Ayurveda: The science of long life in contemporary perspective. In A. Sheikh & K. Sheikh (Eds.), *Eastern & Western approaches to healing.* (pp. 3–32). New York: Wiley.

Darussyifa Online. (2008). *Persatuan Kebajikan dan Pengubatan Islam Malaysia.* Retrieved October 20, 2008, from http://www.darussyifa.org/index.php

Department of Statistics Malaysia. (2007). *Population: Summary statistics.* Retrieved February 20, 2007, from http://www.statistics.gov.my/eng/index.php?option=com_content&view=article&id=50:population&catid=38:kaystats&Itemid=11

Feit, S. S., & Lloyd, A. P. (1990). A profession in search of professionals. *Counselor Education and Supervision, 29,* 216–219.

Hashim, A. H. (1994). *Keperluan bimbingan dan kaunseling di sekolah-sekolah menengah: Satu tinjauan* [Needs of guidance and counseling in secondary schools: A review] [Monograph]. Serdang: Putra University of Malaysia.

Hussin, H. (1999). *Keperluan bimbingan dan kaunseling pelajar di dua buah sekolah menengah di Kelantan* [Guidance and counseling needs of students from two secondary schools in Kelantan]. Unpublished research report for Master of Counselling, Faculty of Education, University of Malaya, Kuala Lumpur, Malaysia.

International Work Group for Indigenous Affairs. (2008). *The political system and government policy.* Retrieved April 15, 2008, from http://www.iwgia.org/sw18355

Johari, M. J. (2001). *Etika profesional* [Professional ethics]. Skudai: Penerbit Universiti Teknologi Malaysia Press.

Kok, T. (2007). *Shrink numbers bad news for mental health.* Retrieved August 29, 2008, from http://teresakok.com/2007/04/23/shrink-numbers-bad-news-for-mental-health/

Lloyd, A. P. (1987). Counselor education in Malaysia. *Counselor Education and Supervision, 26,* 221–227.

Magid, I. (2007). *Islamic perspective of counseling.* Retrieved April 13, 2008, from http://www.isna.net/Resources/articles/community/Islamic-Perspective-of-Counseling.aspx

Malaysia Ministry of Foreign Affairs. (2007). *About Malaysia.* Retrieved February 20, 2007, from http://www.kln.gov.my/?m_id=1&s_id=45

Ministry of Health Malaysia. (1998). *National mental health policy.* Kuala Lumpur, Malaysia: Author.

Ng, K. S. (2003). Family therapy in Malaysia. In K. S. Ng (Ed.), *Global perspectives in family therapy: Development, practice, and trends* (pp. 31–38). New York: Brunner-Routledge.

Ng, K. S., & Steven, P. (2001). Creating a caring society: Counseling in Malaysia before 2020 AD. *Asian Journal of Counseling, 8*(1), 87–101.

Othman, A. H. (1971). *A fresh look at guidance in Malaysian schools.* Paper presented at the seminar on educational psychology, University of Hawaii, Honolulu.

Othman, A. H. (2000). *Kaunseling untuk kesejahteraan Insan—satu pengalaman di Malaysia* [Counseling for human wellness: Malaysian experience]. Inaugural professorial lecture. University of Malaysia, Kota Kinabalu, Sabah, Malaysia.

Othman, A. H., & Aboo Bakar, Sh. Bee. (1993). Guidance, counseling, and counselor education in Malaysia. In A. H. Othman & A. Awang (Eds.), *Counseling in the Asia-Pacific region* (pp. 1–25). Westport, CT: Greenwood Press.

Raguram, P., Venkateswaran, A., Ramakrishna, J., & Weiss, M. G. (2002). Traditional community resources for mental health: A report of temple healing from India. *British Medical Journal, 325,* 38–40.

Salim, S. (2004, January). *Perkhidmatan kaunseling di Malaysia: Perkembangan, cabaran dan halangan* [Counseling services in Malaysia: Development, challenges and obstructions]. Inaugural professorial lecture, University of Malaya, Kuala Lumpur, Malaysia.

SAMHSA National Mental Health Information Center. (2007). *National strategy for suicide prevention: Goals and objectives for action.* Retrieved February 20, 2007, from http://mentalhealth.samhsa.gov/publications/allpubs/SMA01–3517/appendixe.asp

See, C. M. (2007). *Doing well, feeling worse.* Inaugural professorial lecture, School of Educational Studies, University of Science Malaysia, Penang, Malaysia.

Standard and Qualification of Counselor in Training. (2003). Malaysia Board of Counselors.

Stavovy, T. (1996). *Idioms of psychosis in Papua New Guinea.* Unpublished master's thesis, Monash University, Carlton, Victoria, Australia.

Usha, K. N. (2000). *Kesedaran pelajar sekolah menengah di Mentakab terhadap perkhidmatan bimbingan dan kaunseling* [Awareness of students about the guidance and counseling services in a secondary school in Mentakab]. Unpublished master's thesis. Faculty of Education, University of Malaya, Kuala Lumpur, Malaysia.

SOUTH ASIA

15

Counseling in Pakistan

An Eastern Muslim Perspective

پاکستان میں کونسلنگ : مشرقی اسلامی نقطۂ نظر

KAUSAR SUHAIL AND M. ASIR AJMAL

Counseling as a modern discipline is still in its infancy in Pakistan. Whereas the need for counseling is being felt like never before, the infrastructure to provide training and appropriate qualifications simply does not exist. There are, however, traditional models of counseling that seem to have worked quite well until recently. As Pakistani society changes, the demands of modernization have placed additional stress on the individual, who, as a citizen of a developing nation, is already struggling with myriad pressures. In this chapter, we look at attempts in Pakistan to introduce counseling in different spheres of life. We will also examine the different services that have included counseling in their programs. Traditional models of counseling are described and examined. The relative success or failure of modern therapeutic approaches is assessed. It is important, however, to have a sense of the historical context of Pakistan to appreciate the challenges and opportunities connected to the development of counseling services in this country.

BACKGROUND AND HISTORY OF PAKISTAN

Pakistan separated from India in 1947 as a result of the independence movement against the rule of the British Empire. Bordering India, China, Tibet, East Turkestan, Afghanistan, and Iran, Pakistan's 796,095 square kilometers of territory strategically straddles the ancient trade routes between Asia and Europe (http://www.geographia.com/pakistan). Pakistan has a population of 160 million, with the rural population constituting 70% of the total population. The current literacy rate of Pakistan is estimated at 43% of the total population; urban literacy is about

65%, whereas rural literacy is approximately 34%. Pakistan's gender disparity regarding literacy is among the highest in the world; 57% of men are literate, whereas only 28% of women (http://www.raheems.org/statics.htm) are literate. However, the distinct gender gap in education favoring males seems to shrink at a higher education level. Despite this, a vast majority of the population still sees female education as a means to perpetuating traditional roles and statuses. Anwar and Ijaz (1990) pointed out that Pakistani women, by and large, are trained to be docile, dependent, and submitting to the institution of patriarchy. The authors also concluded that on the whole Pakistani women are marginal to the whole process of development in Pakistan.

Social and economic development has remained slow in Pakistan since its inception, and inequality between social classes, genders, and rural and urban areas has led to widespread poverty (Syed, Hussein, & Yousafzai, 2007). Because of continuously rising inflation rates, unemployment, social and economic deprivations, rapidly changing social and cultural values, large-scale political and economic unrest, fragmentation of the family system, and loss of religious values, there has been a corresponding increase in indicators of psychological and social unrest—suicide and violence (Khalid, 2002; Suhail & Qurat-tul-Ain, 2004).

Pakistan as a nation is at the crossroads of tradition and modernity. In fact, each individual is torn between the two and leads two lives that seem to run parallel to each other. One stream is that of the traditional and religious beliefs and practices that have survived colonization. The other is the modernist rationalist way of being that has come about as a result of colonization and Western education. This split is easily visible in the cities, where children get a modern education and also learn about traditional and religious values in school. The Islamic studies teacher defends the creationist perspective that human life began with Adam and Eve, whereas the biology teacher teaches the evolutionist perspective that humans are the result of millions of years of the evolutionary process. This split alone is responsible for a major psychological conflict. Every time one does something where tradition says something different from the modernist perspective, one has a problem to solve in Pakistan (Badri, 1979).

MENTAL HEALTH SERVICES

Tracing the history of psychiatric services in the region, the available evidence indicates that the first recorded incident of treating mental illness is that of Dr. Johann Martin Honiberger starting psychiatric treatment in 1839 for Maharaja Ranjit Singh in Alshifa Hospital outside Delhi Darwaza (gate) at Lahore. In 1854, Robert Montgomery, Judicial Commissioner of Punjab, floated the idea of constructing a mental hospital in Lahore, and in 1900, Mental Hospital Lahore's doors were opened for the public (Sheikh, 2007). Apart from the Mental Hospital Lahore, at the time of independence (1947), Pakistan inherited two other mental hospitals, one each in Hyderabad and Peshawar, as well as a psychiatric unit at the Military Hospital in Rawalpindi. The late 1960s and 1970s were years of expansion for psychiatric services throughout Pakistan. Replacing the mental health act of 1912–1926, the new mental health law, which embodies the modern concept of mental illnesses, treatment, rehabilitation, and civil and human rights, was enacted on February 20, 2001 (Mubbashar & Saeed, 2001). Under this new ordinance, the nomenclature of mental hospitals was changed. Mental Hospital Lahore, the biggest hospital in Pakistan, was renamed in 2002 as Punjab Institute of Mental Health (PIMH). Since acquiring its new status, the institute has been providing a number of services to patients, including emergency services, inpatient facilities (200 beds for men and 60 for women), and daily outpatient department (OPD) services (with an attendance of 250–350 patients each day). The Family Counseling Clinic of PIMH also provides career support and guidance. In all major cities of Pakistan, including Lahore, Karachi, Rawalpindi, and Peshawar, there are separate psychiatric units in major public hospitals, mostly headed by a psychiatrist with a subordinate team of clinical psychologists. Only 0.4% of the national health budget is allocated to mental health (Mubbashar & Saeed, 2001).

There are 25 separate departments of psychiatry in 33 combined military hospitals across the country. Each department is headed by a psychiatrist, but there are no permanent positions for clinical or counseling psychologists, and usually clinical psychologists work on contract for military personnel and their families (Rehman, 2004). Despite the existing mental health services, the imbalance between demand and supply of mental health care is staggering. For example, the ratio of trained clinical psychologists with a postgraduate diploma to the population is approximately 1:400,000 (Gadit & Khalid, 2002).

PERCEPTIONS OF MENTAL ILLNESS AND HELP SEEKING

In Pakistan, mental illness is one of the major health care concerns, with an estimated 10% to 16% of the general population suffering from mild to moderate mental illness, and 1% from severe mental illness (Mubbashar & Saeed, 2001).

Based on a survey in four psychiatric units of Lahore and three units in Karachi, depression was found to be the most frequently occurring mental health problem (35%), followed by schizophrenia (20%), obsessive compulsive disorder (19%), anxiety (14%), conversion disorder (11%), and drug abuse (8%). Although depression appeared to be the leading problem, these figures may not be truly representative of the incidence of this illness in Pakistan because depression often manifests somatically in headaches, stomach problems, aches, and pains, particularly in Pakistani women (Suhail, 2004a).

In Pakistan, the stigma associated with mental illness discourages patients and their families from getting the help they need due to the fear of discrimination. People affected with mental health problems are considered crazy, mad, and dangerous, not being able to think or behave rationally (Qidwai & Azam, 2002; Suhail & Anjum, 2004; Suhail & Chaudhry, 2004). The root causes of discriminatory attitudes are illiteracy, indifference, intolerance, and ignorance, which are meshed in the social fabric of the

society (Syed et al., 2007). There is evidence that in Pakistan, patients with mental disorders, especially those seeking help, are perceived to be socially incongruent and bizarre as compared with those who seek help for physical illnesses (Suhail & Anjum, 2004). With mental problems, patients and their families conceal the illness because of the fear of losing jobs, public repulsion, disapproval, and rejection (Suhail & Chaudhry, 2004).

Cultural perceptions about the possible role of the patient in the etiology of illness may also influence the underuse of mental health services. Most Pakistani households preach the virtue of self-restraint and self-control, and through the socialization process, the child learns that it is wicked to lose control over oneself (Ajmal, 1969). A mental health literacy survey of 1,750 people in Pakistan showed that weakness of character is considered a legitimate, though stigmatized, explanation for mild and severe mental illnesses (Suhail, 2004b).

Help seeking is also influenced by one's willingness to disclose, which in turn is largely determined by one's affiliation with a guilt- or shame-based society. The Western guilt-based individualistic community is primarily internally oriented. Autonomous decision making, control over one's choices, and responsibility to self are highly desirable (Moazam, 2000). Eastern shame-based societies focus on "not jeopardizing relationships." When the goal is to preserve the family name, rather than the individual (Hofstede, 1980), disclosing mental illness can bring a shame to the family and restrict the prospects of marriage, work, and socialization.

Asian cultures with strong familial ties and extended family systems may reduce the need to seek help outside the family as well. Birchwood et al. (1992) demonstrated that South Asians (e.g., with Pakistani, Indian, or Bangladeshi origin) may have a natural protection from distress because of the social support inherent in their cultures.

CONSTRUCTIONS OF MENTAL ILLNESS AND HELPING

The sociocultural construction of mental illness needs to be considered in light of Pakistan's low literacy rate (Miles, 1992) since the two are connected (Mubbashar & Farooq, 2001). Consistent with the relatively low literacy rate in Pakistani villages, mental health literacy levels have also been shown to be similarly low in these areas (Suhail, 2004b). Kausar and Sarwar (1997) found that the majority of their respondents living in Pakistani villages explained the main reasons (culturally and religiously genuine) for mental disorders as possession by ghosts and magic. Misconceptions about the causation of mental disorders included visiting graveyards, visiting gardens during night, being influenced by an evil eye, and eclipses. The researchers pointed out that these misconceptions are cultural and not religious as Islam forbids people from holding such beliefs. Amulets (magical or holy writings on paper) were used for both causing trouble and treatment.

Consistent with the above-mentioned studies, a large-scale survey conducted involving 1,750 Pakistani people showed that magical spells and paranormal phenomena are considered as plausible causes of mental illness by subgroups of the population. A sizeable proportion of that survey believed that the symptoms of depression and psychosis were manifestations of some physical illness such as fever or cancer (Suhail, 2004b).

Choosing someone to help when facing a psychological problem is determined by how the causation is explained. If magical spells are considered as a likely cause for the psychological symptoms, the preferred treatment will be religious or magical. When psychological symptoms are associated with physical problems, general physicians are considered the right choice for treatment.

Alternate forms of treatment closer to cultural beliefs may capture better the attention of people living in rural areas in Pakistan. Faith healers are a major source of care for people with mental health problems in Pakistan, particularly for women and those with little education. Saeed, Gater, Hussain, and Mubbashar (2000) observed and recorded the work of faith healers in rural areas of Pakistan with 139 persons receiving the services. The results indicated that the classifications used by faith healers were based on mystic causes of disorders: *Saya* (evil

spell; 27%), *Jinn* (spirit) possession (16%), or *Churail* (witch; 14%), with little agreement between the faith healers' classification and various *DSM-III-R* diagnoses. Faith healers used powerful techniques of suggestion and cultural psychotherapeutic procedures for treatment. The procedures included *Taawiz* (amulets), *Dua* (prayer), exorcism, and *Dumm* (blowing verses from the Holy Quran on the client). These procedures are described later in this chapter.

THE ROLE OF RELIGION IN UNDERSTANDING PSYCHOLOGICAL PROBLEMS AND HELPING

Religious values and beliefs, particularly those connected with Islam, intersect with culture in understanding and dealing with psychological problems in Pakistan. The universe of Islam includes various classes of beings besides humans, such as *Jinn* (spirits), *Shaitan* (satanic beings), and *Farishtay* (angels). The existence of these beings has been acknowledged very clearly in Al-Quran, the holy book of Muslims (Bose, 1997), encouraging people to visualize and believe in culturally and religiously sanctioned images and ideas. In *Rehman* (Surah 55 of Al-Quran), God directly addresses both humans and Jinn, and *Al-Jinn* (Surah 72) reveals that both creatures are endowed with special abilities but are answerable to God for their deeds. Humans and Jinn have been created by different material, mud and smokeless fire, respectively, and as a result, each is capable of performing different tasks.

Al-Quran acknowledges that magical spells can be exercised on human beings (Surah 113 & 114), though magic can only be employed with the use of holy books (Torah, Bible, Al-Quran) if the content does not have anything evil and when the purpose is to benefit rather than harm others (Surah 2, *Al-Baqar,* Verse 102). The Prophet Mohammad himself treated his own disorientation by reciting Surah 113 and 114 (jointly called *Muawezataen*), requesting shelter from God. In the case of mental illness, exorcism is also practiced in Pakistan, and the evil spirit, the jinn, is cast out by reciting verses from the Holy Quran or through magic spells. For a Muslim, belief in magical forces may serve the purpose of putting the responsibility of misfortune on some culturally accepted external source.

Pakistani practitioners of magic perform either white or black magic. Black magic is performed to harm an enemy; typically, it is the mother-in-law or the husband's mistress in the case of female patients in Pakistan (Suhail & Cochrane, 2002). White magic is performed to undo the effects of black magic on someone, typically on one's husband. There are no hard data available about the practice of magic, but in most town centers, large signboards can be seen inviting people to "conquer your love" and "destroy your enemies." In the town centers, there are also a large number of practitioners of magic who offer to help solve people's problems. They also use a lot of spells from the Hindu tradition. Despite widespread chicanery and quackery, people turn to a large number of spiritually gifted *peers* (spiritual healers) for counseling. The peers offer help in terms of listening, offering advice, guidance, and prayers.

In addition to concepts of magic derived from Islam, the Pakistani culture, especially in rural areas, is infused with Sufism, the Islamic mystical tradition. Like most other mystical traditions, Sufism is based on a one-to-one master-disciple relationship. The peer, the master, teaches the *mureed,* the disciple, how to transcend the illusion of the material world and its suffering, which is caused by attachment. The disciple submits to the will of the master, allowing him or her to experience mystical realities.

Muslim thinkers also developed their theories about the causation and treatment of mental disturbances based on Quranic teachings and the sayings of Prophet Mohammad. Humans, society, and Allah (God) are united; all psychological distance between humans and between humans and nature is commensurate with the distance between humans and Allah. Therefore, alienation from Allah leads to mental illness (Ajmal, 1986). Rizvi (1991) further elaborated that mental disease is largely a flight from responsibility, and an individual is mentally disturbed when she or he becomes subservient to impulses and desires. A renowned Muslim scholar, Ghazali (n.d.), maintained that functional disorders

are due to ignorance and they lead to deviation from God. Ghazali enumerated various types of spiritual disease, including malice, ignorance, cowardice, desires, doubt, envy, jealousy, and greed. Treatment, in most of these cases, is the cleansing of *Qalb* (a spiritual heart found in the physical heart) by total submission to the will of Allah.

INTERSECTIONS OF ISLAMIC TEACHINGS AND WESTERN COUNSELING THEORIES

Muslim scholars such as Razi, Al-Ghazali, Ibn-e-Miskwayh, and Ashraf Ali Thanvi emphasized the development of the whole person, with common therapeutic goals of changing an individual's relationship with God and society. Muslim thinkers preached, in theory and practice, tolerance and respect for others and acceptance of nature as a part of life. Various individual therapies were developed along these lines (Rizvi, 1989). Maulana Ashraf Ali Thanvi, a revered saint of the early 20th century, is considered a great psychotherapist/counselor, and his methods of treatment are very similar to modern counseling approaches. Consistent with the humanistic model, Thanvi (n.d.) believed the cure depended on the client's own cooperation and determination. Like Carl Rogers, he also believed there must be psychological contact between the counselor and the client. In line with behaviorism, Thanvi believed that the job of the therapist was to guide and advise. His ideas were also consistent with the psychoanalytic tradition in explaining the roots of mental illness. Believing that most disorders originate in childhood and the mother plays the major role in shaping a child's personality, he wrote *Bahishti Zaiwar* (Heavenly Ornaments; Thanvi, 1981) for the training of mothers. As in psychoanalysis, Thanvi used therapeutic sessions to make clients' ideas more explicit by reflecting on them. Thanvi believed that the ability to differentiate between voluntary and involuntary behavior is half the treatment. He further elaborated that all commands and prohibitions are voluntary and therefore everyone is responsible for them. For instance, one is not responsible for the content of one's dreams or hallucinations, whereas one is supposed to be accountable for deliberate behavior. His major methods of treatment included reading therapy and "cure by company." His therapeutic philosophy was humanistic, but his approach was directive, like that of a behaviorist. He would invite clients with complex psychological disorders to come to his place, *Khanqah-e-Imadia,* to meet after noon prayers either individually or in a group. At noon, after the prayer, he would also deliver a lecture and explain solutions to various problems and conflicts. As in behaviorists' bibliotherapy, Thanvi would recommend readings to his patients, either from his own writings (he wrote some 800 large and small books to serve this purpose) or from other Muslim writers. He required written reports from the clients about their problems, actions, and experiences leading to catharsis to be shared retrospectively with the therapist (Rizvi, 1989).

Farooqi (2006) indicated that years back, Muslim scholars and physicians endorsed many contemporary psychotherapeutic techniques. She cited Ghazali, Al-Razi, Ibn-e-Sina, Rumi, and Thanvi and explained how their therapies resembled modern therapeutic approaches. Both Al-Ghazali and Al-Razi, for example, acknowledged that environmental conditions could reinforce desirable and undesirable behaviors. Hence, they stressed the modification of unhealthy parental attitudes. Akin to a behaviorist, Ibn-e-Sina suggested the use of aversive conditioning or related procedures, such as the withholding of reinforcement to eliminate a specified behavior, for example, social boycott and depreciation. Modeling one's self after a religious leader has been recommended and used by Rumi and Thanvi. Farooqi pointed out that Muslim scholars were similar to Jung in emphasizing the constructive role of religious faith, spiritual experiences, and revelations and inspiration in the development of a mature and healthy personality.

The spiritual bond between the Muslim saints and their followers is also similar to the modern client-therapist alliance. Though this tradition has lost much of its spiritual significance, the peer has become a hereditary position that is revered by the general public in the rural areas. People approach the peer typically for solutions to their problems.

Not surprisingly, given what has been discussed thus far, the analysis of pathways to mental health services indicates that many people in Pakistan consult faith healers and spiritual leaders before visiting mental health professionals. Under these circumstances, professionals faced with the task of developing mental health services in Pakistan are confronted with a number of challenging issues (Syed et al., 2007).

As previously discussed, since the Middle Ages of Europe, guidance and counseling were offered by many Muslim philosophers, faith healers, and religious leaders. During the period between the downfall of the Greek empire and the Renaissance of Europe, the Muslims kept up these medical and psychotherapeutic traditions. Muslim philosophers put forward a radical humanistic approach (giving respect to the individual and believing that humans have the potential to grow by using their inner resources) toward persons with mental disorders. Subsequently, Europe benefited by this treasure of knowledge (Farooqi, 2006). The great national poet and philosopher Dr. Mohammad Iqbal (1978) believed Muslim scientists and thinkers were predominantly humanists in the essential sense and that contemporary values generated by humanism are those derived from Islamic culture. Iqbal further indicated that neither Europeans nor Muslims acknowledged the Muslim contribution because the extant work of Muslims still lies scattered and unpublished in the libraries of Europe, Asia, and Africa.

CONTEMPORARY COUNSELING IN PAKISTAN: BRINGING TOGETHER EAST AND WEST

The contemporary practice of counseling has emerged and developed in Pakistan as a North American product of the 20th century. However, mental health professionals in Pakistan tend to adapt modern counseling approaches to cultural and religious values and norms in their country.

Assessment and Diagnosis

Twenty percent to 30% of applied psychology and counseling faculty members in Pakistan universities earned their PhDs in Europe and the United States, bringing Western technology, knowledge, and practices with them. Those who acquired their doctoral degrees from Pakistan are also trained in similar ways. Prevalent diagnostic, assessment, and treatment models are often very much the same as those that are used in the West, though efforts have been made to adapt to local culture and draw in indigenous healing traditions.

All psychology departments in universities as well as hospital psychiatric units have the *DSM-IV-TR* and *ICD-10* available in their libraries. In the mid-1970s, a large amount of money was invested and ambitious test construction programs for counseling were initiated (Dar, 1982). Afterward, two organs of the Ministry of Education, the Curriculum Wing and the National Institute of Psychology (NIP), Islamabad, were engaged in activities related to test development.

University psychology departments at Lahore and Karachi have been involved in the adaptation and development of local norms for standardized intelligence, aptitude, and personality tests. Considering the fact that Western measures may not be able to detect distress in Asian cultures due to differences in symptoms, the presentation of illness, and self-disclosure, a few attempts have also been made to develop indigenous scales in the Urdu language for diagnosing mental distress and assessing intellectual abilities. In the armed forces and civil services, at both the provincial and federal levels, Western psychological tests have been adapted and indigenous tests have also been designed to assess the ability, aptitude, and personality of the candidates applying for positions in the armed forces of Pakistan. Although assessment remains primarily Western in orientation, many indigenous approaches have been developed or adapted to meet the needs of Pakistani clients.

Counseling Models and Approaches

Traditional psychoanalytic therapy is practiced infrequently in Pakistan due to its relatively rigid and formalized approaches. Ahmad and Jaleel (1983) pointed out that the vast majority of nonelite Pakistani clients lack "various qualifications" for benefiting from psychoanalysis. Qureshi, a pioneer in the field, started practicing gestalt therapy in 1981. He maintained that gestalt therapy needed to be tailored according to the needs of a Pakistani client, particularly in establishing rapport and in designing methods of working with the individual in making choices without having to abandon or lose the support of his or her extended family and other support systems (Qureshi, 1991).

A few therapists use eidetic imagery psychotherapy (Shaukatullah, 1994), designed and developed by a Pakistani, Akhtar Ahsen, currently editor of the *Journal of Imagery*. The fundamental premise of eidetic psychotherapy as described by Ahsen is ISM, a three-segment experience consisting of an eidetic image (I), a somatic experience involving emotional and physiological states (S), and a meaning (M) of a given experience. The major advantage of the eidetic approach is that it surpasses the elaborate network of defense structures and helps the client come directly to the experience itself (Ahsen, 1985).

Due to their simplicity, practicality, and application to a wide range of psychological and behavioral problems, behavioral approaches work more successfully with the vast majority of Pakistani clients. Behavioral and cognitive behavior therapies (CBT) have been effectively used for a variety of psychological problems, for example, for reducing anxiety of infertile couples (Nilforooshan, Ahmadi, Abedi, & Ahmadi, 2006), anxiety and low confidence (Asad, 1994), and the problems related to the rehabilitation of mentally handicapped children (Suhail, 2001). Although CBT is the most popular therapeutic model worldwide, it cannot be used in its pure form with Pakistani clients because CBT requires clients to take personal responsibility for their own emotional change, whereas in non-Western cultures beliefs in spirits and fate indicate external attributions for illness. Mental health professionals in Pakistan generally agree that CBT works more effectively when the therapy is structured and planned, keeping in view cultural and religious variables. For example, when CBT is presented in light of sayings of Prophet Mohammad and the teachings of Al-Quran, it becomes more understandable to common folk and diminishes their resistance. Many therapists have incorporated Islamic beliefs and practices in the counseling process (Hamdan 2007; Jahangir, 1995). In fact, many teachings of CBT are consistent with Islamic fundamentals, for example, patience, tolerance, agreeableness, and kindness. The essential ingredients underlying the therapeutic efficacy of counseling, hope and faith, are very powerful for a Muslim client when these beliefs are connected to a supreme source.

Similarly, rational emotive therapy (RET) and the teachings of Islam have common ground. For example, both acknowledge the fallible nature of humans, encourage accepting responsibility for one's own actions, and emphasize not indulging in extremes. Rehman (1991) discussed differences between Islamic teachings and RET. Religion is based on faith, and so there are clear-cut *shoulds, oughts,* and *musts.* However, RET is based on the basic premise that this world we live in is fallible and not perfect; thus, *shoulds, musts,* and *oughts* are counterproductive. Moreover, guilt is perceived as positive in Islam but negative in RET. Due to the lack of social justice in Pakistan, pressing physical needs, cultural and religious conflicts between being a Muslim and a therapist, and competing priorities in decision making, Rehman (1991) pointed out that RET has a comparatively limited scope in Pakistan.

In spite of the ongoing debate about the effectiveness of RET with Pakistani clients, a Muslim counselor can adopt a middle way. For example, a counselor can provide unconditional positive regard to the client irrespective of the nature of disclosures of the client. Counselors may condemn problematic behavior as defined by religious and cultural values, but not the person. A Muslim counselor may suggest to the client that humans are prone to make mistakes, but the doors of forgiveness from God are always open.

Shah (2005) criticized the use of value-free Western approaches to psychotherapy with Muslim clients. The Islamic view of humans is based on the innate goodness and divine guidance of humans called *Fitrah,* which supports and emphasizes family and social bonds rather than individuality and self-concern. The Islamic approach follows the principles of self-restraint and self-realization rather than the Western concepts of liberalization and self-actualization. Farooqi (2006) rightly indicated that in the aftermath of the 9/11 tragedy there has been a growing need to understand the Islamic perspective of mental health and gain insight into the followers of this faith, otherwise perceived as "mysterious and Far Eastern."

Apart from the amalgamation of modern Western models of counseling with Islamic teachings, a few indigenous models of treatment deeply embedded in Islamic teachings are also in practice. Rizvi (1989) stated that mental health could be secured by being close to God, whereas mental illness is caused by distance from God. Employing a similar philosophy, Jahangir (1995) has effectively treated clients exhibiting various symptomatology, such as manic-depressive psychosis, depression, and panic attacks. All three types of clients improved within 6 months when their atheist beliefs were modified and they were gradually, undemandingly, and unobtrusively encouraged to renew their connections with God. According to Rizvi (1991), the primary pillars of Islam—prayer, fasting, *zakat* (donation given to poor in the month of Ramadhan), and pilgrimage—offer means of providing spiritual food for developing feelings of love, cooperation, sympathy, sacrifice, tolerance, and sister/brotherhood of humankind among people. These are the ingredients of mental health. Similarly, regular religious meetings and congregations in a mosque foster mental health and provide an opportunity for collective social interaction.

Zikr Allah (remembering God) is another indigenous model of counseling. Awan (as cited in Rehman, 2004) indicated that it is based on a meditation technique practiced by early Islamic Sufis. Purifying the Qalb (spiritual heart) requires invoking and chanting certain of Allah's 99 names, which represent His qualities, accompanied by rapid and deep breathing. For example, when inhaling, one repeats or imagines the word *Allah* while penetrating deeply into one's Qalb; when exhaling, one repeats or imagines the word *Hu* (Him alone). This exercise is practiced repeatedly for a minimum of 15 minutes twice daily. In some psychiatric wards of public and private hospitals, one very important *Surah Rehman* (one of Allah's names meaning the one who is very kind; No. 55) is recited, and many patients report experiencing peace and well-being after listening attentively to this Surah. Reading other holy verses of Al-Quran as well as formal and informal prayers is also highly recommended as a self-help tool for mental distress. Research has shown the effectiveness of *Tahajjed Sawlaat* (late night prayer), *Zikr* (invocation; Majid, 2001), and the recitation of Quranic verses (Rana, 2006) in curbing depression. Similarly, dumm (blowing religious verses on the afflicted or water) and *taweez* (amulets) are used by religious healers during consultations.

Muslim scholars have recommended treatment by books and company since long ago. Many people find solace and peace while reading Al-Quran. Specific verses of the Holy Quran are read by a large majority for diverse problems, such as attaining physical and psychological health, reversing curses and magical spells, increasing financial resources, and improving family relationships. According to Al-Quran, God is the sole, self-subsisting, and all-pervading, eternal, and absolute reality. His 99 names, or essential attributes, such as Life, Eternity, Unity, Power, Truth, Justice, Love, and Goodness, are also recited for attaining psychological health, peace, and contentment (Rizvi, 1982). Treatment by company has been growing rapidly in recent years in Pakistan because of the tremendous increase in psychosocial problems, alienation, and lack of meaning in life. Many people, both highly educated and uneducated, report finding solace in the company of a *Sufi* or *Murshed* (spiritual guide).

The traditional models just discussed remain popular, but the need for modern approaches to counseling has been felt particularly for specialized populations, such as students, individuals with chronic illness, and torture victims.

COUNSELING SPECIALIZED POPULATIONS

Although the traditional model still appeals to a large number of people, the importance of modern approaches and techniques for counseling specialized populations is being recognized. Students are one such group. Some Pakistani universities have set up career and guidance centers for helping students with subjects and career selection, and some also address student adjustment problems. To our knowledge, currently more than 20 career placement centers are located in different universities in Pakistan.

The area of rehabilitation counseling is not very functional in Pakistan, but in a few good hospitals, counseling is provided to cancer and AIDS patients. Drug abuse, on the rise since the late 1970s, is another focus of rehabilitation counseling in Pakistan. A large number of nongovernmental organizations and private clinics provide services in this area. Most service providers are psychology graduates with a basic degree. The drug abuse centers usually rely on a 12-step drug treatment program consisting of spiritual and moral steps to help the abusers recognize the supremacy of a higher power. This method of treatment works quite well as it is congruent with the religious and cultural beliefs of Muslim clients. Organizational assistance is another area where the need for counselors has been recognized recently. Counselors help clients manage stress in work situations and enhance workers' motivation to improve productivity and performance.

Changing circumstances cause new challenges and opportunities, and with these comes a new kind of stress where counseling might be considered helpful. Changing family and gender roles are examples of such difficulties faced by women in Pakistan.

GENDER-SPECIFIC COUNSELING ISSUES

Women in Pakistan, like anywhere else in the world, are faced with new challenges in the modern era. The conflict of tradition and modernity is, for the most part, being played out in the arena of changing gender relations. Traditional gender roles are being questioned, mainly in urban areas, and women are increasingly being employed in the workforce. Women's enrollment in colleges and universities has risen dramatically in the past 50 years, and the numbers are ever increasing. However, for the most part, women constitute an oppressed and discriminated-against group, with little say in how they run their own lives. Counterexamples do exist, but they are exceptions rather than the rule.

In 1979, after the imposition of martial law in Pakistan, the status of women deteriorated dramatically, and the rights granted to them under the constitution were withdrawn under the Islamization project undertaken by the military regime. Archaic laws and their retrograde interpretations were enforced, with devastating consequences for many women, particularly victims of rape. According to these laws, if the victim was unable to produce four male witnesses of the rape, the case was not only thrown out but a new case was registered against the victim for adultery. In 2006, the parliament repealed rigidly interpreted Islamic laws against women.

Many new NGOs were formed during the martial law period (1979–1988) to resist the oppression of women. These include Shirkat Gah, Aurat (woman) Foundation, the Women's Action Forum, and War Against Rape (WAR). Many older associations, such as All Pakistan Women's Association (APWA), kept a low profile and continued to work on women's economic and social empowerment. WAR not only resisted oppressive laws and attitudes but also worked on educating both men and women on rape. They started providing counseling to rape victims in the late 1980s by initiating a confidential telephone service, accompanying the survivors to the hospital, police station, or court, explaining the steps involved (medical, police, and legal) in reporting cases of sexual violence, and referring women to health care professionals (http://www.war.org.pk).

Female sex workers (FSWs) are a particularly vulnerable group in Pakistan. Sex work has been identified as a high-risk occupation for contracting HIV/AIDS. Comprehensive countermeasures need to be taken by the government to regulate prostitution and to prevent HIV infection through community economic development campaigns, shaking off poverty, and inculcating awareness on reproductive health and sex education. In addition, the provision of FSW-friendly health care services near sex workers' dwellings is essential.

Although counseling is still in its infancy in Pakistan, the needs of specialized populations necessitate a profession that is acknowledged and practiced.

PROFESSIONALIZATION OF COUNSELING IN PAKISTAN

During the 1970s, a full-fledged sector dealing with counseling and training was established in the curriculum wing of the Ministry of Education. Despite this, no specialized courses were offered in counseling until 2008, when GC University initiated an MS program in counseling. The program is still being developed, and it is hoped that it will be launched in September 2009.

People working as counselors in schools, universities, and NGOs are generally trained in clinical psychology. Due to this mixture of roles, this section of the chapter will elaborate on the developments occurring in the fields of both counseling and clinical psychology.

National Mental Health Programs in Primary Care and Schools

The national mental health program of Pakistan was the first one in the Eastern Mediterranean Region of the World Health Organization to be developed in 1986 at a multidisciplinary workshop. This program, incorporated in the seventh to ninth 5-year national development plans, emphasized the universal provision of mental health and substance abuse services through their incorporation into primary health care (PHC; Planning Commission, Government of Pakistan, 1998). For the integration of mental health into PHC, the government of Pakistan has allocated a separate budget of more than 22 million Pakistani rupees ($1 U.S. = about 80 Pakistani rupees). Under this program, more than 2,000 primary care physicians, 40,000 health workers, and 78 junior psychiatrists have been trained in community mental health. In the year 2000, a mental health component was included in the teacher training programs at the national level (Mubbashar & Saeed, 2001).

National Guidance and Counseling Programs

Guidance and counseling in Pakistan have emerged as a result of the formal establishment of the Institute of Educational and Vocational Guidance and Counseling for Women in July 1974. This institute resulted from the joint efforts of the Pakistan Federation of University Women (PFUW), the International Federation of University Women (IFUW), the Federal Ministry of Education of Pakistan, and the United Nations Educational, Scientific and Cultural Organization (UNESCO). The Institute was established to provide guidance and counseling through personnel training and to help women who might not be able to adequately evaluate their own potential to prepare themselves for a meaningful career (Ibrahim & Almas, 1983).

During 1977–1978, the National Institute of Psychology (NIP) of Quaid-i-Azam University, Islamabad (capital of Pakistan), initiated a pilot project of guidance and counseling, and trained teachers from 50 schools of Islamabad and the surrounding rural areas to provide counseling in their schools. Starting in 1979, the program expanded for the next 5 years and involved the following work: the development of psychological tests, training of teachers, development of training material, including manuals and handbooks, development of student problem checklists and cumulative record cards.

University-Based Training

In northern Pakistan, Dr. Muhammad Ajmal set up the first psychology department in Lahore at Government College Lahore. Counseling is offered as one course of study within the 4-year degree rather than as a professional degree. Government College University (GCU), the oldest academic institution in the country, initiated the only MS program in clinical psychology in the country in 2005. Postgraduate diplomas in clinical psychology have been set up by two of the most senior female psychologists, Dr. Farrukh Z. Ahmad and Dr. Rafia Hasan.

Licensing and Legislation

There is no organized system of licensure for either practicing counseling or clinical psychologists. Despite a degree or diploma requirement for the practice of clinical psychology, the illegitimate practice of psychology is quite common. Many people with only a graduate degree in psychology advertise themselves as psychotherapists and clinical psychologists. Often, they engage in practice after attending a few seminars or workshops on clinical psychology. There are two professional associations for psychologists, the Pakistan Psychological Association (established in 1968 in Dhaka, Bangladesh, former East Pakistan) and the Pakistan Association of Clinical Psychologists (formed in 1988). However, both organizations are struggling with internal political wrangling with little emphasis on academic preparation and research. Both organizations need to work toward operating according to a well-established code of ethics.

FUTURE CHALLENGES

Although counseling is one of the effective means for developing human potential and a source of social development, it has been evolving very slowly in Pakistan. As discussed earlier, counseling as a profession does not exist as a separate entity. There are programs in clinical psychology offered by some universities, but these are mostly hospital centered and do not cater to the needs of the vast majority of people and their problems. The greatest need, therefore, is to initiate professional courses in counseling focusing on various important areas, including rehabilitation counseling, drug abuse counseling, school counseling, gender empowerment, child abuse, chronic and terminal illness, and reproductive health. This step simultaneously requires the need to legalize the profession by clearly establishing licensure requirements and an ethical code of conduct for those researching and practicing counseling. A total reengineering of the system requires the setting up of counseling and guidance centers in schools, colleges, and universities. These centers can offer professional help to students on campus and maintain a close liaison with NGOs dealing with social and psychological problems.

Since general literacy and mental health literacy are closely linked, an increase in literacy will help reduce the stigma associated with mental illness. Moreover, large-scale campaigns need to be initiated by the government, NGOs, and the media to modify people's help-seeking attitudes and their beliefs and attitudes about persons with mental disorders. Great efforts are particularly warranted for enhancing individuals' acceptance concerning "mere talking" treatment. Finally, there is a need for ongoing efforts to tailor Western counseling paradigms to the cultural and religious beliefs, traditions, and value systems of Pakistan.

As mentioned earlier, women's organizations are contributing positively in the area of gender empowerment, and counseling is one of the means they are using to achieve this end. But there is still a lot more to be done. Additional high-quality counseling help lines, camps, and workshops are needed, given that women constitute 52% of the 160 million people in Pakistan.

Pakistan, as the land of Sufi saints, has an age-old tradition steeped in the mystical love of God and compassion for fellow humans based on the Islamic principles of love and mercy. This spiritual tradition has long served to alleviate emotional problems. Some psychologists are currently attempting to adapt Sufi methods to modern settings. These efforts should be supported, and the needs for spirituality should be acknowledged. As a developing nation with strong Islamic traditions, Pakistan must strike a balance between the challenges of modernity and retaining its traditions. Modern approaches to counseling can play a positive role in the empowerment of women, religious minorities, and other marginalized groups. A counseling orientation that is homegrown but does not neglect the realities created by progress and development is the need of the hour.

REFERENCES

Ahmad, F. Z., & Jaleel, S. S. (1983). The scope of psychoanalytic therapy in Pakistan. *Pakistan Journal of Psychology, 14,* 3–22.

Ahsen, A. (1985). *Eidetic psychotherapy: A short introduction.* Lahore, Pakistan: Nai Matbooat.

Ajmal, M. (1969). Cultural presuppositions and mental disease. *Psychology Quarterly, 3*(4), 25–29.

Ajmal, M. (1986). *Muslim contributions to psychotherapy.* Islamabad, Pakistan: National Institute of Psychology.

Anwar, M., & Ijaz, K. (1990). Women and the development process in Pakistan: Some hurdles. *Journal of Behavioral Sciences, 1*(1), 39–51.

Asad, N. (1994). The effect of cognitive behavior therapy on anxiety. *Proceedings of the Ninth International Conference of Pakistan Psychological Association* (Vol. 3–5, pp. 85–91). Lahore, Pakistan: M. Ilyas.

Badri, M. (1979). *The dilemma of Muslim psychology.* London: MWH.

Birchwood, M., Cochrane, R., Macmillan, F., Copestake, S., Kucharska, J., & Criss, M. (1992). The influence of ethnicity and family structure on relapse in first-episode schizophrenia. *British Journal of Psychiatry, 161,* 783–790.

Bose, R. (1997). Psychiatry and the popular conception of possession among the Bangladeshis in London. *International Journal of Social Psychiatry, 43,* 11–15.

Dar, I. S. (1982). Test development for vocational counseling in Pakistan: Problems and issues. *Pakistan Journal of Psychology, 13,* 25–31.

Farooqi, Y. N. (2006). Understanding Islamic perspective of mental health and psychotherapy. *Journal of Psychology in Africa, 16*(1), 101–111.

Gadit, A. A., & Khalid, N. (2002). *State of mental health in Pakistan.* Karachi, Pakistan: Hamdard University Hospital Press.

Ghazali, A. H. (n.d.). *Keemiyae Seadat* [The alchemy of happiness]. Lahore, Pakistan: Mektabay Rehmania.

Hamdan, A. (2007). A case study of a Muslim client: Incorporating religious beliefs and practices. *Journal of Multicultural Counseling and Development, 35*(2), 92–100.

Hofstede, G. H. (1980). *Culture's consequences: International differences in work-related values.* Beverly Hills, CA: Sage.

Ibrahim, F. A., & Almas, I. (1983). Guidance and counseling in Pakistan. *International Journal of Advanced Counseling, 6,* 93–98.

Iqbal, M. (1978). *Letters of Iqbal* (B. A. Dar, Eds.). Lahore, Pakistan: Iqbal Academy.

Jahangir, S. F. (1995). Third force therapy and its impact on treatment outcome. *International Journal for the Psychology of Religion, 5*(2), 125–129.

Kausar, R., & Sarwar, F. (1997). A study of misconceptions in Pakistani population about etiology and treatment of mental disorders. *Journal of Psychology, 24,* 73–81.

Khalid, K. (2002). *Temporal variations in rates of murders.* Unpublished master's thesis, Government College University, Lahore, Pakistan.

Majid, A. (2001). Healing power of faith and prayer: Religious and scientific perspectives. *Journal of Hazara Society for Science-Religion Dialogue.* Retrieved September 10, 2007, from http://www .hssrd.org/journal/spring2003/healing.htm

Miles, M. (1992). Concepts of mental retardation in Pakistan: Towards cross-cultural and historical perspectives. *Disability and Society, 7*(3), 235–255.

Moazam, F. (2000). Families, patients, and physicians in medical decision making: A Pakistani perspective. *The Hastings Center Report, 3*(6), 28–37.

Mubbashar, M. H., & Farooq, S. (2001). Mental health literacy in developing countries. *British Journal of Psychiatry, 177,* 396–401.

Mubbashar, M. H., & Saeed, K. (2001). *Development of mental health services in Pakistan.* Retrieved September 15, 2007, from http://www.emro.who.int/ mnh/whd/TechPres-Pakistan1.pdf

Nilforooshan, P., Ahmadi, A., Abedi, M. R., & Ahmadi, M. (2006). Counseling based on international cognitive subsystems and its effects on anxiety of infertile couples. *Pakistan Journal of Psychological Research, 21*(3/4), 95–103.

Planning Commission, Government of Pakistan. (1998). Report of the Subcommittee on Mental Health and Substance Abuse. In the *Ninth Five-Year Plan (1998–2003), respective plan 2003–2013.* Islamabad, Pakistan: Author.

Qidwai, W., & Azam, S. I. (2002). Psychiatric morbidity and perceptions on psychiatric illness among patients presenting to family physicians in April 2001 at a teaching hospital in Karachi. *Asia Pacific Family Medicine, 1*(2/3), 79–82.

Qureshi, N. (1991). Gestalt therapy: Cultural perspective and personal experience. *Proceedings of the Eighth International Conference of Pakistan Psychological Association* (Vol. IV, pp. 119–121). Islamabad, Pakistan: Print Style.

Rana, S. A. (2006). *The positive psychology of happiness.* Unpublished doctoral dissertation, University of Leicester, UK.

Rehman, N. K. (1991). Rational emotive therapy and its application in Pakistan. *Proceedings of the Eighth International Conference of Pakistan Psychological Association* (Vol. IV, pp. 110–118). Islamabad, Pakistan: Print Style.

Rehman, N. K. (2004). Psychology in Pakistan. In M. J. Stevens & D. Wedding (Eds.), *Handbook of international psychology* (pp. 243–260). New York: Brunner-Routledge.

Rizvi, A. A. (1982). Ghazali on functional disorders. *Psychology Quarterly, 15,* 12–15.

Rizvi, A. A. (1989). *Muslim tradition in psychotherapy and modern trends.* Lahore, Pakistan: Institute of Islamic Culture.

Rizvi, A. A. (1991). Religion, faith and psychotherapy. *Proceedings of the Eighth International Conference of Pakistan Psychological Association* (Vol. IV, pp. 133–135). Islamabad, Pakistan: Print Style.

Saeed, K., Gater, R., Hussain, A., & Mubbashar, M. (2000). The prevalence, classification and treatment of mental disorders among attenders of native faith healers in rural Pakistan. *Social Psychiatry and Psychiatric Epidemiology, 35*(10), 480–485.

Shah, A. A. (2005). Psychotherapy in vacuum or reality: Secular or Islamic psychotherapy with Muslim clients. *Pakistan Journal of Social and Clinical Psychology, 3,* 3–18.

Shaukatullah, R. (1994). An exposition of eidetic psychotherapy based on a case study. *Proceedings of the Ninth International Conference of Pakistan Psychological Association* (Vols. 3–5, pp. 92–96). Lahore, Pakistan: M. Ilyas.

Sheikh, I. A. (2007). *Punjab Institute of Mental Health: Brief Year 2007.* Lahore, Pakistan: Research & Development Cell, PIMH.

Suhail, K. (2001). Effectiveness of token economy in rehabilitation of mentally retarded. *Journal of Psychology, 25,* 39–48.

Suhail, K. (2004a). Psychology in Pakistan. *The Psychologist, 17*(11), 632–634.

Suhail, K. (2004b). A study investigating mental health literacy in Pakistan. *Journal of Mental Health, 14*(2), 167–182.

Suhail, K., & Anjum, S. (2004). Stigma towards help-seeking behaviour and mental health problems. *Bangladeshi Psychological Studies, 14,* 55–70.

Suhail, K., & Chaudhry, H. R. (2004). Impact of fears and perceived stigma on psychosocial problems in patients with epilepsy. *Pakistan Journal of Social and Clinical Psychology, 2*(1), 51–65.

Suhail, K., & Cochrane, R. (2002). Effect of culture and environment on the phenomenology of delusions and hallucinations. *International Journal of Social Psychiatry, 48*(2), 126–138.

Suhail, K., & Qura-tul-Ain. (2002). Changes in rates of reported suicides over two decades: A content analysis study. *Journal of Behavioural Sciences, 13*(1/2), 33–48.

Syed, E. U., Hussein, S. A., & Yousafzai, A. W. (2007). Developing services with limited resources: Establishing a CAMHS in Pakistan. *Child and Adolescent Mental Health, 12*(3), 121–124.

Thanvi, A. A. (1981). *Behishti Zaiwar* [Heavenly ornaments]. Karachi, Pakistan: Dar-ul-Selam.

Thanvi, A. A. (n.d.). *Tarbiat-ul-Salik* [Training of disciple]. Lahore, Pakistan: Jamia Ashrafia.

16

Tradition and Modernity

The Cultural-Preparedness Framework for Counselling in India

முற்கால பாரம்பரியங்களும் தற்கால வாழ்வும்:
இந்தியாவிற்கு ஆலோசனை ஆயதங்கள்

GIDEON ARULMANI

The practice of counselling in India has a short history but an ancient past. I begin this chapter with a brief overview of the present status of counselling needs and the challenges that confront the practice of counselling in India. A significant portion of the chapter is then dedicated to examining a frame of reference that could inform the development of a model of counselling for the Indian context. An attempt at gaining insights into the field of counselling in India would do well to take into account the impact that philosophy, religion, and spirituality have had on Indian culture. Indian philosophy is replete with concepts and constructs, all of which could in some way be related to assumptions that surround emotional well-being. This chapter introduces the notion of cultural preparedness as a theoretical construct to examine assumptions that influence the practice of counselling in India. I attempt to do this by delineating key philosophic constructs, drawing on illustrations from field research and my own case records.

COUNSELLING IN INDIA: PRESENT STATUS

Western, academic psychology was introduced to India about 75 years ago, and at the last count, 63 universities were listed as offering degrees in psychology, at the undergraduate or postgraduate level. The focus of these courses has largely been on the educational, clinical, industrial, and developmental branches of psychology. Counselling psychology is a more recent addition to the group of subjects taught under the rubric of psychology.

Counselling was recognised as an important service in India from as early as 1938, when the Acharya Narendra Dev Committee underlined the importance of counselling and guidance in education.

Subsequently, various commissions from the early 1950s have made strong recommendations for the formalisation of counselling services at a national level. Bhatnagar (1997), in her review, pointed out that counselling and guidance thrived and grew in India during the 1960s and 1970s. Guidance and counselling were considered to be new and emerging forces that were vitally important to the education system. The same vigour was not seen between the late 1980s and 1990s, and interest in guidance and counselling diminished. Evidence of this decline in interest is seen in the number of research studies available for review. While approximately 160 studies were identified between 1974 and 1987, barely 13 studies were identified for the period between 1988 and 1992 (Bhatnagar, 1997). The recent past, however, has seen a significant increase in the demand for counselling services at the national level. For example, strong recommendations have been made for policy action to support counselling services for adolescents (National Planning Commission, Government of India, 2001). Counselling was also identified as an essential service by the national framework curriculum review in 2005 (National Council of Educational Research and Training, 2001, p. 48). The strongest attention towards counselling has emerged from the school sector. During its 2001 national conference, the Central Board for Secondary Education (one of the largest education boards in the country) resolved that it would be mandatory for all its schools to have trained school counsellors.

Training opportunities have become available over the past few years and range from full-time postgraduate degree programmes to certificates and diplomas. Postgraduate degrees in counselling are offered only by a small number of university departments of psychology, education, and social work. The National Council for Educational Research and Training (NCERT, Government of India) offers a postgraduate diploma in guidance and counselling. Private organisations offer postgraduate diplomas and certificates in specific branches of counselling. Certificate courses in counselling are available through the distance education mode. In length,

these programmes range between short 10-day certificate and diploma courses to full-time 2-year postgraduate courses. Students have the option of specialising in a specific client group. Some common specialisations are marital therapy, counselling adolescents, career counselling, and educational counselling. The better courses require students to obtain internship experiences in organisations that deliver counselling services. In addition to facing written examinations, a common requirement is for students to submit detailed case reports of a prescribed number of clients they have seen.

Against the backdrop of burgeoning counsellor training courses is a worrying neglect of quality. India has not as yet defined the parameters for counsellor qualifications, and *counselling* is a term that is loosely used. The nature and scope of counselling itself remains poorly articulated. Monitoring of counsellor training does not occur in a systematic manner. Someone who has gone through a 3-day "counselling skills workshop" could be referred to as a counsellor just as easily as someone else who has gone through a 2-year programme. At present, there is no licensing system for counsellors.

A recent evaluation of the cultural sensitivity of existing curricula revealed that very little has emerged in terms of Indian models for counselling (Arulmani, 2007a). The attempt seems to have been to adopt (or at best adapt) Western concepts with little or no consideration for "discovering" new approaches and validating them for the Indian situation. On a more positive note, an emerging trend is a gradual move towards more varied approaches to counselling. Although these courses are few and far between, they have set valuable training objectives "to sensitise learners to the possibilities and availability of alternate methods of healing with focus on indigenous and culturally accepted/practiced therapeutic methods" (extract from course objectives, MSc Holistic Counselling, Bangalore University, 2007). The course content includes skills to use yoga, reiki, acupressure, and meditation as counselling techniques.

Access to counselling services, however, is a matter of serious concern. Our survey (Arulmani & Nag, 2006) of 12 different Indian regions, reaching a sample of over 7,000 young people, revealed that fewer than 10% of this sample had access to any form of counselling. These findings echo trends from the preceding decade, in which Bhatnagar and Gupta (1999) found that formal counselling services were available only in 9% of schools in India.

There is also a lack of clarity regarding the role of a counsellor. Referrals to counsellors cover the entire gamut of mental health needs, ranging from severe psychotic problems to issues such as parenting concerns, childhood disorders, adolescent difficulties, and reproductive health (including HIV- and AIDS-related issues). Marital discord, interpersonal problems, scholastic and educational difficulties, stress-mediated disorders, substance abuse, counselling for career development, and questions about sexual orientation are other kinds of referrals a counsellor might receive.

Finally, the need for counselling in modern India manifests itself against a background of social change, the nature and pace of which is unprecedented. A decade of economic reforms has pushed India towards becoming one of the world's fastest growing economies. This in turn has given the need for counselling a new complexion. The ripple effect of a rapidly globalising world, increasingly coming under the control of the free market economy, has also arrived at the doorstep of the Indian counsellor. Economically empowered Indian women, for instance, no longer need to silently accept abuse and disregard. Age-old values are now questioned. The belief that marriage is a lifelong commitment, for better or for worse, for example, is no longer as unshakable as it was. Marital discord is on the increase, as are divorce rates. The Indian middle-class high school student is typically required to put in almost 16 hours of study a day to beat the competition and win a seat in a course leading to a degree in engineering or medicine. Counsellors are repeatedly presented with young people who were forced to choose careers that were popular and "in demand" but who soon discovered that their real interests and talents lay elsewhere. Increasing numbers of young workers show flagging motivation and often express the desire for a career shift within the first year of working.

On another plane, "development" has become a double-edged sword, benefiting a few but exploiting a large number only for the "cheap labour" they offer. Aggression and violence fed by resentment are increasingly seen. These are examples of the complexities that the counsellor practicing in India faces today. I examine the issues that surround the practice of counselling in contemporary India in further detail in a later section.

COUNSELLING IN INDIA: QUESTIONS OF RELEVANCE AND SUITABILITY

Counselling, as it is understood within the framework of Western psychology, is of recent advent in India. Indian scholars have consistently pointed out that modern Western psychotherapy and counselling have at best a tenuous foothold in India (e.g., Neki, 1975). One of the reasons for the apparent failure of counselling to "take" in Indian soil could be that the development of psychology in India has been a largely Euro-American enterprise (Dalal & Misra, 2001). These arguments point to deeper questions related to the relevance and appropriateness of Western counselling frameworks to non-Western contexts.

Historically, psychology in the West actively sought to distinguish itself from theology and metaphysics, separated itself from its earlier preoccupation with the "soul," and oriented itself instead to the study of "behaviour." It committed itself to the epistemology of logical positivism and chose as its tool the inductive process of scientific reasoning. The discipline of counselling psychology emerged from within this framework, in direct response to psychological needs that had their roots in the Western sociocultural milieu. This continues to be an ethos that is founded on materialistic individualism: a culture that celebrates the individual's freedom for self-determination.

The notion of *cultural preparedness* is critical here. Methods of counselling that emerged in the West were created by members of a particular culture in response to needs expressed from within this culture. The approaches were in effect developed by a people, and for a people, with certain cultural orientations. One of the reasons for the success of these approaches could be that both the creators of the service and the consumers of the service have been culturally prepared in a very similar manner to offer and partake of the service. They share a similar vocabulary of values and cherish a particular approach to life. It is against this background of cultural preparedness that counselling techniques could be developed and were necessary and sufficient for the Western context. The key point to be noted is that the same conditions may be neither necessary nor sufficient for a people from a different cultural heritage. A counselling approach that is empirical and individualistic in its orientation, for example, may not find resonance amongst Indians, whose culture has prepared them over the ages to approach their existence in an intuitive, experiential, and community-oriented manner. To flourish in the contemporary, globalised context, counselling psychology cannot be viewed solely or even primarily as a Western specialty (Savikas, 2007). If these critiques are to be addressed, it would be necessary to examine subjectivist versus objectivist epistemologies with a view to building bridges that would allow counsellors from different persuasions to function in tandem (Laungani, 2005). This chapter argues that cultural preparedness must be considered to sharpen the relevance of a counselling approach to a specific context.

SOCIAL RELATIONS IN INDIA: THREE KEY CHARACTERISTICS

Culturally Prepared to Abide Contradiction

A discussion pertaining to counselling in India would do well to concern itself with the questions that surround diversity. The source of this diversity has its roots in India's ancient past. The landmass that today is called India was gradually populated over 2,000 years by people from diverse backgrounds through a natural process of migration and trade relations, as well as through numerous aggressive invasions. As groups of people from other regions of the world settled in India, they brought with them their own traditions, social norms, rituals, and ways of living (Thapar, 1966). Notably, diverse groups seem to have learned to coexist rather than merge. Terms such as *encompass* (Dumont, 1988, pp. 92–97) and *enfold* (Sinha & Tripathi, 2001) have been used to describe this process, whereby people retained their cultural characteristics while simultaneously living in accord with those whose cultures were dissimilar from their own. Over the ages, this has led to the gradual evolution of a cultural atmosphere that has allowed for the coexistence of contradictions (Marriot, 1989; Sinha & Tripathi, 2001). This deeply ingrained toleration of ambiguity seems to be the thread that draws together the diverse elements that compose Indian culture. The following detail in the history of India's independence struggle provides an apt illustration.

It was August 8, 1942. The Quit India resolution had been passed by the All India Congress Committee, marking another phase in the civil disobedience movement across the country. Massive strikes were organised that brought the vast calico textile industry in western India to a grinding halt. Factories were closed. Workers refused to join duty. Tension was in the air. Within this environment, charged with discord and hostility, occurred an interaction between two men. One of them— the owner of a textile mill that had been shut down—took it on himself to care for the well-being and ease and even sought the counsel of the very man who was responsible for his worries. And the instigator of all the trouble on his part lavished praise and expressed his admiration of the mill owner. This instigator was Mohandas Karamchand Gandhi, revered in India as the "Father of the Nation." The viewpoints that these two men held were contradictory and perhaps irreconcilable. They were in fact adversaries. Yet they seem to have been able to compartmentalise their sharp disagreements and sustain a meaningful personal engagement. The interaction between Mahatma Gandhi and the mill owner reflects a cultural process that allowed (or perhaps required) them to abide contradictions. Interactions between individuals and groups in India are embedded within a cultural matrix that allows relationships to be formed and maintained despite ambiguities and oppositions.

Culturally Prepared for Individualism, Collectivism, or Something Else?

Indian culture is commonly described as being collectivistic. However, Indian studies throw a different light on this view. Sinha and Tripathi (2001) moved away from the individualism-collectivism (I/C) dichotomy and created a questionnaire that offered three alternative statements. The first and second alternatives addressed I/C, respectively, and the third alternative offered the respondent a mixture of individualistic and collectivistic elements. Their findings indicated that the majority of their participants demonstrated mixed orientations. Similarly, Arulmani and Nag (2006) found that Indian orientations were not individualistic *versus* collectivistic but were in fact a combination of the two. To illustrate, I present below extracts from the responses of two participants from our surveys (Arulmani & Nag, 2006) to the sentence stub "I want to be . . ."

A perfect woman as well as a perfect architect. First I am a girl and then an architect. I will achieve this. . . . (p. 48)

—17-year-old girl, middle-class family, from a midsized town in eastern India.

I want to be a police officer. This will realize my dream and the dream of my father of seeing me in uniform. We are four sisters. I want to give "something" to my parents as a "son" might have given. People should not sympathise with them for not having a son. . . . (p. 49)

—16-year-old girl, low-income family, from an urban slum, in a large South Indian city.

The point that seems to emerge is that Indians are collectivistic with reference to certain cultural constructions but are individualistic with reference to other engagements with life. The primacy of the

family and caste and kinship bonds could be examples of collectivist orientations. Beyond this, individualism seems to dominate. The common thread that runs through the responses of the young people cited above is their struggle to blend the assertion of self on the one hand with family values on the other.

The Centrality of Religion and Spirituality

Religion occupies a central position in Indian culture. Almost all aspects of life have religious connotations and are coloured by religious beliefs. For example, most forms of classical Indian art have been inspired by religious themes. Almost all initiations (e.g., building a house, beginning a business venture, opening a university) would invoke the gods and ask for their blessing. India is home to some of the major religions of our civilisation and is a religiously diverse country. Each religion, surrounded by its own unique culture, propagates a certain way of life. The objective of this chapter is not to look for the interface between religion and counselling. My attempt instead is to derive principles that could be integrated into a counselling approach that is sensitive to cultural preparedness by examining how common cultural practices prime a person to engage with life. Hinduism predates the advent of other religions in India and is today practiced by more than 80% of the population. Several aspects of the Hindu way of life have permeated the Indian peoples' engagement with life, irrespective of their religious persuasion. Ideas and constructs that originated in Hindu thought have over time been assimilated into Indian epistemology and today have a strong influence on Indian culture. The following section uses some of these ideas to articulate culturally attuned counselling approaches for India.

Five Key Constructs Related to Counselling From Indian Epistemology

Self and the Other: Separate but Interrelated

The most fundamental aspect of the Indian view rests on the postulation that boundaries between the self and the other are porous. The individual and the cosmos, the self and nature, the person and society are all perceived as being a part of a single continuity. Such a worldview presents a platform on which separateness as well as interdependence can be simultaneously expressed.

Dharma: The Code of Duty

Relationships between self and other are governed by the principle of *dharma*—an ancient concept that seems to have been first articulated two millenniums ago in the *Rigveda*. In a cosmic sense, dharma underlies the harmony seen within the natural world. In its most common usage, dharma is understood as the "appropriate way of living" and the "correct conduct" to be exhibited in different situations. Disturbance of dharma or the lack of adherence to dharma leads to psychological and physical discomfort and distress.

Varna and Guna: Occupational Classification Based on Personality Types

Varna is the precursor of caste and was originally intended to be a system of occupational role allocation. Allocation of work responsibilities was originally based on a fourfold classification of occupational roles: *brahmin, kshatriya, vaishya,* and *shudra.* The *triguna* theory is a three-factor description of personality types. Accordingly, the human personality comprises three *gunas* or qualities—*sattwa, rajas,* and *tamas.* This was the basis for guiding young people towards occupations for which they were suited.

The Ashrama System: Developmental Stages

The *ashrama* system describes a stagewise unfolding of an individual's life. This system takes a life span approach and provides guidelines for fulfilling specific aspects of one's dharma and varna as one progresses through the stages of life.

Samsara and Karma: Cyclical Conceptions of Personal Responsibility

Samsara describes the cycle of life and depicts the manner in which life begins, progresses, ends, and begins once again. The doctrine of *Karma Yoga* qualifies the manner in which the individual engages with his or her duties, roles, and responsibilities. Accordingly, engagement must be complete but must be characterised by *nishkama*—the absence of passion. The motivation to work is not what one gains from it. Instead, one is required to perform one's duty with the highest degree of effectiveness, without being driven by self-centered desires. Taken together, samsara and karma describe life as being a cycle that perpetuates itself (Pedersen, 1979). Karma is a thread that draws the past, present, and future together. The actions of the past qualify the present, and the actions of the present qualify the nature of the individual's future existence.

Philosophic Notions or Realities in Daily Living?

Indian scholars have found that these concepts have a significant bearing on everyday life in the Indian context. Sinha (2000) examined the aspirations of rural Indians. He reported that when asked to describe a "happy life," his respondents referred initially to materialistic endeavours but quickly began to equate happiness with religion and spirituality. Roy and Srivastava (1986) conducted a series of open-ended interviews with individuals and groups from rural backgrounds in North India. The sample included different castes as well as a cross section of Muslim groups. Content analysis of the responses revealed that although these were semiliterate people with no access to philosophic texts, their view of life was a reflection of *dharma, karma, samsara,* and *nishkama,* which seemed to be integral to their orientations to life, work, and interpersonal relationships. For example, one of the respondents, a farmer, held the view that total "immersion in dharma" would lead to contentment. Another is reported to have said, "God gives rewards and punishments according to a man's karma. . . ." Concepts such as these have their roots in India's ancient past and represent traditional India. The question that surfaces then is, Does this traditional approach to life continue to influence lifestyles in modern India?

Contemporary India

Contemporary India evokes images of a booming information technology industry and an economy that is growing at an unprecedented rate. Economic development has triggered tremendous social change. The need for counselling in contemporary India manifests within a social, cultural, and economic ethos that this country has not experienced before. I present an excerpt from my case notes to illustrate the challenges that face the discipline of counselling psychology in India.

This was an interaction with a 24-year-old woman working as a call centre agent in a business process outsourcing company. She came from a traditional Indian middle-class home and had grown up in an urban environment. She held a bachelor's degree in commerce. Given below are excerpts reconstructed from my case notes of my first (and only) session with her.

Client: Some of my friends have come to you for help to leave their job as call centre operators. But I don't want to leave. I am happy with the job. I earn well. I want to know how to come up in this job and reach the top in this job.

Counsellor: How have you done at your job so far?

Client: Average. I should have risen higher by now. I am more or less where I started. My performance appraisal said I get irritated with callers. That's why I have come to you.

Counsellor: What makes you irritated?

Client: I don't like answering only to people's complaints. The whole time I have to listen to the complaints of someone from another country. You are a psychologist. You know how to change my personality to suit my job requirement.

Counsellor: Changing a person's personality is difficult and most often not necessary. Your physical and emotional health are far more important than your job.

Client: I can't leave this job. I have taken many loans based on my income. I will not earn as much as I am earning now in any other job. I can't quit. If you can't help me change my personality, then I will go to some other expert.

Counsellor: Do you know of any one who can do that?

Client: Yes! There are many experts. I know an astrologer who can do that.

Counsellor: I can only help you learn to help yourself. I do believe that you can learn to help yourself. What this means is that I am willing to work with you, but you are the one who is really at the centre of our interactions. Think about what I have said and let me know if you would like to continue.

The session ended on this note. The client did not return. Routine telephonic follow-up a month later indicated that she had indeed visited her astrologer who through his divinations found that she was unsuited for the job that she held. He had advised her to look for another job. My client took his advice, found employment as a receptionist in a hotel, and was now quite happy!

This case study provides an insight into psychological needs manifested in contemporary India. It raises the question of a counselling paradigm that could respond to these needs with effectiveness. It raises again the issue of cultural preparedness. In this case, clearly, a therapeutic relationship was not forged, and a number of questions surface: How could the counsellor have been more effective? Would it have been possible at all to establish a counselling relationship with this young person on her terms, rather than on the terms dictated by the school of counselling to which the counsellor was committed? I was stung in the first instance by my client's rejoinder that she would rather go to her astrologer to find answers to her situation. And then my chagrin knew no bounds when I learned that she had followed the astrologer's advice! My initial response of course was one of indignation. However, I gradually realised that this client was embedded in a culture that was different from the culture that had spawned the form of counselling I was trained to administer. I could (and did) of course say that the suitability of this client was low for counselling! What I failed to consider was the possibility that it was in fact the suitability of my form of counselling that was questionable for her. It dawned on me that my client did in fact receive a type of "counselling" from her astrologer. This form of counselling did not have its cultural orientation in the tenets of Western psychology. It was rooted in Indian tradition—a tradition of which both the counsellor (astrologer) and counselee were a part. The astrologer delivered a form of counselling for which the young woman was culturally prepared. It was to answer the numerous questions that surfaced in my mind in response to experiences such as these that I visited the consulting rooms of traditional healers. I briefly report below my experiences in an attempt to further illustrate the notion of cultural preparedness.

Traditional Approaches to "Counselling": A Personal Experience

My approach was to first ask my client group the following question: "To whom do you turn when you or your family are in distress?" Their responses in fact reflected the findings of a comprehensive survey that at some point in their lives more than 90% of Indians use the services of the priest, the faith healer, the astrologer, the "holy man," the guru, and a wide range of others who are sanctioned representatives of religion, including practitioners of traditional methods of healing (Voluntary Health Association of India, 1991). I presented myself as client to six of the most well-known astrologers in south India. Although there were individual variations in the approach taken, the common principles in their method pointed once again to a shared matrix of cultural preparedness. My objective here is not to comment on the validity of these services. It is instead to interpret my experiences within the framework of Western counselling to arrive at insights that could be relevant to the practice of counselling in modern India.

The consulting chambers of each of these persons were filled with representations of culture, religion, and the particular specialisation of the astrologer, immediately creating an ambience of tradition and spirituality. In all cases, I noticed that these persons had gone through many years of rigorous training that began in their late teens and went well into their early adulthood. Training was usually under a *guru* (teacher) who was a part of this tradition. The astrologer also had at his or her disposal a compendium of astrological charts and ancient texts to which constant references were made. In one case (the *nadi* form of astrology), the texts were beautifully handwritten on thousands of palm leaves. Each compilation referred to a certain "category," "personality type," or "type of ailment." The nadi astrologer had inherited his set from his guru. This body of knowledge was itself an object of veneration to which both the astrologer and I were required to pay obeisance. All interactions were in the vernacular.

My first impression was that right from the outset, interactions were directive. The astrologer presented himself or herself as an expert in the field. The initial objective seemed to be diagnostic in nature. I was asked a series of questions that included my biographical details and religious persuasion. My ambiguity regarding my religious persuasion was accepted and classified with equanimity as a type of persuasion! Interestingly, I was never asked what my difficulties were. Arriving at a diagnosis was taken as the astrologer's responsibility as well as a demonstration of his or her skill. In all cases, the astrologer did arrive at a fairly accurate description of my life situation. The astrologer listened carefully and, through a series of successive approximations based on the skilled use of leading questions, gleaned the information he or she required. Given below is an edited excerpt from one of these interactions (translated from the Tamil, a south Indian language) that illustrates the interview technique.

Astrologer: Your facial expression tells me that you are stressed about something. Correct?

Gideon: Yes.

Astrologer: One can be stressed about many things. You are stressed about your work duties. Is that correct?

Gideon: Yes.

Astrologer: You have studied a lot for many years. Your work is not an "outside" type of work. It is in an office. It is with people and not so much with machines. Am I right?

Gideon: Yes, I work mainly with people.

Astrologer: Working with people could be of many types. For example, you could work as a teacher or doctor. Your job is like what a doctor does.

Gideon: Yes. It is like a doctor, but I am not a medical doctor.

Astrologer: Alright. Are you saying that you work with people who have different kinds of problems?

Gideon: Yes. But that is not the source of my difficulty.

Astrologer: Do you work on your own or do you have an office?

Gideon: I work on my own. I also have an office.

Astrologer: Are you doing two jobs or one?

Gideon: I do many jobs.

Astrologer: You are doing too many jobs. That could be the reason for your stress.

Gideon: I don't think so. I like all the jobs I am doing.

Astrologer: We may like all the jobs we do. It is true you are in the stage of life when you must work hard. But if we do not have a way of getting back our energy, we will feel tired and stressed. This is a law of the universe. I have an idea of the source of your difficulties now. Please come back after 3 days. I will meditate about you and check the texts for the best solutions. There are solutions to all types of problems. Do not worry. I am here to help you discharge your dharma.

The second step in the process was to present me with a description of my physical and psychological vulnerabilities. I was given a concise diagnosis and prognosis. The final step was devoted to curative and corrective aspects. A series of *pujas* (religious exercises) were read out from the texts and explained to me. Some of them were performed on my behalf by the astrologer. The interaction ended with a prescription of a list of pujas to be performed with regularity for the next few months. Almost all the interactions were interspersed with stories and folk tales to explain my life situation.

This report of my experiences highlights different aspects of cultural preparedness. Each of the persons I met was a member of the community, commanded a high degree of respect, was revered, and was held in awe. Their methods tapped into processes that are already an integral part of this culture. For example, the approach was directive and oriented to giving advice. It was closely linked to religion. It was deterministic in its orientation but at the same time laid emphasis on personal effort. It was not oriented to the client's problem but instead to his personhood both as an individual and as a member of his community.

Cultural Preparedness: Implications for Counselling

Religion and Spirituality

The primacy accorded to religion and spirituality is perhaps the foremost representation of cultural preparedness in the Indian context. The almost invariable first step for which the Indian is culturally prepared is to seek, in times of distress, the emotional succour offered through religion and representatives of religion. The implications of this aspect of cultural preparedness are profound for the development of a relevant counselling strategy. The common Western understanding that these traditional approaches are primitive and unscientific reflect a suspicion of methods that are culturally alien. The loyalty of the masses to these methods has been routinely attributed to ignorance and the lack of knowledge. Some scholars, however, have attempted to draw a balance and argue that it is the scientists who are not able to transcend the boundaries of their education to examine these alternate methods with equanimity (e.g., Watts, 1975). Others have pointed out that these are ancient practices, distilled over hundreds of years from the collective experience of the community, that in fact have a high degree of efficacy at the practical and everyday level (e.g., Kakar, 2003).

The Indian who approaches a healer comes from a background that venerates this profession and views healers as representative of what is considered spiritual and sacred. The nature of cultural preparedness, therefore, is that the individual is oriented to being advised, directed, and guided towards the solution of his or her difficulties. The Indian would most certainly respond to exhortations that one should help oneself. But the Indian is relatively less prepared to engage with a nondirective form of counselling that does not give advice. The astrologer's approach reported above was directive and advice-oriented, emanating from a cultural matrix that *expected* this approach.

Abiding Contradiction

The Indian is culturally prepared to juxtapose opposites, strive to achieve a synthesis, and thereby create the space to tolerate dissonance. Culture-sensitive counselling will build this capacity and help the Indian counselee cope with situations that are incongruous. For example, an Indian healer will use illustrations from parables, stories from the holy books and folk tales that depict the gods, folk heroes, and other characters whom the Indian counselee is already culturally prepared to revere and respect. The attention of the help seeker will be drawn to the principles that the characters in the stories use to deal with contradictions, and the help seeker will be exhorted to emulate them. The counsellor, who is responsive to the client's cultural preparedness, will draw on the wit and wisdom enshrined in the stories told by court jesters, poets, and itinerant bards of ancient India. Tenali Ramakrishna, for example, was a famous poet and court jester in the 16th century AD, and his stories are a wonderful blend of humour and satire rooted in the cultural ethos of south India (Sastry, 2002). Raja Birbal was the Wazīr-e Azam (grand vizier) of the Mughal court in the 16th century AD, and his stories reflect the culture of north India and offer simple but deeply meaningful insights into the complexities of life (Moseley, 2001). Indian epics, folk tales, and proverbs are excellent repositories of a folk approach to dealing with the incongruities of life. They are a part and parcel of everyday life in India and have not been adequately tapped as counselling tools.

Holistic Conception of Life

Traditional Indian approaches to healing perceive the person as a "whole." This would include the physical being as well as the individual's mind, emotions, beliefs, spiritual inclinations, occupational status, and all aspects of his or her existence. It would also include the nature of the individual's linkages with society and the relationships to which he or she is bound. Ayurveda, an ancient and well-established form of traditional Indian medicine, provides detailed descriptions of how emotions are linked to physical illnesses and how health is a function of maintaining the correct balance between the individual's physical self and aspects of his or her social interactions (e.g., Das, 1974). In the Indian context, an approach to counselling that separates mind from body and the individual from family would most likely fail to address the felt need.

Determinism

The philosophic constructs of karma and samsara are often described as a fatalistic approach to life. The postulation that the present is determined by past actions could evoke a sense of inevitability. However, an often ignored dimension of these constructs is the emphasis on volition and effort. The notions of karma and samsara do not negate the action of the free will. The exercise of effort in the present is linked to future gain and development. Accordingly, the quality of future life could be influenced and shaped by the manner in which one lives one's present life. This emphasis on personal responsibility offers a valuable pointer to counselling techniques that draw on the client's cultural preparedness.

Life Stage Approach

The ashrama system links life's *purpose* to life stages and offers a framework within which to plan one's progress through life. This concept has been drawn into an Indian career counselling programme (Arulmani, 2007b). The programme has been named *Jiva*, which means "life" in most Indian languages. Career is portrayed as an extension of life and is described as a process that unfolds based on previous development starting from childhood. The counselling method provides the young person with tools for introspection that help him or her ponder over the purpose of work, one's role as a worker, and the manner in which one could engage with the world of work. It culminates with the counselee plotting a career development chart that describes the different kinds of jobs he or she will consider at different stages in life and the different duties he or she will discharge as a working member of society as he or she grows through life. The Jiva programme is an illustration of applying the principles of cultural preparedness to develop career counselling for the Indian adolescent.

CONCLUSION

My own decade-long practice of the discipline makes me wonder if counselling as it is practiced today has any relevance outside urban, westernised India, which is a minuscule proportion of this vast and culturally diverse nation of more than 1 billion souls. Although counselling in India may not have existed as a specialised discipline, there has existed a form of counselling that is ages old. It is essential that this fact be acknowledged and accepted. If the attempt to establish counselling in India is merely an exercise to fit into predefined descriptions of counselling, the resulting outcome would not only be irrelevant to felt needs but would most likely fail to take root. In light of the forces of globalisation and the nature of social change today, the promotion of one method as superior to another is ill-advised. Instead, the urgent need is to look for bridges between epistemologies, always keeping the felt need in sharp focus. This writing has attempted to point to the rudiments of a method that could build these bridges, suggesting that understanding cultural preparedness offers a scaffolding for the implementation of counselling

in India. This would require us to search existing epistemologies in the spirit of discovery, to articulate concepts and methods in the language of contemporary India.

Staying within the theme of religion, I conclude with a personal story. Being of the Christian faith, I went to the venerable institution of the church to be married. Since my bride was from a different religious persuasion, the pastor sat us down and in a warm and genuine manner asked her, "Are you willing to become a Christian?" We went away to ponder over the implications of converting from one religion to another. In the meantime, I met my wife's grandmother. She had weathered the loss of everything she held dear by the devastations wrought by the partition of India. She was seated in her tiny puja room, her little temple at home surrounded by many representations of god: little idols, intricate paintings, incense, and vermilion. I presented my case to her with trepidation. Would I encounter religious norms once again? She gave me a long, searching look and asked me three questions: Will you learn Bengali (the family language)? Do you eat fish (the primary diet of the Bengali)? Will you ask for dowry (bride price)? What a dramatic difference between the questions the pastor and this 80-year-old conservative Hindu woman had asked. One set of questions laid down the law. The other drew from the wisdom of the ages and confronted me with life.

If counselling is to flourish and grow in India, we first need to begin with humility, set aside our assumptions, and acknowledge that a given culture has been already prepared in a certain way over aeons of time to engage with the counselling process. This would lay the foundations for a service that would blend naturally with the orientations of a people.

REFERENCES

Arulmani, G. (2007a). Counselling psychology in India: At the confluence of two traditions. *Applied Psychology: An International Review, 56*(1), 69–82.

Arulmani, G. (2007b). *Jiva: The livelihood and career planning programme: Project implementation manual.* Bangalore, India: The Promise Foundation.

Arulmani, G., & Nag, S. (2006). *Work orientations and responses to career choices: Indian regional survey.* Bangalore, India: The Promise Foundation.

Bangalore University. (2007). *Master of science in holistic counselling: Course outline and curriculum.* Bangalore, India: Author.

Bhatnagar, A. (1997). Guidance and counselling. In M. B. Buch (Ed.), *Fifth survey of educational research 1988–92* (Vol. 1, pp. 216–234). New Delhi, India: NCERT.

Bhatnagar, A., & Gupta, N. (1999). *Guidance and counselling: A theoretical perspective* (Vol. 1). New Delhi, India: Vikas.

Dalal, A. K., & Misra, G. (2001). Social psychology in India: Evolution and emerging trends. In A. K. Dalal & G. Misra (Eds.), *New directions in Indian psychology* (Vol. 1, p. 20). New Delhi, India: Sage.

Das, B. (1974). *Fundamentals of Ayurvedic medicine.* New Delhi, India: Bansal & Company.

Dumont, L. (1988). *Homo hierarchicus: The caste system and its implications.* New Delhi, India: Oxford University Press.

Kakar, S. (2003). Psychoanalysis and Eastern spiritual traditions. *Journal of Analytical Psychology, 48*(5), 659–678.

Laungani, P. (2005). Building multicultural bridges: The Holy Grail or a poisoned chalice? *Counselling Psychology Quarterly, 18*(4), 247–259.

Marriott, M. (1989). Constructing an Indian ethnosociology. In M. Marriott (Ed.), *India through Hindu categories* (pp. 1–39). New Delhi, India: Sage.

Moseley, J. (2001). *The ninth jewel of the Mughal crown: The Birbal tales from the oral traditions of India.* Pasadena, CA: Summerwind Marketing.

National Council of Educational Research and Training. (2001). *Position paper of National Focus Group on Work and Education.* New Delhi, India: Author.

National Planning Commission, Government of India. (2001). *Report of the Working Group on Adolescence for the 10th five year plan.* New Delhi, India: Author.

Neki, J. S. (1975). Psychotherapy in India: Past, present and future. *American Journal of Psychotherapy, 29,* 92–100.

Pedersen, P. (1979). Non-Western psychology: The search for alternatives. In A. J. Marsella, R. G. Tharp, & T. J. Cibordwski (Eds.), *Perspective on cross-cultural psychology* (pp. 76–89). New York: Academic Press.

Roy, R., & Srivastava, R. K. (1986). *Dialogues on development.* New Delhi, India: Sage.

Sastry, K. A. N. (2002). *History of South India from prehistoric times to the fall of Vijayanagar.* New Delhi, India: Oxford University Press.

Savikas, M. (2007). Internationalisation of counseling psychology: Constructing cross-national consensus and collaboration. *Applied Psychology: An International Review, 56*(1), 182–188.

Sinha, D. (2000). Psychology and poverty: A fresh look at the researches. In K. A. Mohanty & G. Misra (Eds.), *Psychology of poverty and disadvantage* (pp. 60–71). New Delhi, India: Concept Publishing.

Sinha, D., & Tripathi R. C. (2001). Individualism in a collectivistic culture: A case of coexistence of opposites. In A. K. Dalal & G. Misra (Eds.), *New directions in Indian psychology* (1st ed., Vol. 1, pp. 241–255). New Delhi, India: Sage.

Thapar, R. (1966). *A history of India* (Vol. 1). New Delhi, India: Penguin Books.

Voluntary Health Association of India. (1991). *India's health status.* New Delhi, India: Author.

Watts, A. (1975). *Psychotherapy East and West.* New York: Vintage Books.

Central Asia

17

The Status of Counseling
and Psychology in Kyrgyzstan

Психологиялык жардан: илим менен салттын айкалышында

ELENA MOLCHANOVA, ELENA KIM,
SHARON HORNE, GULNARA AITPAEVA,
NARYNBEK ASHIRALIEV, VLADIMIR TEN, AND DIANA POHILKO

The main goal of the current chapter is to describe the past, present, and future status of counseling and psychology practice and research in Kyrgyzstan. The authors consider psychological counseling to be an evolving profession mirroring changes in the structure of the nation, as well as social transformations and conflicts. The development of mental health service in Kyrgyzstan is an example of how the interaction of traditional culture and the modern state have influenced contemporary mental health service in a very complex way. Although the future directions of psychology and counseling in Kyrgyzstan cannot be envisaged with certainty, it is our intention to highlight in this chapter current trends in the fields of counseling and psychology and make a prediction on the course of these developing fields in Kyrgyzstan.

COUNTRY BACKGROUND

The field of psychology in Kyrgyzstan cannot be understood without a full exploration of the historical and social context. Kyrgyzstan's ambiguous relationship with Russia before the Communist Revolution of 1917, its shared communist history, its unexpected independence after the collapse of the Soviet Union in 1991, and its current political chaos have greatly influenced the development of a national character, a complex identity informed by a hierarchy of values representing the Self in a sociocultural context. All these circumstances contribute to societal expectations of when it is appropriate for a Kyrgyz person to seek psychological help. General attitudes toward mental health reflect complex interrelations among the historical background, cultural diversity, political situation, economic status of the country, and even its landscape.

Geographic and Economic Data

Kyrgyzstan is a physically beautiful landlocked country in Central Asia, with an important geopolitical position for main world powers, such as Russia, China, and the United States. The extent of the Kyrgyz Republic (KR) is 199,900 square kilometers, spreading over 900 kilometers from east to west and over 425 kilometers from north to south. Mountains constitute about 90% of the land, which is on average 1,500 meters above sea level. Kyrgyzstan is located in the northeast of Central Asia and borders Uzbekistan in the west, Kazakhstan in the north, and Tajikistan in the south and southwest, with a wide border with Eastern Turkistan in the southeast.

Demographic Situation

As of May 2008, the population was 5,309,000 (latest data); 65% are of a Kyrgyz ethnic background, whereas Russian, Uzbek, Korean, and other Central Asian ethnicities are represented by smaller percentages. The population growth is low, which can be explained by historical events, migration processes, and decreasing rates of fertility. During the national liberation movement in 1916, prior to Kyrgyzstan becoming a Soviet Republic, approximately 54% of the adult population of Kyrgyzstan was killed; in some rural places (Naryn and Issyk-Kul provinces), this percentage was even greater, at 72%. During the Second World War, approximately 370,000 Kyrgyz people were sent to the battlefront to fight for the Allied Forces, and a fourth of them were killed. Therefore, there is a sense of durability and stamina among the Kyrgyz citizens who survived such hardships. This power of endurance is not compatible with help-seeking behaviors associated with contemporary psychology and counseling. Migration has also negatively affected Kyrgyzstan. In 2001, there were 27,200 emigrants from Kyrgyzstan, mostly ethnic Russians (62%). Although the average life expectancy is 68.1 years, the level of maternal and infant mortality is quite high (22.7 infants per 1,000 people) despite a birth rate consistent with other Asian states, where the number of children is the sign of health and happiness of the family. Public health efforts have been focused on children's health and reducing infant mortality; therefore, we may expect the fields of counseling and psychology to increasingly emphasize child development and mental health.

Political Structure

The official political structure of Kyrgyzstan is defined by the constitution of 1993. According to this framework, Kyrgyzstan is an independent, unitary, democratic, judicial state, which has a single constitution, as well as legislative, executive, and judicial systems. The legislative power is held by the parliament (*Jogorku Kenesh*), executive power by the prime minister and his cabinet, and judicial authority by the constitutional, supreme, and regional courts. There has been some decentralizing of power and transfer of authority to the municipal structures of cities and countries. The constitution has been changed four times since 1993. The official political structure covers informal clan and tribal relationships, which play an important role in power structures in Kyrgyzstan. Some years ago the term *kyrgyzchylyk* came into popular usage to criticize a system of promoting relatives in the sphere of public administration or bribing top officials. The public health system, which includes mental health, is part of the system that was considered corrupt.

Cultural Diversity

One of the main characteristics of the geographical, political, and cultural context of Kyrgyzstan is "splitting," sometimes referred to by mental health professionals as "social schizophrenia." There are two regions (the North and the South) of Kyrgyzstan that are quite different historically, religiously, politically, and even psychologically. The capital of the Kyrgyz Republic is Bishkek, which is situated in the North. It is still heavily influenced by Russian culture, and the majority of the Russian population in

Kyrgyzstan is concentrated there. Kyrgyz people who live in Bishkek and its surrounding areas (the "urban Kyrgyz") use Russian as their first language. The southern capital of Kyrgyzstan, Osh, is mostly under Uzbek influence, which makes it quite different from the North in tradition, cuisine, and dress. In addition, a middle class is only just forming, and the gap in socioeconomic level and quality of life between the Kyrgyz sociopolitical elite class and lower-income citizens is immense. The official cost of groceries per person per month is 3,000 som (about $80) though official salaries on average range from 2,000 to 3,500 som.

Shifting gender roles in modern Kyrgyzstan are of great interest to international and local social organizations. Traditional Kyrgyz culture dictates a patriarchal family structure and minimal involvement of women in the political and social life of the state. The strict hierarchical structure of a Kyrgyz family allows "mild" forms of domestic violence that are considered necessary for keeping order among women and children, who are in subordinate roles. The expression *kizil kamcha* (bloody lash) is often used to describe a man who maintains a tight control over his wife. The Russian proverb "He beats her when he loves her" is also a popular saying in Kyrgyzstan and reinforces societal acceptance of violence to maintain order in relationships.

After the collapse of the Soviet Union, the majority of men became unemployed and women became financially responsible for the family. During the transitional period following independence from the Soviet Union, women were generally more flexible than men in adjusting to the new market system. It was not uncommon to find a woman who was a secondary schoolteacher during Soviet times becoming an entrepreneur or a small business owner posttransition; such innovation by women contributed significantly to the economic stability of families.

This reversal of gender roles has caused a tension between traditional and progressive views on the family; it has contributed to the perception of Kyrgyz women as potential leaders in the social development of the country as well as to strong resistance from those wishing to retain traditional family and social structures. Until the elections of January 16, 2007, there was an evident discrepancy between the number of nongovernmental organizations (NGOs) devoted to women's rights and the absence of women in the Kyrgyz government. However, following a recent election, the number of women in the Kyrgyz parliament is now 25.4%, up from 0%.

Splitting also exists between modern and official mental health services and ancient healing practices, between science and traditional understandings of consciousness, and between official organized religions and shamanism, which we discuss below.

CULTURAL AND EPISTEMOLOGICAL ASSUMPTIONS AND HISTORY OF THE COUNSELING AND PSYCHOTHERAPY PROFESSIONS IN KYRGYZSTAN

There are two quite different streams of epistemological assumptions of psychotherapy and counseling in Kyrgyzstan: The first is closely connected with traditional healing practice and is referred to as "natural Kyrgyz folk psychotherapy." The second is recognized by the official government and is rooted in universities and training academies and has its origins in Soviet and now Russian psychotherapy, which is less popular than folk psychotherapy among Kyrgyz people.

One of the main challenges for specialists in psychology and counseling is the prestige of folk healing in Kyrgyzstan. For example, 89% of patients who visit the Psychotherapeutic Clinic and approximately 100% of patients in the other mental health wards of the Kyrgyz Republic Center of Mental Health have met traditional healers prior to seeking psychotherapy (Molchanova & Aitpaeva, 2008). Official Kyrgyz medical organizations try to discourage access to traditional healers by portraying "shamanism" as negative in the mass media, but statistical data show this to be ineffective: The number of traditional palm readers in the sacred sites of Issyk-Kul and Talas has doubled since 2005, and psychological problems have been the main reasons cited by individuals seeking help (Molchanova & Aitpaeva, 2008).

Folk Healing

Folk healing is so embedded in the culture and appears so natural that its effectiveness does not require any proof or scientific explanation; people simply *believe* the methods of folk healers. Belief in folk healing is supported by the apparent positive effects of healing therapies at *mazars* (sacred sites), described in oral histories of miraculous healings (Aitpaeva, 2006). Shared beliefs about the world, passed on through myths and oral histories, are typical ways of perceiving reality among Kyrgyz people and inform social attitudes and behaviors.

A unique combination of ancient beliefs and Islam is a characteristic feature of contemporary spiritual life in Kyrgyzstan (Light, 2008). Religious ideas of the ancient Middle East penetrated deep into Central Asia and significantly influenced Siberian and Central Asian shamanism, contributing to its contemporary practice. With the arrival of Islam as the main religion in Central Asia, the peoples of Kyrgyzstan chose to merge the two influences; there was a fusion of the official religious ideological system of Islam with local pagan religious philosophical systems. The overwhelming majority of rural Kyrgyz people and spiritual leaders consider themselves Muslims although they also practice a shamanistic spiritual life. This type of Islam blended with shamanism is typical and widespread in Kyrgyzstan but not commonly recognized or acknowledged. Current Islamic leaders, however, consider this type of Islam "impure."

Traditional healing in Kyrgyzstan is very heterogeneous. It includes ancient Turkic beliefs of shamanism within the traditional spiritual practices of *Umai-Ene* (Mother), *Khan-Tegri* (Father), a daemonic being called *Albarsta*, worshiping spirits of predecessors and their mazars, and fetishization (worshiping) of traditional objects. The Kyrgyz continue to have some religious beliefs specific to paganism. Rites, rituals, and relics from prehistoric times as well as elements of totemism, animism, and shamanism are still preserved in Kyrgyz traditional

culture. To this day, there are several types of healers, practicing at mazars (Adylov, 2008).

A *Kuuchu*, which literally means "the one who chases away," is similar to a shaman in his shared use of rituals. Shamans are able to communicate with spirits by using altered states of consciousness to enter a "different" reality of the spirits. The ancient Kuuchu was a combination of a *pagan* (priest) and a *daryger* (doctor), but unlike a shaman, a Kuuchu did not differ from other members of society in the clothes he wore or in his daily activities. Yet the Kuuchu was required to wear white clothing to be able to fully communicate with spirits during rituals. The Kuuchus are keepers of the Kyrgyz shamanistic traditions and are subdivided into "white," associated in traditional Kyrgyz culture with purity, high status, and good health, and "black," which does not have positive associations. The Kuuchus use a variety of symbols in their work. Stripes and pendants symbolize an image of the *arbak*, the protector. Pendants in the form of tails (*candoleck*) symbolize a strong mythical beast resembling a bear. A knife and a *kamcha* (whip) are symbols of protection from evil spirits. The Kuuchus set rhythms during collective magic rituals with an *asataiyak*—a special stick, symbolizing life. Different household items and foods symbolize change. Kuuchus are rare and live almost exclusively in rural areas.

Bakshys consider healing to be their main profession; they are religious men and women who observe all rites and teachings of Islam. Like the Kuuchus, Bakshy men wear white robes with long sleeves that cover the body and use an asataiyak; however, they also have beards. Female patients frequently give presents such as headscarves to Bakshys in appreciation of their healing power. When engaged in healing processes, a Bakshy must wear a long white robe, which is the traditional national style. Men frequently wear a white *tiubeteika* (an embroidered skull cap) even when wearing ordinary clothes, whereas Bakshy women wear white headscarves. At times, they wear medical robes. Wandering Bakshys (*Duvana*) dress in old clothes, sometimes in rags. Like Kuuchus, Bakshys use oral folk stories, messages, or poetry; develop their own style of language; and are known for skillfully introducing unique proverbs into their speech. These healers are believed to be endowed with eloquent poetic skills by the spirits. Many healers believe the first appearance of a spirit is indicated when a person gains the gift of poetic improvisation. Among the Kyrgyz, poetic talent is considered a gift endowed from above. Combining poetry and the knowledge of myths and healing folklore, Bakshy and Kuuchu shamans are skillful healers. Music and rhythm are important in healing rituals as well. The rhythm is set by an asataiyak, and many healers play the *kumuz,* which is a traditional three-stringed instrument. The healing process starts with calling for spirits, and music and *motet* (singing songs) are used.

Asian medical traditions, such as the Chinese, Korean, Tibetan, and other traditions strongly influenced the healing practices of the *Tabybs.* A *Tabyb* or *znahar* (doctor) is a healer who uses medication alongside traditional and Islamic cures and is able to heal dislocated bones and fractures using a diagnostic procedure based on testing the pulse. The Tabybs have their own classification of diseases ("cold and hot ones"), medications to cure them, and nonmedicinal methods (such as acupuncture).

A *Kioz-achyk* ("the one who sees visions") is a clairvoyant man who is considered able to foresee the future, solve something from the past, and diagnose diseases. He works with people who are having difficulty making choices, who have been robbed, who struggle with interpersonal problems, and those who have been diagnosed with a disease or illness. Kioz-achyk engage in healing only on a part-time basis. Healers of this group are not considered by traditional healers to have as comprehensive a practice as Bakshys or Tabybs. Typically, they have an "opening" (disclosing) by spirits during their sleep or in a trance with a more experienced healer, but they have insufficient knowledge of mythology and of the basics of pagan Turkic and Islamic traditions for interpretation. Some engage in new forms of practice, actively studying with more advanced healers, whereas others who may have completed training actively practice healing without sufficient experience and knowledge (Adylov, 2008). According to an ancient Turkic belief, all healers possess an arbak (the spirit of an ancestor), who perceives by using a third eye and "sees" human diseases.

Folk Healing Methods in Kyrgyzstan

The healing process proceeds in two directions—one is aimed at the patient, the second is aimed at the healer himself. It is not surprising that most frequently healers are the healthiest members of their community. A vital element of a healer's practice with a client is mysteriousness, which has several components. In the healer-patient dyad, the former is the main source of information and emotional support, whereas the latter is in need and may be unsure and anxious. The healer reads prayers in Arabic, which are mysterious for Kyrgyz patients, whose language is Kyrgyz. The healer's use of mythology, talismans (*tumars*), special places of healing (e.g., *yurts*), and ritual costumes are common and may contribute to the placebo effect of folk psychotherapy.

Exorcisms take place with the use of hypnotization. A healer looks closely into the left eye of a patient. This method has been in practice for a long time, and it helps the healer concentrate completely on expressing particular phrases while watching the patient. Fixing the gaze of the patient on the bridge of the healer's nose produces the same effect. Experienced psychotherapists also use these methods when moving patients into a trance. Other methods include fixing a patient's gaze on a burning candle, a sparkling item, or beads or having a patient maintain a certain pose. For enhancement of the hypnotic impact, a healer can apply a touch.

Views on Psychopathology Among Kyrgyz Citizens

Several cognitive models inform different views on psychopathology in Kyrgyzstan (Solojenkin, 1997). The first, a "natural model of reality," includes a belief in the interconnectedness of human beings with nature. Humans and nature are considered inseparable, and so if a separation appears to occur, the results are psychologically damaging. This model of reality includes a strong belief in the close connection between the health of Kyrgyz people and their spiritual practices. For example, talented poets, such as *akyn*, recite improvisational poetry, whereas tellers (*manaschi*) of the ancient Kyrgyz epic *Manas*, the guardians of sacred sites, are considered able to connect to the unseen world through different states of consciousness and work within a sacred time (e.g., Thursdays are traditionally considered to be sacred days) marked by rituals and symbols. Akyn, manaschi, and the guardians of sacred sites understand this work as a call to accept a spiritual mission, which diverges from the modern rational understanding of reality embedded in contemporary Western counseling. According to many folk stories, people who do not accept their spiritual mission are afflicted with serious disorders or even death.

The "natural model" of reality also maintains that there exist a minimum of two worlds (Adylov, 2008). The first is our natural one, which is considered accessible to everyone. The second world is the reality of spirits (*arbaktar*), and only a few persons are able to communicate with them. Those persons have to exist between two realities and mediate communication between spirits and common people. According to these beliefs, psychopathology is the "result of a misunderstanding of the spirits' demands." For example, hypochondriasis is often interpreted as the spirit's desire to help a person in the process of self-actualization, and the spirits' task is to bring the person around to the right way. In some cases, the person with a conversion disorder is considered to be "punished" by the spirits or to have the "devil eye on him or her." An initial psychotic episode is usually considered a "spiritual emergence," and a patient generally has to visit a number of traditional healers before a psychiatrist takes care of him or her.

The mechanical model considers psychopathology to be a result of brain malfunction (Solojenkin, 1997). Diagnosing psychopathology in such cases is quite difficult due to the presence of alexithymia and a general denial of psychological problems. For example, depressive symptoms are considered laziness, and people who believe in this model seldom become clients of a psychotherapist. The quality of memory is perceived to be the main sign of human psychic health or disability. Those who subscribe to the "mechanical model" of reality and struggle with memory problems prefer to seek the help of neurologists rather than psychotherapists.

A "distress-model" of psychopathology (Solojenkin, 1997) is often subscribed to by urban citizens in Kyrgyzstan. According to the distress-model, psychopathological symptoms are the result of traumatic or stressful events in everyday life. People who believe this particular model often use psychological terminology to describe their conditions (i.e., stressful event, depression, anxiety). The common expression "all disorders are due to feeling upset" highlights the root of psychopathological symptoms as resulting from stressful periods in life.

Presenting Problems and Attitudes About Help Seeking and Help-Seeking Behaviors

Clients presenting problems, such as with languages, reflect cognitive structures in the human mind: What people consider to be psychological disorders or problems are closely related to what they are capable of understanding. Language structures are a way of thinking and perceiving the world, according to Sapir and Whorf (Kay & Kempton, 1984), so presenting problems depend on the available lexicon.

The Kyrgyz language reflects the history and the complexity of the Kyrgyz people. For instance, Kyrgyz people have more than 130 definitions of ages of horses, cattle, and sheep; many definitions for weather; and a rich lexicon for defining family relationships and qualities of family members. Perhaps due to a history of manual labor, Kyrgyz people find it difficult to express emotional states in their own language. There are no equivalent words for *mood*, *depression*, or *anxiety* in Kyrgyz; all these concepts are captured by "I feel badly" without any clear definition of what, where, and why this sense of feeling badly is. This phenomenon can be considered a cultural alexithymia, a lack of ability to express emotions verbally (Nemiah & Sifneos, 1970), and makes diagnosing mental disorders difficult.

In combination with the cognitive models of reality previously discussed, the help-seeking behavior of Kyrgyz individuals is quite predictable. The first (and often the last) person they would like to see is a traditional healer. In some cases, a traditional healer is the one person who can refer the client to a specialist in the mental health field. The types of psychological problems people present to traditional healers reflect the most important values of Kyrgyz society today (Adylov, 2008). The main cluster of problems is family difficulties, for example, complicated relationships between mothers and daughters in law, and infertility. Other presenting problems are alcohol-related or business failures. Somatic (or somatoform) symptoms often serve as the impetus for people to go to a traditional healer after receiving ineffective treatment from general medical specialists. Psychotic symptoms rarely send a person to visit a traditional healer. But if there is a case, a qualified specialist in "natural folk medicine" usually advises a patient to see a mental health specialist. Based on a long-term study of healers and their occupational activities, Adylov described the professional conduct of healers. The first and most important criterion is that healers refer to medical doctors if medical intervention is warranted.

The situation in official psychotherapy, however, is different. The usual client of a psychotherapist or counselor is an urban citizen who believes that he or she has a "psychological problem." It's important to say that this idea, so common in Western culture, has only recently become a part of Kyrgyz contemporary usage, mainly due to the influence of mass media. Before the dissolution of the Soviet Union, people rarely used terms such as *stress*, *frustration*, or *breakdown*. These terms were rare in Soviet culture. For example, the words of a very popular Soviet song states that a Soviet person should have "a fiery motor instead of heart." In other words, to be depressed or anxious means having a weak will, which is abnormal and shameful. Understandably, during Soviet times, psychotherapists were the least likely choice for individuals with affective symptoms. Typically, help-seeking behavior included an initial visit to a medical doctor, then a neurologist, and then a medical specialist such as an endocrinologist or an oncologist. As the "last hope," an individual might seek out a healer followed by a psychotherapist when he or she believed "I have nothing to lose." Close relatives of a patient usually initiated visits to mental health specialists on behalf of the patient.

The situation has been changing during the past 10 years. The terms *emotional stress*, *feelings*, *psychological problems*, and even *intrapsychic conflict* have become more and more popular, and the professions of the psychologist and psychotherapist are increasing in social prestige. Now, there is a social need for qualified counselors, although a discrepancy exists between the clients' expectations that their problems will be immediately solved by hypnosis and the actual outcomes and goals of counseling.

OFFICIALLY RECOGNIZED PSYCHOTHERAPY AND PSYCHOLOGICAL COUNSELING

There are two main psychotherapeutic schools of thought in post-Soviet Russia—the Moscow and St. Petersburg traditions. The differences between these approaches to mental health services mirror the difference between these two capitals of the former Soviet Union. The fundamentally scientific and centralized Moscow school is relatively traditional in its approach, whereas the St. Petersburg school, the "window" to Europe, is reasonably open to new approaches in psychiatry and psychotherapy.

The development of psychotherapy in Kyrgyzstan was influenced mainly by the St. Petersburg school and mostly associated with two individuals, Nikolay Kantorovich and Valery Solojenkin. To this day, there is no well-developed psychological counseling service in Kyrgyzstan; until the early 1980s, the concepts of psychotherapy and psychological counseling were synonymous to what was referred to as "small psychiatry," which was created by dividing disorders into "severe" and "mild" ones. Specialists in "small psychiatry" were dealing with "mild" or "neurotic" psychopathology, which mostly included neuroses, connected with stress and somatoform disorders (F4 of ICD-10), personality disorders (F6), and eating disorders (F5). "Big" psychiatry includes schizophrenia (now F2), dementia (F0), bipolar affective disorder (F3), mental retardation (F7), and those disorders associated with aging processes such as dementia, depression, and paranoia. Now, they are referred to as recurrent depressive disorder (also in F3) and chronic paranoid disorder (F2). Until 15 years ago, there was a clear distinction between "neurosis" and "psychosis" in the Kyrgyz mental health system.

Nikolay Kantorovich was the head of the Department of Psychiatry at the State Kyrgyz Medical University in the 1960s and 1970s and was a true follower of the St. Petersburg approach. His focus was on the psychological underpinnings of symptom formation. And he became the author of the first two monographs in psychology published in the Kyrgyz Republic, *Medical Psychology* (Kantorovich, 1966) and *Psychogenesis* (Kantorovich, 1972). Proper psychotherapeutic treatment during Kantorovich's era included hypnotherapy, meditation, and so-called rational therapy, a Soviet prototype of cognitive therapy, including Socratic dialogue and other methods of changing patients' cognitive structures. Kantorovich also founded the first psychotherapeutic department in the Republic Center of Mental Health. His former student, Galina Glotova, became the first head of this department, which was focused on "small psychiatry" or "neurosis." The transformation of psychotherapy over time is reflected in the evolving terminology used to describe the psychotherapeutic department for the more than 40 years it has been in service. Originally referred to as a "sanatorium and spa treatment department," it was later transformed into the "department for hypnotization." In the 1990s, the renamed "psychoanalytic department" was informally referred to as the "psychotherapeutic department," that term being used to this day. However, there is still no difference between the concepts of "hypnotization," "psychoanalysis," and "psychotherapy" in most people's minds.

Sultan Usupov, another follower of Kantorovich, introduced group therapy methods into psychotherapy. He used Joseph Moreno's psychodrama approach (Moreno, 1999) for the treatment of neurotic disorders and was one of the founders of "collective and group psychotherapy." The name of this particular method reflects the interactions between the group (collective) and the individual during Soviet times. An individual was considered part of the group (Soviet collective), and adaptation processes were thought impossible without the development of collective interest. One can note some similarities between the concepts of "collective interest" and "social interest" in Alfred Adler's theory (Adler, 1999). However, during the Cold War period, there was no available information about mainstream world psychotherapy, so the psychotherapeutic approaches of the first specialists in Kyrgyzstan were based primarily on their own experience and partly on tidbits of accessible information about Western psychotherapeutic methods (Solojenkin, 1997).

The most important changes in the structure of Kyrgyz official psychotherapy were initiated by Solojenkin. At the beginning of the 1990s, psychotherapy services were centralized in the only psychotherapeutic department of the Republic Center of Mental Health. Solojenkin, who was the chief psychiatrist and psychotherapist of the Kyrgyz Republic, was instrumental in the creation of psychotherapeutic centers in both urban and rural regions of Kyrgyzstan. He developed the first theoretical model of psychotherapy in Kyrgyzstan—the concept of personality-environment interaction (Solojenkin, 1989)—based on his own work with patients with psychosomatic disorders, primarily myocardial infarction. This model emphasizes the reciprocal influences of various social factors on the development and functioning of the person as well as his or her ability to self-disclose and engage in self-reflection. During psychotherapeutic work, the main focus is on changing lifestyle and personal behavior, working with the "I-concept" and the individual's perspective of the world. The client-therapist relationship is characterized by collaboration.

Models of Official Psychotherapy and Counseling Employed in Modern Kyrgyzstan

Currently, the state psychotherapeutic service is still perceived to be a part of psychiatry. Counseling is in the early stages of development, and there is no clear distinction between counseling and psychiatry or between "psychotherapist" and "psychiatrist," although differences are understood by professionals.

During the past several years, there have been several trends in the development of modern psychotherapy in Kyrgyzstan. Gestalt therapy has become more popular in Kyrgyzstan within the past 8 or 9 years. The group of psychotherapists working from this approach have been trained both in theory and practice by Gestalt psychotherapists of GATLA (the Gestalt Association of Los Angeles), Russian Gestalt practitioners from the Moscow Institute of Gestalt and Psycho Drama, directed by Nikolay Dolgopolov, and the Gestalt Institute of St. Petersburg, headed by Elena Ivanova. The Society of Gestalt Therapy Development in Kyrgyzstan is led by Alexander Eremeev, a GATLA-certificated Gestalt therapist.

Neurolinguistic programming (NLP) has become increasingly popular in Kyrgyzstan in the past several years. The use of NLP is common for drug abuse problems, psychological dependencies, obsessive-compulsive disorders, phobias, and other disorders. The faculty of psychiatry and psychotherapy at the Kyrgyz Medical Academy and Slavic University and the majority of practicum sites offer training courses in NLP.

In Kyrgyzstan, there are no official training opportunities in the fields of spiritual psychology and transpersonal psychology although there are therapists who practice from these approaches. The largest private psychotherapeutic center in Kyrgyzstan ("Doctor Nazaraliev's Center") specializes in alcohol and drug abuse problems and has been using transpersonal psychology for the past 2 years. Though the preliminary results of its treatment program, "The Seventh Sky," are very encouraging, research on its effectiveness is at the beginning stages.

Professional Issues

Nikolay Kantorovich founded the Society of Kyrgyz Psychiatrists and Medical Psychologists in 1966. Renamed the Kyrgyz Psychiatry Association (KPA), it has a division of medical psychology and psychotherapy. Solojenkin was the president of KPA from 1996 to 2006, followed by Abdjalal Begmatov, the Director of the Republic Center of Mental Health. As a nonprofit organization, KPA is devoted to the destigmatization of patients with mental health disorders and to the development of mental health services in Kyrgyzstan, primarily through educational activities. Certification, licensure, and other processes are under the control of the powerful Ministry of Health, which presents significant bureaucratic challenges for counselors seeking professional licensure. Psychotherapists in private practice or private centers must become licensed. Those working in public mental health institutions only need medical or specialist degrees. There is no private psychiatry practice, but many psychiatrists have a private practice as psychotherapists.

The first professional psychological (nonmedical) association was founded in 1968 by Aaron Brudny (PhD), but with the collapse of the Soviet Union, the society discontinued its activities due to a lack of financial and social support. The association was called the Kyrgyz Department of Psychological Science of the USSR. It held regular meetings to discuss different issues of the science of psychology. Currently, the Kyrgyz psychological community is reviving the psychological association, which needs renewal as an association and new sources of funding.

Training Paradigms

In the absence of universal training paradigms for psychotherapy and counseling psychology, each university in Kyrgyzstan has its own training model and curriculum, and they differ significantly from one another. The proliferation of universities, academies, and schools is quite common in the post-Soviet states. Bishkek alone has 18 universities, 20 institutes, and 9 academies for higher education. Eight of them have their own psychology departments. National State University, Slavic University in Kyrgyzstan, American University in Central Asia, and the Kyrgyz State Medical Academy are worthy of special attention because these four represent the main training paradigms.

Both National State University (NSU) and Slavonic University (SU) offer courses leading to specialist degrees in psychology (5 years of study), which are different from a Bachelor of Arts degree. After graduating from the universities, the individual may continue his or her study at a graduate level (*Aspirantura*) or begin to work as a psychologist in the field. The training focus is primarily on psychological theories and research, and less attention is given to practice. There is no specialization in counseling.

The Kyrgyz State Medical Academy offers a specialization in psychotherapy on graduation from a 2-year course of postgraduate training following 6 years of general medical education. The psychology department of the American University in Central Asia (AUCA) offers a Bachelor of Arts course in psychology modeled on an American system; it includes three main tracks: counseling, industrial/organizational, and general psychology. AUCA graduates work in organizations (e.g., crisis and AIDS centers and the Republic Center of Mental Health) and in graduate programs in psychology, gender studies, and psychiatry in the United States, Russia, and Central Asia.

Status of Psychological Research

The collapse of the Soviet Union isolated local psychologists from the academic and research centers in Russia and opened up access to specialists from the West. As a result, Kyrgyz psychologists have had opportunities to visit their international counterparts, participate in international conferences, engage in joint research projects, and increasingly publish their work in Western scholarly journals. Despite obstacles such as a lack of language skills and a lack of knowledge of how to publish in Western journals (e.g., APA style, ethical standards and procedures), scholarly work by Kyrgyz psychologists has contributed to the general pool of knowledge in counseling and psychology, including in the West. In the development of psychology as a science in the Kyrgyz Republic, influential studies have been published that have made their authors well-known locally and abroad. Among them is Aaron Brudny, who has published more than 300 articles, reports, and books, including *The Semantics of Language and Human Psychology* (Brudny, 1972), *A Science to Understand* (Brudny, 1996), *A Space*

for Opportunities (Brudny, 1999b), *A Psychology of Hermeneutics* (Brudny, 1999a), and *Personetika* (Brudny, 2003).

Other famous psychologists include Nina Palagina, well-known for her work in child psychology and the psychology of ethnicity. Her publications include *The Psychology of Ethnicity: Theory and Methods* (Palagina, 2001), *Multi-Ethnic Education in Kyrgyzstan* (Palagina, 2003), *Games and Exercises in Early Childhood* (Palagina, 1985), *Preschool Play* (Palagina, 1989), and *Imagination at its Source* (Palagina, 1997). Other prominent Kyrgyz researchers include Aigul Aldasheva, Erik Orozaliev, Sergey Fateev, and Chinara Shakeeva.

Common Research Methodologies in Kyrgyzstan

The current academic psychological community in Kyrgyzstan faces many challenges in conducting research. In some universities, all the professors are required to publish a certain number of academic articles, whereas in others there is no such minimum. It is common for a university professor to break his or her own dissertation into smaller pieces and publish them as separate articles to fulfill the requirement. Thus, one research project may span a number of publications despite the lack of original data. This common occurrence may be attributed to a lack of financial support to conduct new research and a lack of time due to high teaching loads. The Kyrgyz faculty typically teach four or five 2-hour classes per day, including Saturdays, excluding preparation time or research.

Research is firmly rooted in positivism in Kyrgyzstan, which explains the prevalence of quantitative research studies over qualitative ones. A very small percentage of research is based on experimental methods. Again, this is understandable given the lack, if not absence, of resources, including well-equipped laboratories.

Diagnostic and Assessment Tools

Chapter F of the 10th edition of *International Statistical Classification of Diseases* (World Health

Organization, 1994) has been the basic diagnostic and assessment system of mental disorders in Kyrgyzstan since 1991. Other diagnostic and assessment instruments include a wide range of psychodiagnostic tools, which are available in Russian or were created by Russian psychologists. The most popular psychodiagnostic techniques that measure the level of affective symptoms include the Zung Depression Scale, the Spielberger-Khanin Anxiety Scale, and Hamilton's clinical scales. Common personality assessment tools, adapted for the Russian-speaking population by the V. Bekhterev Scientific Research Center in St. Petersburg are the MMPI (Minnesota Multiphasic Personality Inventory), adapted by Sobchik (1990), the PF-16 (Cattell's 16 Personality Factors), and projective techniques, including the Rosenzweig Frustration Test, the Lusher Farbwahi Test, and the Draw a Person Test.

The absence of standardized, reliable, and valid diagnostic and assessment tools in Kyrgyzstan means that Kyrgyz psychologists resort to (a) working with nonverbal projective techniques and (b) performing the procedure of back-to-back translation of the available tests while adhering to ethical guidelines.

Ethical Issues

The Kyrgyz psychological community has only recently started making efforts to establish an ethical framework for teaching, practice, and research. However, it is too early to speak about any significant impact of these efforts on guiding the ethical practice of research and clinical work in Kyrgyzstan. Kyrgyz research in psychology, as well as in other social sciences, is not bound to any institutional ethical regulations. Exceptions are those local research projects being managed or led by international scholars, who abide by the requirements of their in-country institutional review boards. Local researchers rely on their own conscientiousness and awareness of research ethics in conducting their studies. To date, no professional psychological agency or association in the country has taken a leadership role in developing and implementing a code of ethics for the psychological community, and

so there is no guarantee that psychologists abide by international standards.

To establish an ethical culture of research in psychology, a 2-year project (August 2005–June 2007) was initiated by a group of psychologists from Kyrgyzstan (representing psychology departments from different universities, practicing psychologists, students, and others) with facilitation by an American colleague and psychologist, Sharon Horne. Drawing on existing and developing ethical codes in Canada, the United Kingdom, the United States, and Turkey, the group developed a draft version of the Kyrgyz Code of Ethics. This code is based on five general principles: respect for the rights of man, privacy, professionalism and competency, responsibility, and integrity. The working group constructed an action plan to further advance this document, ensure its effectiveness, and, as an ultimate goal, create an organization (association, committee, or agency) to put it into effect.

PREDICTIONS ABOUT THE FUTURE OF PSYCHOLOGY AND COUNSELING IN KYRGYZSTAN

Trends in the evolution of Kyrgyz psychotherapy and counseling make it possible to speculate about future developments that incorporate both Western and Eastern models of helping. The first trend is the development of cognitive and eclectic approaches to counseling as integration between different branches of psychological counseling in modern Kyrgyzstan continues. The appearance of a new generation of Kyrgyz counselors with Western educational degrees facilitates connections with Western specialists in psychotherapy and their entry into world psychological societies. Therefore, Kyrgyz psychology will continue to be shaped by Western developments.

A second trend is the conflict over how to resolve the presence of two healing traditions. "Folk counseling" (traditional healing practice) and official psychology and psychotherapy are sometimes viewed as opposing poles of how mental phenomena are perceived and understood. A rapprochement of the two different perspectives has been considered problematic. There have been movements to render the official mental health service the dominant approach in Kyrgyz society and relegate traditional healing practice to the past. Given the popularity of traditional healing in Kyrgyzstan, however, this seems to be an impossible aim for the near future.

One of the ways of solving this problem is known well by the patients of the Republic Center of Public Health, who are typically comfortable seeking help from both doctors and traditional healers. They separate the cause of a disorder from its symptoms. The cause of the disorder is usually explained within the framework of a traditional mystical paradigm (e.g., as the disturbance of the connection between nature and humans), and so only a traditional healer is able to help with the initial suffering. The symptoms of the disorder, however, continue even after a healer's intervention, thus necessitating the help of a mental health professional. Patients make sense of this by maintaining that the cause of their disorder is spiritual but that the medical practitioner or psychotherapist may be able to help with the "extracted roots" of the disorder. This compromise between folk and official psychotherapy is important in treatment for patients who find themselves in both worlds.

Another way of integrating the two is using the methods of traditional healers in scientific applications of mental health treatment. Milton Erickson's method of informational overload, for example, has its roots in Latin American "magic" techniques. This method is used by psychologists today and is considered to be effective. Inclusion of folk methods within contemporary psychotherapy requires comprehensive research of the treatment components of folk psychotherapy before they can be applied in official applications of psychotherapy. This method is far from ideal, however, because it removes a major component of the healing process, the mystical belief system of the healer and his or her healing rituals. For example, if a psychiatrist in a formal counseling session were to use the rhythmic knocks of an *asatayak* (special stick) in therapy, he or she may not be taken seriously.

Another possibility is to appreciate the positive aspects of folk counseling and to try to use them in contemporary mental health practice (Koss-Chioino, Leatherman, & Greenway, 2003). For example, The Therapist-Spiritist Training Project in Puerto Rico (Koss-Chioino, 2005) brings together two worldviews on healing: a traditional one, used by folk healers, and an official medical approach. One of the results of the project was the development of the emotional regulation mechanisms that are used during the interaction between a medium-healer and patient. This confluence of different perspectives on treatment resulted in a new system of training far richer than the sum of its two parts and allowed the preservation of both approaches in the healing process. This approach could lead to the dissolution of false borders between "natural" and "formal" counseling in Kyrgyzstan and create a culturally relevant form of helping for Kyrgyzstan.

CONCLUSION

Psychological counseling is a rather new branch of mental health service in Kyrgyzstan. During the Cold War period, Soviet academic psychology and Western psychotherapeutic approaches were developing separately. The concept of "psychological counseling" did not exist until the middle of the 1990s. The influence of the official Russian school, on the one hand, and the prestige of traditional folk healing practice, on the other, are creating a unique prototype of Kyrgyz psychological counseling, which is a product of both psychotherapy and traditional healing.

The integration of contemporary Kyrgyz helping methods with modern scientific applications dictates the development of new and progressive techniques of psychological help. For example, crisis phone lines, which are nonexistent in Kyrgyzstan, should be developed. Such new helping methods will require cooperation between Kyrgyz and Western health care specialists, who have greater experience in this area.

Another area of development is the growing importance of PTSD treatment. Centers that can help with the treatment of PTSD will be important due to the unstable political situation in Kyrgyzstan and because the country serves as a place of refuge for people escaping the political crises of Afghanistan, Tajikistan, and Chechnya. Domestic violence is increasingly being viewed as a psychological issue; several crisis centers were established during the last couple of years in Bishkek, and they are gaining in popularity among Kyrgyz citizens.

The status of counseling in Kyrgyzstan has been evolving over the last few years. This sphere of mental health service is facing many challenges connected with its cultural specificity and the Soviet past. Counseling is in a good position to move forward as an important field in Kyrgyzstan because it is less stigmatized than psychiatry or psychotherapy and it integrates aspects of folk counseling and Western approaches. In addition, because of its rich tradition in informing Soviet and post-Communist science, Kyrgyz counseling and psychology will continue to make important contributions to psychology worldwide.

REFERENCES

Adler, A. (1999). *The practice and theory of individual psychology.* New York: Routledge.

Adylov, D. (2008). Healing at mazars: Sources of healing, methods of curative impact, types of healers and criteria of their professional qualifications. In Egemberdieva, & M. Toknogulova (Eds.), *Mazar worship in Kyrgyzstan: Rituals and practitioners in Talas* (pp. 377–395). Bishkek, Kyrgyzstan: Aigine Research Centre.

Aitpaeva, G. (2006). The phenomenon of sacred sites in Kyrgyzstan: Interweaving of mythology and reality. In United Nations Educational, Scientific and Cultural Organization, *Conserving cultural and biological diversity: The role of sacred natural sites and cultural landscapes* (pp. 118–123). Paris: UNESCO.

Brudny, A. (1972). *The semantics of language and human psychology.* Frunze, Kyrgyzstan: Kyrgyzpechat'.

Brudny, A. (1996). *A science to understand.* Bishkek, Kyrgyzstan: Fund Soros.

Brudny, A. (1999a). *A psychology for hermeneutics.* Moscow: Labyrinth.

Brudny, A. (1999b). *A space for opportunities.* Moscow: Labyrinth.

Brudny, A. (2003). *Personetika.* Moscow: Kniga.

Kantorovich, N. (1966). *Medical psychology.* Frunze, Kyrgyzstan: Kyrgyzpechat'.

Kantorovich, N. (1972). *Psychogenii* [Psychogenic disorders]. Frunze, Kyrgyzstan: Kyrgyzpechat'.

Kay, P., & Kempton, W. (1984). What is the Sapir-Whorf hypothesis? *American Anthropologist, 86,* 65–79.

Koss-Chioino, J. (2005). Spirit healing, mental health and emotional regulation. *Zygon, 40,* 409–421.

Koss-Chioino, J., Leatherman, T., & Greenway, C. (2003). *Medical pluralism in the Andes.* London: Routledge.

Light, N. (2008). Participation and analysis in studying religion in Central Asia. In G. Aitpaeva & M. Toknogulova (Eds.), *Mazar worship in Kyrgyzstan: Rituals and practitioners in Talas* (pp. 476–498). Bishkek, Kyrgyzstan: Aigine Research Centre.

Molchanova, E., & Aitpaeva, G. (2008). Traditional Kyrgyz rituals and modern psychological practice: Meeting compromise. *Academic Review of American University in Central Asia, 5,* 75–87.

Moreno, J. (1999). Ancient sources and modern applications: The creative arts in psychodrama. *Arts in Psychotherapy, 26*(2), 95–101.

Nemiah, J. C., & Sifneos, P. E. (1970). Psychosomatic illness: Problem in communication. *Psychotherapy and Psychosomatics, 18,* 154–160.

Palagina, N. (1985). Games and exercises in early childhood. *Voprosi Psychologii, 85*(3), 187–195.

Palagina, N. (1989). Preschool play. *Voprosi Psychologii, 89*(5), 12–25.

Palagina, N. (1997). Imagination at its source. *Voprosi Psychologii, 97*(5), 31–40.

Palagina, N. (2001). *Theory and methods.* Bishkek, Kyrgyzstan: Kyrgyz-Russian Slavonic University.

Palagina, N. (2003). *Multi-ethnic education in Kyrgyzstan.* Bishkek, Kyrgyzstan: Kyrgyz-Russian Slavonic University.

Sobchik, L. N. (1990). *Standardized multiphasic method of the research of personality.* Moscow: Agenstvo.

Solojenkin, V. (1989). *Mechanizmi psihicheskoi adaptacii pri gipertonicheskoi bolezni I IBS* [Ego-defenses and coping mechanisms among patients with arterial hypertension and ischemic heart disease]. Dissertation written in partial fulfillment of the requirements for the postdoctoral degree, St. Petersburg, Russia.

Solojenkin, V. (1997). *Psihologicheskie osnovy vrachebnoi deyatelnosty* [Introduction to psychology for health care specialists]. Moscow: Planeta Detey.

World Health Organization. (1994). *International statistical classification of diseases and related health problems* (10th ed.). St. Petersburg, Russia: Author.

EUROPE

18

"Blowin' in the Wind"

Holding on to Values in the Face of Regulation in Britain

RALPH GOLDSTEIN

Now is a particularly interesting, although far from auspicious, time to consider the nature of British Counselling Psychology. Having apparently reached a kind of adult maturity, we now face major upheaval. The imminent changes are critical in the sense of the ancient Chinese paradox; may you live in interesting times! The specific interest referred to here is the advent of state regulation.

What we in Britain are interested in representing is rather less to do with a syllabus and more to do with a value system. Our group identity is still the key issue, it seems, and this identity ultimately rests on a philosophical basis. This position will be brought out as the chapter develops, but we begin with an historical overview. This system of values is also under great pressure as we will see.

BEGINNINGS

The Counselling Psychology Section of the British Psychological Society was established in 1982 (see Woolfe, 2006, for a witty historical summary). A brief history is outlined, which includes developments in the context of mainstream psychology as well as *counselling* psychology. The section ends with an overview of the framework of current structures within which counselling psychology operates.

The British Psychological Society (hereafter BPS), incorporated by Royal Charter, attained its centenary in 2001 and is still the body responsible for academic and applied psychology in the United Kingdom. We see later in the chapter how state regulation is about to change this. Historically, a number of people with graduate qualifications in psychology and experience in counselling and psychotherapy wished to be allowed to establish a professional Division within the BPS, concerned with professional standards and services in psychotherapy and counselling. Historically, there was always a resistance to psychotherapy within the BPS and so the name of this new Section, and subsequently Division, was limited to "Counselling."

In professional terms, academic psychologists may belong to the Division of Teachers and Researchers in Psychology, but other practising specialisms have their professional home in their own specialist

Divisions. These Divisions, such as the Clinical and the Educational Divisions, which have been established for many decades and somewhat resemble the American Psychological Association's Divisions, have been the source of professional standards. To practise as a clinical or counselling psychologist does in effect require membership of one or other Division, although such a position has no *legal* force.

Each Division provides members to its training committee, which is, in turn, responsible to the Membership and Training Board of the BPS for sending teams to accredit university-level departments offering programmes that qualify graduates for the status of *chartered psychologist* in all specialities, including counselling psychology. Each Division produces at least one publication, which reports on professional developments, often including developments in research. The binding force across the BPS is not only, or mainly, the subject matter but also the empirical orientation to extending knowledge, including knowledge of the outcomes of psychological interventions of all kinds. This emphasis on research training is one factor differentiating *Counselling Psychology* from counselling and psychotherapy more generally.

The level of training recognised by the BPS as conferring eligibility for the status of *chartered psychologist* is a professional doctorate, and the minimum time to train is three years full-time. Under the Royal Charter, the BPS may publish a Register of appropriately qualified psychologists—those who are chartered—and this list may be consulted by the public. Proceedings under the auspices of the Professional Conduct Board may result in being struck off the Register. These procedures are designed to protect the public but do not have the full effect of Civil Law, as already noted, and so do not currently protect the title "Chartered Psychologist."

Against this background, we can see that the Division of Counselling Psychology, with some 1,500 members currently, is on an equal footing with other Divisions. It has its own training syllabus and its own statement of values and philosophy of practice, based on notions of intersubjectivity (BPS, 2003). The Division has also established extensive guidelines on supervision (BPS, 2007), based on the BPS *Code of Ethics and Conduct* (2006).

In attempting to convey what Counselling Psychology is, I can do no better than reproduce the philosophical preamble to the training syllabus. This preamble is brief but reflects the distinctiveness of the discipline, whilst outlining its connections to many forms of psychology and psychotherapy:

Counselling Psychology is embedded in the discipline of psychology and concerns itself with applied areas of psychological work, which overlap with the provinces of psychotherapy, clinical psychology, generic counselling and psychiatry. Therefore, Counselling Psychology is situated at the interface between scientific and clinical enquiry. It derives insights about psychological functioning from the study of the full range of human life, including that manifest in clinical practice, whilst also being open to influence from complementary perspectives. Although it is subject to current scientific investigation, it derives knowledge from sources of insight into the mind that are based on evolving paradigms. In this way Counselling Psychology can also contribute to the pursuit of psychology in general.

Counselling Psychology emphasizes the exploration of the meaning of events and experiences, especially emotionally. Counselling Psychologists, therefore, focus on people's mental representations of events, and the particular significance of these for relationships with themselves and with others. This view opens up a wide range of philosophical and theoretical questions for psychologists, pure and applied, and entails diverse approaches to research and inquiry. Whilst acknowledging the diversity of effective therapeutic approaches, Counselling Psychologists will seek to demonstrate a coherent integration of theory, practice, and inquiry:

More specifically, Counselling Psychologists recognise the pivotal role of intersubjective experience and collaborative formulation between those participating in deriving understanding and approaches to people's often profound psychological distress. As a vital balance to these intersubjective experiences, Counselling Psychologists emphasise the value of maintaining external consultation with experienced members of this and related professions, for their ethical and clinical sensitivity. This stance is embodied in the notion of the reflective practitioner, emphasising, as it does, the joint creation of meaning within the therapeutic alliance.

Counselling Psychologists bring aspects of themselves to this shared enterprise, derived both from their training and their wider knowledge. This personal history is combined with an explicit use of psychological theories to analyse the process of a particular therapy or counselling situation. This partly differentiates Counselling Psychology from psychological therapies practised by non-psychologists. (BPS, 2003)

In summary, then, the BPS provides a professional home for a reflective, but scientifically inclined, practitioner. This home is maintained by parents called psychologists and shared with other specialisms. This system has worked pretty well so far, but what if a new *legal* authority takes over, not an organisation specialising in psychotherapy, say, but a legalistic body that wants to oversee all that we hold important? Is this to risk going back to the beginning again? Before we can answer this question, we need to consider what activities counselling psychologists typically engage in and how these activities are shared with other psychologists, psychotherapists, and counsellors. We also need a sense of the cultural context within which people seek professional help for psychological issues.

CULTURAL CONTEXT

The famous British "stiff upper lip" has lately begun to quiver. In particular, those generations born since 1945 are often willing to consider that various emotional problems, including problems of relationship, may be discussed in exchange for a fee or as part of the Health Service provision. This trend is particularly clear in the acceptance of the diagnosis of posttraumatic stress disorder (PTSD) as no longer a shameful consequence of a weak nervous system exposed to the battlefield but something that can happen to anyone faced with a potentially violent death.

A second trend, almost as powerful, is the trend towards believing that childhood sexual abuse does indeed happen and may not be very rare. People of all ages have sought counselling or psychotherapy, privately or in the Health Service, and what is striking is the number of people born before 1945 who have sought help. Often such memories have surfaced in a period of depression, and a real question remains whether it is truly helpful to delve deeply into these memories. However, acknowledgement that such things happened through no fault of the person-as-child may indeed be helpful. These are still open research areas.

A third trend is very clearly tied to cultural developments, namely, changes in collective attitudes to marriage and divorce. A major source of emotional troubles arises in relationships and the establishment of organisations, chiefly Relate, to provide help specifically geared to relationship conflicts has changed the landscape of British emotional secrecy.

The consequences of these trends at a cultural level are difficult to quantify, but concrete effects are apparent. For example, people demonstrating more or less low levels of PTSD and seeking compensation for accidents through the legal process will often be referred to psychologists and psychiatrists. Many are willing to consider whether therapy may indeed be helpful, whereas only a few decades ago such a suggestion would have met with vehement rejection. Similarly, mention of childhood sexual abuse produces many emotional reactions, but one of the more positive reactions is usually the suggestion to seek therapy. Occasionally, even alleged perpetrators of sexual abuse are encouraged to enter psychotherapy.

These processes are mutually reinforcing; more people hear about the *potential* benefits of psychotherapy and so are more likely to seek out counselling, psychotherapy, and other related services. As part of the same process, more people put themselves forward for training in some form of counselling, leaving us to contemplate the very interesting question of where the asymptote of growth will lie!

CURRENT ISSUES

What, then, is our relationship to our housemates who specialise, for example, in health, forensic, educational, and clinical psychology? For example, clinical psychologists in training are funded for three years by bursaries from the National Health Service (NHS), but counselling psychologists and most others are not funded. Trainees pay their own way to qualification. One consequence is that those specialising in clinical psychology expect—and are expected—to work in the NHS, whereas counselling psychologists expect to work in a variety of settings, such as private psychotherapy, from earlier on in their careers. There is, in fact, a long history of clinical psychologists and psychiatrists working alongside each other in the Health Service.

This introduces us to the question of our near neighbours, such as the Royal College of Psychiatrists' Psychotherapy faculty, the United Kingdom Council for Psychotherapy (UKCP), and British Association for Counselling and Psychotherapy (BACP)[1] and the British Association for Cognitive and Behavioural Psychotherapy. One could go further and list all the psychoanalytic associations, in order to make the point that there are a very large number of organisations concerned with the training and regulation of counselling, psychotherapy, and psychoanalysis in addition to the BPS. And there is indeed something that unites these organisations, besides a profound concern for psychotherapy and counselling, and that is a strong move towards making common cause in the face of a greater external threat, namely, government regulation. One might say that my enemy's enemy is now my friend in league against the Health Professions Council, which represents government control.

The question of "common cause" was highlighted in the work of an official liaison group set up specifically to explore common ground between medical psychotherapists (i.e., psychiatrists by original training), counselling psychologists, and clinical psychologists. But more dramatic common cause was made between the BPS, UKCP, and BACP in making submissions to the government to establish a Psychotherapy Professions Council as a regulatory body. However, this notion has been rejected out of hand by the government. There is a certain irony to this rejection, given the history of warring factions amongst schools of psychotherapy and counselling, which the

UKCP was established to counteract by providing an umbrella organisation for all psychotherapies.

Hence, we can see that the various modes and models of psychotherapy and counselling still get in the way of progress both in the political arena and in the arena of public perception. A person with psychological needs seeking professional assistance has rather few clues as to whom to choose as an appropriate practitioner. As far as I am aware, only one body, the BPS, has made significant and innovative progress in addressing both the issue of schoolism, on the one hand, and the question of training and development beyond initial qualification, on the other hand. It is worth noting that counselling psychologists have played a major role in these developments. The BPS has established a postqualifying *Register of Psychologists Specialising in Psychotherapy* (2001/2005), which resolves these tricky issues and is appreciated as a pioneer in Europe.

Any psychologist who has achieved chartered status within the BPS may have their specialised training in psychotherapy considered for entry onto this Register. In practice, mainly counselling and clinical psychologists have been entered on the Register as foundation members or members with senior status. Senior practitioners will have contributed something to the field and should make suitable supervisors or lead researchers in addition to their competence as therapists.

The fact that individuals who were—amongst other identities—counselling psychologists contributed so much to the establishment of the Register and its six principles tells us something profound about the identity of Counselling Psychology: It is essentially psychotherapeutic in nature. This is of course borne out by looking at our syllabus, which is essentially psychotherapeutic, with a strong research element and psychological base. But all schools of psychotherapy and counselling surely need a theory, and this theory should surely have some empirical underpinning, else we cannot discriminate our endeavours in the clinic from what we might term "crystal-gazing." By this I mean that people can and do set themselves up with a variety of titles and proceed to offer their services to the public with a minimum of training. Such persons may have attended a 3-month course in counselling and despite the fact that the course may have been publicly offered only as an introduction, its "diplomates" cannot be prevented from hanging out a notice to the public. This is one fundamental reason the government wishes to legislate in such a manner that the Health Professions Council, its chosen instrument, retains control of training standards as well as disciplinary matters. I discuss these issues further in the section headed "State Regulation."

However, before we can adequately discuss state regulation, we must get to know the identity of counselling psychology in greater detail.

IDENTITY AS COUNSELLING PSYCHOLOGISTS

One may readily problematise the scientist-practitioner identity (Lane & Corrie, 2006)—is the practitioner a consumer of science, a generator of science, or neither when actively practising? But if we take the description as an identifier of a *grouping*, then we necessarily expect significant variation in the behaviours of those constituting the grouping. (This might be considered a primitive application of evolutionary psychology.)

The more interesting problem is reconciling the descriptor of reflective-practitioner with scientist-practitioner and here changes and advances in methodologies of inquiry have been of profound importance. Phenomenological inquiry and other *qualitative* methods provide us with a publicly shareable means of reflection. None of these methods were invented by counselling psychologists, as far as I know, but by social and developmental psychologists, and others outside psychology, who were thoroughly dissatisfied by the products of the *Cognitive Revolution* or sufficiently provoked by current philosophical problems of knowledge to invent something new.

The other aspect of reflection (faces-in-the-mirror) is found in arrangements for supervision and Continuous Professional Development (CPD). The fundamental assumption guiding arrangements for CPD is that a psychologist should reflect on their

developmental needs for the coming year and then undertake activities to meet these goals. The degree to which goals have been met will be self-evaluated, thus completing the reflective cycle. It is the move towards universal CPD for psychologists that has been formative in allowing the notion of reflective-practitioner to move first from Counselling Psychology then towards clinical psychology and now across Divisions. I do not claim this is an invention of Counselling Psychology, merely an influence on our colleagues who, of course, have also influenced us through the scientist-practitioner identity in particular.

In the field of Counselling Psychology, we do seem to expect our practitioners to be remarkable in their all-round skills. For example, Hammersley (2003), a former chair of the Division, wrote as follows:

> As well as being a scientist, philosopher and researcher, the counselling psychology practitioner needs also to be an artist in order to be creative and innovative to produce the particular moments of change or internal shift which should result from the deep engagement with the client in a therapeutic relationship.[2] (p. 638)

How are we going to support this remarkable range of attributes, in order to help our profession and our clients thrive? The odds appear to be stacked against us because our professional identity is currently under very sharp examination from several angles. A brief list reads as follows:

- Statutory regulation by the government
- Institutional governance issues in NHS
- Efficacy and effectiveness questions; do our interventions benefit our clients?
- Academic, research, and training issues, some of which have already been discussed
- Cost of salaries in public (i.e., government) employment
- More subtle politico-economic issues such as privatisation
- Ethics, a matter of principles rather than rules

There is not space to deal with all these issues extensively, so I will concentrate on those problems which are most immediate in their impact on the field. This impact arises predominantly from the structures set up by the government. As seen from the government's Department of Health, the dominant public mental health need is for relatively easy access to affordable and equitable psychological therapies which are known to work (in some sense). If we look at the needs of the public, we professionals should support these kinds of developments for they represent progress compared to the situation of uneven provision geographically, long waiting lists, and uncertainty over the outcomes, or benefits, to the public. A service that is supported by taxation should, surely, be concerned with both the benefits to individuals as well as the benefits to society at large. A careful study of health economics might try to show that the costs of treating anxiety, depression, and other personal difficulties and disorders are to some extent balanced by the benefits to society of restoring people to productive and socially engaged lives. Counselling Psychologists are by no means alone in not having given sufficient thought to these issues (see review by Thatcher & Manktelow, 2007).

How can more and better psychological therapy for anxiety and depression, in particular, be provided by the NHS without inflating the costs of the service? Salaries in the NHS are by far the main cost to be publicly funded through taxation. At least two linked steps are required: (1) the prescriptive use of short-term therapies (2) applied by people whose salaries are controlled. Obviously, there is a direct correlation between length of treatment and cost, and the longer the treatment times, the more therapists are required to keep waiting times in check. Furthermore, if the number of sessions is controlled, then costs can be accurately forecast, as can the number of patients who will be treated. Finally, a means needs to be found to keep salary costs under control. Therefore, there needs to be an authoritative body prescribing effective treatments, which can be administered by people whose training costs and salaries are cheaper than those of doctors and psychologists.

All these developments are in effect part of state regulation, by virtue of providing the *setting conditions* for working in the public sector. The following section describes these linkages and how they are currently evolving at the time of writing. Many of the issues concerning evidence of efficacy will be familiar to readers of the *American Psychologist* (APA Presidential Task Force, 2006), in which the findings of the President's Task Force on evidence-based practice are reported.

STATE REGULATION

Whilst it should not be forgotten that state regulation will affect private practice profoundly, in terms of training, CPD, and registration costs, I focus on the public provision of health, which accounts for the great majority of mental health provision in Britain.

Regulation of psychologists and, shortly, psychotherapists and counsellors, is potentially linked to institutional governance issues in the NHS. Specifically, this linkage is mediated by the pressure to adopt treatments approved by the National Institute for Clinical Excellence (NICE). This is a body set up by the government to maintain standards of evidence—and latterly of affordability—in medical treatments, and it approaches this task by erecting an hierarchy of types of evidence with randomised control trials, and meta-analyses thereof, as the top of this hierarchy. Cognitive-behavioural therapy (CBT) has been subject to rather more such trials and analyses than other schools of psychotherapy. Therefore, CBT is the clear winner in this race between schools and even gains extra distance by virtue of the fact that cognitive therapists tend to nominate in advance the number of sessions needed to treat anxiety and depression. No other brand makes this seductive claim, despite the fact that the number of sessions nominated in treatment manuals for CBT has no empirically tested basis (see Westen, Novotny, & Thompson-Brenner, 2004).

Thus, we can see the pressure in a resource-limited institution such as the NHS is to favour recruitment of cognitive therapists[3] but what is the nature of the link to *state regulation* which I am claiming here?

The linkage is to be found in the particular form of regulation adopted in England and Wales, which will cover *training standards* as well as conduct and disciplinary procedures. It is very unusual amongst the professions, including medicine, accountancy, and law, for training standards to be conflated with regulatory and inspection issues. Nevertheless, the government has decided that it wishes to establish a unitary body covering those professions contributing to health care, other than doctors, dentists, and nurses. The Health Professions Council (HPC) will become the regulatory body for applied psychologists; we are expecting an Order to this effect to be laid before Parliament in the autumn of 2008. The HPC sets up standards of education and training which are generic and fit all accredited courses. Currently, these minimal, or threshold, standards have been set at Master's degree level, which is not consistent with the current requirements that Chartered Psychologists should be trained to professional doctorate level, as already described. The HPC is also setting up *statements of proficiency* that are specific to each profession or division within a profession.

Thus, if there are eight varieties of applied psychologists to be regulated, then there will need to be eight different statements of proficiency, which overlap to varying extents. Clinical, health, and counselling psychologists all attain competencies with a significant degree of overlap when compared with, say, sports and exercise psychologists and forensic psychologists.

Currently, the BPS has a training committee for each Division, which is responsible to the Membership and Training Board for sending teams to accredit courses offering programmes which lead to the status of chartered psychologist in all specialities, including counselling psychology. It is clear that in future, HPC will send at least one representative to accompany accreditation visits to institutes of higher education. What is quite unclear at this stage is who, in the long run, will have ownership of the syllabus. Currently, this ownership lies with each Division within the BPS, as already described.

One candidate for this role is a body set up at arm's length from government called Skills for Health. This body has already become involved in developing a syllabus and statements of competencies for CBT, specifically, for the kinds of CBT which might be required in the NHS, in order to facilitate access to psychological therapies. This requirement for certain kinds of cognitive therapist has arisen through a programme specifically called Improving Access to Psychological Therapies, and clinical and counselling psychologists have been actively involved in these developments.

A great number of those being trained to implement these forms of CBT in the NHS are mental health nurses by background and so will *not* be regulated by the HPC. A number of others, especially clinical supervisors, are psychologists and they will be regulated by the HPC. Thus, some control is being exerted on the costs of salaries. But in the longer term, some rationalisation will be called for here. And is it not likely, therefore, that the HPC will increase its grip on training standards, thus meeting the government's twin requirements for regulating standards of professional conduct and competence in the provision of therapies approved by NICE?

Such a potential loss of all its roles in professional training would leave the BPS as merely a learned Society. Would members of this learned society still be conducting competent clinical research? It seems as if funded clinical research will be restricted still to a few centres of excellence and thus continue its relative disconnection from the way clinical work is actually conducted in practice. We will continue to have an academic base of research conducted by the few people who are researchers recognised as potential fund holders—which means holding a research doctorate (PhD) rather than a professional doctorate.

RESEARCH

Such an outcome bears directly on the distinction between *effectiveness* and *efficacy* and on the related distinction between *evidence-based practice* and *practice-based evidence.* The former term refers to the scientific basis of treatment; for example, only drugs shown to achieve results in randomized control trials should be prescribed. The question of whether these research results really generalize to the way clinical work is conducted day-by-day is ultimately a matter of *practice-based evidence,* involving the need to check whether the care of patients is improved *locally.* Clinical practice needs to be audited and compared with the data of published evidence. But in practice, as we know, trials of both pharmaco-therapy and psychotherapy rely on carefully selected samples of pure diagnostic categories and tend to have significant numbers of people dropping out from such studies. Cost is not a major consideration at this stage of testing. It is an inescapable fact that such differences between research and practice make comparisons almost impossible because we are attempting to compare two quite different kinds of validity: internal validity—internal to the research study—in the case of efficacy studies, and external validity in the case of the clinic—someone should leave treatment and maintain any benefit in their community.

However, in our clinical practice we may find numbers of those dropping out of treatment vary considerably; indeed, unexplained drop-out is often a key indicator in clinical supervision (e.g., Goldstein, 2008). The questions we really might wish to research might include, on the one hand, what happens to people who reject treatment? Do they recover spontaneously, or will they enter treatment again some time, somewhere? On the other hand, we might want to know what the characteristics are of therapists, who have a very low number of dropouts? These kinds of questions would seem particularly pertinent to the design of a service that responds to the needs of clients effectively.

It may be that those psychologists who will attain supervisory roles in the Health Service and elsewhere—for example, the Prison Service—might be contracted to conduct research. In theory, depending perhaps on how one views clinical supervision, it is possible for clinical supervisors to collect significantly large samples of data concerning outcomes and even the therapeutic process.

I have already made the claim that part of the identity of psychology in general and counselling psychology in particular is to be found in the dimension of research and inquiry. This mutually inquiring relationship between psychology and psychotherapy is one of the six principles forming the basis of the *Register of Psychologists Specialising in Psychotherapy*. Will our future identity still incorporate this fundamental principle or will we have a two-tiered profession of consumers of research outcomes, on the one hand, and a renewed elite of old-fashioned research-based technicians with doctorates on the other hand, who are more familiar with statistical procedures than with seeing patients?

ETHICS

The final topic listed above is the question of ethics, which is again an area likely to be affected by state regulation. The BPS has recently published a *Code of Ethics and Conduct* (2006), whose title itself suggests the *potential* for a distinction between a *code* and *an ethical system of thought*. The specific distinction is this: Laws are codified, systems of ethics are not. This question is absolutely central for a practitioner because it determines their degree of autonomy—just that human potential we are supposed to be fostering in our clients!

The distinctive aspect of the Society's position is this: The BPS adopts just four ethical *principles* and an associated statement of *values*—the moral philosophy—from which are derived a list of standards of behaviour, which psychologists *should* adopt. Reflexively, these include a standard of awareness of professional ethics (2006, p. 14).

This framework makes for an impressive structure, which appears simple because of its hierarchical nature. By using the term *should*, the Society avoids forcing behaviour down fixed paths but also avoids directly explicating the current Law, where the relevant behaviour may come into contact with statute. Any attempt to explicate statute law could obviously be outdated overnight by new developments in Law. But what is clear is that the adoption of an *ethical stance* puts us in a position of making decisions for ourselves. So there are Codes which are the "shoulds" and there is an ethical system that is the principle (e.g., competence) and an associated set of values.

This new *Code* (2006) has therefore perpetuated the central tenet of previous BPS requirements—that psychologists should not attempt to practise beyond their competence and that it is an individual psychologist's own responsibility to decide what evidence demonstrates their claimed competencies.

It is not yet clear how state regulation by the HPC will affect this most elegant code, but at the time of writing, the Trustees of the BPS believe that the Society will continue to require its members to comply with its own *Code of Ethics and Conduct,* and for those who are required to register with the HPC, that compliance would be in addition to the Code adopted by the Regulator. Measures would be put in place to avoid overregulation of any member.

CONCLUSION

We have seen how the identity of counselling psychology evolved in relation to the parent discipline, and we have seen something of the roles of research and inquiry in that identity, an identity founded on an ethical autonomy. However, the future is quite unclear as we wrestle with the changes brought about by government in formulating a regulatory framework. Many members of the Division of Counselling Psychology believe that we are moving away from our deeply held philosophical values without obviously providing a better and more effective framework for helping those in distress.

NOTES

1. I feel I should apologise to the reader for all these acronyms!

2. Personally, I would add that they should have played cricket when young . . . this would be in line with C. G. Jung's admiration of the value of British games.

3. For the present purpose, I ignore the fact that there are many schools of cognitive therapy.

REFERENCES

APA Presidential Task Force. (2006). Evidence-based practice in psychology. *American Psychologist, 61*(4), 271–285.

British Psychological Society. (2001, 2005). *The register of psychologists specialising in psychotherapy: Principles and procedures.* R. Goldstein, A. Newell, M. Mair, & M. Watts (Chair). Leicester, UK.

British Psychological Society. (2003). *Criteria for the accreditation of postgraduate training programmes in counselling psychology.* Leicester, UK.

British Psychological Society. (2006). *The code of ethics and conduct.* Leicester, UK: Author.

British Psychological Society. (2007). *Division of counselling psychology: Guidelines for supervision.* Leicester, UK: Author.

Goldstein, R. (2008). Supervision: Who needs it and for what purposes? [Occasional papers on supervision]. *Counselling Psychology Review, 23,* 3–12.

Hammersley, D. (2003). Training and professional in the context of counselling psychology. In R. Woolfe, W. Dryden, & S. Strawbridge (Eds.), *Handbook of counselling psychology* (2nd ed., pp. 637–655). London: Sage.

Lane, D. A., & Corrie, S. (2006). Counselling psychology: Its influences and future [Special edition: The first 10 years]. *Counselling Psychology Review, 21*(1), 12–24.

Thatcher, M., & Manktelow, K. (2007). The cost of individualism. *Counselling Psychology Review, 22*(4), 31–43.

Westen, D., Novotny, C. M., & Thompson-Brenner, H. (2004). The empirical status of empirically supported psychotherapies: Assumptions, findings, and reporting in controlled clinical trials. *Psychological Bulletin, 130,* 631–663.

Woolfe, R. (2006). A journey from infancy to adulthood: The story of counselling psychology [Special edition: The first 10 years]. *Counselling Psychology Review, 21*(1), 4–7.

19

Career Counseling in Italy

From Placement to Vocational Realization

Orientamento in Italia:
Dall'inserimento lavorativo alla realizzazione professionale

SALVATORE SORESI AND LAURA NOTA

This contribution briefly illustrates the history of career counseling in Italy and proposes how this discipline might change to respond to today's requests and needs. Unlike what happened in Italy some years ago (when it was mainly middle school students who contacted the vocational guidance services), in recent years these services have been increasingly approached by individuals in difficulty, and those with learning difficulties, physically challenged people, and those with sociocultural disadvantages. Vocational guidance programs should become more available for these individuals, at the same time taking on a preventive role, which to be more efficacious should involve significant others. An important study under way in Italy is focused on enhancing parents' and teachers' abilities to help them detect and overcome the barriers that hinder the satisfactory attainment of professional and personal goals of their children or students.

VOCATIONAL GUIDANCE WITHIN THE SOCIOCULTURAL CONDITIONS AND GOVERNMENTAL LEGISLATION

Italy is a parliamentary democracy within the European Union—it was one of its founders—and develops its 30,000 square kilometers boot-shaped territory in the heart of the Mediterranean Sea. It has about 60 million inhabitants, with a population density of 197 inhabitants per square kilometer. Average yearly income per person is $31,791. The Catholic religion is the most widespread and is followed by 88% of the population; this religious culture supports self-determination and has promoted

291

personal counseling over the years; the first training schools for counselors and the first vocational guidance services in Italy were run within the Catholic universities.

Historically, Italy has always had an important place within Western culture, adopting the principles of democracy, equality, and freedom, which it shares with the other countries of Western Europe and with the United States. In addition, its geographical position has allowed it for centuries to approach and establish relationships with other civilizations, especially the Arab cultures. The right to work, the right to education, and freedom of speech, together with social solidarity and respect for diversity, are at the core of its constitution.

Because of historical and political events, social and economic differences are still being recorded between northern and southern Italy. This is due to the north being characterized as an industrial setting, with a host of medium and small businesses concentrating on entrepreneurial development, and the south being mainly an agricultural economic setting. Over time, these different socioeconomic conditions have become associated with cultural differences: In the north, there is a propensity to give emphasis to the individual and the possibilities of seeking professional success, whereas in the south, the tendency is to give importance to family and social relationships as useful means to handle a more rural economy and higher unemployment and to a stable job, preferably in the public administration service (Gentili, 2004). Differences can also be found in the social and health services provided throughout Italy, which, though being public and run by the state, are of better quality in the north than in the south of the country.

Among the state services aiming at guaranteeing the health and well-being of the population are some specifically devoted to infancy, families, social and school inclusion, and supplying psychological counseling interventions. Alongside this array of public services, there has also been an increase, especially over the past decade, of privately run psychological well-being and vocational guidance services.

Specifically with regard to vocational guidance, the first services were started between the two World Wars, but it was not until the 1950s that, thanks to scholars such as Gemelli and Marzi, specific services devoted to vocational guidance were established in different districts of the country (Groppelli, 2005). Toward the end of the 1960s, a group of vocational guidance practitioners founded the UNIO (Italian acronym for the Italian National Association for Vocational Guidance); besides bringing together practitioners of the sector, the association also began a national research on vocational guidance services. The UNIO also started to request specific legislation on the matter, which is, however, lacking even today. Among the pioneers who contributed greatly to the diffusion of vocational guidance in Italy and to training the professional figures who wished to work in this field, the names of Gemelli, Meschieri, Quadrio, Marzi, Chiari, and Scarpellini cannot be forgotten. More details on the early history and development of vocational guidance in Italy can be found in Scarpellini and Strologo (1976).

In the 1960s and 1970s, vocational guidance took on particular importance in schools within the larger school reform under way then. In 1962, the *unified middle school*, explicitly defined as a guidance and development school, was set up and made compulsory for all children aged 11 to 14. After the 1968 crisis, the university system also experienced significant changes, with increased economic help being granted to students of low SES (socioeconomic status) and with the opportunity for students to choose disciplines in degree courses based on their own interests. These innovations led many to conceptualize vocational guidance as a strategic instrument for the promotion of the right to study and to the conscious and autonomous planning of personal vocational development projects.

After the intense activity of the 1960s and 1970s, the next two decades witnessed a decreased interest in vocational guidance issues, which were placed at the periphery of the actions scheduled to be implemented in schools and in society (Castelli & Venini, 1996).

Since the end of the 1990s, however, there has been a revival of vocational guidance related to a number of social factors. In Italy, as well as in other

European countries, the efficacy and effectiveness of the educational services was examined relative to the capacity of our labor market to respond to the new challenges and competition that globalization created—and is still creating—for economies all over the world. Moreover, there was growing awareness that the Western world is showing the typical signs of a postindustrial society, that people are working less and less "with their hands" and more and more "with their brain," so that even the more "repetitive" intellectual activities are increasingly being entrusted to machines. A research study (Fischer, 2004) that examined the characteristics of districts considered as the "engines of Europe" (Baden Württemberg, Germany; Rhône-Alpes, France; Catalonia, Spain; Lombardy, Italy) has clearly shown that career services providers should focus on the human resources necessary to carry out multiple, flexible, collaborative working roles.

Subsequently, especially in the educational systems, differentiated educative courses were encouraged, and at the same time the "same-for-all" pathways that seem to promote rather than reduce the dropout rate were discarded (Gentili, 2004). In Italy, in line with other European countries, a law was passed that made schooling compulsory until the age of 18, introduced school-work alternation, and the division of the educational pathways over two different settings: *lycées* (scientific, classic, artistic and psychoeducational, economic and technological) and vocational schools. Lycées have a 5-year duration and provide specific preparation for those who intend to go on to university education; vocational schools have a 3- and 5-year duration (with the latter awarding a high school diploma) and provide specific training for the world of work. Italian youth typically graduate from high school at the age of 18 or 19, and their diploma, whether from a Lycée or from a vocational school, allows them to enroll in university courses. This reform links with the University Reform Bill (1999), which envisages two consecutive cycles of studies: a 3-year degree course (corresponding to a bachelor's degree) and a further 2-year course leading up to a specialized degree (corresponding to a master's degree).

As to the labor market, a recent legislative decree has brought about some changes by stressing the characteristics of flexibility that the legislator thinks are necessary to enhance work opportunities, guaranteeing everyone equal access to a regular quality occupation and fighting unemployment (which is around 10% in Italy), especially youth unemployment, in the south of Italy.

Changed socioeconomic conditions and the education and labor reforms that have been started in the last few years have given career counseling renewed centrality and salience, so much so that an increasing number of people either ask for this type of support or are encouraged to benefit from it. It follows that many adults in Italy can today obtain public vocational guidance services, usually in their district or region, through various job agencies, occupational training bodies, temporary work and/or selection agencies, counseling offices, schools, and universities (Sarchielli, 2000).

In sum, a wide range of social, political, and economic issues, not only in Italy but in Europe and around the world, have led to a number of governmental legislative acts and resources that have at different times enhanced or inhibited the development of vocational guidance over the past 60 years.

CURRENT PROFESSIONAL AND SOCIETAL CHALLENGES

The changes above resulted in a proliferation of initiatives by agencies and practitioners differently engaged in the fields of training, economics, and work, who very likely have in common only the wish (more or less authentic and apparent) to help individuals in their school and career choices. However, these "aids" are often short, sporadic, and "last-minute" interventions whose counseling objectives are often quite vague, aiming at giving information or at realizing an equally superficial person-environment matching. These interventions are mainly standardized, making it impossible to consider the cultural background of individuals (Soresi, 2007).

All this is made worse by the fact that the majority of career service providers do not have specific training in the field and often work with individuals at great risk. One particular at-risk group are the youth who do not even wish to attend a vocational school or have been expelled because of poor commitment or bad behavior (more than 25% of students attending vocational schools experience this type of failure, even in greatly developed economic areas such as Italy's rich northeast) and those who have learning difficulties and long histories of school failures (about 15% of the school population in Italy). It is important to note that in Italy, dropping out of school is associated with increased probability of maladjustment and with an unsatisfactory work inclusion; moreover, poor academic achievement is related to levels of indecision about one's future, which already characterizes between 11% and 12% of both middle school and high school students. Countless young people are in great need of interventions in support of the difficult school-to-work transition (Soresi, Nota, & Ferrari, 2005).

Another category at risk is that of individuals with sensory motor disabilities, which involves 5% to 6% of the population in Italy, and individuals with intellectual disabilities (2% of the population). Data published by the ISTAT (Italian Institute of Statistics) indicate that only 21% of working age individuals with such disabilities are employed (for individuals with more than one disability or with intellectual disabilities, the percentage goes down to 12%); these numbers are in stark contrast to the 54.6% employment of their peers without any disability. Besides the issue of unemployment, limitations, and the considerable amount of time devoted to rehabilitation (physical, linguistic, etc.), these activities may likely decrease exploratory behaviors during development, thus diminishing the knowledge one can have about professional activities and work settings and the efficacy of decisional processes (Ferrari, Nota, & Soresi, 2008; Soresi, Nota, Ferrari, & Solberg, 2008).

And then there are the immigrants and their children who are starting to attend Italian schools. Immigrants are about 5.2% of the population in Italy; they are young, mostly (70%) between 15 and 44, with minors representing a fifth of them and

almost 5% of the total student population (ISTAT, 2007). For a variety of reasons, thousands of immigrant youth do not take the offer of education available to them, sometimes resulting in a propensity toward illegal actions, as well as social and cultural marginalization. Inclusion in Italian schools is made more difficult also for different ethnic groups and cultures from Eastern Europe, Albania, erstwhile Yugoslavia, China, central and north Africa, and India, cultures little known to teachers and with linguistic differences often underlying poor school achievement (ISTAT, 2007). Although Italy has a particularly enlightened legislation related to integration, stereotypes and prejudices about immigrants and their children do exist, and these are also held by teachers who too often tend to have low expectations for these children's schooling or career and envision them as unskilled and not having very satisfactory occupations, similar to their parents (Maselli, 2007). Moreover, the immigrants' competencies tend to be regarded as "no good" for the Italian labor market; when they are considered good enough, they are hardly ever recognized. In other words, the immigrant must in any case start all over again and be "happy" to carry out jobs that no longer attract autochthonous workers (Mistri, 2004). In addition, certain occupations tend to be taken up by individuals from the same ethnic group (e.g., Eastern European women very frequently care for the elderly), and this contributes to creating a stereotyped view of that ethnic group. The family situations that are thus created, the marginalization, and the life conditions on the border of illegality that may characterize the children of immigrants can negatively affect the optimism with which they look to the future, as well as lower their expectations. This should certainly be an "emergency" for vocational guidance services and practitioners.

Three other social conditions in Italy are currently presenting additional challenges for vocational guidance centers. In the wake of the economic changes, occupations nowadays seem much less stable, specific, and clear-cut than they used to be, showing not only the "vertical" development that occurred until a few decades ago but a "horizontal" development as well. Subsequently, adults and young adults in Italy can experience higher levels of discomfort in their vocational development and have to cope, more frequently than in the past, with changes and revisions of their planning for the future. Another factor is the small number of students who choose science majors at universities and the marked gender differences in occupational choices, with girls still being more "interested" in and encouraged toward more traditional educational and vocational pathways (Nota, Ferrari, Soresi, & Solberg, 2007). The third is the recognition that research has long been insubstantial and that a considerable gap between research and application still exists today in vocational guidance. The psychology of vocational guidance in Italy is definitely weaker than other fields of psychological research and appears to suffer from an inferiority complex.

In sum, all these "differences" and special features require personalized vocational guidance interventions that take into consideration and strengthen the hope these individuals have in their future and in the possibility of their achieving satisfactory professional goals.

BROADENING THE CONCEPTUALIZATION OF CAREER INTERVENTIONS

In 2004, university professors and practitioners interested in promoting and spreading vocational guidance and professional standards in this profession, taking inspiration from the International Association for Educational and Vocational Guidance, founded the SIO, the Italian Society of Vocational Guidance. Its members must either have specific postgraduate qualifications granted by an Italian university (or equally valid credentials) or be university professors carrying out their institutional activity in the vocational guidance field. The SIO was born because there are no national laws in Italy specifying the type of curriculum and competences required of those who deal with career counseling. Its practitioners must have high levels of professionalism and be able to implement action at personal, social, and

political levels; to do so, they must have a broad range of creative and effective problem-solving skills. Subsequently, since 2000, the university professors who founded the SIO have been teaching postgraduate courses in career counseling and guidance (initially of 120 hours' duration, and later master's courses of 1,500 hours, with at least 350 hours devoted to counseling practice at organizations operating with the university). These courses are open to graduates with university degrees in any branch of learning because vocational guidance can benefit from the contributions of diverse disciplines. The courses examine a number of theoretical models: the social cognitive model (Lent, Brown, & Hackett, 1996); Super's life-span, life-space model (Super, Savickas, & Super, 1996); Holland's (1997) theory of vocational personalities and environments; the information processing model (Peterson, Sampson, Reardon, & Lenz, 1996); the social learning model (Mitchell & Krumboltz, 1996); the theory of work adjustment (Dawis, 1996); the life career development model (Gysbers, Heppner, & Johnston, 1998). These approaches have not faced any problems of adaptability to the Italian culture, which has always been sensitive to the need of connecting individuals to the environment and to the issues of learning the skills necessary to one's own accomplishment. As regards other cultures, Italy has only recently had to face the issue of immigration, and research and application within vocational guidance are taking their first steps.

The aim is to train experts who will try to change the realities of their clients, especially those with great disadvantages and experiencing severe discomfort, via interventions structured in such a way as to plan a better future, with self-determination, self-efficacy, problem solving, social skills, and empirically validated instruments, both Italian (e.g., Soresi & Nota, 2001, 2003) and from the United States (CDMSE-Short form, Betz & Taylor, 2000; PSI, Heppner, 1988; CBI, Krumboltz, 1999; Interests and Competencies Beliefs, Gore & Leuwerke, 2000; Lent, Brown, Soresi, & Nota, 2003; Career Search Efficacy scale, Solberg et al., 1994; ICA-R, Tracey & Ward, 1998). They are encouraged to see themselves as change facilitators, able to decide whom to ultimately privilege with their interventions, for which socialization agencies are "cultural mediators" to have an effect on situations with great risk for uncertain and hardly livable "future constructions" (Soresi, 2007).

Moreover, the SIO gives special emphasis to the distribution of scientific knowledge and best practices and organizes national and international conferences and seminars to provide continuing education to its members. The number of scientific publications appearing on vocational guidance has also greatly increased in the past few years, thanks to the birth of a specific scientific journal (*GIPO, the Italian Journal of Vocational Psychology*), and to a series of monographs (Vocational Guidance Pathways), which offer practitioners bibliographic updates and operational guidelines with the aim of reducing the gap existing between research and application.

Scholars and researchers from a number of Italian universities (particularly Padua, Pavia, Rome, Milan, Florence, Cagliari, Catania, and Palermo) are devoting more time to research and collaborate with international scholars. It is hoped that career research will become methodologically stronger and finally reduce the marginalization relegated by the stronger sectors of the psychological and social disciplines.

The aim is to achieve a type of research that not only examines basic phenomena but also proposes and empirically tests action modalities to increase people's self-efficacy and empowerment across levels of career decision making and planning. The aim is also to involve and train those individuals who could facilitate the successful personal and vocational construction of adolescents and youths, to influence juvenile policies, and to improve working conditions for all individuals. The aim is to also examine the impact of different modalities of contextualized interventions. Moreover, a broad range of modalities are to be examined, such as "intelligent" television programs, films, advertising campaigns, and books targeting children, adolescents, and adults. Finally, the aim is to promote research as suggested by Brown and Krane (2000) and Heppner (2006) to

examine vocational guidance within a cross-cultural perspective and increase the cultural sensitivity and thereby effectiveness of a program or counseling session across a broad range of populations.

Over the past few years, efforts have been made to give specific attention to training and research in many Italian universities and to encourage and strengthen the professionals seriously engaged in this field with the setting up of the SIO.

RESEARCH: THE NEW FRONTIERS OF CAREER INTERVENTIONS

To reduce the obstacles and barriers that some people perceive in planning their own futures, primary (searching for and eradicating causes), secondary (early diagnosis of at-risk situations), and tertiary (timely intervention on the diagnosed situations) prevention interventions are necessary. To implement these interventions, Italian career counselors need favorable economic, social, and political conditions and some allies (Hage et al., 2007), such as parents and family members, on the one side, and teachers, on the other. We are convinced that all of them must, in any case, be adequately trained and supported.

The latter issue has been the object of special attention at the University of Padua, and, more specifically, activities that involved teachers and parents have been implemented and tested. For example, a training activity of 650 hours was developed (250 hours of traditional lectures; 250 hours of laboratory activities, practice lessons, drills, and supervision; 100 hours devoted to private study; 50 hours for the drafting of a final paper). The training program was intended to (a) increase teachers' knowledge on some important dimensions of the school-career choice, (b) improve teachers' abilities to implement and realize educational interventions of vocational guidance, and (c) expand teachers' professional self-efficacy beliefs about their ability to realize significant vocational guidance interventions aiming at decreasing the difficulties experienced by their students. Our results suggest that at the end of training, teachers had mastered, at least from a cognitive point of view, the most important pieces of knowledge about the school-career choice and had higher levels of self-efficacy in understanding clients' career problems, promoting academic success through educational counseling, dealing with problems of indecision and choice, and providing career information. In addition, 80% of the teachers implemented activities involving assessment and analysis of students' characteristics, preparing personalized reports for the students, and conducting individual interviews. About 50% of them conducted interventions lasting about 25 to 30 hours with indecisive individuals with the aim of increasing either decision or self-efficacy beliefs and problem-solving abilities. About 60% had planned educational interventions and had obtained the approval of the school council for implementing them the following academic year (Nota, Soresi, Solberg, & Ferrari, 2005).

It has been strongly suggested in the international literature that parents must also be given a significant role in the vocational development of their children (Ferrari, Nota, & Soresi, 2007). For example, consider how often in a family all its members are exposed to behaviors and aspects associated to work, from morning, when people get ready to go to work, until evening, when they return and talk about their job and those of other people, the adequacy of their income—or lack of it—and of their working conditions, the reliability of colleagues and employers, and so on. From these discussions, young people construct their idea of education and work, and of their vocational lives, even before their formal education begins. Consequently, it seems critical that parents need to be involved very early on in preventive actions of vocational guidance. The training for parents does not need to be special but should involve dimensions useful for youth to lead satisfactory personal and vocational lives. At the Larios (Laboratory of Research and Intervention in Vocational Guidance), at the Faculty of Psychology in Padua, a group of parents participated in an experimental program that consisted of the following 10 didactic units: overview of the course; career choice and vocational development; self-efficacy beliefs and interests; how to make decisions; how and when to speak of vocational guidance in the family; how to

help one's children to focus on their career goals; irrational ideas; how to help one's children to get information on vocational options; how to help one's children to choose among options; and how to support one's children's self-determination. The results indicated that parents had not only derived increased knowledge on some important dimensions of career decision making and positive interaction styles with their children on career issues but had also revised their own concept of vocational guidance and of the world of work. Together with their children, they were able to realize a series of specific supports, such as analyzing and sustaining interests; efficacy beliefs and exploration; strengthening commitment in career decision making; and facilitating professional goal setting (Ferrari et al., 2007).

Such interventions for teachers and parents have been devised based on teaching and learning theories and on models of prevention and counseling that emphasize people's strengths and the need to increase their strategies, abilities, and knowledge. They take place in small groups where teachers and parents are asked to elaborate their viewpoints and experiences, and to apply to their own family and professional contexts the modalities of help and support of the school-career choice. These efforts intend to turn parents and teachers into allies of career service providers, with the idea that only in this way can standardized and traditional working ways be abandoned in favor of more personalized modalities sensitive to contextual characteristics.

CONCLUSION

At this time in Italy, a new and promising type of vocational guidance seems to be increasingly taking hold among both researchers and career service providers. Increasingly, vocational guidance cannot be conceptualized as a simple operation of diagnosis and classification or of too superficial and often belated prognoses; rather, vocational guidance should promote individuals' actions capable of producing changes in their vocational lives. Moreover, vocational guidance should leave its mark and be clearly recognized as having a preventive role involving not only professional career counseling but other people who play critical roles in the development of children. The efficacy of vocational guidance, in other words, could be measured by considering its ability to produce significant changes in the conclusions of the life histories of many individuals and, in particular, of those that seemed already predestined or that could be easily predicted or anticipated (Soresi, 2007).

Efforts in that direction must be intensified so that vocational guidance can acquire scientific and ethical depth, legitimization, social relevance, and preventive value. For this it must (a) be started very early in life, with gradual but continuous programs; (b) be adequately planned so as to actually be congruent with the different worldviews or contextual environments of the target individuals and respectful of the characteristics of the participants; (c) be able to lessen the inhibiting power of obstacles, to remove both personal and social barriers and difficulties; (d) be respectful of individual and cultural differences, adjusting to them without hegemonic pretence and with the paramount objective of promoting empowerment, self-determination, and quality of life; and (e) anticipate and stimulate the involvement and participation of those that, because of their own authentic interest (parents and teachers foremost) or because of their own or institutional goals (social and work agencies), could contribute to the spreading of a preventive view of vocational guidance. We believe that these conditions are the most important challenges that vocational guidance must face at the beginning of this new century if we do not wish our role to be confined to giving support to individuals who could probably manage fairly well on their own or who, in any case, have the resources necessary to turn to private tutors and counselors, which has historically been the case as far back as ancient Greece and Rome.

Signs of change encourage us to think with optimism of the future of vocational guidance in Italy because research and training opportunities in this field have actually increased over the past few years. The political world seems to look at these issues with favor and to see the need to reform (even through new legislation) the services that can be put at the disposal of the public for their professional and personal development.

REFERENCES

Betz, N. E., & Taylor, K. M. (2000). *Manual for the Career Decision Self-Efficacy Scale and CDMSE–Short Form*. Unpublished instrument, Ohio State University, Columbus.

Brown, S. D., & Krane, N. E. (2000). Four (or five) sessions and a cloud of dust: Old assumptions and new observations about career counseling. In S. D. Brown & R. W. Lent (Eds.), *Handbook of counseling psychology* (3rd ed., pp. 740–766). New York: Wiley.

Castelli, C., & Venini, I. (1996). *Psicologia dell'orientamento scolastico e professionale* [Vocational psychology]. Milan, Italy: Franco Angeli.

Dawis, R. V. (1996). The theory of work adjustment and person-environment-correspondence counseling. In D. Brown, L. Brooks, & Associates (Eds.), *Career choice and development* (3rd ed., pp. 75–120). San Francisco: Jossey-Bass.

Ferrari, L., Nota, L., & Soresi, S. (2007). Il ruolo della famiglia e del supporto percepito sullo sviluppo professionale [Family role, perceived support and career development]. In S. Soresi (Ed.), *Orientamento alle scelte: rassegne, ricerche, strumenti ed applicazioni* [Vocational guidance: Reviews, research, instruments and interventions] (pp. 314–330). Florence, Italy: Giunti-O.S. (Organizzazioni Speciali).

Ferrari, L., Nota, L., & Soresi, S. (2008). Conceptions of work in adults with intellectual disability. *Journal of Career Development, 34*, 438–464.

Fischer, L. (2004). Società della conoscenza e riforme scolastiche italiane [The society of knowledge and the Italian education reform]. *Magellano, 21*, 15–20.

Gentili, C. (2004). Il riformismo formativo europeo e la riforma Moratti [European reformism and the Moratti reform]. *Magellano, 21*, 5–14.

Gore, P. A., & Leuwerke, W. C. (2000). Predicting occupational considerations: A comparison of self-efficacy beliefs, outcome expectations and person-environment congruence. *Journal of Career Assessment, 8*(3), 237–250.

Groppelli, A. (2005). *Studenti verso l'università* [Students and university]. Rome: Edizioni Borla.

Gysbers, N. C., Heppner, M. J., & Johnston, J. A. (1998). *Career counseling*. Boston: Allyn & Bacon.

Hage, S. M., Romano, J. L., Conyne, R. K., Kenny, M., Matthews, C., Schwartz, J. P., et al. (2007). Best practice guidelines on prevention practice, research, training, and social advocacy for psychologists. *The Counseling Psychologist, 35,* 493–566.

Heppner, P. P. (1988). *The Problem-Solving Inventory: Manual.* Palo Alto, CA: Consulting Psychologists Press.

Heppner, P. P. (2006). The benefits and challenges of becoming cross-culturally competent counseling psychologists. *The Counseling Psychologist, 34,* 147–172.

Holland, J. L. (1997). *Making vocational choices: A theory of vocational personalities and work environments* (3rd ed.). Odessa, FL: Psychological Assessment Resources.

Italian Institute of Statistics. (2007). *La popolazione straniera residente in Italia al 1° gennaio 2007* [Immigrants in Italy on January 1, 2007]. Rome: National Institute of Statistics. Retrieved October 11, 2007, from http://www.istat.it/salastampa/comunicati/non_calendario/20071002_00/

Krumboltz, J. D. (1999). *Career Beliefs Inventory: Applications and technical guide.* Palo Alto, CA: Consulting Psychologist Press.

Lent, R. W., Brown, S. D., & Hackett, G. (1996). Career development from a social cognitive perspective. In D. Brown, L. Brooks, & Associates (Eds.), *Career: Choice and development* (3rd ed., pp. 373–422). San Francisco: Jossey-Bass.

Lent, R. W., Brown, S. D., Soresi, S., & Nota, L. (2003). Testing social cognitive interests and choice hypotheses across Holland types in Italian high school students. *Journal of Vocational Behavior, 62,* 101–118.

Maselli, R. (2007). *Le idee degli insegnanti sul futuro degli studenti extracomunitari* [Teachers' ideas on the future of immigrant students]. Unpublished doctoral dissertation, University of Padua, Italy.

Mistri, M. (2004). Il nodo della formazione professionale degli immigrati in Italia [The problem of training immigrants in Italy]. *Giornale Italiano di Psicologia dell'Orientamento, 5*(3), 11–15.

Mitchell, L., & Krumboltz, J. D. (1996). Krumboltz's learning theory of career choice and counseling. In D. Brown, L. Brooks, & Associates (Eds.), *Career choice and development* (pp. 233–280). San Francisco: Jossey-Bass.

Nota, L., Ferrari, L., Soresi, S., & Solberg, S. V. H. (2007). Career search self-efficacy, family support, and career indecision with Italian youth. *Journal of Career Assessment, 5,* 181–193.

Nota, L., Soresi, S., Solberg, S. V. H., & Ferrari, L. (2005). Promoting vocational development: Methods of intervention and techniques used in the Italian context. *International Journal for Educational and Vocational Guidance, 3,* 271–279.

Peterson, G. W., Sampson, J. P., Jr., Reardon, R. C., & Lenz, J. C. (1996). A cognitive information processing approach to career problem solving and decision making. In D. Brown, L. Brooks, & Associates (Eds.), *Career: Choice and development* (pp. 423–462). San Francisco: Jossey-Bass.

Sarchielli, G. (2000). Orientatore: Una professione emergente. Rappresentazioni, esigenze del compito e sistemi di competenza [Career service providers: An emergent profession. Representations, tasks and competences]. In S. Soresi (Ed.), *Orientamenti per l'orientamento* [Guidance for vocational guidance interventions] (pp. 9–21). Florence, Italy: Giunti-O.S. (Organizzazioni Speciali).

Scarpellini, C., & Strologo, E. (1976). *L'orientamento: problemi teorici e metodi operativi* [Vocational guidance: Theoretical issues and operational methods]. Brescia, Italy: Editrice La Scuola.

Solberg, V. S., Good, G. E., Nord, D., Holm, C., Hohner, R., Zima, N., et al. (1994). Assessing career search expectations: Development of the Career Search Efficacy scale. *Journal of Career Assessment, 2,* 111–123.

Soresi, S. (2007). Competenze, formazione e deontologia dei professionisti dell'orientamento [Competences, training and deontology of practitioners]. In S. Soresi (Ed.), *Orientamento alle scelte: Rassegne, ricerche, strumenti ed applicazioni* [Vocational guidance: Reviews, research, instruments and interventions] (pp. 239–249). Florence, Italy: Giunti-O.S. (Organizzazioni Speciali).

Soresi, S., & Nota, L. (2001). *Portfolio Optimist per l'orientamento dagli 11 ai 14 anni* [Portfolio Optimist for vocational guidance from 11 to 14 years of age]. Florence, Italy: ITER-O.S. (Organizzazioni Speciali).

Soresi, S., & Nota, L. (2003). *Portfolio Clipper per l'orientamento dagli 15 ai 19 anni* [Portfolio Clipper for vocational guidance from 15 to 19 years of age]. Florence, Italy: ITER-O.S. (Organizzazioni Speciali).

Soresi, S., Nota, L., & Ferrari, L. (2005). Counseling and prevention activities with adolescents at risk for health and adjustment problems in Italy. *Journal of Mental Health Counseling, 3,* 249–265.

Soresi, S., Nota, L., Ferrari, L., & Solberg, S. V. H. (2008). Career guidance for persons with disabilities.

In J. A. Athanasou & R. Van Esbroeck (Eds.), *International handbook of career guidance* (pp. 405–418). Amsterdam: Springer Science.

Super, D. E., Savickas, M. L., & Super, C. M. (1996). The life-span, life-space approach to careers. In D. Brown, L. Brooks, & Associates (Eds.), *Career choice and development* (3rd ed., pp. 75–120). San Francisco: Jossey-Bass.

Tracey, T. J. G., & Ward, C. C. (1998). The structure of children's interests and competence perceptions. *Journal of Counseling Psychology, 45,* 290–303.

20

"Our Aspirations Are Our Possibilities"[1]

Growth and Features of Counselling Psychology in Ireland

ELEANOR O'LEARY AND EOIN O'SHEA

Ireland—or *Eire*, to use the country's Irish name—is a small nation nestled on the northwestern fringe of Western Europe. The country has a population of slightly less than 4.5 million (Central Statistics Office [CSO], 2008). Ireland's history contains a number of civil uprisings over the centuries, and even relatively recent problems have emerged as a consequence of the partitioning of the country as part of the Treaty of 1921. Under the terms of this treaty, six of the northern counties of Ireland became politically part of the United Kingdom, whereas the other 26 counties constituted what came to be legally described as the *Republic of Ireland* (ROI Act, 1948). Despite Ireland's turbulent history, the past two decades have seen significant social change and economic growth.

The introduction of free second- and third-level education in the latter half of the past century has resulted in a highly educated people. Furthermore, Ireland scores highest internationally on the Quality-of-Life Index (Economist Intelligence Unit [EIU], 2008). Ireland's traditionally Catholic background may relate to certain struggles within Irish society

that influence the manner in which counselling psychologists work with certain client groups. Abortion, for instance, has been a much debated issue in Irish politics and society in recent times. The Eighth Amendment of the Constitution Act (1983) represented a solidifying of the Irish government's stance against abortion, with its proponents concerned that the Irish Supreme Court might face challenges allowing abortion in certain circumstances—similar to those issues encountered in the U.S. Supreme Court's 1973 case of *Roe v. Wade* (Craig & O'Brien, 1993). The Eighth Amendment was passed by referendum (approximately 67% to 33%), effectively making the procurement of an abortion in Ireland illegal. However, since its introduction, this amendment has been narrowed in interpretation by subsequent ones (the Thirteenth and Fourteenth amendments—both in 1992) to guarantee both a pregnant mother's freedom to travel to countries where abortion is legal and information about abortion services provided abroad. However, from a counselling perspective, services for women experiencing crisis pregnancy still present challenges for counselling professionals. For instance, one such service in Ireland—Positive Options—allows counsellors of women facing crisis pregnancy to provide information and discussion regarding abortion only in the context of fully exploring the other two options available (i.e., keeping the child following birth or offering him or her up for adoption). The second author's experience of working within a community counselling setting (which employed some counsellors trained in the Positive Options system) exemplified the difficulties and controversy surrounding such issues. At the centre, a member of the administrative staff refused (for religious/moral reasons) to accept calls from people wishing to avail of the Positive Options service. She did so because if a woman were to decide to continue on the course of procuring an abortion, the staff member would feel partially responsible for facilitating her. It is apparent that challenges exist for counselling professionals in the handling of such matters.

A major health problem in Ireland relates to alcohol. Though the cultural stereotype of the Irish as hard-living, hard-drinking "characters" is often generalised to an inaccurate—and sometimes offensive—extent, problematic drinking continues to constitute a major problem in Irish society. A European Commission Report (Anderson & Baumberg, 2006) highlighted the fact that the Irish spend more of their disposable income on alcohol than do the citizens of any other European country and that they are the most frequent "binge drinkers" in Europe. Ireland ranked third in the European Commission report in terms of annual per capita consumption of alcohol. Some authors (e.g., Kirby, Gibbons, & Cronin, 2002) have highlighted the Celtic Tiger—Ireland's economic boom during the 1990s—as a possible (though decidedly complex) influence on increasing levels of alcohol consumption among the Irish. However, it seems clear that binge drinking represents one of the more serious problems associated with alcohol. O'Farrell, Allwright, Downey, Bedford, and Howell (2004) found that, between the years 1997 and 2001, acute alcohol intoxication admissions rose by 80%.

Research by Moran, Dillon, O'Brien, Mayock, and Farrell (2001) and Van Hout and Connor (2006) suggested that alcohol (and other illicit drug use) may be resulting in increased antisocial behaviour in classrooms, including fighting, poorer academic performance, and other social problems. Of 4,500 people attending general practitioner services in the eastern area of the country, Anderson (2003) found that 17% were categorised as harmful or dependent in terms of their drinking behaviour and were offered counselling. A 3-month follow-up showed that, of those who accepted this service, one third maintained abstinence and another third showed substantial improvement. The only complaint was that the service was restricted to six hours per week.

Given Ireland's sizable emigrant population, it is not surprising that Pointon (2007) attested to the culturally specific needs often required—but all too often missed—by people of Irish descent living in Britain. Ireland saw numerous catastrophic events (one of the worst being the Great Famine between 1845 and 1848) that sent millions of Irish abroad to live and work over the past 164 years. Research in the United Kingdom over the past decade (e.g., Sproston & Nazroo, 2007) suggested that people of Irish origin suffer the highest incidence of common mental disorders, with Irish men specifically suffering the highest rates of anxiety disorders. This finding may be in line with evidence that suggests that young people—and men in particular—are often less likely to engage in help-seeking behavior (Oliver, Pearson, Coe, & Gunnell, 2005). The Irish diaspora comprises a sizeable number of people worldwide, some of whom may benefit from counselling services that are culturally sensitive to the needs of that group. An example of one such service is Immigrant Counselling and Psychotherapy (ICAP)—a London-based counselling service for minority (though primarily Irish) clients in Britain. Andrew Samuels, a consultant with ICAP, suggested that support for ethnic minority services in health care systems can often face prejudice (Pointon, 2007). Samuels referred to Said's (1979) notion of *orientalism* and explained that this occurs as follows:

You idealise the exotic other, but in so doing you give him or her qualities that are undermining. So you say "oh, the Irish are so spontaneous, they're emotional, they let their hair down and they have lovely parties and Guinness"—but actually, what about the contributions of the Irish to literature in the English language? (Pointon, 2007, p. 6)

Such stereotyping—regarding both what it is to be Irish as well as how this is handled in therapy—is a likely complication of work with both Irish emigrants and Ireland-based Irish in some instances.

Traditionally, help-seeking behaviour in Ireland was pastoral in nature in that those experiencing difficulties or problems frequently approached the clergy. Prayer and other religious rituals were commonly used coping mechanisms. Indeed, some research results (e.g., Robbins & Francis, 2005) suggested this to be the case still. However, given the relative decline in organised religious participation in much of the Western world—including Ireland (Fahey, Hayes, & Sinnott, 2005)—increasing numbers of Irish people are seeking help through counselling. Possible explanations for this have been explored by O'Kane and Millar (2002) in a Northern Irish study that found that pastoral counselling sessions often involved only one session, that an emphasis was placed on problem solving within this time, and that a "lack of awareness of counselling skills, techniques, models of helping, and the need to establish boundaries and effect referral indicated an absence of any significant theoretical understanding of pastoral counselling" (p. 189). Furthermore, considering the increasing move towards professionalization of counselling in Ireland, the authors found that "formal supervision for Catholic priests was not evident, and many of them spoke of the pressure and isolation they felt" (p. 189). Although in the past there was often a stigma associated with seeking help from such professionals, it is much less today. A study by the Health Service Executive (HSE; 2007) suggests that 81% of people surveyed perceived counselling or psychotherapy as a helpful resource for mental health.

PROFESSIONAL ORGANIZATION

The professional development of psychology in Ireland is overseen and regulated by the Psychological Society of Ireland (PSI), which has a membership of more than 2,000 (see PSI, 2008b). For the purpose of the statutory regulation of psychologists (and 11 other professions), the Irish government passed the Health and Social Care Professionals Act 2005 (HSCPA, 2005). This piece of legislation led to the establishment of a Health and Social Care Professionals Council, the functions of which include overseeing and coordinating the activities of the registration boards, providing administrative support to boards and committees, establishing committees of enquiry into complaints against members, and making decisions regarding disciplinary sanctions. It is hoped that this legislation will ensure greater quality-assurance of services by psychologists in Ireland. In terms of publications, the major journal of the PSI is *The Irish Journal of Psychology* (a peer-reviewed, quarterly research journal).

The emergence of counselling psychology in Ireland began with the formation of the Counselling and Therapy Group of the PSI in 1983. This group was headed by the first author as chairperson and, in 1995, was renamed the Counselling Psychology Interest Group. At that time, the group had almost 80 members. Division status was achieved by 1997 (with John Broderick as chairperson). Currently, the membership is more than 200, with members working in a range of locations including educational settings, private practice, voluntary agencies, and governmental health settings.

The aims of the Division are to promote the development of counselling psychology as a legitimate body of psychological knowledge and as a professional field of psychological activity; to encourage scientific research in counselling psychology and to promote the dissemination of existing knowledge; to maintain high ethical and professional standards among counselling psychologists; to develop public awareness of the nature, aims, and practical applications of counselling psychology; and to liaise with relevant bodies at national, European Union, and international levels in the promotion of counselling psychology (PSI, 2008a). Cunningham (2004) found that promotion and development of the profession was viewed by 62.7% of the membership of the

Division as one of its functions, while provision of professional information was identified by 46.3%, provision of ongoing training/professional development by 44.8%, and the representation of counselling psychologists to both the PSI and the public by 37.3%. Only 7.5% of members identified the promotion of research as a function of the Division. This is not surprising, given the relatively small number of counselling psychologists who work in universities in Ireland.

Counselling psychologists are required to have initially completed an undergraduate degree in psychology or its equivalent. Applicants holding professional qualifications gained outside the Republic of Ireland must apply directly to the Department of Health and Children for validation of their qualification to work as a counselling psychology practitioner. Two master's degrees in counselling psychology are offered by Trinity College Dublin and University College Cork and are recognised by the PSI as professional training courses. Both are two-calendar-year, full-time programmes and are based primarily on a "humanistic-integrative" framework.

The perception of counselling psychologists among the general public has developed in tandem with a greater overall recognition of psychology and counselling in general. The publication of Irish books in the 1980s (e.g., O'Farrell, 1988; O'Leary, 1982) promoted interest in counselling psychology. The establishment of the Division of Counselling Psychology has provided members of the public with opportunities to contact counselling psychologists based on their individual needs and to seek redress should ethical abuses or other problems arise in the provision of high-quality psychological services.

THEORETICAL AND RESEARCH DEVELOPMENTS

A major thrust in counselling psychology in Ireland in recent years has been the move towards integration in the development of new frameworks and theoretical integrations and the incorporation of these developments in training. The integrative framework of O'Leary and Murphy (2006a) was considered by Stricker

(2007) as contributing appreciably to current discourse regarding integration in the psychotherapeutic literature in relation to the humanistic perspective. These authors view the internal integration of clients as consisting of four main dimensions, namely, feelings, behaviour, bodily sensations, and cognitions, and emphasise the importance of attention to all four within clients so that holistic healing can occur. These dimensions are also viewed as primary modalities of communication, with the identification of the primary modality aiding in the establishment of empathy. The internal integration of clients is viewed as occurring in the context of their lives, including family, social relationships, emotional relationships, and culture. Stricker stated that the model goes beyond most cognitive-behavioural approaches in its integration of the affective and bodily sensation dimensions and can be differentiated from traditional psychodynamic work by not placing historical determinants at its centre. This integrative framework—along with those mentioned below—is detailed in O'Leary and Murphy (2006b).

Two new theoretical integrations are those of person-centred gestalt therapy by O'Leary (2006) and gestalt reminiscence therapy by O'Leary and Barry (1998, 2006). Person-centred gestalt therapy is firmly rooted in a humanistic and existential view of human nature that emphasises present experiencing, choice, personal responsibility, and freedom. It uses the core conditions of empathy (Rogers, 1961), unconditionality (Barrett-Lennard, 1962), and authenticity together with eight task-outcomes. These task-outcomes are so called because they simultaneously constitute the tasks and outcomes of counselling. They include the sharing of stories, developing the capacity to express and accept feelings, becoming aware of bodily experiencing, building a holistic awareness of experiences through internal processing, increasing in self-responsibility, growing progressively towards interdependence rather than maladaptive dependence on others, acquiring the ability to centre and ground oneself, and resolving feelings relating to unfinished experiences of the past (O'Leary, 2006). These task-outcomes are pursued within the context of three major phases of therapy, namely, orientation, middle, and final. In his review in PsycCRITIQUE,

Stricker (2007) stated that this integration of humanistic and gestalt approaches represents a major addition to the literature on psychotherapy integration.

The second theoretical integration, gestalt reminiscence therapy (O'Leary & Barry, 1998, 2006), based on reminiscence and gestalt therapies, views ongoing personal growth as occurring until death and contextually influenced. The approach has been developed with a view to increasing subjective quality of life and well-being and to living more satisfying lives. Three specific goals have been identified: raising self-esteem, living in the present, and increasing self-support. Primarily used as a group approach with older adults (which lends itself to greater interpersonal contact and feedback), gestalt reminiscence therapy challenges individuals to continue to develop themselves in the emotional, social, and spiritual dimensions of their lives.

Since gestalt reminiscence therapy is at an exploratory stage of development, research has used qualitative methods. Three such studies (O'Leary & Nieuwstraten, 1999, 2001a, 2001b), all of which used discourse analysis, provide support for the use of gestalt reminiscence therapy. In a systematic review of counselling with older adults, Hill and Brettle (2005) initially identified 2,646 potential studies for inclusion. O'Leary and Nieuwstraten's (2001b) study was one of two conducted by the first author and her colleagues that were among the final 47 that met the specified criteria (the other being that of O'Leary, Sheedy, O'Sullivan, & Thoresen, 2003).

Four further areas of research investigation in Ireland by counselling psychologists relate to an investigation of Rogers's (1961) person-centred hypothesis with adolescents; counsellors' views regarding barriers, benefits, personal qualities, and necessary types of preparation for cross-cultural counselling; client-identified helpful moments in therapy; and a needs assessment of Irish counselling psychologists.

With respect to the investigation of Rogers's (1961) hypothesis, O'Leary (1982) conducted a longitudinal study of the core conditions and outcomes of his approach with 123 adolescents. Four main findings were obtained: (1) Empathy was the most significant condition; (2) empathy was established early in the counselling relationship or not at all; (3) an increase in self-acceptance emerged as the primary criterion for successful counselling; and (4) those who terminated counselling early in the relationship (45%) were low in acceptance of others. To the authors' knowledge, this research is the only longitudinal study that has explored the core hypothesis of the person-centred approach with adolescents and falls within the type of research advocated by Elliott (2007) concerning the effects of the facilitative conditions on the outcomes of person-centred therapy.

Fitzgerald and O'Leary (1990) explored counsellors' views regarding barriers, benefits, personal qualities, and necessary types of preparation for cross-cultural counselling with 32 counsellors. Differences in culture and values, as well as language difficulties, were the most frequently encountered barriers (see below), while the objectivity of counsellors and greater clarity were most frequently mentioned in relation to benefits. Reported personal qualities included an openness to difference on the part of counsellors as well as conveyance of the core counselling qualities of Rogers (1961). Familiarity with clients' culture and a grasp of their language were the most frequently recommended forms of preparation. The study provides support for the core conditions of person-centred gestalt therapy.

The investigation of moments in therapy that clients typically find most empowering and helpful was undertaken in a series of studies by Timulak (Timulak, 2007; Timulak & Elliott, 2003; Timulak & Lietaer, 2001). Timulak's studies were of a qualitative and discovery-oriented nature. In an investigation of six university students, Timulak and Lietaer found three main categories of positively experienced episodes, namely, empowerment, safety, and insight. Further taxonomy of positive episodes indicated four themes relating to strengthening of the therapeutic alliance and five themes concerning empowerment of the client. While the authors of the study were careful to point out the necessity of distinguishing between positively experienced, in-the-moment episodes in therapy and those that will actually result in lasting therapeutic change, they suggested nevertheless that "such moments may carry in themselves the potential for deeper engagement in therapeutic endeavour and/or hopeful therapeutic end" (Timulak & Lietaer, 2001, p. 72). In a further study, Timulak and Elliott (2003) identified five different types of empowerment events, namely, poignant, emergent, decisional, empowerment, and accomplishment, which occurred across three domains (i.e., client processes, therapist processes and interaction, and therapeutic impact). Therapist interventions were associated with several types of empowerment, including empathic understanding, empathic affirmation of client growth-promoting aspects, and two-chair work. Timulak (2007) further investigated moments in therapy identified by clients as having a helpful impact employing a qualitative, meta-analytic procedure. Nine categories were identified: awareness/insight/self-understanding; behavioural change/problem solution; empowerment; relief; exploring feelings/emotional experiencing; feeling understood; client involvement; reassurance/support/safety; and personal contact. The study lends support to O'Leary and Murphy's (2006a) integrative framework.

A needs assessment of the members of the Division of Counselling Psychology (PSI) was undertaken by Cunningham (2004). Sixty-seven of 160 members responded, giving a 42% overall response rate. More than half (53.8%) considered that the Division met their professional needs, while 46.3% did not. However, more than three quarters (76.2%) reported that the activities and services provided by the Division were relevant to them, while 19.4% disagreed. With respect to priorities and needs for the future, the three most important were considered to be achieving equality in the employment field, ensuring representation on all public bodies relevant to counselling psychology, and providing ongoing input to continuing professional development. It is not surprising that equality in the employment field was identified as a priority for the future, given the traditional predominance of clinical psychologists within the HSE. Representation on all public bodies is likely to depend on the public profile of the Division, whereas continuing

professional development became an essential requirement of the PSI in January 2005.

FUTURE DIRECTIONS

The PSI was much later than professional psychological associations in other countries, such as the APA (American Psychological Association) in the United States and the BPS (British Psychological Association) in the United Kingdom, in establishing a Division of Counselling Psychology. Heppner, Casas, Carter, and Stone (2000) conducted a review of challenges for counselling psychology in the future and identified 10. These included maintaining unity within a varied discipline, increasing collaboration among counselling organisations, being an "active player" by collaborating with organised psychology, supporting and enhancing member involvement, furthering meaningful international collaborations, bettering the integration of science and practice in counselling psychology research, practice and training, and narrowing the gap between training and the needs of practising counselling psychologists. With respect to increasing Irish collaboration, a 2008 joint conference of the British Psychological Society and the Psychological Society of Ireland's Counselling Divisions occurred for the first time in Dublin. Furthermore, Cunningham's (2004) research found that the majority of Irish Division members were also members of at least one other counselling organisation.

At the time of writing, a three-year doctorate in counselling psychology has been announced by Trinity College Dublin, commencing in October 2009. It is likely that the other course in counselling psychology in Ireland (at University College Cork) will progress in a similar direction, particularly in light of the increasing number of such doctoral-level courses in Britain. This trend is likely to result in improved employment opportunities for counselling psychologists as trainers and academics in third-level education as well as basic grade and senior psychologists in the HSE (the largest employer requiring psychological services in the country). The recently increased placing of counselling psychology trainees in health settings will further add to the latter likelihood. This initiative may pose challenges for counselling psychologists, given the developmental origins of counselling psychology in Ireland. Since the majority of principal psychologists within the HSE are clinical psychologists, trainee counselling psychologists are likely to become part of multidisciplinary teams upon graduating.

The expansion of the counselling service for those of school-going age is also desirable. In Northern Ireland, McElearney et al. (2007) obtained highly positive findings in relation to the provision of a widespread counselling service for this age group, including a high incidence of self-referral from students themselves. Most secondary schools in the Republic rely on the work of guidance counsellors who—though well-trained— often lack the resources (e.g., an adequate number of sessions due to other work-role demands) necessary to provide comprehensive personal counselling.

The portents for the future are encouraging. Cunningham's (2004) research found that almost two thirds (64.9%) of the members of the Division of Counselling Psychology became members between 1997 and 2004. A future challenge for the Division is the establishment of a peer-reviewed *Irish Journal of Counselling Psychology*. Although the annual conference of the PSI provides a platform for the sharing of developments and research in counselling psychology, the absence of such a journal has frequently resulted in these endeavours being published in peer-reviewed journals abroad, with many members of the Division not being aware of their existence.

With the founding of the European Association of Counselling Psychology in 2006, further collaborative opportunities between Irish counselling psychologists and their European counterparts are likely and desirable. A welcome development was the recommendation by the Irish College of General Practitioners that GP intervention programmes for alcohol problems—including relevant counselling services—be provided by more practices throughout the country (Anderson, 2003). Such a demand provides an opportunity for counselling psychologists

to be part of the solution to a cultural problem that is both widespread and highly destructive.

NOTE

1. Quotation from Samuel Johnson (1709–1784), English poet, critic, and writer (Granat, 2003).

REFERENCES

Anderson, P., & Baumberg, B. (2006). Alcohol in Europe—Public health perspective: Report summary. *Drugs: Education, Prevention, and Policy, 13*(6), 483–488.

Anderson, R. (2003). *Alcohol aware practice pilot survey: Final report.* Irish College of General Practitioners.

Barrett-Lennard, G. T. (1962). Dimensions of therapist response as causal factors in therapeutic change. *Psychological Monographs, 76, 562.*

Central Statistics Office. (2008). *Population and migration estimates.* Retrieved August 20, 2008, from http://www.cso.ie/releasespublications/documents/population/current/popmig.pdf

Craig, B. H., & O'Brien, D. M. (1993). *Abortion and American politics.* Chatham, NJ: Chatham House.

Cunningham, S. (2004). *Informing strategic planning: A needs assessment of members of the Division of Counselling Psychology of the Psychological Society of Ireland.* Unpublished master's thesis, Trinity College, Dublin, Ireland.

Economist Intelligence Unit. (2008). *The Economist Intelligence Unit's quality-of-life index.* Retrieved August 27, 2008, from http://www.economist.com/media/pdf/QUALITY_OF_LIFE.PDF

Eighth Amendment of the Constitution Act. (1983). Retrieved August 27, 2008, from http://www.irishstatutebook.ie/1983/en/act/cam/0008/index.html

Elliott, R. (2007). Person-centred approaches to research. In M. Cooper, M. O'Hara, P. F. Schmid, & G. Wyatt (Eds.), *The handbook of person-centred psychotherapy and counselling* (pp. 327–340). New York: Palgrave Macmillan.

Fahey, T., Hayes, B., & Sinnott, R. (2005). *Consensus and conflict: A study of values and attitudes in the Republic of Ireland and Northern Ireland.* Dublin, Ireland: Institute of Public Administration.

Authors' Note: The authors acknowledge the generous permission given by Sharon Cunningham to report findings from her study and the comments of Elizabeth Behan.

Fitzgerald, K., & O'Leary, E. (1990). Cross-cultural counselling: An investigation of counsellors' views on barriers, benefits, personal qualities and necessary preparation. *Irish Journal of Psychology, 11,* 238–248.

Granat, H. (2003). *Wisdom through the ages: Book two.* Victoria, Canada: Trafford.

Health and Social Care Professionals Act. (2005). Retrieved February 5, 2008, from http://www.oireachtas.ie/documents/bills28/acts/2005/a2705.pdf

Health Service Executive. (2007). *Mental health in Ireland: Awareness and attitudes.* Report commissioned by the HSE National Office for Suicide Prevention (NOSP). Retrieved December 15, 2008, from http://www.nosp.ie/ufiles/news0003/mental-health-in-ireland—awareness-and-attitudes.pdf

Heppner, P. P., Casas, M. J., Carter, J., & Stone, G. L. (2000). The maturation of counseling psychology: Multifaceted perspectives, 1978–1998. In S. D. Brown & R. W. Lent (Eds.), *Handbook of counseling psychology* (3rd ed., pp. 3–49). New York: Wiley.

Hill, A., & Brettle, A. (2005). The effectiveness of counselling with older adults: Results of a systematic review. *Counselling and Psychotherapy, 5*(4), 265–272.

Kirby, P., Gibbons, L., & Cronin, M. (2002). *Reinventing Ireland: Culture and the Celtic tiger.* London: Pluto.

McElearney, A., Adamson, G., Shevlin, M., Tracey, A., Muldoon, B., & Roosmale-Cocq, S. (2007). Independent schools counselling: Profiling the NSPCC service experience. *Child Care in Practice, 13*(2), 95–115.

Moran, R., Dillon, L., O'Brien, M., Mayock, P., & Farrell, E. (2001). *Overview of drug issues in Ireland: A research document.* Dublin, Ireland: Health Research Board.

O'Farrell, A., Allwright, S., Downey, J., Bedford, D., & Howell, F. (2004). The burden of alcohol misuse on emergency in-patient hospital admissions among residents from a health board region in Ireland. *Addiction, 99,* 1279–1285.

O'Farrell, U. (1988). *First steps in counselling.* Dublin, Ireland: Veritas.

O'Kane, S., & Millar, R. (2002). A qualitative study of pastoral counselling of Catholic priests in Northern Ireland. *British Journal of Guidance & Counselling, 30*(2), 189–206.

O'Leary, E. (1982). *The psychology of counselling.* Cork, Ireland: Cork University Press. (Reprinted 1986, 2002, 2003)

O'Leary, E. (2006). The need for integration. In E. O'Leary & M. Murphy (Eds.), *New approaches to integration in psychotherapy* (pp. 3–11). London: Routledge.

O'Leary, E., & Barry, N. (1998). Reminiscence therapy with older adults. *Journal of Social Work Practice, 12*(2), 159–165.

O'Leary, E., & Barry, N. (2006). Gestalt-reminiscence therapy. In E. O'Leary & M. Murphy (Eds.), *New approaches to integration in psychotherapy* (pp. 50–60). London: Routledge.

O'Leary, E., & Murphy, M. (2006a). A framework for integrative psychotherapy. In E. O'Leary & M. Murphy (Eds.), *New approaches to integration in psychotherapy* (pp. 12–24). London: Routledge.

O'Leary, E., & Murphy, M. (Eds.). (2006b). *New approaches to integration in psychotherapy.* London: Routledge.

O'Leary, E., & Nieuwstraten, I. (1999). Unfinished business in gestalt reminiscence therapy: A discourse analytic study. *Counselling Psychology Quarterly, 12*(4), 395–413.

O'Leary, E., & Nieuwstraten, I. (2001a). Emerging psychological issues in talking about death and dying: A discourse analytic study. *International Journal for the Advancement of Counselling, 23,* 179–199.

O'Leary, E., & Nieuwstraten, I. (2001b). The exploration of memories in Gestalt reminiscence therapy. *Counselling Psychology Quarterly, 14*(2), 165–180.

O'Leary, E., Sheedy, G., O'Sullivan, K., & Thoresen, C. (2003). Cork Older Adult Intervention Project: Outcomes of a gestalt therapy group with older adults. *Counselling Psychology Quarterly, 16*(2), 131–143.

Oliver, M. I., Pearson, N., Coe, N., & Gunnell, D. (2005). Help-seeking behaviour in men and women with common mental health problems: Cross-sectional study. *British Journal of Psychiatry, 186*(4), 297–301.

Pinkney, M. (2008). *The complete pocket positives: An anthology of inspirational thoughts.* Australia: Five Mile Press.

Pointon, C. (2007). Out of Ireland: Stories of migration. *Therapy Today, 18*(3), 4–6.

Psychological Society of Ireland. (2008a). *Division of counselling psychology.* Retrieved February 10, 2008, from http://www.psihq.ie/members_div_counselling.asp

Psychological Society of Ireland. (2008b). *An overview of PSI.* Retrieved February 8, 2008, from www.psihq.ie/about_overview.asp

Republic of Ireland Act, Section 2 (1948).

Robbins, M., & Francis, L. J. (2005). Purpose in life and prayer among Catholic and Protestant adolescents in Northern Ireland. *Journal of Research on Christian Education, 14*(1), 73–93.

Rogers, C. R. (1961). *On becoming a person.* Boston: Houghton Mifflin.

Said, E. (1979). *Orientalism.* New York: Vintage.

Sproston, K., & Nazroo, J. (Eds.). (2007). *Ethnic Minority Psychiatric Illness Rates in the Community (EMPIRIC).* London: Stationery Office.

Stricker, G. (2007). Psychotherapy integration (halfway) around the world. *PsycCRITIQUES, 52,* 10.

Timulak, L. (2007). Identifying core categories of client-identified impact of helpful events in psychotherapy: A qualitative meta-analysis. *Psychotherapy Research, 17*(3), 305–314.

Timulak, L., & Elliott, R. (2003). Empowerment events in process-experiential psychotherapy of depression: An exploratory qualitative analysis. *Psychotherapy Research, 13*(4), 443–460.

Timulak, L., & Lietaer, G. (2001). Moments of empowerment: A qualitative analysis of positively experienced episodes in brief person-centred counselling. *Counselling and Psychotherapy Research, 1,* 62–73.

Van Hout, M. C., & Connor, S. (2006). Drug use and the Irish school context: A teacher's perspective? *Journal of Alcohol & Drug Education, 52*(1), 80–91.

21

In the Crossing Currents of the United States and Scandinavia

Counseling and Psychology in Iceland

Í miðju ólíkra strauma úr vestri og austri:
Sálfræðileg ráðgjöf og meðferð á Íslandi

STEFANÍA ÆGISDÓTTIR AND SIF EINARSDÓTTIR

Counseling psychology as a special psychological discipline does not exist in Iceland. Yet the main focuses endorsed by the discipline in the United States, such as developmental concerns, vocational issues, human strength, person-environment fit, and prevention (Leong & Leach, 2007), are performed to some degree by psychologists and other human service professionals in the country. In this chapter, we focus on two of the many applied settings influenced by theory and research in counseling psychology: mental health services and career counseling services. This discussion is interwoven with descriptions of the cultural traditions and trends in Iceland.

ICELANDIC CULTURE

Iceland is a country of around 300,000 people, with about 60% of the population residing in the capital city, Reykjavík, and surrounding areas. It is a northern European island, 103,000 square kilometers in size, located between Greenland and Europe. It is the most sparsely populated country in Europe. Norwegian and Celtic immigrants settled in Iceland during the 9th and 10th centuries. Following 300 years of independence, Iceland was subsequently ruled by Norway and then Denmark but gained complete independence from Denmark in 1944 (Ministry for Foreign Affairs, n.d.). At the beginning of the 20th century, Iceland was largely a rural society with about 78,000 inhabitants and had on several occasions endured enormous hardship caused by plagues, volcanic eruptions, and famine. During the course of about half a century, however, Iceland changed from a poor, mostly undeveloped country into a progressive, mostly capitalistic society with an extensive welfare system (e.g., state insurance, free hospitalization), low unemployment, and a relatively even distribution of income. Due to its hydro- and geothermal resources it is nearly energy independent. In the last decade, the income per capita has been among the highest in the world, as are the standards of living and levels of technology and education (Hjálmarsson, 1993; Ministry for Foreign Affairs, n.d.). Currently, life expectancy in Iceland is among the highest in the world (men 79.4 years and women 83 years) and infant mortality is among the lowest (Ministry for Foreign Affairs, n.d.).

Recently, however, Icelanders have been facing a tremendous uncertainty about the future. This time, though, it is not due to plagues or famine. In fall of 2008, in the wake of the global financial crisis, Iceland was in the headlines of the international press due to the collapse of its banking system. The collapse along with the rapid depreciation of the Icelandic currency "krona" resulted in an unprecedented economic and financial crisis (Ministry for Foreign Affairs, n.d.). As of March 2009, unemployment had risen to 9% from less than 1.3% 6 months earlier (Vinnumálastofnun, n.d.). Yet the foundation of the Icelandic economy remains relatively strong (e.g., natural resources, strong infrastructure, well-educated workforce), and Icelanders are determined to recover from this economic crisis as they have recovered from prior crises they have endured throughout history.

Icelanders are a homogeneous mixture of the descendents of the original Nordic and Celtic settlers. Iceland is a republic, with a written constitution and a parliamentary form of government. The executive power rests mostly with the government, which is elected separately from the presidential elections every 4 years. *Althingi* is the Icelandic legislative body of 63 members elected every 4 years by popular vote. The most prevalent religion is Lutheran (about 85%) (Ministry for Foreign Affairs, n.d.).

The language and culture of Iceland have predominantly Scandinavian roots. Icelandic is the national language, and it has not changed much since the settlement. In spite of strong ties to Scandinavia, however, Icelandic culture also has some distinctive characteristics setting it apart from the other Nordic countries. Individual freedom (individualism), equality,

and democracy are strongly valued in all these countries. In Iceland, however, equality beliefs seem less absolute (Ólafsson, 2003). Equality is emphasized in relationships and people's rights and opportunities but less so in distribution of resources and power. Icelanders tend to have greater tolerance for meritocracy (Ólafsson, 1985) than do Scandinavians, who have been criticized for restricting individual achievement through welfare protectionism (Ólafsson, 2003). This greater emphasis on self-reliance as against social protection may be seen in Icelander's strong belief in the merits of hard work (Magnússon, 1989; Ólafsson, 1996), which is reflected in a longer work-week among Icelanders than among other Scandinavians (Organisation for Economic Co-operation and Development [OECD], 2007) and its employment participation, which is among the highest there is (Ólafsson, 2003). In fact, a study of 2,000 Icelanders revealed that hard work/diligence (*dugnaður*) was the fifth most important value of Icelanders, preceded by honesty, frankness, positive attitude/optimism, and trust. These values were followed by family and friendship ties, and health (Proppé, 2000). Also reflecting the emphasis on self-reliance in Iceland is a more liberal version of the social welfare system compared with neighboring countries, a system that is not as tightly knit, with lower compensations and less governmental spending (Njáls, 2006; Ólafsson, 1999).

Also setting Iceland apart is the fact that it has more in common with the United States than do the other Nordic countries. Iceland is, for instance, considered a settlers' or pioneer society just like the United States. Some common characteristics identified in settlers' societies are a strong sense of individualism, importance of self-reliance and independence, absence of rigorous status distinction, and resentment of authority and government (Ólafsson, 2003). Some of these characteristics have been identified in Iceland. In addition, Iceland may be open to U.S. cultural influences because of its geographic location being midway between Europe (Scandinavia) and the United States. Furthermore, many Icelanders obtain graduate degrees from U.S. universities and bring with them to Iceland new ideas and thoughts. There is also a U.S. influence from the popular media and from the long-term existence of the U.S. naval base in Iceland from the end of World War II until the year 2006.

In sum, Icelandic culture seems to share characteristics from both the neighboring Nordic countries and the United States. The strong emphasis on equality and social welfare is shared with the other Nordic countries, while its self-reliance and tolerance for meritocracy are shared with the United States. This creates an interesting mix of individualistic and equalitarian worldviews, placing Icelanders somewhere halfway between Scandinavians and Americans, both socially and geographically.

PSYCHOLOGICAL EDUCATION AND LICENSURE

The education system in Iceland is similar to that of the Scandinavian and some European countries, and its psychological education and licensure laws follow the European and Scandinavian model. Education is compulsory through the 10th grade. Following compulsory education (16 years old), students have the opportunity to attend a 4-year program of study at the upper-secondary school level, from which they complete a university entrance exam (*stúdentspróf*). After this, students may attend university. Most psychologists in Iceland begin their program of study in psychology at a university in Iceland. Currently, two universities offer a BA degree in psychology: the University of Iceland (since 1971) and University of Akureyri (since 2003). These are 3-year, 90-credit-hour (180 European Credit Transfer System [ECTS]) programs focusing on general psychology. Until recently, Icelanders who wanted to practice psychology in Iceland had to pursue graduate studies abroad (e.g., the United States, the United Kingdom, Nordic countries, Germany, France) (Pind, 2003), seeking an MA, a Candidatus Psychologiae Diploma (Cand Psych), or a PhD-level education.

In spite of psychology being among the few disciplines offered when the University of Iceland was founded in 1911 (Pind, 2003), it was not until 1976 that psychology was acknowledged as a formal profession by the Icelandic government. The Icelandic Ministry of Health handles licensure of psychologists

following an evaluation process of candidates by the Icelandic Psychological Association (Sálfræðingafélag Íslands [SÍ]). The SÍ standards are modeled on Scandinavian and European regulations and follow the European Framework for Psychologists' Training. To be licensed, persons need to have either an MA or a PhD degree, depending on the country of education, or a Cand Psych diploma with appropriate academic, internship/practicum, and research training (Icelandic Psychological Association, n.d.). The SÍ has no subdivisions for the various psychology disciplines but treats licensed psychologists as a unified whole. The SÍ also acts as a trade union negotiating minimal pay for practicing psychologists.

Besides the license to practice psychology in Iceland, in 1990 an additional specialist or expert (*sérfræðingur*) endorsement was offered for licensed psychologists in one of four areas of psychology: clinical, rehabilitation/disability, educational/developmental, and social/organizational. This endorsement requires specialized academic and practical training and significant scholarship for at least 4 years beyond completion of a degree (MA, PhD, Cand Psych). To date, (2009), there are about 300 licensed psychologists in Iceland, of which around 30 have an additional specialist endorsement. In 1996, the Icelandic government recognized psychologists as health service providers (Icelandic Psychological Association, n.d.).

Although historically Icelandic psychologists have received graduate training in psychology abroad, in 1999 the University of Iceland (UI) began offering a 60-credit-hour (120 ECTS) Cand Psych program tailored around the Icelandic psychology licensing requirements. Also, in 1991, the UI began offering a 1-year diploma program in career counseling and guidance, which was expanded to a 2-year master's degree in 2004. This is also a 60-credit-hour (120 ECTS) program, accepting students from the social sciences and education.

COUNSELING AND COUNSELING PSYCHOLOGY

Counseling psychology is not recognized as a specialty or an area of psychological expertise in Iceland. One reason for this might be the small numbers of Icelandic counseling psychologists and the consequent lack of pressure on the legislative body to include counseling psychology as a specialty. However, and because of the wide range of areas covered in a typical counseling psychology training, common services offered by counseling psychologists are provided in the country. Mental health services are, for instance, offered by licensed psychologists with Cand Psych–, MA-, and PhD-level education, usually obtained abroad. Career counseling services are typically offered by diploma- or MA-level career counselors, most of them trained in Iceland and a few abroad.

We were able to identify six individuals trained in the United States as counseling psychologists, two of whom are the current authors. As a reflection of the breath of a typical counseling psychology training, these individuals are employed in diverse settings (e.g., hospital, industrial organization, academia, private practice). An interview with three of them revealed that they were very satisfied with the breadth of education and training that they had received and its applicability to numerous applied settings in Iceland. All three of them noted a general lack of identity as counseling psychologists.

Mental Health Services

Research indicates that Icelanders have a positive view of psychological services. One study performed more than a decade ago (Kristjánsdóttir & Guðmundsdóttir, 1994) found that 66% of 247 participants from the general adult population reported a positive attitude toward psychologists and their services, whereas 34% were neutral or expressed a negative attitude. Also, 71% believed in psychotherapy helpfulness, whereas 29% were neutral or did not believe that counseling was helpful. A more recent study on the general population (Ægisdóttir & Einarsdóttir, 2008) also indicated a positive attitude toward psychologists and their services. Of those participating ($N = 352$), 63% indicated a willingness to seek psychological services in the future and found these services available. The

positive attitude toward and willingness to seek psychological services is not surprising, given that the discipline is rooted in thoughts originating from Western individualistic points of view shared in Iceland. Furthermore, Icelanders are known for open-mindedness and are quick to adapt to new ideas and technology, as is evident in its speedy modernization over the past 50 years.

Iceland has a socialized medical system, as do the other Nordic countries. Therefore, Icelanders are hospitalized free of charge for mental and physical problems and can seek outpatient medical treatment for a minimal fee (15% of cost) at health service centers (*heilsugæslustöðvar*) financed by the municipality and the state. These centers are staffed by family physicians, nurses, midwives, and support staff; they offer general medical treatment, examination, home nursing, and preventive services, such as family planning, maternity care, and child health care. The Icelandic Ministry of Health oversees services provided at these centers.

Psychologists do not generally work in the health service centers, and their services (except for children, since 2008) are not covered by the social security insurance. Instead, Icelanders mainly seek mental health services from psychologists in private practice, for which most need to pay the full fee out-of-pocket. The high cost may act as a major barrier for Icelanders seeking psychological services. In fact, a study on psychological help seeking (Ægisdóttir & Einarsdóttir, 2008) indicated that 64% of those participating considered psychological services unaffordable. In some instances, though, the cost involved is shared by the client's trade union or, for low-income persons, the municipal social services. Icelanders with serious or acute conditions can seek services from psychologists in hospital settings (outpatient or day treatment) for less than what they have to pay for private practice. Although some persons seek services from psychologists in private practice, Icelanders seek a great deal of their mental health services from their family physicians in the health service centers because of the low cost. For instance, a study by Agnarsdóttir (1998) found that family physicians had determined that 35% ($N = 499$) of their patients had mental health issues. Similarly, according to the General Health Questionnaire completed by the patients, about 46% of them had mental health issues. The physicians prescribed psychotropic medication to 55% of the patients they had determined had mental health problems, mostly for depression, anxiety, and sleep disturbances. Furthermore, only 3% of these patients were referred to a psychologist. Thus, medication seems more commonly provided to persons with mental health problems than are psychological services. This corresponds with data from 1997 indicating that Icelanders use more antidepressant medication than do people in the other Nordic countries (Heilbrigðis og Tryggingamálaráðuneytið, 1998).

With Icelandic psychologists' diverse training backgrounds from all over the Western world, it is hard to assess the preferred or general theoretical orientation. It is the authors' belief, though, that behavioral and cognitive behavioral approaches are more prevalent compared with psychodynamic ones. In fact, since 1986, those adhering to cognitive behavioral approaches have worked together closely and formed an organizing body (*Félag um hugræna atferlismeðferð*) advocating for this treatment approach. In 2007, the membership was 48. Also indicating this are studies on Icelandic college students' counseling expectations. Ægisdóttir and Gerstein (2000, 2004) found that Icelandic students expected psychologists to be more directive and offer more advice than did the U.S. students, who in essence expected to be more involved in the counseling process. The authors suggested, based on these data, that directive approaches, such as solution-focused and cognitive behavioral approaches, be employed as they fitted with clients' expectations and other help-seeking traditions. It can also be argued that directive approaches fit closely with some of the common Icelandic worldviews discussed earlier, namely frankness, honesty, and hard work.

Mystical beliefs that can be traced back to the Viking era still exist in modern Iceland alongside the Western, predominantly scientific view. These mystical beliefs influence help seeking. According to a recent survey (Gunnell, 2007), around 80% of Icelanders believe in the possibility of mystical powers, such as extrasensory perception (ESP), the ability to forecast the future through dreams and fortune-tellers, and the ability to make contact with the dead. Interestingly, these beliefs have not changed in the past 30 years, since the last survey was conducted, despite increased modernization. Not surprisingly, then, Icelanders have a long tradition of going to fortune-tellers and psychic mediums and healers to relieve stress and to get direction in ambivalent situations. For instance, Kissman (1990) suggested that for many Icelandic women, seeking support from someone who can look into the future minimized conflict and provided a sense of hope and optimism and offered direction for the future. Furthermore, the Icelandic Lutheran church has traditionally offered help, especially regarding grief and loss.

Career Counseling and Guidance Services

In Iceland, formal career counseling and guidance services began in the 1980s (Félag náms- og starfsráðgjafa, 1998). The career counselors' organizing body is the Career and Guidance Counselor Association (Félag náms- og starfsráðgjafa [FNS]), which currently includes 200 members. FNS was founded 25 years ago by a few counselors, who were educated abroad. As of today, FNS is working toward legalizing the career and guidance profession in Iceland and has recently established its own ethical code of practice (Félag náms- og starfsráðgjafa, 2007).

In comparison with the other Nordic countries, the history of career counseling and guidance in Iceland is shorter. Setting Iceland further apart is the U.S. influence on the discipline. Although career counseling in many Nordic countries is rooted in social justice, with the aim of providing a societal safety net for those in need, in Iceland, although there is an emphasis on equalitarian values, there is a stronger influence from the U.S. emphasis on individual differences and testing (Plant, 2003). In fact, it can be argued that Icelanders' emphasis on self-reliance and freedom embraces the focus on the individual endorsed in the study of individual differences. In addition to this ideological fit to the Icelandic culture, U.S. influences on the career and guidance movement in Iceland can be traced to the impact of institutional connections between Icelandic and U.S. universities. For example, Dr. Carol Pazandak, a counseling psychologist from the University of Minnesota (UM), participated in the development of a 1-year diploma program in career counseling and guidance at the UI. Since the early 1980s, courses in vocational psychology, career counseling, and career assessment were offered in both the education and psychology programs in the Social Science Department at UI by visiting U.S. scholars (e.g., Pazandak, Jack Darly) and Icelanders educated in the United States. In 1991, a fully developed program was launched in the Social Science Department at the UI, and Guðbjörg Vilhjálmsdóttir, trained in vocational and educational guidance in France and the United Kingdom, was hired as a training director and the only full-time faculty. This diploma program has now evolved into a 60-credit-hour (120 ECTS) MA program with two full-time faculty. In addition to the strong U.S. influences on the career counseling program in Iceland, European influences (e.g., French, U.K., and Scandinavian) can be seen as well (e.g., Vilhjálmsdóttir & Arnkelsson, 2003).

U.S. influences are also apparent in career counseling research and practice in Iceland (Plant, Christiansen, Lovén, Vilhjálmsdóttir, & Vuorinen, 2003). Early on, career and guidance counselors working in the schools had access to interest inventories and other career tools developed in the United States. Dr. Sölvina Konráðs, a PhD in counseling psychology from UM, for instance, translated and validated the Strong Interest Inventory (SII) for use in the country (Konráðs, 1987; Konráðs & Haraldsson, 1994). She and others have used the Icelandic SII with good results. U.S. theories have also stimulated career counseling research in Iceland (e.g., Einarsdóttir, Rounds, Ægisdóttir, & Gerstein, 2002; Kristinsdóttir, Ægisdóttir, & Haraldsson, 1991), with the Bendill (Einarsdóttir & Rounds, 2007) Project perhaps being the most ambitious initiative.

Recent Developments in Career Counseling and Guidance: The Bendill Project

The vocational interest inventories (e.g., SII, Self-Directed Search [SDS]) that were translated and validated for use in Iceland were well received by both career counselors and clients. Holland's theory, on which these inventories are based, was highly appreciated as well and seemed to fit the Icelandic cultural context (e.g., Einarsdóttir et al., 2002). Despite these important steps in career services to Icelandic clients, there were drawbacks. First, until recently, the SII had to be sent abroad for scoring, resulting in a 2- to 6-week waiting period for clients. Second, whereas interest inventories had been in use for almost two decades in Iceland, very little occupational information was available for clients' career exploration (Félag náms- og starfsráðgjafa, 1998). Finally, being U.S.-based, the occupational categories in the SII and SDS did not fully fit the Icelandic work environment. These challenges were the main driving forces behind the Bendill Project.

Bendill is a Web-based Icelandic interest inventory and occupational information system (Einarsdóttir & Rounds, 2007) in which persons' interests are matched to Icelandic occupational categories based on the person-environment fit ideology. It is based on Holland's theory of occupational types (RIASEC [realistic, investigative, artistic, social, enterprising, and conventional]), Prediger's (1982) data-ideas and people-things dimensional representation, and Rounds and Day's (1999) suggestion of a flexible model of a vocational interest circle.

Prior to the beginning of the Bendill Project, Óskarsdóttir (1990, 1996, 2001) had published occupational descriptions for about 250 occupations in Iceland that were modeled by the *Dictionary of Occupational Titles* (U.S. Department of Labor, 1991). Thus, one of the first steps in developing Bendill was to establish Holland's (1997) RIASEC codes for these occupations using expert ratings. These were then used to develop a Web-based information system with the occupational descriptions organized by their Holland code. Based on a governmental classification of the Icelandic job market, occupational titles (e.g., elementary schoolteacher) were selected, and the Icelandic job descriptions were used to write work-related activity items (e.g., paint a house). Around 300 occupational and activity items were developed representing the Icelandic world of work. Furthermore, 140 school subjects (e.g., history) representing the curriculum of the upper-secondary school system (age 16–20 years) were selected to develop a special version of the inventory for students transitioning between compulsory education and upper-secondary school.

Bendill provides students aged 15 to 20 years with an opportunity for exploration of occupations directed by the results of interest assessment. Bendill is unique in Iceland for many reasons. It is the first vocational interest inventory for use in career counseling and guidance employing an indigenous item pool. Also, it is the first one to form a foundation for a Web-based occupation information and assessment system similar to the O*NET system in the United States (U.S. Department of Labor, 2004). The representation of interests for clients and their matching work environment has a graphic representation for ease of understanding and has been partially adjusted to the specific landscape of vocational interest and the world of work in Iceland (see Einarsdóttir & Rounds, 2007). Finally, Bendill is an inexpensive and easily accessible interest assessment tool largely reflecting the world of work in Iceland, which is theoretically grounded in well-known and established models of vocational interests.

CHALLENGES AND PROSPECTS OF COUNSELING PSYCHOLOGY IN ICELAND

An important question to ask is what the counseling psychology discipline has to offer in Iceland. Its influences on career counseling and guidance are obvious, and the Icelandic clientele has benefited from the insight offered by interest assessment and person-environment fit approaches to counseling. In fact, it can be argued that formal and systematic career guidance did not exist in Iceland prior to the introduction of U.S. theories and interest inventories in Iceland. Furthermore, the development of Bendill was greatly influenced by U.S. theory and research. The influences on mental health services, in contrast, are not as clear. It can be argued, though, that counseling psychology's emphasis on persons' development and optimal functioning, in contrast to the medical approach (treat people when they are ill),

may be gaining greater attention now in Iceland than before. For instance, in 2007 the Ministry of Health announced that prevention would be the main emphasis in a new health care policy (see Heilbrigðis og Tryggingamálaráðuneytið, 2007). Furthermore, as the cost of psychological services seems to be a barrier for persons seeking services (e.g., Ægisdóttir & Einarsdóttir, 2008), greater pressure needs to be placed on policymakers to include psychological services for clients of all ages in the social security insurance program.

Furthermore, career counseling practices are growing extensively in the country, influenced by the emphasis on lifelong learning and social inclusion in Europe. As a result of this emphasis, the Icelandic government has established employment and lifelong learning centers in all major urban areas in the country. Therefore, it is likely that this new government's emphasis on human growth and lifelong learning will be a great avenue for counseling psychology to contribute. Moreover, counseling psychologists may be included in the unique municipal work schools (*vinnuskóli*) of Iceland. In these summer programs operating in most towns in Iceland, youth aged 13 to 16 years are hired during the summer months by municipalities to attend to and beautify their environment. In these programs, besides doing service for their hometown for minimal pay, the youth are taught to work with tools, respect their environment, and develop work ethics, responsibility, and cooperation.

It is apparent that the generalist training of counseling psychologists has given the few Icelandic PhD counseling psychologists an opportunity to work in and influence Icelandic society through many different settings (e.g., health care, business, private practice, academia). The question still remains, though, as to how counseling psychology can serve the Icelandic people best. Should counseling psychologists in Iceland push for a specialist endorsement and form academic programs to train more people in the counseling psychology tradition? Or should counseling psychologists continue their work in diverse settings alongside other professionals? An answer to this question rests largely on the future number of counseling psychologists in Iceland and on whether counseling psychology will ever be an academic discipline in Icelandic universities.

The lack of professional identity as counseling psychologists among the three counseling psychologists that we interviewed may be a reflection of the current status in Iceland. It is, for instance, hard for other professionals and the public to understand what the counseling psychology tradition has to offer and how that is different from other psychology and related disciplines when there is no unifying body and a strong identity. Greater knowledge about the range of services offered by counseling psychologists (and career counselors for that matter) and how these services differ from those offered by other helping professionals may ensure better informed choices by the public. Until now, the emphasis in the Icelandic health care system has been on those who have serious psychological problems and need hospitalization and/or medication. This is in sharp contrast with the recent importance placed on preventive measures in health care. Therefore, this new emphasis offers exciting challenges for Icelandic counseling psychologists in cooperation with other psychology and health care professionals to highlight these discrepancies and offer solutions. Having said this, it is crucial to keep in mind that for any approaches or interventions from U.S counseling psychology to be effective in Iceland, careful attention must be paid to testing, adapting, and tailoring them to fit the social and cultural context of Iceland. There is still much work to be done toward the indigenization of psychology in Iceland.

REFERENCES

Agnarsdóttir, A. (1998). *An examination of the need for psychological counseling services in primary health care in Iceland*. Unpublished doctoral dissertation, University of Surrey, Guilford, UK.

Einarsdóttir, S., & Rounds, J. (2007). *Bendill, rafræn áhugakönnun: Þróun og notkun* [Bendill, a Web-based interest inventory: Development and utility]. Reykjavík, Iceland: Háskólaútgáfan.

Einarsdóttir, S., Rounds, J., Ægisdóttir, S., & Gerstein, L. H. (2002). The structure of vocational interests in Iceland: Examining Holland's and Gati's RIASEC models. *European Journal of Psychological Assessment, 18,* 85–95.

Félag náms- og starfsráðgjafa. (1998). *Afmælisrit* (15th anniversary publication of the Career Counseling and Guidance Association in Iceland). Reykjavík, Iceland: Author.

Félag náms- og starfsráðgjafa. (2007). *Afmælisrit* (25th Anniversary publication of the Career Counseling and Guidance Association in Iceland). Reykjavík, Iceland: Author.

Gunnell, T. (2007). "Það er til fleira á himni og jörðu, Hóras..." Kannanir á íslenskri þjóðtrú og trúarviðhorfum 2006–2007 ["There is more to the heavens and the earth, Hóras..." Surveys on Icelanders' folk beliefs and spirituality 2006–2007]. In G. Þ. Jóhannesson (Ed.), *Rannsóknir í félagsvísindum VIII* [Social science research VIII] (pp. 801–812). Reykjavík, Iceland: Félagsvísindastofnun Háskóla Íslands.

Heilbrigðis og Tryggingamálaráðuneytið. (1998). *Stefnumótun í málefnum geðsjúkra* [Policy regarding matters of the mentally ill]. Retrieved July 23, 2005, from http://www.heilbrigdisraduneyti.is/utgefid-efni//nr1178

Heilbrigðis og Tryggingamálaráðuneytið. (2007). *Innflytjendur og geðheilbrigði* [Immigrants and mental health]. Retrieved November 25, 2007, from http://www.heilbrigdisraduneyti.is/radherra/raedur-og-greinarGTT/nr/2605

Hjálmarsson, J. R. (1993). *History of Iceland: From the settlement to the present day*. Reykjavík, Iceland: Iceland Review.

Holland, J. L. (1997). *Making vocational choices: A theory of vocational personalities and work environments* (3rd ed.). Englewood Cliffs, NJ: Prentice Hall.

Icelandic Psychological Association. (n.d.). *Sálfræðingafélag Íslands* [Icelandic Psychological Association]. Retrieved July 23, 2005, from http://www.sal.is

Kissman, K. (1990). The role of fortune telling as a supportive function among Icelandic women. *International Social Work, 33,* 137–144.

Konráðs, S. (1987). *Cross-cultural cross-validation of the lawyer and engineer scales for linguistically equivalent forms of the Strong-Campbell Interest Inventory*. Unpublished doctoral dissertation, University of Minnesota.

Konráðs, S., & Haraldsson, E. (1994). The validity of using U.S. based interest norms of the Strong Interest

Inventory for Icelandic college population. *Scandinavian Journal of Educational Research, 38,* 65–76.

Kristinsdóttir, H., Ægisdóttir, S., & Haraldsson, E. (1991). *Prófkvídakvardi Spielbergers (vidhorf til prófa): Handbók* [Spielberger's Test Anxiety Inventory (attitudes toward tests): A manual]. Reykjavík, Iceland: Author.

Kristjánsdóttir, A., & Guðmundsdóttir, M. Í. (1994). *Viðhorf til sálfræðinga og starfa þeirra* [Attitudes toward psychologists and their services]. Unpublished BA thesis, University of Iceland, Reykjavík, Iceland.

Leong, F. T. L., & Leach, M. M. (2007). Internationalizing counseling psychology in the United States: A SWOT analysis. *Applied Psychology: An International Review, 56,* 165–181.

Magnússon, F. (1989). Work and identity of the poor: Work load, work discipline, and self-respect. In E. P. Durrenberger & G. Pálsson (Eds.) *The anthropology of Iceland* (pp. 140–156). Iowa City: University of Iowa Press.

Ministry for Foreign Affairs. (n.d.). *The official gateway to Iceland.* Retrieved April 15, 2009, from http://www.iceland.is/

Njáls, H. (2006). *Velferðarastefna—markmið og leiðir* [Social welfare policy—goals and methods]. Reykjavík, Iceland: Félagsvísindastofnun Háskóla Íslands.

Ólafsson, S. (1985). *Hvernig eru Íslendingar? Nokkrar vísbendingar um gildi í menningu Íslendinga* [How are Icelanders? A few hints about Icelandic cultural values]. Unpublished report.

Ólafsson, S. (1996). *Hugarfar og hagvöxtur* [Cultural values and economic affluence in Western countries]. Reykjavík, Iceland: Félagsvísindastofnun-Háskólaútgáfan.

Ólafsson, S. (1999). *Íslenska leiðin: Almannatryggingar og velferð í fjölþjóðlegum samanburði* [The Icelandic welfare model: Social security and welfare in an international comparison]. Reykjavík, Iceland: Félagsvísindastofnun-Háskólaútgáfan.

Ólafsson, S. (2003). Contemporary Icelanders: Scandinavian or American. *Scandinavian Review, 9,* 6–14.

Organization for Economic Cooperation and Development. (2007). *Factbook 2007: Economic, environmental, and social statistics.* Paris: Author.

Óskarsdóttir, G. G. (1990). *Starfslýsingar: Sérfræði-, tækni- og stjórnunarstörf* [Job descriptions: Professional-, technical-, and administrative occupations]. Reykjavík, Iceland: Iðnú.

Óskarsdóttir, G. G. (1996). *Starfslýsingar II: Sérgreinar í iðnaði og þjónustu* [Job descriptions II: Specialized occupations in industry and service]. Reykjavík, Iceland: Iðnú.

Óskarsdóttir, G. G. (2001). *Starfslýsingar III: Almenn störf í framleiðslu og og þjónustu* [Job descriptions III: General occupations in production and service]. Reykjavík, Iceland: Iðnú.

Pind, J. (2003). Sálfræðikennsla í Háskóla Íslands 1911–2001 [Psychology education in the University of Iceland 1911–2001]. *Sálfræðiritið, 8,* 9–19.

Plant, P. (2003). Five swans: Educational and vocational guidance in the Nordic Countries. *International Journal for Educational and Vocational Guidance, 3,* 85–100.

Plant, P., Christiansen, L. L., Lovén, A., Vilhjálmsdóttir, G., & Vuorinen, R. (2003). Research in educational and vocational guidance in the Nordic Countries: Current trends. *International Journal for Educational and Vocational Guidance, 3,* 101–122.

Prediger, D. J. (1982). Dimensions underlying Holland's hexagon: Missing link between interests and occupations? *Journal of Vocational Behavior, 21,* 259–287.

Proppé, J. (2000). Dyggðirnar og Íslendingar [The virtues and Icelanders]. *Tímarit Máls og Menningar, 61*(2), 6–16.

Rounds, J. B., & Day, S. X. (1999). Describing, evaluating, and creating vocational interest structures. In M. L. Savickas & A. R. Spokane (Eds.), *Vocational interests: Their meaning, measurement and use in counseling* (pp. 103–133). Palo Alto, CA: Davies-Black.

U.S. Department of Labor. (1991). *Dictionary of occupational titles* (4th ed). Washington, DC: Government Printing Office.

U.S. Department of Labor. (2004). *Occupational information network resource center.* Retrieved August 15, 2004, from http://www.onetcenter.org

Vilhjálmsdóttir, G., & Arnkelsson, G. (2003). The interplay between habitus, social variables and occupational preferences. *International Journal for Educational and Vocational Guidance, 3,* 137–150.

Vinnumalástofnun. (n.d.) http://www.vinnumalastofnun.is/files/apr09_1976467205.pdf

Ægisdóttir, S., & Einarsdóttir, S. (2008). *Icelanders' psychological help-seeking patterns.* Unpublished manuscript.

Ægisdóttir, S., & Gerstein, L. H. (2000). Icelandic and American students' expectations about counseling. *Journal of Counseling and Development, 78,* 44–53.

Ægisdóttir, S., & Gerstein, L. H. (2004). Icelanders' and U.S. nationals' expectations about counseling: The role of nationality, sex, and Holland's typology. *Journal of Cross Cultural Psychology, 35,* 734–748.

22

Applied Psychology in Sweden

A Brief Report on Its Role, Ambitions, and Limitations

Tillämpad psykologi i Sverige:
En kort rapport om dess roll, ambitioner, och begränsningar

JOHANNA E. NILSSON AND THOMAS LINDGREN

In this chapter, we discuss the history and the contemporary role of psychology in Sweden, including education and training, current workforce, and the role of professional organizations. Additionally, data from recent studies on the mental health of Swedes and the status of psychological services are provided.

HISTORY AND DEMOGRAPHICS

Sweden, located in northern Europe, is the largest of the Scandinavian (Nordic) countries (Denmark, Finland, Iceland, Norway, and Sweden) with a population of more than 9 million. Sweden is also in a transition, from being a country that has been highly homogeneous to one that is increasingly diverse. Today, approximately one fifth of the population is foreign born or has a foreign-born parent.

About a fourth of the foreign-born individuals are from the other Scandinavian countries, a third from other European countries, and the remaining from countries outside Europe. Early immigration waves in the 1950s and 1960s were due to a great labor need, whereas later immigrant waves are associated with refugee and family immigration (Svensson, 2003; U.S. Department of State, 2007). Furthermore, Sweden has Europe's proportionally largest elder population, with 5% of the population over the age of 80 (Swedish Institute, 2007b).

Sweden is a constitutional monarchy, where the king, Carl XVI Gustav, is the head of state but without any formal political power. Three levels of government exist: federal, regional, and local. There are seven main parties: the Left Party (Vänsterpartiet), the Social Democrats (Socialdemokraterna), the Liberal Party (Folkpartiet), the Christian Democrats

321

(Kristdemokraterna), the Center Party (Centern), the Conservatives (Moderaterna), and the Green Party (miljöpartiet). On the federal level, Sweden has a unicameral legislature (riksdag) of 349 members who are elected via a system of proportional democracy. Elections for the federal government are held every 4 years, and all individuals over the 18 years of age have the right to vote. Sweden had a high voter turnout of up to 90% in some elections (Svensson, 2003). Since 2006, a coalition of the center right parties (Folkpartiet, Centern, and Moderterna) under the head of state, Prime Minister Fredrik Reinfeldt (Moderaterna) has governed the country (U.S. Department of State, 2007).

During the 20th century, Sweden evolved from a country with widespread poverty and a rigid class system to a country committed to equality and high standards of living (Svensson, 2003; U.S. Department of State, 2007). Some of this effort was set in place by The Social Democratic Party, which came to power in 1920 and governed Sweden for much of the 20th century. The party's slogan, People's Home (Folkhem) was created in the late 1920s to ensure that Swedes would not suffer again from extreme poverty but experience social and economic equality (Svensson, 2003). Today, Swedes benefit from subsidized medical, dental, and elder care; housing and unemployment benefits if needed; free medical and dental care for children; and a year's paid parental leave (Svensson, 2003). Equality is also evident in the workforce, which includes 48% women. High taxes, especially in the 1960s and 1970s (currently, they are more similar to other European nations) helped pay for this welfare, which has declined somewhat since a financial crisis in the 1990s (Svensson, 2003; U.S. Department of State, 2007).

Sweden is a secular country. Only about 5% of the population attends church services regularly. Even though religion does not seem to influence daily life in Sweden, some Lutheran principles, adopted by King Gustav Vasa in the 1500s, are evident in the current society. These principles are reflected in values and work ethics, such as obedience to authority, diligence, and responsibility in work and life (Svensson, 2003). Other values that influence Swedes are the laws by Jante (Jantelagen) that were proposed in a novel by Sandemose in 1933. This law fosters the values that one should not believe that one is better than anyone else and that one should not strive to stand out socially or economically. Hence, it is suggested that this "law" helped contribute to the Swedish welfare state by stabilizing social and economic forces (Jante Law, 2008; Svensson, 2003). As a group, Swedes have also been described as reserved, serious, industrious, liberal, reliable, and honest (see Svensson, 2003).

PSYCHOLOGY AND PSYCHOLOGICAL TREATMENTS

Similar to many other European countries during the first half of the 20th century, mental health treatments were influenced by psychoanalysis. However, by midcentury, other treatment orientations, such as cognitive and behavioral therapy, began to gain acceptance and are today commonly used (Armelius, 2005). In Sweden, the word *psychotherapy* often serves as an umbrella term for different types of psychological treatment orientations (e.g., dynamic, cognitive), type of client (e.g., individual, group, family), and duration of treatment (Riksförenining PsykoterapiCentrum, 2007). Terms such as *counseling psychology*, *counseling*, and *counselor* are not readily translated into Swedish and do not exist as established psychological specialties. Furthermore, in contrast to the United States, which divides applied psychology training into three major fields (clinical, counseling, and school psychology), only one formal applied psychology training, called *Psykologprogrammet* (psychology program), is offered in Sweden.

Education

Until World War II, psychology in Sweden was the academic responsibility of philosophy faculties. In 1943, the first psychotechnical institute was created at the Högskola of Stockholm (Stockholm Institute of Higher Education; Hysen, 1997). By the end of the 1950s, a more formal training for psychologists was established at universities (Lundberg, 2005). Currently, students complete a 5-year, full-time national curriculum with a focus on applied psychology. This training program (Psykologiprogammet) is offered at eight universities in Sweden (Universities of Gothenburg, Linköping, Lund, Stockholm, Umeå, Uppsala, and Örebro, and at the Karolinska Institute). Students can be admitted to this program following high school graduation. Admission is highly competitive; the psychology program is one of the most popular degree programs in Sweden. Students graduate with a master's of science (MS) degree in psychology. In 2006, 371 students were awarded such a graduate degree (Verket för Högskoleservice/National Agency for Service to University Colleges, 2007). After completing 5 years of academic training, students must enroll for a 1-year internship of supervised, regulated practice to become licensed as a psychologist. A license is required for employment within the health care system in Sweden and is awarded by the National Board of Health and Welfare (Socialstyrelsen).

The Swedish National Agency for Higher Education (Högskoleverket) oversees the quality of the psychology programs and holds the right to disaccredit programs failing to meet expected standards. In the past few years, the psychology programs along with all other university programs have been involved in revising their programs to meet the standards of the Bolonga 1999 Declaration. The purpose of this declaration is to make the diverse system of higher education in Europe more compatible across countries, hence, promoting quality assurance and mobility. In Sweden, this has involved revising the degree levels, grading system, and admission processes. For example, for two semesters of study (40 weeks), students will now earn 60 credits rather than the 40 credits they did in the past (Swedish Institute, 2007a).

Many psychologists continue their education. In actuality, Swedish psychologists further their training to a greater degree than any other group of professionals in the country, including medical doctors, university professors, and engineers (Svensson, Research Report 126, Gothenburg University, cited

in Ahlroos, 2003). Many psychologists enroll in an advanced psychotherapy training program where they receive in-depth training in one of the following treatment orientations: psychoanalytic/psychodynamic, behavioral, cognitive, cognitive behavioral, group, or family therapy. These programs are offered at universities and a few other approved training institutions. Graduation from these programs provides a license of psychotherapy, awarded by the National Board of Health and Welfare (Socialstyrelsen). Most (54%) of the licensed psychotherapists in Sweden are psychologists, but other professionals such as social workers (20%), medical doctors (10%), and nurses (4%) can enroll in this program as long as they meet the basic training requirements (Samrådforum för Psychotherapi, 2007).

Psychologists can also further their training through the National Specialist Certification program, which was created by the Swedish Psychology Association to provide a training model similar to the medical field's residence training programs. This 3-year-long training program is open for licensed psychologists allowing the participants to develop a specialty in one of three areas: clinical, occupational, and educational psychology (Ahlroos, 2007; Nyman, 2002).

Some psychologists complete a doctoral degree. Sweden offers a doctorate of philosophy degree in psychology with a primary focus on research and research training. Only a few students are admitted every year. For example, at Stockholm University, between 10 and 16 students are accepted every year (A. Johnson, personal communication, September 14, 2000).

Current Workforce and Professional Structures

There are about 8,000 psychologists in Sweden, and most of them are members of the Swedish Psychological Association (Sveriges Psykologiförbund). This association has functioned as the union for Swedish psychologists since 1955. Today, it serves its members via its work on salary and employment issues and questions regarding the role of psychology in contemporary society, education, and research

(Sveriges Psykologiförbund, 2007; S. Bertman, personal communication, September 19, 2007).

Based on the Swedish Psychological Association's membership data, 13.6% ($n = 856$) members are employed by the federal government, 50.6% ($n = 3,186$) by the regional government (responsible for medical health care), 16.4% ($n = 1,032$) by the local government (community services, schools, care for the elderly, social services), and 10.8% ($n = 537$) are employed in commercial enterprises. In addition to the 8.5% ($n = 680$) psychologists solely employed in private practice, an additional 300 psychologists have private practice on a part-time basis secondary to their main employment (S. Bertman, personal communication, September 19, 2007). Between 65% and 70% of employed psychologists are women (Strömberg, 2001). In 2007, the average gross income per month was 31,000 kronor (which equals to about $3,674 based on 2009 U.S. and Sweden currency exchange rate). Although not vastly different, the average salary of women was slightly below men's (Örn, 2007).

Research, Grants, and Journals

Research and Grants

Some of the most popular areas of psychology research in Sweden are in the fields of cognitive and neuropsychology, developmental psychology, and clinical psychology. Although grant money for such research can be derived from many different sources, the Swedish Research Council (Vetenskapliga rådet), the Swedish Council for Working Life and Social Research, and the Bank of Sweden Tercentenary Foundation are some of the major funders (L. Rönnqvist, personal communication, October 7, 2007).

Journals

There are several refereed psychology journals in Sweden. Some of them have English as their printed language, and several are published jointly by the Scandinavian countries. Perhaps the most well-known journal is the *Scandinavian Journal of Psychology*, which is published by the Psychological Associations of Denmark, Norway, Finland, and Sweden. Other journals include *Cognitive Behaviour Therapy* (formerly *Scandinavian Journal of Behaviour Therapy*), published by Taylor & Francis and Routledge, and *Scandinavian Journal of Psychoanalytic Review*, published by the University Press of Southern Denmark and sponsored by the Psychoanalytic Societies of Denmark, Finland, Norway, and Sweden.

NATIONAL DATA ON MENTAL HEALTH AND TREATMENT

Several recent studies have been conducted on the mental health of the Swedish population (e.g., Damell & Modig, 2004; Socialstyrelsen, 2007). Data from these studies generally indicate that the well-being of Swedes continues to improve compared with the previous decade, evidenced by decreased use of alcohol and drugs, fewer sick days, and a stabilization of the number of children and adults presenting as overweight and obese. However, concerns about the mental health of young women, ages 15 to 24, have been reported, suggesting that they present with more anxiety, higher rates of suicide attempts, and greater alcohol consumption than they did in the mid-1990s (Socialstyrelsen, 2007). Concerns have also been raised regarding individuals with psychological problems, such as anxiety and depression, suggesting that these individuals may not receive the psychological care they need.

In Sweden, less severe forms of psychiatric conditions, such as depression without a comorbid personality disorder, are often referred to as psychological problems in contrast to psychiatric problems and are viewed with less urgency in terms of treatment. Treatment for mental health and physical problems that are considered medically relevant or motivated are provided by the Swedish medical health care system, which is almost entirely financed through taxes. As of 2008, adult patients in the greater area of Stockholm, which constitutes the most populated area in Sweden, pay a maximum of 900 kronor per year (equivalent to roughly US$107) regardless of actual health care consumption (Vårdguiden, 2008). A similar pay plan covers most types of prescribed medication.

However, it can be difficult to determine what conditions are medically relevant. In 1995, a national legislation was approved, titled the *Treatment Guarantee*, making health care, including psychotherapy, a right for the population. This legislation was created to enforce equality of health care across all parts of Sweden and made regional governments responsible for meeting this treatment guarantee. The caveat for psychotherapy treatment is that it is only guaranteed and subsidized when considered medically motivated, which it tends to be in the cases of more severe psychopathology that require medication.

Individuals with psychological problems, such as anxiety, depression, and life transitions and crises, often seek treatment at the nation's primary health care units (health centers). However, few psychologists are employed in these primary health care units. Of the 1,100 primary health care units in Sweden, about 100 employ psychologists. This results in that most individuals seeking treatment for psychological problems at these settings only receive medication as a form of treatment (Lindgren, Sandell, & Ahlin, 2006). Therapy provided by a psychologist in a private practice setting may be an option for individuals with psychological problems, however, such treatment typically costs between 600 kronor and 1,000 kronor per session (equivalent to roughly US$71 to US$118) and is generally not subsidized. Results from a recent study, based on interviews with a selected group of 204 psychologists employed in private practice, revealed that 80% of the psychologists had denied individuals services due to the individuals' inability to finance their own treatment (Damell & Modig, 2004).

In the same study, Damell and Modig (2004) also surveyed 1,000 adults from the general population. The results from this study highlight some of the problems associated with access of care for individuals with psychological problems. Specifically, 10% of the participants in the study reported experiencing psychological problems, such as depression, burnout, or other serious life crisis. About two thirds of all participants reported that if they were in need of mental health services, they would prefer therapy over medication. Only 12% reported wanting medication as a sole method of treatment, indicating a great desire for talk-oriented treatment. Notably, a majority of all participants (60%) reported to believe that individuals with psychological problems would not obtain the treatment they desired from the available subsidized mental health services.

It should be noted that it is not only the primary health care system that employs a low number of psychologists, this problem is apparent in the school system as well. The number of school psychologists in Sweden (0.3 per 1,000 children) is lower than in many western European countries (e.g., Switzerland with 2 and France with 1.5 school psychologists per 1,000 students; Palmer, 2002). Overall, these data suggest some problems with the availability of affordable treatment options for Swedes presenting with psychological problems. In addition, the low number of psychologists in primary health care and school settings may contribute to the lack of visibility of the profession and the perception that psychological services are only for the more severely mentally ill.

CONCLUSION

The field of psychology has existed in Sweden for more than 100 years. The current workforce of psychologists complete 5 years of academic training in the area of applied psychology followed by 1 year of supervised internship. The desire among this professional workforce for advancing their training and developing a specialization is noteworthy (Ahlroos, 2003). This desire may be a reflection of a dedicated and responsible workforce, eager to advance their skills to respond to the differing psychological needs of the Swedish population. It may, however, also be a response to the psychology training program, Psykologprogrammet, suggesting that is it too generalized and may not adequately prepare students to work with specific populations and problems.

Based on employment and client data, it appears that most individuals served by psychologists in Sweden present with more severe forms of psychopathology and that they tend to be treated in medical settings. In contrast, the Swedish health care system appears less able to meet the treatment needs of individuals presenting with milder forms of mental illness. Although this group may prefer therapy, medication seems to be a more available treatment option for them. Private practice might be another option, however, it is costly and in most cases not subsidized. Middle-income Swedes are unlikely to afford such services for a longer period of time. So what do people in Sweden do when they are in need of or desire a psychologist to talk to due to depression or some kind of life crises? Based on our knowledge, Swedes do not generally engage in some common type of indigenous practice to decrease their suffering other than talking to family and friends. The Swedish culture emphasizes responsibility, independence, and emotional control, and when it comes to managing mental health problems such values may prevent individuals from getting both the informal and formal support they are in need of. In addition, such cultural values may prevent people from demanding changes to the health care system to provide greater access to subsidized mental health treatment, including therapy. In other words, mental health problems compared with medical problems appear quite stigmatized.

Although it is difficult to compare one country with another to suggest changes in provisions of medical and mental health services due to political, historical, and economical differences, the Swedish system would possibly be able to learn something from the field of counseling psychology as it is practiced in the United States. Counseling psychologists in United States are trained to work with less severe forms of psychopathology, provide briefer types of treatment, and focus on the person-environment interaction as well as human diversity in all its forms (Gelso & Fretz, 2001). By developing such a psychology specialty in Sweden, the availability of psychological resources for individuals with psychological problems might increase. Not only would it be likely that such a group of professionals would develop service provisions similar to the ones in the United States, but they may also become needed advocates or spokespersons for individuals presenting with psychological problems. The zeitgeist in Sweden seems ready for such a development. There appears to be an increasing awareness of the need for psychological health care in form of therapy and the Swedish Psychological Association seems determined to develop a workforce with expertise areas. Yet a fundamental requirement for such development may be an amendment in federal policy in how mental health care is funded and without that other changes—in workforce and treatment—seem less certain.

REFERENCES

Ahlroos, M. (2003, October 19). Fortbildning vanligast bland psykologer [Continuing education is most common among psychologists]. *Psykologtidningen, 7–8*, 18.

Ahlroos, M. (2007, May 15). Få invändningar mot nya specialistordningen [Few objections against the new specialist certification program]. *Psykologtidningen, 7*, 9.

Armelius, B.-Å. (2005). Psykoterapi [Psychotherapy]. In P. Hwang, I. Lundberg, J. Rönnberg, & A.-C. Smedler (Eds.), *Vår Tids Psykologi* [The psychology of our time] (pp. 321–346). Stockholm, Sweden: Natur & Kultur.

Damell, C., & Modig, A. (2004). *Psykisk hälsovård och psykologiska behandlingsmetoder* [Mental health care and psychological treatment methods]. Stockholm, Sweden: TEMO AB.

Gelso, C., & Fretz, B. (2001). *Counseling psychology* (2nd ed.). Belmont, CA: Wadsworth & Thomson.

Hysen, T. (1997, November 17). I psykologins backspegel [In the rearview mirror of psychology]. *Psykologtidningen, 21*, 14–15.

Jante Law. (2008). Retrieved February 28, 2008, from http://www.enwikipedia.org/wiki/Jante_Law

Lindgren, T., Sandell, R., & Ahlin, L. (2006, May 24). Sjukvården främjar inte psykologisk problemlösning [Our health care system does not promote psychological problem solving]. *Dagens Medicin, 21*, 41.

Lundberg, I. (2005). Vår tids psykologi växer fram [The psychology of our time grows into being]. In P. Hwang, I. Lundberg, J. Rönnberg, & A.-C. Smedler (Eds.),

Vår Tids Psykologi [The psychology of our time] (pp. 23–48). Stockholm, Sweden: Natur & Kultur.

Nyman, E. (2002, January 28). Så söker du specialistutbildning [This is how you apply for the specialist certification program]. *Psykologtidningen, 2,* 12.

Örn, P. (2007, March 10). Medellönen nu över 30000 kronor [The average salary is now above 30,000 crowns]. *Psykologtidningen, 4,* 7–9.

Palmer, I. (2002). Gemensam policy for skolpsykologer i Europa [Common policy for school psychologists across Europe]. *Psykologtidningen, 6,* 11.

Riksförening PsykoterapiCentrum. (2007). *Om psykoterapi* [About psychotherapy]. Retrieved July 27, 2007, from http://www.riksforeningenpsykoterapicentrum.se/psykoterapi.htm

Samrådforum för Psychoterapi. (2007). *Samrådforum för Psychoterapi* [Consultation for psychotherapy]. Retrieved November 15, 2007, from http://www.samradsforum.se/samradsforum.htm

Socialstyrelsen. (2007). *Folkhälsa—Lägesrapport 2006* [People's health—2006 report about the current situation]. Retrieved August 5, 2007, from http://www.socialstyrelsen.se/Publicerat/2007/9489/Sammanfattning.htm

Strömberg, U.-B. (2001). Djupdykning i lönestatestiken: Försprånget for statligt anställda minskari [A deep dive in the salary statistics: The lead of state government employees decreases]. *Psykologtidningen, 14,* 4–8.

Svensson, C. R. (2003). *Culture shock! A guide to customs and etiquette. Sweden* (Rev. ed.). Portland, OR: Graphic Arts Center.

Sveriges Psykologiförbund. (2007). *Om psykologförbundet* [About the Psychological Association]. Retrieved October 11, 2007, from http://www.psykologforbundet.se

Swedish Institute. (2007a). *Higher education and research in Sweden (2007).* Retrieved September 30, 2007, from http://www.sweden.se/templates/cs/FactSheet___16958.aspx

Swedish Institute. (2007b). *Swedish healthcare.* Retrieved September 30, 2007, from http://www.sweden.se/templates/cs/FactSheet___15865.aspx

U.S. Department of State. (2007). *Background note: Sweden.* Retrieved September 30, 2007, from http://www.state.gov/r/pa/ei/bgn/2880.htm

Vårdguiden. (2007). *Högkostnadsskydd for patientavgifter* [Protection for high costs for patient fees]. Retrieved March 3, 2008, from http://www.vardguiden.se/Article.asp?c=2901

Verket för Högskoleservice/National Agency for Service to University Colleges. (2007). *Statistik* [Statistics]. Retrieved September 28, 2007, from http://www.vhs.se/templates/Page.aspx?id=1444

23

Career Counseling in France

A Growing Practice Among Diverse Professional Groups

Le counseling de carrière en France: Une pratique en développement dans des groupes professionnels divers

VALÉRIE COHEN-SCALI, JEAN GUICHARD,
AND JEAN-PHILIPPE GAUDRON

To outline the status of counseling and counseling psychology in France at the beginning of the 21st century is a task that can be either very simple or infinitely complicated. The task would be simple if it consisted only of observing that France does not have a specific subdivision of psychology called counseling psychology (Bernaud, Cohen-Scali, & Guichard, 2007). As these authors noted, there is extreme heterogeneity across counseling practitioners, their practices, and their theoretical field of reference, as well as a lack of specific degree programs in counseling psychology. Therefore, this chapter provides first a brief account of the recent rise of the various counseling professions in France. The second section of this chapter is centered on a subset of these professions: those relating to school and career

counseling. Finally, we describe some innovative practices in the field in France.

A STRONG PRESENCE OF COUNSELORS IN THE CONTEXT OF A DIFFICULT SOCIAL AND ECONOMIC CONJUNCTURE

Some Evolutions of French Society

The development of counseling practices and professions cannot be discussed without outlining first the French economical situation and mentioning two of the transformations French society has undergone in the past 20 years. France is the sixth economical power in the world and the fourth leading exporting country, with 63.4 million inhabitants. France essentially has a services economy, which involves 72% of the 27.6 million working people. France is a cofunding country of the European Union and the eurozone.

Despite a certain economical dynamism, unemployment has remained around 10% since 1975. Thus, unemployment has become a widespread condition, particularly among the poorly educated population, youth, and women. At the same time, the general level of education training in France has increased. For example, in 1980, 30% of any age group had obtained a high school diploma, whereas in 1990 this number was about 60% and the number of university students had multiplied. Research found a tendency of youth impoverishment and a growing anxiety concerning the future in spite of the increased education level. Additionally, the family, one of the bases of society, has also undergone major transformations in France. Some authors even speak of "a major transformation of the family in its 'traditional' form," that is, "married couple with children, raised by the unemployed wife" (Déchaux, 2007, p. 74). In 1999, 20% of families in France were single-parent ones compared with 13% in 1990. These general trends reveal more precarious living conditions that have resulted in feelings of uncertainty and chronic concerns. These conditions have several consequences: (a) multiple and complex transitions, (b) obligations for continuous training and development of one's competencies, and (c) the weakening of traditional identity anchors, which makes daily life situations more difficult to confront.

The Diversity of Counseling Practices

The living conditions the past 20 years have led to an increased societal need for counseling. There has been an increased number of counselors in France, with either very diverse or more specialized professional practices. The counseling professions may be linked to diverse professional fields, such as education, transition to work, social work, and health and career development. Although for the majority of counselors in France counseling constitutes

the heart of their profession (as is the case for career counseling psychologists, marriage counselors, and career counselors), other professionals have developed more or less formalized counseling activities without these constituting the core of their trade (e.g., nurses, teachers, welfare workers). The professional status, salaries, working conditions, and training of counselors differ greatly as well. For example, some are civil servants, others are attached to organizations, and still others work in companies or are self-employed. In short, counselors in France do not form a homogeneous unit.

Only a small number of professionals have received training centered specifically on counseling services. A majority of counselors have obtained a master's degree in social sciences, supplemented by brief training periods specific to the institutions for which they work. However, some counselors have not had any specific training but have acquired certain competences through practice or from brief training courses (e.g., neurolinguistic programming, transactional analysis), which they use in their daily counseling practice. Additionally, there are no university programs in France leading to a master's degree in counseling, just as there are handbooks in French in this field (except in career counseling, as noted in the following paragraph).

One of the major consequences of this diversity of membership and conditions and of the lack of common counseling training is that counselors perceive themselves above all as a part of a structure or institution rather than belonging to the same occupational group. Furthermore, counselors in France do not consider themselves to be members of a true specific profession sharing the same professional identity.

TRADITIONAL PROFESSIONS AND PRACTICES OF VOCATIONAL GUIDANCE

In this particularly heterogeneous group, the 30,000 school and career counselors constitute, to a certain extent, an exception. Though they do not consider themselves as belonging to the same professional family, a certain number of them have received university training in vocational guidance and use relatively uniform methodologies and techniques. Among these counselors, a distinction is made between those who work with young people and those whose main clientele is made up of adults.

Vocational Guidance and Transition to Work for Young People

Vocational guidance intended for high school students is ensured by 4,700 school and career counseling psychologists (or COP, Conseillers d'Orientation-Psychologues). These professionals work in 600 Information and Guidance Centers (or CIO, Centres d'Information et d'Orientation), which were created in the 1920s and are managed by the Ministry of Education (Guichard & Huteau, 2005). These counselors serve about 8.3 million high school and university students. For most of them, their services are provided in CIO locations in town centers and in the schools. In a CIO, counselors, for instance, conduct an assessment interview of those seeking services (sometimes associated with tests or questionnaires), help young people search for information about existing training fields and professions, and manage career workshops. In the schools, the counselors inform students about training courses and trades, offer preparations and follow-ups of practicums in companies, prepare meetings with professionals and career education programs, and participate in staff meetings (Cohen-Scali, 2004). These counselors have a diploma specialized in vocational counseling, which corresponds to a master's in psychology, offered by the National Institute of Studies on Work and Vocational Guidance (INETOP, Institut National d'Etudes sur le Travail et l'Orientation Professionnelle). INETOP was created in 1928 by a psychologist, Henri Piéron, a disciple of one of the pioneers of vocational guidance in France, Emile Toulouse. In addition to ensuring the initial and continuous training of school and career counselors, INETOP undertakes research on the psychological techniques of individual appraisal. INETOP has also been publishing (since 1928) the only French scientific review dedicated to vocational psychology and counseling, *L'Orientation Scolaire et Professionnelle*. Most COPs are members of a professional organization, the Association of the School and Career Counseling Psychologists of France (ACOP-F, Association des Conseillers d'Orientation-Psychologues de France).

Once students have left the school system, those with little or no learning certification are serviced by another group of vocational counselors, occupational integration counselors, whose role is to help them find employment or to steer them toward a new training (Cohen-Scali, 2004). These counselors are mainly employed by two associative structures (financed from public funds) that were created in 1982 and whose missions are equivalent: "local missions" (ML, Missions Locales) and local reception offices for information and guidance (PAIO, Permanences d'Accueil d'Information et d'Orientation). A total of 7,000 occupational integration counselors work in 357 ML and 244 PAIO. The objective of these institutions, whose size is variable, is to help young people overcome difficulties that hinder their occupational and social inclusion. These professionals have generally graduated with a master's degree in social sciences. Even if they are organized in networks, these occupational integration counselors have an unclear identity, and many of them consider themselves as being at the intersection of several professions, such as social work, youth work, and psychology.

In addition to these two sets of counselors concerned with the public sector, lately there have been an increasing number of professionals working in private consultation companies offering school support and school and vocational counseling for students for a fee. For example, the press group L'Etudiant now offers vocational coaching.

Career Counseling for Adults

Specialized counselors work with employees or with work applicants who seek to be trained or want to change their career path. Two public institutions, founded in the 1960s, employ these professionals. The National Agency for Employment (ANPE, Agence Nationale Pour l'Emploi) comprises

862 local agencies and 17,000 employees, of whom 15,000 offer counseling services. These counselors inform and advise job applicants, age 25 and older, concerning transition to work, career development, employment search, and recruitment. They are also in charge of developing and implementing training courses, which could lead individuals in a process of transition to work toward sustainable employment. Therefore, these counselors rely on methodologies and steps that are often developed within the institution. These counselors, who generally have a university degree in human or social sciences, are recruited competitively and become civil servants (or equivalent). Similarly, the Employment Agency of Executives (APEC, Agence Pour l'Emploi des Cadres) provides this same service for executive work applicants.

The second important institution is the National Association for Adults Vocational Training (AFPA, Association Nationale pour la Formation Professionnelle des Adultes), which constitutes one of the largest centers of vocational training in France. Since its creation, the AFPA has developed a network of 10,000 employees, including more than 700 psychologists all over France in nearly 200 career counseling centers. The vocational guidance services of the AFPA are in charge of recruiting applicants for the trainings proposed by the AFPA and helping them search for employment. Career counseling services are offered by graduate-level psychologists.

Finally, we will mention the counseling practices offered by certain organizations specialized in training and occupational integration. Some of them function as service providers for public agencies (such as the ANPE) that subcontract part of their activities to these organizations (because of their difficulty in coping with the increasing charges for services associated with certain public schemes aimed at helping people in their occupational integration). Others were developed within the framework of a militant action and are intended for specific populations (e.g., women, immigrants). Finally, other public divisions also offer their own services: the Ministry of Justice created vocational guidance centers intended for prisoners, and the Ministry of Defense manages services for soldiers.

Recent Developments in Career Counseling for Adults

Three main changes have influenced adult vocational guidance in France. The two first changes are linked to new political guidelines on adult training. The third one is related to evolutions in companies' human resources management.

The first change corresponds to French innovative legislation about vocational training, which, since the 1970s, has provided a framework common to all career counseling professionals. The second influential force stems from the European Council meeting held in Lisbon in 2000, whereby an objective, set for 2010, is an increased employment rate, development of social cohesion, and greater emphasis on lifelong education and training (Tessaring & Wannan, 2004). Finally, the third change has to do with the increased development of counseling practices among certain company executives. A large number of enterprises provide support for specific employed populations that are perceived as important for their economic development: apprentices, new recruits, managers, and company creators.

In this context, two phenomena particularly marked the field of adult career counseling. On the one hand, since the 1980s, new laws in the field of vocational training—one on competencies elicitation career counseling (Bilan de Compétences) and another on validation of experiential learning (Validation des Acquis de l'Expérience)—deeply transformed the practices of vocational guidance in the public sector. In addition, certain companies started to become essential actors in their employees' career counseling. More and more company executives were encouraged to develop activities of career development counseling. These practices aim at helping employees to manage their occupational situation better and to develop new competences.

Counseling Practices Aiming at Recognizing and Validating Professional Competencies

The intervention named Competencies Elicitation Career Counseling (CECC) is based on law and several statutory orders initiated by authorities, unions, and management. It enables employees to analyze their abilities, skills, and motivations to build a career plan. It must be undertaken with the consent of the employee, who is also the sole recipient of the results. The employee is entitled to a 24-hour leave from work with no loss of salary. The expenses are covered by his or her firm or a continuing education fund, and the CECC session must take place in one of the 900 official centers.

A CECC procedure is composed of three steps: (1) a preliminary phase, which aims at reinforcing the involvement of the clients, clarifying their needs, and acquainting them with procedures; (2) an investigating phase to analyze the clients' motives, competencies, and professional and personal abilities through self-report measures and interviews, and to determine different possibilities in career development with the development of occupational knowledge; and (3) a final phase, during which the results are observed, the different projects are reviewed, and the steps of the selected project are defined. Since its creation in 1991, an average of 60,000 employees per year have gone through this process.

However, a wide variety of tools, methods, and activities are used, reflecting both the existence of different theoretical backgrounds and schools of thought, and the heterogeneous profiles of the counselors (Bernaud et al., 2007). The counselors offering these services must have a university degree, but it is seldom in vocational or counseling psychology.

Research has been performed on the effectiveness of the CECC procedures (see Gaudron & Croity-Belz, 2005, for a review). For instance, a longitudinal and experimental study analyzed the effects of the CECC intervention on several criteria such as participants' self-esteem, self-analysis, self-concept, and situation (work, training, or unemployment) (Bernaud, Gaudron, & Lemoine, 2006). Compared with a control group and measured at three time periods (pre- and postintervention and 6 months later), the positive effects of the intervention were significant. In fact, the effect size of all the criterion variables was .62 or greater, which is similar to the effects reported by meta-analytical studies carried out in the United States for career counseling outcomes (Whiston, Sexton, & Lasoff, 1998).

The validation of experiential learning (VEL) procedure aims at helping individuals valorize their experiential learning in relation to their professional expectations (Aubret, 2005)—as does the CECC intervention. The VEL procedure gives a right to any person (a law was passed in 2002) to obtain a diploma registered in the National Directory of Professional Qualifications (Répertoire National des Certifications Professionnelles) via a validation of his or her professional abilities. At present, it covers almost 15,000 diplomas, including 11,000 for higher education (Centre Inffo, 2005). As for CECC, an employee can benefit from the same 24-hour leave and guarantees.

The VEL procedure depends on various institutions (Public Department of Education, Public Department of Health and Human Service, etc.). Nevertheless, the main steps are relatively similar regardless of the diploma sought. The first step—called information counseling—helps the candidate develop his or her VEL plan and choose the most suitable diploma. In the second step, the candidate builds a report to describe his or her activities and to produce the relevant documents attesting to at least 3 years of experience directly related to the content of the diploma he or she expects to obtain. A validation step follows, in which an examining board assesses the candidate's report. In most cases, an interview with the candidate takes place as well. The board can deliver a full or an incomplete diploma or no diploma at all. In the case of an incomplete validation, the candidate has to obtain additional training to receive a diploma.

Various institutions offer support (individual counseling interviews or group sessions) for candidates to build up their report and be prepared for the interview with the examining board. Unlike the counselors carrying out the CECC intervention, the ones who work in these institutions are not required to have a degree. There is very little research on VEL, but authorities regularly provide statistics. For example, in 2005, 21,379 reports were examined by the boards of public departments (Health, Education, etc.). In 2007, 59% of candidates received a full diploma, whereas 12% received no validation at all.

Counseling Practices Within Companies

Since the 1990s, human resource departments in some companies have offered career counseling services for their employees. The main objective is helping employees face increasingly difficult work situations and enabling them to remain in the labor market (De Peretti, 2003). These counseling services are generally implemented by human resources professionals, who have varied job titles (career counselors, human resource assistants, etc.) and education (e.g., law, management, psychology).

In addition to human resource departments performing these new functions, some company executives are increasingly being made to add career development counseling to the activities of their daily work. These services are intended either for the employees of their company or others, such as company creators and work applicants. These counseling activities involve three new professional figures: the tutor, the godfather, and the company creation assistant.

The Tutor

The company tutor has been in existence since 1982, following an interprofessional agreement. The tutor is an employee appointed by the company for guiding and supporting young trainees or vocational school students in practical training. In addition to teaching and management, tutors have an essential function of socialization and providing social accompaniment to youth. They must promote learning of standards of behavior in a group, clarify the rules of collective life in a professional environment, and initiate new recruits into employment (Gérard, Steiner, Zettelmeier, & Lauterbach, 1998). Thus, a significant part of the tutor's time is devoted to career development counseling: providing information about occupational opportunities, clarifying rules of promotion, and identifying the young trainee's assets and weaknesses. The tutor, however, is not specialized in human relations issues; he or she

is a specialist in a given professional field. The function of the tutor has been the subject of much discussion regarding the competencies that tutoring requires and the training it calls for (training of tutors that the official texts have recommended since 1992). (See, e.g., Guillerme, Chatelet, & Guegen, 1997.)

The Godfather

The godfather function appeared in France around 1993, following a report on the difficulties of certain young people without a diploma (young people of the suburbs and young people born of immigrants) to find employment. The godfather is an experienced worker, whose purpose is to voluntarily help a young person having difficulties in finding a job. This generally unpaid function is performed outside a company but within the framework of organizations specializing in occupational integration of youth. The godfathers are mainly small company managers, company executives, trade union employees, or professionals from the occupational integration and training sectors. These professionals must develop competencies in the field of psychological counseling and career development. They guide youth in their occupational choices by helping them look for information on trades, analyze their strengths and weaknesses, and develop professional plans. They also offer emotional support as well as a regular and continuous avenue for talk (Damerval, 2003). Nevertheless, godfathers sometimes feel incompetent to carry out these counseling tasks and to interact with young people, who can sometimes appear to be aggressive or, in contrast, poorly motivated. Up to now, very little work has been carried out on this new function in France.

The Company Creation Assistant

The field of sustainable and solidarity economics has developed considerably during the past 5 years. Within this framework, certain people seek to share their knowledge and their competencies. In France, since 1983, an original concept of supporting company creation has emerged with the Club of Investors for an Alternative and Local Management and Solidarity

Savings (CIGALES, Club d'Investisseurs pour une Gestion Alternative et Locale et l'Epargne Solidaire) (Russo, 2007). CIGALES consists of groups of 5 to 20 people who contribute part of their savings for the establishment of a company within the framework of solidarity economy. Each member participates for 5 years and saves between 7 and 450 euros each month. This sum, put to common use, is invested in the creation of companies with a high social value, which the club then sponsors. During the past 20 years, 400 companies have been created. They consist of employees, company managers, liberal professionals, elected officials, retired people, and so on. The projects can be quite diverse: creation of an insertion company (an economically viable enterprise, the activity of which is organized specifically to facilitate the reintegration of individuals in a difficult situation— the company gets public funding intended only to help these persons in their career development), a store for equitable clothing distribution, and a company for nonallergenic food, to name just a few.

The activities of the members of these clubs consist of voluntary "technical aid" (assistance with the management and organization of information, drafting communications, accounting and financial management, etc.) and psychosocial counseling. Psychosocial counseling aims, for instance, to help the company creators to manage their stress, analyze their situation, locate people or institutions that can help them, evaluate the difference between what is envisaged and what is carried out, and argue, convince, and interact in a professional framework. Certain members of these clubs can receive a brief training in listening and group dynamic techniques.

CONCLUSION

In conclusion, we would like to highlight five current issues in France. First, there has clearly been a significant rise in counseling activities in France during the last decades of the 20th century. This rise can be observed in all counseling fields (e.g., health, personal relationships, family, work and social integration, career development).

Second, there are a number of very notable innovations in the fields of transition to work and career

development in particular. For example, there are the CECC and VEL interventions and the development of schemes and programs aimed at helping youth in their transitions to work.

Third, characterizing all counseling activities (and thus not only those related to employment and careers) is the development of new activities, which sometimes give rise to new professional functions. These functions often lie within the scope of existing trades, of which they form a new dimension (which is the case with tutors, for example), or carried out through voluntary help or militant actions (as in the case of CIGALES).

Fourth, in relation to the mode of emergence of these new forms of intervention, some of the new counseling activities do not refer to an established corpus of knowledge. To put it bluntly—a great majority of the people carrying out counseling activities in France still remain without any specific training in this field and appear to be unaware of the fact that, for many years, some reference knowledge has existed in the fields of counseling psychology and vocational psychology. However, in recent years, many books and short essays about counseling have been published. Nevertheless, the majority of these books deal more with the concepts of support (e.g., Paul, 2004) or coaching rather than the concept of counseling (see, e.g., Moral & Angel, 2006). Of course, there are a few exceptions (e.g., Lhotellier, 2001, on counseling and Guichard & Huteau, 2006, on career counseling).

Finally, there is an ignorance of counseling psychology and vocational psychology in the psychology departments of the French universities. Indeed, it is often in the departments of educational sciences or human resources management that concerns related to the practices of counseling can be found. The question of counselor training, particularly of the new counselors not trained in the human sciences, constitutes a major economic, social, and human stake. In France, with rare exceptions, a person receiving counseling services is guaranteed little concerning the quality of the interventions offered. Lacroix (2004), for instance, underlined the existence of drifting tendencies: Some cults or fundamentalist movements have intervened in counseling practices at the expense of scientific approaches. For this reason, it appears essential to constitute in France, in the next few years, a professional organization similar to Division 17 of the American Psychological Association or Division 16 of the International Association of Applied Psychology. Today, such an organization seems to be necessary not only for the development of rigorous interventions but also research and debates on the processes, the stakes, the objectives, and the finalities of the career counseling profession.

REFERENCES

Aubret, J. (2005). Accompagnement éducatif et place de l'expérience [Educative counseling and the place of the experience]. In S. Gaulier & E. Golhen (Eds.), *Accompagnement et pédagogie de l'alternance* [Counseling and pedagogy of alternation] (pp. 14–24). Paris: MFR éditions.

Bernaud, J.-L., Cohen-Scali, V., & Guichard, J. (2007). Counseling psychology in France: A paradoxical situation. *Applied Psychology: An International Review, 56,* 131–151.

Bernaud, J.-L., Gaudron, J.-P., & Lemoine, C. (2006). Effects of career counseling on French adults: An experimental study. *Career Development Quarterly, 54,* 242–255.

Centre Inffo. (2005). *La validation des acquis d'expérience: Mode d'emploi* [The competencies elicitation career counseling: Directions for use]. Paris: Centre Inffo-DGEFP.

Cohen-Scali, V. (2004). *Les métiers en psychologie sociale et du travail* [Working with social and work psychology diploma]. Paris: In Press Editions.

Damerval, C. (2003). *Autour du parrainage* [About work godfathering]. Paris: L'Harmattan.

Déchaux, J. H. (2007). La famille en mutation: imbroglio ou nouvelle donne [Changes in families: Imbroglio or new deal?]. In O. Galland & Y. Lemel (Eds.), *La société française* [French Society] (pp. 73–117). Paris: Armand Colin.

De Peretti, J. M. (2003). *Gestion des Ressources humaines* [Human resource management]. Paris: Vuibert.

Gaudron, J.-P., & Croity-Belz, S. (2005). *Bilan de compétences (BC): Etats des recherches sur les processus psychologiques en jeu* [Competencies elicitation career counseling: State of research on the psychological process implied]. *Psychologie du Travail et des Organisations, 11,* 101–114.

Gérard, F., Steiner, K., Zettelmeier, W., & Lauterbach, U. (1998). *Profils professionnels, formation et pratiques des tuteurs en entreprise en Allemagne, Autriche, Espagne et France. Rapport de synthèse* [Professional profiles and practices of tutors of enterprises in Germany, Austria, Spain, and France. Synthesis report]. Saint-Denis, Paris: Centre Inffo.

Guichard, J., & Huteau, M. (2005). *L'orientation scolaire et professionnelle* [School and vocational guidance]. Paris: Dunod.

Guichard, J., & Huteau, M. (2006). *Psychologie de l'orientation* (2ème édition revue) [Counseling psychology, 2nd Rev ed.]. Paris: Dunod.

Guillerme, A., Chatelet, G., & Guegen, E. (1997). *Guide méthodologique de l'alternance à l'usage des formateurs et des tuteurs d'entreprises* [Methodological booklet on alternation for trainers and tutors of enterprises]. Paris: La Documentation Française.

Lacroix, M. (2004). *Le développement personnel: Du potentiel humain à la pensée positive* [Personal development: From human potential to positive thought]. Paris: Flammarion.

Lhotellier, A. (2001). *Tenir conseil; délibérer pour agir* [Take counsel: Deliberating for action]. Paris: Seli Arslan.

Moral, M., & Angel, P. (2006). *Coaching: Outils et pratiques* [Coaching: Tools and practices]. Paris: Armand Collin.

Paul, M. (2004). *L'accompagnement: une posture professionnelle spécifique* [Counseling: A specific professional attitude]. Paris: L'Harmattan.

Russo, P. D. (2007). *Les CIGALES: notre épargne, levier pour entreprendre autrement* [The CIGALES: Our savings, lever to undertake]. Hautes-Alpes, Gap: Editions Yves Michel.

Tessaring, M., & Wannan, J. (2004). *La formation et l'enseignement professionnels: une clef pour l'avenir. Etude de Maastricht* [Professional training and teaching: A key for the future. Study of Maastricht]. Luxembourg: Office des publications officielles des Communautés européennes.

Whiston, S. C., Sexton, T. L., & Lasoff, D. L. (1998). Career-intervention outcomes: A replication and extension of Oliver and Spokane (1988). *Journal of Counseling Psychology, 45,* 150–165.

24

Counseling in Countries Experiencing Political, Cultural, and Economic Transition

The Case of the Former USSR

Консультативная Работа в Странах
Проходящих Политические, Культурные и
Экономические Изменения: Пример Бывшего СССР

OKSANA YAKUSHKO,
TANYA RAZZHAVAIKINA, AND SHARON HORNE

The fall of the Soviet Union resulted in extraordinary changes in the lives of millions of people. These changes have been especially significant for the field of counseling. This chapter provides an overview of the historical and social realities that have influenced Soviet and post-Soviet psychology and counseling in the countries that constituted the Union of Soviet Socialist Republics (USSR) and changes that are occurring within the mental health field. Throughout this chapter, psychology is referenced typically as an academic discipline, whereas counseling is related to the training and practice of applied psychology. Although counseling psychology as a specific subfield of psychology does not formally exist within the former USSR, the training and practice of counseling in it more closely resembles the field of counseling psychology in the United States than it does other areas of psychology. Thus, our focus is primarily on the history and current training and practice of counseling within the former USSR. Additionally, this chapter highlights the unique focus of counselors and psychologists on addressing human trafficking.

BRIEF DESCRIPTION OF THE GEOGRAPHIC AND CULTURAL DIVERSITY OF THE FORMER SOVIET COUNTRIES

Before its breakup, the USSR was the largest country in the world, with one of the most diverse populations. It spanned 11 time zones and included individuals from more than 130 ethnic groups, who spoke more than half of the known languages in the world. Although individuals in Western countries tended to refer to the Soviet Union as "Russia" and people from the USSR as "Russians," such references were not only inaccurate but also offensive to a vast majority of individuals who were neither ethnic Russians nor residents of the Russian Federation (or Republic) (Yakushko & Razzhavaikina, 2007).

The late 1980s and early 1990s brought tremendous changes to this union of the republics, which had been joined by the ideals of socialism and communism. Initiated by the USSR's General Secretary, Mikhail Gorbachev, *perestroika* or "rebuilding" of the economic socialist system by retreating from a centralized system did not succeed. Instead it ended in popular revolts in many parts of the country and, later, a military coup. A majority of the republics broke away from Russia in more than just political or administrative ways. Many of the newly independent states experienced revivals of cultural and religious nationalism that demanded a clear dissolution of the bonds with Russia.

The former USSR included 15 republics, which became independent countries following the events of the late 1980s and early 1990s: Russia, Belarus, Ukraine, Moldova, Tajikistan, Kazakhstan, Turkmenistan, Uzbekistan, Kyrgyzstan, Azerbaijan, Armenia, Georgia, Latvia, Lithuania, and Estonia. The majority of cultures within the former USSR can be described as collectivistic and family oriented. For example, the vast majority of individuals within these communities remain tied to their cities and homes, and it is common for several generations within families to live together. In addition, spiritual worldviews and practices may be openly discussed in a public sphere. It is imperative to note that the former USSR republics and their cultures are far from homogeneous. Russia, or more accurately the Russian Federation, still represents a vast landmass and a great number of culturally diverse people. Although ethnic Russians are the cultural majority, the country also has individuals from indigenous groups such as the Inuits and Koreans. The mobility of people within the former Soviet Union as well as contacts with other prosocialist countries, especially from Africa, also contributed to the ethnic and racial diversification of the former Soviet nations. Furthermore, within each of the former Soviet states, people differ in terms of their religious practices, socioeconomic class, and rural versus urban home environments. For example, Russia, Belarus, and Ukraine are countries with Slavic linguistic and historical heritage. Moldova is also located on the western edge of the former USSR and shares linguistic and cultural similarities with Romania. Tajikistan, Kazakhstan, Turkmenistan, Uzbekistan, Azerbaijan, and Kyrgyzstan are located in the south-central and the south Caucasus regions of the former USSR. These nations are culturally close to both Middle Eastern and Asian cultures and have recently experienced a revival of Islam. Georgia and Armenia, the other two former Soviet republics in the Caucasus region, also share some cultural characteristics with Middle Eastern and Asian cultures but are affiliated with the Christian Eastern Orthodox tradition. Last, Latvia, Lithuania, and Estonia, typically known as the Baltic states, retained more connections with Western Europe and are culturally and linguistically more similar to their Scandinavian neighbors.

Despite the remarkable diversity of its people and civilizations, the former USSR brought together these various cultures under one banner, that of communism. Their health and school systems were governed by the same centralized government regulations. Last, the mass media were typically uniform in presenting cultural messages, such as those about mental health and counseling. Thus, individuals from the former Soviet Union may share worldviews that uniquely distinguish them from all other groups of people around the world.

HISTORY OF COUNSELING IN THE FORMER USSR

Although psychology as a science was well developed in pre-revolutionary Russia and during the Soviet era, which lasted from 1917 to 1991, counseling and psychotherapy were not commonly available or sought in Soviet times. Counseling and psychotherapy as practices were and continue to be viewed primarily as applied subjects, whereas psychology was and continues to be typically associated with biological sciences and medicine. The primary setting for mental health services was medical, and it was controlled by psychiatry (Roth, 1994). Nevertheless, counseling practice has a relatively long-standing tradition in the former Soviet Union. Prior to the Bolshevik Revolution of 1917, individual psychotherapy and especially psychoanalytically influenced counseling were highly developed in Russia. Many of Freud's works were translated into Russian, and Freud himself paid great attention to Russia (Sosland, 1997). Starting in the 1930s, however, the work of Freud and later other Western counseling scholars and practitioners was prohibited and considered reactionary (Havenaar, Meijler-Iljina, van den Bout, & Melnikov, 1998). At that time, critiquing ideas in psychology became common. The major criticism focused on the fact that psychological ideas did not help the Communist Party raise "socially appropriate" personality characteristics (such as job effectiveness) in Soviet citizens (Nalchajian, Jeshmaridian, & Takooshian, 1997). Books and articles on Western counseling practices were distributed only illegally, and information about Western mental health ideas could only be learned through "black market" books. Moreover, many psychologists who showed interest in psychology outside what was officially sanctioned by the former Soviet government lost their jobs and, on occasion, their lives.

Scientific approaches to counseling remained somewhat undeveloped. Vasilyeva (2006) described the main schools of counseling and psychotherapy that became active during the Soviet times. Specifically, she highlighted that the first school of psychotherapy was based on Pavlovian principles regarding brain-behavior patterns. The Kharkov School of Psychotherapy at the Ukrainian State Institute for the Postgraduation Training of Medical Doctors was the first department offering training in counseling within the USSR (founded in 1962). The main methods of psychotherapy used and developed in this school were focused on medically based hypnosis practices.

During the Soviet era, individuals with mental illness were treated solely by psychiatrists within a medical setting. Mental illness was typically associated with prison-like mental institutions, where psychobiological treatments of political dissidence or religious differences were common (Daw, 2002). The "paternalistic models of the State and of psychiatry" (Korinteli, 2003, p. 374) led many of the clients to see their psychiatrists and counselors solely as figures representing Soviet authorities. Psychiatrists were not trusted with less clinically severe counseling issues such as mood disorders (Mokhovikov, 1994), and less severe difficulties, if treated, were addressed by medical professionals through a focus on psychosomatic concerns (Roth, 1994) as well as rational (e.g., convincing, explaining, distracting) and suggestive (e.g., hypnosis) techniques (Havenaar et al., 1998).

Additionally, alternative treatments based on beliefs in energies and spirituality were severely restricted under the Soviet scientific atheism and thus were underground. For example, one of the common causes of bad mental health was believed to be a "bad or evil eye," a type of negative energy inflicted by others on a suffering individual. The treatment by medicine women or men could include listening to the person's concerns, asking for a detailed family and relationship history, scanning the person's body for bad energies with hands or sacred objects, and giving advice on how to deal with particular difficulties. In addition, the indigenous healers were likely to suggest herbs, spiritual practices, and cognitive exercises, such as practicing positive affirmations or reciting a protective prayer or statement to help their clients heal from a particular mental illness. For example, Siberian shamans addressed mental health difficulties during Soviet times especially by supporting the cultural and psychological survival of victims of Stalinist purges, which resulted in the death and imprisonment of an estimated 20 to 50 million people (Conquest, 1986; Yakushko, 2005). During the Soviet era, seeking mental health help from these nonofficial and non–medically based healers appeared to be more appealing to individuals who were suspicious of the role that psychiatrists represented. In addition, those who resided in rural rather than metropolitan areas were more likely to have access to traditional healers rather than to medical doctors.

RECENT DEVELOPMENTS IN COUNSELING IN THE FORMER SOVIET STATES

After the fall of the Soviet Union in 1991, the former USSR and its people have experienced tremendous political, social, and economic transitions. These transitions have negatively affected the medical infrastructure, which is the primary setting for mental health services. Psychiatry, which is still viewed as a primary source for mental health management, has continued its focus on psychosomatic treatment of psychological difficulties, but the larger society has remained ambivalent toward the treatment of mental illness (Roth, 1994). For example, many people can recall the times when psychiatric counseling included forcible treatments through medications and hypnosis to control and change individuals' political views or religious practices (Daw, 2002).

On the other hand, since the mid-1990s, interest in counseling has been booming (Havenaar et al., 1998). Universities and colleges are increasingly offering training in counseling in addition to traditional scientific psychobiology. For example, in the last decade of the 20th century and in the beginning of the 21st century, Makarov played an important role in the development of the Russian school of psychotherapy and developed training courses and advanced trainings for psychotherapy in different regions of Russia (Vasilyeva, 2006). The scientific journal *Voprosy Psihologii* (*Psychological Inquiry*),

produced in Russia, became more active in publishing a wide range of scholarly works by Russian-speaking psychologists. Interest in behavioral and cognitive modification therapies has decreased, and new schools that emphasize psychoanalytic, Jungian, transpersonal, Gestalt, humanistic, neurolinguistic programming (NLP), body-focused, art, and music therapies have been highly popular (Havenaar et al., 1998; Sosland, 1997). Havenaar and his colleagues suggested that such interest in nondirective, insight-oriented counseling methods reflects the societal movement away from what are perceived as authoritarian therapeutic traditions associated with the Soviet era. Moreover, these approaches are more consistent with many cultural traditions within the former USSR that emphasize the role of relationships, spirituality, and community. For example, in describing the rise of interest in psychology in Russia, Brothers (1993) emphasized the key significance of the concept of "Russian soul," which she related to a yearning toward higher spiritual commitments and truths found among many Russians.

A particularly unique response to the past authoritarian models of dealing with mental health difficulties is the growing number of nongovernmental organizations that address specific mental health needs. Issues such as domestic violence, trafficking of women, and rights of individuals with severe mental illnesses are addressed through individual and group counseling by centers, organizations, and active hotlines (see Horne, 1999). Increasingly, people who are in need of mental health services reach out to hotlines, often supported by grants or volunteers, to talk with someone about their concerns. With only a few hotlines on specialized issues (e.g., domestic violence, sexual assault, gay and lesbian issues), hotline counselors find themselves managing a wide array of mental health concerns. This has caused many institutes and centers to begin to offer counseling training, both from Western-trained therapists and from local centers that have emerged to address mental health needs (e.g., the Gestalt Institute).

In addition, many of the nondirective approaches to counseling are based on Western theories, which appeal to both lay and professional individuals from the former USSR because of the general influence of Westernization (Havenaar et al., 1998). In metropolitan areas, an interest in counseling has been on the rise in part due to the influx of Western values through Western media. For example, magazines such as the *Ladies Home Journal* are now printed in many native languages, with content similar to that of their Western parent-magazines (e.g., advice on how to choose a therapist, mental health, sex, and diet). Counseling is often presented as a new and high-status practice; that is, individuals who are wealthy and Westernized can avail themselves of these new counseling services at a growing number of private counseling centers. Counseling costs at these centers may be as much as US$100 a session (by comparison, a typical monthly salary for an individual may be approximately between US$200 and $300).

Individuals also continue to seek mental health services from more traditional indigenous healers. Many psychiatrists trained during the Soviet era have abandoned their previous medical focus and have turned their practice to indigenous healing, including guided meditation and psychological imagery. These renewed and modified indigenous traditions have become more visible through a growing media attention to their practices. For example, most daily Ukrainian papers include sections on traditional healing methods that can help individuals deal with issues such as anxiety, depression, substance abuse, and relational concerns (e.g., divorce, family conflict, intergenerational misunderstanding) (Yakushko, 2005). The methods presented in the paper typically include advice about protective prayers and charms or herbal remedies.

It is important to note that the growing interest in counseling training and mental health services in the former USSR, however, has not resulted in a rapid change in tendencies and attitudes toward seeking professional help. Given all the aforementioned historical and cultural influences, it is not surprising that many individuals within the former USSR continue to hold negative stereotypes of mental health services and may not choose counseling as a valuable and appropriate option to deal with their emotional and relational concerns. Because most

cultures within the former USSR can be described as collectivistic and family oriented, mental health support is almost always first sought within a close circle of families and friends. Individuals are also more likely to speak with their medical doctor or to seek help from indigenous healers prior to deciding to engage in counseling. In addition, the public continues to lack information about counseling as a field, and the field itself tends to suffer from a lack of organization, structure, laws, and regulations.

Thus, although it is rapidly emerging, counseling as a profession in the former USSR continues to face a number of profound challenges. Training in psychology within traditional academic institutions remains heavily focused on psychobiology and psychological theories and not clinical applications. Moreover, due to the lack of financial support and other factors, universities that provide training in counseling do not typically have a training clinic where students can practice theoretical principles they learn in classes. Additionally, there seems to be a lack of connection between universities and organizations that provide counseling to the public. This disconnect results in very limited opportunities for students to have field placement or externship experiences prior to graduation. Training in applied counseling is unregulated and widely varied. A person can claim to be a counselor or a psychologist after completing several months of a course in psychology as well as after a 5-year educational process through training at universities or institutes (Daw, 2002). No licensing regulations exist. It is not uncommon in cities to see someone seated with a sign reading "Counseling Services by a Psychologist," which invites people passing by to take a seat on a bench and receive a brief "counseling" session for a small fee. Across the former USSR, programs in counseling have no accreditation process, and to date there are no ethical statutes or regulations that govern the work of those who practice counseling. Because of this lack of standards, abuses can easily occur, and there is no mechanism for educating professionals or imposing sanctions against counselors' nonprofessional or harmful behavior. Anecdotal evidence indicates that dual and sexual relationships between therapists and their clients are not uncommon and are encouraged by some counselors. Last, counseling help is often available only to those who can afford high fees because the former USSR, with its history of socialized free medicine, does not have a developed system of third-party payments for health or mental health (Daw, 2002).

WORKING WITH VICTIMS OF HUMAN TRAFFICKING

Although sex trafficking is not a new phenomenon, it is only recently that it was acknowledged as a significant problem (Monzini, 2005). A major factor in the explosion of the international sex trade, in the late 20th century and after it, is attributed by many to the globalization movement sweeping the world (International Organization for Migration [IOM], 2005). Women from the former USSR constitute some of the highest numbers of women forced or lured into sexual slavery—legally (through mail-order marriages) or illegally, by various means that include violence or entrapment (kidnapping; promises of lucrative employment or glamorous careers). For example, between 1991 and 1998, 500,000 Ukrainian women were trafficked to Western countries, and the corresponding number has dramatically increased in the past decade (Huges & Denisova, 2003; Scholes, 1999).

Women who are entrapped in sex-trafficking rings often come from small towns or villages, in other words, depressed rural or semirural communities (Skrobanek, Nataya, & Chutima, 1997). Paradoxically, however, women coming from higher rungs of the economic and social ladder are increasingly inclined to succumb to the promise of a glamorous, luxurious, or more prestigious lifestyle. These women prove willing, even eager, to take risks to reach that promised utopia. Once sold, lured, or tricked into the industry, women are brutally forced into prostitution: They can be raped, bludgeoned, even starved (Monzini, 2005). Women who are rescued from such harrowing situations are often arrested and deported, returned to the very communities they sought to escape, which are likely to shame them for their choices (Huges & Denisova, 2003).

In countries such as Ukraine, the response to trafficking has been fueled through networking by multiple agencies. For example, multiple local, national, and international organizations that have a counseling focus have conducted preventative work by organizing media campaigns as well as school visits to educate youth about the risks associated with participation in "international job opportunities." These preventative campaigns refer individuals to agencies such as LaStrada, which offers phone help lines to verify whether job advertising agencies are legitimate. Their hotline volunteers are trained in counseling skills and supervised by psychologists in providing phone-based counseling for callers who may be vulnerable to being lured into trafficking situations.

In addition, a network of organizations that provide counseling and rehabilitation to victims of trafficking has been developed across many post-Soviet states, especially Ukraine and Russia (Bezpalcha, 2003). These nongovernmental organizations usually include psychologists and counselors as well as lay counselors and often work in partnerships with organizations such as the IOM and the United Nations (UN). Counseling issues addressed by these organizations usually include psychosomatic reactions to trauma, psychological concerns such as posttraumatic stress disorder, depression, anxiety, psychoactive substance abuse and dependence, social and vocational adjustment, and physical consequences of sexually transmitted diseases or injuries (IOM, 2004).

The challenges in providing psychological services to victims of human trafficking are many. Because of the lack of a broad system and established tradition of counseling and psychotherapy across the former USSR, many communities, especially in rural areas, cannot provide any assistance to women and girls who have experienced trafficking. Where such services exist, burnout among professionals is common (IOM, 2004), and training or continuing education resources are minimal. As the campaign to eradicate trafficking and educate the public continues, a greater number of individuals in many communities across the former USSR are beginning to come forth as victims of trafficking, whereas psychological resources for them remain quite limited. However, it is often those individuals who are trained in psychology and counseling who are developing new and innovative ways to prevent and rehabilitate those who were trafficked.

CONCLUSION

Psychology and counseling in the former USSR has a long, varied, and unique history. The political and social changes that occurred after the fall of the socialist government also heralded a new era for the field of psychology and counseling. We believe that interest in counseling will continue to grow and better-trained counselors will provide much needed help for mental health services, such as those for victims of trafficking. As we have discussed, this relatively new field of counseling is facing tremendous challenges, such as the rehabilitation of victims of human trafficking. These developments, however, will continue to be hampered by a lack of professional training programs and organizations, as well as ethical standards. As countries of the former USSR recover from their periods of political transition, we expect to see a greater number of innovative and exciting psychology and counseling–related developments emerge.

REFERENCES

Bezpalcha, R. (2003). *Helping survivors of human trafficking*. Kiev, Ukraine: Winrock International.

Brothers, B. J. (1993). From Russia, with soul. *Psychology Today*. Retrieved December 20, 2007, from http://wwwpsychologytoday.com/articles/pto-19930101

Conquest, R. (1986). *The harvest of sorrows: Soviet collectivization and the terror-famine*. New York: Oxford University Press.

Daw, J. (2002). Russian psychology fights to bring psychotherapy to a needy but wary public. *Monitor in Psychology, 33*, 23–25.

Havenaar, J. M., Meijler-Iljina, L., van den Bout, J., & Melnikov, A. V. (1998). Psychotherapy in Russia. *American Journal of Psychotherapy, 52*, 501–514.

Horne, S. (1999). Domestic violence in Russia. *American Psychologist, 54*, 55–61.

Huges, D. M., & Denisova, T. (2003). The transnational political criminal nexus in trafficking of women from Ukraine. *Trends in Organized Crime, 6*, 47–64.

International Organization for Migration. (2004). *The mental health aspects in trafficking in human beings*. Geneva, Switzerland: Author.

International Organization for Migration. (2005). *Second annual report on victims of trafficking in South-East Europe*. Geneva, Switzerland: Author. Retrieved June 15, 2007, from http://www.iom.int/jahia/

Korinteli, R. (2003). On the psycho-social conditions of psychotherapy in post-Soviet Georgia. *Journal of Analytical Psychology, 48*, 371–380.

Mokhovikov, A. N. (1994). Suicide in the Ukraine. *Crisis, 15*, 137.

Monzini, P. (2005). *Sex traffic: Prostitution, crime and exploitation* (P. Camiller, Trans.). New York: Zed Books.

Nalchajian, A. A., Jeshmaridian, S., & Takooshian, H. (1997). Post-Soviet psychology: What is ahead? *Eye on Psi Chi, 1*, 22–24.

Roth, L. H. (1994). Access to and utilization of mental health services in the former Soviet Union. *Journal of Russian and Eastern European Psychiatry, 27*, 6–18.

Scholes, R. J. (1999). *The "mail order brides" industry: Its impact on the U.S. immigration* (Report No. COW-8-P-0233). Washington, DC: Immigration and Naturalization Service. Retrieved November 10, 2004, from http://www.uscis.gov/files/article/MobRept_AppendixA.pdf

Skrobanek, S., Nataya, B., & Chutima, J. (1997). *The traffic in women: Human realities of the international sex trade*. London: Zed.

Sosland, A. (1997). The state of psychotherapy in Moscow. *International Journal of Psychotherapy, 2*, 229–234.

Vasilyeva, A. V. (2006). The development of Russian psychotherapy as an independent medical discipline in the second half of the twentieth century. *International Journal of Mental Health, 34*(4), 31–38.

Yakushko, O. (2005). Mental health counseling in Ukraine. *Journal of Mental Health Counseling, 27*, 161–167.

Yakushko, O., & Razzhavaikina, T. I. (2007). Counseling international students from the former USSR. In H. D. Singaravelu & M. Pope (Eds.), *A handbook for counseling international students in the United States* (pp. 273–282). Alexandria, VA: American Counseling Association.

25

Psychology and Counseling in Greece

Rapid Contemporary Development
in the Context of a Glorious Past

Η Ψυχολογία και η Συμβουλευτική στην Ελλάδα:
Ραγδαία σύγχρονη εξέλιξη στο πλαίσιο ενός ένδοξου παρελθόντος.

GEORGIOS K. LAMPROPOULOS AND ANASTASSIOS STALIKAS

Although ancient Greece is often regarded as the cradle of Western civilization, which gave birth to many contemporary political, philosophical, scientific, cultural, and psychological concepts, the modern history and current status of psychology and counseling in Greece is perhaps less well-known. Indeed, psychology and mental health have grown rapidly in the past two decades. This chapter begins with an overview of the demographic, historical, and cultural background of the country to set the context for the description of the fields of psychology, counseling, and mental health. A summary of the history of psychology, as well as the current status of undergraduate and graduate training in psychology and psychotherapy, is provided. A discussion of professional issues follows, along with an analysis of the mental health system and the provision of psychological services. The chapter concludes with a description of

psychological testing and psychological research, as well as priorities and recommendations for improving psychology and counseling in Greece.

COUNTRY BACKGROUND AND CULTURAL INFORMATION

Basic Statistics

Greece (Hellenic Republic) is situated in the southeastern edge of Europe, at the crossroads of Europe, Asia, and Africa. It occupies an area of 131,957 square kilometers (51,146 square miles) and has a population of approximately 11 million (National Statistical Service of Greece, 2006). Its territory is largely mountainous, with coastal plains, an extensive coastline, and more than 3,000 islands. The climate is temperate/Mediterranean, with mild

345

winters and hot dry summers. The majority of the population resides in coastal cities (only 25% lives in rural areas), with approximately 4 million inhabitants living in the Greater Athens Area (National Statistical Service of Greece, 2006).

Historical and Political Background

Greece has a long history of thousands of years that expands from antiquity to the Hellenistic and Roman times, to the Byzantine Empire and the occupation by the Ottoman Empire, all of which exerted cultural influences on the country and its people. Following the war of independence in 1821 against the Ottoman Empire, and the subsequent involvement in the Balkan wars and World Wars I and II, the modern Greek state has evolved into its current geographical borders. Politically, Greece experienced a tumultuous 20th century, with two military dictatorships (1936–1941 and 1967–1974) and a civil war (1946–1949). Since 1974, the restored modern parliamentary democracy has provided political stability, and Greeks report the highest interest in politics among young adults in Europe (Flash Eurobarometer, 2007).

Economy and Society

The Greek society and economy have significantly grown in the past several decades, with Greece joining the European Union (EU) in 1981. The economy is primarily based on the service sector and secondarily on manufacturing and agriculture. Presently, the Greek population is employed in trade (14%), agriculture/livestock (13%), manufacturing (12%), construction (8%), real estate/finance (8%), public administration/defense (7%), tourism (6%), transport/communication (6%), education (6%), health care (4%), and other services (3%), with unemployment at 9% (National Statistical Service of Greece, 2006). Greece ranks high (24th out of 177 countries worldwide) on the Human Development Index, a measure of well-being that combines assessments of life expectancy, education/literacy, and standards of living (United Nations Development Program, 2007). It also ranks 22nd on a similar but broader index of quality of life that includes additional factors, such as

family/community life, climate, job security, political freedom/stability, and gender equality (Economist Intelligence Unit, 2005).

Education

The educational system is unified, national, and run by the state. Free at all levels, it has a structure similar to those of other Western educational systems (e.g., primary, secondary, and tertiary). Entrance in state universities is achieved via a national examination. Higher education is strongly valued, which often creates high parental expectations and pressure for their children to succeed academically (Hatzichristou, Polychroni, & Georgouleas, 2007).

Culture and Diversity

The official language of the country is Greek, and 98% of Greeks identify themselves as Greek Orthodox in their religious beliefs. The Greek Orthodox Church has historically played a major role in preserving the Greek culture and language and continues to have a significant influence on people's life in the present day. In fact, the religious beliefs of Greeks are among the strongest in the EU (Special Eurobarometer, 2005). Although the Greek population has been largely homogeneous in terms of ethnicity, language, and religion, in the past two or three decades there have been a significant and diverse number of Greek expatriates or individuals of Greek descent who have returned to Greece from a variety of Western and Eastern European countries (Sidiropoulou-Dimakakou, 2003). Furthermore, a large number of economic immigrants (and political refugees) from the Balkans, Asia, and Africa have moved to Greece, creating a more diverse picture in the contemporary Greek workforce (15–20% immigrants), schools (9% children of immigrants), and society (7% noncitizens; Baldwin-Edwards, 2004; Hatzichristou et al., 2007; Psalti, 2007; Sidiropoulou-Dimakakou, 2003).

Cultural and Family Values

Greek society is thought to be in the midpoint in terms of a collectivist versus individualist orientation (i.e., emphasis on individual vs. family/group values and goals) and moving toward the latter (Georgas, 1989, 1991). The traditional extended and nuclear Greek family has been patriarchal, typically with the father being the breadwinner and the mother being the housewife (Mylonas, Gari, Giotsa, Pavlopoulos, & Panagiotopoulou, 2006). However, with the support of gender equality legislation enacted during the past several decades and various socioeconomic changes, the position of women in the family and society has changed (Mylonas et al., 2006). Currently, Greece ranks 24th in the world in gender-related development (i.e., gender equality in life expectancy, education, and income), and 37th in gender empowerment (gender equality in access to political and economic power; United Nations Development Program, 2007). Although studies have shown that modern Greeks reject the traditional hierarchical roles of men and women in the family, they do preserve other traditional familial values, such as the responsibility of the children to take care of the parents when they get older and the value of staying connected with one's family (Georgas, 1991, 2006b; Mylonas et al., 2006). Furthermore, multinational studies have shown that Greeks are among the people with the most frequent contact (as well as closest geographical proximity) with relatives (Georgas et al., 2001; Mylonas et al., 2006). According to Georgas (2006b), comparative data from the EU indicated that Greece has the highest number of three-generation households and the lowest number of single-parent households (as well as the lowest divorce rate—less than 20%; Eurostat, 2006), which also support the idea of close family ties.

In summarizing some of the unique historic, socioeconomic, demographic, and cultural characteristics of Greek society that bear relevance to counseling today, it seems that the relatively recent political stability, in the context of a long, turbulent, and glorious history, has provided the opportunity for rapid social and economic development. Such development entails a continuous shift from a collectivistic to an individualistic societal orientation and possibly creates adjustment/identity issues at both the individual and systemic levels (see also Georgas, 1991; Haritos-Fatouros & Hatzigeleki,

1999). Greeks still struggle with their changing cultural and familial values, including changes related to family relationships, gender roles and gender equality, the cultural diversification of the society, and the role of religion. At the same time, the improvement of the socioeconomic conditions in Greece is compounded with a relatively high unemployment rate (particularly among women [13%] and young adults), which is reportedly the number one concern of Greeks today (Eurobarometer Special Surveys, 2007). Although these are obviously complex issues that could not be fully examined here, we have provided a glimpse and a context for the discussion of counseling and mental health in Greece that follows.

HISTORY OF PSYCHOLOGY AND TRAINING PARADIGMS

History of Psychology

The ancient Greek philosophers (e.g., Aristotle, Plato, Socrates, Epictetus) have been credited as the pioneers of studying a variety of psychological phenomena that are currently recognized as the precursors/foundations of many modern psychological theories/fields, such as empiricism/behaviorism, cognitive psychology, social psychology/attitude change, psychoanalysis, and cognitive therapy (Georgas, 1995, 2006a). Although the first psychological laboratories were established in the early 20th century at the universities of Athens and Thessaloniki, for historical reasons psychology remained tied to philosophy in Greece for most of the 20th century and was taught in schools of philosophy and education (Georgas, 1995, 2006a). The first department of psychology was founded at the University of Crete in 1987, followed in the early 1990s by three more departments of psychology at the University of Athens, University of Thessaloniki, and Panteion University of Social and Political Sciences. Today, these four departments enroll approximately 1,000 new students annually.

Undergraduate Training

The undergraduate degree in psychology (*ptychio*) is a 4-year degree, requires between 148 and

207 credit hours (somewhat varying by university), and typically includes 50 to 60 courses, a brief practicum (total of 120–200 clock hours), and an undergraduate thesis. At least 75% of the courses are in psychology, covering a wide area of course work (e.g., cognitive/experimental, developmental/ school, clinical/counseling, vocational/organizational, personality/social, and health/medical psychology, as well as research methods/statistics and neuro-psychology/psychopharmacology), with the remaining courses in related fields (e.g., education). Given the heavy requirements of the Greek undergraduate degree, it usually takes 4 to 6 years to complete and leads to a professional license to practice psychology, issued by the Ministry of Health.

Graduate Training

Graduate studies in psychology are offered by the four aforementioned departments of psychology, with graduate (master's) programs in the areas of clinical, school, health, cognitive, and organizational psychology; psychology and media; and psychology of addictions. Graduate training typically comprises 2 years of course work, 2,000 to 2,500 hours of supervised practicum/internship, and a thesis and usually takes 3 years to complete. Graduates with a master's degree can continue and get the PhD degree in the aforementioned specialties. In fields where there are no master's level degrees offered, students can pursue doctoral studies directly after completing their bachelor degrees. This requires the completion of a doctoral thesis without any further course load requirements, and the minimum duration of studies is 3 years. Additional master's degrees are offered to various mental health professionals by related departments (e.g., departments of education or psychiatry) in fields such as career counseling and social psychiatry. Furthermore, several British and American universities operate campuses and offer undergraduate and graduate training in psychology and counseling. These programs are not currently recognized as equivalent (to those offered by the Greek universities), but their recognition and accreditation are imminent, with new legislation having been proposed.

Psychotherapy Training

In addition to training provided by graduate programs in psychology, training in counseling/ psychotherapy in Greece is also provided separately by at least 29 different private and public training centers (Stalikas et al., 2003). Most of these centers, affiliated with Greek or international psychotherapy societies, were established between 1990 and 1995 and cover most theoretical orientations. Trainees are usually professionals from various mental health specialties but may also come from other backgrounds. Training usually lasts 3 to 4 years, includes theory and practice under supervision, and often requires personal therapy/development and occasionally a thesis (Stalikas et al., 2003). However, the quality of these training programs varies significantly and is difficult to assess. The most prominent schools of psychotherapy training represented in Greece are psychoanalytic/psychodynamic, family systems, and cognitive-behavioral, followed by humanistic/Gestalt and others (art therapy, integrative therapies, etc.). Finally, in the past decade there has been an interest in positive psychology, with the establishment of several research initiatives. Interested readers can learn more about the history and current status of psychotherapy practice and training in various modalities in Greece in Assimakis (1999), Brouzos and Mouladoudis (2004), Georgas (1995), Haritos-Fatouros and Hatzigeleki (1999), and Softas-Nall (2003).

PROFESSIONAL ISSUES

Legislation

Before 1987, the majority of psychologists in Greece were trained in various European countries (mostly France, Germany, and the United Kingdom) and North America (Georgas, 1995; Macri, 2001). With the emergence of psychology departments in Greece, there have been thousands of new graduates with bachelor degrees in psychology. According to the Greek law governing the practice of psychology (passed in 1979 but enacted in 1993), psychologists are licensed at the (Greek) bachelor level. However, there is an ongoing debate and serious questions regarding the adequacy of this preparation for the independent practice of psychology (Dafermos, Marvakis, & Triliva, 2006), as well as efforts to promote legislation for the certification of psychological specialties, based on master's-level training. Unfortunately, given that Greek psychologists (before and after 1987) have been trained in different countries and types of undergraduate and graduate programs, developing common and acceptable standards for certification and licensure has been a complex issue (Georgas, 1995; Macri, 2001). Other complicating factors for the legislation of specialties might be the lack of sufficient graduate programs in clinical/counseling/school psychology and the lack of a clear professional identity of different specializations.

Professional and Scientific Organizations

The professional organizations for psychologists in Greece are the Association of Greek Psychologists (founded in 1963) and the Panhellenic Psychological Association (founded in 1998), which both require a psychology license for membership. The main scientific society in the country, the Hellenic Psychological Society (HPS; founded in 1990), requires a PhD in psychology for membership and has approximately 600 members (including student members). It has 10 divisions, including clinical/ health psychology, counseling psychology, and school psychology. HPS, particularly the divisions of clinical/health, counseling, and school psychology, is very involved and influential in the discussion of professional/licensure/specialty issues in psychology.

Psychology Practitioners

The majority of psychologists in Greece are employed as clinical psychologists in private practice or in psychiatric units of state general hospitals, state or private psychiatric hospitals, and state or private community mental health centers (Georgas, 1995; Macri, 2001). They often work as part of multidisciplinary teams, in which psychiatrists typically have the ultimate authority in terms of admission/treatment/discharge decisions. Psychologists are also increasingly employed in university counseling centers or in general or specialized hospitals (e.g., for oncology patients) as health psychologists. Other common employment settings include private and public schools, and special education for school psychologists, and private businesses for organizational psychologists (Georgas, 1995; Hatzichristou et al., 2007). A major issue for psychologists in private practice in Greece is that neither private nor state insurance programs reimburse psychological treatment to private practitioners (Macri, 2001).

In a first effort to provide a glimpse into the educational profile of psychologists who practice psychotherapy in Greece, Stalikas et al. (2003) surveyed 1,100 psychologists from around the country (128, or 12%, responded). The picture that emerged showed a very varied profile of undergraduate and graduate training, as well as varied levels of practical training and supervision. Although there were several limitations to this study, there were notable findings—for example, only 36 of the 128 respondents reported that they had master's-level training in clinical or counseling psychology (and only 13 of the 128 had a PhD in clinical/counseling psychology).

MENTAL HEALTH AND COUNSELING SERVICES

Mental Health System

Until the early 1980s, the mental health system in Greece was characterized by a lack of sufficient community mental health services, understaffing, overcrowding, and limited national coverage (Madianos, Tsiantis, & Zacharakis, 1999; Madianos, Zacharakis, & Tsitsa, 2000). During that time, mental health and psychiatric services were primarily based in nine large state psychiatric hospitals. From 1984 to 1996, with the support of the EU, a major reform of mental health services was undertaken at the national level, adding 388 new mental health facilities throughout the country (Madianos et al., 2000; Madianos, Tsiantis, et al., 1999). This reform led to the establishment of community mental health centers, psychiatric units within general hospitals, outpatient and child clinics, rehabilitation centers, short-stay and crisis units, and related facilities. These major efforts significantly contributed to the deinstitutionalization of mental health and dramatically improved the quality and quantity of mental health services throughout Greece (Madianos et al., 2000; Madianos, Tsiantis, et al., 1999).

Some major improvements achieved during those years include the dramatic increase in relevant personnel of all specialties in state mental hospitals (psychiatrists, psychologists, occupational therapists, social workers, nurses), coupled with a decrease in patient length of stay. Although the profile of mental health services in Greece is now comparable with that of other southern European countries, further improvements are needed in the areas of rehabilitation and outpatient services, partial hospitalization and short-term psychiatric care in general hospitals, and mental health coverage at the regional level (Madianos, Tsiantis, et al., 1999). Additional benefits of the mental health reform of the 1980s and 1990s include advances in mental health training and patient legislation, as well as some improvement in public attitudes toward mental illness (Madianos, Economou, Hatjiandreou, Papageorgiou, & Rogakou, 1999). Specifically, surveys of the stigma associated with mental health conducted in 1979 and 1994 have shown reduced social discrimination and more positive attitudes over time regarding the integration of the mentally ill in the community (Madianos, Economou, et al., 1999). Older and lower SES (socioeconomic status) individuals expressed more negative attitudes toward mental illness in these surveys, indicating a need for further awareness raising and reduction of mental health stigma.

Another particularly positive recent change is the establishment of University Counseling Centers (UCCs) at various institutions of higher education during the past two decades (Malikiosi-Loizos, 2007a). These UCCs provide individual, group, and outreach services to students while also offering psychological training and conducting counseling research (e.g., Kalantzi-Azizi & Karademas, 2003; see also Kalantzi-Azizi, 1997; Malikiosi-Loizos, 2007b). Most of these UCCs are at early stages of their development and operate with limited resources and staff. Some Greek universities still lack such counseling services.

Help-Seeking Behaviors

With the increasing presence of mental health facilities and professionals and with the stigma associated with mental health problems decreasing (Madianos, Economou, et al., 1999), it seems that Greek society is becoming more comfortable with the concept of professional counseling. In a recent study focusing on help-seeking attitudes in a rural area, respondents were found to be more likely to prefer psychological to psychiatric treatment for anxiety and depression and to recommend family and social support as an adjunct or only treatment for anxiety (Zissi, 2006). Although such findings may reflect some concern over the (greater) stigma of seeking psychiatric help (see also Macri, 2001), they are also consistent with our anecdotal experience that Greeks, depending on their collectivist orientation, will often use informal help and social support from family members and friends to deal with distress. Greeks feel intimate and open to share their everyday difficulties in handling issues such as work stress, financial anxiety, sadness over a separation, and mourning for the loss of a loved one. In line with these observations, a study of female college students found that, compared with Americans, Greeks are more likely to have a "best friend" and more reciprocal friendships and to be more distressed in the absence of such relationships (Malikiosi-Loizos & Anderson, 1999).

The culturally indigenous help-seeking behavior of Greeks may include not only the social support of family and friends but also informal help seeking from the Greek Orthodox Church, a powerful and well-organized presence in Greece. Devout individuals with psychological difficulties may commonly invest in receiving help from God, following religious methods (e.g., reading the scripture, praying, attending services, and seeking consultation from the clergy or priests and monks with a reputation of enlightenment or divine healing powers), and experiencing their psychological problems as a test of their faith and part of a divine plan. In fact, there is some research supporting the idea that religious participation/behaviors among Greeks are predictive of some indicators of health and mental health, such as physical activity, healthy nutrition, life satisfaction, and feeling relaxed (Chliaoutakis et al., 2002).

Professional Help Seeking and Services

Partly because of the cost involved and a prevailing, yet declining, social stigma, professional help is frequently sought out only when the functioning of the individual is impaired (e.g., severe panic attacks, inability to work). Although empirical data are lacking, anecdotal experience suggests that psychotherapy and counseling clients in Greece can be grouped in two broad categories. The first includes people with serious, chronic, and debilitating psychological or psychiatric illnesses, such as severe depression, anxiety, and schizophrenia. These individuals have typically already visited a psychiatrist and receive—or have received—medication, yet their problems persist. Seeking psychotherapy represents their "last resource" in alleviating psychological pain. The second category includes clients who are more psychologically minded, usually younger and better educated, and with some affiliation or interest in mental health issues (e.g., teachers, psychology students, nurses, and mental health professionals). Their motivation for seeking psychotherapy and counseling is guided by their understanding that psychological problems can grow over time. They are better informed and less concerned with the stigma of mental health.

Counseling and psychotherapy in Greece is practiced along the same lines as in the rest of the Western hemisphere. Sessions are planned weekly, last an hour, and follow the same ethical guidelines of confidentiality. Most psychotherapists employ a listening, client-centered attitude along with some psychoeducational interventions rooted in the cognitive-behavioral tradition. Analysts follow the same principles of analysis as practiced in Western Europe.

Diversity Counseling

Last, a special mention of the status of counseling for diverse populations, such as women and minorities,

is warranted. Despite the reported progress in terms of gender equality and empowerment, the traditional hierarchical roles of men and women in the family and society are entrenched in Greek culture, particularly in rural areas. Antonopoulou (1999) has examined domestic violence in Greece in the context of gender inequality, reporting that the perpetrators of violence against women are either husbands (two thirds of cases) or fathers (one third of cases). The results of this study also confirmed that female and male views regarding the desirability and actual progress of gender equality in Greece differ somewhat. Notably, half of the respondents perceived the need of women for equality and independence as a contributor to domestic violence, with one third of men expressing the opinion that women should be submissive to men (Antonopoulou, 1999). Founded in 1999, the Division of Counseling Psychology of the HPS has promptly recognized and responded to the need for gender-sensitive counseling in Greece by devoting its entire first national conference (in 2003) to the psychology and counseling of women (Malikiosi-Loizos, Sidiropoulou-Dimakakou, & Kleftaras, 2006), with its second national conference (in 2006) focusing on the psychology and counseling of men.

Equally important is the need for culturally sensitive counseling services as Greek society tries to cope with the sudden and substantial change in its cultural composition (ethnic, religious, etc.) over the past two decades. Minority groups in Greece are very diverse, represent many different countries, diverge in degree of prior connection to the Greek culture, and vary significantly in current acculturation status (Baldwin-Edwards, 2004; Sidiropoulou-Dimakakou, 2003). Many of them are illegal immigrants, which further complicates assessment and counseling efforts. Common difficulties they face (somewhat varying by group) include discrimination, poverty, mental health/adjustment issues, and limited access to education, employment, health care, and other resources (Sidiropoulou-Dimakakou, 2003). Contemporary multicultural counseling efforts in Greece have focused on cultural awareness, career counseling, and the psychosocial adjustment of multicultural populations (Papastylianou,

2005; Psalti, 2007; Sidiropoulou-Dimakakou, 2003; Voulgaridou, Papadopoulos, & Tomaras, 2006). Examples include developing and testing cultural awareness/skills training programs for primary and secondary school teachers (Psalti, 2007) and adapting traditional family therapy approaches for use with refugee families (e.g., by including individuals from the refugee community as cultural mediators; Voulgaridou et al., 2006). However, professionals involved in providing psychosocial services to multicultural populations in Greece report that a well-organized context for the provision of such services is lacking (Yiotsidi & Stalikas, 2004).

DIAGNOSTIC AND ASSESSMENT SYSTEMS

The development, standardization, and use of psychological assessment measures in Greece have been relatively limited and slow, partly due to the limited support from the Ministry of Education as well as the limited interest from the private sector (because of the small financial market of Greece; Triliva & Stalikas, 2004). An edited volume of psychological measures used in Greece lists 135 tests (15 of which were developed in Greece); however, most of them are research instruments (Stalikas, Triliva, & Roussi, 2002). Yet, in a forthcoming edition of the aforementioned volume, there is a sharp increase in the number of tests available in the Greek language, with more than 400 tests presented (Stalikas, Triliva, & Roussi, in press). However, a survey of 150 private practice psychologists showed that only 1% used psychological tests, and then only occasionally (Triliva & Stalikas, 2004). Tests are more frequently used in organized mental health settings (e.g., community mental health centers, hospitals and rehabilitation centers, and special schools and child/adolescent settings), with 27 tests being used in at least 5% of the settings. The MMPI (Minnesota Multiphasic Personality Inventory) is the most commonly used instrument (almost 60% of settings), followed by the WAIS (Wechsler Adult Intelligence Scale) and WISC (Wechsler Intelligence Scale for Children) (around 45% of settings), the TAT (Thematic Apperception Test) and the Rorschach (between 30% and 40% of settings), and the *Athina* test[1] for learning difficulties (used in more than 20% of settings; Triliva & Stalikas, 2004). This survey also found that tests were more frequently used for diagnostic purposes and less frequently for treatment planning or other reasons. Other interesting findings of the study included the complete lack of use of achievement tests, as well as the use of unofficial translations of tests that have not yet been standardized in Greece, such as the WAIS (Triliva & Stalikas, 2004). It is worth noting that, in terms of the standardization process of major tests in Greece, the MMPI-II and the WISC-III have been standardized in Greek samples, whereas the WAIS-III is still in the standardization process.

PSYCHOLOGICAL RESEARCH IN GREECE

Since its establishment, the HPS has held 12 national conferences on psychological research and has been involved in or has organized many smaller scientific meetings or international conferences. HPS publishes the premiere peer-reviewed psychology journal in the country, *Psychologia* (*Psychology: The Journal of the Hellenic Psychological Society*). A second major peer-reviewed psychology journal, the *Hellenic Journal of Psychology*, is published by the Psychological Society of Northern Greece. Several other Greek journals in psychology, psychiatry, and education also exist.

Psychological research in Greece has substantially grown in quantity and quality in recent years and extends to many different fields of psychology (for a sample description see Georgas, 1995). A recent search in PsycINFO revealed 4,042 publications with an author affiliation in Greece, and this does not include an overwhelming majority of the numerous journal articles and books published in Greek. Some representative areas of recent research related to the field of counseling include health psychology and coping, psychotherapeutic interventions, psychological assessment, and the psychology/counseling of diverse populations.

PRIORITIES AND RECOMMENDATIONS FOR PSYCHOLOGY/COUNSELING IN GREECE

The fields of psychology and mental health have experienced significant development and transformation during the past two decades in Greece. However, considerable challenges and areas for growth remain. In closing, based on our experiences with psychological training (as students, clinicians, and faculty) in Greece, Canada, and the United States, the authors would like to highlight the following priority issues and recommendations regarding the future of psychology and counseling in Greece.

First, as the psychology profession is still in its early stages of development in Greece, there is a continuous need to define and implement the desirable standards of undergraduate/graduate training and, most important, related licensing procedures. This is a critical step to ensure that psychologists have proper and adequate preparation to practice competently (see also Dafermos et al., 2006). This goal is likely to be achieved in the context of licensing psychology specialties at the graduate level (e.g., clinical, counseling, school) and in accordance with the European Diploma of Psychology common qualifications proposed in the EU (see also Georgas, 2006a).

Next, although counseling psychology is a vibrant division of the HPS, there are very few faculty members and no graduate programs in counseling psychology in the country. Furthermore, UCCs are understaffed or not available in all Greek universities. We believe that these are priority issues for the development of counseling psychology in Greece, along with promoting the unique identity of counseling psychology as a psychological specialty.

And finally, given that a lot of psychological theory/training/practice has been hastily imported from Western psychology and often uncritically applied to the cultural context of Greece (Dafermos et al., 2006), there is a need for evaluation and cultural adaptation of existing psychological practices and training, as well as the development of specific counseling models based on the needs and characteristics of Greek society. Of course, this needs to accommodate the evolving multicultural landscape of Greece. Most important, additional attention is needed in assessing the problems of vulnerable populations in Greece (e.g., religious and ethnic minorities, immigrants, LGBT [lesbian, gay, bisexual, transgender] individuals, and single mothers) and developing specific psychological models and psychosocial interventions to assist them.

NOTE

1. The *Athina* test is a Greek diagnostic instrument with several subscales developed to identify reading, writing and verbal comprehension abilities and difficulties.

REFERENCES

Antonopoulou, C. (1999). Domestic violence in Greece. *American Psychologist, 54*, 63–64.

Assimakis, P. (Ed.). (1999). *Sygxrones psychotherapies stin Ellada* [Contemporary psychotherapies in Greece]. Athens, Greece: University of Indianapolis Athens Press.

Baldwin-Edwards, M. (2004, January). *Immigration into Greece, 1990–2003. A southern European paradigm?* Paper presented at the European Population Forum, Geneva, Switzerland. Retrieved February 10, 2008, from http://www.mmo.gr/pdf/publications/publications_by_mmo_staff/UNECE%20paperV3.pdf

Brouzos, A., & Mouladoudis, G. (2004). Past, present and future of the person-centered approach in Greece. *Person-Centered and Experiential Psychotherapies, 3*, 256–267.

Chliaoutakis, J. E., Drakou, I., Gnardellis, C., Galariotou, S., Carra, H., & Chliaoutaki, M. (2002). Greek Christian Orthodox ecclesiastical lifestyle: Could it become a pattern of health-related behavior? *Preventive Medicine, 34*, 428–435.

Dafermos, D., Marvakis, A., & Triliva, S. (2006). (De)constructing psychology in Greece. *Annual Review of Critical Psychology, 5*. Retrieved February 15, 2008, from http://www.discourseunit.com/arcp/arcp5/arGreece%20ARCP%205.doc

Economist Intelligence Unit. (2005). *EIU's quality of life index*. Retrieved February 10, 2008, from http://www.economist.com/media/pdf/QUALITY_OF_LIFE.pdf

Eurobarometer Special Surveys. (2007). *European social reality: Greece*. Retrieved February 11, 2008, from http://www.ec.europa.eu/public_opinion/archives/ebs/ebs_273_fiche_el.pdf

Eurostat. (2006). *Eurostat yearbook 2006–2007: Population*. Retrieved February 10, 2008, from http://www.epp.eurostat.ec.europa.eu/cache/ITY_OFFPUB/KS-CD-06-001-01/EN/KS-CD-06-001-01-EN.PDF

Flash Eurobarometer. (2007). *Young Europeans*. Retrieved February 11, 2008, from http://www.ec.europa.eu/public_opinion/flash/fl_202_sum_en.pdf

Georgas, J. (1989). Changing family values in Greece: From collectivist to individualist. *Journal of Cross-Cultural Psychology, 20*, 80–91.

Georgas, J. (1991). Intrafamily acculturation of values in Greece. *Journal of Cross-Cultural Psychology, 22*, 445–457.

Georgas, J. (1995). Psychology in Greece. In A. Schorr & S. Sarri (Eds.), *Psychology in Europe: Facts, figures, realities* (pp. 59–75). Gottingen, Germany: Hogrefe & Huber.

Georgas, J. (2006a). The education of psychologists in Greece. *International Journal of Psychology, 41*, 29–34.

Georgas, J. (2006b). Families and family change. In J. Georgas, J. W. Berry, J. R. Van de Vijver, C. Kagitçibasi, & Y. H. Poortinga (Eds.), *Families across cultures* (pp. 3–50). New York: Cambridge University Press.

Georgas, J., Mylonas, K., Bafiti, T., Christakopoulou, S., Poortinga, Y. H., Kagitçibasi, C., et al. (2001). Functional relationships in the nuclear and extended family: A 16-culture study. *International Journal of Psychology, 36*, 289–300.

Haritos-Fatouros, M., & Hatzigeleki, S. (1999). The family and family therapy in Greece. In U. P. Gielen & A. L. Comunian (Eds.), *International approaches to the family and family therapy* (pp. 43–56). Padua, Italy: Unipress.

Hatzichristou, C., Polychroni, F., & Georgouleas, G. (2007). School psychology in Greece. In S. R. Jimerson, T. D. Oakland, & P. T. Farrell (Eds.), *The handbook of international school psychology* (pp. 135–145). Thousand Oaks, CA: Sage.

Kalantzi-Azizi, A. (Ed.). (1997). *Psychologiki symvoyleytiki foititon: Europaiki diastasi—Elliniki empeiria* [Psychological counseling for students: European dimensions and Greek experiences]. Athens, Greece: Ellinka Grammata.

Kalantzi-Azizi, A., & Karademas, E. C. (2003). A pilot programme for group management of student stress: Description and preliminary findings. *Psychology: The Journal of the Hellenic Psychological Society, 10*, 330–342.

Macri, I. (2001). Medical psychology in Greece. *Journal of Clinical Psychology in Medical Settings, 8*, 27–30.

Madianos, M. G., Economou, M., Hatjiandreou, M., Papageorgiou, A., & Rogakou, E. (1999). Changes in public attitudes towards mental illness in the Athens area (1997/1980–1994). *Acta Psychiatrica Scandinavica, 99*, 73–78.

Madianos, M. G., Tsiantis, J., & Zacharakis, C. (1999). Changing patterns of mental health care in Greece (1984–1996). *European Psychiatry, 14*, 462–467.

Madianos, M. G., Zacharakis, C., & Tsitsa, C. (2000). Utilization of psychiatric inpatient care in Greece: A nationwide study (1984–1996). *International Journal of Social Psychiatry, 46*, 89–100.

Malikiosi-Loizos, M. (2007a). Psychological counseling in Greek higher education institutions. *International Section Newsletter, APA Society of Counseling Psychology, 1*, 16.

Malikiosi-Loizos, M. (Ed.). (2007b). *Symvoyleytiki Psychologia: Syxrones Proseggiseis* [Counseling psychology: Contemporary approaches]. Athens, Greece: Atrapos.

Malikiosi-Loizos, M., & Anderson, L. R. (1999). Accessible friendships, inclusive friendships, reciprocated friendships as related to social and emotional loneliness in Greece and the USA. *European Psychologist, 4*, 165–178.

Malikiosi-Loizos, M., Sidiropoulou-Dimakakou, D., & Kleftaras, G. (Eds.). (2006). *I symvoyleytiki psychologia stis gynaikes* [Counseling in women's issues]. Athens, Greece: Ellinika Grammata.

Mylonas, K., Gari, A., Giotsa, A., Pavlopoulos V., & Panagiotopoulou, P. (2006). Greece. In J. Georgas, J. W. Berry, J. R. Van de Vijver, C. Kagitçibasi, & Y. H. Poortinga (Eds.), *Families across cultures* (pp. 344–352). New York: Cambridge.

National Statistical Service of Greece. (2006). *Concise statistical yearbook*. Retrieved February 10, 2008, from http://www.statistics.gr/Documents/yearbook-06.pdf

Papastylianou, A. (Ed.). (2005). *Diapolitismikes diadromes: Palinnostisi kai psyxokoinoniki prosarmogi* [Multicultural journeys: Repatriation and psychosocial adjustment]. Athens, Greece: Ellinika Grammata.

Psalti, A. (2007). Training Greek teachers in cultural awareness. *School Psychology International, 28*, 148–162.

Sidiropoulou-Dimakakou, D. (2003). *Epaggelmatiki symvoyleytiki kai polytismiki diaforetikotita* [Career counseling and cultural diversity]. *Psychology: The Journal of the Hellenic Psychological Society, 10,* 399–413.

Softas-Nall, B. (2003). Reflections on forty years of family therapy, research, and systemic thinking in Greece. In K. S. Ng (Ed.), *Global perspectives in family therapy: Development, practice, and trends* (pp. 125–143). New York: Brunner-Routledge.

Special Eurobarometer. (2005). *Social values, science and technology.* Retrieved February 10, 2008, from http://www.ec.europa.eu/public_opinion/archives/ebs/ ebs_225_report_en.pdf

Stalikas, A., Roussi, P., Hatzigelleki, S., Triliva, S., Kalantzi-Azizi, A., Malikiosi-Loizou, M., et al. (2003). *Katagrafi kai parousiasi ton symperasmaton tis ypoepitropis gia ton kathorismo ton kritirion tou ergou tou psychologoy-psychotherapeyti* [Assessment and presentation of findings of the subcommittee for the definition of the criteria for the practice of psychology-psychotherapy]. Unpublished manuscript.

Stalikas, A., Triliva, S., & Roussi, P. (Eds.). (2002). *Ta psychometrika ergaleia stin Ellada* [Psychometric instruments in Greece]. Athens, Greece: Ellinika Grammata.

Stalikas, A., Triliva, S., & Roussi, P. (Eds.). (in press). *Ta psychometrika ergaleia stin Ellada (anatheorimeni ekdosi)* [Psychometric instruments in Greece] (Rev. ed.). Athens, Greece: Ellinika Grammata.

Triliva, S., & Stalikas, A. (2004). The use of psychological tests and measurements by psychologists in the role of a counsellor in Greece. *Counselling Psychology Review, 19,* 32–39.

United Nations Development Program. (2007). *Human development report 2007/2008.* Retrieved February 10, 2008, from http://www.hdr.undp.org/en/media/ hdr_20072008_en_complete.pdf

Voulgaridou, M. G., Papadopoulos, R. K., & Tomaras, V. (2006). Working with refugee families in Greece: Systemic considerations. *Journal of Family Therapy, 28,* 200–220.

Yiotsidi, V., & Stalikas, A. (2004). *I diapolitismiki symvoyleutiki kai psychotherapeia se prosfyges: Psychokoinonikes anagkes kai politismikes diafores* [Cross-cultural counselling and psychotherapy for refugees: Psychosocial needs and cultural differences]. *Psychology: The Journal of the Hellenic Psychological Society, 11,* 34–52.

Zissi, A. (2006). Community perceptions of mental disorders: A Greek perspective. *Journal of Community & Applied Social Psychology, 16,* 136–148.

THE AMERICAS AND THE CARIBBEAN

26

Counseling in the Canadian Mosaic

A Cultural Perspective

Le counseling dans la mosaïque Canadienne: Une perspective culturelle

RICHARD A. YOUNG

Counseling psychology in Canada is a dynamic and growing professional practice. In its various forms and iterations, counseling has been known there for more than 50 years. Its history has been largely influenced by parallel developments in the United States, including immigration, industrialization, the mental health movement, World War II, the rise of psychological testing for selection and placement, and the provision of vocational guidance in schools. At first glance, counseling psychology in Canada may appear as the mirror image of its sister in the United States. But as Bowman (2000) pointed out, Canada is unique in many ways that affect the development and practice of professional psychology, including counseling. These differences include the size of the population, income, government spending on social programs, education, health, families, crime and corrections, and cultural diversity. Thus, the commonalities between counseling psychology in Canada and the United States, as well as

their differences, contribute to the uniqueness of Canadian counseling psychology.

To address this unique Canadian counseling psychology, I take a cultural perspective in this chapter. This perspective begins with understanding counseling as primarily a practice comprising goal-oriented and intentional human action. In turn, human action embodies the cultures in which it is enacted. Following Boesch (1991), culture is seen as the field of human action, pointing to the close connection between culture and counseling practice. What happens in counseling, as in many other human processes such as education and child rearing, is to help the person discover and construct the possibilities of his or her culture. Counseling expands the range and focus of the fields of human action. Rather than narrowly focusing on a particular ethnic, gendered, or other group, this cultural perspective is integrative and inclusive.

This perspective is important because it suggests that culture is not simply the context in which counseling occurs. Counseling isn't simply a practice that happens in this or that culture. Counseling actually helps the person discover and construct the possibilities of action within cultures. The link between counseling and culture is much more significant than is commonly believed; however, this is not a view that is espoused explicitly by Canadian counseling psychologists. Rather, it is often assumed that culture provides a backdrop for the counseling process. In contrast, in this chapter, culture is approached as the field of action that clients and counselors construct and create in counseling.

As a field of action, the Canadian culture is multifaceted and layered, suggesting that describing counseling psychology in Canada is a complex and challenging task. The Canadian culture offers possibilities for counseling practice in various forms, modalities, agencies, programs, and policies, implemented through a variety of human agents. In turn, this practice is informed by conceptualizations, research, popular discourse, media, and human needs and wishes as constructed in this society. Ideally, one would examine the specifics of this or that counseling practice to see what field of human action it represents. However, in this chapter, a broad-brush approach is taken to portray counseling psychology in Canada as cultural practice. It can be addressed by answering two questions:

1. How is counseling psychology understood as a fairly generalizable domain of professional practice applied in Canada? That is, what are the broad parameters of the culture in which it evolved and continues to evolve and what is counseling psychology's current status and identity?

2. Can the possibilities for practice be illustrated by addressing several important issues in counseling psychology in Canada? A subquestion is, in taking up these illustrative issues, what unique contributions does Canadian counseling psychology have to offer this field, particularly in light of global developments and multicultural perspectives?

HISTORY AND CONTEXT: THE CANADIAN MOSAIC

The title of this chapter suggests Canada is a mosaic. Its population of 33 million comprises people who themselves or their ancestors originated in virtually all parts of the world (Martel & Caron-Malenfant, 2007). It has an Aboriginal population of approximately 1.3 million (i.e., about 4% of the total population compared with the United States, where American Indians and Alaskan Natives constitute 0.9% of the population). The Aboriginal population is further divided into First Nations, Inuit, and Métis. Canada has one of the highest net migration rates among Western countries (5.62 per 1,000 population, compared, e.g., with 2.52 in the United States and 3.72 in Australia) (Index Mundi, 2008).

Canada is constituted as a federal system composed of 10 provinces and 3 territories, all of which have substantial self-governing rights and responsibilities in areas such as health, education, and labor. Furthermore, Canada is a mosaic geographically. After Russia, it is the country with the largest landmass in the world, bordering the Arctic, Pacific, and Atlantic oceans, with very distinct geographical regions. There are also significant regional linguistic and historical differences.

Mosaic is also an important term in understanding the Canadian experience. Ethnic diversity continues to increase. Following the Aboriginal peoples, who established a number of distinct nations in what is now Canada before recorded history, the French and English explored and colonized Canada beginning in the 16th century. Subsequently, the past 100 years have seen considerable immigration from all parts of the world. Mosaic, however, does not imply equality. Porter (1965) used the term *vertical mosaic* to reflect the historical domination of people of British origin in government and economic spheres. More recent legislation and political changes, including significant immigration from non-European countries, have shifted the power balances in Canada such that French Canadians are better represented in the power elites, and Aboriginal peoples continue to advance, despite acknowledged economic and social disparity and the significant impact on First Nations peoples by the Indian Act of 1867 and the residential school system (Royal Commission on Aboriginal Peoples, 1996).

The diversity of the Canadian people was reflected in the federal government policy of multiculturalism in 1971. Subsequently, this policy developed over several years to the Canadian Multiculturalism Act of 1988, in which the federal government recognized "the importance of preserving and enhancing the multicultural heritage of Canadians" (Canadian Multiculturalism Act, 2006). In its various iterations, multiculturalism has focused on cultural sensitivity, employment equity, human rights, social justice, and global security. Multiculturalism is considered important in the Canadian discourse and is seen by many as a distinct way of addressing diversity compared with more assimilative policies regarding immigrants and ethnically diverse groups. It is also seen as reflective of Canadians as a tolerant people. In contrast, multiculturalism can also be seen as a fluid concept that may not have kept pace with the realities of globalization; that it is a smoke screen for human rights abuses and social injustices; and that social forces of assimilation are just as present in Canada as they are in other countries, despite the rhetoric.

Generally, Canadians appear to value the traditions and principles of Western societies and countries, including the rule of law, democratic institutions, the freedom of religion, gender equality, respect for diversity, and individual liberty. A large number of Canadians support universal health care, gun control, noncapital punishment, and gay marriage, which are included in federal and provincial legislation. However, one may question whether these are the values that hold the Canadian society together. Heath (2003), for example, argued that both freedom and cultural diversity suggest a much greater differentiation of values in Canadian society than is often believed to be the case. Both positions have implications for counseling. The first position suggests that counseling could serve, and probably has served, to help people internalize values that were perceived to be held by all Canadians and thus serves a highly assimilative function. In contrast, it may be the particular strength of counseling to be able to assist people in integrating in a harmonious society, at the same time recognizing their ethnic uniqueness and value differences. This position accords a more accommodative role to counseling. It is likely that over time there has been a shift in counseling practice from the first to second position, but both are tacit attitudes that are played out in the client's and counselor's constructions of action possibilities in counseling.

Canada is an economically prosperous country. A recent International Monetary Fund report suggested that its economic policies are to be envied (Klyuev, Bayoumi, & Mühleisen, 2007). Although it may be a common perception outside that Canada's prosperity is based on Canadians being hewers of wood and drawers of gas and oil, economically, Canada is more like diversified modern economies than many people realize. For example, in 2007 only 7% of Canada's GDP came from mining, gas and oil, agriculture, forestry, and fishing (Statistics Canada, 2008). Rather, it is the financial and real estate sectors that are driving economic growth in Canada. Economic prosperity allows services such as counseling to be available to the population. At the same time, the prosperity itself brings its own challenges that heighten the need for counseling services, including counseling related to employment, work, and family adjustment, and particularly the broad range of concerns of migrant and immigrant workers and their families. The Canadian occupational profile also suggests a dependence on a sophisticated system of, and participation in, higher education, which has concomitant implications for the provision of counseling services as well as for the kinds of problems presented by clients.

Religion is another domain in which Canadian uniqueness is reflected. Although approximately 70% of the population nominally identify themselves as either Roman Catholic or Protestant, a 2003 Gallup poll indicated that only 23% of Canadians considered religion as very important in their own lives, compared with, for example, 60% of Americans (Ray, 2003). The shift away from the importance of religion for Canadians has resulted in the rise of a secular humanism, and greater emphasis on the therapeutic, including counseling, medical, and other interventions, as a means to address individual challenges and difficulties.

HISTORY AND CURRENT IDENTITY OF COUNSELING PSYCHOLOGY

It was in this Canadian mosaic that counseling as a practice made substantial gains in the 1950s and

1960s. Paralleling developments in the United States, formal education for school counselors was introduced in Canadian universities, and the work of Carl Rogers added a significant therapeutic component to counseling. In the 1960s, the Canadian Guidance and Counselling Association (now the Canadian Counselling Association, CCA) was founded, as was its bilingual journal, the *Canadian Journal of Counseling/Revue Canadienne de Counseling* (formerly *Canadian Counsellor*). The CCA now has more than 2,900 members, most of whom are trained at the master's level and work as counselors in a range of educational institutions, government and social agencies, corporations and businesses, and private practice (CCA, 2008). The *Canadian Journal of Counselling* serves as the primary Canadian vehicle for publication of scholarly work in counseling and counseling psychology.

By the 1980s, counseling psychology began to distinguish itself from the more generic practice of counseling with the formation of the counseling psychology section in the Canadian Psychological Association (CPA) and the accreditation of doctoral programs in counseling psychology by the CPA (Young & Nicol, 2007). Lalande (2004) described a range of definitions of counseling psychology used in Canada. These definitions refer to helping reasonably adjusted people enhance and improve normal functioning, accomplish life tasks, solve problems, make decisions, and cope with the stresses of everyday life.

Nonetheless, questions of identity persist. Although counseling psychology in Canada has benefited from the developments in the United States, the history of counseling and counseling psychology in Canada, as well as the effect of a population about 1/10 the size of the American population, has resulted in a greater overlap between counselors and counseling psychologists than is the case in the United States. This led Hiebert and Uhlemann (1993) a decade and a half ago to ask, "Are we counsellors or psychologists?" More recently, a high degree of similarity was found between practicing counseling and clinical psychologists (Linden, Moseley, & Erskine, 2005). The identity of counseling psychology in Canada is also substantially influenced by the

integration of Canadian and American professional psychology in North America. Although each country has distinct professional associations, namely, the Canadian Psychological Association and the American Psychological Association, there are several significant North American associations and groups, such as the Association of State and Provincial Psychology Boards (ASPPB) and the Association of Psychology Postdoctoral and Internship Centers (APPIC), that contribute to greater similarities than differences in counseling psychology in Canada and the United States.

At the same time, this brief history of counseling in Canada has alluded to some of its unique aspects. For example, the development of counseling psychology as a discipline in francophone Quebec has not paralleled its development in anglophone parts of the country. Specifically, training in counseling psychology (*la psychologie de counseling*) is not available in the French language universities in Quebec. Rather, guidance counseling (*l'orientation*) has been well-established in Quebec for several decades, with its own legislated professional and regulatory bodies.

The identity of counseling psychology can also be seen from the perspective of the presenting concerns of clients, which are, in fact, quite broad. Clearly, a number of client concerns address the staple issues counseling psychology clients face elsewhere. These include relationships, occupational choice and adjustment, and transitions of various sorts. Counseling psychologists also address issues of depression and social anxiety. Less common but nevertheless important in the Canadian context are the following client presenting concerns: the aftermath of residential school abuse for Aboriginal Canadians, issues that arise from geographic mobility for work, immigrant adjustment, and substance abuse and addiction.

Client presenting problems have to be considered in the context of help-seeking attitudes of Canadians, which appear to differ by ethnic group as well as other factors. A recent report by the Canadian Medical Association pointed to the negative attitudes that many Canadian have about mental illness. For example, 46% of Canadians think that mental illness is an excuse for bad behavior (Sullivan, 2008). This attitude is reflected in help seeking among Canadians with a mental disorder. Park and Nelson (2006) reported that more than half the Canadians in this category have not sought help for their problems, with men and younger Canadians (aged 15–24 years) manifesting higher rates of non-help-seeking. Ethnic background and recent migration to Canada are also factors in help seeking. Recent immigrants often compare the type of social support with what is available in their homelands. Factors such as practical social support, reciprocity and friendship with the counselor, and a nonbureaucratic setting may influence whether immigrants seek help from counselors and the type of help that is sought (Simich, Mawani, Wu, & Noor, 2004).

NEW POSSIBILITIES FOR PRACTICE

Canadian counseling psychologists are addressing a range of issues that reflect new and enhanced possibilities for counseling practice. These include issues such as social justice (e.g., Arthur, 2005), spirituality (e.g., Wong & Fry, 1998), and counseling process (e.g., Greenberg & Watson, 2006). Particularly noteworthy among these issues are diversity, health, career development, and qualitative research.

Diversity

In previous decades, diversity and multiculturalism were not mentioned as areas of concern or defining characteristics of Canadian counseling psychologists (Hiebert & Uhlemann, 1993). However, partly reflecting the growth of multiculturalism as a third force within counseling psychology more generally (e.g., Pedersen, 1991) as well as the view of Canada as a multicultural country, described earlier, there has been significant recognition of multiculturalism as an important factor in Canadian counseling psychology recently. Several developments are indicative of this shift, notably attention by Canadian counseling psychologists to various aspects of counseling in a multicultural context (e.g., Collins & Arthur, 2005; Ishiyama & Arvay, 2003; James & Prilleltensky, 2002; Moodley & West, 2005; Wong & Wong, 2006).

Young, Marshall, and Valach (2007) elaborated on one of the challenges of counseling in the context of cultural diversity as the risk involved in considering cultural characteristics as static variables rather than understanding how culture is constructed as an active, dynamic process, both within and outside counseling. Considering cultural variables as static may have the unintended consequence of *othering* clients from ethnic, racial, gender, or age groups that are not the same as the counselor's. When culture is considered as a dynamic and ongoing process in which both counselor and client are engaged, the opportunity of creating the *I-Thou* relationship Buber (1958) addressed is increased. The experience of the other in dialogue, that is, in process, is what makes the I-Thou relationship possible.

Of particular note in the field of diversity is attention to the influence of alternate and integrated forms of cultural healing that have arisen among the First Nations peoples in Canada (McCormick, 1995). These forms of healing, which include empowerment, cleansing, balance, discipline, and a sense of belonging, have not assumed any degree of primacy in the practice of counseling psychology. However, they represent integrative and spiritual dimensions as well as ways in which an increased symbiosis between counseling and traditional forms of healing can occur. For example, Blue and Darou (2005) have documented several counseling processes that reflect a First Nations worldview. These processes include storytelling, talking circles, healing circles, the advice of elders, and ceremonies such as drumming, dancing, sweat lodges, and vision quest. There is a growing literature on the uniqueness of counseling and other mental health issues among First Nations peoples in Canada (e.g., Chandler, Lalonde, Sokol, & Hallett, 2003; Guilmette & MacNeil, 2004; Heilborn & Guttman, 2000), and recently a university-based First Nations and Aboriginal counseling degree program has begun (Brandon University, 2008).

Health

Heretofore, the focus of counseling psychology practice has largely been remedial, relying largely on individual counseling and psychotherapy (Hiebert & Uhlemann, 1993), despite the rhetoric of developmental and preventive models. However, counseling psychology is well situated, at least in principle, to respond to the emphasis in Canada on population health (e.g., Evans, Barer, & Marmor, 1994; Keating & Hertzman, 1999).

The emphasis in population health on the capacity of people to respond well to life challenges and changes reflects a perspective shared with counseling psychology. The key to population health is the recognition of health as a process rather than a state—"which corresponds more to the notion of being able to pursue one's goals, to acquire skills and education, and to grow" (Public Health Agency of Canada, 2008). The overlap with the aims of counseling psychology is significant. Although counseling psychology has traditionally had a role in the factors involved in population health, it is only beginning to capitalize on this very broad policy base for health as a new area of practice.

Valach, Young, and Lynam (1998) addressed the challenge of translating population health policies into practice. One shift they proposed is to reconceptualize health-related processes. Population health is not about analyzing the social conditions of a healthy population. Rather, "The basic health processes are conceived in a dialogic, interpersonal, joint and supra-individual manner" (p. 2). Evidence of this reconceptualization is available for health domains such as recovery from addiction (Graham, Young, Valach, & Wood, 2008) and family health promotion (Valach, Young, & Lynam, 1996). A parallel reconceptualization has occurred in the field of career psychology.

Career Psychology

A challenge for counseling psychology in Canada and elsewhere is the place that it assigns to vocational psychology. In its training programs and among its graduate students, there is clearly a wavering of interest in vocational topics. At least one doctoral program in counseling psychology accredited by the CPA does not require a course in vocational psychology or career counseling. In Canada, there has been a hiving off of persons interested in career development into their own professional associations and training programs, the latter usually at the level of diplomas and community college programs. We have also witnessed a phenomenal growth in the practice of career coaching.

In contrast, there has also been considerable interest in and financial support available for research, policy development, and practice in areas related to career development. Specifically, Human Resources and Social Development Canada, a department of the federal government, and the Canadian Career Development Foundation have, over the past several decades, contributed significantly to Canada's global leadership in policy development in the field of career development.

The particular advantage of career development is the potential conceptual framework that it holds for the practice of counseling psychology once practitioners and researchers let go of the tight bond between career and occupation. As Young and Valach (2000) pointed out, career can be linked directly to human action over the long-term, rather than exclusively to occupation. In this way, it provides a conceptual framework for counseling practice. It addresses the meaning of human action and fits with the foundation for a global psychology that "gives priority to meaning-making over behavior" (Moghaddam, Erneling, Montero, & Lee, 2007, p. 189). Attention to meaning and meaning making in counseling psychology research and practice has given rise to the development of qualitative research.

Qualitative Research

Qualitative research and methods have been a particular strength of counseling psychology programs in Canada. Rennie, Watson, and Monteiro (2000) found that the lion's share of 44 Canadian qualitative researchers identified in the PSYCINFO database were in counseling psychology programs. However, Rennie (2004) also found that Canada is more similar to the United States in its reliance on positivist epistemologies in counseling and psychotherapy research than is the case in the United Kingdom. Nevertheless, counseling psychology researchers in Canada seems less reluctant to depart from accustomed research practices compared with other psychology programs and areas. In addition, qualitative research methods are particularly suited to emerging areas such as cultural diversity and spirituality.

What is frequently attractive about qualitative research methods is their closeness to the lived experience of clients, and thus their capacity to describe, if not explain, issues of culture (Young et al., 2007), diversity (Offet-Gartner, 2005), globalization (Stead & Young, 2007), spirituality (Miller & Crabtree, 2000), and the processes of counseling and other life processes. These methods also have the advantage of being able to describe experience and represent the voices of the researched in ways not available in quantitative methods.

CONCLUSION

The uniqueness of counseling psychology in Canada, and in any country for that matter, is highlighted when one considers that counseling is primarily a practice. As such, it involves over short and long periods of time the intentionality, goals, purposes, and actions of those involved in it directly and those more distant from it. As part of the field of human action in Canada, it captures, reflects, and constructs the Canadian culture. In turn, culture is also transformed by counseling practice. Counseling sessions or programs expand in various ways to include different clients, training institutions, research, conferences, networks, and modalities of practice to eventually result in a collective process and structure. As such, counselors and clients enter a preestablished environment that itself is evolving and developing. The possibilities offered by counseling practice are open to both client and counselor. As a person grows up in Canada, or comes to Canada, he or she becomes more aware of the possibilities in and for counseling. Importantly, counseling practice can assist in opening possibilities in one's own life.

At the same time, it is important to note that counseling, or any human process, does not have these possibilities hidden in a box in the counselor's office to be unwrapped during counseling. Rather, it is the engagement between counselor and client itself that constructs and realizes these possibilities.

REFERENCES

Arthur, N. (2005). Building from diversity to social justice competencies in international standards for career development practitioners. *International Journal for Educational and Vocational Guidance, 5,* 137–148.

Blue, A., & Darou, W. (2005). Counselling First Nations peoples. In S. Collins & N. Arthur (Eds.), *Culture-infused counselling: Celebrating the Canadian mosaic* (pp. 303–330). Calgary, Alberta, Canada: Counselling Concepts.

Boesch, E. E. (1991). *Symbolic action theory and cultural psychology.* Berlin, Germany: Springer-Verlag.

Bowman, M. L. (2000). The diversity of diversity: Canadian-American differences and their implications for clinical training and APA accreditation. *Canadian Psychology, 41,* 230–243.

Brandon University. (2008). *First Nations and Aboriginal Degree Counselling Program.* Retrieved July 17, 2008, from http://www.brandonu.ca/Academic/FNAC/

Buber, M. (1958). *I and thou* (2nd ed., R. G. Smith, Trans.). New York: Scribner.

Canadian Counselling Association. (2008). *What is CCA?* Retrieved March 18, 2008, from http://www.ccacc.ca/aboutus.html

Canadian Multiculturalism Act. (2006). Retrieved April 16, 2009, from http://www.parl.gc.ca/information/library/PRBpubs/936-e.htm

Chandler, M. J., Lalonde, C. E., Sokol, B. W., & Hallett, D. (2003). Personal persistence, identity development, and suicide: A study of native and non-native North-American adolescents. *Monographs of the Society for Research in Child Development, 86,* 1–128.

Collins, S., & Arthur, N. (Eds.). (2005). *Culture-infused counselling: Celebrating the Canadian mosaic.* Calgary, Alberta, Canada: Counselling Concepts.

Evans, R. G., Barer, M. L., & Marmor, T. R. (1994). *Why are some people healthy and others not?* New York: A. de Gruyter.

Graham, M. D., Young, R. A., Valach, L., & Wood, R. A. (2008). Addiction as a complex social process: An action theoretical perspective. *Addiction Research and Theory, 16,* 121–133.

Greenberg, L. S., & Watson, J. C. (2006). *Emotionally-focused therapy for depression.* Washington, DC: American Psychological Association.

Guilmette, A. M., & MacNeil, M. S. (2004). Preventing youth suicide: Developing a protocol for early intervention in First Nations communities. *Canadian Journal of Native Studies, 24*(2), 343–355.

Heath, J. (2003). *The myth of shared values in Canada.* Ottawa, Ontario, Canada: Canadian Centre for Management Development.

Heilborn, C. L., & Guttman, M.-A. (2000). Traditional healing methods with First Nations women in group counselling. *Canadian Journal of Counselling, 34,* 3–13.

Hiebert, B., & Uhlemann, M. R. (1993). Counseling psychology: Development, identity and issues. In K. S. Dobson & D. J. G. Dobson (Eds.), *Professional psychology in Canada* (pp. 285–312). Toronto, Ontario, Canada: Hogrefe & Huber.

Index Mundi. (2008). *Country comparison: Net migration rate.* Retrieved July 31, 2008, from http://www.indexmundi.com/g/r.aspx?v=27&1=en

Ishiyama, I., & Arvay, M. (Eds.). (2003). Multicultural counselling: Embracing cultural diversity [Special issue]. *Canadian Journal of Counseling, 37,* 171–231.

James, S., & Prilleltensky, I. (2002). Cultural diversity and mental health: Towards integrative practice. *Clinical Psychology Review, 22,* 1133–1154.

Keating, D. P., & Hertzman, C. (Eds.). (1999). *Development health and the wealth of nations: Social, biological, and educational dynamics.* New York: Guilford Press.

Klyuev, V., Bayoumi, T., & Mühleisen, M. (2007). *Northern star: Canada's path to economic prosperity* (Occasional Paper No. 258). Washington, DC: International Monetary Fund.

Lalande, V. M. (2004). Counselling psychology: A Canadian perspective. *Counselling Psychology Quarterly, 17,* 273–286.

Linden, W., Moseley, J., & Erskine, Y. (2005). Psychology as a health-care profession: Implications for training. *Canadian Psychology, 46,* 179–188.

Martel, L., & Caron-Malenfant, E. (2007). *Portrait of the Canadian population in 2006: Findings.* Ottawa, Ontario, Canada: Statistics Canada. Retrieved March 18, 2008, from http://www.12.statcan.ca/english/census06/analysis/popdwell/index.cfm

McCormick, R. M. (1995). The facilitation of healing for First Nations people of British Columbia. *Canadian Journal of Native Education, 21,* 251–322.

Miller, W. L., & Crabtree, B. F. (2000). Clinical research. In N. K. Denzin & Y. S. Lincoln (Eds.), *Handbook of qualitative research* (2nd ed., pp. 607–643). Thousand Oaks, CA: Sage.

Moghaddam, F. M., Erneling, C. E., Montero, M., & Lee, N. (2007). Toward a conceptual foundation for a global psychology. In M. Stevens & U. Gielen (Eds.), *Toward a global psychology: Theory, research, intervention, and pedagogy* (pp. 179–206). Mahwah, NJ: Lawrence Erlbaum.

Moodley, R., & West, W. (Eds.). (2005). *Integrating traditional healing practices into counseling and psychotherapy.* Thousand Oaks, CA: Sage.

Offet-Gartner, K. (2005). Research across cultures. In S. Collins & N. Arthur (Eds.), *Culturally-infused counseling: Celebrating the Canadian mosaic* (pp. 263–300). Calgary, Alberta, Canada: Counselling Concepts.

Park, J., & Nelson, C. (2006, August). *Help-seeking behaviour of individuals with mental disorder in Canada.* Paper presented at the annual meeting of the American Sociological Association, Montreal, Quebec, Canada. Retrieved August 21, 2008, from http://www.allacademic.com/meta/p105531_index.html

Pedersen, P. B. (1991). Multiculturalism as a generic approach to counseling. *Journal of Counseling and Development, 70,* 6–12.

Porter, J. (1965). *The vertical mosaic: An analysis of social class and power in Canada.* Toronto, Ontario, Canada: University of Toronto Press.

Public Health Agency of Canada. (2008). *What is the population health approach?* Ottawa, Ontario, Canada: Author. Retrieved August 11, 2008, from http://www.phac-aspc.gc.ca/ph-sp/approach-approche/index-eng.php

Ray, J. (2003). *Worlds apart: Religion in Canada, U.S., and Britain.* Washington, DC: Gallup. Retrieved July 31, 2009, from http://www.gallup.com/poll/9016/Worlds-Apart-Religion-Canada-Britain-US.aspx

Rennie, D. (2004). Anglo-North American qualitative counseling and psychotherapy research. *Psychotherapy Research, 14,* 37–55.

Rennie, D. L., Watson, K. D., & Monteiro, A. (2000, June). Qualitative research in Canadian psychology. *ForumQualitative Sozialforschung/Forum: Qualitative Social Research.* Retrieved March 25, 2008, from http://www.qualitative-research.net/index.php/fqs/article/view/1098

Royal Commission on Aboriginal Peoples. (1996). *Report of the Royal Commission on aboriginal peoples* (Vols. 4 and 5). Ottawa, Ontario, Canada: Author.

Simich, L., Mawani, F., Wu, F., & Noor, A. (2004). *Meaning of social support, coping, and help-seeking strategies among immigrants and refugees in Toronto* (CERIS Working Paper No. 31). Toronto, Ontario, Canada: Joint Centre of Excellence for Research and Settlement.

Statistics Canada. (2008). *Gross domestic product at basic prices, by industry.* Retrieved July 30, 2008, from http://www.40.statcan.ca/101/cst01/econ41.htm?sdi=mining

Stead, G. B., & Young, R. A. (2007). Qualitative research methods for a global psychology. In M. Stevens & U. Gielen (Eds.), *Toward a global psychology: Theory, research, intervention, and pedagogy* (pp. 207–232). Mahwah, NJ: Lawrence Erlbaum.

Sullivan, P. (2008). *Stigma attached to mental illness a "national embarrassment": CMA.* Ottawa, Ontario, Canada: Canadian Medical Association. Retrieved August 21, 2008, from http://www.cma.ca/index.cfm/ci_id/10042907/la_id/1.htm

Valach, L., Young, R. A., & Lynam, M. J. (1996). Family health promotion projects: An action theoretical perspective. *Journal of Health Psychology, 1,* 49–63.

Valach, L., Young, R. A., & Lynam, M. J. (1998). Social, critical and ethical issues in health psychology. In R. Schwarzer (Ed.), *Advances in health psychology research* (CD-Rom, Vol. 1). Berlin, Germany: Freie Universität.

Wong, P. P. T., & Fry, P. S. (Eds.). (1998). *The quest for human meaning: A handbook of psychological research and clinical applications.* Mahwah, NJ: Lawrence Erlbaum.

Wong, P. P. T., & Wong, L. C. J. (Eds.). (2006). *Handbook of multicultural perspectives on stress and coping.* New York: Springer.

Young, R. A., Marshall, S., & Valach, L. (2007). Making career theories more culturally sensitive: Implications for counseling. *Career Development Quarterly, 56,* 4–18.

Young, R. A., & Nicol, J. J. (2007). Counselling psychology in Canada: Advancing psychology for all. *Applied Psychology: An International Journal, 56,* 20–32.

Young, R. A., & Valach, L. (2000). Reconceptualizing career psychology: An action theoretical perspective. In A. Collin & R. A. Young (Eds.), *The future of career* (pp. 181–196). Cambridge, UK: Cambridge University Press.

27

After *la Violencia*

The Psychology Profession in Colombia

Después de la violencia:
Un análisis de la profesión de psicología en Colombia

EDWARD A. DELGADO-ROMERO, EDUARDO E. DELGADO POLO, RUBÉN ARDILA, AND COREY SMETANA

This chapter addresses the history, practice, and future challenges of the profession of psychology in the South American country of Colombia. We first review the relevant demographic information, provide an overview of the educational system relative to psychology, and then review the history of psychology as a profession in Colombia. We then examine the global presence and influence of Colombians and conclude with challenges for the future development of counseling psychology.

BACKGROUND AND CULTURE

Colombia is located in northwestern South America. The capital is Bogotá. Colombia is bordered by Venezuela, Brazil, Ecuador, Peru, and Panama and by the Caribbean Sea and North Pacific Ocean.

Colombia has a tropical climate along the coastline and Eastern Plains and a cooler climate inland. Colombia's main exports are petroleum, coffee, coal, and apparel (Delgado-Romero, Rojas, & Shelton, 2007). Colombia is a large (1.14 million square kilometers) and populous (42,888,592 inhabitants in 2007) country with a population growth projected to be 1.8%. Colombia is the third most populous country in Latin America, after Brazil and Mexico (U.S. Department of State, 2007). Spanish is the main language spoken in the country. Famous Colombians include the writer Gabriel García Márquez, neuroscientist Rodolfo Llinás, medical researcher Elkin Patarroyo, physicist Eduardo Posada, artist Fernando Botero, entertainer Shakira, and sports figures Juan Pablo Montoya (NASCAR) and Camilo Villegas (professional golfer).

Colombians are a diverse mixture of races and cultures. The population represents *Mestizo* (Indian and Spanish, 64%), white (22%), *Mulato* (black and Spanish, 6.5%), Afro-Colombian (4%), and Amerindian (3.5%) heritage (CIA, 2007). The country is divided into urban and rural areas, with factors such as literacy varying widely by area (e.g., 94.2% literacy rate in urban areas, 67% in rural areas; U.S. Department of State, 2007). The majority of people live in cities (urban population 70% in 2007). The Colombian economy has improved in recent years, yet 49.2% of Colombians live below the poverty line. There is a large disparity in wealth and resources among Colombians, and the middle class often appears to be small (Delgado-Romero et al., 2007). Ninety percent of the population is baptized as Roman Catholics (CIA, 2007), and 61% state that they are practicing Catholics.

Politically, Colombia is a republic, and Álvaro Uribe Velez has been president since 2002. Colombia is emerging from a four-decade period of internal war termed *la violencia* (the violence). The conflict was between the government, antigovernment insurgent forces, and paramilitary groups (CIA, 2007). Complicating matters further was the consolidation of Colombian drug lords into organized cartels that created an extensive and lucrative drug trade that peaked during the 1980s. The influx of wealth made the cartel leaders rich and fueled both insurgent and paramilitary groups. During the violence that ensued, government leaders and judges were kidnapped and assassinated, and torture and murder became commonplace. Widespread loss of life and migration occurred as a result.

EDUCATION

Colombia has a long tradition in education, in particular the arts and humanities. There are many colleges and universities in Colombia, with a university education being a status symbol. The value of education has caused the proliferation of universities and service and health programs, such as in medicine, law, business administration, and psychology (Ardila, 2004). The Colombian tertiary education system consists of both public and private institutions, with 86% of students enrolled at universities and the remaining 14% enrolled in technological and technical training institutions. In 1996, less than 15% of students at the master's level were enrolled in the natural sciences, engineering, and agricultural sciences, while 73% of graduate students in Colombia were enrolled in the social sciences. This situation is the inverse of what one typically finds in the region (World Bank, 2003).

During the 1990s, enrollment in tertiary education mushroomed. However, inequalities in tertiary education persisted, with the poorest Colombians lacking access. Only 11% of Colombian workers have attended some form of tertiary education—compared with 24% of the labor force in industrialized countries. This lack of access is predicted to have a significant economic impact in the future. Improving access to tertiary education for lower- and middle-income groups is therefore an important remedy to mitigate future inequalities (World Bank, 2003).

For those Colombians who are able to enroll in a university, the typical curriculum for undergraduate training in psychology lasts 5 years. Psychology training is professionally oriented and resembles European professional training or master's-level psychology training in the United States (Ardila, 2004). During the last three semesters of study, Colombian undergraduate psychology majors focus on a single area of psychology (e.g., clinical, industrial/organizational, health, educational, experimental, neuropsychology, sport, forensic psychology). A generic degree of "Psychologist" is awarded at the undergraduate level after a thesis and supervised professional practice. Despite the dominance of the European training model, currently Colombian psychology is heavily influenced by psychology in the United States as regards popular theories, models, textbooks, authors, and approaches. Major theoretical approaches used in Colombia include cognitive-behavioral, systemic, behavioral, and psychoanalytic ones. The writings of Piaget, Vigotsky, and Skinner are influential in psychological practice in counseling areas. It should be noted that specific, indigenous, and original models of counseling have yet to be widely articulated (R. Ardila, personal communication, October 31, 2007).

Ardila (2004) reported that in 2003 there were an estimated 12,000 graduated psychologists, 20,000 students of psychology, and 77 professional training programs in Colombia. The overwhelming majority of Colombian psychologists who practice were trained in the undergraduate training model described earlier. Psychology has been traditionally a female profession, with two thirds of Colombian psychologists being women. In the master's and doctoral programs that exist, the curriculum is very specialized and is oriented toward scientific research. It is expected that a graduate student will master an area of psychology (e.g., clinical, social, forensic, behavior analysis, neuropsychology, health) and go on to conduct scientific research in that area. Those few psychologists who have a PhD or PsyD degree have usually been trained abroad in the United States, Belgium, Mexico, Russia, or Spain (Ardila, 2004). At the time of writing this, only two psychology doctoral programs exist in Colombia, and a few more are in the processes of being established.

HELP-SEEKING BEHAVIOR

The need for psychological services in Colombia is robust. In general, the interest in seeking psychological help has increased in the past few decades in Colombia. Urban, young, and female Colombians tend to be the ones who primarily seek help for psychological difficulties. In high schools and universities, psychological services are often in demand, and long wait lists are common. Common presenting issues in Colombia include family issues, sexual abuse, depression, stress and anxiety, and a need for vocational guidance (R. Ardila, personal communication, October 31, 2007). Given that 90% of the population is Catholic, many Colombians consult clergy for personal problems, and in turn, clergy often consult with or refer to psychologists. The relationship between Catholicism and psychological practice in Colombia is an intriguing area that should be examined further.

Although the need for psychological services can be robust in some areas and with certain populations,

cultural norms developed during years of conflict also inhibit help seeking. As a result of years of dealing with violence and corruption, Colombians have learned to keep a skeptical distance between themselves and others (E. Delgado Polo, personal communication, July 31, 2008). Colombians, therefore, are likely to build trust in others slowly and deliberately, taking great care to be sure of the intentions and trustworthiness of others. In addition, this caution in interpersonal relationships has resulted in an emphasis on individualism, working alone versus with others, and a valuing of confidence in one's own ability. Consequently, many Colombians will only reactively turn to others for help in times of crisis. Thus, psychologists must be trained to deal with cultural values productively to promote the value of prevention and ensure a successful working alliance.

ASPECTS OF PSYCHOLOGY IN COLOMBIA

History

Ardila (1973, 1993, 2004) summarized the development of Colombian psychology. He stated that modern Colombian history is marked by the arrival of the Spaniards in 1492, which led to three centuries of colonization. A part of the colonization process was the creation of an educational system based on the European model. The 19th century led to many scientific advances, including the advent of scientific psychology. The professionalization of psychology began in 1947 with the creation of the first professional training program at the National University of Colombia. Ardila (1993, 2004) noted the important role that psychologist Mercedes Rodrigo (1891–1982) played in establishing professional psychology in Colombia. In 1947, she created the Institute of Applied Psychology at the National University of Colombia in Bogotá for the purpose of training professional psychologists, bringing in the first professional psychology program in South America. The first psychologists graduated in 1952. Psychology in Colombia is Western oriented, and scientific principles are accepted as universal and not necessarily unique to the people or the culture of Colombia (Ardila, 2004). Given the decades of violence that have marred the country's recent history, much of the work of Colombian psychologists has dealt with research regarding rehabilitation, posttraumatic stress, and grief. Recently, psychologists have begun to focus on protective factors for children, adolescents, and families faced with trauma. Concurrent with the end of widespread violence, there has been an increased focus on civil rights, civil participation, and community development.

Professional Organizations

The most prominent professional organization is the Colombian Society of Psychology (*Sociedad Colombiana de Psicología* [SOCOPSI], http://www.socopsi.com). The society was founded in 1979, and its mission is the academic and professional fortification of the community of psychologists in Colombia. The society is a scientific and professional association, and it also provides a forum for communication and networking between students and professionals in psychology in the country (SOCOPSI, 2007). The society is composed of divisions such as the following: clinical, community, experimental, educational, industrial/organizational, and sport psychology. Counseling psychologists tend to join either the educational psychology or clinical psychology divisions of the Colombian Society of Psychology (R. Ardila, personal communication, October 31, 2007).

The code of ethics for Colombian psychologists was updated in 2006. The code is composed of 93 articles that address the practice of the profession of psychology in Colombia. The professional practice of psychology requires a degree (usually the 5-year undergraduate degree) and registration by the secretary of health. Licensing and certification are based on one's professional training. The major continuing education event is the biannual Colombian Congress of Psychology (Ardila, 2004). The 13th congress was held in Bogotá in 2008 (http://www.13congreso.socopsi.com/).

Colombians Abroad

It is estimated that more than 300,000 Colombians have fled the country because of narcotics-related activities, guerilla warfare, and paramilitary activities and that there are between 1.8 and 3.8 million Colombian emigrants and internally displaced persons (CIA, 2007). In 2007, the net migration rate for Colombian was estimated to be −0.29 migrants per 1,000 persons (meaning there are more emigrants than immigrants as opposed to countries with more migrants than emigrants, such as the United Kingdom and the United States; CIA, 2007). Given the large number of Colombian emigrants, it should not be surprising to note that as Colombians migrate to other countries there may be a considerable amount of posttraumatic stress, loss, and concern for relatives left behind. For example, Colombians make up the largest South American population in the United States. During the 1950s and 1960s in the United States, Colombians were stereotyped as successful and wealthy, but that stereotype was supplanted by the stereotype of the Colombian drug lord by the 1980s (Delgado-Romero et al., 2007; Delgado-Romero & Rojas, 2004).

CHALLENGES FOR THE FUTURE

Colombian psychologists are faced with multiple possibilities and challenges for the future. A basic problem is the Colombian educational system, in which there is a high dropout rate (estimated at 50% in undergraduate education) and uneven preparation for higher education coupled with persistent labor and economic problems (Delgado Polo & Sandoval, 2002). Another challenge is the number, quality, and direction of psychology training programs. This challenge is tied to the popularity of psychology as a major in Colombia, which leads to an oversupply of psychologists at the undergraduate level (Ardila, 2004). The small number of master's and doctoral-level training programs compounds this problem as further graduate training in psychology is limited.

At the same time, the popularity of psychology as a major provides the profession with a critical mass of people invested in the development of this profession. As the political situation in the country continues to stabilize, psychologists (both immigrants and Colombians trained abroad) may come to the country and help create an infrastructure for master's and doctoral-level training and help the science and applications of psychology develop further. With an increase in participation in the international psychological community, Colombian psychologists will continue to develop the profession and embrace, adopt, and create technological innovations related to the science and practice of psychotherapy.

Our hope is that Colombian psychologists will also develop theories and models (and reflect those theories and models in research and practice) specific to the relevant social realities of Colombian society as there is currently a lack of indigenous or local models. For example, given the realities of a racially mixed society and the existence of marginalized communities of color (e.g., Afro-Colombians, Amerindians), specific counseling applications such as identity development models and related research (e.g., health disparities) should be developed. In addition, given the long history of civil war and related trauma, Colombian psychologists could articulate theories and models of treatment grounded in the strengths of Colombian history and culture. For example, during the writing of this chapter, Colombia took center stage internationally as two hostages, held for almost 6 years, were released by a rebel group. The hostage release, followed by a dramatic hostage rescue, made headlines and reminded the world of the ongoing struggles in Colombian society. Colombian psychologists could examine and expound on how Colombians coped and adapted to a social situation where kidnapping, terrorism, and random violence were a daily reality. Psychologists could focus on the resilience and protective factors in Colombian families rather than focus on pathology, such as increased rates of substance abuse.

Our second hope is that Colombians will embrace the positive values that counseling psychology has advanced as a specialty in psychology. These include an emphasis on normal human development, vocational development, multiculturalism, and social justice in training, practice, and research (see Brown & Lent, 2008). For example, Colombian psychologists could move beyond etic applications of psychology to Colombian people and examine the emic implications of the diversity of Colombian cultures. The profession of counseling psychology in the United States has provided a model—addressing the necessary multicultural competencies and guidelines with resultant implications for research, measurement, and training—that Colombians might apply to their specific situation. This model is not limited to cultural or ethnic minority issues and includes relevant issues such as social class, gender, sexual orientation, and disability. Without a doubt, these issues are already emerging in Colombian psychology; however, we would like to see the specific development of the subfield of counseling psychology, which has an explicit emphasis (and established clinical and research base) on these values. One of the authors (Delgado Polo), a Colombian psychologist and educator, points to the development of university counseling centers and the development of doctoral programs as positive signs that counseling psychology may be poised to emerge as a specialty in its own right in Colombia.

It is our hope that, as Colombia continues to emerge from decades of civil war, the discipline of psychology will continue to grow and reflect the unique aspects of Colombian culture and history. We believe that counseling psychology is an ideal discipline to facilitate the "Colombianization" of psychology, and we encourage counseling psychologists from around the world to exchange knowledge, research, and best practices with Colombian psychologists.

REFERENCES

Ardila, R. (1973). *La psicología en Colombia, desarrollo histórico* [Psychology in Colombia: Historical development]. Mexico City, Mexico: Editorial Trillas.

Ardila, R. (Ed.). (1993). *Psicología en Colombia, contexto social e histórico* [Psychology in Colombia: Social and historical context]. Bogotá, Colombia: Editorial Tercer Mundo.

Ardila, R. (2004). Psychology in Colombia: Development and current status. In M. J. Stevens & D. Wedding (Eds.), *Handbook of international psychology* (pp. 169–177). New York: Taylor & Francis.

Brown, S. D., & Lent, R. W. (2008). *Handbook of counseling psychology* (4th ed.). Hoboken, NJ: Wiley.

Central Intelligence Agency. (2007). *The world factbook: Colombia.* Retrieved July 27, 2007, from htp://www .cia.gov/library/publications/the-world-factbook/ geos/co.html

Delgado Polo, E., & Sandoval, S. (2002). *Maestro: Contextos y horizontes en su formación professional. El oficio de Investigar* [Professor/teacher: Context and horizons in professional formation. Office of investigations]. Research Center, National Pedagogical University of Colombia, Bogota, Colombia.

Delgado-Romero, E. A., & Rojas, A. (2004). Other Latinos: Counseling Cuban, Central and South American Clients. In C. Negy (Ed.), *Cross cultural psychotherapy: Toward a critical understanding of diverse client populations* (pp. 139–162). Reno, NV: Bent Tree Press.

Delgado-Romero, E. A., Rojas, A., & Shelton, K. L. (2007). Immigration history and therapy considerations with Hispanics from Cuba, Central and South America. In C. Negy (Ed.), *Cross cultural psychotherapy: Toward a critical understanding of diverse client populations* (2nd ed., pp. 133–160). Reno, NV: Bent Tree Press.

Sociedad Colombiana de Psicología [The Colombian Society of Psychology]. (2007). *Mission of the society of Colombian psychology.* Retrieved April 15, 2009, from http://www.socopsi.com/institucional.html

U.S. Department of State Bureau of Western Hemisphere Affairs. (2007, March). *Background note: Colombia.* Retrieved July 27, 2007, from htp://www.state.gov/ r/pa/ei/bgn/35754.htm

The World Bank. (2003). *Tertiary education in Colombia: Paving the way for reform.* Washington, DC: Author. Retrieved July 27, 2007, from http://www.bc.edu/bc_ org/avp/soe/cihe/ihec/regions/WorldBank_Colombia.pdf

28

Psychological Counseling in Venezuela

Culture, Change, and Challenges

Asesoramiento Psicológico en Venezuela:
Cultura, cambios y retos

PEDRO E. RODRÍGUEZ, ALCIRA TEIXEIRA, AND EMMA MEJÍA

Venezuela is a Latin American country in northern South America. It is bordered to the west by Colombia, to the south by Brazil, to the east by Guyana, and to the north by the Caribbean Sea. It is approximately 916,480 square kilometers in area, and its territory shows significant contrasts in climate and geography. It is divided into four large natural regions: the Andean region, the Caribbean region, the *Llanos* (flat plains) region, and the Amazonian region. The country is administratively divided into 23 states, the Capital District, and the federal dependencies, which comprise 311 islands, keys, and islets. The government system is defined as "participative-democratic," and the official language is Spanish.

The ethnic makeup includes *mestizos*[1] (67%), whites (21%), blacks (10%) and indigenous people (2%). There are also other minority groups, predominantly of Middle Eastern and Chinese descents. According to the latest national census, the population in 2001 was 23,232,553. The estimate for 2007 was 27,600,000. According to the same census, 87.7% of Venezuelans lived in urban areas, whereas 11.5% lived in rural areas.

In 2005, the life expectancy was 73.43 years, literacy was 95%, and per capita income was $4,102. In total, the Human Development Index was 0.81 (National Statistics Institute, 2007). For the first semester of 2002, the percentage of households in poverty or extreme poverty (according to the poverty line method) was 41.5%, whereas the percentage above the poverty line was 58.5% (National Statistics Institute, 2007). It is in this social context that psychology emerges as a social science practiced by licensed professionals since approximately 50 years ago.

COUNSELING IN VENEZUELA

There are at present eight schools of psychology in Venezuela. Only one of them is affiliated with a public university; the rest are privately funded. The most widespread approach to training professionals is the "psychology as science and profession" model, which involves two stages or cycles. The first, which may vary in length, consists of course work with theoretical and foundational content; the second is a final cycle of applied training. This applied training can be organized according to one of two modalities. One option is "a generalist" training, which requires the student to take courses in all areas of psychology. The second modality consists of a basic training common to all candidates, followed by training in a specialty area. The psychology specialties offered in Venezuela are clinical psychology, industrial psychology, school psychology, and psychological counseling (León, Matos, & Campagnaro, 2007). It takes 5 years to complete a psychology degree.

Training in psychological counseling at the undergraduate and graduate levels usually includes the following content: (a) models of psychological intervention, such as the psychodynamic, humanistic-experiential, and cognitive-behavioral models; (b) training in career and educational counseling; (c) individual and group psychotherapy; and (d) preventive and community-based intervention. Theoretical training is frequently accompanied by a practicum, typically at a university or high school counseling center.

According to the country's legislation, every psychologist, on graduation, is legally qualified to practice psychology, performing services such as evaluation, diagnosis, and intervention. Although there is a high demand for new professionals in the education sector (especially in schools and universities), this high demand is greatly compromised by the scarce availability of opportunities for professional development and the relatively poor conditions of graduate studies in the field.

Historically, the main difference between graduate and undergraduate programs is that in the former there are many more academic requirements for completing the course of study and a richer exposure to supervised counseling experience in a variety of contexts. However, at present, only two universities—both located in Caracas, the country's capital—offer graduate programs in educational counseling. Although such programs include psychologists as faculty members, these programs are mainly directed toward educators and therefore do not offer extensive training in psychological counseling. It is for this reason that most young professionals who work as counselors choose to enter graduate programs in clinical psychology, which can be completed in 2 to 3 years. The education received in these programs is frequently complemented with nonformal training, such as training in group therapy or in specific psychotherapeutic models (e.g., Gestalt therapy, psychoanalysis, humanistic psychology, family counseling). The fundamental requirement for admission into these programs is a degree in psychology.

BRIEF HISTORY OF PSYCHOLOGICAL COUNSELING IN VENEZUELA

It is widely agreed that psychological counseling in Venezuela has been systematically plagued by a confusion about its objectives and strategies. The diversity of the academic levels of its practitioners has plagued it as well. This predicament has led to a confused professional identity, afflicted by poorly defined roles and functions (Rodríguez, 2003, 2006). This situation might perhaps be better understood in light of the specialty's history.

Psychological counseling started in Venezuela as a discipline with a strong educational bias (Casado, 1995; Rodríguez, 2006). Its beginnings were tied to the creation of the Orientation Division (*División de Orientación*) of the Ministry of Education, which was in charge of planning, coordinating, and supervising the practice of counseling in the country. As a result of this origin, psychologists enjoyed little discretionary power during this initial stage, and their functions were basically reduced to evaluation. It was not until later, with the arrival of psychologists trained in the United States and Europe during the 1960s, that some universities began to offer graduate programs in psychological counseling. This increased the opportunities for professional improvement. In particular, it resulted in an increased awareness of psychotherapeutic theories and models, which allowed psychologists to distinguish themselves from educators. This fact was readily noticed by employers in private institutions, and as a result, counseling psychologists began occupying the majority of the positions in private secondary education institutions. Another important source of employment for counseling psychologists was (and still is) student services at both public and private universities. There are various roles and functions for counseling psychologist in these settings: interventions connected to academic counseling, therapy, group therapy, and community-based programs.

In spite of the fluctuations experienced over time by the specialty, there are three elements that currently characterize the practice of psychological counseling in Venezuela. The first is the fact that it has been systematically and directly associated with the practice of psychology in educational contexts. The second is the strong influence that humanistic and experiential models have had on the development and philosophy of intervention techniques. The third is the effort to establish a psychologically based approach to counseling in the educational contexts in which most psychological counselors work.

Counseling Professionals

By 1996, there were approximately 5,800 psychologists in Venezuela, of whom 75% were professionally active. By 1999, there were 10,000 psychologists registered in the Venezuelan Federation of Psychology, only 10% of whom reported having pursued graduate studies (Rodríguez & Sánchez, 1996). It is certain that a significant proportion of professionals dedicate themselves to diverse areas, such as school psychology, clinical psychology, health psychology and, of course, counseling psychology. Nevertheless, it is important to recognize that there is no information available on how many psychologists actually are counseling psychologists.

As can be expected, the lack of opportunities for professional training, together with the constant sharing of functions with educators, has brought about a decline in the counseling specialty's standing within the wider context of the professional practice of psychology. Also, psychologists who occupy positions as psychological counselors come from different training traditions. Some have barely completed their undergraduate studies. Others have a background in school psychology, family therapy, or clinical psychology.

Models of Intervention in Venezuela

Psychological counseling in Venezuela has developed on the basis of two models: the psychotherapeutic and the psychoeducational models. Each model has its respective epistemological, theoretical, and methodological consequences.

The psychotherapeutic model, commonly referred to in Spanish as *Asesoramiento,* has been heavily influenced by the medical approach in psychology. It assigns a preeminent role to individual and group interventions, in both their remedial and preventive modalities. It has been also the predominant approach in counseling centers at universities and private educational institutions.

The psychoeducational model, typically called *Orientación,* is strongly influenced by the educational approach and is most frequently found in public schools. It is characterized by activities such as guidance, academic and vocational information sessions, and selective attention to individual and group cases from an educational perspective.

Although these models characterize the current practice of psychology in Venezuela, they are far from constituting a "homegrown" psychology. In fact, there is no such thing as an indigenous psychology in the country. The models, strategies, and activities in use have been shaped by the (sometimes uncritical) incorporation of developments and resources from other countries, especially the United States. This is hardly surprising since, as Alarcón (2002) pointed out, Latin American psychology has developed from foreign models that originate from the world's knowledge centers.

The following are among the most frequent interventions performed by professionals in the discipline.

Academic Counseling. This mode of intervention is a chief element in the country's education-oriented tradition in counseling. Typical activities within this modality are vocational counseling, academic performance counseling, personal-social counseling, and coaching, among others.

Psychotherapy. This approach (as can be expected) is at the heart of the psychotherapeutic model. Among the strategies employed in this modality are brief psychotherapy, topic- and process-focused psychotherapy (e.g., focusing on dispersed symptoms of depression and anxiety, social phobias, and eating disorders), and developmental tasks (e.g., fear of development, adaptation, developmental changes, psychosocial stress).

Family Psychotherapy. This is not just another intervention modality but an integral approach in its own right. It focuses on family dynamics across the life cycle, taking into account the cultural heritage and identity of the Venezuelan people.

Crisis Intervention. This model has gained prominence in recent years. Among the activities that characterize this modality are individual-, group-, and community-level interventions; facilitator training; development of psychoeducational materials; talks; and so on.

Community-Level Interventions. These include work with institutions, as well as the development of programs for the promotion of psychological well-being in high-risk populations.

THE PREVALENCE OF PERSONS SEEKING HELP

Venezuela is a country with a deeply rooted collectivist tradition (e.g., Triandis, 2001). Before the development and expansion of formal psychological practice, many of the popular care practices were (and still are) associated with nonformal strategies that relied on elements already present in the community. Among these were social and family relationships, as well as institutions with strong social roots, such as the church and the practice of medicine. Occasionally, other significant people in the community were also involved, such as professionals who were not trained in the helping professions and folk healers. All these informal practices are based on idiosyncratic criteria, which range from mere commonsense interventions to complex naïve theories. Unfortunately, there is no information about the practices of noncounseling trained professionals and folk healers.

Venezuelans are usually reared in tightly cohesive Catholic families. People have a legacy of supporting each other in the family, and the value of solidarity is most describing of the culture. In a way it helps under crises since it mobilizes resources in nuclear and extended families and even in friend-networks known as *compadres*. Therefore, seeking help outside one's network is considered risky. The risk involves separation from family of origin and its legacies, and a detachment from religious principles. Ethics is seen as very tightly connected to morality and religion, and professionals and scientists even social scientists are people who are not always completely trustworthy. There is fear that the heritage of family cohesion, the needed cohesion that has historically been developed to face poverty, and migration from the land to the cities in search of improved health, housing, income, education, and job stability with the surge of the oil industry in the past century could be endangered if cohesion is not preserved. Thus, issues of differentiation from family of origin are hard to deal with, and within that context, searching for help away from the traditional religious system is perceived as a threat to both cohesion and moral standards.

By the same token, Venezuelans have faced adversity by working hard and even assuming self-sacrificing attitudes. Because of this, the possibility of being relieved by counseling without searching for family or religious support is against some of the legacies and family mandates. A virtuous person in

Venezuelan culture and religion chooses first to maintain togetherness regardless of how dysfunctional a family situation may be. One example is domestic violence.

Unfortunately, there are no up-to-date data at the national level about the reasons why people seek help in counseling centers; however, and in spite of the population's heterogeneity, there are firmly established help-seeking tendencies among populations in higher education institutions. In these settings, persons seek services to relieve affective and interpersonal issues. This tendency is similar to those reported by researchers in other countries. Besides these types of issues, there is also demand for vocational counseling and the development of study skills (Rodríguez, 2006; Romero, 1993). To these we must add the significant presence of overwhelming, multifaceted cases (e.g., domestic violence, sexual abuse) that sometimes seem to go beyond the objectives of counseling centers. It has been often reported that mental disorders have surpassed the capacity of several centers, especially at the university level (Romero, 1993).

In fact, there are multidimensional cases that challenge the additional complexities posed by the contexts in which the specialty is practiced. Some of the most interesting challenges and opportunities are, in the first place, the challenges posed by educational contexts. In Venezuela, the majority of students drop out of the formal education system and only a small percentage reach higher education. This fact—which has not received enough attention on the profession's part—poses significant difficulties for psychological interventions since educational institutions constitute the usual context for the practice of counseling in the country.

Second, there are challenges posed by the use of psychological tests. The available vocational tests are typically oriented toward prospective university students and not toward those seeking training in trades and technical professions, which constitute the fundamental goal of a broad section of the population. Third are the challenges posed by looking for help and challenging social issues. Recently, there has been an increase in people seeking counseling services for psychopathological and multiproblematic contents, arising from conditions of violence, poverty, and exclusion. Many of those presenting with these severe issues do not receive adequate attention at the health care centers due to the limitations and inadequacies in the public health care system. These challenges are even greater for those psychologists who are not adequately trained in psychopathology, crisis intervention, and other emergency areas.

Finally, there are challenges posed by the political climate. Since the beginning of the 21st century, Venezuela has undergone a complex process of political polarization between those who support the country's president and those who oppose him. In some cases, this conflict has had terrible social repercussions, such as demonstrators' deaths and politically motivated layoffs of public and private employees. There is also a generalized sensation of fear and threat, which has resulted in the most important migration in the country's modern history. This has had consequences for the kind of situations faced by psychological counselors, in the wake of the recent increase in the number of high school and university students who are assaulted or detained under irregular conditions by the government's security agencies. Some of these students have then requested help from counseling centers in their schools or universities. This has meant a heavier presence of political factors in the day-to-day practice of professionals in the field, and at the same time, it has presented them with new opportunities for action.

PERCEPTION OF COUNSELING

Few studies in Venezuela have addressed the question of how counseling is perceived. Among those few is a study conducted by Rodríguez (2003), which explored the social representation of the educational counselor from the students' perspective. Rodríguez found that the social representation built its figurative core around the "professional" and "friend" figures. About 68% of the sample described *counselors* on the basis of socioaffective features, such as kindness, willingness to listen, patience, cordiality, and friendliness. This contrasts with the additional finding that, among students in public schools, the counselor's *role* was in general negatively perceived. By and large, the study shows that the students' perceptions of counselors tend to highlight the curative or remedial role, at the expense of the rest of the counselor's proper functions, such as prevention and planning. Broadly speaking, it appears that the students' perception of counseling is largely based on the skills needed for providing intensive care in situations of conflict or hardship.

CONCLUSION

The future of counseling in Venezuela is at an interesting crossroad. We could say (at the risk of seeming too optimistic) that it is one of the psychological specialties with the widest opportunities for development. Psychological counseling assigns primary importance to the rescue of the person's healthy part, and in so doing, it emphasizes the development of individual and group resources, competencies, and strengths. Moreover, in addition to offering *direct* attention to clients, it also offers *indirect* attention to the community by providing training to agents who will themselves become trainers (e.g., parents, teachers, health care professionals, key members of the community). This indirect action multiplies the number of people who can benefit from psychological services and also bestows a social character on the profession as it allows a wide range of institutions and communities to be reached. However, the specialty also faces significant threats, the most important of which is perhaps a decline in the opportunities for graduate training in the area, in the prospect for growth and, indirectly, in the country's general conditions for the practice of psychology as a science and a profession.

Some of the challenges facing professional counseling are also challenges faced by the Venezuelan people. The culture and history of the Venezuelan people merge more and more with a globalized world. There are also greater life cycle challenges in a political and socioeconomic context that result in increased stress among the people and not necessarily better social support, despite Venezuela's paradoxical success with the oil industry.

Counselors have to respect, acknowledge, and validate these complex dynamics to help individuals deal with the more complex life cycle tasks without being disloyal to their history, family, and culture. Values must be acknowledged and respected in the process of counseling. A culturally respectful intervention incorporates a full acknowledgment of the ethics, values, and spirituality of the population in a nonjudgmental counseling and therapeutic context, in consonance with the challenge of postmodernist and indigenous approaches.

NOTE

1. Persons of racially mixed parentage.

REFERENCES

Alarcón, R. (2002). *Estudios sobre psicología latinoamericana* [Studies on Latin American psychology]. Lima, Peru: Universidad Ricardo Palma.

Casado, E. (1995). Orientación y educación [Counseling and education]. In E. Casado (Ed.), *De la orientación al asesoramiento psicológico: una selección de lecturas* [From advice to psychological counseling: A selection of readings] (pp. 17–20). Caracas, Venezuela: Universidad Central de Venezuela.

León, C., Matos, M., & Campagnaro, S. (2007). School psychology in Venezuela. In S. R. Jimerson, T. D. Oakland, & P. T. Farrell (Eds.), *The handbook of international school psychology* (pp. 427–435). Thousand Oaks: Sage.

National Statistics Institute. (2007). *Reporte del instituto nacional de estadística* [Report of the National Statistical Institute]. Retrieved November 11, 2007, from http://www.ine.gov.ve/

Authors' Note: A special thanks to Edison Barrios, PhD, Ana Beatriz Sapene, and Swelen Andari for their help in the translation of this document.

Rodríguez, M. A. (2003). *Representación social del orientador desde la perspectiva de los alumnos (caso colegio universitario Francisco de Miranda)* [Social representation of orientation from the perspective of students: Case of University College Francisco de Mirada]. Maestría Educación, Mención Orientación [Master of education, Advice mention], UCV, Venezuela.

Rodríguez, P. E. (2006). Asesoramiento psicológico [Counseling psychology]. In G. Peña, Y. Cañoto, & Z. Santalla (Eds.), *Una introducción a la psicología* [An introduction to psychology] (pp. 505–530). Caracas, Venezeula: UCAB.

Rodríguez, P. R., & Sánchez, L. (1996). La psicología en Venezuela [Psychology in Venezuela]. *Papeles del psicólogo, 66,* 45–50.

Romero, J. C. (1993). Atención psicoterapéutica a estudiantes universitarios [Psychotherapeutic assistance to college students]. *Revista de psicología clínica, 1,* 16–27.

Triandis, H. (2001). Individualism-collectivism and personality. *Journal of Personality, 69*(6), 907–924.

29

Psychology in Argentina

In Search of New Paradigms and Professional Identities

La Psicología en Argentina:
En Busca de Nuevos Paradigmas e Identidades Profesionales

SUSANA VERDINELLI AND CARLOS M. DIAZ-LAZARO

This chapter explores different aspects of the field of psychology in Argentina. It begins with an overview of general characteristics of the country, followed by a description of the activities psychologists perform and an exploration of historical events that shaped this field, education of psychologists, research, professional licensing, and different models of healing. Finally, a discussion on the future direction of psychology in Argentina is provided.

ARGENTINA: AN OVERVIEW

Argentina is South America's southernmost country and has a population of more than 36 million inhabitants. It is the eighth largest country in the world and the main language is Spanish. The racial composition of its population is 85% white, 10% *mestizo* or mixed, and 5% indigenous or other. Most

Argentineans are of European descent since in addition to early Spanish conquistadors, waves of European settlers principally from Italy and Spain came to Argentina from the late 19th to mid-20th century. Indigenous populations survive in small groups, and only a few tribes practice traditional lifestyles (Ministerio de Relaciones Exteriores [Ministry of Foreign Affairs, International Trade and Worship], 2007). The early extinction of the native population and the subsequent settlements of European immigrants generated an Argentine culture widely influenced by a European heritage.

THE FIELD OF PSYCHOLOGY

The field of psychology in Argentina has grown tremendously since the first programs of psychology were established in the country. Psychology is present in many aspects of everyday life both in academic circles and pop culture. Argentina is considered one of the countries with the largest number of psychologists in the world. In 2005, there were 62,760 graduates of psychology. A projection indicates that there will be 70,000 graduates by the year 2010. Between 1995 and 2005, there were an average of 2,376 graduates per year. There is one psychologist for every 754 inhabitants (Alonso & Gago, 2006), and about 80% of psychologists are females (Instituto Nacional de Estadística y Censo [National Institute of Statistics and Census], 2001). Unfortunately, there are no clear politics or regulations regarding the number of psychologists needed to serve the needs of the Argentine population (Alonso & Nicenboim, 1997), and there is no regulation on the number of students who can attend graduate psychology programs. This results in an oversupply of young professionals, who experience difficulties finding jobs (Castro Solano, 2004).

Argentine psychologists work primarily in clinical settings. It is estimated that around 85% of psychologists work in the clinical field, primarily providing psychotherapy to adults, adolescents, children, and families (Alonso & Nicenboim, 1997; García & de Barbenza, 2006; Gentile, 1989). Clinical practice also involves consultation, diagnostic interviews, psychological evaluations, and report writing. School psychology has also been through considerable development. It involves the practice of educational and vocational guidance, early diagnosis of learning problems, testing, and the provision of therapy and psychological services to children, adolescents, and their families within the school setting. To a lesser extent, forensic psychology and industrial-organizational psychology have emerged in the country. The main duty of forensic psychologists is the provision of expert reports in trials, whereas industrial psychologists work in recruitment and personnel selection, training programs, and prevention of work-related injuries (Castro Solano, 2004). In Argentina, the field and degree of counseling psychology as it is defined in the United States (Munley, Duncan, & McDonnell, 2004) does not exist. Among psychologists, the concept of counseling psychology is paired with that of clinical psychology.

Early Development of Psychology

The development of psychology in Argentina can be categorized into two main stages: the preprofessional and the professional stages (Vilanova, 1990). The preprofessional stage, which began at the end of the 1800s, is also called a period of "psychology without psychologists" (Vezzetti, 1988). At the end of the 1950s, the professional period began with the creation of psychology programs at the universities. Paradoxically, psychology as a science had its strongest development and growth during the preprofessional stage. Since their inception, psychology programs have emphasized the role of the psychologist as a practitioner and not as a researcher (Vilanova & Di Doménico, 1999).

During the preprofessional stage, different experimental psychology laboratories were founded. In 1891, Victor Mercante founded an experimental laboratory to measure psychophysical phenomena. During this time, the first psychology courses taught were in law and social sciences programs (Klappenbach & Pavesi, 1994). In its early years, psychology was strongly influenced by positivistic ideas, and it was markedly European in origin. In 1906, Felix Krueger, who trained in Germany in Wundt's experimental laboratory, organized an experimental psychology laboratory in an educational institution in Buenos Aires. At the same time, Horacio Piñero and other scholars who contributed to the development of psychology professed a great admiration of the French intellectual elite. Despite this positivist influence, economic conditions prompted the advancement of applied psychology mainly in the fields of psychometrics and school guidance (Klappenbach, 1996). The movement toward a greater clinical emphasis was further highlighted in 1954 by the First Argentine Congress of Psychology, which recommended the creation of the first schools of psychology in the country. This event initiated the beginning of the professional stage (Klappenbach, 1995).

Education of Psychologists

There are 9 public universities and 30 private universities that offer a degree in psychology. The number of schools offering this degree has been steadily increasing in the past 10 years. Argentina's degree system differs from that of the United States. In Argentina, university degrees center on a single field of knowledge or profession and not on arts or sciences as is typically the case in the United States. There are no courses leading to a bachelor's degree. The university degree in psychology is named *licenciatura en psicología* (graduate in psychology) or *psicólogo* (psychologist). Students can enroll in psychology programs after finishing high school. The program of psychology requires 5 or 6 years of study. Completing the requirements of the *licenciatura* allows the professional to practice in any field of psychology, including clinical, educational, organizational, and forensic psychology, which are the main areas of specialization practiced in the country. Thus, the licenciatura is the only university degree required for the professional practice of psychology. Education in public universities is free of charge, whereas the fees of private schools are affordable for middle-class citizens. Considering the breadth and depth of the licenciatura, this degree is comparable with a master's degree in the United States. However, in the United States, the homologation of the licenciatura is considered equivalent to an undergraduate degree in psychology.

The licenciatura takes typically 5 to 6 years, and most schools require attending an average of 35 courses, which is equivalent to 3,400 hours. The programs are usually divided into three cycles: an introductory or basic one, which contains courses in general psychology, philosophy, anthropology, or sociology and biology of human behavior; a core cycle, which includes courses in developmental psychology, with an emphasis on childhood and adolescence, psychological assessment, systems of psychotherapy, psychopathology, and research methodology; and a third specialized cycle, which includes courses in the areas of educational, clinical, forensic, and organizational psychology (Alonso, 1994).

The profile of the graduate in psychology depicts a professional with generic skills and abilities and an emphasis on the training of clinical psychology and mental health (Paolucci & Verdinelli, 1999). Psychoanalytic conceptualizations have been embedded in the training of psychologists since the inception of the degree. Some programs in psychology include up to five-course sequences in psychoanalysis. Indeed, it has been argued that most psychology programs teach all courses from a psychoanalytic perspective (Piacente, 1998; Vilanova, 1993). In recent years, other theoretical orientations have been included in the training of psychologists, such as systemic, cognitive, behavioral, Rogerian person-centered, integrative, and humanistic approaches.

Research

There was a strong emphasis in psychological scientific research until 1930, but around the beginning of the professional stage, the interest in conducting research diminished significantly. Presently, around 10% of psychologists concentrate their activities on research (García & de Barbenza, 2006). In 1995, the National Laws in Education offered monetary incentives to professors in public universities, which resulted in more psychologists becoming interested and engaging in research. Most research centers and teams depend on the National Council for Scientific and Technical Research and are housed in public universities. The National Council for Scientific and Technical Research is a government-funded agency that hires researchers and provides grants to fund diverse research topics.

Most research in psychology is done with human subjects and concentrates on descriptive and correlational research studies rather than experimental or basic processes research. The results are usually published in national journals; thus, most of the findings do not reach an international scientific audience (Mustaca, 2006). Despite the difficulties associated with conducting research, there is an increased interest in developing this area.

Professional Licensing and Other Administrative Regulatory Practices

Most Argentine provinces have *Colegios de Psicólogos* (professional associations of psychologists) that regulate the practice of psychology by administering licenses and supervising the ethical professional practice. To obtain licensure and be able to practice, psychologists are mandated to join these professional associations. At the national level, the FePRA (Federation of Psychologists of the Argentine Republic) is the most important association of psychologists, and it organizes all provincial associations of psychology. FePRA is the representative of psychologists both nationally and internationally. For example, it represents psychologists in the Committee of Psychologists of the Mercosur and associated countries (FePRA, 2007).

Schools and departments of psychology are organized under the AUAPsi (Association of Academic Units of Psychology), which began its functions in 1991. The AUAPsi has analyzed comprehensively the state of the education of psychologists at public universities, making recommendations to improve the training of psychologists (AUAPsi, 2007). A similar association, the AUAPri (Association of Academic Units of Psychology at Private Universities) develops and recommends education standards for private psychology departments and schools. AUAPsi recommended that all programs at public universities guarantee a core curriculum with similar basic content areas, promote quality training in the teaching of psychology in needed areas, and create a more specific scope of the psychological practice in the country. FePRA and AUAPsi recently presented a document to the Ministry of Education containing the standards of accreditation for psychology programs, the core curriculum, and the scope of practice (FePRA, 2008).

MODELS OF HEALING

Psychotherapy

In general, people in Argentina associate mental health services with long-term psychoanalytic treatment. It has been argued that the influence of psychoanalysis has come to permeate contemporary Argentine urban culture, and references to psychoanalysis can be traced in TV shows, newspapers (some which have weekly sections devoted to psychoanalysis), and popular knowledge on specific psychoanalytic terms derived from people attending

psychoanalytic therapy (Bass, 2006). Fernández-Alvarez, Scherb, Bregman, and García (1995) investigated the social representation of psychotherapy in the city of Buenos Aires surveying 410 people. They found that most of the survey respondents (72.8%) were familiar with psychotherapy. This survey also identified psychologists as the main providers of psychotherapy, and more than 50% indicated that they either received or had an acquaintance who had received psychotherapy. Additionally, they evaluated the results of psychotherapy as beneficial or very beneficial, and only occasionally respondents indicated that psychotherapy had a negative effect.

García and de Barbenza (2006) surveyed a representative sample ($N = 226$) of psychologists from different regions of the country about their theoretical orientations and clinical practice. More than 40% of psychologists reported that they ascribe to psychoanalysis; 20.8% to eclectic and integrative approaches; 16.8% to cognitive-behavioral models; 10.6% to systemic, gestalt, and existential models of psychotherapy; 8.8% to no theoretical model; and 2.2% to other models. Other studies showed the same tendency, with psychoanalysis as the first theory of choice and an eclectic or integrative approach the second (Müller, Fondacaro, García, & Rodríguez, 2005; Müller, Oberholzer, Iglesias, Flores, & Bugiolocchi, 2004; Müller & Palavezzatti, 2005). Among the group of therapists who integrate different theories, the majority mentioned that psychoanalysis was the theoretical basis for integration and cognitive theory the second (Müller & Palavezzatti, 2005). These percentages represent the variety of theoretical orientations used in Argentine psychotherapeutic practice.

Understanding the introduction, development, and maintenance of psychoanalytic thought in a country that has the world's second largest community of psychoanalysts affiliated to the International Psychoanalytic Association (second only to the United States) and the world's second largest Lacanian psychoanalytic community (second only to France) (Bass, 2006; Plotkin, 2001) is a complex matter. Klappenbach (2005) identified three influential forces on the history of psychoanalysis in Argentina:

(1) the establishment of the Argentine Psycho-analytical Association in 1942; (2) the writings of Jacques Lacan in the middle of the 1970s; and (3) multilayered processes stemming from various intellectual, cultural, social, and political forces that shaped psychoanalysis in Argentina. Of note is the fact that psychoanalytic thought was introduced in the first psychology programs in the country in the 1950s (Klappenbach, 2003). To varying degrees, the developers of the programs believed that knowing about psychoanalysis was essential in the training of psychologists. Some of these psychology trainers equated *psychologist* with *psychoanalyst* and perceived psychoanalysis as a theory, a therapeutic approach, and a research methodology (Klappenbach, 2000). Since then, psychoanalysis has permeated both the academic training and the psychotherapeutic practice of psychologists.

In sum, psychotherapy has been a significant component of popular culture in Argentina for a long time, which has resulted in there being little stigma attached to seeking out psychological services. Although Argentinean society can be categorized as patriarchal, and the values of competence, achievement, and success are quite strong, attending therapy is not necessarily seen as a sign of weaknesses. Although most Argentineans are not unaware of the fact that many attend therapy for serious, chronic mental health problems, they perceived psychotherapy as an opportunity for personal growth resulting from their tackling of their intrapsychic conflicts. As a result, most Argentineans' expectations of therapy involve emotional cathartic components typically associated with psychoanalytic perspectives. The Argentinean population has a high rate of attendance in therapy, which they expect to be a long-term process.

Chamanismo and Curanderismo: Nontraditional Models of Healing

Along with the practice of psychotherapy and the provision of mental health services, other models of healing exist. Psychologists often ignored and did not study the alternative models of healing present in Argentina. Two main expressions of these alternative models are *chamanismo* and *curanderismo*. *Chamanismo* is the traditional medicine of the aboriginal societies of Argentina. As with curanderismo, chamanismo has taken different forms among aboriginal groups of Latin America. Depending on each tribe, the chaman has different roles and characteristics. In all cases, the chamanes have the power to heal, and this makes them important and respected persons in their communities. The chamanes can heal, they know the sacred prayers, and they have a magic-religious power. The therapy they provide is cost free (Carbonell, 2003). The other alternative model of healing is *curanderismo*, which is a common expression of Latin American folk medicine and assumes specific characteristics in the country where it is practiced. *Curar* is a Spanish verb that means "to heal," and curanderismo is interpreted as a system of healing. In Argentina, curanderismo blends religious beliefs and rituals, which are mainly rooted in Catholic practices, indigenous idiosyncrasies, and knowledge brought by European immigrants about the diagnosis and treatment of diverse illnesses, such as the evil eye (*ojeo/mal de ojo*) and the fright disease (*susto*). The belief in witchcraft and the application of ancient medicine, particularly the humoral one, are also main components of curanderismo (Idoyaga Molina, 2002; Viotti, 2002).

The *curanderos*, the healers, existed for centuries and initially lived in rural areas. They are capable of treating physical and mental illnesses. Illness or sickness is understood as an imbalance between the person and his or her environment affecting the person's harmony. The imbalance can be organic, social, religious, environmental, or personal (Idoyaga Molina, 2000). The rural population acknowledges a variety of illnesses that the curandero treats, such as the evil eye, the fright disease, envy (*envidia*), the goat's foot (*pata de cabra*), and witchcraft (*brujería*), among many others. These illnesses are also common in other Latin American countries (Disderi, 2001). The rituals the healers use to treat people include praying, invocations, petitions, burning of candles for Christian deities, the use and drinking of holy water, the triple repetition of actions (the number 3 is considered a holy number associated with the divine Trinity), the use of water and oil, and the making of the sign of the cross, which is the symbol of life (Idoyaga Molina, 2001).

An example of a traditional illness is the fright disease. It is more common among children, and the rural people do not consider it a mental disorder. However, among adults, this disease may manifest as a mental disorder (Idoyaga Molina, 2002). Among its most common symptoms are physical weakness, crying, sleep problems, and a startled state. Other physical symptoms may include diarrhea, cough, and vomiting. It is believed that this disorder is caused by a great shock resulting in the soul abandoning the body. The goal of treatment is to regain the lost soul (Korman & Idoyaga Molina, 2002).

Mental health providers usually misunderstand these types of beliefs expressed by the rural population and often diagnose those afflicted with fright disease with depression and psychosis, which are treated in public hospitals. References to witchcraft or the effects of envy or mythical persons are usually diagnosed as psychosis. Psychologists and psychiatrists do not generally consider the fright disease or any other traditional illnesses in the context of cultural dimensions. Instead, they categorize them using Western diagnostic criteria such as the *Diagnostic and Statistical Manual of Mental Disorders,* 4th edition, text revision (*DSM-IV-R*) or the World Health Organization's *International Classification of Diseases*–10th revision (*ICD-10*). In fact, the *DSM-IV-TR* is a formal requirement in most institutions, but the psychotherapeutic practice in public institutions still employs the more traditional psychoanalytic diagnostic criteria, such as psychosis, neurosis, and perversion. Neither the *DSM* nor the psychoanalytic diagnostic criteria allow the exploration of cultural meanings and contexts of the traditional illnesses that the rural population experiences. Psychological services offered to this population are oftentimes inadequate, resulting in high dropout rates (Korman & Idoyaga Molina, 2002). Psychologists in Argentina lack the appropriate training to conceptualize the interactions of culture and mental health and therefore struggle to offer effective psychological services integrating culturally relevant alternatives to traditional psychotherapy and medicine (Arrúe & Kalinsky, 1991).

The practice of curanderismo and alternative ways of healing do not only belong to the rural population. Persons in urban contexts embrace a variety of alternative medicines due to internal migration from rural to urban areas in the past 60 years. The expansion of a variety of healing practices in urban settings resulted as a consequence of the economic crisis, which led to the deterioration of the public health system (Gonzalo, 2002). Idoyaga Molina (2005) provided a classification of the different ethnomedical systems and their therapeutic practices. She identified the categories of biomedicine, traditional medicines, religious medicines, alternative medicines, and self-treatment. In any case, this reflects the richness and variety of healing methods that along with formal and academic therapeutic practices coexist in urban contexts.

Not surprisingly, psychological therapies are the most rejected by the rural population, and curanderismo is the preferred therapeutic choice. The native population believes that mental disorders originate in external actions or intentions, and mental problems are the result of witchcraft or fright. Formal mental health services that are offered contradict the rural population's perceptions about the origin, manifestation, and treatment of mental disorders (Korman & Idoyaga Molina, 2002). Moreover, curanderos are cost free or inexpensive; they operate in the patients' natural environment, and these healers establish a close relationship with their clients (Fernández-Alvarez & Nicenboim, 1998).

CONCLUSION AND FUTURE DIRECTIONS

The major contribution and development of psychology in Argentina in the last decades has been in the clinical field. Enrique Pichón Riviere, one of the founders of the Argentinean Psychoanalytic Association, developed a theoretical model that bridged the gap between therapy and prevention through group work. Another influential figure was

Guillermo Vidal, who contributed to the establishment of networks between experts from different countries through his editorship of the journal *Acta Psiquiátrica y Psicológica de América Latina* for more than 40 years (Fernández-Alvarez & Nicenboim, 1998). Jorge Colapinto, Celia Jaes Falicov, Cloé Madanes, Salvador Minuchin, and Carlos Sluzki constitute a group of Argentine therapists established in the United States who have made great contributions to systemic and family therapy in Argentina.

The influence of the counseling psychology specialty in the United States cannot be understated. Counseling psychologists in the United States have provided a unique perspective from which the field of psychology, and the populations it serves, has tremendously benefited. As we seek to understand how the major philosophical assumptions and practices of counseling psychology are displayed internationally, it is important to understand the sociocultural and historical contexts that drive the development of a field such as psychology in each of the countries in which the profession is practiced. In the United States, counseling psychology developed from the guidance and vocational movements and later expanded to focus on the well-being of persons across the life span. This expansion of the role of counseling psychologists formally took effect in 1951 with the change in name of the Division of Personnel and Guidance Psychologists to the current Division of Counseling Psychology (Roger & Stone, n.d.). However, it was not until 1954 that the creation of schools of psychology was even recommended in Argentina by the First Argentine Congress of Psychologists. Whereas in the United States the field of psychology has seen a significant expansion in the number of specializations and interest groups as exemplified by the number of divisions (i.e., 54) of the American Psychological Association, in Argentina, the field has not seen such a trend. It could be argued that the clinical psychologist in Argentina is quite similar to what in the United States is known as a psychologist with a generalist perspective. The scope of practice in Argentina is much more general and less specialized. As a result, no distinction is made between vocational/career and clinical issues. Clinical psychologists in Argentina serve not only in the traditional role of clinical psychologists in the United States but also in the roles that counseling psychologists serve. While writing this chapter, we asked several of our psychologist friends in Argentina to define *counseling* and *counseling psychology*. The most common reaction was a confused look and a reply such as, "What do you mean?" In Argentina, the word *counseling* does not share a meaning with the term *psychotherapy* as it does in the United States. Another difference in how psychology is perceived in Argentina compared with the United States relates to the concept of normality. For counseling psychologists in the United States, one of the core aspects differentiating counseling psychology from clinical psychology is the emphasis on the well-being of normal populations throughout the life span. However, in Argentina, the line separating normal from abnormal is not as well delineated as it is in the United States. *Clinical* is most of the time associated in the United States with "abnormal." By that definition, a significant proportion of Argentines could be categorized as abnormal, as indicated by the number of Argentines who have been treated by clinical psychologists. However, the high numbers of Argentines attending therapy more realistically reflects a significant number of persons seeking help for less severe issues than are commonly treated by clinical psychologists in the United States.

Notwithstanding cultural as well as professional differences in the way psychology has evolved in Argentina and the United States, we strongly believe that the psychological practice in Argentina can benefit from what counseling psychology has to offer. Professional psychological practice in Argentina can be strengthened in three ways: (1) by reinforcing the use of diverse theoretical orientations, (2) by generating culturally sensitive interventions, and (3) by developing subfields in psychology, such as counseling psychology, health psychology, and rehabilitation psychology. The psychoanalytic theoretical framework has dominated the practice and training of psychologists in Argentina. In the past 20 years, the use of systemic, cognitive, humanistic, and integrative approaches has increased. It is our belief that a more open position toward diverse theoretical orientations will allow a pluralistic view of psychology and human beings. Additionally, psychologists need to broaden their perspective around the concept of health and incorporate new methodologies in the treatment of diverse populations. To lower the attrition rate and respond better to the needs of the native and rural populations, it is necessary to develop culturally sensitive interventions. For example, it would seem appropriate to create a list of culture-bound syndromes or vernacular illnesses such as the evil eye, the goat's foot, and envy among others experienced by the rural Argentine population and make this available to mental health professionals.

Incorporating other subfields in the current professional landscape of psychology in Argentina will enrich its practice. Counseling psychology, for instance, may focus on working with healthier, less pathological populations and on career and vocational assessments. The philosophical framework of counseling psychology implies working within a developmental perspective across the full range of psychological functioning, which may lead to a less pathological view of mental health problems (Munley et al., 2004). It also pays special attention to human diversity (e.g., gender differences, sexual orientation, ethnic and cross-cultural issues, women's issues), which is an area that needs further development in Argentina. Furthermore, the use of briefer counseling approaches and an emphasis on prevention and psychoeducational interventions could prove as useful alternatives to the needs of the Argentine population. In addition, the areas of health and rehabilitation psychology will enrich mental health services by identifying the behaviors and experiences that promote health, lead to illness, and influence the effectiveness of health care. The conceptualizations of a biopsychosocial model that includes biological characteristics, behavioral factors, and social conditions in the concepts of health and illness need to be incorporated in the training and work of psychologists in Argentina.

The training of psychologists in Argentina faces many challenges. Although in the past 15 years there have been attempts to modify the programs and emphasize research and reach international academic standards, much improvement is still needed.

Resources available to faculty and students in psychology programs are inconsistent at best. One of the main obstacles faced by public universities is the impoverishment of material conditions. Libraries do not have an adequate supply of materials, and access to full-text articles from online database services is unusual. Facilities do not have enough capacity to hold the large number of students. The faculty's salary is generally low. The psychology curriculum emphasizes the development of a practitioner over a scientist identity. As mentioned earlier, the curricula in most clinical psychology programs have a strong psychoanalytic influence leaving very little room for the inclusion of alternative theories. Furthermore, although the scope of practice for psychologists tends to focus on a generalist perspective as opposed to a specialized one, the field could benefit from what the counseling psychology specialty has to offer. Finally, international scientific and professional collaborations could further enhance the field by providing a needed critical lens and exchange of ideas and practices through which to assess and improve the state of psychology in Argentina.

REFERENCES

Alonso, M. (1994). Los psicólogos en la Argentina: Datos cuantitativos [Psychologists in Argentina: Quantitative data]. *Acta Psiquiátrica y Psicológica de América Latina, 40,* 50–55.

Alonso, M., & Gago, P. (2006). Algunos aspectos cuantitativos de la evolución de la psicología en Argentina 1975–2005 [Some quantitative aspects of the evolution of psychology in Argentina 1975–2005]. *XII Jornadas de Investigación.* Facultad de Psicología–UBA.

Alonso, M., & Nicenboim, E. (1997). La psicología en la República Argentina. Aspectos académicos y profesionales [Psychology in the Republic of Argentina. Academic and professional aspects]. *Papeles del Psicólogo, 67.*

Arrúe, W., & Kalinsky, B. (1991). *De la Médica y el Terapeuta. La Gestión Intercultural de la Salud en el Sur de la Provincia del Neuquén* [About the doctor and the therapist. The intercultural health initiative in the South of Neuquén province]. Buenos Aires, Argentina: Centro Editor de América Latina, Colección Universitarias.

Asociación de Unidades Académicas de Psicología. (2007). *Asociación de Unidades Académicas de Psicología* [Association of Academic Units of Psychology]. Retrieved November 15, 2007, from http://www .auapsi.org.ar/mardel.htm

Bass, J. (2006). In exile from the self: National belonging and psychoanalysis in Buenos Aires. *Ethos, 34*(4), 433–455.

Carbonell, B. (2003). Cosmología y chamanismo en Patagonia [Cosmology and shamanism in Patagonia]. *Gazeta de Antropología, 19.*

Castro Solano, A. (2004). Las competencias profesionales del psicólogo y las necesidades de perfiles profesionales en los diferentes ámbitos laborales [The psychology professional comptencies and the needs of professional profiles in the different job areas]. *Interdisciplinaria, 21*(2), 117–152.

Disderi, I. (2001). La cura del ojeo: Ritual y terapia en las representaciones de los campesinos del centro-oeste de Santa Fe [The cure of the evil eye: Ritual and therapy in the representations of the rural population from western Santa Fe]. *Mitológicas, 16*(1), 135–151.

Federación de Psicólogos de la República Argentina [Federation of Psychologists of the Argentine Republic]. (2007). *Institución* [Institution]. Retrieved November 15, 2007, from http://www.fepra.org.ar

Federación de Psicólogos de la República Argentina [Federation of Psychologists of the Argentine Republic]. (2008). *Acciones reservadas al título* [Scope of practice]. Retrieved March 20, 2008, from http://www .fepra.org.ar

Fernández-Alvarez, H., & Nicenboim, E. (1998). "Native" psychotherapy in Latin America: The case of Argentina. *Revista Interamericana de Psicología/Interamerican Journal of Psychology, 32*(1), 113–122.

Fernández-Alvarez, H., Scherb, E., Bregman, C., & García, F. (1995). Creencias sobre extensión y eficacia de la psicoterapia en la población de la ciudad de Buenos Aires [Beliefs about the extension and efficacy of psychotherapy in the city of Buenos Aires]. In J. P. Jiménez, C. Buguña, & A. Belmar (Eds.), *Investigación en Psicoterapia: Procesos y Resultados* [Research in psychotherapy: Processes and results] (pp. 89–107). Santiago de Chile: Corporación de Promoción Universitaria.

García, H., & de Barbenza, C. (2006). Modelos teóricos de psicoterapia en Argentina: Actitudes y creencias de sus adherentes [Theoretical models of psychotherapy in Argentina: Psychologists' attitudes and beliefs]. *International Journal of Psychology & Psychological Therapy, 6,* 381–396.

Gentile, A. (1989). La carrera de psicología en Rosario y el proceso de profesionalización [The psychology degree at Rosario and the professionalization process]. *Intercambios en Psicología, Psicoanálisis y Salud Mental, 1,* 12–13.

Gonzalo, J. (2002). La búsqueda de la salud perdida: Los otros terapeutas [The search of the lost health: The other therapists]. *Scripta Ethnologica, 24,* 81–131.

Idoyaga Molina, A. (2000). La calidad de las prestaciones de salud y el punto de vista del usuario en un contexto de medicinas múltiples [The quality of health service delivery and the user's point of view in the context of multiple medicines]. *Scripta Ethnologica, 22,* 21–85.

Idoyaga Molina, A. (2001). Lo sagrado en las terapias de las medicinas tradicionales del NOA y Cuyo [The sacred in the therapies of traditional medicines at the Northwest of Argentina and Cuyo]. *Scripta Ethnologica, 23,* 9–75.

Idoyaga Molina, A. (2002). *Culturas, Enfermedades y Medicinas. Reflexiones sobre la Atención de la Salud en Contextos Interculturales de Argentina* [Cultures, illnesses, and medicines. Reflections about the health services in intercultural contexts of Argentina]. Buenos Aires, Argentina: CAEA-CONICET.

Idoyaga Molina, A. (2005). Reflexiones sobre la clasificación de medicinas. Análisis de una propuesta conceptual [Reflections about the classification of medicines. Analysis of a conceptual proposal]. *Scripta Ethnologica, 27,* 111–147.

Instituto Nacional de Estadística y Censo [National Institute of Statistics and Census]. (2001). *Población de 20 años y más que completó el nivel universitario por división político territorial según disciplina y área de estudio* [Population of 20 years and older who completed graduate education by geographical area and field of study]. Retrieved August 20, 2007, from http://www.indec.mecon.ar

Klappenbach, H. (1995). Antecedentes de la carrera de psicología en universidades Argentinas [Precedents of the psychology degree in Argentine universities]. *Acta psiquiátrica y Psicológica de América Latina, 40,* 237–243.

Klappenbach, H. (1996). Prólogo a la psicología experimental en la República Argentina de Horacio Piñero [Prologue to the experimental psychology in the Republic of Argentina by Horacio Piñero]. *Cuadernos Argentinos de Historia de la Psicología, 2,* 239–268.

Klappenbach, H. (2000). El título profesional de psicólogo en Argentina: Antecedentes históricos y situación actual [The psychologist's professional degree in Argentina: Historical precedents and current situation]. *Revista Latinoamericana de Psicología, 32,* 419–446.

Klappenbach, H. (2003). La globalización y la enseñanza de la psicología en Argentina [The globalization and the teaching of psychology in Argentina]. *Psicología em Estudo, Maringá, 8*(2), 3–18.

Klappenbach, H. (2005). Book review: Mariano Ben Plotkin. Freud in the pampas: The emergence and development of a psychoanalytic culture in Argentina. *Isis, 96*(4), 674–675.

Klappenbach, H., & Pavesi, P. (1994). Una historia de la psicología en Latinoamérica [A history of psychology in Latin America]. *Revista Latinoamericana de Psicología, 26,* 445–482.

Korman, G., & Idoyaga Molina, A. (2002). Alcances y límites de la aplicación del manual diagnóstico y estadístico de las enfermedades mentales (*DSM-IV*) en contextos interculturales del gran Buenos Aires [Scope and limits of the application of the *Diagnostic and Statistical Manual of Mental Disorders (DSM-IV)* in intercultural contexts of Buenos Aires Metropolitan areas]. *Scripta Ethnologica, 24,* 173–214.

Ministerio de Relaciones Exteriores, Comercio Internacional y Culto [Ministry of Foreign Affairs, International Trade and Worship]. (2007). *La República Argentina* [The Republic of Argentina]. Retrieved November 10, 2007, from http://www.mrecic.gov.ar

Müller, F., Oberholzer, N., Iglesias, M., Flores, M., & Bugiolocchi, T. (2004). Psicoterapia en la Argentina: Modelos teóricos y práctica clínica en el interior del país [Psychotherapy in Argentina: Theoretical models and clinical practice]. *Acta Psiquiátrica y Psicológica de América Latina, 50,* 218–228.

Müller, F., & Palavezzatti, M. (2005). Modelos teóricos y práctica clínica en la Argentina: Psicoterapia en Capital Federal [Theoretical models and clinical practice in Argentina: Psychotherapy in Capital Federal]. *Revista Argentina de Clínica Psicológica, 14,* 73–82.

Müller, J., Fondacaro, P., García, M., & Rodríguez, F. (2005). Modelos Teóricos y Práctica Clínica en la Argentina: Psicoterapia en las provincias de Santa Fe, Buenos Aires y Chubut [Theoretical models and clinical practice in Argentina: Psychotherapy in the provinces of Santa Fe, Buenos Aires, and Chubut]. *Investigaciones en Psicología, 10,* 73–88.

Munley, P., Duncan, L., & McDonnell, K. (2004). Counseling psychology in the United States of America. *Counselling Psychology Quarterly, 17,* 247–271.

Mustaca, A. (2006). La psicología científica y el análisis del comportamiento en Argentina [Scientific psychology and behavioral analysis in Argentina]. *Avances en Psicología Latinoamericana, 24,* 13–27.

Paolucci, C., & Verdinelli, S. (1999). La psicología en Argentina [Psychology in Argentina]. In C. Di Doménico & A. Vilanova (Eds.), *Formación de Psicólogos en el MERCOSUR* [Training of psychologists in the MERCOSUR] (pp. 15–32). Mar del Plata, Argentina: Universidad Nacional de Mar del Plata.

Piacente, T. (1998). Psicoanálisis y formación académica en psicología [Psychoanalysis and academic training in psychology]. *Acta Psiquiátrica y Psicológica de América Latina, 44,* 278–284.

Plotkin, M. (2001). *Freud in the pampas: The emergence and development of a psychoanalytic culture in Argentina.* Stanford, CA: Stanford University Press.

Roger, P., & Stone, G. (n.d.). *What is the difference between a clinical psychologist and a counseling psychologist?* Retrieved October 14, 2008, from http://www.div17. org/students_differences.html

Vezzetti, H. (1988). *El Nacimiento de la Psicología en la Argentina* [The birth of psychology in Argentina]. Buenos Aires, Argentina: Puntosur.

Vilanova, A. (1990). Historia de la psicología clínica [History of clinical psychology]. *Boletín Argentino de Psicología, 3*(6), 7–19.

Vilanova, A. (1993). La formación de psicólogos en América Latina [The training of psychologists in Latin America]. *Acta Psiquiátrica y Psicológica de América Latina, 29,* 193–205.

Vilanova, A., & Di Doménico, C. (1999). *La psicología en el Cono Sur. Datos para una historia* [Psychology in the south. Data for a history]. Mar del Plata, Argentina: Editorial Martin.

Viotti, N. (2002). La moral y sus contextos. Reflexiones sobre los límites de la acción dañina entre curanderos del Noroeste Argentino (NOA) [The moral and its contexts. Reflections about the limits of harmful actions among healers in the northwest of Argentina]. In A. Colatarci (comp), *Folklore Latinoamericano* [Latin American folklore]. (Vol. VI). Buenos Aires, Argentina: Confolk.

30

Diversity, Hegemony, Poverty, and the Emergence of Counseling Psychology in Ecuador

Diversidad, Hegemonía, Pobreza y Surgimiento de la Consejería Psicológica en el Ecuador

MARÍA-CRISTINA CRUZA-GUET, ARNOLD R. SPOKANE, CARLOS LEÓN-ANDRADE, AND TERESA BORJA

Ecuador is a country of 13.75 million (65% *mestizo* or mixed indigenous-white, 25% indigenous or Amerindian, 7% Spanish, and 3% black; 95% Roman Catholic) lying directly across the equator (*Ecuador* means equator) with an area about the size of Nevada. Bordered by Colombia to the north and Peru to the south and east, Ecuador is a small (by South American standards) but highly diverse country. Ecuador encompasses three geographically and climatically distinct regions (i.e., the Coast, the Andean Highlands, and the Amazon), as well as the Galapagos Islands, an ecosystem with more than 480 species of marine life alone. Indeed, Ecuador is the birthplace of the term *diversity of species* by way of Charles Darwin's laboratory on the Galapagos.

Because the geography of Ecuador is so diverse, the lifestyles, principal work, and economic status of its population are also diverse. There are fishermen along the coasts, cattlemen in the southern highlands, farmers on central highland slopes, and oil workers in the Amazon. The country exports some 400,000 barrels of oil daily in addition to coffee, bananas, flowers, and other marine and agricultural products that form the basis of its developing economy. In its metropolitan areas, there are zones that resemble European communities for the appearance of their construction and the lifestyles of their residents; in stark contrast, there are also urban slums in the major cities, such as in Quito and Guayaquil, where many Ecuadorians live in putrid conditions.

Despite these differences, several cultural values unite the Ecuadorian population. Among these values, *familism,* or the maintenance of strong interdependent ties with nuclear and extended family members, is perhaps the most important (Zubieta, Fernandez, Vergara, Martinez, & Candia, 1998). Similarly, Ecuadorians strive to maintain harmony in their relationships as their sense of well-being is so closely connected with the support and appreciation of their social network. As such, Ecuadorians have been characterized not only for the polite manner in which they communicate (Placencia, 2007) but also for their tendency to perceive the "expression of individual character . . . [as] transgressive" (Tousignant & Maldonado, 1989, p. 900). Furthermore, Ecuadorians' social organizations are eminently patriarchal. Men are typically the breadwinners of their households, whereas women largely function as housewives and caretakers.

In addition to these values, one of the enduring influences on Ecuadorian life is the resistance against the historical domination or hegemony of outside cultural groups. The native peoples of Ecuador were first conquered by the Inca Empire and thereafter, in the 1500s, became a colony of Spain following Francisco Pizarro's invasion and conquest. Although Ecuador became an independent democracy in 1809 with help from Simon Bolivar, traces of these two conquests remain significant and have discernable effects on many aspects of everyday life, not least on the practice of mental health (León-Andrade & Lozano, 1997). Indeed Ecuadorian culture, including the attitudes and behaviors of its population with respect to mental health issues, reflects a pervasive tension between what is foreign and what is perceived to be authentically Ecuadorian. Although the majority of the population identifies itself as *mestizo* or *mestiza,* a racial admixture of Spanish and native Indian, there is no universal agreement on what mestizo values are or on how to promote them at different levels (Beck & Mijeski, 2000) despite efforts made by multicultural activists to embrace a mestizo worldview.

On one hand, there has been a powerful movement directed toward "modernizing" the country (Whitten, 1981) by abandoning everything that is aboriginal and adopting secular and Western values. This movement has influenced the emergence of imported models of psychological practice as well as more tolerant attitudes toward seeking help from formally trained mental health professionals—particularly with respect to youth conduct learning difficulties or when a mental health referral is made by a physician. In contrast, there has been an ongoing struggle by the indigenous population living in rural areas to both "assert . . . (their) dignity and autonomy as . . . member(s) of a proud ethnic group" (Beck & Mijeski, 2000, p. 120) and strive to preserve their native cultural customs and spiritual beliefs. Religious influences, a mixture of Incasic and pre-Incasic polytheistic creeds and Roman Catholic beliefs, are, in fact, often evoked by Ecuadorians, both indigenous and mestizos/as, to explain life and health outcomes. The success of even the most advanced and highly specialized medical procedures, such as in vitro fertilization, is commonly attributed to God's presence in the laboratory (Roberts, 2006). Thus, the roots of local healing practices can be traced to an amalgam of precolonial and Catholic doctrines and rituals (León-Andrade & Lozano, 1997), where either the priest or the *curandero* (i.e., healer) is sought to provide help and treatment for psychological problems. It is in the context of these two seemingly antagonistic attitudes toward mental health issues that Ecuadorians tend to navigate, frequently holding ambivalent feelings about seeking help from either source or at times mixing forms of treatment.

Another critical social issue that has hindered the development of psychology in Ecuador is the country's overall low socioeconomic status. According to estimates from the World Bank (2007), 40.8% of Ecuadorians lived on less than $2 a day between 1990 and 2005. Moreover, Ecuador has the highest population density in South America, along with related urban crowding and substandard living conditions. Ecuadorian's governmental resources are therefore allocated to support the most basic needs (i.e., nutrition, physical health, elementary education) of a majority of it inhabitants, with little left to invest in mental health programs.

MENTAL HEALTH PROFESSIONS EVOLVING

As is typical in most developing nations and was the case in the United States in the early 1900s, psychology in Ecuador evolves as mental health issues in need of focused attention appear. A few of these issues, particularly those for which published data exist, are addressed in the following paragraphs. Additionally, we provide information about Ecuador with respect to the three major domains of contemporary counseling (education and training, professional practice, and research) (Leong & Ponterotto, 2003). Finally, we briefly describe indigenous healing practices, and we discuss the potential emergence of counseling psychology in Ecuador and the implications of this emergence for American counseling psychology.

Mental Health Issues in Ecuador[1]

In Ecuador, work and unemployment concerns, migration-related problems, teen suicide, and women's issues appear to be the major mental health issues motivating the emergence of the counseling professions.

Unemployment

Vocational and career counseling has received limited attention within Ecuador's psychology professions; paradoxically, work-related concerns have become one of the main presenting problems among those who seek counseling in Ecuador. This is due to the high rates of unemployment and underemployment that ascend to 10.6% and 47%, respectively (U.S. Central Intelligence Agency, n.d.), and force many Ecuadorians to migrate in search of job opportunities.

Migration-Related Problems

In response to an ongoing economic crisis that deepened during the late 1990s, hundreds of thousands of Ecuadorians, hopeful of improving the socioeconomic status of their families, have moved from rural to urban areas or left the country. It is estimated that in 2001 more than 500,000 individuals emigrated (Saad, Saad, Cueva, & Hinostroza, 2004). As a result, countless families have disintegrated and many children have been left to be cared for by their grandparents. This, in turn, has led to a number of dysfunctional behaviors among those separated by migration, including alcoholism, domestic violence, youth gangs, and depression, particularly among adolescents (Saad et al., 2004).

Teen Suicide

Adolescents in Ecuador are not only the victims of depression but also the victims of suicide. In a recent investigation of global suicide rates among 15- to 19-year-olds, only a handful of countries (among the 90 that were studied) reported higher suicide rates in women than in men; Ecuador was among them (Wasserman, Cheng, & Jiang, 2005). Despite uncertainty as to the root causes for the high rate of suicide among young Ecuadorian women, there is speculation that separation from family due to migration, underreporting of suicide for males due to *machista* attitudes, and conflicts that stem from gender issues contribute to the problem.

Women's Issues

Ecuadorian women, especially mothers, hold a revered status within their home (Mealy, Stephan, & Abalakina-Paap, 2006). Yet concurrently they are subject to discriminatory practices and face considerable impediments to educational and economic opportunities. Moreover, women are victims of violence from parents or partners. Indeed, violence against women in Ecuador is a problem that is both rampant and underrecognized. Estimates suggest that among women between the ages of 15 and 49 who have been married or cohabit with a partner, the prevalence of psychological, physical, and sexual abuse reaches 40.7%, 31%, and 11.5%, respectively (Center for Population Studies and Social Development [CEPAR], 2004). These gender-related problems as well as the other issues previously described (i.e., unemployment, migration-related problems, and teen suicide) may shape the way psychology in Ecuador is taught, applied, and researched. We describe the current status of these domains—training, practice, and research—in the following section.

Major Domains of Contemporary Counseling

Education and Training

In Ecuador (as in other South American countries—notably Colombia, Argentina, Brazil), imported theoretical counseling paradigms have influenced the practice of psychotherapy and training available for mental health professionals (Ardila, 2004). Most educational programs embrace psychoanalysis (i.e., Freudian, Ego Psychology, Lacanian and Jungian orientations), behaviorism, and, more recently, systemic and humanistic theories as the core for curriculum development. Though more than 25 specialties in psychology exist across Latin America (Sierra & Bermudez, 2005), three areas have dominated the field in Ecuador: clinical, educational/school, and organizational/industrial. "Counseling psychology," as conceived in the United States, does not yet formally exist in Ecuador.

As in the European educational system, the typical training program, in any of the three specialties just described, admits students immediately after high school. Most of these programs consist of approximately 5 years of course work (Hereford, 1966; Sierra & Bermudez, 2005), the first 3 of which are devoted to general psychology, followed by 2 years of specialized mental health education, professional practice (internship), and thesis work. On completion of these requirements, trainees are certified to perform the same professional tasks (i.e., individual, group and family counseling) as graduates with a U.S. master's degree in clinical psychology or counseling. They may also conduct psychological testing (including personality, cognitive, and projective assessments) at the level of a U.S. doctorate in psychology. These trainees obtain the title of either *Psicólogo*

(psychologist)[2] or *Licenciado en Psicología* (degree in psychology) and are commonly referred to as *psicoterapeutas* (psychotherapists). The term *consejero* (counselor) is not used to describe university graduates with a degree in mental health, and it is not part of the psychology vernacular. Nonetheless, as previously mentioned, Ecuadorian mental health professionals perform functions comparable with those of counselors in the United States.

There are approximately 15 psychology programs in the clinical area, 14 in organizational and industrial psychology, and more than 30 in the school or educational specialization (Consejo Nacional de Educacion Superior [CONESUP], 2008; El Universo, n.d.). Very few schools offer master's degrees in psychology, and doctoral degrees are a rare occurrence; they are offered by certain schools on a periodic basis only. Currently, only one university offers a doctorate in clinical psychology (El Universo, n.d.). This doctorate is the equivalent of a PsyD. Programs awarding the degree of doctor of philosophy in psychology do not exist.

In most of the existing educational programs, multicultural issues are not integrated as a core aspect of the curriculum. In general, students become proficient in the use of assessment tools normed in other Spanish-speaking countries and learn the theories and techniques of the psychotherapeutic model adopted by a particular training program. Typically, however, these programs incorporate neither information about the values and needs of Ecuador's diverse cultural groups nor a discussion of how these values and needs be addressed in the therapeutic milieu. Moreover, in these educational contexts, indigenous healing practices tend to be ignored, and those who seek this type of service are regarded as "ignorant."

Although little is known vis-à-vis the efficacy of the imported models of therapy as it pertains to the Ecuadorian population, it seems reasonable to conceive that practices that disregard clients' worldviews may also hinder the therapeutic process. Interventions rooted in individualistic values, for instance, may conflict with the interdependent relationships that Ecuadorians maintain with nuclear and extended family members. Similarly, therapeutic strategies that overlook clients' faith in indigenous healing may be regarded with distrust or reluctance or interpreted as a sign of rejection. By and large, the schism previously described between interventions and clients' worldviews recapitulates the history of subjugation of Ecuadorians to the Inca and the Spaniard, and the ensuing imposition of foreign values brought about by these two conquests. Unfortunately, in the absence of a multicultural perspective in the educational field, this schism is perpetuated in professional mental health practices, to which we now turn.

Psychological Practice in Ecuador

In this section, we summarize information on the practice of adopted forms of psychotherapy (i.e., those conducted by psychology professionals) as well as those of indigenous healing practices—as both represent the types of mental health treatments used by Ecuadorians.

Professional Practice

Graduating from a program that is accredited or legitimized by the Ecuadorian Ministry of Education is a prerequisite for practicing all the psychological specialties. On graduation, psychology professionals have the option to join one of several regional or national associations of psychologists (i.e., Asociación Ecuatoriana de Psicología, Federación Ecuatoriana de Psicología Clínica, Colegios de Psicólogos, etc.) that exist in Ecuador. These organizations promote the rights of psychology professionals and provide their members with opportunities for educational advancement and professional networking. Nonetheless, they do not play a formal regulatory or licensing role over practitioners. In the absence of any such regulatory agencies, it is difficult to accurately estimate the sum total of psychology professionals currently in practice. According to World Health Organization (WHO, 2005) statistics, however, there are approximately 29.1 psychologists per 100,000 inhabitants in Ecuador.

In general, psychologists with clinical expertise are either hired by health (i.e., general hospitals and community mental health centers) and nonprofit organizations or are self-employed. A major challenge that most of these professionals face relates to the scarcity of financial resources, which limits the availability of both job options and career opportunities. A majority of the population is medically insured by the Instituto Ecuatoriano de Seguridad Social (Ecuadorian Institute of Social Security), which hires a marginal number of psychology professionals and pays only for those services provided by their network of hospitals. Access to private insurance is limited to the upper-middle and upper-socioeconomic strata, and in most cases, insurance does not cover the cost of mental health services. As a result, psychological treatment is mostly self-paid and generally regarded as a luxury. Consider that while the minimum monthly wage in Ecuador is only $170 (Ministerio de Trabajo y Empleo [Ministry of Labor and Employment], n.d.), the cost of an hour of psychotherapy session ranges between $10 and $20. Under these circumstances, establishing and sustaining profitable private practices becomes possible only for those very few psychology professionals who have access to the resources (i.e., loans) needed to invest in a practice and who successfully market their services among high socioeconomic status groups.

Most clinical practitioners reside and provide their services in metropolitan areas. Even though 40% of the Ecuadorian population lives in rural zones (United Nations Populations Fund [UNFPA], 2005), there are few incentives for psychology professionals to relocate outside the country's major cities, thereby leaving the countryside with limited access to formal mental health services. It is in these rural areas, where the majority of the indigenous peoples, who preserve close cultural links with their pre-Hispanic roots (León-Andrade & Lozano, 1997; Pribilsky, 2001), live and, consequently, where indigenous healing practices are the most popular.

Indigenous Healing Practices

These forms of treatment, rooted in the spiritual beliefs of the Amerindian population, are known as *curanderismo* and *chamanismo,* given that they are performed by popular aboriginal leaders—the *curandero* and *chaman*, respectively. Although there are variations among indigenous groups, healers in general reason that mental illnesses are caused by either (a) supernatural causes, which refer to the intrusion of negative energies or evil spirits into a person's body (León-Andrade & Lozano, 1997), or (b) a disruption of an individual's harmony within himself or herself or with his or her natural and/or social environment (Chelada, 2007). Thus, treatment is viewed as a process that purifies the individual and restores his or her harmony with the cosmos (Chelada, 2007; León-Andrade & Lozano, 1997). This is attained through a combination of practices, such as the use of herbal medicines and hallucinogenic beverages, revered ritual objects, suggestions that invoke spiritual or sacred meanings, and even interpersonal interventions that involve the sufferer's community (Chelala, 2007; León-Andrade & Lozano, 1997; Tousignant & Maldonado, 1989). Curandero and chaman provide basically the same types of treatment; however, they differ in that the latter, typically a male, is supposed to naturally posses divine powers that allow him to foresee the future (*chaman*—the one who knows), whereas the curandero or curandera attains his or her skills through learning ("Ecuador entre brujas," 2006).

Examples of mental ailments (i.e., culture-bound syndromes) that are treated by chamans and curanderos or curanderas are *espanto* (fright) and *pena* (sorrow), among many others. Espanto is a condition characterized by a state of fright that afflicts children who have gone through a haunting or shocking experience, such as witnessing a serious fight between their parents (McKee, 1987). Symptoms of espanto include emotional lability, noise intolerance, hypersensitivity to certain stimuli, night terrors, insomnia, social isolation, trembling and sweating, heart palpitations, anorexia, and gastrointestinal disturbances (León-Andrade & Lozano, 1997). Pena, on the other hand, is a syndrome that resembles the Western diagnosis of clinical depression (Tousignant & Maldonado, 1989) but presents other peculiar somatic symptoms, such as *ataques* (convulsions not related to epilepsy) and upper chest sensations; the

latter have a metaphorical meaning: heart pain. Indeed, the indigenous peoples of highland Ecuador associate pena with some sort of loss, particularly with that which entails a social reciprocity failure as it occurs in the context of marital problems, the death of a loved one, and so on (Tousignant & Maldonado, 1989).

The treatment of pena exemplifies the multidimensional nature of the healing practices used in the aboriginal communities of Ecuador. On one hand,

> The healer rubs the patient's body with eggs, flowers, plants, a young guinea pig and other miscellaneous objects. Calls are made to mountains, springs of water and Christian saints. Suctions in the epigastric area lead to the extraction of impurities like black frogs and tadpoles, and bloody secretions mixed to the healer's saliva. (Tousignant & Maldonado, 1989, p. 903)

On the other, the sufferer of pena is encouraged to improve his or her relationships with family and friends, an intervention that is endorsed by both the indigenous healer and the entire community in light of the underlying social significance of this ailment (Tousignant & Maldonado, 1989). Furthermore, in some severe cases, individuals afflicted with pena are referred to a psychologist or a psychiatrist who can prescribe antidepressants.

It is not uncommon for those who seek the assistance of an indigenous healer to also consult with a psychology professional about the same problem. In general, however, the provision of traditional healing practices and provision of Westernized treatments have been independent of one another. Recently, an integrative approach that blends indigenous and modern practices has been proposed as a feasible alternative that could better meet the needs of the Ecuadorian population. At least one community organization, the Jambi Huasi (House of Health) in Otavalo, a predominantly indigenous town located 70 miles north of Quito, the capital, has already implemented this new modality and claims to be producing positive outcomes (Chelala, 2007). It is worth noting, nonetheless, that with the exception of case study reports, information about the efficacy of indigenous healing practices, imported models of psychotherapy, or a combination of the two with Ecuadorian populations is scant. In fact, there has been limited mental health research in Ecuador, as will be made evident in the following paragraph.

Research

Of the three major domains of contemporary counseling (education, practice, and research), research has received the least attention, in large part due to a lack of funding and given that psychology in Ecuador has emerged as an applied field rather than as an investigative one (Ardila, 2004). Nonetheless, there are a few research initiatives under way conducted by some of the major hospitals (i.e., Hospital Psiquiátrico Lorenzo Ponce, Hospital Carlos Andrade Marin), by university faculty, and by independent researchers—oftentimes in collaboration with American scientists. Examples of these initiatives include studies on the mental health consequences of migration (Saad et al., 2004), disasters (Lima et al., 1989), alcoholism (Ayala Loor & Galera, 2004), and smoking (Ockene, Chiriboga, & Zevallos, 1996; Ramirez Ruiz & Andrade, 2005). Results of a selected number of these investigative endeavors were summarized earlier in the section "Mental Health Issues in Ecuador."

EMERGENCE OF COUNSELING PSYCHOLOGY IN ECUADOR AND IMPLICATIONS FOR U.S. COUNSELING PSYCHOLOGY

Given Ecuador's diversity, its long-standing social issues, and the pervasive dissociation between its professional mental health practices and its cultural values and indigenous forms of healing, there seems to be a profound need to develop a model of counseling that addresses the necessities of its varied populations. Such a model may need to take into account Ecuadorians' collectivistic orientation and long-standing socioeconomic plight so as to conceptualize human behaviors as the byproduct of familial and

societal influences (i.e., unemployment, migration, etc.). In the context of such a model, psychologists could intervene at multiple levels of the social environment and act as agents of social change. Moreover, Ecuadorian psychology may benefit from establishing a model of psychotherapy that recognizes Ecuadorians' deep-rooted spiritual beliefs and reliance on indigenous healing practices. This may be possible by developing an interdisciplinary mode of community practice that incorporates the chaman or curandero (León-Andrade & Lozano, 1997). Furthermore, there is a need to develop a research plan that evaluates the therapeutic efficacy of this and other models of counseling, thereby promoting the advancement of a true Ecuadorian psychology.

In the milieu of Ecuador's rich and deep-rooted complexity, counseling psychology may find fertile ground to develop. Because of its emphasis on multiculturalism and social justice practices (Heppner, Casas, Carter, & Stone, 2000; Toporek, Gerstein, Fouad, Roysircar, & Israel, 2006), counseling psychology could contribute to the development of a model of counseling that, as we have proposed, is consistent with the worldviews and social problems of the Ecuadorian population. In such a way, counseling psychology could assist Ecuadorian mental health professionals in finding appropriate ways of meeting the needs of their clients. Furthermore, as the economy in Ecuador grows, life options and choices will increase as well. As Amartya Sen (2000) has so eloquently observed, development both presages and produces freedom. As development progresses, individuals and families are increasingly faced with more complex and vexing educational, occupational, marital, and lifestyle choices—precisely the day-to-day issues about which counseling psychology is most concerned (Tyler, 1961). Thus, we can expect that counseling psychology may spread in developing nations, such as Ecuador, much as it did in the United States and Europe during the past century. The unique culture and social ecology of Ecuador will shape this emergence in predictable ways (e.g., more family and community emphases, less expert and more indigenously derived forms of assistance). Although models, theories, and interventions will need to be adapted, revised, and in some cases discarded entirely, much of what we know in counseling psychology may have applicability and value in countries such as Ecuador.

In a similar vein, the professional worldviews and practices of Ecuadorian psychology practitioners may serve U.S. counseling psychologists not only "to counter the dominance and hegemony of Western psychology" (Leong & Ponterotto, 2003, p. 384) but also to improve the efficacy of their treatment and assessment models with the rapidly growing Hispanic immigrant populations. The use of psychological treatments that combine indigenous healing practices with modern forms of psychotherapy (i.e., the model adopted in the Jambi Huasi community center) provides, in this sense, a unique learning opportunity for U.S. psychologists. The emergence of counseling psychology in Ecuador can indeed be a source of potential growth for Ecuadorian psychology as well as for this specialty in the United States.

NOTES

1. There is a dearth of empirical and epidemiological information describing the types of psychological disorders that are most prevalent among the Ecuadorian population. Informal data provided by several mental health professionals reveal that the most common problems include depression, anxiety disorders (particularly panic attacks), and substance abuse and employment concerns. According to Pan American Health Organization (PAHO, 1998), the prevalence of alcoholism is 7.7% among individuals older than 15.

2. In Ecuador, the term *psychologist* is not specific to those who have obtained a doctorate degree.

REFERENCES

Ardila, R. (2004). La psicología latinoamericana: El primer medio siglo [Psychology from Latin America: The first half century]. *Revista Interamericana de Psicología, 38,* 317–322.

Ayala Loor, E., & Galera, S. A. F. (2004). Percepción sobre el uso de alcohol y tabaco en familiars de niños enfermos. Consulta externa del hospital materno infantil del Guasmo Sur, Guayaquil [Perceptions about the use of alcohol and tobacco in families of sick children. Outpatient services of the mother and infant hospital from South Guasmo, Ecuador]. *Revista Latino-am Enfermagem, 12,* 340–344.

Beck, S. H., & Mijeski, K. J. (2000). Indigena self-identity in Ecuador and the rejection of Mestizaje. *Latin American Research Review, 35,* 119–137.

Center for Population Studies and Social Development. (2004). *Encuesta demográfica y de salud materna e infantil—ENDEMAIN* [Demographic and mother and infant health survey]. Retrieved January 30, 2008, from http://www.cepar.org.ec/publicaciones/publi.htm

Chelala, C. (2007, July 7). Health in the Andes. *Américas.* Retrieved January 10, 2008, from http://www.mywire .com/pubs/Americas/2007/07/01/4352070/print/

Consejo Nacional de Educación Superior. (2008). *Counsulta de Carreras—Universidad* [Career: University consultation]. Retrieved April 25, 2008, from http://www .conesup.net/buscar_carreras_universidad.php? pagina=7

Ecuador entre brujas, magias y hechiceros [Ecuador between witches, magic and wizards]. (2006, December 10). *Noticias del Ecuador y del Mundo Hoy Online.* [News from Ecuador and the *Mundo Hoy* Online]. Retrieved October 7, 2007, from http://www.hoy .com.ec/NoticiaNue.asp?row_id=253075

El Universo. (n.d.). *Guía de Carreras Universitarias y Postgrados—Ecuador 2006* [Guide to university and graduate careers—Ecuador 2006]. Retrieved November 14, 2007, from http://especiales.eluniverso.com/ especiales/guiadeCarreras/listadoPosgrados.asp

Heppner, P. P., Casas, J. M., Carter, J. A., & Stone, G. L. (2000). The maturation of counseling psychology: Multifaceted perspectives, 1978–1998. In S. D. Brown & R. W. Lent (Eds.), *Handbook of counseling psychology* (pp. 3–49). New York: Wiley.

Hereford, C. F. (1966). Current status of psychology in Latin America. *Latin American Research Review, 1,* 97–108.

León-Andrade, C., & Lozano, A. (1997). Raíces culturales de la psiquiatría en el Ecuador [Cultural roots of psychiatry in Ecuador]. *Revista Electrónica de Psiquiatría.* Retrieved June 28, 2007, from http://www.psiquiatria .com/psiquiatria/v011num2/artic_2.htm

Leong, F. T. L., & Ponterotto, J. G. (2003). A proposal for internationalizing counseling psychology in the United States: Rationale, recommendations, and challenges. *The Counseling Psychologist, 31*, 381–395.

Lima, B., Pai, S., Santacruz, H., Lozano, J., Chavez, H., & Samaniego, N. (1989). Conducting research on disaster mental health in developing countries: A proposed model. *Disasters, 13*, 177–184.

McKee, L. (1987) Ethnomedical treatment of children's diarrheal illnesses in the highlands of Ecuador. *Social Science & Medicine, 25*, 1147–1155.

Mealy, M., Stephan, W. G., & Abalakina-Paap, M. (2006). Reverence for mothers in Ecuadorian and Euro-American Culture. *Journal of Cross-Cultural Psychology, 37*, 465–484.

Ministerio de Trabajo y Empleo de la República del Ecuador [Ministry of Labor and Employment of the Republic of Ecuador]. (n.d.). *Salario Mínimo* [Minimum salary]. Retrieved December 1, 2007, from http://www.mintrab.gov.ec/MinisterioDeTrabajo/index.htm

Ockene, J. K., Chiriboga, D. E., & Zevallos, J. C. (1996). Smoking in Ecuador: Prevalence, knowledge, and attitudes. *Tobacco Control, 5*, 121–126.

Pan American Health Organization. (1998). Ecuador. *Health in the Americas.* Retrieved January 28, 2007, from http://www.paho.org/english/hia_1998ed.htm

Placencia, M. (2007). Studies on politeness in Colombian, Ecuadorian, and Peruvian Spanish. In M. Placencia & C. Garcia (Eds.), *Research on politeness in the Spanish-speaking world* (pp. 59–89). Mahwah, NJ: Lawrence Erlbaum.

Pribilsky, J. (2001). Nervios and modern childhood: Migration and shifting contexts of child life in the Ecuadorian Andes. *Childhood: A Global Journal of Child Research Special Issue: Capitalizing on Concern, 8*, 251–273.

Ramirez Ruiz, M., & Andrade, D. (2005). Family and risk factors related to alcohol consumption and smoking among children and adolescents (Guayaquil-Ecuador). *Revista Latino Americana Enfermagem, 13*, 813–818.

Roberts, E. F. S. (2006). God's laboratory: Religious rationalities and modernity in Ecuadorian in vitro fertilization. *Culture, Medicine & Psychiatry, 30*, 507–536.

Saad, E., Saad, J., Cueva, E., & Hinostroza, W. (2004). La emigración masiva en el Ecuador como factor etiológico de la depresión en los adolescentes [The mass migration in Ecuador as an etiological factor of depression in adolescents]. *Interpsiquis.* Retrieved June 28, 2007, from http://www.psiquiatria.com/articulos/psiqsocial/15139/

Sen, A. (2000). *Development as freedom.* New York: Anchor.

Sierra, J. C., & Bermudez, M. P. (2005). Hacia el título Iberamericano de psicología: análisis de los programas docentes de las carreras de psicología en Iberoamérica [Toward the Iberoamerican degree in psychology: Analysis of teaching programs in Iberoamerican careers in psychology]. *Revista Mexicana de Psicología, 22*, 224–242.

Toporek, R. L., Gerstein, L. H., Fouad, N. A., Roysircar, G., & Israel, T. (2006). *Handbook for social justice in counseling psychology: Leadership, vision, and action.* Thousand Oaks, CA: Sage.

Tousignant, M., & Maldonado, M. (1989). Sadness, depression and social reciprocity in highland Ecuador. *Social Science and Medicine, 28*, 899–904.

Tyler, L. (1961). Research explorations in the realm of choice. *Journal of Counseling Psychology, 8*, 195–201.

United Nations Population Fund & Population Reference Bureau. (2005). *Country profiles for population and reproductive health, policy developments and indicators.* Retrieved January 24, 2008, from http://www.unfpa.org/worldwide/countryprofiles.html

U.S. Central Intelligence Agency. (n.d.). *CIA world factbook.* Retrieved November 1, 2007, from http://www.indexmundi.com/ecuador/unemployment_rate.html

Wasserman, D., Cheng, Q., & Jiang, G. (2005). Global suicide rates among young people. *World Psychiatry, 4*, 114–120.

Whitten, N. E. (1981). *Cultural transformations and ethnicity in modern Ecuador.* Urbana: University of Illinois Press.

World Bank. (2007). *World development indicators 2007.* Washington, DC: Author.

World Health Organization. (2005). *Mental health atlas.* Retrieved January 27, 2008, from http://www.who.int/mental_health/evidence/atlas/profiles_countries_e_i.pdf

Zubieta, E., Fernandez, I., Vergara, A. I., Martinez, M. D., & Candia, L. (1998). Cultura y emoción en América [Culture and emotion in America]. *Boletín de Psicología, 61*, 65–89.

31

Counseling From the Subversive

The Development of Psychotherapy in Puerto Rico

Consejería de la Subversión:
El Desarrollo de la Psicoterapia en Puerto Rico

LUIS RIVAS QUIÑONES

The Spanish psychologist and Jesuit priest Ignacio Martín Baró and the Venezuelan psychologist Maritza Montero popularized the term *la psicología social de la liberación,* or *the social psychology for liberation,* to describe the model of psychology that evolved from the social processes of Latin American countries in the 1970s (Dussel, 1998). This model aims to promote social justice by validating the reality of all marginalized groups, particularly victims of state and government oppression. While indigenous to Latin America, this model has been slow to develop in Puerto Rico due in part to the inability of its people to fully experience independence and autonomy as a country.

The development and practice of counseling and psychotherapy in Puerto Rico is best understood from the background of the colonization process that Puerto Rico and its people have lived through for more than 500 years. The colonial situation, as described, for example, by Fanón (1963) and

Memmi (1969), involves a systematic negation of the colonized by fostering constant challenges and distortions of the collective and individual sense of identity, resulting in an internalization of oppression, subjugation, perceived social inferiority, negative self-definition and self-esteem, and intragroup conflicts and violence among other individual and collective dynamics. The colonization process has left native psychologists in a bind: A number of positive aspects have come from the influence of the colonizing culture on the field of psychology, including increased access, a more organized infrastructure and resources, and opportunities for growth. Nevertheless, this influence has also limited the processes inherent to the social psychology for liberation (e.g., conscientization—or exposing social/political contradictions and taking action against the oppressor—and de-ideologization—or screening out what serves the interests of the oppressor by making native ideas seem natural) (see Aron & Corne, 1996;

403

Vázquez, 2000), ultimately hindering the development of its own indigenous model of psychotherapy. Rather than simply listing statistics and events, the author of this chapter will attempt to provide the necessary historical context to genuinely comprehend the cultural aspects involved in the practice of psychotherapy in Puerto Rico—including its current status and future directions.

CONTEXTUAL BACKGROUND FOR THE DEVELOPMENT OF PSYCHOLOGY AND PSYCHOTHERAPY IN PUERTO RICO

Location and Demographic Overview

Puerto Rico is an archipelago consisting of a larger island and several smaller ones that lie in the Caribbean Sea directly east of the Dominican Republic. It measures approximately 110 miles long and 40 miles wide. Census figures from July 2008 estimate the population at 3.95 million inhabitants (U.S. Census Bureau, 2008a). The median age for males and females is 33.4 and 36.8 years, respectively. Life expectancy for males and females is 74.6 and 82.7 years, respectively. San Juan is the capital city of Puerto Rico. An additional 3.99 million Puerto Ricans live in the continental United States (U.S. Census Bureau, 2008b) for a total population of almost 8 million Puerto Ricans.

Original Inhabitants

The Taíno Indians were the original inhabitants of Puerto Rico—or Borikén, as it was named in their language. The word *taíno* literally means good or noble. Their main focus was on the land, the family, and the community. They lived in formally established town and social-class structures. Town leaders, called *caciques,* could be either females or males. Taínos were also very spiritual and prayed to two supreme gods as well as several minor gods. The colonization of Puerto Rico began with the arrival of Christopher Columbus on the island in 1493. Dressed in shining armor and speaking a foreign language, the Spaniards were initially perceived by the Taínos as gods. Despite some resistance, the

Taínos were significantly outnumbered and underprepared; their defeat paved the way for 400 years of Spanish control.

Spanish Colonization Period

An important consequence of Spanish governance in Puerto Rico was the introduction of the African race to the island through slavery. The geographical limitations of an island caused the ethnicities to mix, and most Puerto Ricans can trace their ethnic roots to a mixture of Africans, Taíno Indians, and Spaniard caucasians—and their skin color is a continuum ranging from black to white in appearance. For years, this mixture of ethnicities was the main argument against the existence of racism in the country. A popular folk saying in Puerto Rico is "*y tu abuela . . . ¿a 'onde etá?*" ("and your grandmother . . . where is she?") referring to the notion that those who espouse racism or discrimination need only look at their grandmother's generation to find their black heritage. Nevertheless, Puerto Ricans have become increasingly aware of the subtle racism, primarily based on class and socioeconomic status differences, present on the island.

The Spaniards also implemented Roman Catholicism as the only accepted religion. The Taínos adapted quickly to this change because of their polytheist beliefs. The resulting practice of Taíno and African interpretations of Catholicism is a religion with some unique characteristics, some of which are taboo in present-day culture. Many Puerto Ricans, particularly—but not exclusively—those with more limited financial and educational means, place credibility on the work of *santeros* or *curanderos*. These are folk healers who perform *despojos* (or "rid-dances" of negative energies) through elaborate ceremonies and rituals that often employ religious amulets and other symbols. These healers trace their origins to the Taíno *behikes* or *buhitíes* (e.g., the village historians, priests, doctors, and healers) (see González Rivera, 2007) and have been referred to as the "psychiatrists of the poor" (Núñez Molina, 2005). Their importance has also been augmented by their high level of accessibility (due to their low cost of services, residence in the community served, reliance on familiar concepts of religion), in contrast to the more expensive and to some extent still stigmatized mental health professionals.

The stigma associated with seeking help from mental health professionals has decreased to some extent in present-day Puerto Rico due to the influence of U.S. culture and the normalization of mental health concerns stemming from increased awareness due to media coverage and the Internet. While people in general seek psychological services on a more formal basis and in an openly accepted manner now (due in part to an increase in the availability of trained professionals), they still will often informally seek guidance from clergy, healers, and other spiritual guides. Those who do not may occasionally make statements such as "I do not believe in that stuff, but I respect it." Spiritual and religious beliefs continue to play an important role in Puerto Ricans' perceptions about health, treatment, and general help-seeking behavior, and such beliefs help maintain a cultural bond with their African, Taíno, and Spanish heritage (Comas-Díaz, 2006; Núñez Molina, 2005).

Taíno and African culture placed great importance on the family and the community. Catholicism reinforced the sanctity of the family structure and the marriage bond. The cultural values of *machismo* (e.g., the belief that males are superior to females and must act as such) and *marianismo* (e.g., the belief that females must be submissive and emulate the Virgin Mary) prescribed double standards with regard to sexuality and reinforced patriarchal social roles for men and women. Religion also dictated Spanish political structure, as all towns followed the same structural design: The town hall (where "the Law of Man" was made) was directly across from the Church (where the "Law of God" was taught), with a plaza for community gatherings separating the two. This blueprint can be found in many of the Latin American countries that fell under Spanish rule and remains in use to date (having the ultimate effect of encouraging the accessibility of important town figures, such as the mayor and the clergy, to their people thus further promoting a sense of community).

Arguably, the most significant remnant of the Spaniards' colonization of Puerto Rico is the Spanish language. The Spanish language played an important role in the second colonization period of Puerto Rico, which began with the invasion of the United States during the Spanish-American War of 1898. The original intent of the United States was to turn this strategic military post into a full-fledged state of the union, and reeducating the local population was identified as a way to accomplish this. English became the mandatory language in all schools. Other rituals, such as singing the U.S. national anthem and reciting the pledge of allegiance to the U.S. flag, were implemented in schools. Puerto Ricans were also granted U.S. citizenship under the Jones Law of 1917 (Picó, 1986; Silén, 1973). This allowed all individuals who were born on the island to migrate freely between the United States and Puerto Rico.

Transition Into a U.S. Territory

The country was ill-equipped to cope with the implementation of some of these policies. The cultural divide was further widened by the continuous assignment of U.S.–born military governors who had little command of the Spanish language and limited knowledge of Puerto Rican culture. Although the attempt to turn Puerto Rico into an English-speaking state of the union was eventually discontinued, an important consequence of this was that it facilitated the solidification of several hundred years of an evolving Taíno-African-Spanish culture into a Puerto Rican culture.

As the differences between the Puerto Rican and U.S. cultures became more apparent, the United States officially approved the Commonwealth of Puerto Rico—the current political status of the island—in 1952. *Free-associated state, U.S. territory,* and *U.S. protectorate* are some of the many terms that have been used to describe a colonial relationship with the United States in which Puerto Rico maintains self-governance over local, everyday matters, while the United States maintains final control in federal and international affairs. For more than 50 years, Puerto Ricans have been able to participate in federal government programs (such as social security and the military), but have not been able to vote for the president of the United States (who, as the head of state, retains ultimate sovereignty over the island) or challenge any of the House and Senate laws that have to be implemented on the island. The country does not function as a state of the union nor does it function independent of the union.

Many Puerto Ricans colloquially agree that the most popular "sport" in the country is politics, a subject that can come up in any kind of conversation on any topic. Puerto Rico has one of the highest rates of voter participation in the world, and its model of running elections has been studied and attempted in other countries. The three primary political ideologies define themselves by their stance on the island's relationship with the United States. Some mental health professionals informally theorize that a way to assess the level of ethnic identity of Puerto Ricans is to ask for an individual's political beliefs. Puerto Ricans who hold to the belief that Puerto Rico should become a state of the United States manifest high levels of acculturation and a lower sense of ethnic identity. Those who profess allegiance to the independence of Puerto Rico from the United States manifest a high sense of ethnic identity and lower levels of acculturation. Finally, those who support the notion of maintaining the current commonwealth status manifest higher levels of assimilation and conformism.

For more than 500 years, Puerto Ricans have always had to consider the influence of a ruling country in the development of their own identity as a nation. The ability to engage in the conscientization process of the social psychology for liberation has remained limited, and the ability to achieve self-actualization and a sense of self as a human being has always been at least partly "other defined." This is readily apparent when considering how individuals interact with each other, for example, the value on a sense of family and community that comes down from Taíno times (and the dignity and "face" that must be preserved through any type of adversity) and the need for achievement and recognition to prove worth (thus the significant value Puerto Ricans place on success at any type of international event—from boxing matches and international sporting events to music awards and Miss Universe). This also becomes evident at the systemic level when

considering the history and development of the field of psychology and the practice of psychotherapy in Puerto Rico. As Bernal and Martínez-Taboas (2005) stated, "Clearly, psychotherapy in Puerto Rico responds to its 'circumstances' as a colonized country in its political, social, and economic relations with the United States" (p. 4).

HISTORY OF PSYCHOLOGY AND PSYCHOTHERAPY IN PUERTO RICO

A brief overview of the history of psychology in Puerto Rico underscores the difficulties that professionals have struggled with in developing an indigenous model of psychology in the face of the larger, external influence and the opportunities for development that have come with it. Different forms of counseling and guidance have always been present throughout Puerto Rican history, although early knowledge in these areas is limited. Documented efforts to formally address mental health during Spanish rule date back to the 1800s. The Casa de Beneficiencia in 1844 was an early treatment facility (run in part by the clergy), and the Sociedad de Estudios Psicológicos La Caridad in 1888 was the first professional organization to address psychological and spiritual concerns (Bernal, 2007; Rosselló, 1975).

The transition to U.S. government coincided with the establishment of the University of Puerto Rico in 1903, which included psychology among its first course offerings (Alvarez, 2007). Military involvement by Puerto Ricans in the U.S. army also brought the need for mental health treatment services beginning in 1925 (Bernal, 2007). Led by the fields of medicine and psychiatry, treatment facilities (e.g., Clínica Juliá in 1925) and hospitals (e.g., Hospital de Psiquiatría de Río Piedras in 1929) began to emerge. U. S. citizenship under the Jones Law as well as benefits earned through participation in the military allowed for some of the forefathers of Puerto Rican psychology (e.g., Carlos Albizu Miranda, Jorge Dieppa, Juan Nicolás Martínez, and Pablo Roca de León) to complete their doctorates in U.S. institutions (e.g., Columbia University, New

York University, Purdue University, and the University of Texas).

The 1950s marked the beginning of the integration of the field of psychology as a discipline in Puerto Rico (Bernal, 2007). The consequences of U.S. involvement in World War II on the island were manifold. There was an increase in the demand for psychological assessments and intelligence testing as well as individual and group counseling. The approval of the GI Bill accounted for increased access to education by war veterans (Mettler, 2005). Furthermore, these events coincided with the approval of Puerto Rico's status as a Commonwealth (and the ensuing economic boom triggered by the Operation Bootstrap project of the Puerto Rican government), which increased both the accessibility of mental health resources for the general population as well as the financial means for the government to develop them.

The Puerto Rico Psychology Association was formed in 1954 and immediately became affiliated with the American Psychological Association (APA), becoming the 41st association to do so (Roca de Torres, 2007). Soon after, a counseling and rehabilitation program began at the University of Puerto Rico in 1958 (Bernal, 2007). The psychology department was established as a separate program in 1963 and 3 years later began conferring master's degrees (Rivera & Maldonado, 2000). The psychologists Carlos Albizu Miranda and Norman Matlin also founded the free-standing Instituto Psicológico de Puerto Rico in 1966—known as the Centro Caribeño de Estudios Postgraduados since 1970 and as Universidad Carlos Albizu since 2000. In 1970, the Instituto Psicológico became the first institution of higher learning in Puerto Rico to confer doctoral degrees in psychology (Alvarez & Vélez-Pastrana, 1995; Auger & Quintero, 2005).

With the advent and proliferation of psychology training programs in the 1960s and 1970s and increased funding from the government, the availability of psychological services expanded beyond the confines of hospitals and private practice (Hernández, 1985). Different populations were now being served through government programs and institutions (Rosselló, 1988). Some of these included people with substance abuse problems, police officers, university students, and people with developmental disabilities.

Hogares CREA (Comunidad de Reeducación de Adictos) [Community for the Reeducation of Addicts]—a grassroots, community-based organization whose residential model of strict rules and spiritual guidance to treat addictions has been exported throughout six Latin American countries as well as the United States—was founded in 1968 (Hogar CREA, 2009). U.S. participation in the Vietnam War also spurred the forming of the Psychological Services program at the San Juan Veterans Affairs Medical Center in 1970, removing it from under the umbrella of Psychiatric Services. The Society of Psychoanalysts of Puerto Rico was formed in 1973. The Puerto Rican Association of Counseling Professionals was formed in 1977 (currently affiliated with the American Counseling Association). In 1978, Lucy López-Roig and Associates took psychology to the private sector through consultation services to the business and education community (Lucy López-Roig & Associates, 2009). However, it was not until 1995 that the Society for Industrial/Organizational Psychologists of Puerto Rico was established.

The area of investigative research developed some consistency in the 1980s and into the 1990s as more ongoing research programs began to emerge. This was partly due to the continuous development of the training programs associated with different universities. The University of Puerto Rico began conferring doctoral degrees in psychology in 1986. The investigative branch of the Centro Universitario de Servicios y Estudios Psicológicos (CUSEP) and the Insitituto de Investigación de Ciencias de la Conducta, institutions affiliated with the University of Puerto Rico, as well as the Centro de Investigación y Evaluación Sociomédica (CIES) were founded in 1986, 1990, and 1982, respectively (Bernal, 2007). The Puerto Rico Psychology Association published the first volume of its journal *Revista Puertorriqueña de Psicología* in 1981 (Martínez-Taboas & Pérez

Pedrogo, 2007). Finally, Santiago (2007) has recently documented the research efforts of students in pursuit of master's and doctoral degrees in psychology by accounting for more than 1,500 theses and dissertations defended since 1966.

PRESENT-DAY PRACTICE OF PSYCHOLOGY AND PSYCHOTHERAPY IN PUERTO RICO

As has previously been stated in this chapter, Puerto Ricans have always had to consider the influence of a ruling country in the development of their own identity as a nation. Some of this has been delineated above in addressing the history of the field of psychology in Puerto Rico. It follows, then, that this is also true in the current practice of counseling and psychotherapy.

The Work of Carlos Albizu Miranda

A veteran of the U.S. army and Purdue University graduate, Carlos Albizu Miranda is considered one of the pioneers of Puerto Rican psychology because of his early work for an inherently Puerto Rican model of psychology. Framed within that ubiquitous "other-defined" stance, he argued that "psychology from the United States does not work in Puerto Rico" (Albizu Miranda & Matlin, 1967, p. 78).

In support of this argument, Albizu Miranda and Matlin (1967) pointed out that the implementation of early models of counseling and psychotherapy in Puerto Rico was done by native psychologists returning to Puerto Rico after having been trained in the United States. Albizu Miranda and Matlin analyzed the distinction between the cultural values of guilt and shame to highlight what they perceived as problematic examples of the implementation of these foreign models in clinical work with Puerto Ricans. They argued that psychopathology in the United States was "guilt" driven, or stemming from what present-day psychology has theorized as an individualistic or idiocentric culture. Albizu Miranda and Matlin proposed that psychopathology in Puerto Rico was more "shame" driven, or a

manifestation of what we now associate with a collectivistic or allocentric culture. They analyzed the examples of handshakes and gift giving as behaviors used by Puerto Ricans to invite their therapists to form an alliance with clients and individuals in exploring their problems, taking an interest in them, and expressing appreciation for their behavior/initiative (as opposed to the U.S. models, at the time, which taught therapists to see these as secondary-gain behaviors to be analyzed rather than shared). Their analyses of the cultural values and degree of importance associated with extended families also evoke the modern-day cultural practice of assigning distinct, endearing terms for extended families (e.g., *suegra, yerno*) in Puerto Rico, whereas these relationships in the United States are primarily legal (and theoretically more distant) in nature (e.g., mother-*in-law*, son-*in-law*).

Albizu Miranda, Matlin, and Stanton (1966) also criticized the utility of employing psychological tests based on foreign models in Puerto Rico. They noted that nearly a third of the people of Puerto Rico could be classified as mentally retarded according to the different tests' designed cutoff scores—a statistically and theoretically impossible result when based on the norms of intelligence tests in which only 2% of the population can fall in that range. It thus followed that if psychological tests were to be performed in Puerto Rico, they needed to be normed and designed on the basis of the cultural reality of Puerto Ricans.

Psychological Testing

As first formally documented by Albizu Miranda et al. (1966), psychological testing is a domain that has long been a focal point of controversy among psychologists in Puerto Rico. Herrans (2000) has thoroughly tracked attempts to implement intelligence measures in Puerto Rico, beginning with the Stanford-Binet Intelligence Scale in 1937 and the Wechsler Intelligence Scale for Children (WISC) in 1951. These early versions were literal translations of the English language scales and resulted in more than half the population tested performing in the mental retardation range (Vázquez, 1987). Ensuing attempts to use intelligence measures (e.g., the Wechsler Adult Intelligence Scale [WAIS] in 1962 and 2006, the WISC in 1975 and 1988) have incorporated the practice of standardizing and normalizing tests with the Puerto Rican population (with mixed results). Nevertheless, the lack of development of assessment instruments with a local population, several decades after this was identified as a concern, continues to be a criticism of psychology in Puerto Rico. Furthermore, other tests continue to be used without having proper normalization or validation processes completed. For example, the Minnesota Multiphasic Personality Inventory (MMPI-2) currently used in Puerto Rico is the Hispanic version developed by García-Peltoniemi and Azán (1993) that was normed on a Mexican population (the only modifications being a change in the wording of eight items to be more congruent with the Puerto Rican use of the language).

Professional Licensure and Training Programs

The role of testing by psychologists has also had a great influence in the current licensure process. The early participation of psychologists in government institutions and psychiatric hospitals was limited to test administration and interpretation, with psychology as a profession under the umbrella of psychiatry (Rosselló, 1988). However, the advent of World War II brought a high demand for psychological testing. The low numbers of prepared psychologists led to the commissioned use of bachelor's-level staff and other technicians to administer psychological tests. These individuals were then encouraged to pursue advanced degrees in psychology. Law 96 (LexJuris Puerto Rico, 2009), the first state regulation to oversee the practice of psychology in Puerto Rico, was approved in 1983. The law established the Puerto Rico Psychologist's Examining Board; specified that candidates for licensure, at both masters and doctoral level, be required to pass a written examination; required the adoption of rules and a code of ethics; established continuing-education requirements for professional

recertification; and stated criteria and procedures for disciplinary enforcement. The psychology law in Puerto Rico is generic in nature and psychologists are credentialed without reference to a specialty practice (Maldonado Feliciano & Rivera Alicea, 2007; Rivera & Maldonado, 2000). An amendment to Law 96, approved in 1990 and still in effect, stipulates that all psychologists seeking licensure must have a doctoral degree only if their specialization is in clinical psychology; all other specialties in psychology must have a master's degree to become licensed (Boulón-Díaz, 2007).

The former licensing board president Dr. Frances Boulón-Díaz (2007) reported that a total of 1,057 psychologists were "grandfathered" into licensure from 1984 through 1989. A total of 2,923 licenses have been awarded by the board from 1984 until September of 2007 (Boulón-Díaz, personal communication, September 26, 2007). Approximately 2,000 of these are currently active (Boulón-Díaz, personal communication, September 26, 2007). It should be noted that psychologists in Puerto Rico are licensed in the area of general psychology and not all active, licensed psychologists perform clinical work. The most recent statistics available through the Puerto Rico Department of Health (Departamento de Salud de Puerto Rico, 2004) indicate that by 2004 a total of 1,036 psychologists with active licenses perform clinical work (e.g., clinical, counseling, and school psychology). These data also document psychologist gender ratios at 70% females and 30% males. The average age for female psychologists is 43.7 years and for male psychologists, 48 years. For psychologists, 84% completed their training in Puerto Rico, while 11% did so in the United States and another 4% in Latin American or at European institutions.

Psychologists in Puerto Rico become licensed by achieving a passing score (70%) on the licensure exam, a 200-item (170 scored items and an additional 30 experimental items), multiple-choice test that comprises 10 sections related to general psychology (i.e., ethics, measurement, statistics, psychophysiology, social psychology, development, learning, personality, motivation, and psychopathology). The test is offered twice per year and has been made available electronically through computer administration since November of 2008. The pass rate has remained between 44% and 50% for the past 5 years (Boulón-Díaz, personal communication, September 26, 2007). More than 400 candidates took the test in 2005, while 514 candidates completed it 2 years later. There is no limit on how many times the test can be taken, so candidates can continue to take it until they pass.

A proliferation of training programs in recent years has produced a greater applicant pool for the licensure exam (known in Puerto Rico as *la reválida*). The academic system in Puerto Rico closely resembles that of the United States in terms of structure and organization. There are a total of 13 undergraduate programs, 15 master's programs, and 18 doctoral programs in psychology. A number of different specialty areas are taught at the graduate level. These include academic-research psychology, clinical psychology, counseling psychology, industrial-organizational psychology, school psychology, social-community psychology, and general psychology.

Currently, there are three doctoral-level (two PhD and one PsyD) and four master's-level programs in counseling psychology and six doctoral-level (three PhD and three PsyD) programs in clinical psychology. Three doctoral programs in clinical psychology are accredited by the APA. These are offered through Universidad Carlos Albizu (accredited since 1994) and Escuela de Medicina de Ponce (Ponce School of Medicine; accredited since 2004). One predoctoral internship training program, offered through the Veterans Affairs Caribbean Healthcare System, has been accredited by the APA since 2001. With a total of four full-time slots (increased from two beginning in the 2008–2009 academic year), the internship program is fully accredited until the year 2012. At present, none of the counseling psychology programs are accredited by the APA. Master's degree programs in counseling psychology require the completion of 52 to 63 graduate credits, supervised practicum, and presentation of a research project. Doctoral-level programs in counseling psychology require from 83 to 103 graduate credits and clinical psychology

programs require from 80 to 96 graduate credits beyond the bachelor's degree, comprehensive exams, supervised practicum, dissertation, and a 1-year predoctoral internship. Students in these graduate programs may complete their clinical hours of supervised practicum or internship requirements at mental health community centers associated with the institutions.

CHALLENGES AND FUTURE DIRECTIONS OF PSYCHOLOGY AND PSYCHOTHERAPY IN PUERTO RICO

The Colonization Process and the Ongoing Struggle to Solidify a Native Model of Psychology

Velázquez et al. (2006) proposed that the significant use of translated textbooks in academia and the use and pursuit of accreditation by the APA as the measuring stick for training curricula represent examples of the influence of the colonization process. This is true of the majority of the doctoral programs in the country, several of which model themselves after APA curriculums and training sequences despite not being accredited by the APA. Predoctoral internships are more varied in terms of their similarity to APA-approved internships and vary greatly with regard to the amount and level of supervision received and areas of specialization addressed. Therefore, the hundreds of psychologists who become licensed every year represent very diverse backgrounds in a continuum of training and exposure to APA rules and regulations. A solid critical mass is thus present to work toward a native model of psychology.

Velázquez et al. (2006) also argued that the use of imported models of testing and psychopathology is another example of the influence of the colonization process that needs to be addressed. This has been well documented and remains an area for growth in the field. Nevertheless, it should be noted that some groundwork has already been laid to address this. The WAIS was normed with a Puerto Rican population and published as the *Escala de*

Inteligencia Wechsler para Adultos (EIWA) (Wechsler, 1968). The WISC-R was also normed with a Puerto Rican population and published as the *Escala de Inteiligencia Wechsler para Niños—Revisada de Puerto Rico* (EIWN-R-PR) (Herrans & Rodríguez, 1992). The WAIS-III is also in the advanced stages of being translated and normed with a Puerto Rican population (Pons Madera et al., 2007). Other tests normed with a Puerto Rican population include the Cognitive Assessment System (CAS) (see Rodríguez-Arocho, 2007) and the Tell-Me-A-Story (TEMAS) (see Constantino, Dana, & Malgady, 2007). Finally, other assessment instruments have been developed in their entirety in Puerto Rico, and have even been adopted for use by professionals in other countries, such as the *Inventario Cirino de Intereses Vocacionales* (ICIV) (see Cirino, 1992). Funding, securing representative samples, the standardization of the test administration process, and getting participants to genuinely participate remain some of the main challenges for the further development of this area (Sharon Pérez-Arroyo, personal communication, August 4, 2008).

Velázquez et al. (2006) underscore the need for a critical look at the current psychology ethics code in Puerto Rico, emphasizing that it originated from a translation of an outdated 1979 APA code (p. 3). The APA's ethical principles for psychologists and code of conduct have primarily been based on a Western model of psychotherapy and fail to take into account some of the cultural differences that affect clinical work with clients from a Puerto Rican population. For example, Velázquez et al. (2006) stated the following about the APA ethics code:

> Professionals . . . teach most of their students to keep a certain distance from the person who solicits services, to not initiate any physical contact, and to not receive any gifts from their part. This type of behavior, although framed in a professional context, goes against the cultural nature of Puerto Ricans. (p. 3)

The code of ethics has been a topic of heated debate among psychologists in Puerto Rico. Law 96

afforded legal power to the newly created governing body, and a code of ethical conduct was adopted in 1992. Revisions to this code were proposed in 2002, but no changes were made (Junta Examinadora de Psicólogos de Puerto Rico, 2008). The Puerto Rico Psychology Association also has its own recently revised code of ethical conduct, which applies only to its members (Asociación de Psicología de Puerto Rico, 2008a). It is similar to but not the same as the current APA ethical standards for psychologists (which also apply to those Puerto Rican psychologists who are members of the APA). Legally bound by one (outdated and culturally inconsistent) code and ethically bound by possibly one or two more codes is a challenge that mirrors the confusion of being caught between two cultures and merits attention and clarification in the future.

Research

Martínez-Taboas and Pérez Pedrago (2007) have argued for the need to develop a culture of research among psychologists in Puerto Rico. Martínez-Taboas (1999) reported that 90% of psychologists in Puerto Rico have never published an article in a professional journal. There are two primary professional journals in Puerto Rico. *Ciencias de la Conducta* is affiliated with Universidad Carlos Albizu and was established in 1985 in part to help disseminate the research of its students. In recent years, this journal has become more diverse in breadth and scope and has consistently included contributions by professionals not affiliated with the university, as well as a regular section on art and culture (e.g., poetry, narratives, cultural analyses, etc.). *Revista Puertorriqueña de Psicología* is affiliated with the Puerto Rico Psychology Association and was established in 1981. Its mission is to promote the development of psychology as a scientific and responsible professional practice that contributes to the health and well-being of Puerto Rican society (Asociación de Psicología de Puerto Rico, 2008b). The journal has had an erratic publication history (15 volumes between 1981 and 2004) and a high acceptance rate (80%) (Martínez-Taboas &

Pérez Pedrago, 2007). The mission of the Association is also promoted through a number of other initiatives (e.g., a newsletter, an annual convention, an electronic group, a biweekly column in a major local newspaper, and a continuing education program). While there is some innovative and groundbreaking research being conducted as part of master's and doctoral theses, dissemination of the results of these remains mostly limited to presentations at the annual convention of Puerto Rico Psychology Association (which is usually loaded with student projects as presentations).

Several research institutions, some affiliated with different universities, have produced a solid research base. Some of these include CUSEP, established in 1986, and the Instituto de Investigacion Científica, established in 1978. Some of the topics that have been addressed by different investigators in the country include HIV and AIDS prevention, depression (particularly among adolescents), test translation and validation, attention deficit hyperactivity disorder, drug use and prevention, cognitive processes, and family/community interventions. Funding remains one of the key challenges in the development of more programmatic research. The government supports some efforts by state agencies, and additional funding has recently been secured through grants from institutions of the federal government. The development and solidification of research opportunities will, it is hoped, provide more students with exposure to the scientist aspect of their profession and thereby stimulate interest in it.

During his recently completed tenure as the president of the Puerto Rico Psychology Association, Dr. Alfonso Martínez-Taboas promoted the development of a task force to study evidence-based mental health practices in Puerto Rico (Martínez-Taboas, 2006). While some specific systems of psychotherapy have traditionally been associated with specific training programs (e.g., the University of Puerto Rico and psychoanalysis, Universidad Carlos Albizu and cognitive-behavioral therapy, the Ponce School of Medicine and the biopsychosocial model), no research programs have been developed to investigate the specific impact of these approaches on the

Puerto Rican population. These developments represent a promising start on these concerns and an important area of growth for the field of applied research in Puerto Rican psychology.

Training

Education represents the first formal avenue for the introduction of psychology in Puerto Rico, beginning with the founding of the University of Puerto Rico in 1903. Training remains one of the keys for the further development of the field, and the growth of training programs in recent years is a hopeful sign. Additional training programs and experiences help bring new ideas into the fold. The development of more university-affiliated research programs will have the added side-effect of generating opportunities for students to gain exposure to the publication process and possibly stimulate the development of much needed Spanish textbooks and research paradigms based on the needs of the Puerto Rican population.

The active pursuit of APA accreditation will also need to be balanced with the possible development of a standard curriculum that is designed to meet the training needs of the local student population. It is interesting to note that the APA has come to Puerto Rico three times for its accreditation study of the country's internship site, and they have always commented on what they perceive to be a lack of diversity in the site's staff. Each time they have made recommendations for this to be addressed. These observations, which seem to be based on racial background and the emphasis on cultural diversity so salient in the United States, do not seem to reflect other important aspects of cultural diversity (such as the ethnic makeup of most Puerto Ricans, as well as within-group staff differences) and the actual needs of the population served (primarily Spanish speaking and almost exclusively of Puerto Rican descent).

The training of more psychologists will continue to develop the researchers necessary to further the work of Abigail Díaz Concepción, Efraín Sánchez Hidalgo, Miguelina Nazario de Hernández, Pablo

Roca de León, and Alba Nydia Rivera, among others, and continue to develop the field of psychology in Puerto Rico to get closer to an indigenous model of psychotherapy. Carlos Albizu Miranda and Norman Matlin were instrumental in this process because they took their intellectual knowledge regarding the need to develop alternatives to the imported models used at the time and put it to use. Initiatives such as the Instituto Psicológico de Puerto Rico (the first institution to confer doctoral degrees in psychology in Puerto Rico and site of the first clinic for training and supervision in the provision of psychological services in the country) directly respond to the specific needs of the Puerto Rican population. Such work needs to continue.

Practice

Practice represents the other formal avenue for the introduction of psychology in Puerto Rico. However, it has developed in the shadow of the more respected and established field of psychiatry, with initial work opportunities limited to testing responsibilities in hospital settings. Some lingering conflict remains between the two fields with regard to credibility and practice. Meanwhile, testing continues to be one of the primary roles that the public associates with psychologists, as well as one of psychologists' main sources of income (primarily in forensic and school settings).

Students would be well served with the development of more applied clinical experiences to further develop their clinical skills. Opportunities for training and practice in clinical supervision are even more limited or virtually nonexistent. Licensed psychologists would be well served by diversifying their roles to increase their marketability with regard to the general population. The responsibility for this rests on their shoulders.

Law 96, which allows candidates to take the licensure exam as many times as they need to, has the advantage of licensing more psychologists, which ultimately facilitates the growth and visibility of the profession. However, this also has the unintended consequence of generating a greater supply for what is at the moment a very limited demand in terms of employment opportunities for psychologists. The most recent statistics from the Department of Health indicate that during the 2001 to 2004 reporting period, 45% of psychologists with active licenses worked in the private sector, 41% worked in the public sector, 13% were self-employed, and 0.6% worked in voluntary positions (Departamento de Salud de Puerto Rico, 2004). Boulón-Díaz (2007) listed institutions of higher education as one of the primary places of employment for psychologists in Puerto Rico. Other specific employment settings for psychologists include government agencies (e.g., health, education, corrections, family services, addictions, the police, etc.), private industries (e.g., banks, hospitals, consulting firms, etc.), and the continuously growing private practice alternative. Health care and medical insurance, at the moment, do not reimburse for services received by counseling psychologists; only licensed clinical psychologists are subject to any type of financial support (Julio Ribera, personal communication, September 7, 2006). With a little more than 2,000 licensed psychologists for a population of nearly 4 million, the need for more psychologists to improve the mental health of the population is certainly present. However, the venues to meet those needs remain rather scant.

Puerto Rican American Psychology

An overview on the development of Puerto Rican psychotherapy would be incomplete without mention of Puerto Rican American psychology. It is important to note that the Puerto Rican population living in the continental United States (e.g., Puerto Rican Americans) has outnumbered the mainland Puerto Rican population since 2003. This phenomenon has evolved through years of different migration patterns and is unique in the Western hemisphere, bringing about its own consequences in terms of the development of a native model of psychology. While mainland Puerto Ricans have struggled to develop their own identity and sense of self, the identity of Puerto Rican Americans as a "minority" group in the United States has been provided to them. Their struggle to overcome years of prejudice and discrimination has prompted the necessity to explore ways to address mental health concerns specific to their own cultural needs.

Gherovici (2003) documented an example of this phenomenon in her book *The Puerto Rican Syndrome*. This term was coined by U.S. army medical officers during the 1950s in their treatment of Puerto Rican soldiers participating in the Korean War. The Puerto Rican syndrome linked culture to alleged mental illness by attributing to a particular nationality a set of symptoms that could not be explained through traditional neurological or psychiatric means.

Experiences like this have facilitated the development of some interventions indigenous to the Puerto Rican American population. *Cuento therapy* (Constantino, Malgady, & Rogler, 1986) was originally developed as an intervention with young Puerto Ricans to affirm their cultural identity. It relies on traditional, Spanish language folktales (e.g., cuentos) to relay rules, values, social norms, and customs, the conceptual model behind this being that psychological problems are the result of acculturation stress, weak traditional cultural values, and loss of ethnic pride (Ramírez & Flores-Torres, 2006). The TEMAS test (Constantino, Dana, & Malgady, 2007) and *dicho therapy* (Zuniga, 1991) have similarly been developed and studied as applicable to the Puerto Rican American population, following the same model of cultural affirmation and the need to reclaim a sense of ethnic pride.

CONCLUSION

Paralleling its own sociopolitical history, psychology in Puerto Rico has struggled throughout the years to find its own identity and direction. Rivera Ramos (1984) stated that "psychology in Puerto Rico has been dominated by the influence of North America" (p. 4), while Bernal (2007) referred to the development of psychology in Puerto Rico as "doing psychology from the subversive" (p. 378). This partly reflects some of the confusion and ambiguity that the people of Puerto Rico live on a daily basis, part of the bicultural political status that comes with being a U.S. commonwealth. This is evident in the fact that Puerto Rican psychology has not developed solely in the context of Western psychology models—contrary to Puerto Rican American psychology.

Counseling psychology has equally struggled beneath the shadow of clinical psychology. Its history as a specialty area is significantly less extensive. The coming years could see the solidification of a sense of identity as a field separate from clinical psychology. Similarly, future years could also see the further development of the Puerto Rican Association of Counseling Professionals and increased visibility of counseling psychologists in the areas of research, training, and practice. The possibility remains that a counseling psychology training program could pursue accreditation by the APA. Nevertheless, APA accreditation is a relatively recent phenomenon and has been met with mixed reactions from psychologists in terms of its impact on the actual needs of the Puerto Rican population. More research is clearly needed to determine the extent to which the APA promotes or interferes with the development of a Puerto Rican model of psychology.

In conclusion, the practice of psychotherapy in Puerto Rico has experienced significant growth in recent years in the number of practicing psychologists, training programs available, research production, and employment opportunities, as well as the development of a governing body and the beginnings of a process to regulate the field. The search for a native model of psychology has been slow to develop, but the groundwork has been laid and the progress continues.

Author's Note: The author wishes to thank Leslie E. Maldonado Feliciano, PhD, for his significant contribution to the development of this manuscript.

REFERENCES

Albizu Miranda, C., & Matlin, N. (1967). La psicología en Puerto Rico: Apuntes sobre el estado del arte [Psychology in Puerto Rico: Notes on the state of the art]. *Revista de Ciencias Sociales, 9,* 71–80.

Albizu Miranda, C., Matlin, N., & Stanton, H. R. (1966). *The successful retardate.* San Juan, Puerto Rico: Vocational Rehabilitation Administration.

Alvarez, A. I. (2007). La enseñanza de la psicología en la Universidad de Puerto Rico, Recinto de Río Piedras: 1903–1950 [The teaching of psychology at the University of Puerto Rico, Río Piedras Campus: 1903–1950]. *Revista Puertorriqueña de Psicología, 17,* 93–113.

Alvarez, V., & Vélez-Pastrana, M. C. (1995). La profesión de la psicología en Puerto Rico [The profession of psychology in Puerto Rico]. *Revista Puertorriqueña de Psicología, 10,* 175–185.

Aron, A., & Corne, S. (1996). *Writings for a liberation psychology.* New York: Harvard University Press.

Asociación de Psicología de Puerto Rico. (2008a). *Código de ética de la asociación de psicología de Puerto Rico* [Code of ethics of the Puerto Rico psychology association]. Retrieved August 28, 2008, from http://www.asppr.net/pdf/codigo_etica_appr_07.pdf

Asociación de Psicología de Puerto Rico. (2008b). *Historia-misión-visión-metas* [History-missionvision-goals.] Retrieved August 28, 2008, from http://www.asppr.net/index.php?option=com_content& view=article &id=5&Itemid=2

Auger, C., & Quintero, N. (2005). Modelo de adiestramiento clínico de la Universidad Carlos Albizu [Clinical training model of Carlos Albizu University]. In G. Bernal & A. Martínez-Taboas (Eds.), *Teoría y práctica de la psicoterapia en Puerto Rico* [Theory and practice of psychotherapy in Puerto Rico] (pp. 357–370). Hato Rey, Puerto Rico: Puertorriqueñas.

Bernal, G. (2007). La psicología clínica en Puerto Rico [Clinical psychology in Puerto Rico]. *Revista Puertorriqueña de Psicología, 17,* 341–388.

Bernal, G., & Martínez-Taboas, A. (2005). Teorías de psicoterapia en Puerto Rico: Una introducción [Psychotherapy theories in Puerto Rico: An introduction]. In G. Bernal & A. Martínez-Taboas (Eds.), *Teoría y práctica de la psicoterapia en Puerto Rico* [Theory and practice of psychotherapy in Puerto Rico] (pp. 2–7). Hato Rey, Puerto Rico: Puertorriqueñas.

Boulón-Díaz, F. (2007). La psicología como profesión en Puerto Rico: Desarrollos y nuevos retos [Psychology as a profession in Puerto Rico: Developments and new challenges]. *Revista Puertorriqueña de Psicología, 17,* 215–240.

Cirino, G. (1992). *Manual: Inventario Cirino de intereses vocacionales, Forma E* [Manual: Cirino inventory of vocational interests, Form E]. San Juan, Puerto Rico: Author.

Comas-Díaz, L. (2006). Latino healing: The integration of ethnic psychology into psychotherapy. *Psychotherapy: Theory, Research, Practice, Training, 43*(4), 436–453.

Constantino, G., Dana, R. H., & Malgady, R. G. (2007). *TEMAS (Tell-me-a-story) assessment in multicultural societies.* Mahwah, NJ: Lawrence Erlbaum.

Constantino, G., Malgady, R. G., & Rogler, L. H. (1986). Cuento therapy: A culturally sensitive modality for Puerto Rican children. *Journal of Consulting and Clinical Psychology, 54*(5), 639–645.

Departamento de Salud de Puerto Rico. (2004). *Psicólogos: Noveno registro, 2001–2004* [Psychologists: Ninth registry, 2001–2004]. San Juan, Puerto Rico: Author.

Dussel, E. (1998). *Ética de la liberación en la edad de la globalización y de la exclusión* [Liberation ethics in the age of globalization and exclusion]. Madrid, Spain: Trotta.

Fanón, F. (1963). *Los condenados de la tierra* [The condemned of the land]. México D.F., México: Fondo de Cultura Económica.

García-Peltoniemi, R., & Azán, A. (1993). MMPI-2: Inventario multifásico de la personalidad-2, Minnesota [MMPI-2: Minnesota Multiphasic Personality Inventory-2]. Minneapolis: University of Minnesota Press.

Gherovici, P. (2003). *The Puerto Rican syndrome.* New York: Other Press.

González Rivera, S. (2007). Apuntes sobre las ideas psicológicas en Puerto Rico: Desde el periodo precolombino hasta el siglo XIX [Notes on psychological ideas in Puerto Rico: From the precolombian period until the 19th century]. *Revista Puertorriqueña de Psicología, 17,* 3–26.

Hernández, R. (1985). Historia de los programas en salud mental en Puerto Rico [History of mental health programs in Puerto Rico]. *Homines, 3,* 22–31.

Herrans, L. L. (2000). *Psicología y medición: El desarrollo de pruebas psicológicas en Puerto Rico* (2da ed.) [Psychology and measurement: The development of psychological tests in Puerto Rico (2nd ed.)]. México D.F., México: McGraw-Hill.

Herrans, L. L., & Rodríguez, J. M. (1992). *Manual for the Escala de Inteligencia Wechsler para niños: Revisada de Puerto Rico (EIWN-R PR)* [Manual for the Wechsler Intelligence Scale for Children: Revised Puerto Rico (PR EIWN-R)]. San Antonio, TX: Psychological Corporation.

Hogar CREA. (2009). *Datos importantes* [Important facts]. Retrieved April 23, 2009, from http://www.hogarcreapr.org/Datos_Imp/datos_imp.html

Junta Examinadora de Psicólogos de Puerto Rico. (2008). *Revisión del Código de Ética* [Revision of the Code of Ethics]. Retrieved August 28, 2008, from http://psic.uprrp.edu/Politicas/codigo_etica_junta.pdf

LexJuris Puerto Rico. (2009). *Ley para Reglamentar el Ejercicio de la Profesión de la Psicología en Puerto Rico* [Law to regulate the practice of the profession of psychology in Puerto Rico]. Retrieved April 23, 2009, from http://www.lexjuris.com/lexmate/profesiones/lex103.htm

Lucy López-Roig & Associates. (2009). *Welcome*. Retrieved April 23, 2009, from http://www.lucylopezroig.com/Welcome.html

Maldonado Feliciano, L. E., & Rivera Alicea, B. E. (2007). *Reglamentación de especialidades para la práctica de la psicología en Puerto Rico: Consideraciones legales y profesionales* [Regulation for specialty practice of psychology in Puerto Rico: Legal and professional considerations]. *Revista Puertorriqueña de Psicología, 17,* 297–337.

Martínez-Taboas, A. (1999). *La publicación de artículos profesionales: Reflexiones, anécdotas, y recomendaciones de un editor* [The publication of professional articles: Reflections, anecdotes, and recommendations from an editor]. *Ciencias de la Conducta, 16,* 63–78.

Martínez-Taboas, A. (2006). *Mensaje del Presidente* [Message of the president]. Retrieved April 24, 2009, from http://www.asppr.net/mensajepresident.htm

Martínez-Taboas, A., & Pérez Pedrogo, C. (2007). Las revistas de psicología en Puerto Rico: Una breve mirada histórica [Journals of psychology in Puerto Rico: A brief historical outlook]. *Revista Puertorriqueña de Psicología, 17,* 571–589.

Memmi, A. (1969). *Retrato del colonizado* [Portrait of the colonized]. Buenos Aires, Argentina: Ediciones de la Flor.

Mettler, S. (2005). The creation of the G.I. Bill of Rights of 1944: Melding social and participatory citizenship ideals. *Journal of Policy History, 17*(4), 345–374.

Núñez Molina, M. (2005). Acercamiento transpersonal: El espiritismo puertorriqueño como terapia [Transpersonal approach: Puerto Rican spiritism as therapy]. In G. Bernal & A. Martínez-Taboas (Eds.), *Teoría y práctica de la psicoterapia en Puerto Rico* [Theory and practice of psychotherapy in Puerto Rico] (pp. 36–65). Hato Rey, Puerto Rico: Puertorriqueñas.

Picó, F. (1986). *Historia general de Puerto Rico* [General history of Puerto Rico]. Río Piedras, Puerto Rico: Ediciones Huracán.

Pons Madera, J., Rodríguez, J. M., Herrans, L. L., Matías Carrelo, L., Medina, G., Rodríguez, M., et al. (2007, October). *Traducción, adaptación y normalización de la EIWA-III en Puerto Rico: Resultados preliminares, estudios de validez y confiabilidad y proyecciones para el psicodiagnóstico* [Traduction, adaptation, and norming, of the WAIS-III in Puerto Rico: Preliminary results, validity and reliability studies, and projections for the psychodiagnostician]. Paper presented at the Puerto Rico Psychological Association Annual Convention, Ponce, Puerto Rico.

Ramírez, S. Z., & Flores-Torres, L. L. (2006). Indigenous treatments: Cuento therapy. In Y. K. Jackson (Ed.), *Encyclopedia of multicultural psychology* (pp. 248–249). Thousand Oaks, CA: Sage.

Rivera, B. E., & Maldonado, L. (2000). Revisión histórica de la reglamentación de la psicología en Puerto Rico: 1954–1990 [Historical review of the regulation of psychology in Puerto Rico: 1954–1990]. *Revista Interamericana de Psicología, 34*(1), 127–162.

Rivera Ramos, A. N. (1984). *Hacia una psicoterapia para el puertorriqueño* [Toward a psychotherapy for Puerto Ricans]. San Juan, Puerto Rico: CE-DEPP (Centro para el Estudio y Desarrollo de la Personalidad Puertorriqueña).

Roca de Torres, I. (2007). La Asociación de Psicología de Puerto Rico: Una perspectiva histórica (1954–2005) [The Psychological Association of Puerto Rico: A historical perspective (1954–2005)]. *Revista Puertorriqueña de Psicología, 17,* 241–276.

Rodríguez-Arocho, W. C. (2007). Estudio de los procesos cognitivos en Puerto Rico: Antecedentes, actualidad y perspectivas [Study of cognitive processes in Puerto Rico: Antecedents, actualities, and perspectives]. *Revista Puertorriqueña de Psicología, 17,* 517–549.

Rosselló, J. (1975). *Historia de la psiquiatría en Puerto Rico: Siglo XIX* [History of psychiatry in Puerto Rico: 19th century]. Río Piedras, Puerto Rico: Universidad de Puerto Rico.

Rosselló, J. (1988). *Historia de la psiquiatría en Puerto Rico: 1898–1988*. [History of psychiatry in Puerto Rico: 1898–1988]. San Juan, Puerto Rico: Relaciones Humanas.

Santiago, J. (2007). Apuntes sobre la investigación psicológica en Puerto Rico: Tesis y disertaciones [Notes on psychological research in Puerto Rico: Theses and dissertations]. *Revista Puertorriqueña de Psicología, 17,* 487–516.

Silén, J. A. (1973). We, the Puerto Rican people: A story of oppression and resistance. In F. Cordasco & E. Bucchioni (Eds.), *The Puerto Rican experience: A sociological sourcebook* (pp. 186–197). Totowa, NJ: Rowman & Littlefield.

U.S. Census Bureau. (2008a). *Table 1: Annual estimates of the resident population for the United States, regions, states, and Puerto Rico: April 1, 2000 to July 1, 2008* (NST-EST2008–01). Retrieved April 24, 2009, from http://www.census.gov/popest/states/ tables/NST-EST2008–01.xls

U.S. Census Bureau. (2008b). *Table B03001: Hispanic or Latino origin by specific origin–universe: Total population* (Data set: 2006 American community survey). Retrieved August 5, 2008, from http://www.factfinder .census.gov/servlet/DTTable?_bm=y&-geo_id=0100 0US&-ds_nam'e=ACS_2006_EST_G00_&-mt_name =ACS_2006 _EST_G2000_B03001

Vázquez, J. J. (2000). *Psicología social y liberación en América Latina* [Social psychology and liberation in Latin America]. México D.F., México: Universidad Autónoma de México.

Vázquez, M. (1987). *El asilo sin paredes: Apuntes sobre la provisión de servicios al enfermo mental* [Asylum without walls: Notes on the provision of services to the mentally ill]. Unpublished master's thesis, Universidad de Puerto Rico, Río Piedras, Puerto Rico.

Velázquez, J., Millán, F., Colton, M., Cabiya, I., Rodríguez, K., Miranda, Y., et al. (2006). Una nueva mirada a la psicología en Puerto Rico: Apuntes sobre el estado de un arte [A new look at psychology in Puerto Rico: Notes on the state of the art]. *Glossa— Ambilingual Interdisciplinary Journal, 1*(1), 1–14.

Wechsler, D. (1968). *Escala de inteligencia Wechsler para adultos* [Wechsler Adult Intelligence scale]. San Antonio, TX: Psychological Corporation.

Zuniga, M. E. (1991). "Dichos" as metaphorical tools for resistant Latino clients. *Psychotherapy: Theory, Research, Practice, Training, 28*(3), 480–483.

SOUTH AND WEST AFRICA

32

The Quest for Relevance

Counseling Psychology in South Africa

Die Soeke na Relevansie: Voorligtingsielkunde in Suid Afrika

ANTHONY V. NAIDOO AND ASHRAF KAGEE

South Africa is one of the few countries on the continent of Africa in which counseling psychology as a discipline has gained a substantive presence. In South Africa, counseling psychology is formally recognized as one of the main subdisciplines in psychology, representing one of five major areas of specialization for students pursuing a career as a psychologist. Credentialing for any of the psychology specializations, including counseling psychology, requires an accredited master's level qualification, offered by several universities, and leading to registration or licensing as a counseling psychologist. In spite of its long history, counseling psychology continues to struggle with issues of sociopolitical relevance and identity as South Africa grapples with serious social questions of escalating crime, unemployment, the HIV/AIDS pandemic, and other challenges (Leach, Akhurst, & Basson, 2003; Watson & Fouche, 2007).

In this chapter, in contextualizing the genesis, scope, and application of counseling psychology in South Africa, we discuss how the sociopolitical history of apartheid has shaped the emergence of the discipline (Anonymous, 1986; Whitaker, 1991). We describe the professional organization of psychology amidst the changing social context as South Africa evolves from being a racially segregated society to a new democratic order. Several salient contemporary issues are highlighted, including the search for relevance, the relationship between counseling and clinical psychology, and the poor uptake of counseling services. We further examine the difference in paradigms between South African and U.S. counseling psychology and some of the challenges facing the discipline.

THE PERVASIVE AND DEEPLY ENTRENCHED SOCIOPOLITICAL CONTEXT OF APARTHEID

The development of psychology in South Africa is entwined with the country's history of racial separation and discrimination (Cooper, Nicholas, Seedat, & Statman, 1990; Holdstock, 1981). In April 1993, South Africa officially inaugurated Nelson Mandela as its first democratically elected president. This marked the beginning of a new period in South Africa's history, bringing an end to an oppressive era of white rule that had become embodied by the term *apartheid*. While discriminatory practices have been evident in South Africa's history since 1652 and the first arrival of Europeans, the formalization of racial segregation into legislation and social policies coalesced when the National Party, representing the interests of the Afrikaner[1] constituency, came into power in 1948. Despite deep differences and tensions between Afrikaans-speaking and English-speaking white South Africans as a consequence of the Anglo-Boer war during which thousands of Afrikaner women and children died in British concentration camps, their combined numerical minority relative to the black majority was the basis of the political compromise to ensure white domination of the social and economic order (Kagee, Naidoo, & van Wyk, 2003).

Apartheid encompassed an evolving system of legislation and social policies that forcefully segregated and codified the South African population into one of four racial categories:[2] (1) white, (2) colored (mixed heritage), (3) Asian, and (4) African (black). According to the mid-2007 estimates from Statistics South Africa (2007), the country's population stands at some 47.9 million. Blacks are in the majority at just over 38 million, making up 79.6% of the total population. The white population is estimated at 4.3 million (9.1%), the colored population at 4.2 million (8.9%), and the Indian/Asian population is just under 1.2 million (2.5%).

The social engineering of apartheid not only separated the designated "nonwhite" groups (as they were perjoratively termed) physically and socially from the white group but, by its divide-and-rule strategy, gave the white minority group political and economic control and domination over the majority of the disenfranchised South African population. Differential dispensations for the nonwhite groups by the white government also created divisions and tensions among these groups. These racial categories and structures were reinforced by often violent enforcement of a draconian set of apartheid laws that racialised all aspects of an individual's (and a designated group's) life from birth to death. Apartheid determined, for instance, which hospital or clinic could be accessed (segregated public facilities and differential services), place of residence (strictly racially based neighborhoods), school and further education and training (institutions were racially segregated and very disparate in terms of facilities and academic programs), job opportunities (racial discrimination was rampant in favor of white job reservation), whom the individual could marry or have sex with (sexual intercourse between white and nonwhite individuals was prosecuted under the Immorality Act), and even where the individual was allowed to be buried.

The entrenched system of racial segregation and the increasingly oppressive measures used to maintain the system (for instance, the pass [identity document] system used to regulate the movement of black workers, banning, house arrest, detention-without-trial mechanisms, imprisonment, and also the torture and murder of political detainees) inflicted deep, traumatic, and pernicious injuries to the social and psychological fabric of South African society (Nicholas, 1990a). From mid-1970s to the early 1990s, the intense political conflict threatened to rapidly escalate into a civil war. Opposition to white rule was violently suppressed, and the human rights of most South Africans were violated. Restrictions were imposed on citizens' rights of association, movement, and political expression to preempt any threat to the apartheid regime. This system of political domination of white over black South Africans resulted in oppression, social upheaval, impoverishment, and the social and cultural marginalization of the majority of the country's population (Kagee et al., 2003).

The apartheid divide manifested in very disparate First world and Third world social realities for white and black South Africans, respectively. This was evident in mental health provision as well: Whereas whites enjoyed excellent facilities and well-resourced and staffed services, mental health services for the disenfranchised groups were inferior, inadequate, difficult to access, inappropriate, and discriminatory (Lazarus, 1988). Notwithstanding the relatively peaceful negotiated political transition in 1994, apartheid has left an indelible legacy of trauma, racial disparity, and deeply entrenched racial stereotypes and prejudice that continue to have a negative impact on race relations throughout the country (Mda & Mothata, 2000). The economic disparities between the white and black sectors of the population are among the most extreme in the world (World Bank, 2002, cited in Kagee et al., 2003). South Africa's per capita income is that of a middle-income country. Yet only 13% of the population have access to first-world living conditions, whereas 53% of the population are exposed to extreme hardship and poverty (World Bank, 2002, cited in Kagee et al., 2003).

PSYCHOLOGY IN SOUTH AFRICA

South African psychology has been accused of playing a duplicitous role. Under the guise of scientific neutrality, it has been accused of colluding with and maintaining apartheid (Anonymous, 1986; Nicholas, 1990a, 1990c). Foster (2004) noted that psychology has, since it began in South Africa as a discipline in the 1920s, offered little resistance to racism. Moreover, psychological research was used strategically by the government to bolster its racist policies. Because of both this silence and direct complicity, the psychology profession has been accused of being a willing partner in the apartheid system by reinforcing and serving the interests of white minority rule (Watson & Fouche, 2007). Indeed, for most of the 20th century, psychology was essentially in white and male hands (Seedat, 1997, cited in Foster, 2004), reflecting the privileged white minority position and serving the needs of mainly white clients.

Since the early 1980s, psychology as a discipline and a profession in South Africa has been subjected to increasing scrutiny as South African society experienced considerable political turbulence (Cooper et al., 1990; Naidoo, 2000). Increasingly, critical voices decried racism in psychology (Duncan, 2001;

Duncan, van Niekerk, de la Rey, & Seedat, 2001; Durrheim & Mokeki, 1997) and psychology's complicity with apartheid (see Lambley, 1980; Nicholas, 1993; Nicholas & Cooper, 1990). They critiqued the imposition and hegemony of Western and Eurocentric psychology (Anonymous, 1986; Bulhan, 1990), called for social relevance (Dawes, 1985; Holdstock, 1981; Stead & Watson, 2002), and emphasized the need for more critical engagement within the discipline (Painter & Terre Blanche, 2004; Whitaker, 1991).

APARTHEID AND COUNSELING PSYCHOLOGY

Since 1974, counseling psychology has been one of five recognized disciplines or categories in South African psychology and, as such, has been deeply affected by the interplay of racism, ideology, and politics. The emergence of applied psychology and its early links to implicit and explicit racist ideologies in South Africa reflects the overall development of psychology as a field and counseling psychology in particular (Watson & Fouche, 2007). The impetus for the emergence of applied psychology in South Africa is linked to the ascendance of the mental-testing movement in the United States, after intelligence testing was used to identify mentally retarded individuals circa 1916 (Stead, 2004). Various psychological tools and technologies were imported and adapted for application in education and industry. During the 1920s and 1930s, psychometric testing burgeoned, with a particular social-Darwinian slant toward research into racial differences in mental abilities. Lower performance of blacks relative to whites generally was attributed to heredity or environmental deprivation (e.g., poverty, culture, and education) or both (Stead, 2004). There was also a particular focus on the testing and placement of black workers for the mining industry. Broader social contexts at the time included the labor challenges of the industrial revolution, migration from rural areas to the cities, the need to jumpstart the economy after the end of the World War I, the attention focused on "the poor white problem,"[3] race relations, mental hygiene, and the rise in

Afrikaner nationalism (Painter & Terre Blanche, 2004). (See Nicholas, Naidoo, & Pretorius, 2006, for an understanding of how this social context influenced the beginnings of career psychology in South Africa).

Similar wellsprings of psychometric testing and vocational guidance, which shaped counseling psychology in the United States, also influenced the early beginnings of this discipline in South Africa. The Carnegie Commission, appointed to investigate the plight of the economically challenged white group, made recommendations that were readily harnessed to demonstrate psychology's usefulness in the solution of social problems (Louw, 1986). Leach et al. (2003) contended that the appointment of H. F. Verwoerd, who was later to become prime minister and the chief architect of apartheid, to the position of professor of applied psychology at Stellenbosch University in 1927 was significant and served to align counseling psychology with Afrikaner nationalism and racist ideologies (Cooper et al., 1990). This new discipline, distinct from the clinical psychology emphasis in English-speaking departments, could focus on career issues, job opportunities, health development, prevention of psychological disorders, and economic empowerment approaches directed specifically at Afrikaans-speaking students and their constituencies thereby serving the purpose of bolstering Afrikaner nationalism (Leach et al., 2003).

Shortly after legislation was passed in 1974 formalizing the registration of psychologists into five registration categories (i.e., clinical, counseling, educational, industrial, and research), counseling programs were established at the Afrikaans-speaking universities of Stellenbosch, the Orange Free State, Port Elizabeth, Rand Afrikaans, and at the English-medium university of Natal (Leach et al., 2003). Visits by the psychologists Carl Rogers and Donald Super to South Africa in the 1980s, while controversial at the time because of the call for international sanctions against the apartheid state, served to provide a new impetus to the counseling discipline, with several psychology departments adopting Rogers' person-centered therapy as their training orientation. Individuals who played a prominent role in the early development of counseling psychology were

H. G. van Niekerk, A. G. Botha, J. M. du Toit, and Bodley Van der Westhuijsen (1992) at Stellenbosch University and A. van Aarde at the University of Port Elizabeth (Dr. H. Brand, personal communication, October 29, 2007).

With the establishment of counseling psychology programs at black institutions (e.g., the University of the Western Cape [UWC] in the late 1980s) and other progressive white institutions, the political focus of counseling psychology began to shift toward greater social relevance and addressing the needs of the disenfranchised groups (Naidoo, 1996; Nicholas, 1990b, 1995). There was growing opposition to apartheid despite increased state repression. Prior to the 1980s, black students had severe limitations placed on them if they wished to attend white universities and were rarely admitted to graduate programs in psychology. Many of the first cohort of black counseling psychologists received their training in the United States through externally funded scholarship programs. Nicholas and his colleagues were particularly active in providing this impetus at UWC by hosting two important international conferences: the Apartheid and the Crisis in Psychology Conference in 1990 and the Psychology and Societal Transformation Conference in 1994. In the Eastern Cape, Mark Watson and Graham Stead began to play prominent roles by advocating a contextualized career psychology in South Africa (Stead & Watson, 1998, 2006a, 2006b, 2006c; Watson & Stead, 2002).

THE PROFESSIONAL ORGANIZATION OF PSYCHOLOGY

The first official body for psychology, the South African Psychological Association (SAPA), was established in 1948, the same year the Nationalist Party came to power. Racial agendas and tensions were evident from the onset. After protracted and often acrimonious debate and machinations, a decision to admit a black member in 1956 caused a split in SAPA (Painter & Terre Blanche, 2004). In 1962, many prominent members, followed by other members, disaffiliated from the multiracial SAPA to form the Psychological Institute of the Republic of South

Africa (PIRSA) with exclusively white membership. PIRSA members were largely Afrikaans speaking (Stead, 2004), and its main focus was on psychological research on racial differences (Nicholas, 1990a). It was within this segregated and fragmented context that counseling psychology emerged.

In 1974, the two bodies were forced to engage in discussions on the registration of psychologists and established the Professional Board of Psychology under the auspices of the South African Medical and Dental Council. By 1977, SAPA and PIRSA signed an agreement of cooperation, hosted a joint conference, and launched the *South African Journal of Psychology* (Louw, 1987; Nicholas, 1990a). By 1983, with the government's attempts to disguise some features of apartheid, the two associations disbanded and formed the Psychological Association of South Africa (PASA). While PASA may not overtly have supported apartheid, many psychologists perceived it as being complicit by omission because of its unwillingness to challenge apartheid policies (including detentions, torture, and discrimination) and dereliction of its duty to promote the mental health of all South Africans (Stead, 2004).

The groundswell against apartheid in the decade leading up to the 1994 democratic elections was a catalyst that fomented radical changes within the formal organization of the psychology profession (Naidoo, Shabalala, & Bawa, 2003). Three organizations associated with anti-apartheid movements emerged in which progressive psychologists sought to put into effect the call for the relevance of health and social science disciplines in community settings. These were the Organization for Alternative Social Services in South Africa (OASSSA), established in 1983, a grouping of predominantly white psychologists, psychiatrists, and social workers; the Psychology and Apartheid Group, consisting of black psychologists, which hosted the conferences focusing on the relationship between psychology and apartheid at UWC; and the South African Health and Social Services Organization (SAHSSO), a grouping for interdisciplinary health workers (Painter & Terre Blanche, 2004). These organizations were engaged in challenging the apartheid system, locating mental

health within a political context, and engaging with the emerging mental health challenges the country was facing (Naidoo et al., 2003). They also provided forums to protest the dereliction of the mental health services to the majority of South Africans (Stead, 2004).

In 1994, PASA was dissolved to make way for the multiracial Psychological Society of South Africa (PsySSA). PsySSA is the guild organization of psychologists in South Africa, akin to the American Psychological Association (APA), and has 10 membership divisions. The *South African Journal of Psychology* is its official publication forum. Counseling psychology is one of the major divisions of PsySSA, with its own membership. For a population of 48 million people, there are approximately 8,000 licensed psychologists with 35% registered as counseling psychologists. The majority of registered psychologists (87%) are white, female, and work largely in private practice serving white, middle-class clients (De la Rey & Ipser, 2004). The Southern African Association for Counseling and Development in Higher Education (formerly the Society of Student Counseling in Southern Africa) provides a separate professional forum for counselors working in universities and colleges, of whom an increasing proportion have qualifications other than in counseling psychology.

The credentialing of psychologists in South Africa is through the Board of Psychology, which forms part of the regulatory statutory body called the Health Professions Council of South Africa (formerly the South African Medical and Dental Council). The requirements for registration (licensing) for counseling psychology include completion of an accredited master's level program, followed by a 12-month internship at an approved site in the second year, and passing the board exam. Accredited master's programs in counseling psychology are currently offered at eight local universities, with three programs offering combined clinical and counseling programs at a theoretical level but with differentiated practical and internship training (Leach et al., 2003).

In the 1990s, a new, lower-level counselor qualification—the 4-year Bachelor of Psychology

(BPsych) degree—was introduced at several universities as an initiative to train counselors to work at the community grassroots level in a range of specialization areas (such as trauma, vocational counseling, family counseling, pastoral counseling, HIV/AIDS, and psychometry). However, several difficulties have affected the viability of this training, including the strain on the departments' resources running simultaneous undergraduate and graduate programs, as well as limited employment opportunities for BPsych graduates in the health care system. Many students have used the BPsych qualification as a springboard to gain entry into graduate programs rather than entering the job market. However, given the amount of resources required to teach, supervise, and oversee students enrolled in BPsych programs, several universities have subsequently discontinued the BPsych program.

CONTEMPORARY ISSUES

The Search for Social Relevance

The debate in the 1980s and 1990s about how South African psychology could become more relevant to the local sociopolitical and multicultural context resulted in the field becoming increasingly focused on community issues. Within the South African context, community psychology has become a vehicle for framing this call to relevance (see Ahmed & Pretorius-Heuchert, 2001; Naidoo, 2000; Seedat, Cloete, & Shochet, 1988; Seedat, Duncan, & Lazarus, 2001; Swartz & Gibson, 2001). De la Rey and Ipser (2004) stated that "changing the demographic profile of psychology as a profession and an area of scholarship has also been used as a criterion to assess the relevance of South African psychology" (p. 546). There has been a mandate from the Professional Board of Psychology calling for more diversity among the staff and students. Proposals for how psychology could move away from its white elitist image included adopting more culturally relevant theories and interventions, embracing indigenous knowledge, and encouraging communication between psychological practitioners and traditional

healers. In addition, the issues of prevention, psychoeducation training, mental health promotion, advocacy, and lobbying have been identified as domains as important as individual therapy (Lazarus, 1988; Naidoo, Duncan, Roos, Pillay, & Bowman, 2007).

The Relationship Between Counseling and Clinical Psychology

The division between clinical and counseling psychology in South Africa mirrors the divisions along the fault lines of race and ethnicity. To a large extent, where these divisions are most apparent there is an accompanying hierarchy in which clinical psychology occupies a privileged position above counseling psychology, while both are inferior to psychiatry. The position of psychology under the auspices of the erstwhile South African Medical and Dental Council has contributed to the higher status accorded to clinical psychology. In a society where social division has been carefully cultivated, the clinical-counseling schism is an almost natural consequence. Clinical psychology, with its historical emphasis on diagnosis and assessment, has aspired to the "medical" model while counseling psychology, in its rhetoric if not in its practice, has traditionally eschewed viewing individuals through the lens of pathology and has instead embraced a developmental approach to individual behavior.

Some universities have elected to combine once separate clinical psychology and counseling psychology programs so as to integrate the emphases of both subdisciplines. For example, the new master's program at Stellenbosch University in clinical psychology and community counseling and the University of the Witwatersrand's community counseling program provide training to psychologists to work with individuals, families, groups, and communities. Counseling psychology continues to be a specialization at a handful of universities in South Africa but does not enjoy a distinctive identity as it does in industrially developed countries. Despite the greater relevance of counseling psychology training to community work, only clinical psychology graduates are currently required to do an additional year of compulsory community service under the auspices of the Department of Health. This anomaly reflects the subordinate status accorded to counseling psychology.

Poor Uptake of Counseling Services

While the emphasis for counseling has shifted away from the one-on-one model, there continues to be some stigma associated with seeking and receiving mental health services. Leach et al. (2003) have argued that a significant discrepancy exists between the need for psychological services in South Africa and the fact that the majority of the population is unable to access or use such services, even if they were available. These authors cite two major causes of the limited uptake of services: (1) that psychological services may be perceived as a largely Western way of engaging with psychosocial problems, and (2) that psychology is distrusted because most of its practitioners are white (mistrust of whites is a pervasive sentiment in South Africa, a legacy of apartheid). We offer two more reasons for this phenomenon: (1) the low ratio of psychologists to the population, and (2) the ubiquity and widespread acceptance of indigenous healers in South Africa, particularly in rural areas.

Some authors have suggested that the assumptions of Western psychology are limited in their applicability to African contexts (e.g., Campbell, 2003). However, the assertion that African and Western worldviews and healing systems are separate and self-contained entities has been challenged (Swartz, 1985). As argued by Swartz (1998), "The categories 'Western' and 'non-Western' are our creations and reflect neither the diversity of beliefs (often mutually contradictory) that people hold, nor the commonalities that exist across apparently very different groups of people" (p. 92). At the same time, it has been noted that psychological counseling treatment programs are founded on Eurocentric notions of independence, decision making, self-concepts, and assertiveness rather than people's social circumstances (Mlungwana, 2001). Moreover, the role of spiritual forces, as opposed to individual

agency, in determining psychological status is often not given credence in Western psychology. In South Africa, traditional healers, known as *sangomas* or *inyandas,* usually attend to the medical and psychological needs of many South Africans. Their treatment often includes an invocation of spirits in countering their clients' problems and the dispensing of *muti* (a medicinal remedy).

It has been estimated that there are between 150,000 and 200,000 traditional healers practicing in South Africa (Kale, 1995), and 80% of the South African population consult them (Abdool Karim, Ziqubu-Page, & Arendse, 1994). Reasons for the popularity of traditional healers include inadequate health care services, too few hospitals and clinics, overcrowded facilities, and more significantly, familiarity with and belief in the cultural framework within which the traditional healer works (Walker, Reid, & Cornell, 2004). The interventions provided by a traditional healer are thus comprehensible to consumers of health care and in keeping with a holistic understanding of a human being as having social, physical, and spiritual dimensions. African traditional healing often emphasizes the spiritual aspect of the self (Walker et al., 2004) in which ancestors of the person who is ill or disturbed are invoked as mediators (Comaroff, 1985). Thus in the absence of formal psychological services, which is true of many communities in South Africa, African traditional healers are sought for the resolution of mental health problems. As far as we know, no research has been undertaken to assess the effectiveness of traditional healers for psychological problems. However, the role of cultural factors unique to mental health care should be considered alongside the dearth of psychological services for black South Africans.

In many African countries, including South Africa, traditional healers are seen by many health care consumers as legitimate practitioners (Walker et al., 2004). Leach et al. (2003) have called for counseling psychology to be informed by African traditional healing practices and for both traditional and Western healing approaches to treatment to be emphasized in training programs. As yet, there is only one tertiary psychology training program in which African traditional healing has been introduced as an epistemological and conceptual paradigm. Many counseling psychologists do not speak African languages and have to rely on translators when their clients are not fluent in English, thus creating a further barrier to the uptake of psychological services. This barrier to counseling services is particularly salient for black South Africans living in rural areas, where psychologists are few in number and where fluent English and Afrikaans is spoken only by a minority. Nair (2008) highlighted the ethical imperative of ensuring that students receive substantive multicultural training to be able to work competently and sensitively with clients from diverse backgrounds.

A Paradigmatic Mismatch Between South African and American Counseling Psychology

At least until recently, counseling psychology in the United States has remained rooted in the paradigm of logical positivism. From this basis, it has generally emphasized those attributes of the human experience that can be measured, tested, and manipulated experimentally or quasi-experimentally. In South Africa, counseling psychologists have in large part mimicked their American counterparts, at least at the level of epistemology. However, as mentioned previously, psychology as a whole has seen the rise of alternative epistemologies and paradigms, including feminist and Marxist psychology, postmodern theory, social constructivism, and critical psychology (Painter & Terre Blanche, 2004). South African counseling psychology has, to a large extent, either been silent on these disciplinary epistemological and ontological movements or has followed suit without critical engagement with these influences. The critique of empirical science did not emerge from counseling psychology itself. When counseling psychologists wrote against the dominant epistemological regimes, they did so as psychologists rather than under the umbrella of their subdiscipline—that is, counseling psychology (e.g., Lionel Nicholas, Mark Watson, and others). Nonetheless, the challenge to the dominant epistemological regimes has been felt in South African counseling psychology,

and to this extent, it may be said that there is some epistemological mismatch between the subdiscipline in South Africa and in the United States.

Parallel to the rise of these alternative epistemologies, there has been growing skepticism of psychology as an empirical science with its attendant claim to neutrality. To a large extent, the claim of objectivity has been immune to critique in American counseling psychology, as has the assumption that human cognition, affect, and behavior defy scholarly analysis if they are not operationalized and measured. A corollary of the notion of scientific objectivity is political neutrality, which has been an assumption underlying American counseling psychology. Yet such claims to neutrality stand in sharp contrast to the role that counseling psychology has played, for example, in serving and supporting the United States military whose forays into foreign nations have been ongoing since World War II. Most recently, this claim of neutrality has been called into question by the refusal of the APA to prohibit its members from participating in the interrogation of suspects detained without trial in the so-called war on terror, as it is well-known that detainees have been subjected to physical and psychological torture in locations such as the Abu Ghraib prison in Iraq, Guantanamo Bay in Cuba, and other secret locations. The political neutrality claimed by a subset of South African counseling psychologists during apartheid similarly needs to be juxtaposed against the severe oppression and repression visited on black South Africans by the white regime, including long-term imprisonment of activists, detention without trial, torture, and forced removals, not to mention the variety of other social ills that stemmed from apartheid. Perhaps here it is helpful to distinguish between conservative and liberal psychologists—who were either allied or indifferent, respectively, to apartheid—on the one hand and radical psychologists who agitated for a democratic, nonracist social order.

The Absence of Established Career Paths for Counseling Psychologists

Unlike the United States, where the Veterans Administration, college counseling centers, university academic programs, and Medicare- and Medicaid-funded psychological services provide a natural home for counseling psychologists, South Africa is characterized by the continued absence of counseling psychologists in the public mental health system. Thus, the most common place of employment for counseling psychologists is in private practice, which caters to individuals with private health insurance (Medical Aid) or those able to pay out of pocket. This system effectively excludes the majority of South Africans, including the unemployed (close to 40%), the underemployed, and persons in low-paying jobs. Even more than 15 years after the formal end of apartheid, racial and class fault lines roughly coincide, resulting in a social divide whereby most of the South African poor are black, while whites remain overwhelmingly represented among the affluent. Counseling for persons living in poverty is sometimes available from nongovernmental organizations (NGOs), which are often funded by overseas donors and have very specific mandates, such as to provide counseling to patients living with AIDS or to survivors of trauma, rape, or crime. Yet NGOs have only a few employees who are registered counseling psychologists. Many persons providing counseling services in NGO settings are professional or lay counselors or social workers. In large part, this scenario is due to the often difficult and financially unpredictable nature of NGO work and the fact that psychologists employed in NGOs are often thrust into managerial positions, thus taking them away from the coal-face of service provision.

HIV as an Important Contemporary Issue

No chapter on South African counseling psychology is complete without commentary on the field's application to the problem of HIV and AIDS. AIDS as a public health problem has had a devastating effect on South African society. It is estimated that in 2005, 4.8 million South Africans were living with HIV (Shisana et al., 2005). The trajectory of AIDS is as follows: infection, latency, opportunistic infections, and death. With the availability of antiretroviral therapy, persons living with HIV may live healthy lives for several years. Counseling psychology has

an important role to play at all stages of the disease trajectory:

First, prior to infection, counseling is relevant for helping persons at high risk avoid being infected with the virus. Thus, for school-going adolescents, persons seeking treatment at primary health clinics, and women attending antenatal clinics, counseling can help them avoid behaviors that increase HIV risk. The question of risk behavior is a complex matter in a society where unequal gender relations, transactional sex driven by economic deprivation, and sexual violence, including rape, play a prominent role in the transmission of the virus. Thus, simplistic solutions, such as abstinence or condom use, may have only limited application. Counseling psychology has much to contribute in helping design and implement programs aimed at preventing new HIV infections and thus lowering the incidence of the disease.

Second, following infection persons diagnosed with HIV commonly have to deal with overwhelming psychological distress as they adjust to their status. In understanding the trajectory of psychological responses, counseling psychology—with its emphasis on understanding development and life transitions—is well-placed to offer its expertise in identifying effective tertiary interventions to help people cope with their condition. For persons living with HIV who have access to antiretroviral treatment (ART), the question of adherence has become salient in the provision of health care: Low levels of ART adherence have been observed in many clinics and hospitals in South Africa. Counseling psychology has a role to play in fashioning appropriate psychosocial support for patients whose adherence to treatment is suboptimal and for whom the benefits of treatment are not realized.

Third, at the end-stage of the disease trajectory when patients face impending death, counseling psychology has a contribution to make in helping the patient and family prepare for the death of and life without the patient. Such assistance is of considerable importance as most South Africans dying of AIDS are of childbearing age and, thus, leave behind offspring who have no one to care for them. The phenomenon of "AIDS orphans" and child-headed households after the parents have died is on the increase in South Africa. Counseling psychologists can provide expertise in facilitating the psychological and social development and adjustment of the survivors of the pandemic.

Fourth, at the level of social policy counseling psychologists must influence government spending on HIV prevention, treatment literacy and adherence, and psychosocial adjustment programming. The expertise of counseling psychology is crucial in lobbying for programs and resources for persons who have to cope with difficult life circumstances. The application of counseling psychology principles—with their emphasis on the development of individuals, families, and communities rather than psychopathology—has an indispensable role to play in helping reduce HIV incidence and in ameliorating the effects of the pandemic on South African society (Kagee et al., 2003).

CONCLUSION

Counseling psychology in South Africa is best understood in the context of the complex and difficult political history of the country. The history of counseling psychology within general psychology to a large degree parallels the history of racial oppression that has characterized the South African social and political landscape for the past several decades. It is apparent that the number of psychologists in South Africa is too small for counseling psychology to become independent of psychology, as it has done in the United States. For this reason, most of those who are registered as counseling psychologists identify with psychology in general rather than counseling psychology as a separate or distinctive discipline. Moreover, given the small ratio of psychologists to the number of people requiring services, specialization and the crystallization of subdisciplines within psychology has not occurred in the way it has in the United States and industrially developed countries.

Since the 1980s, psychology has engaged in a self-reflexive search for social relevance with the specific objectives of shedding its elitist image, helping to undo past injustices, and contributing to community development. This quest has prompted the rise of community psychology and a greater focus on validating indigenous knowledge systems and traditional healing. However, the relationship between psychology as a profession and traditional healing is an area that is currently under-researched. The development of psychological theories that are organically derived from the local context is an area that requires particular investigation. For the most part, psychological theories imported from Northern and Western countries remain dominant in counseling psychology practice.

The search for a more relevant paradigm is an ongoing conversation in the social sciences and humanities in South Africa. The critique of logical positivism is particularly strong in South African psychology, possibly because of the perception of psychology's complicity with apartheid and its historical association with conservative political ideologies. Moreover, the success and popularity of radical epistemologies, such as those articulated by structuralist and poststructuralist theorists, have seen scientific psychology come under criticism in favor of reflexive, interpretive, and constructivist approaches. This matter is beyond the scope of the present chapter; suffice it to say that we do not accept that empirical science is inherently ideologically conservative. We believe that empirical research has an important role to play in social transformation. Rather than fostering a polemic debate, we argue for the coexistence of various epistemologies within psychology as it serves to enrich debates within the field.

Despite its history of silence in the context of political oppression, South African counseling psychology has an important role to play in the post-apartheid era. It has been left to critical psychologists as a whole—most of whom do not necessarily identify themselves as counseling psychologists—to assume leadership in the struggle for racial, gender, and class equality and social justice in South Africa. Yet the unique contribution of counseling psychology can play a constructive role in present-day South Africa with its various community needs, addressing areas such as crime, violence, and HIV/AIDS.

NOTES

1. White settlers of Dutch descent took on the identity of "Afrikaners" and evolved their own language, Afrikaans. The Afrikaners' rebellion against British rule led to several battles, culminating in the Anglo-Boer war during which thousands of Afrikaner women and children died in concentration camps. Many farm houses, livestock, and crops were destroyed by the British during the war.

2. Although problematic, these categorizations continue to be used for official purposes to designate racial/ethnic group membership. These categorizations gloss over many ethnic and cultural differences. For instance, while the *white* group comprises descendents of various European origins, there has been animosity between the Dutch settlers and those from England. Similarly, the group designation *African* comprises indigenous people from several tribes, including Xhosa, Zulu, Suthu, Venda, and Ndabeli among others. *Colored* refers to people of mixed heritage, including a significant proportion who are Muslim. *Asian* refers to descendents of the Indian subcontinent who were brought over as indentured workers by the British colonizers. This group comprises Hindu, Christian, and Muslim adherents.

3. The influx of many white settlers into the urban areas highlighted the issue of "the poor white problem," which was perceived as necessitating government mitigation, while black poverty was ignored and regarded as a normal condition of native life.

REFERENCES

Abdool Karim, S. S., Ziqubu-Page, T. T., & Arendse, R. (1994). Bridging the gap: Potential for a health care partnership between African traditional healers and biomedical personnel in South Africa. *South African Medical Journal, 84*(Suppl.), 1–16.

Ahmed, R., & Pretorius-Heuchert, J. W. (2001). Community psychology: Past, present, and future. In M. Seedat, N. Duncan, & S. Lazarus (Eds.), *Community psychology: Theory, method and practice* (pp. 79–80). Cape Town, South Africa: Oxford University Press.

Anonymous. (1986). Some thoughts on a more relevant or indigenous counselling psychology in South Africa: Discovering the socio-political context of the oppressed. *Psychology in Society, 5,* 81–89.

Bulhan, H. A. (1990). Afro-centric psychology: Perspective and practice. In S. Cooper & L. J. Nicholas (Eds.), *Psychology and apartheid: Essays on the struggle for psychology and the mind in South Africa* (pp. 66–75). Johannesburg, South Africa: Vision.

Campbell, C. (2003). *Letting them die: How HIV/AIDS prevention programmes often fail.* Wetton, South Africa: Double Storey Books.

Comaroff, J. (1985). *Body of power, spirit of resistance.* Chicago: University of Chicago Press.

Cooper, S., Nicholas, L. J., Seedat, M., & Statman, J. M. (1990). Psychology and apartheid: The struggle for psychology in South Africa. In L. J. Nicholas & S. Cooper (Eds.), *Psychology and apartheid: Essays on the struggle for psychology and the mind in South Africa* (pp. 1–21). Johannesburg, South Africa: Vision/Madiba.

Dawes, A. (1985). Politics and mental health: The position of clinical psychology in South Africa. *South African Journal of Psychology, 15*(2), 55–61.

De la Rey, C., & Ipser, J. (2004). The call for relevance: South African psychology ten years into democracy. *South African Journal of Psychology, 34*(4), 544–552.

Duncan, N. (2001). Dislodging the sub-texts: An analysis of a corpus of articles on racism produced by South African psychologists. In N. Duncan, A. van Niekerk, C. de la Rey, & M. Seedat (Eds.), *Race, racism, knowledge production and psychology in South Africa* (pp. 127–154). New York: Nova Science.

Duncan, N., van Niekerk, A., de la Rey, C., & Seedat, M. (Eds.). (2001). *Race, racism, knowledge production and psychology in South Africa.* New York: Nova Science.

Durrheim, K., & Mokeki, S. (1997). Race and relevance: A content analysis of the South African Journal of Psychology. *South African Journal of Psychology, 27*(3), 206–213.

Foster, D. (2004). Liberation psychology. In K. Ratele, N. Duncan, D. Hook, N. Mkhize, P. Kiguwa, & A. Collins (Eds.), *Self, community & psychology* (pp. 1–44). Lansdowne, South Africa: University of Cape Town Press.

Holdstock, T. L. (1981). Psychology in South Africa belongs to the colonial era: Arrogance or ignorance? *South African Journal of Psychology, 11*(4), 123–129.

Kagee, S. A., Naidoo, A. V., & van Wyk, S. B. (2003). Building communities of peace: The South African experience. *Journal for the Advancement of Counselling, 25*(4), 225–234.

Kale, R. (1995). South Africa's health: Traditional healers in South Africa: A parallel health care system. *British Medical Journal, 310*(6988), 1182–1185.

Lambley, P. (1980). *The psychology of apartheid.* London: Martin Secker & Warburg.

Lazarus, S. (1988). *The role of the psychologist in South African society: In search of an appropriate community psychology.* Unpublished doctoral dissertation, University of Cape Town, South Africa.

Leach, M. M., Akhurst, J., & Basson, C. (2003). Counseling psychology in South Africa: Current political and professional challenges and future promise. *The Counseling Psychologist, 31*(5), 619–640.

Louw, J. (1986). White poverty and psychology in South Africa: The poor white investigation of the Carnegie Commission. *Psychology in Society, 6,* 47–62.

Louw, J. (1987). From separation to division: The origin of two psychological associations in South Africa. *Journal of the History of the Behavioural Sciences, 23,* 341–352.

Mda, T. V., & Mothata, M. S. (Eds.). (2000). *Critical issues in South African education after 1994.* Kenwyn, South Africa: Juta.

Mlungwana, J. (2001, April). *Cultural dilemmas in life skills education in KZN: Umbonambi primary school project.* Paper presented at the AIDS in Context Conference, University of the Witwatersrand, Johannesburg, South Africa.

Naidoo, A. V. (1996). Challenging the hegemony of Eurocentric psychology. *Journal of Community and Health Sciences, 2*(2), 9–16.

Naidoo, A. V. (2000). *Community psychology: Constructing community, reconstructing psychology in South Africa.* Inaugural lecture, University of Stellenbosch, Stellenbosch, South Africa.

Naidoo, A. V., Duncan, N., Roos, V., Pillay, J., & Bowman, B. (2007). Analysis, context and action: An introduction to community psychology. In N. Duncan, A. V. Naidoo, J. Pillay, & V. Roos (Eds.), *Community psychology in South Africa: Theory, context and practice* (pp. 9–23). Wetton, South Africa: University of Cape Town Press.

Naidoo, A. V., Shabalala, N. J., & Bawa, U. (2003). Community psychology. In L. Nicholas (Ed.), *Introduction to psychology* (pp. 423–456). Lansdowne, South Africa: University of Cape Town Press

Nair, S. (2008). *Psychologists and race: Exploring the identities of South African trainee clinical psychologists with reference to working in multiracial contexts.* Unpublished doctoral dissertation, Stellenbosch University, Stellenbosch, South Africa.

Nicholas, L. J. (1990a). Psychology in South Africa: The need for an openly politically contextualised discipline. In L. J. Nicholas & S. Cooper (Eds.), *Psychology and oppression: Critiques and proposals* (pp. 205–211). Johannesburg, South Africa: Skotaville.

Nicholas, L. J. (1990b). The response of South African professional psychology associations to apartheid. *Journal of Behavioural Sciences, 26,* 58–63.

Nicholas, L. J. (1990c). The response of student counselors in South Africa to racism in higher education. In L. J. Nicholas (Ed.), *Psychology and oppression: Critiques and oppression* (pp. 198–204). Johannesburg, South Africa: Skotaville.

Nicholas, L. J. (Ed.). (1993). *Psychology and oppression: Critiques and oppression.* Johannesburg, South Africa: Skotaville.

Nicholas, L. J. (1995). Patterns of student counselling in South African universities. *International Journal for the Advancement of Counselling, 18*(4), 275–285.

Nicholas, L. J., & Cooper, S. (Eds.). (1990). *Psychology and apartheid.* Cape Town, South Africa: Vision/Madiba.

Nicholas, L. J., Naidoo, A. V., & Pretorius, T. B. (2006). Historical perspective of career psychology in South Africa. In G. B. Stead & M. B. Watson (Eds.), *Career psychology in the South African context* (2nd ed., pp. 1–10). Pretoria, South Africa: J. L. van Schaik.

Painter, D., & Terre Blanche, M. (2004). Critical psychology in South Africa: Looking back and looking ahead. *South African Journal of Psychology, 34*(4), 520–543.

Seedat, M., Cloete, N., & Shochet, I. (1988). Community psychology: Panic or panacea. *Psychology in Society, 11,* 39–54.

Seedat, M., Duncan, N., & Lazarus, S. (Eds.). (2001). *Community psychology: Theory, method and practice.* Cape Town, South Africa: Oxford University Press.

Shisana, O., Rehle, T., Simbayi, L., Parker, W., Zuma, K., Bhana, A., et al. (Eds.). (2005). *South African national HIV prevalence, HIV incidence, behaviour and communication survey.* South Africa: HSRC Press.

Statistics South Africa. (2007). *Population statistics.* Retrieved November 15, 2007, from http://www.statssa.gov.za/publications/populationstats.asp

Stead, G. B. (2004). Psychology in South Africa. In D. Wedding & M. J. Stevens (Eds.), *The handbook of international psychology* (pp. 59–74). New York: Brunner-Routledge.

Stead, G. B., & Watson, M. B. (1998). Career research in South Africa: Challenges for the future. *Journal of Vocational Behavior, 52,* 289–299.

Stead, G. B., & Watson, M. B. (2002). Indigenisation of career psychology in South Africa. In G. B. Stead & M. B. Watson (Eds.), *Career psychology in the South African context* (2nd ed., pp. 181–190). Hatfield, Pretoria: Van Schaik.

Stead, G. B., & Watson, M. B. (Eds.). (2006a). *Career psychology in the South African context.* (2nd ed.). Hartfield, Pretoria, South Africa: J. L. Van Schaik.

Stead, G. B., & Watson, M. B. (2006b). Contextualising career psychology in South Africa: Bringing it all back home. *Journal of Psychology in Africa, 12,* 147–160.

Stead, G. B., & Watson, M. B. (2006c). Indigenisation of career psychology in South Africa. In G. B. Stead & M. B. Watson (Eds.), *Career psychology in the South African context* (2nd ed., pp. 181–190). Hatfield, Pretoria, South Africa: J. L.Van Schaik.

Swartz, L. (1985). Issues for cross-cultural psychiatric research in South Africa. *Culture, Medicine, and Psychiatry, 9,* 59–74.

Swartz, L. (1998). *Culture and mental health: A southern African view.* Cape Town, South Africa: Oxford University Press.

Swartz, L., & Gibson, K. (2001). The "old" versus the "new" in South African community psychology: The request for appropriate change. In M. Seedat, N. Duncan, & S. Lazarus (Eds.), *Community psychology: Theory, method and practice* (pp. 3–14). Cape Town, South Africa: Oxford University Press.

Van der Westhuijsen, T. W. B. (1992). Voorligtingsielkunde: Requiem of vreugdode? In *Proceedings of the 10th Congress of the Psychological Association of South Africa* (pp. 249–259). Stellenbosch, South Africa.

Walker, L., Reid, G., & Cornell, M. (2004). *Waiting to happen: HIV/AIDS in South Africa.* Boulder, CO: Lynne Rienner.

Watson, M. B., & Fouche, P. (2007). Transforming a past into a future: Counselling psychology in South Africa. *Applied Psychology: An International Review, 56*(1), 152–164.

Watson, M. B., & Stead, G. B. (2002). Career psychology in South Africa: Moral perspectives on present and future directions. *South African Journal of Psychology, 32*(1), 26–31.

Whitaker, S. (1991). A critical historical perspective on psychology in Azania/South Africa. In J. Jansen (Ed.), *Knowledge and power in South Africa: Critical perspectives across the discipline* (pp. 55–68). Johannesburg, South Africa: Skotaville.

33

Cross-Cultural Counseling in Nigeria

Iyanju lati asa-de-asa ni ile Naijiria

CHARLES N. UGWUEGBULAM, ALICIA M. HOMRICH,
AND CELESTINE U. U. U. KADURUMBA

This chapter provides a synoptic picture of the practice of guidance and counseling in Nigeria, with this brief sketch of the demographics and history of Nigeria. The indigenous traditions of helping followed by the efforts to formalize the counseling profession in Nigeria's educational system and beyond are also included.

Located on the western coast of the continent, Nigeria is Africa's most densely inhabited country. The populace of approximately 140 million people comprises members from 250 distinct ethnic groups. The largest of these are the Hausa and Fulani, who dominate the north; the Yoruba, who live primarily in the southwest; and the Ibo, the majority of the inhabitants in the southeast. The terrain is diverse and encompasses tropical forest, savanna, and semi-desert ecosystems. The economy is based on mining, agriculture, and petroleum production. Although English is the official language, indigenous languages are widely spoken in addition to English.

Nigeria was created in 1914, when the British colonized several geographic territories encompassing identified indigenous kingdoms. Nigeria's history as an independent republic began in 1960 when the call for self-rule ended British colonial control over the region. The mix of many different cultures and religions led to escalating tensions, and the first republic ended with a military coup in 1966. Violent clashes followed, and in 1967, the Ibo declared eastern Nigeria the independent state of Biafra. Civil war ensued, culminating in the surrender of Biafra 3 years later. After a period of reconciliation and economic growth, there followed alternating periods of military coups d'état and civilian rule. A civilian-run government was created in 1999 under a new constitution. In recent years, regional conflicts related to limited resources, community control, and ethno-religious boundaries have continued (U.S. Department of State, 2008). The nation continues to struggle to strengthen its economy and maintain a stabilized democratic government.

435

Today, the Federal Republic of Nigeria consists of 36 states plus Abuja, the Federal Capital Territory in the center of the country. The median age of the population is 18.7 years and the average life expectancy is approximately 48 years. HIV/AIDS has had a significant impact in Nigeria, affecting life expectancy, infant mortality rates, and population growth (2.38%) (Central Intelligence Agency, 2008).

Islam is practiced by most Hausa and Fulani. A large number of southerners are followers of Christianity. Indigenous religious traditions are practiced by the remaining population; however, religious pluralism is not uncommon (Embassy of the Federal Republic of Nigeria, 2004; U.S. Department of State, 2008). For example, among the Yoruba various combinations of traditional religions, Islam and Christianity have prevailed for more than a century.

Consistent with religious beliefs in Nigeria, the basic view of human nature is that individuals do not exist alone in this world and need the assistance of others to achieve competence. The cultural importance of the larger group takes precedence over personal needs and results in a locus of control that is externally based. In Nigeria, "Group affiliation is so crucial in all their life events—for example, people must support each other because 'paradise without people is not worth living in'" (Akande, 1999, p. 174). The lives of Nigerians are culturally and religiously anchored in the belief that the entities of community and family take precedence over the individual.

TRADITIONAL METHODS OF HELPING

Historical Development of Counseling in Nigeria

Before the advent of formalized guidance and counseling, Nigerians solved problems through what Iwuama (1991) called "traditional guidance," which is any type of assistance given to somebody in need. Helpers were those individuals with accumulated wisdom and experience who helped in resolving challenges within indigenous communities. The World

Health Organization (2002) reported that up to 80% of the population in Africa uses traditional medicine to help meet their health care needs, including mental disorders. Chronicling the development of indigenous helping is challenging because the knowledge is passed from generation to generation through the oral tradition.

In contrast to a Western focus on mind, matter, and science, the Nigerian cultural focus is on heart, spirit, nature, and faith and is based on a holistic/organic worldview. Beliefs about human functioning extend to causes of mental illness. With the exception of mental problems induced by substance abuse, Gureje, Lasebikan, Ephraim-Oluwanuga, Olley, and Kola (2005) discovered that one third of their Nigerian sample believed that supernatural causation, such as possession by evil spirits, caused mental illness. One tenth of their respondents believed that divine punishment from God presented in the form of mental distress. A holistic approach to counseling is necessary because the boundary between the physical and psychological is de-emphasized in the African perspective of functioning, as are the distinctions between the spiritual, natural, and supernatural (Okeke, Draguns, Sheku, & Allen, 1999).

Many authors contend that counseling services have always existed in Nigeria, historically institutionalized in the form of indigenous practitioners who attend to the mental well-being of their clients in the context of traditional approaches to healing (Adekson, 2003, 2005; Ajila, 2004; Alao, 2004; Aluede, McEachern, & Kenny, 2005; Peltzer, 1995). Indigenous methods are viewed by these writers as practices that parallel Western methods in many respects in that they are based on the principles of presence, guiding, assisting, helping, and enlightening in ways that are contextually appropriate to the beliefs of the Nigerian people. As reported by Alao (2004),

It is important to be aware that indigenous African counselling has equivalents for almost all concepts and procedures in Western forms of counselling. A study of African indigenous counselling reveals that from time immemorial, African societies have institutionalized psychological provision for the maintenance of the well-being of all members of society. (p. 250)

Awareness of the importance of Nigerian worldviews extends to the contemporary counseling profession: "The members of the Counselling Association of Nigeria (CASSON) recognize that no guidance practice in the country can be scientific or meaningful if such practice is not based on the value orientation of its people" (Okon, 1983, p. 458).

Methods of Traditional Healing

In Nigeria, traditional counseling practitioners are recognized as those who help people with their problems. They are referred to by various terms, depending on the specific culture. For example, the Yoruba call these practitioners *babaláwo*. Among the Ibibio, indigenous practitioners are known as *uzenapkos*; as *ogbafa*, and *dibia* in the Igbo culture; as *obozi* among the Igala-Tiv of the Benue State; and as *duba* in Hausa land. Spiritual teachers or clerics in the largely Muslim areas of northern Nigeria are known as *mallams*. These counselors/healers are frequently sought as a source of resolution for intricate individual issues, including mental health problems, and they practice a traditional form of community counseling (Adekson, 2005; Makinde, 1983).

Rituals, as well as religious and semireligious ceremonies, are features of traditional healing. According to Ekeopara (2005), traditional healers show their knowledge and wisdom by treating the whole person, soul and body, through religious ceremonies. In cases involving rituals, the spirits of the ancestors are invoked as a source of help that makes the treatment more efficacious. This is based on the recognition that all healing depends on divine intervention. The healer, who has hidden supernatural power, must ask for the authority of the spirits to assist clients in healing. In some cases, healers use the sympathetic or imitative magical approach, based on the belief that like materials produce a like

effect. For instance, a person going to war needs protective medicine and is given a talisman made of the heart or bone of a lion to give the strength and fearlessness of a lion before its enemies. Thus, traditional healers show their knowledge and wisdom by involving physical, spiritual, and psychological means in the treatment of ailments and concerns.

Although practices vary from one ethnic or cultural group to another, the well-documented traditions of the Yoruba are featured in this chapter as one example of how healing practices by indigenous counselors function in Nigeria. Having written extensively on this topic across cultures, Makinde (1974, 1980, 1983, 1987) suggested that the effectiveness of practices used by Nigerian indigenous counselors can be witnessed in the sociocultural context of the Yoruba ethnic group. Adekson (2005) concurred, "Traditional counseling is inherently embedded in Yoruba tradition because people seek help for different problems from traditional healers as a way of living a holistic lifestyle and finding meaning for their lives" (pp. 8–9).

Among the Yoruba, the traditional practitioner is the Ifá priest, known as a babaláwo—a master of ancient wisdom. He or she is a diviner, sage, and traditional doctor possessing the ability to see beyond the here and now as well as interact with the gods for the resolution of human problems. Babaláwo are consulted for direction in social, psychological, physiological, intellectual, and political matters (Adekson, 2005). They help clients through divination, a method of explaining misfortune and solving problems that has existed for thousands of years. Using various rituals, babaláwo establish an atmosphere of positive regard, respect, and care for clients through the use of their physical presence and actions, including listening, encouragement, positive commentary, praying, and advice giving (Adekson, 2005). The traditional Yoruba counselor also uses nonverbal communication techniques to reduce tension and promote optimism that a presenting concern will soon be overcome. Behaviors such as head nodding, warm smiles, shaking hands (if the client is an older person), and therapeutic dance convey respect, acceptance, and approval, and serve to restore the confidence and raise the morale of clients. The combination of movement and the magical sounds of the words in the form of Ifá proverbs are "linked with creative principles of nature" (Makinde, 1983, p. 88) that, when used effectively, awaken consciousness in the client.

The instruments of divination consist essentially of *Opon Ifa*, the divining board, and *Opele*, the divining charm. The opele is a charm of eight double-sided flat objects, usually palm seeds, which are the symbol of Ifá, the God of Divination. When cast on the divining board, there are 260 possible configurations, known as *Odu*, each of which indicates a trend of one life or another. It is the configuration of the seeds that indicates the client's problems and solutions, based on prehistoric precedents recounted in the form of divination poetry. The babaláwo delivers the related incantation from the *Odù Ifá* and applies the message in a manner that addresses the individual's specific problem and context. Divination reveals to the Yoruba the future path for their lives. The *Odù Ifá* is a corpus of 16 volumes of sacred stories of Ifá literature, the compendium of knowledge, wisdom, and philosophy of the Yoruba people. To learn the *Ifá* "is to learn how to understand the problems of men and how *Ifá* could help to guide men in the solution of such problems" (Fabunmi, 1975). The traditional counselor believes that the words and phrases in *Odù Ifá* are inspired by the godhead. The babaláwo typically employs stories, tales, verses, or phrases that have accumulated in the oral tradition of the *Ifá* to create a process of self-realization or self-actualization. This approach parallels the application of metaphors in Western counseling for evaluating the dilemmas of clients and to suggest paths for problem resolution.

Traditional counselors are rich in the knowledge of their clients' histories and contexts and thus approach problems with a shared understanding. They supplement the curative process with words, proverbs, lyrics, and aphorisms that are relevant to the local setting in which they are employed. Unlike modern counselors who work within time structures, babaláwo focus on the healing task as the priority, minimizing attention to clock time.

Additionally, the family system is considered essential in the traditional healing process, taking an active role by their presence, involvement, and belief that if all members are healthy, everyone in the family will be happy. The reassuring cohesion of their extended family, the comforting sense of continuity with their ancestors, and uninterrupted consultation with the babaláwo have social value among the Yoruba in helping facilitate positive life development. Problem resolution occurs when harmony is restored by achieving balance among all levels of existence—spiritual, physical, psychological, supernatural—and is reflected in the intense respect and reverence for life, humanity, and all aspects of being that are prevalent among the Yoruba. These healing processes help release tension and bring clients "home" to their origin.

Training of Traditional Counselors

The extent to which clients come to a babaláwo for assistance with their problems depends on the healer's proven ability as predicated on their experiences and training. Not all elders can be counselors, but individuals who, beginning in early childhood, associate closely with elders of wisdom by following them to meetings and observing the practices of healing, often pursue the career path of a diviner. The period of professional training undergone by a babaláwo is typically at least 7 years long and includes rigor, stress, and thoroughness in practice. Preparation includes memorization of thousands of *Ifá* verses that tell of myths, songs, riddles, proverbs, and rituals in Yoruba society. Babaláwo trainees also receive instruction in traditional medicine, counseling, and human relations culminating in an oral examination before a committee of practitioners. Babaláwo are expected to observe the code of conduct and ethics of their profession and remain transparently honest—an important quality for healers.

Observations and studies by multiple authors affirm that the training and methods of indigenous counselors are sound and that their philosophy and practice have much in common with Western psychotherapy. Indigenous practices include the use of psychological checks and balances to maintain psychological equilibrium (Abimbola, 1968; Akinsanya, 1972; Fabunmi, 1975; Peltzer, 1995). More recently, Adekson (2003, 2005) has conducted detailed analyses of cases to examine the parallels between the practices of indigenous healers and those of Western counselors.

Effectiveness of Indigenous Practice

As is typical of traditional healing practices, the therapeutic effect can be observed but the curative cause is rarely measured. There is a lack of empirical research seeking to validate the effectiveness of traditional counseling or to determine whether it is the words, music, setting, actions, or personality of the healer that changes behavior or prevents problems. Makinde (1974) maintained that the beautiful words and utterances of the babaláwo are irresistibly effective and potent. He also compared specific qualities of the traditional healer with characteristics of Rogerian client-centered therapy (Makinde, 1983). Adekson (2005) detailed nine hypotheses for the efficacy of practices among Yoruba traditional healers and validated them through observations and interviews in a qualitative analysis. Peltzer (1995) compared and contrasted African practices in relation to Western dimensions of the application of psychology, such as time frame, time focus, locus of control, and cognitive/emotional style; however, his report is primarily observational. Alao (2004) proposed that there are therapeutic resources in indigenous African counseling that compare with Western forms of counseling, such as rational emotive therapy, Rogerian therapy, and the use of words as directives and metaphors. Makinde (1987) stated:

> It has been sufficiently demonstrated that the age long system of counselling in Africa . . . can no longer be set aside as unscientific or orthodox. If we believe in counselling as a strategy firmly rooted in the philosophy of the community, then we must base our practices largely on community belief and philosophy. (p. 83)

CONTEMPORARY GUIDANCE AND COUNSELING SERVICES

Utilization of Mental Health Counseling

Mental health care among the Nigerian population, as defined by Western standards, has been identified by the World Health Organization as having an unusually high level of unmet needs. This is likely due to the lack of understanding about mental illness, concerns about the stigma of mental illness, and a shortage of counseling professionals trained to assist with mental health problems (Gureje & Lasebikan, 2006). Okorodudu (2006) also identified a lack of funding, illiteracy, a shortage of ideological support for counseling innovations, and a deficiency of training programs as limitations to the integration of community mental health services in Nigerian society. Additionally, the belief in supernatural causes of mental problems, in conjunction with the finding that only 10% of individuals surveyed believe that biological factors or brain disease could cause mental illness, may influence the reluctance of Nigerians to seek or support formal treatment services (Gureje et al., 2005).

In Nigeria, the mental health delivery system is not developed adequately to meet the needs of clients. Gureje and Lasebikan (2006) in their Nigerian study found that treatment for the largest category of diagnosed disorders, substance abuse disorders, was not pursued most of the time. The majority of disorders that met *DSM-IV* criteria, other than substance abuse, were anxiety disorders followed by mood disorders. Of the entire sample of diagnosable cases, only 1.2% reported receiving treatment, and 94% of those individuals who did receive services had done so from a general-care facility.

The mental health professions as a whole are underrepresented in Nigeria, which is consistent with a World Health Organization (2002) report that mental health services are hampered by grossly inadequate personnel and facilities. Guidance and counseling in Nigeria are isolated professionally from other mental-health-related disciplines, such as psychology, psychiatry, and social work (Aluede, Afen-Akpaida, & Adomeh, 2004), because of counseling's position as a service primarily directed toward school settings. Private practice counseling is seldom available in Nigeria due to the poverty affecting the majority of citizens (Aluede et al., 2005). Individuals who do seek private, professional counseling for mental health problems are likely to be those with financial resources, who live in urban areas, and who come from, or are familiar with, cultures that consider psychotherapy an acceptable source of assistance.

Guidance and Counseling in the Education System

Historical evidence indicates that the profession of counseling started with a vocational guidance point of view. Okon (1983) reported that school-based guidance and counseling in Nigeria began in 1959 as the result of a group of Reverend Sisters in charge of St. Theresa's College Oke-Ado in Ibadan, who were concerned about what would become of their graduates on completion of their secondary education. The Reverend Sisters sought to empower graduating students by giving them occupational information that would facilitate informed decision making about certain occupations. Twenty people from different walks of life were invited to speak about their different professions to the sixty graduating students, which could be likened to a "career day" event. After the exercise, a follow-up study revealed that 54 of the students of St. Theresa's College benefited by being placed in various jobs. This resulted in the formation of the Ibadan Career Council, which offered a model for other major schools in Nigeria.

In 1964, the Federal Ministry of Education organized the first seminar on guidance, counseling, and testing intended to enhance the training of teachers, known as career masters, who were specialized in providing vocational assistance to students. The Vocational Guidance Bureau was also opened in Lagos to organize workshops on guidance and counseling for teachers. The 1977 Nigerian National Policy on Education included provisions for guidance and counseling in schools, specifying the requirement that guidance counselors initiate desirable behavior modification plans and provide career guidance for students in schools (Federal Ministry of Education, 2004). A secondary goal of the policy was to provide assistance to schoolchildren experiencing personality maladjustment. The policy also suggested that schools employ guidance counselors in adequate numbers in each primary and postprimary school. As a result of this policy, tertiary institutions initiated degree and postgraduate programs in guidance and counseling that were supported by government-awarded postgraduate scholarships to those intending to study guidance and counseling.

The Counseling Profession

In 1976, CASSON was formed bringing Nigerian counselors together on the national level. The organization affiliated with the American Personnel and Guidance Association (now the American Counseling Association) in 1977. CASSON is currently building a secretariat in Kuje, Abuja, Nigeria, and some Nigerian states also have chapters. Njoku (2005) summarized the present status of counseling in Nigeria as a professional group that provides training and resources through CASSON aimed at improving guidance and counseling services in the nation's educational system. Additionally, CASSON is working toward certification and licensing of their members and has established a Certificate and Licensure Board (CALB) to professionalize counseling in Nigeria and legitimize it legally through the National Assembly of Nigeria. CALB is also charged with the responsibility of preparing and producing a code of ethics for the Association, the initial draft of which was developed in 2008.

CASSON also established a Web site stating their mission: shaping lives that result in role models; helping individuals, clients, or groups maximize their potentials and find solutions to challenges; providing clientele with an opportunity to share burdens; and providing educational, vocational, and personal counseling within and outside the school setting (Counselling Association of Nigeria, 2007).

Additionally, a committee was established to develop counseling modalities and operationalize them after they received approval by the General Assembly of CASSON. Even with these accomplishments, gains as a professional organization have been slow. According to Aluede et al. (2004), CASSON lags in establishing professional standards, conducting research, and promoting the profession.

Roles and Functions of Counselors in Nigeria

Most professional counselors work in schools as full-time guidance counselors providing orientation programs, familiarizing students with the teaching/learning environment, advising students on how best to cope with various types of problems they may encounter, and showing students how to live cooperatively in the dormitories and relate to each other interpersonally. Counselors also help students educationally by cultivating good study skills and providing academic counseling. Today in Nigeria, there is an alarming number of school dropouts. School counselors assist in providing guidance to encourage students to stay in school as long as possible to become literate and obtain the skills and education necessary for employment. Nigerian counselors also assist students in making vocational decisions consistent with their abilities, interests, and personality characteristics (Gothard & Bojuwoye, 1992). Counselors employ intervention strategies to assist students in coping with adjustment problems and serve as consultants to teachers in the assessment of student performance. Many Nigerian students are aware of and use guidance and counseling services, where they are available, and report benefiting greatly from these services (Njoku, 2005). Guidance counselors are also expected to work within the family and community context to support student success.

Counselor Training and Professional Development in Nigeria

Professional counseling in Nigeria is an emerging profession in the early stages of development.

According to the federal government of Nigeria, the profession of counseling is intended to help youth respond to the social, economic, and vocational changes occurring in the country and provide support within educational settings (Aluede et al., 2005). The majority of Nigerian training programs in counseling and guidance are taught as adjuncts to teacher-training programs, with the philosophy that students may be more likely to access counseling services from individuals with whom they are familiar from the classroom. Thus, the provision of counseling services in schools is typically conducted by classroom teachers who specialize in counseling. This circumstance hinders the perception of counseling as a freestanding profession. An alternative perspective is that guidance counselors should be free of classroom responsibilities and focus solely on rendering the counseling and psychological services needed by students. The Alvan Ikoku Federal College of Education, Owerri, Imo State, which runs the University of Nigeria, Nsukka, program, does not subordinate counselor education as an adjunct to a teaching degree. Programs placing more emphasis on the fieldwork practicum are in the minority of training programs.

Graduate programs that train counselors to provide community mental health services, independent of the school system, are slowly emerging. However, the lack of standardization of the curriculum at the university level and the absence of an accrediting body that professionally regulates training and practice has led to identity confusion for the profession. Currently, counselor education programs are either designed to exclusively meet local needs or they feature Western training models and textbooks that promote the Western-oriented freedom of choice philosophy, which restricts perspectives relative to traditional Nigerian values rooted in collectivist indigenous beliefs (Aluede et al., 2004). Additionally, multicultural counseling is not a standardized part of the curriculum in Nigerian counselor education programs, which is problematic considering the wide range of ethnic and religious differences present in Nigeria as well as emerging trends of global interdependence. Sociopolitical problems facing Nigerians, such as HIV/AIDS, substance abuse, under- or unemployment, violence, youth militancy, and poverty, remain unaddressed by counselor training programs. Ideally, a curriculum that teaches counselors how to incorporate indigenous healers in collaborative practice or referral would result in a system that honors Nigerian traditions and values and is applicable to contemporary problems (Adegoke & Culbreth, 2000; Aluede et al., 2004). Postdegree training and professional development opportunities are available to counselors who belong to professional associations such as CASSON, which organizes annual conferences, skills training, and development opportunities, and produces two scholarly publications annually to contribute to the professional development of its members.

Challenges Encountered by Professional Counselors in Nigerian Society

The profession of counseling in Nigeria is relatively young and is organizing slowly, which affects issues of training, standardization, advocacy, licensure, identity, theory development, and need fulfillment. The primary challenges faced by Nigerian counselors relate to the relative newness of the profession, the small number of practicing professionals, and the general lack of understanding about the services counselors can offer that might assist individual, family, and community development. The role of the professional counselor may also be perceived as inconsistent with traditional helping/healing approaches. Aluede et al. (2004) suggested that guidance and counseling in Nigeria has not responded to the national and international issues that concern the country's citizens, such as issues related to HIV/AIDS, ongoing food shortages, corrupt practices on all levels of society and government, and youth unrest.

The general population has misconceptions about counseling services within the community setting and typically views counseling as a school-based service. The role of community counselors as helpers for personal or family problems is neither

well understood nor taken advantage of in Nigeria. The role of school guidance counselors is widely recognized in relation to academic and school adjustment; however, some Nigerians hold the viewpoint that guidance services are concerned only with vocational adjustment or are restricted to highly maladjusted children. Some Nigerian parents fear that third-person involvement between them and their children may involve disclosure of family secrets. Others believe that guidance involves forcing children to accept and implement what the counselor believes is best for the child, versus the family's or community's views. This is consistent with the opinion that guidance connotes conformity—that is, making children conform to the existing norms and ethics with respect to educational pursuits, job choice, and behavioral expectations. Students often perceive guidance counselors as disciplinarians who will punish them when they offend or violate school rules, which undermines the possibility of their seeking assistance in the future from counselors outside a school setting.

Many schools in Nigeria do not have the funding for the provision of guidance services, resulting in insufficient facilities, support, resources, and scheduling opportunities. Because guidance services are a relatively new innovation in the Nigerian educational system, programs have not been accepted by many school principals, headmasters, and headmistresses because of negative attitudes toward change and the belief that they have been coping with student problems all along without the so-called guidance services. School guidance programs in Nigeria have not found a programmatic approach that has proven to be efficient and comprehensively helpful in counteracting these opinions. Instead of individual counseling, it is suggested that counselors adopt a "whole-school guidance approach" that promotes the goal of student development across multiple levels of the school environment in collaboration with teachers, administrators, the community, and traditional helpers, not just in the form of individual student-oriented casework (Aluede et al., 2004).

BRIDGING WESTERN AND NIGERIAN MODELS

Counseling and psychotherapy in Nigeria necessitate an approach that varies from methods commonly accepted in Western countries. Years ago, both Okon (1983) and Denga (1983) suggested that ideas about the nature of the person and human freedom differ in Nigeria from the European or American views that typically influence core counseling concepts. Specifically, the values of individualism are not congruent with Nigerian views of the group (family, ancestors, village, clan, or nation) as an important influence on decisions such as vocational direction.

> The concept of freedom of choice as viewed from the Western philosophy of guidance does not come to Africa readily. The individual must be willing to sacrifice his freedom and individuality if necessary, in order to meet the needs of the family and the larger society, particularly the needs for economic survival and development. (Denga, 1983, p. 118)

This perspective is applicable today; however, it has yet to be integrated into a contemporary theoretical model of mental health counseling that would serve the Nigerian populace. The development of a counseling approach that incorporates Nigerian cultural values would assist in creation of counseling practices that are more acceptable as a community resource. This is especially important with regard to the European and American tendency to separate somatic and psychological functions. Okeke et al. (1999) suggested that a holistic orientation that deemphasizes the boundaries between the physical and psychological components of experience is important when understanding the nature of distress in Nigerian culture. More recently, others have advocated for an African-centered epistemology and practice of counseling (Alao, 2004; Grills, 2002; Obayan, 1998). It is critical to consider the cultural foundations and different expressions of problems, such as depression or anxiety, among various ethnic groups in Nigeria to know how to uniquely diagnose or approach treatment within a cultural context. The mental health professions in Nigeria, including counseling, have yet to define such an approach.

There is a time-honored tradition of the indigenous approach to helping in Nigeria that is important in the formulation, training, and implementation of contemporary mental health counseling. As the World Health Organization (2000) stated,

> Traditional medicine is the sum total of the knowledge, skills and practices based on the theories, beliefs and experiences indigenous to different cultures, whether explicable or not, used in the maintenance of health, as well as in the prevention, diagnosis, improvement or treatment of physical and mental illnesses. (p. 1)

Denga (1983) wrote that "the present and future of counseling in Nigeria must take cognizance of the modern and the traditional nature of the African society and its clients" (p. 121). He suggested that counselors be trained to make appropriate referrals to indigenous healers as necessary for client healing. Concerns continue today about culturally suitable integration of traditional counseling with the contemporary training of Nigerian counselors.

> There exists a real danger that people who are instrumental in developing counseling within Nigeria could so over-adapt Western-based counseling techniques that they fail to perceive the importance of the need to develop models, techniques and approaches appropriate to Nigerian culture. (Adekson, 2005, p. 36)

As counseling is professionalized in Nigeria, Western perspectives must respectfully adapt to indigenous reality. Ilechukwu (1989) suggested modification of the Western psychotherapeutic approach with consideration for Nigerian clients whose awareness is group based, who express problems somatically in terms of symptoms, and are typically seeking direct advice or direction from helpers. As counseling is professionalized, balancing and integrating the most effective indigenous practices with culturally appropriate Western methods are critical.

CONCLUSION

This chapter presents an overview of counseling in Nigeria from traditional indigenous methods to contemporary efforts to formalize the profession. In its traditional form, indigenous practitioners have assisted with the rebalancing of the psyche in accordance with the spiritual traditions that inform the organization of individuals and communities. Formalized contemporary counseling in Nigeria has grown from vocational guidance in private schools, followed by government support for public school counseling as outlined in the National Policy of Education for Nigeria (Federal Ministry of Education, 2004). In its current state, the profession of counseling in Nigeria is, to a very large extent, tailored to meet the needs of secondary schools. University programs and CASSON are working to establish an identity separate from adjunctive teacher education and secondary school guidance as the primary locations of counselor training and practice.

The future direction of counseling in Nigeria lies in the assimilation of the contemporary and the traditional. Mental health services in Nigeria do not fulfill the needs of the population. Accessible guidance and counseling services in primary schools, universities, employment settings, hospitals, and in the community have yet to become commonplace. There is a need in Nigeria to expand and develop graduate-level counselor education training programs that encompass community counseling practice as well as advancing research that is specific to counseling in Nigeria.

The forthcoming developments in traditional or indigenous methods of counseling will depend on the belief systems of the population. As the Federal Republic of Nigeria makes educational and economic gains in a global context, methods of healing must accommodate the evolving mental health needs of the people. Documentation of traditional healing methods would assist future integration efforts, allowing for the development of models of counseling that uniquely address the psychological delivery of services appropriate for the diverse cultures of Nigeria. In addition, training programs that teach counselors how to incorporate indigenous healers in collaborative practice or referral would result in a system that is true to Nigerian traditions and values and applicable to the problems of contemporary Nigerians (Adegoke & Culbreth, 2000; Aluede et al., 2004).

Well-integrated educational programs and certification courses could be developed and implemented in the areas of mental health counseling, community support, advocacy, counseling in the workplace, and other forums thus fulfilling the counseling needs of a larger majority of Nigerians. With judicious planning, continued development of the professional associations, integration of the traditional approaches, standardization of professional practice through licensure, and cooperation among cultural, social, educational, and governmental institutions, the future of guidance and counseling in Nigeria looks bright (Ugwuegbulam, 2005).

REFERENCES

Abimbola, W. (1968). *Ifá* as a body of knowledge and as an academic discipline. *Lagos Notes and Records, 2*(2), 30–40.

Adegoke, A. A., & Culbreth, J. R. (2000). School counselor preparation in Nigeria and the USA. *Compare, 30*(2), 235–244.

Adekson, M. (2003). Indigenous family work in Nigeria. In K. S. Ng (Ed.), *Global perspectives in family therapy* (pp. 147–160). New York: Brunner-Routledge.

Adekson, M. O. (2005). *The Yoruba traditional healers of Nigeria.* New York: Routledge.

Ajila, C. O. (2004). Hope fostering among the Yoruba-speaking people of Nigeria: The use of proverbs, cognomen, prayers, and names. *Anthropologist, 6*(2), 141–146.

Akande, A. (1999). Intercultural and cross-cultural assessment of self-esteem among youth in twenty-first century South Africa. *International Journal for the Advancement of Counseling, 21*(3), 171–187.

Akinsanya, A. (1972, June 4). The case for traditional medicine and psychiatry. *Daily Times,* p. 7.

Alao, K. (2004). Silver and gold we have none but what we have, we give unto thee: Indigenous African counseling and the rest of the world. *International Journal for the Advancement of Counseling, 26*(3), 249–256.

Aluede, O., Afen-Akpaida, J. E., & Adomeh, I. O. C. (2004). Some thoughts about the future of guidance and counseling in Nigeria. *Education, 125*(2), 296–305.

Aluede, O., McEachern, A. G., & Kenny, M. C. (2005). Counseling in Nigeria and the United States of America: Contrasts and similarities. *International Journal for the Advancement of Counseling, 27*(3), 371–382.

American Psychiatric Association. (1994). *Diagnostic and statistical manual of mental disorders* (4th ed.). Washington, DC: Author.

Central Intelligence Agency. (2008, May). *The world factbook: Nigeria.* Retrieved May 28, 2008, from http://www.cia.gov/library/publications/the-world-factbook/print/ni.html

Counselling Association of Nigeria. (2007). *Our vision and mission statement.* Retrieved May 17, 2008, from http://www.cassonlc.com/vision.htm

Denga, D. I. (1983). The state of counseling in Nigeria. *International Journal for the Advancement of Counseling, 6*(2), 115–123.

Ekeopara, C. A. (2005). *African traditional religion: An introduction.* Calabar, Nigeria: Natos Affairs.

Embassy of the Federal Republic of Nigeria. (2004). *This is Nigeria.* Retrieved May 17, 2008, from http://www.nigeriaembassyusa.org/history.shtml

Fabunmi, M. A. (1975, August). *The efficacy of indigenous counselling in Nigeria.* Speech delivered before the Nigeria Careers Council Conference, University of Ibadan, Nigeria).

Federal Ministry of Education. (2004). *National policy on education* (4th ed.). Lagos, Nigeria: Nigerian Educational Research and Development Council.

Gothard, W. P., & Bojuwoye, O. (1992). Counselor training in two different cultures. *International Journal for the Advancement of Counseling, 15*(4), 209–219.

Grills, C. (2002). African-centered psychology: Basic principles. In T. Parham (Ed.), *Counseling persons of African descent* (pp. 10–24). London: Sage.

Gureje, O., & Lasebikan, V. O. (2006). Use of mental health services in a developing country: Results from the Nigerian survey of mental health and well-being. *Social Psychiatry, 41,* 44–49.

Gureje, O., Lasebikan, V. O., Ephraim-Oluwanuga, O., Olley, B. O., & Kola, L. (2005). Community study of and attitude to mental illness in Nigeria. *British Journal of Psychiatry, 186*(5), 436–441.

Ilechukwu, S. T. C. (1989). Approaches to psychotherapy in Africans: Do they have to be non-medical? *Culture, Medicine and Psychiatry, 13*(4), 419–435.

Iwuama, B. C. (1991). *Foundations of guidance and counselling.* Benin City, Nigeria: Supreme Ideal.

Makinde, O. (1974, October). The indigenous Yoruba Babalawo model: Implications for counselling in West Africa. *West Africa Journal of Education, 18*(3), 325.

Makinde, O. (1980). Indigenous counseling techniques among the Yoruba and Igala people of Nigeria. *International Journal for the Advancement of Counseling, 3*(3/4), 171–184.

Makinde, O. (1983). *Fundamentals of guidance and counselling.* New York: Macmillan.

Makinde, O. (1987). Cultural resources for integrated counselling in Nigeria. *Nigerian Journal of Guidance and Counseling, 3*(1/2), 73–85.

Njoku, L. N. (2005). History and development of guidance and counselling. In N. P. Onyemerekeya & C. N. Ugwuegbulam (Eds.), *Introduction to guidance and counselling* (pp. 34–51). Owerri, Nigeria: Versatile.

Obayan, A. O. I. (1998). Client/family interface in counseling: Challenges for counselor acceptability and performance in Nigeria. *Counseling Psychology Quarterly, 11*(1), 87–94.

Okeke, B. I., Draguns, J. G., Sheku, B., & Allen, W. (1999). Culture, self, and personality in Africa. In Y.-T. Lee, C. R. McCauley, & J. G. Draguns (Eds.), *Personality and person perception across cultures* (pp. 139–162). Mahwah, NJ: Lawrence Erlbaum.

Okon, S. E. (1983). Guidance and counseling services in Nigeria. *Personnel and Guidance Journal, 61*(8), 457–458.

Okorodudu, R. I. (2006). Global citizenship: Implications for guidance and counseling innovations in developing nations. *International Journal for the Advancement of Counseling, 28*(2), 107–120.

Peltzer, P (1995). *Psychology and health in African cultures.* Frankfurt, Germany: IKO-Verlag fur Interkulturelle Kommunikation.

Ugwuegbulam, C. N. (2005). Developing a guidance programme. In L. N. Njoku & C. N. Ugwuegbulam (Eds.), *Effective organization and administration of guidance programmes in schools* (pp. 76–85). Owerri, Nigeria: Versatile.

U.S. Department of State. (2008, April). *Bureau of African affairs: Background note: Nigeria.* Retrieved May 17, 2008, from http://www.state.gov/r/pa/ei/bgn/2836.htm

World Health Organization. (2000). *General guidelines for methodologies on research and evaluation of traditional medicine.* Geneva: Author.

World Health Organization. (2002). *WHO traditional health care strategy, 2002–2005.* Geneva: Author.

THE MIDDLE EAST

34

Context and Diversity in the Provision of Counseling Services in Israel

הקשר ושונות במתן שירותי ייעוץ בישראל

MOSHE ISRAELASHVILI AND BENNY A. BENJAMIN

Israel is a very rich country, albeit not in natural resources, but in its variety of people, landscapes, cultures, and its endless stream of social, political, military, and religious turbulence. All these have created a state that offers a rich kaleidoscope of phenomena that challenges any exploration of human behavior. Nevertheless, some preliminary insights can be derived regarding the issue of counseling in Israel. This chapter begins by describing the historical and phenomenological context of the State of Israel, including the evolving counseling agencies and their current status. This is followed by two examples of the implications of multiculturalism in the Israeli society on the provision of counseling services in Israel. The first example relates to the position of career counseling in Israel. The second refers to the micro-implications of multiculturalism in Israeli society on the development and utility of individual counseling. Finally, several generalizations

from the Israeli experience that may have relevance to professionals in other countries are offered.

THE HISTORICAL AND EVOLVING CULTURAL CONTEXT IN ISRAEL

Israel is a small, dynamic country in the Middle East. Due to its myriad aspects of contrast, it eludes monolithic definition. Historically, largely due to its geographical and theological attraction, it has served as a crossroad and often as a site of conflict and clashes between Eastern and Western civilizations for millennia in the realm of the military, culture, trade, and religion. This exposure has proved a double-edged sword, certainly enriching the land to this day but also exacting a harsh price, given its vulnerability to conflict and stress, both external and internal.

Israel began its modern age resettlement in the last quarter of the 19th century through primarily communal agricultural enterprises (such as the kibbutz) that implemented a predominant socialistic secular European-inspired political ideology. This ideology framed the social structure through the first two decades of statehood. The Holocaust, perpetrated during World War II, resulted in the destruction of more than a third of the world's Jewish population and left the decimated European Jewry homeless, wandering among displaced persons' camps at the war's end, until they procured passage to several international destinations, among them Israel. The 20th century witnessed the inception, birth, and thriving of the modern State of Israel, established in 1948 as a culmination of international declarations, especially that of the United Nations in November 1947. With an area of 22,000 square kilometers, Israel is slightly smaller than New Jersey, slightly larger than Kuwait, and 1/19th the size of California. Its current population of just more than 7 million (Israel Central Bureau of Statistics, ICBS, 2007) comprises 76% Jews, 20% Arabs (Muslims, Christians, and Druze, among other religions), and 4% unclassified. Its ultra rapid growth from just more than 800,000 in 1948 to its current level can be traced to relatively high birthrates among both Jewish and Arab populations, but it is largely due to massive post–World War II Jewish immigration from European countries as well as from Arab countries. Immigration has continued, though less intensively, over Israel's six decades. Other waves of immigrants arrived after the establishment of the state, such as from north Africa and Arab countries in the 1950s, from North America in the 1970s, and from South America in the 1980s. Three recent prominent immigrant groups arrived from the former Soviet Union, from Ethiopia, primarily during the 1990s, and from France more recently, illustrating the broad range of challenges faced by the host culture for proper absorption. Currently, immigrants from the former Soviet Union constitute about 20% of the entire Israeli population.

Compared with Western countries, the population is considered young (28% are between ages 0 and 14, compared with an average of 17% in other Western countries). The country's population is growing at a rate of 1.8%, and with this growth, there is a relatively high population density (overall, 310 people per square kilometer), especially in the center of the country (ICBS, 2007). Ultimately, the very mixed origins of massive immigration could not ensure the socioeconomic homogeneity of the population so that subgroup distinctions have led to alternative political, socioeconomic, and religious models. In recent years, Israel has been evolving from a socialist welfare state to a capitalistic, rapidly privatizing economy.

As a result, if one were to seek a condensed descriptor of Israeli society, it would likely be "diversity." To some extent, the same can be said for the non-Jewish society in Israel. Israeli-Arab citizens' cultural and religious identities are also diverse, ranging from Muslim to Druze, to Christian, and so on. Moreover, some of these individuals have maintained almost double identities as a result of living side by side in mixed Jewish-Arab cities such as Acre, Nazareth, and Jerusalem. As a natural result of being encompassed by four Arab states, a small-scale dynamic of immigration occurs among the Arab-Israeli population due to the migration of Arab residents from other countries to Israel (and vice versa), mainly following intermarriage. Hence, not surprisingly, a glance at an Israeli crowd would reveal a kaleidoscope of faces, colors, clothes, manners, and behaviors.

Diversity is a suitable descriptor of the geographical landscape of Israel as well. A tour of the State of Israel would expose the driver to constantly changing vistas within a short span, starting in the cold and snow-capped (in winter) mountains of northern Israel, continuing south to the Mediterranean coast alongside central Israel, with the Jerusalem hills to the east, and completing the journey in the Negev desert region, which covers the entire southern swath of Israel (about one third of its territory). In contrast to its relative prominence in the world media, the State of Israel is very small. Driving from the north to the south of Israel would take approximately 10 hours (in traffic) and from east to west would take between 30 and 90 minutes. Hence, this limited and changing landscape has major implications for Israeli society; the space is relatively small, and the population is growing. Practically speaking, living in such a density means that the presence of others cannot be ignored; those others, as mentioned, are of all varieties.

Important implications of Israel's diversity are manifested in the labor market as well, on the one hand, by way of high-achieving international high-tech entrepreneurs and on the other hand by sections of society that have distanced themselves from the job market, such as the Haredi ultraorthodox Jewish male population (Barak & Golan, 2000) and the Arab female population. The growing Haredi community has steadfastly adopted an economically austere lifestyle in favor of the religious obligation of learning theological texts and insulating their community by disdaining integration. In addition, Arab females have largely been thwarted from developing careers due to cultural and religious constraints. As a result, Israel is still listed as having among the lowest participatory rates in the job market (56%) among Western countries (ICBS, 2007), a critical factor affecting economic robustness.

Several key issues have framed Israeli society in its 60 years of statehood, including the following:

- The challenge of integrating the various waves of immigration, culturally, economically, and socially, into a coherent society (Krau, 1991).
- Lack of significant natural resources, leading to an emphasis on developing human capital, thus reinforcing personal achievement increasingly in the global arena.
- The ongoing challenge to Israel's existence by the surrounding Arab neighbor countries, with the concomitant socioeconomic focus on defense. Combined with Israel's long, narrow, and uneven borders, large swaths of the population are directly exposed to periodic military and/or terror threats.

Multiple sources of stress and instability (e.g., military and terror threats, immigrant absorption difficulties, family disintegration due to intergeneration conflict, especially among immigrants, and multigenerational despair resulting from long-term poverty) (Kopp, 2006) have manifested themselves in many of the maladies of the modern state, such as violence and abuse among adults and youth, road violence, substance abuse, sexual offences, and unemployment. In turn, the helping professions have been called on to deal with grief, phobia, trauma from historic and recent wars, the treatment of second-generation holocaust survivors, and evolving sexual orientations.

Israel today is characterized as a leading element in the global industrial village, especially in information technology, and research and development, operating within a rich mosaic of religious, ethnic, and cultural subgroups who engage in an approach-avoidance struggle to maintain their traditional integrity in a modern state.

THE ARAB POPULATIONS WITHIN THE STATE OF ISRAEL: A CROSS-CULTURAL PERSPECTIVE

Many would assume that the rich diversity of the Israeli community should be consolidated into two major sectors—the Jewish and Arab populations. Such an assumption would emerge from the many differences that can be clearly discerned while traveling around Israel. The first and most prominent distinction is language; that is, while Jewish citizens speak Hebrew, Arab citizens speak Arabic, both being official languages of Israel. It must be noted that, due to their minority status, more Arabs are functional and even fluent in Hebrew than are Jews in Arabic. Add to that the segregated residential areas for each group, even in mixed cities; the diverse educational systems, under government supervision; the traditional collectivistic habits of the Arab people, such as a strong bonding to one's family and community, versus the more individualistic-oriented character of Jewish citizens; the male-oriented Arab community in comparison with the relatively more democratic and egalitarian status of women among the Jewish community; and so forth. These and other differences paint the Arab community and the Jewish community, living side by side in Israel, as two distinctive cultures.

However, a deeper look at both the Arab community and the Jewish community would quickly lead to two major conclusions: First, *there is diversity among subgroups:* Within each community, there are different subgroups. Altogether, these subgroups form a wide spectrum of different communities. Some Jewish and Arab Israelis consider religion, language, and tradition as irrelevant to their identity and being, whereas others—Jews and Arabs alike—completely isolate themselves, even from those from their own sector, to facilitate what they would consider the very survival of their specific subculture. Interestingly, recent references to the U.S. Arab population also call for a departure from the assumption perceiving the Arab population as a monolithic, collectivistic-oriented culture and consider the differences among Arab Americans who emigrated from different Arab countries (Ajrouch & Jamal, 2007). Diversity needs to be acknowledged between those who wish to be integrated more with the U.S. society and those preferring to maintain their traditional habits (e.g., Haboush, 2007). Second, *gradual change exists:* Data from studies conducted among Jewish and Arab populations living side by side in Israel certainly support the need for a better understanding of the Arab population culture and mentality. For example, Levav and Ben-Ari (2008) found that whereas the structure of life's routine ups and downs is similar for Jews and Arabs, the two groups differ in the impact of those events on the family and on personal life satisfaction. The locus of Israeli Arabs' stress is identified primarily in the sphere of family issues, whereas Jews are likely to complain more about personal and mental health issues (Azazia, 2005). This is especially true for Arab adolescents, who are likely to perceive their family as excessively demanding (Peleg-Popko, Klingman, & Nahhas, 2003).

Differences exist also in help-seeking behavior, with Arab youth more reluctant to seek help (Latzer, Tzischinsky, & Geraisy, 2007), but when confronted with a major problem they prefer procuring help from formal help systems (e.g., school counselor), whereas Jewish youth are more likely to turn to informal help sources (e.g., parents and friends) (Sherer & Karnielli-Miller, 2007). Nevertheless, a growing number of studies have failed to demonstrate

differences between Jews' and Arabs' responses to various social phenomena—for example, in reactions to trauma (Cohen & Eid, 2007) or with regard to occupational decision making (Hijazi, Tatar, & Gati, 2004)—but have highlighted the major impact of other universal distinctions among people, such as gender (Moore, 2004), level of education (Baron-Epel, Weinstein, Haviv-Mesika, Garty-Sandalon, & Green, 2005; Kulik, 2007), religiosity (Shechtman & Tanus, 2006), and national identity (Sherer & Enbal, 2006). According to Azaiza (2005), the gradual de-emphasis of ethnic differences is the result of the processes of globalization and modernization that the Arab population in Israel is undergoing. Thus, cross-cultural differences between Israeli Jews and Arabs should not be analyzed from a simplistic ethnic perspective but rather from a more comprehensive view of each individual's unique characteristics and background. Applying this principle to counseling processes, it mandates more attention to the Arab client's personal, social, and political life circumstances rather than assuming that ethnicity retains the monolithic impact it had in the past, thus avoiding professional interventions based on stereotypes. A similar suggestion has recently been offered to counselors working with Arab Americans (Hakim-Larson, Kamoo, Nassar-McMillan, & Porcerelli, 2007; Read, 2004), and it fits well also with recent theories of cultural identity (Oyserman, Coon, & Kemmelmeier, 2002).

DEVELOPMENT OF COUNSELING SERVICES IN ISRAEL

Historically, Israel's counseling and psychotherapeutic interventions have reflected a medical model school of thought, an outgrowth of their European origins. Therapy was sought for rehabilitative purposes if one could not function due to a psychopathological disturbance.

The massive waves of post–World War II immigration generated other critical psychological services, such as vocational counseling and guidance. Most adult immigrants could not assume their original professions in Israel. Their need for professional retraining led to the establishment of career assessment services by the Hadassah Vocational Guidance Bureau in 1944. Services were adapted to meet changing needs, in light of the waves of immigration of the 1950s and 1960s. The Hadassah Institute was a pioneering force in developing and evaluating its own culturally fair psychometric tests and questionnaires and translating and adapting them into more than a dozen languages. Shortly before its demise in 2006, having been acquired by a private human resource institute, it was renamed the Hadassah Institute for Personal and Organizational Development, again reflecting an expansion of services to address the contemporary professional needs of the public as well as private sector.

In a government-sponsored initiative, the Vocational Guidance Arm of Israel's Ministry of Labor was inaugurated in 1969 to provide a testing and assessment function for candidates of technological training courses. One immediate motive was to help facilitate Israel's economy shift from the heavily loaded service sector to the industrial production sector. Renamed the National Career Counseling Psychological Center by the century's end, it had been incorporated into the Israel National Employment Service since 1977. Prior to its massive overhaul and downsizing in 2006, with the aim of outsourcing most vocational psychological services, the center provided individual and group career counseling, extensive psychological client testing services, and candidate selection services. It conducted job-search skills workshops and produced and distributed occupational information through its extensive occupational libraries and computer applications (Benjamin, 2006). Between the years 1962 and 1967, guidance services in the school system functioned as a joint effort of the Ministries of Education and Labor. Their goal was to deal with a concern that exaggerated social stratification in the wake of large waves of immigration, posing a socioeconomic hazard. Subsequently, each ministry developed its own vocational guidance service.

The psychology profession has undergone steady growth since Israel's inception. Current records reflect the relative prominence of the clinical psychology specialty in Israel, with a total of 2,400 licensed clinical psychologists, 1,400 licensed school psychologists, and only 250 licensed vocational/industrial-organizational psychologists. A graduate program in counseling psychology that had been operating at Tel Aviv University for several years was discontinued, mainly due to Israel's Health Ministry's refusal to accredit its graduating students as members of a distinct psychological specialty. A proposed "psychotherapy law," opposed by clinical psychologists for many years, would acknowledge the reality that psychotherapeutic services are offered by nonclinical psychologists as well as by clinical social workers. This proposal recognizes as "psychotherapy" those personal counseling services that are conducted by helping professionals specifically trained in psychotherapeutic post degree training programs in which clinical therapeutic and diagnostic skills have been acquired (Benjamin, 2007). Hence, it can be anticipated that mental health counseling providers will become more diverse and more broadly visible in Israel. A proposed case management system controlled by health insurance organizations is anticipated to further impinge on the professional autonomy and dominance of clinical psychologists, possibly leading to a significant restructuring of the profession.

Among other identifiable dilemmas that frame the helping professions in Israel today are the following:

- How can the helping professional contribute to the normal functioning of the population in an often abnormal setting? (Israelashvili, 2005). Specifically, how can coping with stress be sublimated in day-to-day life in a way that allows optimal individual actualization in the long-term?
- How can the integrity of ethnic groups be respected while seeking ways to help them actualize their members' individuality? (e.g., Tatar, 1998). And what multicultural skills are needed for this undertaking? (e.g., Shechtman & Tanus, 2006).
- How can a pervasive cultural sense of identity as a "victim" or as a "survivor" of hostile forces (historically and contemporarily) be channeled to constructive paths rather than to acting-out behaviors? For instance, varying narratives have

been identified among Jewish and Arab counselors in describing the current Arab-Israeli conflict, which may have an impact on the provision of counseling services. According to Tatar and Horenczyk (2003), Israeli-Arab counselors conceptualize the key political issue as a minority struggle to attain equality, whereas the Israeli-Jewish counselors perceive the conflict in terms of the survival struggle of Jews in the face of a threatening Arab world.

Over the years, alongside the medical model, a community preventive model of intervention (Caplan, 1961) has developed and dominates today. This community-focused approach fits well into features of Israeli culture (see below), and it can be traced to the 1940s and the 1950s, when large-scale psychological adjustment counseling services were granted to the large numbers of youth who had been placed in out-of-town youth village boarding schools shortly after their immigration to Israel, often without their parents. Implementation of the preventive approach means that particular attention is given to the education of the young as well as to the introduction of a variety of prevention efforts among targeted segments of Israeli society (e.g., newborns, socioeconomically disadvantaged students, recent immigrants). Some of these programs are the outgrowths of collaboration between organizations such as the Ministry of Health and the Israel Defense Forces.

One current example of the preventive/community approach is manifested in the guidelines for the immediate activation of helping professionals, who are directed to sites within the school system in which individuals or families are at risk of being exposed, or have already been exposed, to a traumatic physical or emotional loss (Klingman & Cohen, 2004). According to these guidelines, school staff is directed to carry out several preparatory activities once the potential of a military threat is identified, such as training students to quickly approach the sheltered area, selecting older students to assist the younger classes' teachers in accompanying pupils, and instructing teachers how to respond following a trauma event. Another example is the establishment of telephone hotlines for more normative personal traumas, such as coping with unemployment (Benjamin, 2007). The community approach has been prominent as well in dealing with the trauma of shock and posttraumatic stress disorder (PTSD) during armed confrontations among army personnel as well as civilians. It is already axiomatic that soldiers suffering from shock who are treated in proximity to the field and returned as quickly as feasible to their home unit consistently demonstrate better recovery rates. Alongside the strategy of quick response in dealing with trauma, a nonprofit voluntary organization (Natal) of helping professionals established a decade ago has assisted in the everyday coping of long-term sufferers.

The burgeoning life-coaching revolution has been making its presence securely felt in Israel in the family of helping professions. Coaching is already perceived by many as a legitimate professional tool needed to move the client off-center and to advance the individual's goals for personal accomplishments and for learning new coping styles. It is also an avenue for the manifestation of the growing positive psychology movement in Israel. Whereas many non-counselors have been trained in life and executive coaching, with professional regulation still languishing in the legislature, coaching has begun to be mainstreamed and has been adopted by recognized postdegree professional university programs. This informal specialty is anticipated, on the one hand, to further reduce the stigma associated with seeking outside help and, on the other hand, to further crowd the territory and blur the boundaries of professional counseling specialties.

We have thus far presented a complex aspect of the multicultural challenges confronting the counseling professional in Israel: On the one hand, more commonalities are evident among the various Israeli cultures and subcultures with time, partly due to the forces of globalization, the Internet, and so on, whereas, on the other hand, seemingly similarly oriented clients from these cultures and subcultures are still likely to maintain some very pervasive differences not obvious to the uninitiated. What follows are two examples of the implications of Israeli society's multiculturalism for the provision of counseling services. The first is from the area of career education; the second, from the area of individual counseling.

CAREER EDUCATION IN ISRAEL

Generally speaking, perceptions of career education in different countries vary along a continuum. At one pole, career education is viewed as a discreet event, usually offered by the educational system (mainly in high schools), aimed at helping the student identify the occupation that best fits his or her needs, values, and abilities. This approach highlights the matching of individual attributes to appropriate opportunities (Roberts & Robins, 2004). This process is usually implemented on transition from school to work. The underlying assumptions are that (a) this process expresses the commitment of society to the individual's well-being/achievement of meaning in his or her life and (b) the work domain is a major sphere for achieving a meaningful life. An occupation is seen as the primary site of identity formation, even at the expense of other life roles, such as leisure activities (McCash, 2006). At the other pole of this continuum, career education is seen as a lifelong learning process aimed at enabling people to acquire a range of general employability and adaptability skills so that they can adapt to continuous change in the world of work and make educated decisions and transitions that will determine the course of their career development, thereby helping them manage their own careers (Fuller & Whealon, 1979). This perspective is consistent with the demands of the global market, new technologies, and other changes in the world of work demanding workers to assume more responsibility for the advancement of their careers. The aim of career education is to support, accelerate, and ameliorate this process of managing one's own career (Watts, 2001). Career education is not necessarily limited to the work domain as a source of identity formation and can and ought to be launched at an early age of development.

As a reflection of ethnic diversity, the educational system in Israel comprises several different sectors that represent various values and lifestyles. The secular and national-religious sectors comprise students who face a compulsory 2- to 3-year period of post–high school military service. The transition from school to work for these students is delayed until after military service. Israeli Arabs administer their own education system. The Bedouin sector comprises wandering Muslim extended family tribes living mostly in tent communities. This sector is currently facing the dynamics of transitioning to more permanent city-like settings. Their youth are typically conscripted to military service, whereas Arab students are commonly exempted from serving, thus facing a school-to-work transition at the age of 18. The ultraorthodox population, prizing full-time religious studies for most men, typically seeks and receives military exemptions or at least a delay and minimization of their army service, with most not-active participants in the workforce. Paradoxically, women in the ultraorthodox sector are more likely to participate in the labor market, often being the family's primary breadwinner. Whereas military service is technically compulsory for women as well, they are more easily granted exemptions on the basis of a declaration of the need for religion-mandated modesty.

The professionals engaging in career education are school counselors, school psychologists, and teachers. The Ministry of Education's Psychological Counseling Service (Sheffi) was established in 1971 and received a wider mandate to deal with numerous other development issues, especially the pupils' general well-being (Karayanni, 1996). According to Israel's Ministry of Education, 75% of the schools in the national public school sector are served by school counselors, whereas in the Israeli-Arab sector, only 25% of the schools have school counselors. A school psychologist typically works external to the school team, providing diagnostic and psychological counseling services to several regional schools. A total of 81% of the national public sector institutions and 32% in the Arab sector offer school psychological services (Stein, 2007). Until recently, educational systems within the ultraorthodox sector lacked counselors and psychologists. However, recent years have seen a significant growth in the staffing of mental health professionals within ultraorthodox educational systems, preferring professionals hailing from their sector.

In light of the socializing role expected of the junior high school system, the past decade has seen the school counselor's role distancing itself from traditional guidance interventions toward a greater emphasis on enhancing awareness of society's ills and coping with them. Given the fact that compulsory military service for Jewish students occurs on high school graduation, priority is granted to this transition by the public school system (Israelashvili, 2006).

The Ministry of Education's Psychological Counseling Service emphasizes counselors' responsibility to students' wellness and academic achievements through a healthy school environment. Israeli school counselors are expected to be actively involved in eight major issues: (1) promotion of a healthy school climate and prevention of violence; (2) life skills; (3) prevention of alcohol abuse; (4) sexuality, gender, and family issues; (5) prevention of child abuse; (6) trauma and emergencies; (7) learning disabilities; and (8) at-risk youth (Israel Education Counselors and Psychologists, 2007). Special interventions have been developed for each, with counselors offering seminars and workshops for teachers on these topics. Although each of these important issues can be seen as related in some way to career education, currently there is no accepted statutory program that treats career education as a distinct concept. Rather, the different segments of the Israeli educational system emphasize various academic and pedagogic goals that reflect the different possibilities along the above-mentioned spectrum of career education. In the elementary and preelementary levels, there is a recognition and emphasis on the need to establish personal and academic skills as the basis of further development. Although commitment to the world of work is not addressed, the curriculum comprises units aimed at developing the life skills of knowing and understanding the self as well as the surrounding environment (Israel Education Counselors and Psychologists, 2007). Unlike Israeli high schools, Israeli universities offer vocational services for those needing assistance in selecting or changing their majors, as well as CV-writing workshops and personal counseling for those with adjustment difficulties (Israelashvili, 1997). The career counseling typically offered to university students can be characterized as the single-event matching approach.

Unlike the Jewish common educational sector, the Israeli-Arab educational sector is more committed to the importance of the transition to the world of work since its students are exempt from army duty and need to make career choices on completion of high school. Although this sector lacks the counseling manpower resources relative to the Jewish sector, its approach to the issue of career education is more developed, with special units and programs focusing on helping students find work or continue their studies. However, several cultural characteristics still inhibit the expansion of career counseling for Arab 12th graders. For example, a common phenomenon is the discrepancy between Arab female adolescents' postsecondary aspirations and their parents' vision of their future. In the current era, many Arab female adolescents are eager to continue their studies in higher education. Yet their parents typically expect them to marry rather than study. According to the traditional-collectivistic approach, which still governs much of Israeli-Arab adult society, a female is expected to marry, have babies, and support her husband's career. This type of conflict, between traditional family values and individual career aspirations, is less prominent in urban communities and more evident in the relatively smaller Arab villages, where tradition is more likely to dictate daily life. In one documented case, the (Arab) school counselor initiated a meeting with all 12th graders' parents to discuss post–high school plans. That counselor was known as a "modernist" who had long ago adopted Western customs. However, to convince the parents of his views, he cleverly drew on an even more powerful influence than tradition, namely religion, so that during that meeting the counselor asked the parents "to reconsider the utility of ignoring the need for higher education . . . in light of the Koran's [Muslim's holiest book] praises of learning" (A. Badera, personal communication, June 24, 2001).

According to Watts and Sultana's (2004) review of national career guidance policies in 37 countries, no country has yet developed an adequate lifelong guidance system. This is characteristic of Israel as well. Furthermore, in Israel, the traditional trait-factor matching approach is still the dominant one, with a primary focus on the work role and focusing less on other important aspects of career counseling, such as the family-work relationship. The challenge facing career education in Israel is to design programs that will enable direct engagement with career development learning in a way that will allow students to explore the complex nature of their self-environment in an empowering way.

INDIVIDUAL COUNSELING

On discussing individual counseling, a question arises as to the assumptions that a counselor should hold regarding the client's norms and code of behavior. Few generalizations can be offered regarding the Israeli character since attributes often ascribed to this character hold true only to a limited portion of Israelis. The only characteristics that might be generally applied to a large segment of the population are, again, those that relate to people living in changing and stressful circumstances. These would include attributes such as constant exploration of others, having heightened awareness to changes in others' situations, offering frequent and sometimes defensive comments and advice to others, and directing easily elicited emotional expressions at those who seem to be similar to oneself and different from others. The metaphor traditionally attached to the "archetype" Israeli is the *Sabra* (the prickly pear cactus), which is prickly on the outside but tender and sweet on the inside, providing the image that Israelis may have a tough exterior but, on probing deeper, possess a warm and friendly interior.

Applying these notions to individual counseling means that there is a high probability of the Israeli client being initially very suspicious but becoming more open and cooperative as the session progresses. It is not the phenomenon itself that is unique to the Israeli client (see Kelly, 2000); rather, it is the stark change in behavior that is much more evident among Israeli clients, relative to clients in other cultures.

Given Israel's Jewish majority, a reference to Jewish Israeli characteristics should be made. Be it the Jewish religion that fosters obedience to God, the Jewish heritage that emphasizes the commitment of the individual to the community, Jewish history chronicling a people in exile, or the legendary Jewish mother who is known to intensively care for her children up to the level of interference, it seems that many Israeli Jews share a tendency to explore in a curious fashion, along with possessing a rootless eagerness to progress and achieve (Friedman, Friedlander, & Blustein, 2005). Hence, once the Israeli client moves from a defensive mode to cooperation with the counselor, she or he may be ready to proceed with new experiences and exploration, sometimes even beyond the counselor's initial expectations (e.g., too fast or in too many directions simultaneously).

Examples of going beyond a counselor's expectations would be the well-documented phenomena of sharing and disclosure, which characterize many Israelis. It is only a matter of time until an Israeli will tell you almost everything about his or her personal life, problems, and plans for the future. Some trace the tendency to share to the socialist kibbutz culture, in which family-like sharing was the basic motto of life and people were known to share almost everything, including raising their offspring communally. Others would connect it to the prominence of the Jewish value of communality, whereas several researchers of Israeli society will view it as an example of the phenomenon of a need for affiliation in a stressful environment (Maner, DeWall, Baumeister, & Schaller, 2007; Rofe, 1984). However, the culture of sharing may create a problem for the professional counselor, who is obliged to help the client process the often contradictory pieces of freely dispensed advice she or he has been offered by others. It should be noted that sometimes it is not the professional counselor or therapist who can facilitate the change but rather a nonprofessional helper who can make a significant contribution to solving a problem (Cowen, 1982).

Another example of going beyond the counselor's expectations is the widespread consultation of religious and native healers in Israeli society. Despite the reputation of Israel as a leading global high-tech center, in their private life many Israelis (both Jewish and Muslim, both religious and secular) turn to spiritual healers and/or believe in supernatural powers who can heal numerous mental and physiological ailments (Bilu, Witztum, & Van der Hart, 1990; Praglin, 2005). Hence, many of those who might seek help from a professional counselor would also turn to a religious or spiritual leader to ask for a blessing and/or advice.

Practically speaking, in some cases, a professional counselor's help is sought, whereas many other potential helpers (professional and nonprofessional) are simultaneously consulted regarding the problem and contribute their own goodwill, advice, and knowledge. Hence, it might be difficult to know what really made the difference in resolving a client's problem, whether it was the result of the counselor's formal professional intervention or, perhaps, a blessing from a charismatic religious leader whom the client admires and follows.

Nevertheless, in spite of the culture of sharing and the community orientation of the Israeli population, formal help seeking is still not the first choice of many people (Vogel, Wester, & Larson, 2007). This is especially true for adolescents (Tishby et al., 2001) and for recent immigrants (BenEzer, 2006; Shor, 2006). Israeli adolescents would prefer to ask for help from peers or family (Ben-Ari & Pines, 2002). It should be noted that such a reluctance of Israeli adolescents to seek professional help has been documented also in extreme situations, such as war (Israelashvili, 1999) and terrorist attacks (Tatar & Amram, 2007). A possible explanation for this may be related to the need to avoid admitting to weakness and dependence. As memories of the Holocaust are still very vivid in Israeli society, and adolescents are no exception, it is possible that some believe that no war experience in our day can compare with what their grandparents endured in the Holocaust. Hence, they must be resilient and survive, especially in times of an existential threat to the country. Since Israel's inception, the post-Holocaust self-image of the "New Jew" as

being strong and self-reliant has been prominent, possibly having a role in avoiding professional counseling. Interestingly, the readiness of many Israeli mental health professionals to offer voluntary direct assistance in times of national crisis, such as military conflict, has led to a distorted public impression that counselors and psychologists are out to solicit patients (Raviv & Weiner, 1995).

For completely different reasons, the tendency to eschew formal help seeking exists also among non-Jews, especially Muslims (El Kchirid, 2007). Studies conducted among the Israeli Arab Muslims have demonstrated that they prefer to deal with personal problems within the framework of their nuclear family (Savaya, 1998). The exceptions would be problems that are related, of course, to family issues or in times of a significant economic hardship that accompanies a personal difficulty, in which Arabs would be more willing to reveal their problems to others (Savaya, 1997).

Counseling the Arab or Muslim client, the counselor confronts values that may clash with the Western ideology of individualism, which idealizes the searching for and striving to actualize one's uniqueness. The Muslim client, having been brought up valuing collectivism, would likely hesitate to disclose how he or she differs from the group, especially in relation to affect. Only sophisticated, round about questioning could elicit the self-disclosure that could be a key to the client's progress. For instance, given the client's reticence to share individual feelings, the culturally sensitive counselor would avoid asking the Muslim client, "How does that make you feel?" and rather inquire in a more behavioral context, "What do you do when . . . ?" (M. Faher, personal communication, February 10, 2009). In light of the gradual change in the direction of accommodating Western values within the Arab population, some researchers believe that the major difference between Arab and Jewish Israelis relates to each group's socioeconomic status rather than genuine cultural differences (Nadler & Halabi, 2006). Others call for the establishment of cultural-related models, rather than the use of Western models, in dealing with issues related to help seeking and help providing among the Arab population (Dwairy, 2006; Sherer & Karnieli-Miller, 2007). As a result of this debate, counseling students are exposed to a variety of counseling models in the course of their training, along with a warning about the eclectic pitfalls and the need to approach counseling as a lifelong learning process and with cultural sensitivity.

After completing their training, many counselors and psychologists identify themselves as practicing either humanistic models or dynamic models of counseling. In Israel, the cognitive-behavioral model is not as prominent as in other Western societies, though it is steadily expanding. Fostered by the unique characteristics of Israeli society, a method of counseling that seems to fit well into the Israeli culture is group counseling (Weinberg, 2000). In a well-grounded and well-reported series of studies, Shechtman (2007) has demonstrated that both Jewish and Arab adolescents (Shechtman & Tanus, 2006) collaborate well in group counseling, especially when it is combined with art therapy (Shechtman & Perl-Dekel, 2000). However, it has been observed that separating genders in group counseling among Arab village residents is a precondition to conducting groups (as is the case in ultraorthodox Jewish participants), whereas a mixed-gender group is more acceptable among Arab city residents.

In recent years, alternative counseling modalities have gradually expanded in Israel. These include counseling over the radio (Raviv, Raviv, & Arnon, 1991) or the telephone (Al-Krenawi, Graham, & Fakher-Aldin, 2003), mental health and employment counseling telephone hotlines, and e-counseling (Barak & Bloch, 2006; Gati, Gadassi, & Shemesh, 2006). Many Israelis—Jewish, Arab, adult, adolescent, religious, nonreligious, and so on—express an avid interest in these alternative distance methods of one-to-one help seeking. Thus, several Israeli psychologists have tried their hand at establishing online counseling for local and international clients, using Skype, phone, or e-mail as the mode of communication. Some of these services, such as life coaching, parent counseling, and adjustment counseling, are enterprises that survive, whereas others languish in inactive Web sites. For instance, an Israeli franchise

of an international career counseling service has been recently launched, whereby counseling sessions are to be conducted by phone, and ability and values assessment are to be administered via the Internet. In general, however, Israel lags behind most Western countries in developing professionally viable e-counseling frameworks (A. Barak, personal communication, January 17, 2008). On the other hand, it should be noted that there are many successful moderated Internet forums for personal sharing, some professionally monitored but often only loosely administered, in a myriad categories that are managed like self-help groups in a written format. One might posit a connection of this extensive personal e-sharing to the consistently high per capita usage of cellular phones in Israel.

Although there will always be those who prefer the anonymity of sharing and learning from others, whether by telephone hotlines or by Internet, most of the actual counseling in Israel still takes place in more traditional settings. Israel's size and dynamics of population concentration make distance and e-counseling primarily relevant to the sparsely populated peripheral communities.

Once a client seeks individual counseling, she or he will likely conduct a comprehensive search (Yagil & Israelashvili, 2003) before selecting a counselor. Many cultural and subcultural issues will shape the person's final decision regarding whether and from whom she or he should seek help. For example, the ultraorthodox, in particular, have multiple barriers before seeking the help of professional counselors. This is not due to a de-legitimization of the profession by the community but rather to the fear of individuals of being exposed to non-Jewish and especially nonreligious issues or directives from the counselor (Greenberg, 1991; Schnall, 2006). An example of this would be a question that the counselor might naively pose to the client, such as "How would you describe your relationship with your parents?" The fifth of the Ten Commandments requires honoring his or her parents. Hence, reporting difficulties with parents may be perceived as dishonoring them. In another example, sharing views of others might be perceived as engaging in gossip, a religiously prohibited behavior.

Nevertheless, the ultraorthodox community is becoming increasingly aware of the power and potential positive impact that professional counseling might have on it, and recently its leaders have more easily directed their community members to counsel with a mental health professional and have granted their approval for professional training of school counselors and social workers from within their ranks. The significant issue when a member of this community seeks a counselor is the counselor's behavior and lifestyle: Namely, he or she needs to be dressed modestly, to be generally knowledgeable concerning the code of ethics in the religious community, and to not express disparaging stereotypes about religious people and the religious lifestyle. These "screening" criteria carry two major implications. First, religiously observant clients are likely to intensively examine the counselor's behavior during the session prior to disclosing the real problem. Though such a phenomenon is well documented in the literature (Kelly, 2000), in the case of a religious client, this would have a significant impact on the progress of the sessions. And second, once the counselor has "passed" the examination and has proven himself or herself, the client will likely refer many other religious clients to his or her counselor. However, with the ultraorthodox clients, it might manifest itself more dramatically (e.g., parents who are prepared to travel 2–3 hours in each direction and twice weekly to cooperate with a counselor who "passes muster").

The religiosity of the therapist is only one example of the many cultural factors that might play a significant role in shaping counseling Israeli clients. Due to Israel's diversity and multiculturalism, there are still too many people who have to overcome too many stereotypes before requesting and receiving comprehensive counseling services. In particular, this means overcoming cultural and gender (i.e., masculine) (Kulik, 2005) biases and role types that are sometimes fostered by the stressful war-related circumstances that the State of Israel has been exposed to since its establishment.

CONCLUSION

Israel is a relatively young and diminutive country. Nevertheless, within its limited social and geographical

space, a wide spectrum of multiple religions, cultures, subcultures, and mixed roots live side by side. These people live together in a kind of limited social armistice, though everyone is aware of the differences among the subgroups and wonders if there are any features common to all Israelis. The current review has pointed out some of the many sources of Israel's multiculturalism, both historically and contemporarily, and their implications for the work of the professional counselor. In addition to the notion of differential needs and priorities within the different cultural groups that make up Israeli society, one must also take into account the dynamic political and security situation, such as repeated armed conflicts with neighboring states and terror organizations, which significantly affect daily life in Israel.

As a result of all this, a growing tendency has emerged within the Israeli educational and social systems to focus more on the present (i.e., the general and current well-being and/or achievements of the person) rather than to devote their efforts to a comprehensive and individually oriented life planning and vocational counseling. Practically speaking, with regard to both Jews and Arabs, the Israeli government devotes very limited resources to promoting a proper definition and better organization of its mental health services, including the counseling profession. In response, a sector approach has emerged, whereby different segments of Israeli society pay differential attention and devote differential resources to counseling services. These services, in return, devote more resources and attention to their sector's global needs, sometimes even more than to the individual's needs. An example of that would be the restrictions imposed by religious high school principals, Jewish and Arab, on career counseling to female adolescents.

However, parallel to the differentiation that has arisen, some common features of effective counseling processes for Israeli clients have been reviewed, such as the community-preventive approach, distance counseling (e.g., radio counseling and e-counseling), and group counseling. These three counseling modes can be related to what seems to be a common characteristic of many Israelis—a heightened awareness of others. Referring to individual counseling, most of the universally known phenomena of reluctance to seek help, exploration of the counselor's qualifications before divulging major problems, and so forth also exist in Israel. However, it has been suggested that the magnitude of some of these phenomena is much more prominent in Israel than in other countries. In addition, in relation to the aforementioned propensity to be attuned to others, it was suggested that the Jewish client can become much more forthcoming than those from other cultures to share his or her problems with others and to collaborate with unconventional quasi-therapeutic experiences along the path to healing. Whereas Arab clients might be initially more selective in sharing personal matters with others, once having engaged in such disclosure, they will take professional and community considerations into account. However, there is evidence that cultural gap between Israeli Jewish and Israeli Arab clients are gradually diminishing, especially among urban dwellers from both sectors.

Taking the suggested process of differentiation along with the parallel process of heightened awareness of others, it may be hypothesized that these paradoxical vectors are in fact reflective of a system in Israel that has achieved a status of social equilibrium, that is, culturally mandated mechanisms that respect cultural diversity while acknowledging the existence of out-group people and communities.

In the current era of globalization, where a counselor might face clients with unfamiliar cultural roots, several lessons can be drawn from the Israeli experience: the need to constantly reexamine the relevance of seemingly well-established assumptions on encountering a client from an unfamiliar ethnic group; the vitality of human nature, as evident in Israelis' resilience in the face of continuing armed conflicts; the ongoing tension between a traditional-collectivistic approach and a modern-individualistic approach, especially to positive and negative implications that both might have in changing circumstances; the governmental impact on the development of counseling as a profession, and so on.

In their discussion of cross-cultural counseling, Skovholt and Rivers (2004) advocated the idea that the culturally skilled counselor is expected to be able to respect diversity and explore its implications of the counseling process whenever meeting a new person. Our observations of Israeli society lead us to realize that to some degree, these are also among the major challenges that Israeli society is facing as a whole (i.e., respect for the diversity and exploration of its implications). These challenges are not new to Israeli mental health professionals, as they are constantly forced to find new ways to meet these challenges; otherwise their work would lose its effectiveness. Mental health professionals from other countries are invited to refer to this chapter as an invitation to learn more about the ongoing challenges that cross-cultural counseling is currently facing in Israel and the emerging ways to meet them.

REFERENCES

Ajrouch, K. J., & Jamal, A. (2007). Assimilating to a White identity: The case of Arab Americans. *International Migration Review, 41,* 860–879.

Al-Krenawi, A., Graham, J. R., & Fakher-Aldin, M. (2003). Telephone counseling: A comparison of Arab and Jewish Israeli usage. *International Social Work, 46,* 495–509.

Azazia, F. (2005). Parent-child relationships as perceived by Arab adolescents living in Israel. *International Journal of Social Welfare, 14,* 297–304.

Barak, A., & Bloch, N. (2006). Factors related to perceived helpfulness in supporting highly distressed individuals through an online support chat. *Cyber-Psychology and Behavior, 9,* 60–68.

Barak, A., & Golan, G. (2000). Counseling psychology in Israel: Successful accomplishments of a nonexistent specialty. *The Counseling Psychologist, 28,* 100–116.

Baron-Epel, O., Kaplan, G., Haviv-Messika, A., Tarabeia, J., Green, M. S., & Kaluski, D. N. (2005). Self-reported health as a cultural health determinant in Arab and Jewish Israelis: MABAT—National Health and Nutrition Survey 1999–2001. *Social Science & Medicine, 61,* 1256–1266.

Ben-Ari, A., & Pines, A. M. (2002). The changing role of family in utilization of social support: Views from Israeli Jewish and Arab students. *Families in Society, 83,* 93–101.

BenEzer, G. (2006). Group counseling and psychotherapy across the cultural divide: The case of Ethiopian Jewish immigrants in Israel. *Transcultural Psychiatry, 43,* 205–234.

Benjamin, B. A. (2006). *Career guidance in the MEDA region* [Education and Training for Employment]: *Country report on Israel*. Turin, Italy: European Training Foundation.

Benjamin, B. A. (2007). Counseling psychology in Israel: A virtual specialty in transition. *Applied Psychology, 56,* 83–96.

Bilu, Y., Witztum, E., & Van der Hart, O. (1990). Paradise regained: "Miraculous Healing" in the Psychiatric Clinic. *Culture, Medicine and Psychiatry, 14,* 105–127.

Caplan, G. (1961). *An approach to community mental health.* New York: Grune & Stratton.

Cohen, M., & Eid, J. (2007). The effect of constant threat of terror on Israeli Jewish and Arab adolescents. *Anxiety, Stress & Coping: An International Journal, 20,* 47–60.

Cowen, E. L. (1982). Help is where you find it: Four informal helping groups. *American Psychologist, 37,* 385–395.

Dwairy, M. (2006). *Counseling and psychotherapy with Arabs and Muslims: A culturally sensitive approach.* New York: Teachers College Press.

El Kchirid, A. (2007). *Best practices working with Arab and Muslim clients.* International Institute of New Jersey. Retrieved February 16, 2009, from http://www.culturallycompetentmentalhealthnj.org/docs/Sept07Workshops/best-practices-Arab-and-Muslim/BestPracticesworkingwithArabandMuslimClientsabadul.pdf

Friedman, M. L., Friedlander, M. L., & Blustein, D. L. (2005). Toward an understanding of Jewish identity: A phenomenological study. *Journal of Counseling Psychology, 52,* 77–83.

Fuller, J. W., & Whealon, T. O. (Eds.). (1979). *Career education: A lifelong process.* Chicago: Nelson-Hall.

Gati, I., Gadassi, R., & Shemesh, N. (2006). The predictive validity of a computer-assisted career decision-making system: A six-year follow-up. *Journal of Vocational Behavior, 68,* 205–219.

Greenberg, D. (1991). Is psychotherapy possible with unbelievers? The care of the ultra-orthodox community. *Israel Journal of Psychiatry and Related Sciences, 28,* 19–30.

Haboush, K. L. (2007). Working with Arab American families: Culturally competent practice for school psychologists. *Psychology in the Schools, 44,* 183–198.

Hakim-Larson, J., Kamoo, R., Nassar-McMillan, S. C., & Porcerelli, J. H. (2007). Counseling Arab and Chaldean American families. *Journal of Mental Health Counseling, 29,* 301–322.

Hijazi, Y., Tatar, M., & Gati, I. (2004). Career decision-making difficulties among Israeli and Palestinian Arab high-school seniors. *Professional School Counseling, 8,* 64–72.

Israel Central Bureau of Statistics. (2007). *Annual report.* Retrieved November 1, 2007, from http://www.cbs.gov.il/saka_q/11_01.pdf

Israelashvili, M. (1997). Students' counselling in Israeli universities. *International Journal for the Advancement of Counselling, 19,* 55–63.

Israelashvili, M. (1999). Adolescents' help-seeking behavior in times of community crisis. *International Journal for the Advancement of Counselling, 21,* 87–96.

Israelashvili, M. (2005). Staying normal in an abnormal corner of the world: Mental health counseling in Israel. *Journal of Mental Health Counseling, 127,* 238–248.

Israelashvili, M. (2006). The school-to-army transition: Interventions for high-school students and their families. In P. Buchwald (Ed.), *Stress and anxiety: Application to health, community, work place, and education* (pp. 325–346). Cambridge, UK: Cambridge Scholar Press.

Israel Education Counselors and Psychologists. (2007). *Shefinet.* Retrieved November 1, 2007, from http://www.cms.education.gov.il/EducationCMS/Units/Shefi

Karayanni, M. (1996). The emergence of school counseling and guidance in Israel. *Journal of Counseling and Development, 74,* 582–587.

Kelly, A. E. (2000). Helping construct desirable identities: A self-presentational view of psychotherapy. *Psychological Bulletin, 126,* 475–494.

Klingman, A., & Cohen, E. (2004). *School-based multisystemic interventions for mass trauma.* New York: Kluwer Academic/Plenum.

Kopp, Y. (Ed.). (2006). *Israel's social services—2006.* Israel, Jerusalem: Taub Center.

Krau, E. (1991). *Contradictory immigrant problem: A socio-psychological analysis.* New York: Peter Lang.

Kulik, L. (2005). Predicting gender role stereotypes among adolescents in Israel: The impact of background variables, personality traits, and parental factors. *Journal of Youth Studies, 8,* 111–129.

Kulik, L. (2007). Equality in the division of household labor: A comparative study of Jewish women and Arab Muslim women in Israel. *Journal of Social Psychology, 147,* 423–440.

Latzer, Y., Tzischinsky, O., & Geraisy, N. (2007). Comparative study of eating-related attitudes and psychological traits between Israeli-Arab and Jewish schoolgirls. *Journal of Adolescence, 30,* 627–637.

Levav, Y., & Ben-Ari, A. (2008). The association of daily hassles and uplifts with family and life satisfaction: Does cultural orientation make a difference? *American Journal of Community Psychology, 41,* 89–98.

Maner, J. K., DeWall, C. N., Baumeister, R. F., & Schaller, M. (2007). Does social exclusion motivate interpersonal reconnection? Resolving the "Porcupine Problem." *Journal of Personality and Social Psychology, 92,* 42–55.

McCash, P. (2006). We're all career researchers now: Breaking open career education and DOTS. *British Journal of Guidance and Counselling, 34,* 429–449.

Moore, D. (2004). Gender identities and social action: Arab and Jewish women in Israel. *Journal of Applied Behavioral Science, 40,* 182–207.

Nadler, A., & Halabi, S. (2006). Intergroup helping as status relations: Effects of status stability, identification, and type of help on receptivity to high-status group's help. *Journal of Personality and Social Psychology, 91,* 97–110.

Oyserman, D., Coon, H. M., & Kemmelmeier, M. (2002). Rethinking individualism and collectivism: Evaluation of theoretical assumptions and meta-analyses. *Psychological Bulletin, 128,* 3–72.

Peleg-Popko, O., Klingman, A., & Nahhas, I. A. (2003). Cross-cultural and familial differences between Arab and Jewish adolescents in test anxiety. *International Journal of Intercultural Relations, 27,* 525–541.

Praglin, L. J. (2005). Jewish healing, spirituality, and modern psychology. In W. West & R. Moodley (Eds.), *Integrating traditional healing practices into counseling and psychotherapy* (pp. 170–181). Thousand Oaks, CA: Sage.

Raviv, A., Raviv, A., & Arnon, G. (1991). Psychological counseling over the radio: Listening motivations and the threat to self-esteem. *Journal of Applied Social Psychology, 21,* 253–270.

Raviv, A., & Weiner, I. (1995). Why don't they like us? Psychologists' public image in Israel during the Persian Gulf War. *Professional Psychology: Research and Practice, 26,* 88–94.

Read, J. G. (2004). Family, religion, and work among Arab American Women. *Journal of Marriage and Family, 66,* 1042–1050.

Roberts, B. W., & Robins, R. W. (2004). Person-environment fit and its implications for personality development: A longitudinal study. *Journal of Personality, 72,* 89–110.

Rofe, Y. (1984). Stress and affiliation: A utility theory. *Psychological Review, 91,* 235–250.

Savaya, R. (1997). Political attitudes, economic distress, and the utilization of welfare services by Arab women in Israel. *Journal of Applied Social Sciences, 21,* 111–121.

Savaya, R. (1998). The under-use of psychological services by Israeli Arabs: An examination of the roles of negative attitudes and the use of alternative sources of help. *International Social Work, 41,* 195–209.

Schnall, E. (2006). Multicultural counseling and the orthodox Jew. *Journal of Counseling and Development, 84,* 276–282.

Shechtman, Z. (2007). *Group counseling and psychotherapy with children and adolescents: Theory, research, and practice.* Mahwah, NJ: Lawrence Erlbaum.

Shechtman, Z., & Perl-Dekel, O. (2000). A comparison of therapeutic factors in two group treatment modalities: Verbal and art therapy. *Journal for Specialists in Group Work, 25,* 288–304.

Shechtman, Z., & Tanus, H. (2006). Counseling groups for Arab adolescents in an intergroup conflict in Israel: Report of an outcome study. *Peace and Conflict: Journal of Peace Psychology, 12,* 119–137.

Sherer, M., & Enbal, B. (2006). In the shadow of dispute: Self-esteem of Jewish and Arab youths in Israel. *International Journal of Intercultural Relations, 30,* 287–309.

Sherer, M., & Karnieli-Miller, O. (2007). Intentions for advice and help seeking among Jewish and Arab youth in Israel. *Youth and Society, 39,* 33–53.

Shor, R. (2006). When children have problems: Comparing help-seeking approaches of Israeli-born parents and immigrants from the former Soviet Union. *International Social Work, 49,* 745–756.

Skovholt, T. M., & Rivers, D. A. (2004). *Skills and strategies for the helping professions.* Denver, CO: Love Publishing.

Stein, B. (2007). School psychology in Israel. In P. T. Farrell, S. R. Jimerson, & T. D. Oakland (Eds.), *The handbook of international school psychology* (pp. 189–198). Thousand Oaks, CA: Sage.

Tatar, M. (1998). Counseling immigrants: School contexts and emerging strategies. *British Journal of Guidance and Counselling, 26,* 337–352.

Tatar, M., & Amram, S. (2007). Israeli adolescents' coping strategies in relation to terrorist attacks. *British Journal of Guidance and Counselling, 35,* 163–173.

Tatar, M., & Horenczyk, G. (2003). Dilemmas and strategies in the counseling of Jewish and Palestinian Arab children in Israeli schools. *British Journal of Guidance and Counselling, 31,* 375–391.

Tishby, O., Turel, M., Gumpel, O., Pinus, U., Lavy, S., Winokour, M., et al. (2001). Help-seeking attitudes among Israeli adolescents. *Adolescence, 36,* 249–264.

Vogel, D. L., Wester, S. R., & Larson, L. M. (2007). Avoidance of counseling: Psychological factors that inhibit seeking help. *Journal of Counseling and Development, 85,* 410–422.

Watts, A. G. (2001). Career education for young people: Rationale and provision in the UK and other European countries. *International Journal for Educational and Vocational Guidance, 1,* 209–222.

Watts, A. G., & Sultana, R. G. (2004). Career guidance policies in 37 countries: Contrasts and common themes. *International Journal for Educational and Vocational Guidance, 4,* 105–122.

Weinberg, H. (2000). Group psychotherapy and group work in Israel-1998. *Journal of Psychotherapy in Independent Practice, 1,* 43–51.

Yagil, D., & Israelashvili, M. (2003). Helpers' characteristics and problem intimacy as determinants of emotions associated with help-seeking. *Counselling Psychology Quarterly, 16,* 223–228.

35

Counseling Challenges Within the Cultural Context of the United Arab Emirates

التحديات التي تواجه مهنة الإرشاد في دولة الإمارات العربية المتحدة في ضوء الثقافة السائدة

FATIMA AL-DARMAKI AND MOHAMED ABDELAZIEM SAYED

This chapter describes the counseling profession in the United Arab Emirates (UAE) as well as discussing the influence of cultural ethos and practices on counseling in general and psychotherapy in particular. The role of cultural assumptions and practices will be examined in light of the traditions prevalent in the Emirates culture. An attempt to integrate Western psychology and non-Western practices will be made. The remainder of the chapter highlights issues related to counseling in the UAE as practiced nowadays and the challenges that have ensued in trying to fit Western psychotherapeutic realities into indigenous cultural metaphors, ethos, beliefs, and practices. We will then provide a synopsis of the UAE's sociopolitical and economical realities. These realities help shape the practice of counseling in the UAE, and the burgeoning of the class is setting the stage for even more challenges and opportunities. (Several factors have been shown

to account for the variability and disparity we see in traditional Emirati society as people try to deal with differing therapeutic realities of our time.) In addition, we discuss variables that influence therapeutic realities and assumptions, such as help-seeking behavior, the conceptualization of mental illness, communication styles, the use of metaphors in expressing psychological discomfort, current practices and applications, and barriers and challenges in the provision of mental health services that are consistent with the cultural traditions of the UAE.

UAE CULTURE AND COUNSELING

The UAE occupies an area of 77,700 square kilometers along the southeastern tip of the Arabian Peninsula, and it consists of seven emirates (Abu Dhabi, Dubai, Sharjah, Ajman, Umm Al Quwain, Ras Al-Khaimah, and Fujariah). The population of the UAE is growing fast due to factors such as a strong economy, healthy social development, and political stability. Other factors supporting this growth include the influx of foreign workers, improved health care and other services (e.g., the educational system), and availability of job opportunities (Kjeilen, 2007; Ministry of Information and Culture, 2006). The UAE population is very diverse (e.g., in nationality, religion, and spoken language); only 20% of the population are native Emirati; the majority are Arabs, Asians, and Westerners. The diversity of the UAE population has created a society that is multicultural in nature. Yet the UAE culture, customs, and traditions (e.g., Emirati music, art, dance, poetry, camel racing, clothing, and food) continue to make up the UAE identity. The UAE continues to be a tolerant, open, caring society that cherishes its traditional roots (Ministry of Information and Culture, 2006). When preparing to counsel individuals, the UAE counselors (especially those who are from other cultures or have been trained in Western cultures) need to learn about UAE culture, its impact on the clients, and their ways of presenting and dealing with their issues.

The UAE is predominantly an Islamic society (Kjeilen, 2007). Religion is not only relegated to the practice of faith in the UAE and other Muslim cultures, it is a way of life, as values stem from religious prescriptions and their interpretations. In addition, Muslims believe that all events are controlled by Allah and that sickness and health come from Allah and from Allah only. In therapy, Muslim clients may not only deal with psychological distress but also with guilt feelings stemming from the belief that they must have done something to deserve their distress (Sayed, Collins, & Takahashi, 1998).

The native tongue for Emirati is Arabic. Additional languages that are widely spoken in the UAE are English, Urdu, Persian, and other languages used by Asians. The use of multiple languages in UAE society presents challenges to the counseling situation, such as the impact of using an interpreter on the counseling process. Arabic is rich in metaphor. The use of metaphor plays an important role in communication in the counseling situation. In communicating their suffering and pain, clients may use metaphors such as "my heart is burning" to express sadness or "my blood is boiling" to communicate anger and frustration. The use of such metaphors may reflect the clients' cultural conceptualization of mental processes rather than lack of the ability to express them. Metaphors act as a matrix or bridge that further the working through of thoughts and affect symbolization (Fabregat, 2004) and may facilitate cultural understanding of distress by revealing cognitive variability in their production. This is one instance where understanding, conceptualization, and meaning come together to form a web of interrelationships that promotes understanding and appreciation of the cultural meanings attached to issues of a psychological nature. Therefore, understanding and meaning come together to be both meaningful and efficacious.

The labor market in the UAE is very competitive. The requirements for most occupations have become challenging for college graduates who usually lack necessary skills and training needed by the labor market. As a result, many job seekers may remain unemployed for a long period of time. The UAE workforce is shaped by three main factors: (1) a demand for skills in the face of fast economic growth; (2) a working-age population that is increasingly made up of young people (more than 5% of the total national population is less than 15 years of age); and (3) an increased dependence on foreign labor as a source of skilled and unskilled workers.

These changes in the requirements of the labor market have led to the introduction of career-development and career-counseling concepts in society. Efforts to train job seekers to obtain job-related skills such as English language skills and technical skills or to obtain work-related experience, so as to match job seekers' qualifications with demands of the job market, have received increased attention from decision makers in the UAE as a means of solving the unemployment problem. High school graduates seek career counselors to make the right career decisions before entering college. Annual job fairs are held to offer job seekers opportunities to explore various jobs available to them in the market. Some universities and colleges have started developing career-advising programs or courses and providing career counseling to their students.

The family in the UAE plays an important role in the life of its members. The family (both nuclear and extended) provides support, protection, and guidance to its members. Family-related decisions (e.g., marriage, types of education, career, and medical/psychological treatment) are considered family affairs and usually made by the head of the family (i.e., the father or the older son). Men are responsible for looking after the womenfolk in the family. In counseling, the family may object to sending their children for counseling or may interfere in the counseling process by asking to attend the sessions or to obtain information about them. The relationship between the client and the therapist may be influenced by factors related to the meaning, interpretation, and intervention inherent in traditional healing practices. Consequently, the presence of a family member during therapy sessions, while achieving the cultural expectation of the individual client and family, may lead to questions about the efficacy of such interpretation, intervention, and understanding. A similar challenge is the presence of an interpreter in the therapy room. While such a practice might be helpful in elucidating a more thorough information gathering, it can disrupt normal counselor-client interactions, including transference and countertransference interactions for those therapists who work from a psychodynamically informed model. The presence of a family member or a translator in the therapy process adds complexity to the therapy process and can cause role confusion and role expectations for both therapist and client (Sayed, 2003b). These issues need to be explored and dealt with in therapy. More accurate communication between the therapist and the clients would require understanding of linguistic and cultural variations embedded in the Arab clients' conceptualization of mental illness and health.

The UAE culture encourages individuals to obey authority figures such as parents and those who are in powerful positions such as teachers and doctors. Therefore, in therapy, clients expect physicians and psychotherapists to have the power to cure them or

solve their problems. This is another culture-laden perspective arising from traditional respect for people perceived to be in authority. Doctors should know everything, just as clan or tribal leaders do, and should be able to provide support and authority in different cultural situations (Sayed et al., 1998). Clients are expected to take a passive stance and not challenge what the doctor orders. They conform, as they do with their elders, tribal leaders, and individuals perceived to be powerful, as they are expected to be passive and to accept current psychotherapeutic practices and applications.

Male and female relationships are regulated through marriage according to Islamic principles. Marriage is a family affair, and therefore, individuals have to obtain their family's approval before getting married. The interference of the family in the life of the couple and the lack of premarital counseling for the couples may result in martial conflicts and divorce, especially among young couples. The high divorce rate in the UAE indicates a need for couple and marriage counseling to help protect the unity of new families in the UAE. Currently, those who have marital conflicts can mostly obtain help through marital-guidance offices developed by the courts. Providers of such services typically employ religion-based interventions such as reminding husbands and wives of their responsibilities and rights.

Women in the UAE have received considerable support to play an active role in the development of society. Based on the UAE Constitution, women have been encouraged to seek as high a level of education and career as men. The General Women's Union was established in 1975 with the main objectives of activating women's role and participation in all aspects of life, assisting women by removing obstacles hindering their participation in the development of society, increasing awareness about women's issues and concerns, and advocating that decision makers establish new laws to ensure that women enjoy their full rights as prescribed by law and religion. Women's participation in the workforce is considered low even though female graduates greatly outnumber male graduates. There are several reasons for this phenomenon. First, the number of economically active males over 15 years (2.12 million in 2003) far exceeds the female figure (365,000), mainly due to foreign workers' being predominantly male. Second, some workplaces prefer to hire more males than females. Third, UAE society is patriarchal, and the changing of traditional views concerning a women's place in the family and in society is a slow process that seems to affect women's careers and participation in the labor force. Fourth, women's educational choices and career paths are highly determined by their families. Women usually work in traditional female occupations such as education, the health sector, and social affairs. Recently, women were encouraged to be involved in careers that are considered nontraditional as women's occupations, such as engineering, medicine, finance, information technology, social sciences, police force, and the army (Ministry of Information and Culture, 2006). Working women are expected to balance their roles as personal (as wives and mothers) and professional (as part of the workforce). In addition, they are expected to sacrifice their careers when conflicts arise between work and family obligations.

The diversity in the UAE population, along with globalization, technology, the influence of other cultures (e.g., Western culture), the economical boom, and changes in living, has led the society to experience many changes in response to these factors. Among these changes are changes in social life, gender roles, job requirements and expectations, family structure, values, and attitudes. These changes seem to have created problems for some individuals such as unemployment, stress, depression, relationship issues, marriage and couple issues, behavioral problems, a gap between the generations, and role conflict. The need for counseling and psychotherapy came about as a result of these changes, difficulty adjusting to these changes on the part of some individuals, and the need to seek other methods of treatment that are less stigmatizing than psychiatry. Three types of counseling have gained prominence: career counseling, for helping individuals deal with career issues; marriage and couples counseling, for marital problems; and school counseling, for student behavioral problems.

BUILDING ON A VACUUM: WAYS TO INTEGRATE WESTERN PSYCHOLOGY AND NON-WESTERN PRACTICES

We were both directly influenced by Western perspectives in our training as counseling/clinical psychologists. Our personal and professional journey, navigating simultaneously two or more cultures, has opened our eyes to the fundamental role that culture plays in psychology. With the growing interest in cultural traditions, ethos, and practices, it is especially important to examine potential mismatches between the cultural context of our training and the cultural traditions surrounding our practice of psychotherapy. Our struggle is one of an existential nature and is exhibited in our dealing with concepts ranging from idioms or metaphors and other linguistic phenomena to identity formation and even to the conceptualization of mental distress. There is little evidence that Western communities share Eastern traditions of healing; as such, no claim should be made about Eastern cultures having the same Western cultural underpinnings pertaining to counseling practices, assumptions, and implications.

For example, as counselors in an Arab world, in dealing with our clients from different racial, religious, and tribal backgrounds within the UAE, we have come to question the validity of some of the Western assumptions of psychotherapy and discourse. How can we be of help to our clients who expect us not only to help them with psychopathologies but to be culturally sensitive to their existence, religion, way of life, and societal fabric? In other words, the value of our help is limited by the hybrid identity and acculturation brought about by our exposure to the Western model of healing. In the words of Marsella (2005),

The importation of popular Western culture to Middle Eastern cultures becomes more than "harmless" importation of clothing, food, and entertainment, it becomes a threat to a traditional fabric of life rooted within a culturally constructed reality embedded in a religion that penetrates all aspects of daily life and behavior. (p. 657)

At the same time, there is a vacuum, not within so-called Western psychology, but enveloping efforts to bring other practices of a psychological nature to help deal with the complexity of human existence in cultures with vastly different norms, customs, and values. And at times, there have been seemingly difficult implications arising from the *accidental* ignorance on the part of Western psychologists of other people's cultural traditions, ethos, values, and social construction of reality (however eager these psychologists were to integrate cultural matter into their psychological practices). Obviously, there are more questions than answers to this situation that we have confronted during our cultural journey.

In this chapter, we discuss some of the hurdles that we encountered as Western-trained therapists working with our indigenous populations and how Western therapeutic models fail to generalize to some Middle Eastern cultures such as are found in the UAE. The next section addresses the following distinct yet interrelated strands: (a) help-seeking behavior, (b) conceptualization of mental illness, (c) communication style and the use of metaphors in expressing psychological discomfort, (d) current practices and applications, and (e) barriers and challenges in the provision of mental health services in the UAE culture.

HELP-SEEKING BEHAVIOR

In the Arab culture, individuals may not seek proper professional help due to fear of self-disclosure, as self-disclosure may signify to them a betrayal of the individual's family and/or might be seen as an unequivocal declaration of weakness (Al-Darmaki, 2003a; Sayed, 2002). Whether to seek or not seek psychological help is largely determined by parents and other male members in the family (e.g., older brothers). Seeking professional help is viewed as a family affair, and it is up to the family to encourage or discourage their children to receive counseling or other mental health assistance when needed.

In addition, the lack of awareness of the availability of mental health services, combined with the stigma of seeking psychological help, seems to affect the help-seeking behavior of Arabs from all classes. That is, it is not just the poor, the disadvantaged, and disenchanted who do not enter therapy in the UAE, but also people of the educated class, who typically seek help privately, travel to a different country, or wait until it is too late for intervention to work effectively. In addition, when they do seek therapy, they make it difficult for the counselor to help by employing a negative attitude or by invoking a power differential by virtue of their wealth and status in society. Because of the closely knit family configurations, middle- and upper-class individuals avoid seeing counselors from their own country and opt to see counselors who have little knowledge of the intricate underlying mechanisms of their culture, consequently doing themselves a disservice.

In the UAE, mental health services were established in the mid-1970s, and these services were in the form of psychiatric services in some emirates (e.g., Abu Dhabi, Dubai). In the 1980s, psychological services were viewed as supportive services in the treatment of clients who were receiving psychiatric help at the hospitals (Al-Darmaki, 2004b). The need for the provision of psychological services in UAE society became prominent as a result of the rapid social and economic changes that have taken place within the last 30 years, in addition to the external influences of other cultures. Such changes seem to affect the values, beliefs, and role expectations of individuals, which may, in turn, effect their psychological health, especially for those who may not be able to adjust to these changes (Al-Darmaki, 2003a, 2005). Despite the governmental effort to establish competent mental health services in the UAE, this effort seems to be hindered by the shortage of practitioners who are professionally and culturally competent (Al-Darmaki & Sayed, 2004). In addition, the prevailing medical-treatment model of practice in the UAE, together with the tendency of the public to seek help from religious or faith healers, seems to contribute to the underuse of mental health services in the UAE. This, in turn, impinges on the importance of service delivery in the society at large. Public trust in mental health services and providers seems to be affected by the observed increase in malpractice by individuals who are not professionally competent. The absence of a licensing board, standards of practice, and a professional association to regulate the provision of services seems to contribute to malpractice and to the public's negative attitude toward seeking professional psychological help (Al-Darmaki & Sayed, 2005). Future research needs to explore these issues. However, a recent study on college students from UAE University revealed that students with more education and art-related majors reported more tolerance of stigma and more confidence in the psychological help received from providers (Al-Darmaki, 2003a).

CONCEPTUALIZATION OF MENTAL ILLNESS

In Arab culture, mental illness is viewed within the medical model. Clients suffering from mental health problems are usually treated with pharmacotherapy. Psychotherapy and counseling are considered "just talk" and, viewed as such, are not regarded as curative. Talking to a therapist or counselor is not viewed as a valuable method to bring about the desired change. Seeking the expertise of a psychotherapist is seen as weakness or a shameful event that might bring disgrace to the family (El-Islam, 1998; Okasha, 2000; Sayed, 2003a, 2003b).

A widely used and acceptable method of treatment of sickness in UAE society is traditional healing, which is provided by a religious individual called a *Mutawaa*. This person often employs nonmedical, nonpsychological methods of treatment such as using readings from the *Qur'an* and employing traditional medicine. This method of treatment was the only known method of treatment of mental health illness in the UAE prior to the formation of the seven emirates in 1971 (Al-Darmaki, 2004b). This type of treatment involves the belief that this treatment will drive the "evil spirit" and "evil eye" away and cure the person who is ill. This belief comes from the Arabic conceptualization of mental illness as having a *jinni* (devil) taking over and changing one's life (Sayed et al., 1998). Although modern medical practices are widely accepted, it is

observed that many people in the UAE would consider this traditional method of healing over modern medical or psychological treatment because of its acceptability in the society and the prevailing belief of the evil possession of the ill. Embracing of both traditional healing methods and modern medical practices is termed *cognitive tolerance* by Younis (n.d.). The coexistence of seemingly contradictory values (within the same culture or individual) may account for persons' attitudes toward seeking psychological help from both mental health providers and traditional healers with little discomfort.

Mental illness is also considered as a sign of weakness in the individual's faith. Therefore, a person should strengthen his or her relationship with Allah through prayers and readings from the *Qur'an* to achieve psychological comfort and peace of mind. Therefore, psychological treatment would be considered as the last avenue of treatment or when severe psychopathology is evident. In many cases, individuals are referred to psychiatric care through the emergency room or a general practitioner. This tendency to seek faith or traditional healers is embraced and encouraged by the society at almost all levels. The problem arises when a traditional healer narrows his or her intervention to an understanding that mental illness is caused by demonic possession, and therefore by intervening in a spiritual manner, the cure is subsequently achieved. It has been observed that some of the positive results purportedly gained from going to see a traditional healer are embedded in the type of psychopathology presented and the susceptibility of the individual for cure. It also relieves the individual from the fact that the illness is externally created, and therefore no feeling of shame is experienced. However, for an experienced and money-driven traditional healing practice, the consequences for the individual may reach catastrophic proportions. Almost all our readers are familiar with the simple therapeutic premise: the earlier the intervention, the better the curative outcome. Unfortunately, some people in the UAE who have some psychiatric symptoms (therefore the strong argument for demonic possession) tend to delay seeking proper care or seek care only when it's too late and their condition has begun to take a chronic path. In these situations, families' feeling of shame start to exasperate them and the ensuing conclusion is to leave their "beloved ones" behind in a restricted ward probably for the rest of their life.

The choice of treatment method is usually controlled by the family of the ill, and the family assumes the role of the guardian to explain the symptoms and complaints to the health care providers. The client sits passively while the assigned family member describes to the therapist the major complaints which, from our experience, are communicated as malingering because she or he is not "obedient" or "hangs with the wrong crowd." This issue obviously creates challenges to the treatment of mental illness in the Emirates and other cultures. Sometimes, doctors will use their power differentiation to prescribe a therapeutic intervention, which is culturally accepted, as doctors, or *hakims* (a physician who is a philosopher), are assumed to know everything (if not, why would they be doctors?) (Sayed et al., 1998).

According to the medical model, patients would characteristically communicate their symptoms and complaints to physicians, who would then diagnose the problem(s) and prescribe medication. Individuals who seek mental health services in the UAE would expect the same course of action when visiting other practitioners. Therefore, they may get discouraged or exasperated by the strategies used by psychotherapists, especially if the intervention requires revealing family secrets and self-disclosure. Therapists who treat Arab clients may need to spend more time explaining the therapy process to their clients and explore their role expectations about the process before hand.

In addition, many clients would express their psychological symptoms in the form of physical complaints (somatization) to avoid the stigma attached of being mentally ill. The use of somatization in the face of stigma can serve many purposes. Apart from escaping and being unduly described as mentally ill, this avenue of expression is culturally sanctioned and allows the client to escape from being branded mentally ill. Being mentally ill may have the connotation that one is not following religious practices or is possessed by a jinni. The link between bodily

symptoms and the use of somatization as a metaphor to convey psychological distress in the absence of demonstrable organic bases has been established in some Arabian Gulf countries. For example, in the UAE, El-Rufaie, Abuzied, Bener, and Al-Sabosy (1999) reported a high prevalence of somatized mental disorders as compared with psychological disorders.

COUNSELING IMPLICATIONS AND STRATEGIES FOR ARABS IN THE UAE

Most mental health services in the UAE are provided within hospital settings. Some hospitals in the UAE are dedicated to providing comprehensive mental health services for both inpatients and outpatients. These are located in major cities such as Abu Dhabi, Dubai, and Ras Al-Khaimah. Other hospitals have outpatient clinics and units for hospitalization. These facilities are well established, and their services are professionally trusted because it is viewed that their intervention is emanating from a medical model. Other mental health services are provided within the educational setting (e.g., counseling centers, school psychological services, and community mental health services).

The services provided by these agencies would typically involve individual counseling, group therapy, and other psychological services. However, for the latter, despite their purported approaches to counseling (i.e., employing interventions, orientation to counseling that includes remediation, outreach, and the use of paraprofessionals and consultation), they often lack an integrated, systematic approach to counseling and therefore are not functioning in a meaningful fashion. These agencies typically lack the necessary resources that make them useful to the extent desired (e.g., well-trained practitioners).

According to our experience and observation, and our involvement in the development of such interventions, we have witnessed an increased demand for mental health services as well as a need for a competent mental health system in the UAE. For example, the number of clients seen at the UAE University counseling center is increasing when compared with the number of clients who sought services 6 years ago when the center started providing its services to students. The clients seen at the UAE University counseling center have showed interest in receiving therapy and working with their therapists to achieve their treatment goals. Yet some clients have expressed concerns about confidentiality and interference of their parents in their treatment (e.g., refusing the referral of their children to psychiatric care).

Our experiences highlight the utility of adopting Western perspectives of confidentiality in a culturally different population. How one deals with multiple therapeutic relationships and conforms to the therapists' role in Arab cultures such as the UAE involves a number of cultural nuances, none of which are discussed in Western theoretical models. This seemingly naive posture—from a Western perspective—gives relief to the client who, working from a communal model of healing, sees no contradiction; and their *passivity* is regarded as culturally sanctioned. Psychotherapists would be considered inefficient if they failed to meet clients' expectations.

Helping Arab clients to be active participants in their own therapy and to make them express their feelings and concerns would be very difficult and challenging for many therapists. In general, the UAE culture does not encourage its people to express their emotions or focus on the self. Individuals tend to focus on themselves in relation to others (e.g., the family), and in therapy, they are more comfortable bringing up nonpsychological issues (e.g., academic, career issues).

STATUS OF THE COUNSELING PROFESSION IN THE UAE

The counseling profession in the UAE is relatively new. Counseling has not been seen as a valuable method of mental health treatment until recently, due to some cultural and social factors (e.g., viewing mental illness within the medical model, stigma of mental illness, family interference, and acceptance of traditional methods of healing). Counseling is provided within educational settings, hospitals, and community mental health agencies. Depending on the objectives of each setting, services may involve individual or group therapy, career counseling, couples counseling, and other psychological help. Clients are seen for issues such as psychological concerns, academic difficulties, family-related issues, and career concerns. These settings usually lack resources (e.g., well-trained practitioners). Help providers are mainly social workers and psychology paraprofessionals (Al-Darmaki & Sayed, 2005; Sayed, 2003a).

Counselors in the UAE are trained at the bachelor's level due to many reasons, such as the observed increasing need for the provision of counseling in the society and the unavailability of graduate programs in counseling (Al-Darmaki, 2004a). Graduates of these programs typically work in schools, hospitals, social support services, and university counseling centers.

Counseling research has focused on issues such as counseling training (e.g., Al-Darmaki, 2004a), attitudes toward seeking professional help (e.g., Al-Darmaki, 2003a), and other counseling-related issues (e.g., Al-Darmaki, Al-Etir, & Nassar, 2004; Al-Darmaki & Sayed, 2005). There is no specialized journal for counseling research in the UAE and, to our knowledge, the counseling services we have established at UAE University can be considered as pioneering work (Al-Darmaki, 2003b).

Initial steps toward establishing a professional organization in the UAE have been taken by some counseling practitioners. This initiative seems to reflect an interest in developing counseling as a recognized profession in UAE society, in addition to an awareness of the importance of promoting the role of counseling in dealing with counseling-related issues resulting from globalization, diversity, and rapid changes (e.g., social, economic, cultural) experienced by individuals in UAE society (Heppner, Leong, & Gerstein (2008).

Although the counseling profession in the UAE is promising, it faces many challenges, such as a shortage of professionally and culturally competent practitioners. The absence of a licensure board, accreditation bodies, standards of practice, and a professional association to regulate the provision of counseling services seems to contribute to malpractice and to negative attitudes toward seeking professional psychological help (see Al-Darmaki & Sayed, 2005, for more discussion).

CONCLUSION

There is a limited availability of competent mental health community resources in the UAE despite the increased awareness of the need for mental health services and the increased realization of the impact of mental problems on both the individual and society (Al-Darmaki & Sayed, 2004). Moreover, there is a need for indigenous models of counseling to guide counselors to provide culturally sensitive services based on the customs and values in traditional Emirati society, specifically services that address the role of the family, psychosomatic illness, religion, and emotional control.

The family (Jackson, 1991; Soliman, 1991) in the UAE culture as well as in other Arab cultures plays a significant role in the life of its members. It is the expectation that each member of the family expresses loyalty to the family and protects its honor beyond what is expected from his or her counterpart in other cultures. Moreover, the family is viewed as the main source of emotional, social, and financial support to its members. Males are given the role of heading the family, and most significant decisions and affairs (e.g., marriage, education, career, choice of medical treatment) are typically undertaken by the fathers or the brothers. In the UAE, there is often confusion in therapy with regard to role expectations and the client-therapist relationship (see Sayed, 2003a, 2003b, for more discussion). Consequently, it is more normative for people to express psychological problems in the form of physical concerns in order to avoid the stigma of being mentally ill (Al-Darmaki, 2003a, 2004a; El-Rufaie et al., 1999; Sayed, 2002). Whether to seek or not seek psychological help is largely determined by parents and other male figures in the family (e.g., older brothers). Thus, models of psychological help in the UAE must incorporate the role of the family, and particularly elder males in the family, as well as psychosomatic dimensions, to a much greater degree than Western models of counseling.

The perceived role of religion (Jackson, 1991; Nasser-McMillan & Hakim-Larson, 2003) is not only relegated to the practice of faith in the UAE and other Muslim cultures, it is a way of life, as values stem from religious prescriptions and their interpretations. In addition, Muslims believe that all events are controlled by Allah and that sickness and health come from Allah and from Allah only. In therapy, Muslim clients may not only deal with psychological distress but also with the guilt feelings stemming from the belief that they must have done something to deserve their distress (Sayed et al., 1998). Thus, future models of counseling interventions must include a religious dimension in the UAE.

The cultural code concerning the expression of emotions (Al-Darmaki & Sayed, 2004; Cook, 1990) in general does not lend itself to individuals in the UAE expressing their emotions either publicly or in front of others. Perhaps therapists in the UAE need to encourage clients to express their emotions, teach them how emotions affect their overall well-being, or examine other models of emotional regulation that emphasize emotional control.

Finally, in the UAE, the absence of a governing board or an agency to regulate mental health services through standards of practice in the community seems to have greatly affected the quality of services offered in addition to the occurrence of cases of malpractice.

REFERENCES

Al-Darmaki, F. (2003a). Attitudes towards seeking professional psychological help: What really counts for United Arab Emirates University students? *Social Behavior and Personality: An International Journal, 31*, 497–508.

Al-Darmaki, F. (2003b). *Handbook of the counseling services unit at UAE University*. Al-Ain, United Arab Emirates: UAE University Press.

Al-Darmaki, F. (2004a). Counselor training, anxiety, and counseling self-efficacy: Implications for training of

---

Authors' Note: The authors share equal responsibility for the content in this chapter. A randomization procedure was used to determine the order of authorship.

psychology students from the United Arab Emirates University. *Social Behavior & Personality: An International Journal, 32*(5), 429–440.

Al-Darmaki, F. (2004b). *Mental health care in UAE since the formation of Al-Itihad.* Al-Ain, United Arab Emirates: UAE University Press.

Al-Darmaki, F. (2005). Counseling self-efficacy and its relationship to anxiety and problem-solving in United Arab Emirates. *International Journal for the Advancement of Counseling, 27,* 323–335.

Al-Darmaki, F., Al-Etir, F., & Nassar, K. (2004). Adolescents' problems in Abu Dhabi Emirate in the United Arab Emirates. *Journal of Humanities and Social Sciences, 20*(1), 108–145.

Al-Darmaki, F., & Sayed, M. (2004, July 28–August 1). *Practicing polymorphism in traditional gender-role Emirates: Conflict and challenges.* Symposium conducted at the 112th annual meeting of the American Psychological Association, Honolulu, HI.

Al-Darmaki, F., & Sayed, M. (2005, August 18–21). *Mental health services in the UAE: In search for a paradigm.* Symposium conducted at the 113th annual meeting of the American Psychological Association, Washington, DC.

Cook, E. P. (1990). Gender and psychological distress. *Journal of Counseling & Development, 68,* 371–375.

El-Islam, M. F. (1998). Clinical applications of cultural psychiatry in Arabian Gulf communities. In S. O. Okpaku (Ed.), *Clinical methods in transcultural psychiatry* (pp. 155–170). Arlington, VA: American Psychiatric Press.

El-Rufaie, O. E. F., Abuzied, M. S. O., Bener, A., & Al-Sabosy, M. M. A. (1999). Somatized mental disorder among primary care Arab patients: Possible determinants. *Arab Journal of Psychiatry, 10,* 50–57.

Fabregat, M. (2006, June 21–24). *Metaphor in psychotherapy: From affect to mental representation.* Paper presented at the 37th annual meeting of Society for Psychotherapy Research, Edinburgh, Scotland.

Heppner, P. P., Leong, F. T. L., & Gerstein, L. H. (2008). Counseling within a changing world: Meeting the psychological needs of societies and the world. In W. B. Walsh (Ed.), *Biennial Review in Counseling Psychology* (pp. 231-258). Thousand Oaks, CA: Sage.

Kjeilen, T. (2007). *United Arab Emirates. Encyclopedia of the Orient.* Retrieved February 23, 2007, from http://www.i-cias .com/e.o/uae_5.htm

Jackson, M. L. (1991). Counseling Arab American. In C. C. Lee & B. L. Richardson (Eds.), *Multicultural issues in counseling: New approach to diversity* (pp. 197–206). Alexandria, VA: American Counseling Association.

Marsella, A. J. (2005). Culture and conflict: Understanding, negotiating, and reconciling conflicting constructions of reality. *International Journal of Intercultural Relations, 29,* 651–673.

Ministry of Information and Culture. (2006). *UAE yearbook 2006.* Retrieved February 23, 2007, from http://www.uaeinteract.com

Nasser-McMillan, S. C., & Hakim-Larson, J. (2003). Counseling considerations among Arab Americans. *Journal of Counseling & Development, 81,* 150–159.

Okasha, A. (2000). The impact of Arab culture on psychiatric ethics. In A. Okasha, J. Arboldeda-Florez, & A. Sartorius (Eds.), *Ethics, culture, and psychiatry* (pp. 15–28). Washington, DC: American Psychiatric Press.

Sayed, M. A. (2002). Arabic psychiatry and psychology: The physician who is philosopher and the physician who is not a philosopher: Some cultural considerations. *Social Behavior and Personality: An International Journal, 30,* 235–242.

Sayed, M. A. (2003a). Conceptualization of mental illness within Arab cultures: Meeting challenges in cross-cultural settings. *Social Behavior and Personality: An International Journal, 31,* 333–342.

Sayed, M. A. (2003b). Psychotherapy of Arab patients in the West: Uniqueness, empathy, and "otherness." *American Journal of Psychotherapy, 57,* 445–459.

Sayed, M. A., Collins, D. T., & Takahashi, T. (1998). West meets east: Cross-cultural issues in inpatient treatment. *Bulletin of the Menninger Clinic, 62,* 439–454.

Soliman, A. (1991). The role of counseling in developing countries. *International Journal for the Advancement of Counseling, 14,* 3–14.

Younis, F. (n.d.). *Cultural interference: A reply from psychology.* Unpublished manuscript, United Arab Emirates University, Al-Ain, United Arab Emirates.

36

Counseling in Turkey

A Blend of Western Science and Eastern Tradition

Türkiye'de danışmanlık:
Batı biliminin Doğu geleneğiyle harmanlanması

DENİZ CANEL ÇİNARBAŞ,
FİDAN KORKUT OWEN, AND AYŞE ÇİFTÇİ

Turkey is a young country with a short history of counseling. Perhaps due to their short histories, Turkey and Turkish counseling have been going through several changes and shifts. In this chapter, topics such as culture, mental health, help seeking, indigenous healing methods, and personal and professional issues are discussed as they relate to counseling in Turkey.

BACKGROUND AND CULTURE

Turkey has gone through significant changes in the past 100 years. With the collapse of the Ottoman Empire and the establishment of the new Turkish Republic in 1923, secularism became the official ideology of the state (Çarkoğlu & Toprak, 2000; Engin-Demir, 2003). There have been major historical-cultural influences on Turkish society,

including nomadic-Turkish, Anatolian, Islamic–Middle Eastern, and the Mediterranean (Kağıtçıbaşı, 1982). The establishment of the new Turkish Republic by Atatürk in 1923 accelerated the Westernization trend, which started during the last decades of the Ottoman rule. There are differences in the values brought by Atatürk (e.g., modernism, rationalism, science, secularism, social and legal equality, and justice) and the values inherited from the Ottoman Empire (e.g., seniority, obedience to authority, dominance of traditions, and customs over civil rules) (Köse, 2001). As a result of the Westernization trend, Turkish culture demonstrated a shift from collectivism to individualism (Mocan-Aydın, 2000). According to Hofstede (1980), collectivist societies emphasize emotional dependence, group solidarity, and sharing, whereas individualistic societies emphasize autonomy, emotional independence, and privacy. Despite the cultural shift toward individualism, Turkish cultural values still promote respect toward figures of authority (Mocan-Aydın, 2000).

Turkey has a population of approximately 67 million. Forty four million Turkish people live in the cities, and 23 million live in rural areas and small villages (Turkish Statistical Institute, 2000). The level of education is relatively low in Turkey. In 2000, only 41% of boys and 34% of girls were enrolled in secondary schools (Turkish Statistical Institute, 2000). The figures for university graduates are even lower. Approximately 4.7% of men and 2.6% of women have degrees from higher-education institutions (Korkmaz, n.d.). Cimilli (1997) reported that Turkey has high child death rates and a low energy consumption per capita. The yearly per capita income was $2,160 in 2000 (Turkish Statistical Institute, 2000). Approximately 97% of the population is Muslim (Çarkoğlu & Toprak, 2000), and 90% of those are from the Sunni sect (Engin-Demir, 2003).

According to Cimilli (1997), premodern and modern characteristics coexist in Turkish society. In premodern societies, collectivism is promoted, the extended family system is predominant, and individuals tend to be fatalistic, believing that events are determined by fate. Modernity, on the other hand, promotes determinism, scientific thinking, and individualism. In modern industrialized societies, individuals populate the cities more than they do the rural areas, live in nuclear family units, and emphasize independence and freedom. Turkey, both geographically and culturally, exists between the East and West and combines traditional and modern lifestyles (Cimilli, 1997).

Cimilli (1997) stated that Turkish society has witnessed increased migrations from the rural to the urban areas in the last 50 years. Although migration to the cities has increased social mobility for some, many individuals have experienced difficulty finding jobs and housing and have had little access to education. Thus, the society at large has not yet made the shift to becoming fully industrialized and has continued to display the characteristics of premodern societies.

Although the political structure shifted from autocracy to democracy in 1923, certain characteristics of the governing bodies remained the same. Both the Ottoman Empire, which ruled the area for more than 600 years, and the government of the Turkish Republic were centralist and authoritarian. In authoritarian governments, there is a distinct divide between the ruling cadres and the citizens. The ruling caste does not allow the development of local powers and encourages dependency. The expression of individual views and creativity is discouraged (Cimilli, 1997). The shift to democracy, however, brought a shift toward individualism and modernism. This amalgamation of values shapes current Turkish society as well as the society's understanding of mental health.

MENTAL HEALTH, HELP SEEKING, AND COUNSELING

Cultural and Religious Constructions of Mental Health, Help Seeking, and Helping

In Turkey, mental health services are underused, and there is a paucity of mental health service providers (Demir & Aydın, 1997). For example, there are 398 mental health units and psychiatric wards (Health Ministry of Turkey, 2002) or 1 mental health unit per 168,000 people. In contrast, in the United States, there are 4,546 mental health units and psychiatric wards, or 1 mental health unit per 61,000 people (National Center for Health Statistics, 2004).

Many cultural factors, such as religion, the stigma associated with mental illnesses, and the preference for indirect expression of emotions, may contribute to the underutilization of mental health services in Turkey. Cimilli (1997) discussed the relationship between culture and the mental health problems in Turkey. He indicated that in Turkey individuals are more likely to express depression in terms of somatic (i.e., bodily) symptoms. Similarly, Üstün and Sartorius (1995) stated that depression and somatization are the most common presenting problems among Turkish clients. It can be argued that based on Hofstede's (1991) classification, Turkish society is a "tight society" where consensus, harmony, social context, and indirect expressions of emotions are valued. Therefore, it is not surprising that somatization as an indirect expression of emotion is prevalent in the Turkish society (Üstün & Sartorius, 1995). Moreover, displaying somatic symptoms helps individuals avoid the stigma of mental illness and obtain social support (Al-Issa, 2000). Consequently, individuals tend to seek help from medical practitioners for somatic symptoms rather than seek help from mental health practitioners.

The high prevalence of somatic symptoms among Turkish clients can also be explained by the cultural view regarding the unity of mind and body. According to this view, mind and body interact with one another. In the same way, biological and psychological diseases are parallel to one another (Broom, 2002). Nasr (1987) stated that according to Islam, body and soul are closely related and the state of health is achieved through harmony and equilibrium. Islamic medicine is also holistic and promotes the health of both body and spirit. Similarly, the holy book of Muslims, the *Qur'an*, has a direct healing effect on the body and the spirit (El-Kadi, 1993). Religious leaders often use basic principles of Islam, such as praying and reading the *Qur'an*, to help and support people with mental illness (Koptagel-İlal & Tuncer, 1981). Hence, many Turkish Muslims seek help from religious leaders rather than mental health practitioners.

Islamic humoral theory, which has four elements of air, earth, fire, and water, is salient among Muslim countries and Muslim immigrants in Europe (Al-Issa, 2000). Many Turkish immigrants consider good air and water to be beneficial to their health. They visit hot springs with the understanding that their health will improve.

Moreover, the Muslim worldview emphasizes the notion of receiving illness and death with patience, meditation, and prayers (Rassool, 2000). Muslims believe that illness, suffering, and dying are part of life and a test from Allah. Illness is perceived as atonement for sins, an event that serves to purify and balance people physically, emotionally, mentally, and spiritually (Rassool, 2000). Thus, Turkish individuals tend to view suffering as a purifying process and consider help seeking as a weakness.

Indeed, the stigma of mental illness is quite strong among the general public as well as health care providers. Academicians, resident physicians, and nurses were found to have a negative attitude toward patients with mental illness in spite of their sufficient knowledge and training (Aydın, Yiğit, İnandı, & Kırpınar, 2003). In a similar study, Taşkın et al. (2003) found that the public in rural areas can recognize schizophrenia, yet they tend to have negative attitudes and an increased social distance toward patients with schizophrenia.

There also seems to be a stigma attached to receiving mental health services. Even though people in urban areas are more likely to receive mental health services, the majority of the people in Turkey still rely on their strong family relationships, friendship networks, and indigenous healers for social support and treatment (Bolak-Boratav, 2004). In a study of Turkish individuals' help-seeking behavior carried out by Ünal and colleagues (2001), 12.3% of participants reported having gone to traditional healers, 32.5% had visited medical doctors, and 32.5% had visited psychiatrists for their problems.

In another study, Yaşan and Gürgen (2004) found that 57% of psychiatry clinic patients and 15% of rehabilitation clinic patients sought help from indigenous healers. Relıgous healing methods were most sought after. The most frequent diagnosis was possession by a *cin* (or genie), and the most common treatment recommended was to carry amulets. Cins are believed to be created by Allah. According to the *Qur'an*, although some cins worship Allah, others are associated with the evil spirit (Ateş, n.d.). These findings indicate that seeking help from indigenous and relıgous healers is rather frequent and the stigma against seeking help from mental health professionals is still strong.

Cultural factors also play a role in the kind of help that Turkish clients seek from mental health practitioners. Turkish individuals are taught to respect and obey figures of authority, such as parents, teachers, or professionals such as counselors. Hence, Turkish clients tend to expect the counselors to give specific and concrete advice and are willing to follow such advice. Turkish clients prefer directive, action-oriented counseling approaches, such as cognitive-behavioral therapy (Mocan-Aydın, 2000). Moreover, due to the collectivist nature of the society, Turkish clients prefer group-based interventions (Vassaf, 1983).

Clients from small villages differ in their counseling preferences from clients from metropolitan areas (Vassaf, 1983). Vassaf stated that clients from rural areas preferred counselors with a cultural background similar to theirs. Similarly, clients from rural areas did not feel understood by counselors from an urban background. Vassaf concluded that directive behavioral approaches and preventive mental health interventions are more effective with clients of a rural background. Clients from metropolitan areas, on the other hand, may be more receptive to therapy approaches that focus on emotions, insight, and self-exploration.

In summary, cultural characteristics such as collectivism, religion, and a stigma against mental illnesses shape Turkish individuals' attitudes toward seeking help. Turkish individuals tend to use mental health services only after exhausting all other resources, such as religious services, medical services, friends, and family. On the other hand, Westernization has been a strong trend in Turkish society, and there is a shift toward individualism. Turkish culture can be described as a unique combination of Eastern and Western cultural characteristics. Therefore, Turkish people who are more individualistic and more Westernized may be more comfortable seeking help from mental health service providers. Consequently, a purely Western framework of counseling may still be suitable to meet the needs of some Turkish individuals.

Indigenous Beliefs and Practices in Help Seeking and "Helping"

In addition to religious and cultural factors, pre-Islamic indigenous beliefs and practices shape Turkish people's help-seeking behavior. Indigenous practices such as visiting sacred places, tying ribbons on trees, and carrying amulets are widespread among Turkish individuals. Many Turkish people visit sacred places and tombs to pray and to give *adak* (i.e., to make vows) to a deceased religious leader (Koptagel-İlal & Tuncer, 1981). For instance, according to a common belief among the local people, three Muslim brothers who were leading a war against non-Muslims died and were buried in Sivas, a city located in the central part of Turkey (Gökbel, n.d.). Today, travelers and local people visit their burial place, pray, and sacrifice animals, such as sheep, as *adak*, dedicated to the souls of the deceased leaders. Visitors share the meat of the sacrificial animal with other visitors, friends, and family members.

Çarkoğlu and Toprak (2000) investigated religious practices as well as the use of indigenous healing methods of Turkish individuals. They found that 52.7% of respondents visited sacred places and tombs. Islamic scholars, however, argue that giving *adak* to a deceased person is against Islamic rules and *adak* should only be dedicated to Allah (*Kabirlere Kurban Adamak*, n.d.). In agreement with Islamic scholars, Artun (n.d.) indicated that visiting sacred places and giving *adak* are in fact pre-Islamic practices.

Before adopting Islam, Turks followed shamanistic and animistic belief systems (Artun, n.d.). According to animistic beliefs, all living and nonliving beings have souls. If the soul leaves the body, the body dies. However, the soul stays around the body and continues to live. Thus, people should respect the soul of the deceased and present gifts and food (Tezcan, 1997). Similarly, it was believed that wise leaders' souls continue to help and protect their people after death (Artun, n.d.). Today, Turkish people still pray for the souls of their ancestors and give *adak*.

According to the belief systems of pre-Islamic Turks, trees were symbols of life and eternity. Trees were protected and respected for the power they represented (Artun, n.d.). A current indigenous practice is to tie ribbons and pieces of cloths on trees to make wishes. Another common indigenous practice is having religious leaders write prayers on amulets and carrying these amulets on one's body. It is believed that these amulets bring good luck and protect the wearer from illnesses. Çarkoğlu and Toprak (2000) reported that 11.8% of the participants in their survey of religious practices used amulets. Tying ribbons on trees, visiting sacred places and tombs, and giving *adak* are practiced to heal mental illnesses, to alleviate marital and family problems, and to wish for a job or for marriage. Though the prayers on amulets are usually written by Islamic religious leaders, Islamic scholars argue that such practices are against Islamic rules (*Üfürük ve Muska*, 2004).

Beliefs about psychological health and distress in Turkish society involve a blend of Islamic and indigenous principles and practices. Islam has been the predominant belief system among Turkish people for centuries. Although Turkish people still practice shamanistic rituals, Islamic beliefs tend to be stronger than shamanistic beliefs.

Integration of Western and Indigenous Healing Methods in Counseling

Despite the common use of indigenous and religious healing methods, few mental health practitioners integrate indigenous approaches and Western approaches. A Turkish psychiatrist, Dr. Mustafa Merter (personal communication, September 19, 2000), uses both Western therapy techniques and religious healing methods to help his clients. He organizes retreats and blends breathing techniques and meditation, which are practiced in the Mevlevi order as well as various Sufi traditions (Friedlander, 2003), with guided imagery and talk-therapy techniques. He instructs the clients about breathing techniques and joins his clients in practicing meditation as a group. Following meditation sessions, he instructs his clients to look at their parents' childhood photographs and imagine interacting with their parents as children. He then invites the clients to share their experiences and perceptions of their parents with the group.

Although some Turkish individuals may use both indigenous and Western counseling methods, models that systematically integrate these two methods do not exist. Moreover, no known empirical study has investigated the outcome of indigenous healing methods. Consequently, the gap between the indigenous healing approaches and Western approaches to

mental health is significant. The authors of this chapter believe that many mental health practitioners would favor the use of Western approaches and would frown on the use and integration of indigenous methods. Turkish mental health practitioners are usually trained in Western approaches. They may believe that indigenous healing methods are not grounded in the scientific approach, and, thus, their effectiveness cannot exceed the placebo effect. The authors hope that the therapeutic factors embedded in the indigenous healing methods will be recognized by Turkish mental health practitioners and that research into the outcome of such methods is generated.

AN OVERVIEW OF COUNSELING IN TURKEY

Despite the existence of indigenous approaches to mental health, more recent and scientifically rooted indigenous approaches to psychology and counseling are rare (Kağıtçıbaşı, 1994; Öngel & Smith, 1999), and there does not appear to be a movement toward indigenization of psychology and counseling in Turkey. A content analysis of 152 articles from the *Turkish Journal of Psychology* revealed that Turkish researchers rely on Western models, research paradigms, and theories (Öngel & Smith, 1999). The content analysis also showed that U.S. theories and perspectives are most widely used in Turkish psychology and counseling.

On the other hand, there is evidence of a strong tendency toward empirical studies focusing on Western models and theories. Başaran and Şahin (1990) reviewed 139 articles that were published between 1977 and 1990. They found that 44% of the articles were in the area of clinical psychology, 15% in experimental psychology, 11% in social psychology, and 10% in development psychology. After 1981, research projects focused mainly on social perception, social cognition, attribution, and human development (Kağıtçıbaşı, 1996, as cited in Karakaş & Çakmak, 2001). In addition, there has been an increase in the number of research articles published in international journals. Nevertheless, studies that review counseling-related research are not available.

As stated at the beginning of this chapter, counseling has a rather short history in Turkey. Counseling training programs offer specialization only in school counseling. Almost all counselors work in the education system. There are no programs that offer specialization in counseling psychology or mental health counseling. Several factors may have prevented the emergence of counseling psychology in Turkey. Clinical psychologists are the largest group of psychologists who provide mental health services. There tends to be tension between clinical psychologists, counselors, and psychiatrists as to who should provide mental health services. Clinical psychologists and psychiatrists seem to have more influence over the field of mental health than do counselors. This competitive environment, combined with the underutilization of existing services (Demir & Aydın, 1997), has led counseling to be confined to schools. Therefore, the history of counseling will be discussed in the context of school counseling.

The Turkish counseling movement started in the 1950s and has been influenced by movements and advances in counseling in the United States. Doğan (2000) divided the history of counseling in Turkey into five periods: (1) taking initial steps (1950–1956), (2) formative years (1957–1969), (3) establishing counseling services in schools (1970–1981), (4) establishing undergraduate programs in counseling (1982–1995), and (5) assigning counselors to schools (1996 to the present). During the first period, the Ministry of National Education (MONE) offered scholarships for teachers to study abroad. During the second period, the first educational psychology and guidance department and graduate programs in counseling were established. During 1970 and 1971, the third period, MONE employed counselors to work in secondary schools. During the fourth period (1982–1995), the first undergraduate program in counseling was established, followed by six other universities admitting students to undergraduate programs in guidance and counseling. During the fifth period (1996–present), many significant developments took place. For example, the chairs and cochairs of counseling departments held a meeting regarding the reconstruction of counseling programs. They aimed to standardize counselor education programs at the undergraduate and graduate levels. However, though the standardization process was held back due to legal complications, several universities continued to work toward this goal.

Counselor Training Programs in Turkey

Although there is a strong drive toward standardization, counselor education in Turkey needs an organizational structure within which to establish its professional identity (Doğan, 2000). At present, standardized criteria have not been established for selection of counseling students for counselor education programs. Turkey does not have formally recognized requirements for certification as a professional counselor, and procedures are not yet in place for official accreditation of undergraduate and graduate training programs. Finally, a specialty title and definition for counseling need to be established.

Under current structures, only the Turkish Psychological Counseling and Guidance Association (TPCGA) and Higher Education Council (HEC) are involved in standardization and accreditation activities. In 1995, the TPCGA developed ethical standards for the counseling profession to raise the standards of the profession (Korkut, 2007a). That year, TPCGA members stated that there is a discrepancy between the job descriptions of counselors and the curricula of counselor education programs. Moreover, they agreed that there are disparities among universities in terms of the content of counseling courses (Akkoyun, 1995).

A total of 66 counseling programs are offered in 39 universities. Most of these universities are public universities. Only two private universities offer counseling programs. There are 31 undergraduate degree programs, 21 master's degree programs, and 14 doctorate degree programs (Korkut-Owen, 2007). Although undergraduate training tends to focus on school counseling (Doğan, 2001; Korkut, 2007a), some counselor educators argue that counselor education must be at the graduate level (Kuzgun, 2000). Others, largely because of a desperate need for counselors, advocate that an undergraduate degree is sufficient to practice as a counselor (Akkoyun, 1995). Master's-level training is used as an intermediate step toward doctoral work or as a necessary degree for working as an administrator of guidance services in schools. A doctoral degree is necessary for becoming a counselor educator or a consultant for MONE.

Counselor training in Turkey is somewhat influenced by the American model of counselor education (Doğan, 2000). Graduate and undergraduate counseling programs offer training in developmental approaches, preventive approaches, and cognitive-behavioral theories. Students take many courses in counseling skills and guidance techniques. On the other hand, although counselors who work in the school system are expected to provide career counseling, Korkut (2007b) reported that one out of every four counselors had never taken a formal course in career counseling. In counselor education programs, clinical practice courses are generally limited in scope and fail to provide extensive opportunities for skill development. Efforts are under way to provide more extended practicum opportunities.

In terms of psychologists, members of the Turkish Psychological Association (TPA) founded a commission to initiate the legislative process for accreditation of undergraduate and graduate psychology training programs and the credentialing of professional psychologists. This commission prepared a manuscript for legislation. The manuscript was sent to parliament in 2004, starting the process to legally recognize psychology as a profession ("TPD Yasa çalışması konusunda bilgilendirme," n.d.). The TPCGA also prepared a manuscript for legislation in 2007 and presented it to parliament ("PDR Meslek Odasına Doğru," n.d.).

Contemporary Role of Counselors in Turkey

Counselors play a large role in the Turkish school system. The number of schools that have counseling services has been increasing. There are 42,897 primary and secondary schools, 13,042,247 students, and 12,470 counselors. In addition, 931 counselors work in 148 Guidance Research Centers (Korkut, 2007a). Other institutions, such as the Turkish Employment Organization (İŞKUR), General Directory of Security, Ministry of Justice, Ministry of Health, Ministry of Labor and Security, and Special Education and Rehabilitation Centers, also employ counselors. Private practice is not common among counselors (Korkut, 2007a).

Counselors and school administrators differ in their understanding of the roles and functions of the school counselor (Baker & Gerler, 2004). Several researchers found that the roles and functions of counselors in the school system are not clear (Akbaş, 2001; Deniz, 1993; Paskal, 2001) partially because administrators, who do not know counselors' roles and functions (Nazlı, 2007), define many of the school counselors' tasks and assignments. In their respective studies, Akbaş, Deniz, and Paskal referred to the Turkish MONE's (1985) definition of counselors' roles and functions. According to this definition, the counselors provide consultation to classroom teachers in administering school guidance and counseling programs; provide necessary resources, materials, and tools for measurement; evaluate programs together with other teachers and improve the programs as needed; inform the parents about the programs; and design guidance and counseling programs based on a school's needs and conditions. Baker and Gerler, on the other hand, referred to the American School Counselor Association's (ASCA, 2004) definition of counselors' roles and functions. According to ASCA, some of these roles and functions are implemented in the school guidance curriculum in collaboration with other educators. Furthermore, counselors help students in establishing personal goals and future plans; provide preventive or remedial services to meet students' immediate and future needs; and establish, maintain, and enhance school counseling programs. Despite the existence of such definitions, Turkish counselors frequently assert that they are frustrated because of competing demands and the expectations of the school principals. Therefore, it is important that the counselor and the administrator share a common view of the guidance program and the counselor's role.

Counselors typically work at elementary and secondary schools. Some of the issues and tasks that require counselors' attention are adjustment issues, educational guidance such as guidance and support for the university entrance exam, career guidance, test anxiety, stress, issues surrounding friendships and romantic relationships, Internet addiction, and family issues. Counselors usually conduct guidance programs and psychoeducational programs in groups of 10 or more. They rarely provide individual counseling. If individual counseling is required, it is typically limited to two or three sessions. Solution-focused techniques and cognitive-behavioral techniques are commonly used. Counselors may also meet with the parents and teachers to collaborate in helping students.

On the other hand, psychologists may also work within the educational system and at schools, and they provide similar services as counselors. Due to the lack of established professional standards, the roles and functions of counselors and psychologists may overlap. Yet psychologists typically work at hospitals and mental health clinics and provide therapy to adults and children, whereas counselors are limited to providing guidance and career counseling in school settings.

CROSSING CULTURES: PERSONAL AND PROFESSIONAL ISSUES

Amid legal difficulties and the stigma against mental illness it is somewhat courageous to choose counseling as a profession in Turkey. Moreover, counselors face financial difficulties as well as difficulties in finding jobs. Some of the Turkish universities (such as the Middle East Technical University) require that the academic faculty have a degree or at least 10 months of postdoctoral research/training experience from a Western country (usually the United States). Thus, it is common for graduate students to seek education opportunities abroad. The first and third authors of this chapter have continued their graduate education in counseling psychology in the United States. Although students do go to the United States to pursue academic goals, they also hope to learn a new culture, improve their English, build

relationships with host nationals, and teach others about their own culture (Barratt & Huba, 1994; Yang, Teraoka, Eichenfield, & Audas, 1994).

Being a Turkish psychology student in the United States can be a both enriching and challenging experience. Learning Western counseling and bringing it back to Turkish culture requires continuous adaptation. There are challenging situations in which to decide between culturally sensitive counseling and ethical and appropriate counseling. The emphasis on individualism and an autonomous self is not consistent with Turkish culture. For example, a single adult living with his or her family may be perceived as a well-functioning individual in Turkish culture.

Similarly, a culturally sensitive client-counselor relationship may raise ethical questions according to Western psychology. For instance, due to the collectivist nature of Turkish society and the respect for hierarchy, Turkish clients are likely to expect more permeable boundaries with the counselor. For instance, a Turkish counseling psychology intern at a college counseling center stated that a Turkish client referred to her as *abla* (older sister) and asked for her personal phone number to call for social activities. Similarly, it is customary to bring a gift as a way of showing respect. However, accepting a gift from a client may go against Western ethical guidelines for counseling. Conversely, in Turkish culture it will be perceived as disrespectful to not accept the gift.

After getting training in the United States, the question about whether to go home or stay in the United States can be a challenging one. Whether practicing counseling or teaching at a university, Turkish counseling professionals who go back to Turkey are faced with the difficulty of adjusting their training to Turkish culture. Those who stay in the United States are faced with new challenges, such as negotiating cultural differences (e.g., now from a faculty member perspective) in student-faculty and coworker relationships, language, and workplace norms.

THE FUTURE

The history of counseling in Turkey is filled with legal, financial, and professional obstacles. The future, it is hoped, will be brighter. Yeşilyaprak (2007) expects that counseling in Turkey will continue to change in many ways. Moreover, Yeşilyaprak predicts that there will be an increased focus on developmental issues and the preventive function of counseling, more emphasis on solution-focused therapies, and an increase in the use and acceptance of indigenous models of counseling. The present authors believe that Turkey's European Union membership application will also influence the continuing evolution of counseling in Turkey by accelerating the legal process toward the accreditation of counseling programs and the licensure of mental health practitioners.

The authors also hope that there will be a trend toward the indigenization of counseling. Such indigenization can be accomplished through encouraging and financing research projects that focus on religious and indigenous practices as well as the relationship between cultural characteristics and help seeking. Similarly, psychology and counseling training programs can offer undergraduate and graduate courses that emphasize Turkish cultural values and characteristics and their effect on mental health issues. Ultimately, it is the present authors' hope that Turkish counselors will overcome the obstacles they face and that they will be able to provide help to those in need.

REFERENCES

Akbaş, S. (2001). *İlköğretim ve ortaöğretim okullarındaki rehberlik hizmetlerinin yürütülmesinde oluşturulan işbirliğinin incelenmesi: Adana Örneği* [Cooperation in elementary and secondary schools for counseling and guidance services: The example of Adana]. Unpublished master's thesis, Çukurova University, Adana, Turkey.

Akkoyun, F. (1995). Psikolojik danışma ve rehberlikte ünvan ve program sorunu: Bir inceleme ve öneriler [The problems of job title and training programs in psychological counselling and guidance: A review and recommendations]. *Psikolojik Danisma ve Rehberlik Dergisi, 2*, 1–28.

Al-Issa, I. (2000). The mental health of Muslim immigrants in Europe. In I. Al-Issa (Ed.), *Al-Junun: Mental illness in the Islamic world* (pp. 253–274). Madison, CT: International Universities Press.

American School Counselor Association. (2004). *The role of the professional school counselor.* Retrieved July 31, 2008, from http://www.schoolcounselor.org/content.asp?pl=325&sl=133&contentid=240

Artun, E. (n.d.). *Çukurova konar-göçer Türkmenlerinin halk kültürlerinde eski Türk inançlarının izleri* [Traces of old Turkish beliefs in Çukurova nomadic Turkmens' culture]. Retrieved July 2, 2007, from http://www.turkoloji.cu.edu.tr/HALKBILIM/artun_konar_gocer.pdf

Ateş, S. (n.d.). *Kur'an-ı Kerim ve yüce meali* [Qur'an and its holy meaning]. Ankara, Turkey: Kılıç Kitabevi.

Aydın, N., Yiğit, A., İnandı, T., & Kırpınar, I. (2003). Attitudes of hospital staff toward mentally ill patients in a teaching hospital, Turkey. *International Journal of Social Psychiatry, 49*, 17–26.

Baker, S. B., & Gerler, E. R., Jr. (2004). *School counseling for the twenty-first century* (4th ed.). Englewood Cliffs, NJ: Prentice Hall.

Barratt, M. F., & Huba, M. E. (1994). Factors related to international undergraduate student adjustment in an American community. *College Student Journal, 28*, 422–436.

Başaran, F., & Şahin, N. (1990). *Psychology in Turkey: Country status report. Social and human sciences in Asia and the Pacific* (RUSHAP Series, 34). Bangkok, Thailand: UNESCO.

Bolak-Boratav, H. (2004). Psychology at the cross-roads: The view from Turkey. In M. J. Stevens & D. Wedding (Eds.), *Handbook of international psychology* (Vol. 19, pp. 311–330). New York: Bruner-Routledge.

Broom, B. C. (2002). Somatic metaphor: A clinical phenomenon pointing to a new model of disease, personhood, and physical reality. *Advances in Mind-Body Medicine, 18*, 16–29.

Çarkoğlu, A., & Toprak, B. (2000). *Türkiye'de din, toplum ve siyaset* [Religion, society, and politics in Turkey]. Istanbul, Turkey: TESEV Yayınları.

Cimilli, C. (1997). Depresyonla ilişkileri bağlamında Türkiye'nin sosyal ve kültürel özellikleri [Social and cultural characteristics of Turkey in the context of their relation to depression]. *Türk Psikiyatri Dergisi, 8*, 292–300.

Demir, A., & Aydın, G. (1997). Student counselling in Turkish universities. *International Journal for the Advancement of Counselling, 18*, 287–302.

Deniz, Z. (1993). *Liselerdeki yönetici, sınıf öğretmeni ve ders öğretmenlerinin psikolojik danışma ve rehberlik hizmetlerine ilişkin beklentilerinin bazı değişkenlere göre incelenmesi* [Investigation of high school administrators' and teachers' expectations regarding psychological counseling and guidance services based on certain variables]. Unpublished master's thesis, İnönü University, Adana, Turkey.

Doğan, S. (2000). The historical development of counselling in Turkey. *International Journal for the Advancement of Counselling, 22*, 57–67.

Doğan, S. (2001, September). *Invitation for reconstruction of counseling programs.* Paper presented at the annual National Conference of Counseling and Guidance, Ankara, Turkey.

El-Kadi, A. (1993). Health and healing in the *Qur'an.* In S. Athar (Ed.), *Islamic perspectives in medicine. A survey of Islamic medicine: Achievements and conteporary issues* (pp. 117–118). Indianapolis, IN: American Trust.

Engin-Demir, C. (2003). Secularism and education in Turkey. In E. P. Quntero & M. K. Rummel (Eds.), *Becoming a teacher in the new society: Bringing communities and classrooms together* (pp. 256–278). New York: Peter Lang.

Friedlander, S. (2003). *Rumi and the whirling dervishes.* New York: Parabola Books.

Gökbel, A. (n.d.). *Gürün'deki ziyaret yerleri* [Sacred visiting places around Gürün]. Retrieved November 23, 2004, from http://www.cumhuriyet.edu.tr/akademik/fak_ilahiyat/der62/001.htm#_ftnref4

Health Ministry of Turkey. (2002). *Temel Sağlık İstatistikleri* [Basic health statistics]. Retrieved January 20, 2004, from http://www.saglik.gov.tr

Hofstede, G. (1980). *Culture's consequences: International differences in work-related values.* Beverly Hills, CA: Sage.

Hofstede, G. (1991). *Cultures and organizations: Software of the mind.* London: McGraw-Hill.

Kabirlere kurban adamak [Sacrificing animals at tombs]. (n.d.). Retrieved November 23, 2004, from http://www.sevde.de/Hurafeler/Kabirlerde_kurban.htm

Kağıtçıbaşı, Ç. (1982). *Sex roles, family, and community in Turkey.* Bloomington: Indiana University Turkish Studies 3.

Kağıtçıbaşı, Ç. (1994). Psychology in Turkey. *International Journal of Psychology, 29*, 729–738.

Karakaş, S., & Çakmak, E. D. (2001). Psikoloji bilimi: Ülkemizde, Üniversitemizde ve Dünyada'daki Durum [Psychological science: Status in our country, university, and the world]. In B.Yediyıldız (Ed.), *Atatürk'ün ölümünün 62. yılında cumhuriyet Türkiye'sinde bilimsel gelişmeler Sempozyumu 8–10 kasım 2000* [Scientific developments in Turkish Republic Symposium for 62nd anniversary of Atatürk's death, November 8–10, 2000] (pp. 41–60). Ankara, Turkey: Hacettepe University.

Koptagel-İlal, G., & Tuncer, C. (1981). *Proceedings of the 13th European Conference on Psychosomatic Research.* Istanbul, Turkey: Bozak Basımevi.

Korkmaz, M. (n.d.). *Türkiye'de nüfus artışı ve genç nüfusuneğitim sürecindeki görünümü* [Population increase in Turkey and the young population in the educational process]. Retrieved September 11, 2007, from http://yayim.meb.gov.tr/dergiler/medergi/18.htm

Korkut, F. (2007a). Counselor education, program accreditation and counselor credentialing in Turkey. *International Journal for the Advancement of Counselling, 29*, 11–20.

Korkut, F. (2007b). Psikolojik Danışmanların Mesleki Rehberlik ve Psikolojik Danışmanlıkla İlgili Görüşleri. [Counselor's thoughts and practices related to career guidance and counseling]. *HÜ E itim Fakültesi Dergisi, 32*, 187–197.

Korkut-Owen, F. (2007). Professionalism in counseling and counselor education: Current status in the United States, European Union Countries and Turkey. In R. Özyürek, F. Korkut-Owen, & D. W. Owen (Eds.), *Pathways to professionalism in counseling* (pp. 95–122). Ankara, Turkey: Nobel Yayınevi.

Köse, M. R. (2001). Toplumsal cinsiyet, eğitim ve çocuk işgücü [Gender-based education, employment, and child labour in Turkey]. *ILO-IPOC ve Çalışma ve Sosyal Güvenlik Bakanlığına sunulmuş yayınlanmamış rapor* [Unpublished report of International Programme on the Elimination of Child Labour International (ILO-IPOC) and Turkish Ministry of Labor and Social Security, Ankara, Turkey].

Kuzgun, Y. (2000). *Mesleki danışma: Uygulamalar-Kuramlar* [Career counseling: Practices-theories]. Ankara, Turkey: Nobel Yayınevi.

Ministry of National Education. (1985). Rehberlik Hizmetleri Yönetmeliği [Regulations for guidance services]. *Tebliğler Dergisi, 48*, 2201.

Mocan-Aydın, G. (2000). Western models of counseling and psychotherapy within Turkey: Crossing cultural boundaries. *The Counseling Psychologist, 28*, 281–298.

Nasr, S. H. (1987). *Science and civilization in Islam* (2nd ed.). Cambridge, UK: The Islamic Texts Society.

National Center for Health Statistics. (2004). *Health, United States, 2004: With chartbook on trends in the health of Americans.* Washington, DC: Government Printing Office.

Nazlı, S. (2007). Okul yöneticilerinin rehberlik ve psikolojik danışma hizmetlerini algılamaları [School principals' perception of the guidance and counseling service]. *Eğitim Araştırmaları Dergisi, 26,* 281–290.

Öngel, U., & Smith, P. B. (1999). The search for indigenous psychologies: Data from Turkey and the former USSR. *Applied Psychology, 48,* 465–479.

Paskal, K. (2001). *İlkö retim okulu müdürlerinin bu okullarda görev yapan rehber öğretmenlerin görevleri ve rehberlik hizmetleri ile ilgili bilinçlilik düzeyleri* [Primary school principals' knowledge of school counselors' responsibilities and guidance services]. Unpublished master's thesis, Marmara University, İstanbul, Turkey.

PDR Meslek Odasına Doğru [Toward becoming a legal profession]. (n.d.). Retrieved September 11, 2007, from http://www.pdr.org.tr/tr/?Sayfa=Icerik&Id=18

Rassool, G. H. (2000). The crescent and Islam: Healing, nursing and the spiritual dimension. Some considerations towards an understanding of Islamic perspectives on caring. *Journal of Advanced Nursing, 32,* 1476–1484.

Taşkın, E. O., Şen, F. S., Aydemir, Ö., Demet, M. M., Özmen E., & İçelli, I. (2003). Public attitudes to schizophrenia in rural Turkey. *Social Psychiatry and Psychiatric Epidemiology, 38,* 586–592.

Tezcan, M. (1997). *Kültürel Antropoloji* [Cultural anthropology]. Ankara, Turkey: Kültür Bakanlığı.

TPD Yasa çalışması konusunda bilgilendirme [Briefing about TPA's legislative efforts]. (n.d.). Retrieved September 11, 2007, from http://www.psikolog.org.tr

Turkish Statistical Institute. (2000). *Istatistikler* [Statistics]. Retrieved January 18, 2004, from http://www.tuik .gov.tr

Üfürük ve Muska [Breathing on the person and amulets for healing]. (2004). Retrieved November 24, 2004, from http://www.sozluk.sourtimes.org

Ünal, S., Özcan, Y., Emul, H. M., Çekem, A. B., Elbozan, H. B., & Sezer, Ö. (2001). Hastalık açıklama modeli ve çare arama davranışı [Illness explanatory model and help-seeking behaviour]. *Anadolu Psikiyatri Dergisi, 2,* 222–229.

Üstün, T. B., & Sartorius, N. (1995). *Mental illness in general health care: An international study.* New York: Wiley.

Vassaf, G. Y. H. (1983). Conflict and counselling: Psychological counselling with university students in the emerging nations—Turkey. *School Psychology International, 4,* 31–36.

Yang, B., Teraoka, M., Eichenfield, G. A., & Audas, M. C. (1994). Meaningful relationships between Asian international and U.S. college students: A descriptive study. *College Student Journal, 28,* 198–215.

Yaşan, A., & Gürgen, F. (2004). Psikiyatri ve fizik tedavi polikliniklerine başvuran hastaların geleneksel yardım arama davranışının karşılaştırılması [The comparison of patients who were admitted to psychiatry versus rehabilitation clinics in terms of traditional help-seeking behavior]. *Dicle Tıp Dergisi, 31,* 20–28.

Yeşilyaprak, B. (2007). The role of Turkish Psychological Counseling and Guidance Association in the development of psychological counseling and guidance in Turkey. In R. Özyürek, F. Korkut-Owen, & D. W. Owen (Eds.), *Pathways to professionalism in counseling* (pp. 95–122). Ankara, Turkey: Nobel Yayınevi.

OCEANIA

37

At the Crossroads

Counseling Psychology in Australia

WENDY PATTON

The counseling profession in Australia is still emerging. There is no statutory regulation of counseling practice, and any individual can engage in counseling practice and assume the title of "counselor" (Pelling, Brear, & Lau, 2006). In addition, there are a number of professional associations that purport to promote and develop the profession of counseling, these associations being linked to specific areas (e.g., school counseling, dance therapy) or particular geographical locations (e.g., state-based professional associations). Very little data have been gathered on the profession as a whole, and "as a result, little is known about Australian counselors, who they are, and what they do" (Pelling et al., 2006, p. 205). In contrast, where the practice of counseling is linked with psychology, there is much tighter regulation—as psychology is a legally regulated profession in Australia—and much greater recognition of the professional status of the field. While this is so, counseling psychology itself is at a crossroads in Australia. There have been recent changes in recognition of the work of a psychologist in relation to how government health insurance

rebates are distributed to psychologists; these have resulted in differential funding levels being applied to practitioners in clinical psychology relative to other specialized psychology groups (e.g., counseling psychology, educational and developmental psychology). These changes have marginalized the field of counseling psychology, which is currently working through the challenges of reinvention to create for itself a sustainable place in Australian psychology.

This chapter focuses on counseling psychology in Australia as there are very little data on the general counseling profession. Following a presentation of some relevant background on Australia as a country, this chapter presents a definition of counseling psychology as established by the Australian national peak body for psychologists, the Australian Psychological Society (APS), and outlines the roles of the counseling psychologist in Australia. Major themes within the professional and empirical counseling psychology literature in Australia are discussed, including the impact of the scientist-practitioner model, the relationship between clinical and counseling psychology, and the relationship between counseling psychology and other counseling professional developments (e.g., career counseling). Suggestions for the future viability of the counseling psychologist within the Australian context will be proffered.

THE AUSTRALIAN CONTEXT

The Commonwealth of Australia comprises six states and two internal territories: Queensland, New South Wales, Victoria, South Australia, Tasmania, Western Australia, the Australian Capital Territory, and the Northern Territory. The system of government is a parliamentary democracy with three levels of government: federal, state or territory, and local. There are more than 20 million people in Australia, most of whom live in the major coastal cities and regional centers. Most Australians live within 50 kilometers of the coast, with approximately 66% in major cities, 31% in inner and outer regional areas, and 2.6% in remote and very remote areas (Australian Bureau of Statistics [ABS], 2007c). The indigenous population at June 30, 2001, was 458,500, with the largest proportion of indigenous people living in the Northern Territory (28.8%) (ABS, 2007c). Less than 1% of the indigenous population speaks an Australian indigenous language. English is the official language of Australia, although one in four Australians was either born in a non-English-speaking country or has at least one parent from such a country. At least 16% of the population speaks a language other than English at home. The five most commonly spoken languages other than English are Italian, Greek, Cantonese, Arabic, and Vietnamese. Greek, Arabic, and Italian speakers constitute the largest group of Australian-born, second-language speakers as these languages were largely brought to Australia more than 20 years ago (ABS, 2007c).

Australia has enjoyed positive economic growth for a number of decades, as measured by the gross domestic product, consumption and investment data, housing finance approvals, incomes, and unemployment rates. Currently, Australia's unemployment rate is the lowest for more than 30 years, with a rate of 4.1% at January 2008 (ABS, 2008). In 2005, Australia's labor force participation rate for those aged 15 to 64 years was 76%—above the OECD (Organisation for Economic Co-operation and Development) average (70%) for that year, but below some other OECD countries, including Sweden, Canada, New Zealand, and the United Kingdom. Data from the ABS (2007b) also indicate that life expectancy has increased from 1995 to 2005, that Australia's real net worth per capita rose, and that in the same period, more Australians obtained a nonschool qualification. The recent Adult Literacy and Life Skills Survey (ABS, 2007a) also indicated a slight increase in adult literacy levels.

Locating and Conceptualizing Counseling Psychology in Australia

The APS is the largest professional group of psychologists in Australia. It is the primary voice of Australian psychologists and the body charged with developing and advocating for the profession. It oversees the nine specialist colleges that its members can join. These include clinical neuropsychologists, clinical psychologists, community psychologists, counseling psychologists, educational and developmental psychologists, forensic psychologists, health psychologists, organizational psychologists, and sports psychologists. APS members who are not members of specialist colleges maintain the status of psychologist, albeit without a specialist affiliation. A number of interest groups have also formed under the auspices of the APS. From January 2006, the Australian Psychology Accreditation Council (APAC)—which is a collaboration between the APS and all six Australian states' and two territories' psychologist registration boards—became the body that assesses and approves the minimum qualifications set by recognized schools of psychology in universities for registration as a psychologist (a process that remains with individual geographical states and territories within Australia) and for membership of the APS. Therefore, prospective psychologists who require this dual accreditation must complete accredited programs.

Counseling psychology in Australia is a relatively new profession, with the first recorded discussion within the APS in 1970, prior to the formation of the Division of Counselling Psychologists in 1976 (which became the College of Counselling Psychology in 1993) (Brown & Corne, 2004). The first chairman of the division, Clive Williams, commented that in establishing this specialized branch of psychology, Australia drew on theory and practice models adopted predominantly in the United States (Williams, 1978). Williams noted that the focus of counseling psychology during the 1970s in Australia was based on the triple emphasis in the United States on rehabilitative, educational/developmental, and preventive counseling. He emphasized that Australia's focus was educational/developmental and preventive, and included a focus on the distinctive needs of target populations and procedures. He commented on the move in counseling psychology to become differentiated from clinical psychology and the move "from a focus on sickness to a focus on wellness" (p. 35).

Australian culture tends to favor an "It'll be all right" approach to personal problems, with the preferred strategies being to draw on family and friends or to seek no support rather than access professional intervention. This is changing, albeit slowly. For example, in 1986 Sharpley reported that only 28% of Australians indicated a willingness to pay for services from counselors as opposed to psychologists (counseling and clinical) or psychiatrists. In 2004, Sharpley, Bond, and Agnew reported that this figure had increased to 78% and included counselors and counseling and clinical psychologists, although in this survey, Australians were most likely to see a psychologist for anxiety, phobias, eating disorders, and sexual dysfunction and less likely to see one for family and marital issues and related interpersonal problems. It is these latter areas that are largely the perceived work of the counseling psychologist. The College of Counselling Psychologists (CCP) Web site describes the following as key skills of the counseling psychologist in Australia: counseling and psychotherapy, health and life management, program development and evaluation, conflict resolution, career development, assessment and reports. The definition of the *counseling psychologist* is as follows:

Counselling psychologists employ a wide range of therapeutic methods, each of which places a significant emphasis on the quality of the relationship between the client and the psychologist. They assist individuals, families and groups in areas related to personal wellbeing, interpersonal relationships, work, recreation and health. They are also trained to assist people experiencing both acute and chronic life crises. (APS, 2007a)

Data from the ABS (2003) indicate that settings for the employment of counselors and counseling psychologists include health and community services (39.6%), education (29.5%), property and business services (10%), and government and administrative services (10%). Within these contexts, counselors and counseling psychologists are employed in general counseling, community support services, human resources, employee assistance, and school counseling. Patrick (2005) reported that while the economic contribution of the psychology activity to the overall economy has increased between 1991 and 2001, "individual income for psychology declined over this period, and still lags 9.2% behind related professional groups" (p. 157). That is, income to individuals from the practice of psychology is less than income to individuals in related professions, such as psychiatry, mental health nursing, social work, counseling, and human resources. Patrick argued that psychologists need to stimulate value and demand by advocating for the relevant cost-benefit nature of their work. Recent changes in government health insurance rebates for psychological services, a major change in government policy, have been the result of this advocacy by the national psychological society (the APS). Littlefield (2007) reported that in the first 7 months of the Better Access to Mental Health Care initiative, 595,131 individual psychology items (services) were provided by psychologists to Australians. This initiative may well stimulate the profession of psychology in Australia through the existence of a government rebate to individuals for accessing psychological services. However, the new initiative has only been operational for 1 year, and any detailed data on the increased use of psychology services are not yet available.

Training and Professional Development

To register as a psychologist in Australia, individuals need to complete 4 years of APAC accredited undergraduate study, followed by either an accredited postgraduate program or 2 years of supervised practice as a psychologist. Undergraduate study can comprise either an integrated 4-year qualification, or a 3-year qualification with an additional 4th year. Supervised practice is administered by the Registration Board in each state or territory. There are only a few accredited postgraduate training programs in Australia specifically for counseling psychologists; currently there are only 5 counseling psychology master's programs in the whole country, as compared with 28 master's programs in clinical psychology (APAC, 2007a).

The College of Counselling Psychology, which operates within the APS, has its own additional requirements for membership. Professional development activities, fulfilled annually, have been part of the APS individual colleges' membership requirements since 1997. As of July 1, 2007, for the first time all APS members holding a grade of Associate Member or above are required to formally complete and document professional development activities as part of their ongoing membership, irrespective of whether they are a member of a specialist college. Psychologist registration boards in states and territories around the country have also signaled that there will be professional-development requirements for ongoing registration in the near future. Such requirements enhance the professional accountability of psychologists and are in keeping with the APS Code of Ethics in the area of competence.

Postgraduate training programs in counseling psychology in Australia cover the following areas: (a) developing the therapeutic alliance, including with people from different cultures and indigenous peoples; (b) culturally sensitive and appropriate assessment, especially with a view to acknowledging indigenous and migrant clients; (c) knowledge and skill in applying at least one research-based therapeutic intervention; (d) professional communication skills; and (e) ethics and the importance of ongoing professional development and supervision.

KEY PROFESSIONAL ISSUES

A number of key issues continue to be features of the profession of counseling and counseling psychology in Australia. These include the adherence to, benefits of, and issues associated with the scientist-practitioner model, and the relationship between counseling psychology and clinical psychology. Generally, Australia has adopted North American models in the training of psychologists and the practice of psychology. However, the past decade in psychology has seen a newly emerging focus on indigenous and multicultural approaches. Yet there is still a sparse literature in this area, and many training programs continue without a particular focus on indigenous and multicultural issues at their core (Ford, 2003).

Evidence-Based Practice

The scientist-practitioner model, the basis of the education and training of psychologists and of the practice of psychology, is well established in North America, Australia, New Zealand, and the United Kingdom (Vespia, Sauer, & Lyddon, 2006). Indeed, the standards for accreditation developed by the APAC, the body that assesses and approves the minimum qualifications from schools of psychology, specify that the fifth and sixth years of professional education in psychology "should be based on the scientist-practitioner model" (APAC, 2007b, p. 32). There is a long history to the adoption of this model, and in part it has contributed to the clinical psychology-counseling psychology schism. In discussing the historical background of professional psychology in Australia in the very first issue of the *Australian Psychologist*, Want (1966) commented on the increasing focus on the training of psychologists with what he termed a *psychonomic* orientation: that is, "psychonomes—psychologists with a laboratory orientation" (p. 3) over psychologists—"whose attention is directed towards social behaviour" (p. 3). He noted the greater status afforded the former and commented on the likelihood that degree courses in psychology were likely "to be more efficient in producing psychonomes than psychologists" (p. 6).

This history may partly explain the ongoing tension between "scientists" and "practitioners" in counseling psychology in Australia. This notion of the psychologist as scientist-practitioner implies ideals of disinterested objectivity and technical competence and is often perceived as being at odds with the role of the counseling psychologist. A number of authors have asserted that the role of the counseling psychology practitioner is subsumed by the researcher focus as the attempt to embed practice in science becomes paramount (O'Donovan, Dyck, & Bain, 2001). Indeed, Brown and Corne (2004) have commented that "students who want to become counselling psychologists are frequently trained to become good researchers, particularly to evaluate the therapy that they practice, at the expense of learning therapeutic techniques" (p. 289). This assertion is also supported by a survey conducted of conditionally registered psychologists who overwhelmingly cited the need for more training in psychological testing, interventions, counseling skills, and problem evaluation (Spencer, 2004). The master's-level training program in counseling psychology requires the teaching of therapeutic techniques underpinned by "sound theory and empirical research" (APS, 2000b) for national accreditation. In addition, 25% of the overall course is allocated to research in the form of a research dissertation.

This research-practitioner divide may also be attributed to the historical connection between clinical and counseling psychology, and while clinical psychology has developed a focus on building evidence for particular techniques, counseling psychology has focused more on the therapeutic alliance, which is less evidence based as the quantification of relationships is less straightforward. Denham (2006b) defended the scientific emphasis of counseling psychology training, noting that "counselling psychology is committed to building the scientist/ practitioner guiding notion for our profession by

producing practitioners informed by research findings; (and) a science informed by practice knowledge (reflective practice)" (p. 3). He also argued for a reduction in the gulf between research and practice for counseling psychologists.

However, it is clear that the accountability agenda so closely related to government policy on funding for particular interventions that is evident in the United States (American Psychological Association, 2005) is also prevalent in Australia. Debate continues about the differential role in therapeutic outcomes attributable to the therapeutic alliance versus specific techniques (Andrews, 2000). Public perceptions and funding accountability requirements also emphasize the value of empirically supported therapies (Richards, 2001). While arguments for scientific-based practice focus on the requirement to have evidence before the use of particular psychological interventions, others argue that many treatments are not empirically investigated because existing research paradigms act as limitations to appropriate investigation. Indeed, there has been a diversity of views on evidence-based practices. Charman and Barkham (2005) have argued that evidence be derived from naturalistic practice settings. The policy document released by the American Psychological Association in 2005 emphasizes a threefold approach to evidence: empirical findings, expert opinion, and an understanding of patient characteristics. All in all, irrespective of the requirements of governments, clients, and medical-insurance bodies, the professional psychologist must ensure that the best therapy—as understood by the state of knowledge at that time—is provided.

Clinical and Counseling Psychology

In reviewing the growth of psychology in Australia to 1978, Sheehan (1978) commented, "The Counselling Division (of the APS) found it more difficult to define its competency" (p. 311). "The data in hand indicated that while the Clinical Division emphasized its technical knowledge base more than the Counselling Division, the Counselling Division expressed more concern for the service ethic or collectivity orientation of its professional orientation" (p. 311). In discussing the formation of the establishment of a separate division of counseling psychology in Australia, Williams (1978) commented that "the development of the psycho-educational model . . . has helped clarify the role of counselling psychology" (p. 35). This move was connected to a perspective that counseling psychologists should be involved in developmental work and not only in clinical interventions. As such, counseling psychologists continue to distinguish themselves from clinical psychologists through the former's focus on the development of the therapeutic alliance with attention to the developmental needs of the client as opposed to the latter's focus on specific techniques. Like their counterparts in the United Kingdom and North America, many counseling psychologists in Australia embrace a range of approaches to their practice (Kazantzis & Deane, 1998) choosing to adopt the preferred aspects of different guiding theories for the presenting case. A survey of counseling psychologists by Poznanski and McLennan (1998) identified the following main approaches to counseling psychologists' work: cognitive-behavioral (30%), psychodynamic (17%), family systemic (11%), behavioral (8%), and eclectic (7%).

It is ironic that the separation between clinical and counseling psychologists appears to have contributed to a decline in counseling psychology in Australia. In 1979, there were 172 members in the Division of Counselling Psychology (Penney, 1981), 904 members in 1997 (Browne & Corne, 2004), and a current membership of 700 in the College of Counselling Psychology (APS, 2007b). Conversely, the numbers in the College of Clinical Psychology have continued to grow (1,292 in 2007); in fact, the College of Clinical Psychology is the only one of the nine colleges in the APS where this is the case (Browne & Corne, 2004). Research conducted by Patrick and Pretty (2004) demonstrated the stark difference in the popularity of postgraduate psychology programs: 42.4% of honors' year students preferred clinical psychology, and organizational and educational psychology came ahead of counseling psychology, which is at 7.1%. As discussed

previously, universities have continued to cancel offerings of graduate programs in counseling psychology.

Counseling psychology in Australia has been seen as a profession that is remunerated less lucratively than clinical psychology, and it has not been perceived as of equivalent status to clinical psychology since its very early beginnings (Want, 1966). The decrease in students and resulting decline in the number of university courses and the professional body memberships of the professional colleges also can be attributed to these perceptions. Another related factor in the professional reputation of counseling psychologists is the connection of the professional title with "counselor." As highlighted by Sheehan in 1978, "The main problem counsellors appear to experience is that there is a relative lack of specific skills to demarcate them from other helping professions" (p. 311). Williams (1978) also noted that the attempt to develop a counseling psychology profession distinct from clinical psychology "has led to confusion with other areas within the broad field of counseling" (p. 35), going on to say that "we are a loose mixture of guild members becoming increasingly more divergent in our training, skills, and goals" (p. 36). As discussed previously, the counseling profession in Australia is not a regulated activity, and various individuals (some without accreditation) use the title of counselor. Counseling, as a specific activity, currently has no minimum standard for training and no requirement for ongoing professional development within all professional organizations (Pelling et al., 2006).

The impact of the separation between counseling psychology and clinical psychology and the potential for further decline are exacerbated by a recently established, government mental health service rebate model that has included psychological services under Australia's Medicare (national health insurance) system for the first time, albeit within a medical model (i.e., the Better Access to Mental Health Care Initiative). Within this two-tier model, a higher government rebate is available to clients who access services from a clinical psychologist than to those who access services from a category of "general" psychologist (Littlefield, 2006; Pirkis et al., 2006).

Both the general psychological and clinical psychological services are available for a large range of clinically diagnosable disorders, including psychotic disorders, generalized anxiety, bereavement disorder, dementia, and posttraumatic stress disorder. The list of mental disorders is derived from the World Health Organization (1996) *Classification of Mental and Behavioural Disorders* (*ICD [International Classification of Diseases]-10 Primary Care Version*). The general psychological services include provision of focused psychological strategies, which include psychoeducation, cognitive behavioral therapy, relaxation therapy, skills training, and interpersonal therapy. Clinical psychologists provide these services, in addition to associated assessment with an emphasis on evidence-based techniques and therapies.

Access to psychological services has been provided through private health funds for some time; however, they only became available through the national health system from November 1, 2006. Individuals need to be referred by a medical practitioner and generally are able to receive 12 individual sessions in a calendar year. The APS-recommended fee for a session with a psychologist lasting more than 46 minutes and less than 60 minutes is AU$192 (for the period July 1, 2007, to June 30, 2008). The government schedule fee is AU$88.20 for the session provided by a "general" psychologist with the rebate to an individual currently being AU$75. The government schedule fee for the service provided by a "specialist" clinical psychologist is AU$129.40, and the rebate to the individual for the service is AU$110.

A number of writers have lamented the possible lack of a future for counseling psychology in Australia as the result of this two-tiered national health rebate system (see Denham, 2006a), which comes on top of a long historical battle for recognition. The system undermines the status of counseling psychology and acts as a further disincentive to students undertaking expensive training to enter the field. Both the Australian Psychological Society's College of Counselling Psychologists and the College of Clinical Psychologists are working together to resolve transition opportunities for

members of the Counselling College to qualify for eligibility for the Clinical College.

Indigenous and Multicultural Issues in Australian Counseling Psychology

As previously discussed, much Australian psychology has been derived from North American and European models. More recent initiatives have focused on understanding psychology from the perspectives of indigenous Australians and Australians from other cultures. In a 2004 survey on ethnicity and APS membership conducted by the APS, only 13 psychologists identified themselves as Australians of Aboriginal and Torres Strait Islander (ATSI) descent. Similarly, no more than 400 psychologists in total identified themselves as being from Africa, Asia, Central and South America, and the Middle East. These data indicate that much development of cultural competence in psychologists needs to occur, given the demographic data on Australia's population identified earlier in this chapter.

Data on numerous health and well-being indices (Australian Institute of Health and Welfare, 2005) continue to emphasize the ongoing disadvantage of indigenous Australians. A number of authors have emphasized the important role psychologists play in addressing this disadvantage, in particular in understanding the workings of racism and the generational perpetuation of cultural trauma (Dudgeon, 2000; Sanson & Dudgeon, 2000). These authors emphasize the vast differences between the philosophical underpinnings of modern psychotherapy—individualism, materialism, secularism—and the worldviews of Aboriginal culture—community, spirituality, relatedness, and connectedness (Sanson & Dudgeon, 2000). Psychology is criticized for many practices that continue to treat indigenous issues as a fringe area. Despite the *Guidelines for the Provision of Psychological Services for, and the Conduct of Research with, Aboriginal and Torres Strait Islander People of Australia* published by the APS in 2003b, much coursework in Australian psychology training programs does not take account of indigenous issues (Ford, 2003). Work to increase the indigenous cultural competence of practicing psychologists continues through the activities of the ATSI peoples and the psychology interest group of the APS (Ranzijn, McConnochie, Nolan, Day, & Unaipon, 2007). Integrating indigenous culture worldviews to forge a connected approach to counseling psychology is an important direction for the field to take in Australia. An example of a practice change to incorporate indigenous issues would be accepting that the dichotomous professional/client relationship is not relevant in indigenous culture. What is more important is the development of a relationship with the community. Counseling is akin to "yarning" a narrative, and being available for this conversation at any time is part of the preparation for a psychologist working in indigenous communities. Similarly, ethically appropriate strategies need to be developed for third-person referrals, a process that is in line with the traditional way that Aboriginal people make referrals to their own healers. Other concepts that demonstrate the differences between Aboriginal and Western understandings include suicide, which is understood as being paid back for a transgression; and "sick for country," which might manifest as depression but refers to being removed for long periods from one's birthplace.

An example of the commitment of the APS to increasing the number of psychologists from ATSI backgrounds is the offering of a bursary to alleviate some of the financial concerns involved in completing university study. The bursary is offered in the hope that the funding will make a difference to the numbers of ATSI students who graduate with a postgraduate psychology degree and who are then able to make a commitment to the profession and to the community at large. In addition, those ATSI individuals who feel that they are suffering financial hardship are encouraged to also make application for funding from a Financial Assistance Fund.

While demographic data emphasize Australia's multicultural status, cross-cultural psychology has only recently begun to be a core part of training programs, remaining in many cases an elective area of study. Like the interest group on ATSI peoples and the psychology interest group, the following interest groups work within the APS to develop an increased intercultural understanding and competence among all psychologists: the psychology and cultures interest group, and the psychology from an Islamic perspective interest group.

REINVENTING COUNSELING PSYCHOLOGY IN AUSTRALIA

In response to the challenges identified previously, counseling psychology needs to embrace its role within the broad domains of dealing with development and adjustment issues and psychoeducational approaches. Opportunities for regeneration would appear to exist in a number of areas, in particular in school psychology and in career guidance and counseling. Each of these will be discussed in turn.

The Role for Counseling Psychology in Career Guidance: Being Part of the Action

A number of countries, including Australia, have developed accreditation requirements for career practitioners related to a career-specific tertiary qualification (Career Industry Council of Australia, 2004, 2005). The psychology profession needs to be actively connected with these initiatives in the development of national quality standards for the qualifications and training of career practitioners and related accreditation in the career industry.

Postgraduate programs in career development/career counseling in Australia are almost all located in education faculties and in private colleges. A review of all Australian university psychology department Web sites, conducted by the author in 2004 (see Patton, 2005), found that only three psychology departments in Australia offer any specific studies in career development. As Australia moves toward mandated qualifications for accreditation in career development practice (to be instituted in 2012), the profession of psychology needs to reexamine its relevant graduate programs. Other countries also acknowledge these issues, for example, Dagley and Salter (2004) emphasized that in the United States, "The intensity seems to have been ratcheted upward with the increasing neglect of career counselors' training by graduate programs in counseling and psychology" (p. 38). Developments in Australia leave no doubt that psychologists will be required to have specific postgraduate training in career guidance programs recognized by the national body to be accredited and to work as career development practitioners.

With regard to psychologists' training in Australian career development practice, there are three colleges of the APS (viz., Counselling, Educational and Developmental, and Organisational) that claim career development (variously described) as a professional competency within their respective purviews. Yet a number of authors have raised doubts concerning counseling psychology's coverage of career development (Patton, 2005; Pelling, 2004). In the OECD (2002) review of career services in Australia, the APS's specialist colleges' competencies and training requirements were not identified as being sufficiently comprehensive for entry-level qualifications to the profession of career development.

In light of Patton's (2005) observation on the current postgraduate psychology training system, the relatively limited number of academics claiming career development as an area of expertise, and the APS's general principle for supervision that "members must refrain from offering advice or undertaking work beyond their professional competence" (APS, 2003a), there is a need to consider psychology's training system with regard to career development practice. The APS acknowledges that educational and developmental psychologists provide assistance in career guidance and school-to-work transition to adolescents and adults. Similarly, the CCPs' Web site names career development as one of the six skill areas of counseling psychologists. However, the guidelines developed to assist universities in preparing course submissions for postgraduate programs by the College of Educational and Developmental Psychologists (CEDP) and the CCP are silent on many of the requisite competencies to prepare psychologists to engage in career development work (APS, 2000a, 2000b). For example, the "theoretical content" competency does not include

the very significant body of career development theory, and the "knowledge areas" competency does not include any of the areas identified as required by career practitioners, such as knowledge of updated information on educational, training, employment trends, labor market, and social issues. While the core areas—such as professional issues and skills training in interviewing, counseling, consultation, assessment and planning, implementing and evaluating educational and developmental interventions—are included, any focus on an extensive career-related literature in, for example, career counseling and career assessment, is absent. Similar absences are noted in the equivalent APS guidelines for the CCPs (APS, 2000b), although it is acknowledged that educational and vocational issues may be covered in university programs through formal units or electives.

Students of professional postgraduate degrees in psychology, which are endorsed by the APS, must complete practica under supervision, and while undertaking a practicum must address the professional competencies of their chosen APS specialization. For psychologists aiming to develop career assessment and intervention skills or ultimately work in the career industry, this mandatory practicum situation is complicated by the advent of the Professional Standards for Australian Career Development Practitioners. Not only do psychologists have to comply with the APS requirements but they also have to comply with the career development practitioner professional standards if they are also to belong to a Member Association of the Career Industry Council of Australia. If APS-endorsed postgraduate degrees and the colleges' competencies for specialized psychological practice represent the most advanced form of training for Australian psychologists, then psychologists are at risk of being inadequately prepared for the current changes in the career-development industry. It is in this area that counseling psychology could stake a claim and carve a renewed niche in Australian psychology.

Counseling Psychologists in Schools

More than 2,000 psychologists currently work in schools throughout Australia (Faulkner, 2007). These psychologists are drawn from a range of APS colleges. In addition, they work as part of a larger group of professionals who perform school psychology services who are not registered psychologists, as different arrangements operate in different states across Australia. This latter group includes social workers and school counselors/guidance officers. Historically, professionals who chose to work in school counselor/psychologist roles were teachers undergoing a career change and who undertook a 1-year diploma in counseling, school counseling, or something similar. More recently, some Australian states have been employing 6-year-trained psychologists.

In addition to the variation in title and training, the role of the school counselor can also vary across states. For example, in states where the role is performed by nonpsychologists, there is a limit to the nature of the assessment that can be performed. Similarly, the role performed in the public education system can be different from that performed in a private school. Armstrong et al. (2000) conducted a review of the professional responsibilities of counselors and psychologists in public schools. Responsibilities included individual and group counseling, psychoeducational and vocational assessments and report writing, consultancy with respect to student behavior management and appropriate school-based interventions, liaison with related welfare and medical agencies, parent and family counseling, and crisis response in schools where necessary.

Competencies for practice and accreditation largely have been developed by the CEDP; however, the focus of these competencies is on life span development as opposed specifically to the school context. Frydenberg and McKenzie (2007) have argued that there needs to be a renewed focus on competencies for psychologists working in schools in Australia. Competency standards developed by the National Association of School Psychologists (NASP) in the United States could serve as a reference for the NASP-identified eight domains of competence: (1) interpersonal and collaborative skills, (2) competence in diverse areas, (3) technological skills, (4) professional, ethical, and legal competencies, as well as practice competencies, such as (5) data-based decision making, (6) systems-based service delivery, (7) enhancing

the development of cognitive and academic skills, and (8) enhancing the development of wellness, social, and broader life skills (NASP, 2006).

With the focus on counseling and advocacy in the school psychologist/school counselor role, it would seem that there is scope for counseling psychology to affirm its place in this field. Frydenberg and McKenzie (2007) have asserted that the CEDP needs to reexamine its core competencies to more appropriately prepare psychologists for work in schools; the CCPs could do the same and develop programs that emphasize the core skills that underpin the work of psychologists working in schools.

FUTURE CHALLENGES AND CONCLUSION

Counseling psychology has a distinctive role to play in the overall group of professional bodies in psychology. In Australia, it is at the crossroads, and especially so after the recent change in government medical-rebate arrangements. While students are continuing to choose clinical postgraduate programs over counseling psychology programs and current counseling psychologists seek membership in the APS clinical college, it is vital that a reappraisal and redesign of the profession of counseling psychology be undertaken to resurrect its status. One suggested strategy is to reinvigorate a focus on psychoeducational models to carve a niche in other emerging areas in Australia (e.g., in school psychology and career psychology). Williams (1978) noted that the psychoeducational model had made the distinction between clinical psychology and counseling psychology clearer, and it is to this that counseling psychology needs to return. A preventive focus to mental health and developmental issues through educational interventions aligns the counseling psychologist with its early roots, both in Australia and in the United States, and is in keeping with the skills of the professional counseling psychologist.

REFERENCES

American Psychological Association. (2005). *Presidential task force on evidence-based practice.* Washington, DC: Author.

Andrews, H. B. (2000). The myth of the scientist-practitioner: A reply to R. King (1998) and N. King and Ollendick (1998). *Australian Psychologist, 35*(1), 60–63.

Armstrong, S., Kelly, P., Phillips, J., Royle, B., White, J., & Yates, K. (2000). The status of school counselling and guidance in Australia: A summary report. *Australian Guidance and Counselling Newsletter, 2,* 20–25.

Australian Bureau of Statistics. (2003). *Labour force survey.* Canberra, Australia: Author.

Australian Bureau of Statistics. (2007a). *Adult literacy and life skills survey.* Canberra, Australia: Author.

Australian Bureau of Statistics. (2007b). *Measures of Australia's progress: Summary indicators 2007.* Canberra, Australia: Author.

Australian Bureau of Statistics. (2007c). *Year book Australia.* Canberra, Australia: Author.

Australian Bureau of Statistics. (2008). *The labour force.* Canberra, Australia: Author.

Australian Institute of Health and Welfare. (2005). *The health and welfare of Aboriginal and Torres Strait Islander peoples.* Canberra, Australia: Australian Government.

Australian Psychological Society. (2000a). *Course approval guidelines: APS College of Counselling Psychologists.* Retrieved March 9, 2005, from http://www.psychology.org.au

Australian Psychological Society. (2000b). *Course approval guidelines: APS College of Educational and Developmental Psychologists.* Retrieved March 9, 2005, from http://www.psychology.org.au

Australian Psychological Society. (2003a). *APS ethical guidelines: Guidelines on supervision.* Retrieved June 28, 2007, from http://www.psychology.org.au

Australian Psychological Society. (2003b). *Guidelines for the provision of psychological services for, and the conduct of psychological research with, Aboriginal and Torres Strait Islander People of Australia.* Retrieved April 27, 2009, from http://www.psychology.org.au/membership/ethics/guidelines/

Australian Psychological Society. (2007a). *APS member groups.* Retrieved May 29, 2007, from http://www.psychology.org.au

Australian Psychological Society. (2007b). *College of Counselling Psychologists.* Retrieved May 29, 2007, from http://www.psychology.org.au/community/specialist/counselling

Australian Psychology Accreditation Council. (2007a). *Accredited courses by state.* Retrieved June 8, 2007, from http://www.apac.psychology.org.au

Australian Psychology Accreditation Council. (2007b). *Course accreditation guidelines.* Retrieved June 8, 2007, from http://www.apac.psychology.org.au

Brown, J., & Corne, L. (2004). Counselling psychology in Australia. *Counselling Psychology Quarterly, 17*(3), 287–299.

Career Industry Council of Australia. (2004). *Shaping a career development culture: Quality standards, quality practice and quality outcomes.* Adelaide, Australia: Author.

Career Industry Council of Australia. (2005). *National standards and accreditation of career practitioners project: Stage two final report.* Adelaide, Australia: Author.

Charman, D., & Barkham, M. (2005). Psychological treatments: Evidence-based practice and practice-based evidence. *Inpsych, December,* 8–13.

Dagley, J., & Salter, S. K. (2004). Practice and research in career counseling and development. *Career Development Quarterly, 53*(2), 98–157.

Denham, G. (2006a). Chair's message. *PSI Counselling News, 6,* 1.

Denham, G. (2006b). Counselling psychology: What is it? *PSI Counselling News, 6,* 3.

Dudgeon, P. (2000). Counselling with indigenous people. In P. Dudgeon, D. Garvey, & H. Pickett (Eds.), *Working with Indigenous Australians: A handbook for psychologists* (pp. 249–270). Perth, Australia: Gunada Press.

Faulkner, M. (2007). School psychologists or psychologists in schools. *Inpsych, 29*(4), 10–13.

Ford, S. (2003). Bridging cultures: Psychologists working with Aboriginal clients. *Inpsych, October*(5), 4–10.

Frydenberg, E., & McKenzie, V. (2007). Training of school psychologists: Meeting the needs of the present and future. *Inpsych, 29*(4), 14–15.

Kazantzis, N., & Deane, F. P. (1998). Theoretical orientations of New Zealand psychologists: An international comparison. *Journal of Psychotherapy Integration, 8,* 97–113.

Littlefield, L. (2006). Looking beyond Medicare to 2007. *Inpsych, December,* 6–7.

Littlefield, L. (2007). Accessible Medicare-funded psychological services for all Australians. *Inpsych, 29*(4), 7–8.

National Association of School Psychologists. (2006). *School psychology: A blueprint for training and practice.* Bethesda, MD: Author.

O'Donovan, A., Dyck, M., & Bain, J. (2001). Trainees' experience of postgraduate clinical training. *Australian Psychologist, 36*(2), 149–156.

Organisation for Economic Co-operation and Development. (2002). *OECD review of career guidance policies: Australia country note*. Retrieved November 6, 2004, from http://ezproxy.usq.edu.au/login?url=http://www.oecd.org/dataoecd/17/47/1948341.pdf

Patrick, J. (2005). The economic value of psychology in Australia: 2001. *Australian Psychologist, 40*(3), 149–158.

Patrick, J., & Pretty, G. (2004, September). *Postgraduate market demand survey*. Paper presented at the 39th Annual Conference of the Australian Psychological Society, Sydney, Australia.

Patton, W. (2005). Career psychology in Australia: Where is it and where does it need to go? In M. Katsikitis (Ed.), *Proceedings of the 40th annual conference of the Australian Psychological Society* (pp. 228–232). Melbourne, Australia: Australian Psychological Society.

Pelling, N. (2004). Counselling psychology: Diversity and commonalities across the Western world. *Counselling Psychology Quarterly, 17*(3), 239–245.

Pelling, N., Brear, P., & Lau, M. (2006). A survey of advertised Australian counsellors. *International Journal of Psychology, 41*(3), 204–215.

Penney, J. (1981). The development of counselling psychology in Australia. *Australian Psychologist, 16*(1), 20–29.

Pirkis, J., Stokes, D., Morley, B., Kohn, F., Mathews, R., Naccarella, L., et al. (2006). Impact of Australia's better outcomes in mental health care on psychologists. *Australian Psychologist, 41*(3), 152–159.

Poznanski, J. J., & McLennan, J. (1998). Theoretical orientations of Australian counselling psychologists. *International Journal for the Advancement of Counselling, 20*, 253–261.

Ranzijn, R., McConnochie, K., Nolan, W., Day, A., & Unaipon, D. (2007). Teaching cultural competence in relation to Indigenous Australians: Steps along a journey.

Inpsych, February. Retrieved September 18, 2007, from http://www.psychology.org.au/publications/inpsych/teaching_cultural

Richards, J. C. (2001). Rewriting the agenda for training in clinical and counselling psychology. *Australian Psychologist, 36*(2), 99–106.

Sanson, A., & Dudgeon, P. (2000). Guest editorial: Psychology, Indigenous issues and reconciliation. *Australian Psychologist, 35*(2), 79–81.

Sharpley, C. F. (1986). Public perceptions of four mental health professions: A survey of knowledge and attitudes to psychologists, psychiatrists, social workers and counsellors. *Australian Psychologist, 21*(1), 57–67.

Sharpley, C. F., Bond, J. E., & Agnew, C. J. (2004). Why go to a counsellor? Attitudes to, and knowledge of, counselling in Australia. *International Journal for the Advancement of Counselling, 26*, 95–108.

Sheehan, P. (1978). Psychology as a profession and the Australian Psychological Society. *Australian Psychologist, 13*(3), 303–324.

Spencer, F. (2004). Professional development: What courses do trainee psychologists want. *Inpsych, February*, 36–37.

Vespia, K. M., Sauer, E. M., & Lyddon, W. J. (2006). Counselling psychologists as scientist-practitioners: Finding unity in diversity. *Counselling Psychology Quarterly, 19*(3), 223–227.

Want, R. (1966). Qualification for membership of the Australian Psychology Society: A viewpoint. *Australian Psychologist, 1*(1), 2–12.

Williams, C. (1978). The dilemma of counselling psychology. *Australian Psychologist, 13*(1), 33–40.

World Health Organisation. (1996). *The ICD-10 classification of mental and behavioural disorders: Clinical descriptions and diagnostic guidelines*. Retrieved April 27, 2009, from www.who.int/classifications/icd/en/bluebook.pdf

PART III

Implications and Conclusion

38

A Global Vision for the Future of Cross-Cultural Counseling

Theory, Collaboration, Research, and Training

LAWRENCE H. GERSTEIN,
P. PAUL HEPPNER, STEFANÍA ÆGISDÓTTIR,
SEUNG-MING ALVIN LEUNG, AND KATHRYN L. NORSWORTHY

The chapters in this book have provided a rich perspective on various topics related to the status and challenges of the counseling profession around the world, cultural assumptions about help seeking and counseling, indigenous models of healing, and future directions for the cross-national counseling movement. Chapters 1 through 8 offered an in-depth discussion on the conceptual, philosophical, methodological, and applied issues connected to engaging in cross-national, cross-cultural, and indigenous pursuits relevant to counseling. The dangers and potential benefits of relying on emic and/or etic counseling paradigms were highlighted, as were the consequences of promoting an ethnocentric, Eurocentric, or U.S.-centric model of counseling. Concrete suggestions for addressing these issues and their consequent dangers, challenges, and benefits were introduced as well.

The chapters in Part II of this book revealed the history, innovative developments, challenges, and future directions of the mental health helping profession in nine regions of the world. Furthermore, these chapters introduced the rich cultural context grounding help-seeking behaviors in the targeted countries. Unique models and strategies of modern forms of counseling based on the cultural context as well as traditional approaches to healing were also discussed in many of these chapters.

In this concluding chapter, we identify some common themes found throughout the book as a way to highlight a few similarities and differences in the counseling profession worldwide. Based on these observations, general implications are provided for counseling and psychology in the United States and elsewhere. Additionally, we mention some of the strengths, challenges, and opportunities associated with cross-national collaboration. Ethical issues connected to international counseling activities are highlighted as well. This chapter also introduces some recommendations about how to integrate and infuse international issues into counseling training programs and potential content to include in such programs. Moreover, we discuss some essential cross-cultural and cross-national counseling competencies. Throughout this chapter, we introduce many suggestions for the further development of theory, research, and practice linked with international counseling activities.

COMMON THEMES IN COUNSELING WORLDWIDE

As we come to the end of our journey within the pages of the *International Handbook of Cross-Cultural Counseling,* we are struck by the richness of the collective wisdom represented. Each contributor has shared valuable knowledge, insights, and practices based on years of experience wrestling with important issues and questions related to research and culturally competent applications of counseling and counseling psychology in their home countries and in cross-national activities. There were a number of important themes that emerged in this volume reminding us of the challenges associated with inventing and reinventing a truly relevant counseling profession for the 21st-century global village.

First and foremost, as Pedersen (2003) observed, counseling practices and functions have existed for thousands of years, performed by members of cultural communities holding varied roles, including local healers, spiritual leaders, physicians, teachers, and elders. The formal professions of counseling and counseling psychology, in contrast, are relatively new. For the most part, they have emerged within a Western and primarily U.S. context and from particular social, political, and economic structures that are informed by and reinforce a set of values and worldviews (i.e., individualism, autonomy, competition, logical positivism). As the professionalization process subsumes the functions and practices of counseling, indigenous wisdom and helping can

become marginalized and devalued. This is especially the case when Western counseling and counseling psychology professionals use their power and influence (often unconsciously) to define the standards of practice internationally and when Western models and approaches are uncritically transported to other parts of the world.

This book clearly reveals the presence of an international movement to resist the globalization of Western counseling models and the attendant pressures toward homogenization and the discrediting of local healers, helpers, and wisdom. Authors featured in this book have demonstrated how professionals and community leaders in each of the countries represented are thoughtfully and carefully creating and implementing counseling models that are informed by local cultures and contexts, local wisdom and cosmological perspectives on healing and helping, taking into account the social, political, and psychological dimensions of people's lives. In many chapters, exciting, diverse approaches to the indigenization of counseling were presented, both in terms of the professionalization process as well as in the modalities and applications used from country to country. Also, many contributors noted the challenges involved in transforming Western models, creating their own, and accessing Western venues, such as journals, books, conferences, and research grant funding. Some authors also observed that Western counseling professionals do not frequently publish in or read other countries' scholarly journals, nor do they attend or present at their conferences.

Conversely, there is an increased trend toward international "border crossings" whereby counseling professionals from different parts of the world partner and collaborate in research and practice projects or engage in advanced training as international students. Several of our authors shared their experiences with cross-national and cross-cultural professional relationships, emphasizing the importance of power sharing, reciprocity, and mutual respect as a foundation for growth and learning. A key to cultural competence and successful collaborative projects across cultures involves the development of a critical consciousness about the current global power arrangements in relation to the counseling profession, a humble mind, and devoting considerable time and energy to understanding the local culture and contexts.

International students attending U.S. counselor education and counseling psychology training programs are also increasingly participating in cross-cultural and cross-national partnerships. They bring to light the importance of internationalizing the curriculum and breaking through the cultural encapsulation that characterizes much of the counseling and psychology training in the United States. Yet, while U.S. counseling and psychology have historically been more inwardly focused than internationally focused, the diversity, multicultural, and social justice movements (and the associated awareness, knowledge, and skills) within the professions are probably one of the most potentially important contributions of U.S. counseling to the larger global profession.

We do want to acknowledge that the professional contributions of every country, including the United States, offer crucial information that can be used to respond to local needs. The amalgamation of and access to information gathered worldwide seems to be the pathway to maximum effectiveness in this complex world.

This handbook is a venue for addressing one of the major challenges associated with inventing a counseling profession that reflects and responds effectively to the wide range of human experience globally—that is, the need for the exchange of knowledge and skills across countries and cultures. Since, as we have pointed out earlier in this handbook, diversity is the key to surviving and thriving, we all need one another to cultivate a connected, interactive, international system of counseling professionals through which we can draw on our collective wisdom and experiences to respond to the complexities of life in the 21st-century global village. Thus, we need to develop and nurture cross-national and cross-cultural research and practice partnerships and information exchanges vis-à-vis literature, conferences, and professional exchange/immersion programs. Furthermore, attention and resources devoted to expanding cross-cultural research methods,

focusing on the emic and etic constructs as part of a unified whole and using qualitative and quantitative research approaches, are essential in shedding light on the important questions related to culture, identity, and context in the counseling process.

We strongly echo previous scholars who have observed that counselors and counseling psychologists potentially have the awareness, knowledge, skills, and motivation to participate in addressing many serious challenges faced by people around the world, ranging from trauma resolution to reconciliation and peace building (e.g., Gerstein, 2006; Heppner, 1997; Leong & Blustein, 2000; Norsworthy & Gerstein, 2003). The more we understand one another beyond our own personal and national borders and the more we as counseling professionals share the locally and cross-culturally generated knowledge and skills needed to fulfill our important roles locally and globally, the greater our ability to create a peaceful planet that will sustain life for future generations.

IMPLICATIONS FOR COUNSELING AND COUNSELING PSYCHOLOGY IN THE UNITED STATES

A number of important implications for counseling and counseling psychology professionals in the United States can be gleaned from the chapters in this book. First, it was rather apparent and critical that counseling students and professionals in the United States must become multilingual, or rely on interpreters and translators, if they are to be effective and culturally competent when working with diverse, non-English-speaking populations throughout the world.

Second, it was obvious from the chapters in Part II that psychological help-seeking patterns worldwide are guided by the cultural, historical, and political context of each country and the specific mental health service delivery system operating in each country (also see Cheung, 2000). Thus, it is important that U.S. counselors and counseling psychologists be cognizant of context when assisting persons from other countries and cultures, especially those in which there is a history of mistrust toward mental health professionals. For instance, individuals from the former USSR may still be reluctant to seek mental health services because of memories from the communist era when psychiatrists were believed to use medication and hypnosis to change a person's political views and religious practices. In South Africa, individuals might also be reluctant to seek psychological services as they have been viewed as a Western strategy to solve problems. Moreover, in the past South African mental health professionals, in general, have not been trusted because most are white.

Additionally, in some countries in South and Central America (e.g., Venezuela and Ecuador), the Middle East (e.g., the United Arab Emirates and Turkey), Africa (e.g., Nigeria), and Asia (e.g., Japan, Taiwan, China, Pakistan, India, Korea, and Malaysia) that hold collectivistic values (e.g., social harmony, family cohesion, and saving face), seeking professional mental health services may be perceived as a threat to or a rejection of those worldviews. When working with persons from such countries, therefore, it is essential that U.S. counselors and counseling psychologists be sensitive to and incorporate, when possible, the family and the social network into the counseling process. Similarly, it is extremely important that U.S. mental health professionals working with individuals from other countries carefully assess the attitudes and expectations these persons may have about the counseling process. Information gathered from this assessment can prove extremely valuable when conceptualizing issues and developing and implementing culturally appropriate interventions.

The use of indigenous healing systems was also highlighted in many of the countries represented in Part II. In most of these countries, people have sought out local healers throughout the ages, and continue to do so (e.g., the United Arab Emirates, Pakistan, Malaysia, Nigeria, and Kyrgyzstan). At times, indigenous approaches also have been integrated with U.S. models of counseling. Therefore, to effectively work with individuals from cultures and countries valuing local wisdom in helping and healing, counselors and counseling psychologists might be more successful in taking on the role of a social-change agent or facilitator of indigenous healing systems. This can be accomplished by collaborating, incorporating, and supporting individuals in seeking relief using methods that make sense to them and are culturally valid (e.g., Atkinson, Thompson, & Grant, 1993).

Related to the last implication, numerous chapters in this book discussed the importance of religion and spirituality not only in the general day-to-day lives of people (e.g., in India, Malaysia, Pakistan, and Singapore) but also in the context of counseling. Islam is intimately woven into the fabric of counseling in countries such as the United Arab Emirates, Malaysia, Pakistan, and Turkey, while Buddhism is integrated into models of counseling, for instance, in Japan, Singapore, and also some parts of Malaysia. Hinduism is embedded in various counseling models in Singapore and India. Given the central role of religion and spirituality throughout the world, mental health professionals need to acquire a broad and deep knowledge of the world's religions and, as stated earlier, increase their knowledge of various forms of traditional folk healing. To be effective with individuals from different parts of the world, they must develop the skills to integrate religion and spirituality into their conceptual framework and applied strategies as well. For instance, U.S. counselors and counseling psychologists must be cautious about diagnosing someone as "psychotic" when he or she comes from a highly spiritual country or when she or he has strong spiritual beliefs. Instead, professionals should carefully entertain more than one hypothesis about the causes of "symptoms" thought to be manifestations of a psychological problem. Moreover, all mental health professionals need to recognize and be aware that psychological problems are highly culture laden (i.e., culture-bound syndromes). As such, counselors and counseling psychologists worldwide must be willing to explore a person's cultural beliefs and use the information acquired to tailor unique intervention strategies.

The role and importance of emotions in the cultures and countries discussed in this book was greatly varied. U.S. mental health professionals as well as professionals elsewhere cannot assume that emotions are always openly experienced and verbally expressed. Furthermore, professionals must be aware that emotions can be experienced and expressed in diverse ways (e.g., see the chapter on Turkey). For example, as reported in the chapter on Kyrgyzstan, there are no words for depression or anxiety in this country. A person will simple say, "I feel bad." Also in some countries (e.g., Turkey), emotions might be displayed through physical symptoms and not by language as a way to avoid the stigma of having a psychological problem. For instance, depression in Turkey frequently manifests as somatization of bodily symptoms. Therefore, U.S. counselors and counseling psychologists working with people who come from such countries need to be comfortable with clients who either do not express their feelings or are unwilling to explore and express them. U.S. mental health professionals should realize this reality could be reflective of cultural values and not a form of individuals' resistance.

Another distinctive characteristic of a couple of cultures in countries (e.g., the United Arab Emirates, Turkey, and Kyrgyzstan) discussed in this book was the importance of obeying authority figures, such as parents and doctors. As a result, it is highly likely that individuals from such countries will expect their counselor or counseling psychologist to be very active, directive, and solution focused. Counseling professionals in the United States, therefore, need to be sensitive to this dynamic and adjust their behavior and interventions accordingly. This means, for instance, being comfortable giving advice when appropriate to clients that have this expectation. Similarly, in other cultures with tight relational rules (e.g., Korea) manifesting in strong respect and appreciation for the hierarchical order of society and the family, U.S. mental health professionals would do well to demonstrate an understanding of these rules and to tailor their interventions so as not to violate them.

A major challenge for U.S. counselors and counseling psychologists is assisting women who are experiencing gender-based oppression. In a few of the countries represented in this book (e.g., the United Arab Emirates, Pakistan, and Kyrgyzstan),

the authors shared that women experienced much less social, political, and cultural power than men. Of course, sexism and misogyny are global phenomena; however, the most appropriate methods for counseling women experiencing the effects of gender inequality must take into account their worldviews and contexts. U.S. counseling professionals need to find the most effective ways to support the empowerment and mental health of women clients given their social, political, and cultural contexts.

Counselors and counseling psychologists in the United States can learn a great deal from the models and strategies of social justice employed by counseling psychologists and other mental health professionals in, for instance, South Africa and Israel. As the result of apartheid and the widespread prevalence of HIV/AIDS, South African mental health professionals have generated many innovative and useful social justice programs and techniques that could easily be adapted and implemented in the United States. Similarly, Israeli mental health professionals have designed and implemented numerous creative programs to address violence, conflict, and ethnic disputes that could be modified and used in the United States.

In a number of the countries (e.g., the United Arab Emirates, Pakistan, and Ecuador) represented in this book, unemployment was an important social issue addressed by counseling professionals. For instance, in France, many innovative methods were presented to effectively deal with concerns of unemployment and sustainable employment for French citizens. The authors reported on programs and systemic efforts, such as the Tutor and the Godfather, and different job training centers in which individuals could have their work and life experiences assessed and validated to be more competitive in the job market. Some of these innovative programs may be adapted to work in the United States. Similarly, counseling professionals in the United States working with school-to-work transitions may derive important lessons from Italy. Of special note were the efforts in Italy to empower teachers and parents to be more involved in enhancing the career maturity and effective decision making of youth.

Finally, throughout the chapters contributed by authors from different countries, the use of Western and U.S. counseling theories seemed very prevalent, and the importance of the indigenization of counseling and psychology was noted as an important effort that was needed and foreseeable in the near future. The science and practice of counseling would greatly benefit from indigenization in different countries. In many countries, the effort to indigenize is just in its infancy, while other countries already have unique indigenous models of counseling in place (e.g., Taiwan, Japan, and Singapore). For instance, in Chapter 21 (Iceland), the authors reported on the development of an online career guidance inventory (the Bendill project) in which an etic conceptualization of career interests (Holland's theory) was employed along with indigenous emic items to more accurately represent the Icelandic work environment, and therefore more effectively aid Icelanders' career decision making. U.S. counseling professionals might be in a position to collaborate and get involved in efforts such as these in different countries. There are numerous ways that U.S. counseling theories and conceptual systems may be adapted, modified, and expanded to better fit the cultural context of countries outside the United States. In fact, many of the authors who have contributed to this handbook were involved in, and called for, collaboration with U.S. and other counseling professionals to work on such efforts.

IMPLICATIONS FOR COUNSELING AND PSYCHOLOGY OUTSIDE THE UNITED STATES

We now turn our attention to some important implications for counseling and counseling psychology professionals outside the United States based on the chapters in Part II of this book. These chapters verify that the counseling profession outside the United States is growing and that it has a bright future despite the unique concerns and roadblocks that are experienced in different regions of the world. In all the countries discussed in this book, counseling is closely connected to the needs and cultures of the society. Furthermore, it appears that the counseling profession is accelerating its pace of development in response to such needs. Counseling and psychology have become popular areas of study in many parts of the world, and we foresee that, in time, the strength and size of the counseling profession will increase substantially (e.g., Iceland, Colombia, China, and Sweden).

Counseling professionals worldwide are forming local professional organizations, systems of credentialing, and practice guidelines and identifying counseling practices that can serve individuals within their cultures and communities (e.g., China, Taiwan, and Great Britain). They are also eager to use their indigenous knowledge to promote the well-being of individuals within and across cultures.

The fact that a professionalized approach to counseling is in the early stages of development in many countries outside the United States does not mean that counseling professionals from these countries are playing a secondary role in the international arena. In his book *The World Is Flat: A Brief History of the Twenty-First Century*, Friedman (2006) used the term *glocalization* to denote how small local economies or cultural groups can make an important global impact through the use of available communication and information technologies. This is true for counseling professionals outside the United States as well.

As evidenced by the chapters in Part II of this book, professionals from many countries and cultures outside the United States are finding creative and interesting ways of transforming counseling models and practices into culturally and contextually grounded approaches suited to local cultures and concerns. Indigenizing counseling involves acknowledging and incorporating wisdom and cosmologies from local healing practitioners and spiritual traditions, valuing local worldviews, and recognizing the cultural construction of "psychological disorders." The knowledge produced as the result of this indigenization process will certainly expand and deepen the understanding of counseling professionals around the world and, in so doing, enhance their ability to offer culturally competent counseling services to a diverse range of clients.

Furthermore, opportunities to explore culturally sensitive and effective delivery systems of counseling (e.g., office based vs. community based, etc.) will also lead to an expansion of professionals' knowledge about how to best provide services.

The chapters also suggest that the field of counseling in many countries (e.g., Japan, Korea, Singapore, and Turkey) is closely connected to the education system. Whereas counseling and psychology in the United States is still establishing an institutionalized role in school settings, counseling professionals outside the United States have discovered numerous opportunities to use their knowledge and skills to assist students, to work with other mental health professionals and intervene with students and families, to build resilience, and to engage in various forms of guidance and counseling to promote mental health and well-being. Education is valued in many countries, and schools will continue to be an important theater wherein counseling professionals find recognition for their contributions and a niche where they can continue to grow and expand.

Career interventions have also been identified as a major component of the global counseling profession (e.g., France, Israel, Korea, Great Britain, and Italy). Career development and career guidance are part of the historical roots of counseling and counseling psychology worldwide. These foci are important areas of scholarly inquiry and intervention. Hence, career development is a common topic of inquiry and intervention that connects counseling professionals from different countries and provides an exciting opportunity for new discoveries and developments.

As the counseling profession develops outside the United States, training has certainly become an important area of attention. Educators are increasingly aware of the need to design counseling training programs based on their cultural and contextual characteristics and concerns rather than "copying" the training structure and philosophy of counseling and counseling psychology in other countries, most often the United States. The unique culturally and socially responsive ways that these programs are developed will offer new and diverse approaches to

counselor education and counseling psychology training. At the same time, educators from many countries (e.g., India, Turkey, and China) are struggling with questions and issues related to training, such as how to structure the curriculum and how to contend with the absence of trainers, insufficient resources, and competition from related mental health specialties. Creatively addressing these challenges is critical to supporting the future strength of the counseling profession and also future generations of counseling professionals, who have the potential to continue the mission of the field internationally. One mechanism that can be employed to help address such challenges is cross-national collaboration.

CROSS-NATIONAL COLLABORATION: STRENGTHS, CHALLENGES, AND OPPORTUNITIES

Currently, national and geographic boundaries have been reduced by advances in communication technologies (e.g., e-mail, Internet information technologies, and Skype). There is increased access to a variety of workflow technologies (e.g., word-processing and statistical software) that allow individuals from different corners of the world to collaborate without leaving their offices and homes (see Chapters 7 and 8). This handbook is an example of international collaboration in which close to 100 scholars from different continents participated. This project involved a substantial amount of communication cross-nationally, yet almost all these cross-national efforts were performed within our homes, offices, or communities.

International collaboration is facilitated by the awareness that we are all members of a global village and that despite our differences there is much to learn from each other and much we could do to help one another grow. The stories in this book about the development of the counseling profession in different countries have suggested several consistent themes related to international collaboration: (a) counseling professionals from around the world perceive that such collaboration can strengthen the development of counseling in their own region; (b) international collaboration has and will continue to facilitate the development or adaptation of theories, practices, research, and tools for use in local cultures and contexts; and (c) international collaboration will become increasingly important in an age in which many local concerns could have an international impact (e.g., HIV prevention, terror incidents, and the 2009 financial tsunami). Counselors and counseling psychologists can encourage collaboration among professionals by offering their expertise and working cojointly across national borders. Additionally, cross-national teams of counseling scholars can conduct research and publish important cross-cultural studies, capitalizing on the various strengths that diverse counseling professionals can offer. The consensus on the importance of international cooperation is a valuable strength that will foster greater collaboration on into the future (Heppner, 2006).

There are also many challenges to international collaboration. First, an important challenge is how counseling professionals can collaborate as equals. Historically, counseling professionals from the United States have served as the leaders in developing counseling theories, practice, training, and research. Counseling professionals in other parts of the world, on the other hand, have adapted to varying degree the materials from the United States. As pointed out in many instances throughout the chapters in this book, the new paradigm of international collaboration needs to be bilateral and multilateral in the sense that counseling professionals are coleaders and cofollowers (Leung, 2003) and also are equal in terms of the distribution of formal and informal power (Horne & Mathews, 2006; Norsworthy, 2006). The counseling profession would become more relevant locally and globally if counseling theories and practices were developed to be consistent with the local context (see Chapter 6).

A second challenge of international collaboration is language and communication (see Horne & Mathews, 2006). Ideally, counseling professionals engaged in international collaboration should be multilingual or, at the very least, conversant in the language used by the parties connected to the collaborative activity. This would enhance comprehending the cultural context, increase knowledge about the content connected to the project, and greatly improve communication between all involved parties.

Counseling professionals outside the United States, however, can use their multilingual, cross-cultural, and cross-national knowledge and skills to make scholarly contributions through summarizing and reviewing literature from non–English language sources. In this regard, international collaboration also requires documentation of what has been done locally and within different cultures so that members of the profession can use, adapt, and refine those strategies and outcomes. The content presented in the chapters in Part II illustrate indigenous materials that have been developed in many cultures and regions and not previously published or summarized in the English language counseling and psychology literature. Making indigenous materials developed in different cultures and countries available worldwide will continue to be a challenge to international collaboration, but we hope that bilingual professionals could serve as the bridge to having these "treasures" be known and used in the international counseling community.

The magnitude and size of the problems that the global village is experiencing (e.g., natural and human-created disasters, global warming and weather changes, wars and conflicts, and the financial tsunami) have posed many challenges to the human race, and as much as we do not want these problems to surface and threaten the fabric of our societies, these are also opportunities for counseling professionals to make a difference. Counseling professionals inside and outside the United States are in a unique position to collaborate and provide community-developed solutions for regional and global problems. Such efforts require the concerted and sustained collaboration of multiple professionals. The global financial tsunami is a case in point: Counseling professionals could use their knowledge and skills in mental health and career development to assist individuals experiencing financial and employment uncertainties. There are many ways that counseling professionals could share their experience and resources to promote mental health and well-being at such a challenging time.

Moreover, we suspect that future international collaboration will have the potential to change the face of counseling and counseling psychology forever. For example, as Heppner (2006) predicted, "In the future . . . the parameters of counseling psychology will cross many countries and many cultures" (p. 170). Furthermore, the cumulative knowledge base of the counseling profession will be grounded in information, obtained from all corners of the world, putting "the puzzle together as an extraordinary picture of a worldwide psychology" (Heppner, Leong, & Chiao, 2008, p. 82). International collaboration has a great deal of potential to strengthen our research and practice and greatly enhance our knowledge of the cultural context (see Heppner, 2008), including furthering our understanding of how culture shapes and influences ethical professional behavior.

ETHICAL ISSUES CONNECTED TO INTERNATIONAL COUNSELING ACTIVITIES

The codes of ethics of various mental health professions, such as those developed by the American Psychological Association (APA) and the American Counseling Association (ACA), are designed to provide guiding principles as well as standards for professional conduct. Ethics are not simply proper etiquette (Heppner, Wampold, & Kivlighan, 2008), but rather they are expressions of our values and a guide to achieving them (Diener & Crandall, 1978). Not surprisingly, ethical codes in psychology date back over 50 years (see Golann, 1970). Although the codes are relatively easy to read, their application to specific situations is often complicated by intersecting and competing principles. In essence, complex ethical problems require decisions and actions that often cannot be prescribed by particular principles.

Moreover, ethical codes are intertwined within a context, specifically a cultural context. For example, Pedersen (1995, 1997) asserted that the ACA and

APA ethical codes of the late 1990s were based on the dominant U.S. cultural perspective and minimized or ignored the impact of cultural context in ethical issues. Subsequently, U.S. scholars provided ethical decision-making models that included cultural assumptions, relevant cultural data, and cultural conflicts (Ridley, Liddle, Hill, & Li, 2001). In short, the cultural context is critical in any professional counseling or psychological code of ethics, and more recently, the ethical codes of the ACA and APA have attempted to address context (Pack-Brown & Williams, 2003).

Additionally, some books have been published on various ethical challenges and strategies for psychologists when conducting research with ethnocultural populations and communities (e.g., Trimble & Fisher, 2006). Furthermore, other books have been published on the importance of counseling professionals considering cultural issues when engaged in ethical decision making (Houser, Wilczenski, & Ham, 2006). In fact, Houser et al. (2006) discussed Western (i.e., Native American), Eastern (i.e., Confucius, Taoist, Hindu, and Buddhist), Middle Eastern (i.e., Jewish and Islamic), and southern-hemisphere (i.e., Hispanic/ Latino and Pan-African) theories of ethics in relation to counselor decision making. These chapters are quite revealing and informative, and they offer counseling professionals the opportunity to develop an appreciation and respect for how different philosophical and religious worldviews can influence and guide ethical decision making.

Given the richness of the philosophical and religious worldviews just mentioned, it is not surprising that many countries have developed ethical codes and guidelines to regulate the practice of psychology. For example, Leach (2008) has compiled a listing of 44 ethical codes (mostly in English) of national psychology associations from around the world. As of this writing, Leach is in the process of adding most of the ethics codes of South American national associations of psychology as well. Leach and Oakland (2007) have also compared the ethical standards influencing test development and use across 31 ethical codes, affecting practice in 35 countries.

The General Assembly of the International Union of Psychological Science (IUPsyS), the International Association of Applied Psychology (IAAP), and the International Association for Cross-Cultural Psychology have developed a "universal declaration of ethical principles for psychologists" to address "the common moral framework that guides and inspires psychologists worldwide toward the highest ethical ideals in their profession and scientific work" (Ad Hoc Joint Committee, 2005, p. 2). This is a generic set of moral principles based on shared human values around the world, and it avoids pre- scribing specific behaviors because such conduct is considered relative to the local cultural customs, beliefs, and laws. More specifically, the principles emphasize values, such as respect for the dignity of all human beings; respect for diversity among human beings; working to maximize benefits and minimize harm to individuals, families, and commu- nities; striving for honest, open, and accurate com- munication; and being responsible to society. In essence, the universal declaration provides a shared moral framework for the work of psychologists within a larger social context.

There is a need for greater attention to ethics in national associations in counseling professions throughout the world. Some have suggested a very basic universal declaration of ethical principles in counseling (see Chapter 3). Such delineation could be very useful to underscore our common values and to establish a shared moral framework. In addi- tion, there are currently a range of broad cross- national professional activities (e.g., consultation, training, research, and practice) involving participa- tion across at least two countries that potentially raise an array of ethical issues related to cross- cultural competence, exploration, and the benefits to the larger society. That is, these cross-national issues can be conducted with varying degrees of cul- tural sensitivity. Aware of some of these issues, the APA adopted a "Resolution on Culture and Gender Awareness in International Psychology" (APA, 2004, Appendix 4; see Appendix, Chapter 4, this volume) that addresses some of these important challenges. However, much more attention is needed

to deal with the many complexities related to cross- national collaboration within the counseling profes- sion as well as in psychology in general (Heppner, Leong, & Chiao, 2008; Leong & Lee, 2006). In short, in this closing chapter, we want to remind readers that there are many ethical complexities in crossing national borders, and as responsible mem- bers of the counseling profession, we must carefully attend to these complexities and be knowledgeable about the work being done in this arena.

INTERNATIONALIZING TRAINING OF COUNSELING PROFESSIONALS: CHALLENGES, OPPORTUNITIES, AND COMPETENCIES

Challenges Associated With Training

At the heart of the internationalization process is the preparation of professionals who are truly global citizens and who have the awareness, knowl- edge, skills, and ethics relevant for work across cul- tures, national boundaries, identities, worldviews, and contexts. Culturally sensitive counseling profes- sionals are also truly motivated to question their own assumptions and biases and increase their knowledge and skills to more effectively work with others outside their own culture and comfort zone (Ægisdóttir & Gerstein, in press). As previously dis- cussed in this book, the counseling field has been tremendously influenced by Western, and particu- larly U.S., paradigms, research and professional lit- erature, and models of practice, much of which tends to be ethnocentric and culturally encapsulated. With this in mind, Marsella and Pedersen (2004) warned that internationalizing the training of U.S. counselors might be challenging, specifically due to the existing cultural biases in the U.S. professional literature (e.g., Arnett, 2008); because of the unwill- ingness to acknowledge the need to be more cross- culturally, cross-nationally, and internationally competent; and as the result of the lack of interest among many Western and U.S. academics to inter- nationalize the curriculum. Marsella and Pedersen (2004) argued that to internationalize,

Our training will need to be more multicultural, multisectoral, multinational, and multidisciplinary. We will need constantly to be aware of the importance of developing new Western psychologies, indigenous psychologies, and syncretic psychologies that resist the hegemonic imposition or privileged positioning of any psychology because of its powerful economic, political, or cultural context. (p. 415)

As is evident in the previous chapters, colleagues and students outside the United States are often most likely to recognize the need to invent a 21st-century counseling profession that takes into account local context, worldviews, and practices of healing and helping (e.g., Cheung, 2000; Leung, 2003; Yang, Hwang, Pedersen, & Daibo, 2003). This recognition often occurs during their Western or U.S.-based training process, either at home or in a Western or a U.S. university. On returning to their home countries, they are challenged to find ways to indigenize the Western or U.S.-based counseling models.

Throughout this book, the rich descriptions of the status of counseling worldwide as well as the current challenges point to some logical directions and steps in infusing international perspectives into the training of counselors and counseling psychologists. The following discussion is an effort to further the conversation within our professional organizations, university training programs, and classrooms, recognizing that the internationalization process is ongoing and evolving with ever-changing local and global contexts.

Opportunities Associated With Training

Counseling and counseling psychology training programs can broaden the curriculum to include information about counseling and other forms of psychological helping from various countries and regions of the world, particularly emphasizing the need to understand the social, political, and cultural contexts from which different models arise (Ægisdóttir & Gerstein, in press). As was apparent in the chapters appearing in Part II of this book, in many cultures and countries people in distress, needing guidance and advice, or having significant psychological concerns often seek the assistance of indigenous healers, religious leaders, elders, or other respected members of the community before turning to counselors or psychologists (if these professions even exist locally). Thus, providing training opportunities aimed at exploring the broad array of healing and helping approaches as well as collaborating with such indigenous healing and support systems will enhance culturally sensitive practices (e.g., Atkinson et al., 1993). There must be an effort in counseling training programs to reduce the stigma of the use of indigenous healing systems. Instead, training programs need to focus on ways to investigate and research the effectiveness of such systems on people's well-being as stand-alone treatment options or in combination with more traditional counseling services. Students should also be taught some basic concepts and strategies connected to indigenous forms of healing. Furthermore, a focused discussion in classrooms on cultural constructions of psychological "disorders" would offer trainees ways to understand client diversity and provide more effective psychological and counseling services.

It is our view that focusing on and thereby valuing indigenous healing systems and the cultural contexts of psychological difficulties supports and fosters the development of indigenous psychologies and counseling approaches. In this handbook, many authors discussing the status of counseling and psychology in their home countries pointed to the need for training that integrates traditional Western models with indigenous knowledge and skills. They also spoke about the importance of obtaining training and details on how counseling is being indigenized in cultures and countries in which the profession is developing. Therefore, we urge educators of counselors and counseling psychologists to offer this type of training by providing examples of such efforts. Many chapters in this book presented models of counseling that integrated Western paradigms and indigenous forms of healing (e.g., Ecuador, Turkey, Pakistan, Malaysia, Singapore, Taiwan, and Japan). Additionally, there are a number of books that discuss traditional forms of healing, the integration of these approaches with Western strategies of counseling, and the challenges of employing these models in professional practice (e.g., Adler & Mukherji, 1995; Gielen, Fish, & Draguns, 2004; Hoshmand, 2006; Moodley & West, 2005; Santee, 2007).

It is also important for the training curriculum to incorporate a greater emphasis on issues of cross-cultural research competence introducing students to concepts such as equivalence and bias (see Chapter 5). Developing a richer knowledge about the intricacies of conducting cross-culturally valid research could also contribute to counseling professionals enhancing the indigenization of counseling and psychology in different countries. One example of a successful effort to indigenize the assessment of career interests was presented in the chapter on Iceland.

A primary objective for publishing this handbook was to offer an avenue toward internationalizing the training curriculum in counseling and counseling psychology. Counseling professionals need to realize that they may have very limited and culturally encapsulated information about the models and tools linked with their field. This is especially true of U.S. counseling professionals given the limited information available on international topics and the minimal inclusion of international topics and cross-cultural research in the U.S. counseling and psychology literatures (e.g., Arnett, 2008; Gerstein & Ægisdóttir, 2007; Ægisdóttir, Gerstein, & Çinarbaş, 2008). Moreover, as Draguns (2001) noted, "The development of a truly international psychology is obstructed at this point by the massive disregard of contributions that are published in languages other than English" (p. 1019). Thus, incorporating readings, such as this handbook, and encouraging students to search for journal articles and book chapters providing diverse perspectives and populations relevant to their course topics might help in this regard. Furthermore, it is important for faculty members in counseling and psychology programs around the world to collaborate and explore the use of Web-based conferencing and other available technologies to discuss among themselves and with students course-related issues and how they may be affected by culture.

Another important step toward internationalizing the training of counseling students and professionals is implementing structures and policies that empower international students studying in Western and U.S. universities (e.g., Gerstein & Ægisdóttir, 2007; Heppner, 2006). These students should be strongly encouraged to share their cultures, worldviews, and indigenous knowledge and practices in the classroom and on research teams. They should also be encouraged to critically examine the validity and applicability of theories and methodologies to their home culture and to discuss their ideas with their classmates and their professors (Gerstein & Ægisdóttir, 2007; Ægisdóttir & Gerstein, in press). International students who feel empowered in their programs to critically evaluate Western theories, counseling approaches, and methodologies in relation to their home cultures and countries will not only benefit more from their training, they will enrich their training programs and contribute substantially to the internationalization efforts of university programs. Such critical examination and the discussion of theories, approaches, and methodologies could also be accomplished by using Web-based conferencing technologies to network classrooms of students meeting in different corners of the world.

In research classes in the counseling curriculum, it is critical to encourage the use of emic (within culture) and etic (cross-cultural) constructs and approaches (see Chapter 5). This can help trainees appreciate the fact that these are not separate constructs but instead parts of a larger unified whole. In so doing, it would broaden and deepen students' knowledge about the intersections of culture, identity, and psychological functioning. Including a cross-cultural component in every research methods class or offering a cross-cultural research methods class would greatly enhance students' cultural competence in research.

Important Cross-Cultural and Cross-National Competencies

In addition to the overall suggestions just offered concerning how to train counseling professionals to be effective cross-nationally and in an international context, it is critical to identify a set of competencies that are necessary to engage in such activities. In this section, we discuss some of these competencies. A multicultural and cross-cultural perspective plays a complementary role in promoting culturally competent and sensitive research, interventions, and training in counseling and counseling psychology in the United States and internationally (see Heppner, Leong, & Chiao, 2008; Chapter 2, this volume). Based on existing writings about multicultural (Arredondo et al., 1996; Atkinson et al., 1993; Sue, Arredondo, & McDavis, 1992) and cross-cultural (Heppner, Leong, & Gerstein, 2008; Ægisdóttir & Gerstein, in press) counseling competencies, we want to focus on four main dimensions of cross-cultural competence: *motivation, awareness, knowledge,* and *skills* (C-C MAKS) (Ægisdóttir & Gerstein, in press). A description of these dimensions follows with suggestions about how to acquire such competencies.

Motivation is the driving force behind the effective incorporation of culture and context into the science and practice of counseling and psychology. Many counseling professionals continue to minimize the interdependence of people and nations despite the fact that direct and indirect contact between cultures is increasingly more apparent and subject to both positive and negative consequences. This interrelatedness among cultures confirms the importance of developing an understanding and appreciation for international issues and populations. Given the fact that current psychological knowledge in the United States is only based on a small proportion of the world population (Arnett, 2008) and the fact that there is a widespread and at times uncritical exportation of this knowledge worldwide, it is essential that the knowledge, challenges, and issues faced throughout the world be incorporated into current counseling training paradigms. It is also important that scholars pursue international research and topics to advance the science and practice of counseling. As others have suggested (e.g., Gerstein & Ægisdóttir, 2007; Marsella & Pedersen, 2004; Ægisdóttir & Gerstein, in press), we concur that, to enhance motivation to learn

about and pursue international issues and topics, it is necessary that counseling faculty members and students create informal (e.g., roundtable discussions) and formal (e.g., poster and paper sessions, symposiums, and courses) mechanisms in their departments and at conferences to introduce individuals to international work and research and to provide opportunities for rich discussion about such content. Additionally, to increase the motivation of individuals to engage in international activities, university administrators should be encouraged to offer internal grants to increase faculty and student travel to international conferences and to pursue research and applied projects in other countries. Professional organizations around the world must be urged to provide support as well. Furthermore, networking between students and departments throughout the world may enhance individuals' motivation to pursue international work and explore the role of culture and context in issues relevant to counseling.

The second dimension of C-C MAKS is awareness. This dimension refers to counseling professionals being aware of their own and their clients' worldviews, cultural values and biases, and how one's cultural background and experiences influence help-seeking behavior and beliefs about psychological processes (e.g., Arredondo et al., 1996). To increase awareness, counselors must have an ecological-systems perspective to help understand the influences of culture on attitudes, values, and behavior (Bronfenbrenner, 1979; Heppner, Leong, & Gerstein, 2008; Neville & Mobley, 2001). According to Bronfenbrenner, contextual influences are rooted in five different systems and the interactions between them: microsystem, mesosystem, exosystem, macrosystem, and chronosystem. These systems range from structures in which the individual is directly connected (microsystem; e.g., family, church, neighborhood, and healers) through societal and political structures, norms, and cultural belief systems, to transitions and environmental events influencing individuals over time (chronosystem). Counseling professionals providing services and performing research internationally need to think of themselves and others in the context of the systems influencing individuals' thoughts, feelings, and behavior. Such awareness, therefore, involves being cautious about generalizing findings and constructs across cultures (Pedersen & Leong, 1997; Varenne, 2003; Ægisdóttir et al., 2008), learning from scholars around the world (Heppner, 1997; Leong & Blustein, 2000), and separating observations from interpretations, as interpretations of one's surroundings are heavily influenced by one's values, biases, and experiences (Ægisdóttir & Gerstein, in press).

The third dimension, knowledge, refers to having information about another person's cultural heritage and customs and how such information affects definitions of normal and abnormal behavior and the process of counseling. Obviously, knowledge is an important component of cross-cultural counseling competencies. Knowledgeable counseling professionals understand that culture affects a wide array of behaviors, such as personality formation, career choices, signs and expressions of disorders, help-seeking behavior, and the validity, suitability, and appropriateness of counseling approaches (Arredondo et al., 1996). As stated previously in this handbook, in the United States knowledge about psychology and counseling outside the United States is lacking. Gerstein and Ægisdóttir (2007) found that only 6% of articles published in 4 counseling journals over 5 years focused on an international topic. Also, Arnett (2008) found that in six premier APA journals over a 5-year span, 68% of the samples studied were in the United States, 14% were in other English-speaking countries, and 13% were in Europe. Only 3% of the samples were from Asia, 1% from Latin America, and less than 1% from Africa and the Middle East. To change this trend, we need more articles focusing on international issues in English-language journals (Heppner, 1997).

Additionally, learning more about cultures worldwide may involve students and professionals reading publications in other fields (e.g., cultural anthropology, political science, linguistics, or sociology) (e.g., Ægisdóttir & Gerstein, in press), in languages besides English (Sexton & Misiak, 1984), and from a variety of countries. If students are proficient in multiple languages, they should be urged to read publications from original sources (Sexton & Misiak, 1984). Where multiple-language proficiency is lacking, it might be valuable for bilingual and international students and faculty members in mental health programs worldwide to explore the literature in psychology and anthropology written in languages other than English and share their findings with others in their program (Gerstein & Ægisdóttir, 2007). Faculty members are also encouraged to conduct more cross-cultural and international research, develop interdisciplinary teaching teams (Ibrahim, 1985), mentor students in conducting international research projects, and obtain training experiences relevant to the international arena (Heppner, 2006; Heppner, Leong, & Chiao, 2008; Heppner, Leong, & Gerstein, 2008). Mentoring students is critical to the acquisition of knowledge and competencies connected to working internationally (Ægisdóttir & Gerstein, in press). Leong and Ponterotto (2003) also suggested that a modern-language competency, once again, be encouraged in U.S. counseling programs and that international publications be included in the curriculum. Additionally, counseling professionals must carefully evaluate the cross-cultural validity of psychological concepts, methods, and strategies found in the profession (e.g., Ægisdóttir et al., 2008; Chapter 5, this volume).

Finally, requiring or strongly encouraging students (and counseling professionals, for that matter) to complete international internships, immersion experiences, or home-country practicum placements in community settings serving marginalized and minority communities can bring classroom and textbook learning to life (see also Ægisdóttir & Gerstein, in press). Some authors have predicted that there will be a rise in international internships in the near future (Leach, 2005; Leong & Leach 2007), which is definitely needed in the counseling profession. In fact, according to Leong and Leach (2007), the APA has started a process to explore setting up a group to manage accrediting international internships. Douce (2004) also encouraged establishing international internships and externships. She reported that the APA Society of Counseling Psychology along with the Counseling Psychology Division of the IAAP had plans to pursue such placements. To date, however, this plan has not progressed.

In the community and international "engagement" situations mentioned above, students interact with and humanize those who may have been previously "othered" or completely unknown. They also learn firsthand how to work in partnership and enact power sharing rather than paternalism in transnational and cross-cultural relationships. Cultural immersion experiences, even of a limited nature, can be very powerful learning opportunities (Heppner, Leong, & Chiao, 2008; Chapter 2, this volume). Traveling to different countries, however, is not always possible. Instead, training programs can modify their courses to integrate material from cultures around the world using existing publications and information found on Web sites and by watching movies. Furthermore, Web-based conferencing between counseling training programs around the world may be used to discuss a host of issues relevant to the cultural context of counseling and psychology. Online forums, Web-based bulletin boards, and chat rooms could also be launched to discuss pertinent issues, to post individual professional interests and projects, and to announce opportunities for collaboration and networking.

The fourth dimension of C-C MAKS is skills. Skilled counseling professionals pursue educational, consultation, and training opportunities to become more competent in multicultural and international work (e.g., Arredondo et al., 1996; Ægisdóttir & Gerstein, in press). They also understand the limits of their knowledge about other cultures and collaborate with native persons when working in international settings, ever aware that hierarchies of power and access exist in all countries and need to be considered when deciding on entry points and, thus, whose interests are being served when engaging in cross-national partnerships (Norsworthy, 2006). Counseling professionals must be skilled in diverse "cross-cultural contexts with people who hold differing world views" (Heppner, 1997, p. 7) and hold varying levels of power and privilege in their home countries (see Chapter 7).

As stated earlier, cultural-immersion experiences are effective ways to enhance one's skills to work

and function in an international setting (e.g., Leong & Ponterotto, 2003; see Chapter 8, this volume). Furthermore, as apparent from the chapters in Part II of this handbook, it is important to enhance counseling professionals' skills in the development of indigenous psychology outside the United States. Many of the recommendations mentioned earlier in this chapter and in this handbook (e.g., Chapters 1 through 8) can help accomplish this. We particularly encourage cross-national collaborations involving scholars, practitioners, and students.

While developing skills will contribute to cross-cultural competency, these skills must be combined with a rich philosophical framework. As such, counseling students must be trained to become aware of their own philosophy of life, their own capabilities, "and a recognition of different structures of reasoning and how all these variables affect one's communication and helping style" (Ibrahim, 1985, p. 636).

Based on the Atkinson et al. (1993) model and the work of Ægisdóttir and Gerstein (in press), we also suggest that more emphasis should be placed on counseling and psychology students developing skills in interacting with individuals while holding roles other than counselor or psychotherapist. In many cultures, the helping role needs to be adjusted to each person's level of acculturation to Western culture, the locus of problem etiology, and whether the intervention needs to be preventive or remedial. Given this observation, counseling professionals must be trained and feel comfortable in the roles of adviser, advocate, facilitator of indigenous support or healing systems, consultant, or change agent. In this respect, it is critical that the current schism between scientific psychology or counseling and traditional folk healing be resolved. Achieving an effective resolution may enhance the development of indigenous psychology and counseling worldwide. As part of this resolution, it is important for counseling professionals working internationally to consider how well their interventions and projects fit with cultural values and worldviews and adapt them accordingly.

Obviously, there is much more work to be performed to internationalize graduate training programs in counseling inside and outside the United States. We have provided some recommendations to accomplish this objective. Some writers have suggested, however, that such training should begin at the undergraduate level "with direct exposure to, and contact with, psychology abroad" (Sexton & Misiak, 1984, p. 1028). We agree with this suggestion and also strongly agree with Marsella and Pedersen (2004), who appealed to counseling psychology professionals:

> We call upon counseling psychologists throughout the world to dialogue, to exchange views and actual positions, to learn the challenges facing our world, and in the process, to create a new professional and global consciousness that can advance our field, resolve problems, and restore dignity. (p. 422)

CONCLUSION

The counseling profession around the world is growing rapidly and in unique ways to respond to the specific needs of diverse nations, cultures, people, and situations. Rich conceptual, research, and intervention paradigms have been developed, modified, and employed to address and meet these needs. Counseling professionals worldwide are actively engaged in a reflective and evaluative process to determine the validity, suitability, and applicability of various forms of counseling for their local constituents, cultures, and environment. In many parts of the world, this process has led to both considering and embracing an integration of emic (indigenous) and etic (universal) models of traditional healing and counseling as part of a unified whole. Cross-national collaboration among counseling professionals has contributed in part to the evolution of this exciting development, as has the growing recognition of the importance of designing and implementing paradigms of counseling that honor and respect indigenous cultural values and behaviors. It is hoped that with further cross-national interactions, counseling professionals will provide even greater support for the science and practice of the indigenization of counseling and psychology in all

corners of the world. In this regard, it is relevant to heed the words of Gardner Murphy (1969):

> The study of the human predicament can come from a human race familiar with the method of science, but a human race speaking many tongues, regarding many values, and holding different convictions about the meaning of life sooner or later will have to consult all that is human. (p. 528)

Consistent with Murphy's (1969) decree, counseling professionals can take full advantage of the numerous available technologies that can facilitate intimate and immediate communication. Also, it is essential that more frequent international conferences be scheduled by professional counseling associations to offer opportunities for face-to-face interactions that allow for more in-depth sharing of scientific findings, innovative interventions, training paradigms, and challenges, as well as the potential for networking individuals from various locations around the world. Attending such conferences can greatly increase the possibilities for fostering collaborative activities (e.g., research projects, consulting projects, exchange programs, or jointly sponsored training programs) among counseling professionals living in different countries.

To enhance understanding about counseling in different parts of the world, a Web-based clearinghouse of information easily accessible to all interested individuals would be highly beneficial. This multilingual clearinghouse should contain, for instance, a current listing of all professional counseling and psychology associations, relevant scholarly journals, credentialing bodies, ethical guidelines, and training programs. It should also feature bulletin boards, chat rooms, and networking forums where persons can post interests and dialogue about issues, challenges, and concerns. While there are a couple of Web-based sites that include some of this information, most of the sites are outdated and not comprehensive. Of course, to design, implement, and manage the proposed clearinghouse would be quite difficult; it would require a major investment of time and resources (financial and human) and the ability of professionals to closely and effectively collaborate on a very intricate and complex task. Perhaps professional associations worldwide could select representatives to serve on a steering committee to begin discussing the value, practicality, and usefulness of such a clearinghouse.

As was reported time and again in this book, to increase understanding about counseling in different parts of the world there is also a need to make scholarly journals more accessible to a wider readership. Perhaps editors of counseling and psychology journals worldwide could agree to publish one article in each issue in a language other than the one featured in their own periodical. To accomplish this, editors could establish "article exchange" relationships between their own periodical and one published in a different country. A much simpler task would be for editors to publish at least one abstract per issue of an article from another country's journal. Another option would be to develop a new international counseling journal, and for each issue, have editors from around the world submit one article in their country's primary language. A similar recommendation was offered by Beier (1952). To date, however, we are unaware of any such publication!

Although we could not locate any journals structured in a fashion outlined in the previous paragraph, there are journals that feature content in multiple languages. For instance, *Applied Psychology: An International Review* publishes articles in English and abstracts in English and French. The *International Journal for the Advancement of Counselling* includes articles and abstracts in English and, if the author so desires, an abstract in an additional language. Furthermore, the *Interamerican Journal of Psychology* publishes articles in Spanish and abstracts in both English and Spanish. Last, the *International Journal of Psychology* features articles in English and abstracts in English, French, and Spanish, while the *International Journal of Psychology and Psychological Therapy* publishes articles in English and abstracts in English and Spanish.

One other initiative has the potential to increase understanding about counseling in various countries throughout the world. As we have seen from the chapters in Part II of this book, the definitions and

functions of *counseling, counseling psychology, counselor,* and *counseling psychologist* vary from country to country, if the terms exist at all. Similarly, the credentialing and accreditation systems for counseling also widely differ. What might be helpful, then, is to establish forums or working groups wherein leaders of mental health professional associations from a host of countries could discuss the advantages and disadvantages of developing and implementing, for example, international standards for practice, credentialing, and accreditation. Another strategy to pursue standardized accreditation was recommended by Nixon (1990) who suggested that the IUPsyS and the IAAP might collaborate to assist national professional associations in establishing and accrediting training programs.

Given the complexity of developing and implementing international standards in the counseling profession and the diversity of the unique challenges to accomplish this task, specific tangible outcomes would be difficult to achieve in a short period of time. Regardless, the process of dialoguing about this task would result in greater understanding and, it is hoped, deeper respect for the unique characteristics of the counseling profession in different countries. Furthermore, such a process could generate other types of achievable, collaborative projects between national professional counseling associations and professionals to address shared and unique needs and concerns.

In conclusion, it is rather evident that we are in the midst of a renaissance period in the counseling profession worldwide. Without a doubt, this period of reflection, evaluation, innovation, and cross-national collaboration will continue and evolve for decades into the future. It is difficult to predict how the field of counseling might change, how psychological services may be delivered, and how the texture and content of our collaborative professional relationships might develop and blossom. In the years ahead, however, we are absolutely convinced that new, refined, and creative approaches to counseling grounded in diverse cultural contexts and incorporating traditional forms of healing will continue to emerge and thrive. These approaches will revolutionize how helping professionals around the world conceptualize and offer assistance to individuals, groups, organizations, and nations. They will also dramatically alter how we think about science, philosophy, research, and the human experience. Ultimately, through such discoveries, helping professionals worldwide will be better equipped to effectively assist their clientele, and at the same time, these discoveries can reinforce and promote the indigenous cultures that enrich our lives and also preserve the unique humanity of our species.

REFERENCES

Ad Hoc Joint Committee for the Development of a Universal Declaration of Ethical Principles for Psychologists. (2005). *Interim report: Developing a universal declaration of ethical principles for psychologists.* Retrieved April 29, 2009, from http://www.am.org/iupsys/resources/ethics/index.html

Adler, L. L., & Mukherji, B. R. (Eds.). (1995). *Spirit versus scalpel: Traditional healing and modern psychotherapy.* Westport, CT: Bergin & Garvey.

American Psychological Association. (2004). *Resolution on culture and gender awareness in international psychology.* Washington, DC: Author.

Arnett, J. J. (2008). The neglected 95%: Why American psychology needs to become less American. *American Psychologist, 63,* 602–614.

Arredondo, P., Toporek, R., Brown, S. P., Jones, J., Locke, D. C., Sanchez, J., et al. (1996). Operationalization of the multicultural counseling competencies. *Journal of Multicultural Counseling and Development, 24,* 42–78.

Atkinson, D. R., Thompson, C. E., & Grant, S. K. (1993). A three dimensional model for counseling racial/ethnic minorities. *The Counseling Psychologist, 21,* 257–277.

Beier, E. G. (1952). A problem in international communication. *American Psychologist, 7,* 592.

Bronfenbrenner, U. (1979). *The ecology of human development: Experiments by nature and design.* Cambridge, MA: Harvard University Press.

Cheung, F. M. (2000). Deconstructing counseling in a cultural context. *The Counseling Psychologist, 28,* 123–132.

Diener, E., & Crandall, R. (1978). *Ethics in social and behavioral research.* Chicago: University of Chicago Press.

Douce, L. A. (2004). Globalization of counseling psychology. *The Counseling Psychologist, 32,* 142–152.

Draguns, J. G. (2001). Toward a truly international psychology: Beyond English only. *American Psychologist, 56,* 1019–1030.

Friedman, T. L. (2006). *The world is flat: A brief history of the twenty-first century.* New York: Farrar, Straus & Giroux.

Gerstein, L. H. (2006). Counseling psychologists as international social architects. In R. L. Toporek, L. H. Gerstein, N. A. Fouad, G. Roysircar-Sodowsky, & T. Israel (Eds.), *Handbook for social justice in counseling psychology: Leadership, vision, and action* (pp. 377–387). Thousand Oaks, CA: Sage.

Gerstein, L. H., & Ægisdóttir, S. (2007). Training international social change agents: Transcending a U.S. counseling paradigm. *Counselor Education and Supervision, 47,* 123–139.

Gielen, U. P., Fish, J. M., & Draguns, J. D. (Eds.). (2004). *Handbook of culture, therapy, and healing.* Mahwah, NJ: Lawrence Erlbaum.

Golann, S. E. (1970). Ethical standards for psychology: Development and revision, 1938–1968. *Annals of the New York Academy of Sciences, 169,* 398–405.

Heppner, P. P. (1997). Building on strengths as we move into the next millennium. *The Counseling Psychologist, 25,* 5–14.

Heppner, P. P. (2006). The benefits and challenges of becoming cross-culturally competent counseling psychologists. *The Counseling Psychologist, 34,* 147–172.

Heppner, P. P. (2008). Expanding the conceptualization and measurement of applied problem solving and coping: From stages to dimensions in the almost forgotten cultural context. *American Psychologist, 63,* 805–816.

Heppner, P. P., Leong, F. T. L., & Chiao, H. (2008). The growing internationalization of counseling psychology. In S. D. Brown & R. W. Lent (Eds.), *Handbook of counseling psychology* (4th ed., pp. 68–85). New York: Wiley.

Heppner, P. P., Leong, F. T. L., & Gerstein, L. H. (2008). Counseling within a changing world. In W. B. Walsh (Ed.), *Biennial review of counseling psychology* (Vol. 1, pp. 231–258). New York: Routledge, Taylor & Francis.

Heppner, P. P., Wampold, B. E., & Kivlighan, D. M. (2008). *Research design in counseling* (3rd ed.). Belmont, CA: Thompson Brooks/Cole.

Horne, S. G., & Mathews, S. S. (2006). A social justice approach to international collaborative consultation. In R. L. Toporek, L. H. Gerstein, N. A. Fouad,

G. Roysircar-Sodowsky, & T. Israel (Eds.), *Handbook for social justice in counseling psychology: Leadership, vision, and action* (pp. 388–405). Thousand Oaks, CA: Sage.

Hoshmand, L. T. (Ed.). (2006). *Culture, psychotherapy, and counseling: Critical and integrative perspectives.* Thousand Oaks, CA: Sage.

Houser, R., Wilczenski, F. L., & Ham, M. A. (2006). *Culturally relevant ethical decision-making in counseling.* Thousand Oaks, CA: Sage.

Ibrahim, F. A. (1985). Effective cross-cultural counseling and psychotherapy: A framework. *The Counseling Psychologist, 13,* 625–638.

Leach, M. M. (2005). Internationalization and applied psychology internships. *International Psychology Reporter, 9*(3), 22–23.

Leach, M. M. (2008). *Compendium: Codes of ethics of national psychology associations around the world. International Union of Psychological Sciences.* Retrieved April 29, 2009, from http://www.am.org/iupsys/resources/ethics/index.html

Leach, M. M., & Oakland, T. (2007). Ethics standards impacting test development and use: A review of 31 ethics codes impacting practices in 35 countries. *International Journal of Testing, 7,* 71–88.

Leong, F. T. L., & Blustein, D. L. (2000). Toward a global vision of counseling psychology. *The Counseling Psychologist, 28,* 5–9.

Leong, F. T. L., & Leach, M. M. (2007). Internalizing counseling psychology in the United States: A SWOT analysis. *Applied Psychology: An International Review, 56,* 165–181.

Leong, F. T. L., & Lee, S. H. (2006). A cultural accommodation model of psychotherapy: Illustrated with the case of Asian Americans. *Psychotherapy: Theory, Research, Practice, and Training, 43,* 410–423.

Leong, F. T. L., & Ponterotto, J. G. (2003). A proposal for internationalizing counseling psychology in the United States: Rationale, recommendations and challenges. *The Counseling Psychologist, 31,* 381–395.

Leung, S. A. (2003). A journey worth traveling: Globalization of counseling psychology. *The Counseling Psychologist, 31,* 412–419.

Marsella, A. J., & Pedersen, P. (2004). Internationalizing the counseling psychology curriculum: Toward new values, competencies, and directions. *Counseling Psychology Quarterly, 17*(4), 413–423.

Moodley, R., & West, W. (Eds.). (2005). *Integrating traditional healing practices into counseling and psychotherapy.* Thousand Oaks, CA: Sage.

Murphy, G. (1969). Psychology in the year 2000. *American Psychologist, 24,* 523–530.

Neville, H. A., & Mobley, M. (2001). Social identities in contexts: An ecological model of multicultural counseling psychology processes. *The Counseling Psychologist, 29,* 471–486.

Nixon, M. (1990). Professional training in psychology: Quest for international standards. *American Psychologist, 45,* 1257–1262.

Norsworthy, K. L. (2006). Bringing social justice to international practices of counseling psychology. In R. L. Toporek, L. H. Gerstein, N. A. Fouad, G. Roysircar-Sodowsky, & T. Israel (Eds.), *Handbook for social justice in counseling psychology: Leadership, vision, and action* (pp. 421–441). Thousand Oaks, CA: Sage.

Norsworthy, K. L., & Gerstein, L. (2003). Counseling and building communities of peace: The interconnections. *International Journal for the Advancement of Counseling, 25*(4), 197–203.

Pack-Brown, S. P., & Williams, C. B. (2003). *Ethics in a multicultural context.* Thousand Oaks, CA: Sage.

Pedersen, P. B. (1995). Culture-centered ethical guidelines for counselors. In J. G. Ponterotto, J. M. Casas, L. A. Susuki, & C. M. Alexander (Eds.), *Handbook of multicultural counseling* (1st ed., pp. 34–49). Thousand Oaks, CA: Sage.

Pedersen, P. B. (1997). The cultural context of American Counseling Association Code of Ethics. *Journal of Counseling and Development, 76,* 23–28.

Pedersen, P. B. (2003). Culturally biased assumptions in counseling psychology. *The Counseling Psychologist, 31,* 396–403.

Pedersen, P. B., & Leong, F. (1997). Counseling in an international context. *The Counseling Psychologist, 25,* 117–122.

Ridley, C. R., Liddle, M. C., Hill, C. L., & Li, L. C. (2001). Ethical decision making in multicultural counseling. In J. G. Ponterotto, J. M. Casas, L. A. Susuki, & C. M. Alexander (Eds.), *Handbook of multicultural counseling* (2nd ed., pp. 165–188). Thousand Oaks, CA: Sage.

Santee, R. G. (2007). *An integrative approach to counseling: Bridging Chinese thought, evolutionary theory, and stress management.* Thousand Oaks, CA: Sage.

Savickas, M. L. (2007). Internationalisation of counseling psychology: Constructing cross-national consensus and collaboration. *Applied Psychology: An International Review, 56*(1), 182–188.

Sexton, V. S., & Misiak, H. (1984). American psychologists and psychology abroad. *American Psychologist, 39,* 1026–1031.

Sue, D. W., Arredondo, P., & McDavis, R. J. (1992). Multicultural counseling competencies and standards: A call to the profession. *Journal of Counseling and Development, 70,* 477–486.

Trimble, J. E., & Fisher, C. B. (2006). *The handbook of ethical research with ethnocultural populations and communities.* Thousand Oaks, CA: Sage.

Varenne, H. (2003). On internationalizing counseling psychology: A view from cultural anthropology. *The Counseling Psychologist, 31,* 404–411.

Yang, K. S., Hwang, K. K., Pedersen, P. B., & Daibo, I. (Eds.). (2003). *Progress in Asian social psychology:* *Conceptual and empirical contributions.* Westport, CT: Praeger.

Ægisdóttir, S., & Gerstein, L. H. (in press). International counseling competencies: A new frontier in multicultural training. In J. C. Ponterotto, J. M. Casas, L. A. Suzuki, & C. A. Alexander (Eds.), *Handook of multicultural counseling* (3rd ed). Thousand Oaks, CA: Sage.

Ægisdóttir, S., Gerstein, L. H., & Çinarbaş, D. C. (2008). Methodological issues in cross-cultural counseling research: Equivalence, bias, and translations. *The Counseling Psychologist, 36,* 188–219.

Index

Italy, 293, 296–297
See also Vocational guidance
Career model, Chinese, 200
Carnegie Commission, 424
CAS. *See* Cognitive Assessment System (CAS)
Casa de Beneficiencia, 406
CASSON. *See* Counselling Association of
    Nigeria (CASSON)
Catholicism:
    Puerto Rico, 404–405
    Venezuela, 370, 378–379
Cattell's 16 Personality Factors, 275
CBT. *See* Cognitive behavior therapies (CBT)
CCA. *See* Canadian Counseling Association (CCA)
CCP. *See* College of Counselling Psychologists (CCP)
CCS. *See* Collectivist Copy Styles (CCS) inventory
CDI. *See* Career Development Inventory (CDI)
CECC. Competencies Elicitations Career
    Counseling (CECC)
CEDP. *See* College of Educational and Developmental
    Psychologists (CEDP)
Central Asia, 265–276, 506
Certificate and Leisure Board (CALB), 440
Certification, in Greece, 348–349
Certified counselor designation, 168
Certified psychological designation, 168
Chae-myun (saving face), 165–167, 179
Chamanismo, 7, 387–388, 397–399
Chartered psychologist, 282, 287
Cheung, F. M., 74
Chiao, Hung, 553
Childhood sexual abuse, 283
China, 183–196
    CPS registration document, 192
    development of indigenous counseling in, 194
    economic and social development, 183–184
    establishment of first code of ethics for counseling
        and clinical practice, 188–189
    future destinations, 194–195, 508
    licensure and credentialing of counseling
        professionals in, 185–188
    mental health demands, 183–184
    research in counseling, 189–191
    training programs, 191–194
    Yin and *Yang*, 226
Chinese Association of Psychological Testing, 15
Chinese career model, 200
Chinese Mental Health Association (CMHA), 185,
    190, 192–194
Chinese Mental Health Journal (CMHJ), 189–190
Chinese Ministry of Labor and Social Security Affairs
    (CMLSS), 184–185
Chinese Personality Assessment Inventory (CPAI), 100

Chinese Psychological Society (CPS), 184–187, 192
Chosun dynasty, 178
Christianity:
    former USSR, 338
    Israel, 450
    Malaysia, 222
    Nigeria, 436
    South Korea, 178
    See also Catholicism; Greek Orthodox Church
Chronic paranoid disorder, 272
Churches Counselling Service, 211
Çiftçi, Ayşe, 553
Cin (genie), 477
Çınarbaş, Deniz Canel, 553
CIP. *See* Committee on International Planning (CIP)
CIRP. *See* Committee on International Relations in
    Psychology (CIRP)
Civil disobedience, in India, 254
Civil rights, 47. *See also entries for specific countries*
Civil rights movement, in United States, 35, 41–42
Clawson, Thomas, 553
Clinical psychology:
    Australia, 493–495
    China, 186
    South Africa, 426–427
Clinical psychology licensure, 168
Club of Investors for an Alternative and Local
    Management and Solidarity Savings, 335
CMHA. *See* Chinese Mental Health
    Association (CMHA)
CMHJ. *See* Chinese Mental Health Journal (CMHJ)
CMLSS. *See* Chinese Ministry of Labor and Social
    Security Affairs (CMLSS)
Coaching, 454
Code of Ethics for Counseling and Clinical Practice
    (China), 188
Cognitive Assessment System (CAS), 411
Cognitive-behavioral approach, 315, 459, 494
Cognitive-behavioral counselor, 216
Cognitive behavior therapies (CBT),
    243–244, 286–287
Cognitive Behaviour Therapy, 324
Cognitive psychotherapy, Taoist, 190
Cognitive Revolution, 285
Cognitive therapy, 272
Cognitive tolerance, 470
Cohen-Scali, Valérie, 553
Collaboration:
    challenges to, 510
    cross-cultural, 141–153
    crossing borders in, 125–137
    facilitation of, 112
    See also Internationalization

About the Editors

Lawrence H. Gerstein is a professor of psychology, director of the doctoral program in counseling psychology, and director of the Center for Peace and Conflict Studies at Ball State University in Muncie, Indiana. He is coeditor of the *Handbook for Social Justice in Counseling Psychology: Leadership, Vision, and Action,* and he managed the Tibetan and Chinese translations of the book, *Buddha's Warriors.* He is a fellow of the American Psychological Association, coeditor of *The Counseling Psychologist* International Forum, president of the International Tibet Independence Movement, and a past cochair of the International Section of the Society of Counseling Psychology–American Psychological Association. He has published extensively on international and social justice issues as well as on loneliness, self-monitoring, and employee assistance programs. He received his PhD in counseling and social psychology from the University of Georgia in 1983. Since his teenage years, he has traveled extensively throughout the world. He has been fortunate to collaborate with individuals in numerous countries.

P. Paul Heppner is currently a professor of the Department of Educational, School, and Counseling Psychology at the University of Missouri. He is cofounder of and since 1998 has been codirector of the MU Center for Multicultural Research, Training and Consultation, and he was the inaugural cochair of the International Section of the Society of Counseling Psychology. He has published more than 160 articles or book chapters and eight books; his primary research interests focus on applied problem solving and coping. He has made hundreds of presentations at national conferences and delivered more than 40 invited presentations in 14 countries. In addition, he has served on several national and international editorial boards and as editor of *The Counseling Psychologist.* He is a fellow of the American Psychological Association (Divisions 17 and 52) and the American Psychological Society. In 2005–2006, he served as president of the Society of Counseling Psychology. He has been honored to receive a named professorship and to be the recipient of several awards for his leadership, research, teaching, mentoring, international work, and activities promoting diversity and social justice issues; he has been the recipient of three Fulbright awards, and has been fortunate to live in six countries and have wonderful collaborators in several countries, most notably Taiwan. He received his doctorate in 1979 from the University of Nebraska–Lincoln.

Stefanía Ægisdóttir is a native of Iceland and an associate professor in the Department of Counseling Psychology and Guidance Services at Ball State University, Indiana. She is a former Fulbright scholarship recipient for pursuing doctoral studies in the United States and recently completed a 3-year grant from the Icelandic Research Fund (Icelandic Centre for Research [Rannís]) to study psychological help-seeking patterns of Icelanders. Her primary teaching interests are research methodology, assessment, program development and evaluation, and clinical training. She has written about cross-cultural research methods, attitudes and expectations about counseling, clinical judgment, and international and cross-cultural issues and competencies in counseling research and training. She received her doctorate in counseling psychology in 2000 from Ball State University.

Seung-Ming Alvin Leung is a professor in and chairperson of the Department of Educational Psychology, The Chinese University of Hong Kong. He previously held faculty positions at the University of Nebraska–Lincoln and the University of Houston. His major areas of scholarly interest include career development and assessment; cross-cultural, multicultural, and international issues in counseling; and counseling in educational settings. He is currently the editor of *Asian Journal of Counselling*. He is the first counseling psychologist from outside the United States to serve as associate editor of *The Counseling Psychologist* (1999–2002). He is a fellow of the American Psychological Association (APA) and the Hong Kong Professional Counselling Association. He received the "Distinguished Contributions to the International Advancement of the Counseling Profession" Award at the 2008 International Counseling Psychology Conference in Chicago and the 2009 "Distinguished Alumni Award" from his alma mater, the University of Illinois at Urbana–Champaign. He is one of the three cochairs of the International Section of the Division of Counseling Psychology of the APA (2008–2010).

Kathryn L. Norsworthy is a licensed psychologist, nationally certified counselor, and university professor. She is the Bornstein Faculty Scholar (2008–2009), Graduate Studies in Counseling, at Rollins College, Winter Park, Florida. She currently serves as chair of the international committee of the Division of Trauma Psychology of the American Psychological Association (APA). Since 1997, she has been engaged in activist research and practice projects focusing on trauma, feminist counseling, cross-national collaboration, and peace building in Thailand, Cambodia, and northern India, as well as with refugee and internationally displaced communities of Burma and cross-national groups. Nationally, she received the 2003 American Counseling Association Kitty Cole Human Rights Award, the 2007 Outstanding International Psychologist from the International Division of the APA, and the 2008 Many Faces of Counseling Psychology Award from the APA's Division of Counseling Psychology during its international conference. Author and coauthor of numerous articles and book chapters on her international social justice work and cross-national partnerships, she was featured in the December 2007, issue of the *APA Monitor on Psychology* as a "Humanitarian Hero." She received her doctorate from the University of Minnesota.

About the Contributors

Gulnara Aitpaeva, in 1999, founded the Kyrgyz Ethnology Department at American University–Central Asia in Bishkek, Kyrgyzstan, Kyrgyz Republic, with the mission of developing new social science anthropology. In 2002, she took the initiative of transforming this department into the Department of Cultural Anthropology and Archeology to expand its scope and mission. From 2001 to early 2004, she has been Vice President for Academic Affairs at American University–Central Asia. Her team led the process of transforming the university from a Soviet-style curriculum to a Western credit system of education. In spring 2004, she founded the Aigine Cultural Research Center with the mission of expanding research into lesser known aspects of the cultural and natural heritage of Kyrgyzstan, integrating local, esoteric, and scholar epistemologies relating to cultural, biological, and ethnic diversities. She earned a candidate degree in literature studies at Moscow State University, Russia, in 1987, and a doctoral degree in literature and folklore studies at Kyrgyz National State University, Bishkek, in 1996.

M. Asir Ajmal is a professor of psychology at GC University, Lahore, Pakistan. His father, Dr. Muhammed Ajmal, was a pioneer and helped establish the discipline of psychology in Pakistan. He taught educational psychology to primary schoolteachers in Lahore. In 1999, he moved to the United Kingdom, where he got his statement of equivalence as a clinical psychologist after 3 years of training. He worked as a clinical psychologist in a forensic setting in the United Kingdom. He is active in promoting indigenous qualitative research in Pakistan. His ongoing projects include studying interfaith relations, especially between Muslims and Jews. In 1994, he earned his PhD in psychology at Dartmouth College, Hanover, New Hampshire.

Fatima Al-Darmaki is currently an assistant professor in the counseling program in the Department of Psychology and Counseling, College of Humanities and Social Sciences, United Arab Emirates University, in Al-Ain, United Arab Emirates (UAE). She was the director of the Student Advising and of the Counseling Center of UAE University for 6 years (1999–2005). She developed student counseling services at UAE University according to international standards for college and university counseling services. Her research interests include cross-cultural counseling, help-seeking behavior, women's issues, and counselor training. She is married and has one daughter. She received her PhD in counseling psychology from the University of Missouri–Columbia. She completed her internship at the University of Iowa Counseling Services in 1998.

Rubén Ardila is a Colombian research psychologist and a professor at the National University of Colombia. He has done research on experimental analysis of behavior, history of psychology, and the application of psychology to socioeconomic development. He has published 29 books and more than 250 scientific papers in journals from several countries. Some of his books have been translated into English and other languages. As a visiting professor in several countries, including the United States, Germany, Puerto Rico, Spain, Argentina, and others, he has promoted international psychology.

He has been president of the Interamerican Society of Psychology (SIP), the International Society for Comparative Psychology (ISCP), the Latin American Association for the Analysis and Modification of Behavior (ALAMOC), and others. He founded the *Revista Latinoamericana de Psicologia* (*Latin American Journal of Psychology*) and edited this journal from 1969 to 2003. He was a member of the executive committee of the International Union of Psychological Science (IUPsyS) between 1992 and 2004. He is a member of the Board of Directors of the International Association of Applied Psychology (IAAP, 2006–2010). In 2004, he received the Science Award from Colombia. His most recent recognition is the American Psychological Association Award for Distinguished Contributions to the International Advancement of Psychology (2007). He received a PhD in experimental psychology from the University of Nebraska–Lincoln.

Gideon Arulmani is a clinical psychologist. He is the managing trustee of The Promise Foundation, a charity headquartered in Bangalore, India. He is a consultant to multilateral agencies and has executed assignments on guidance and counseling in Africa and South Asia. He is an honorary research fellow at the University of Portsmouth (United Kingdom), an international fellow of the National Institute for Careers Education and Counselling (United Kingdom), and visiting Senior Lecturer at the University of Canterbury Christ Church (United Kingdom). His core interests lie in developing applications from the behavioral sciences that are in tune with cultural practices. He received his doctoral degree from the University of Portsmouth (United Kingdom).

Narynbek Ashiraliev is an associate professor in the Department of Anthropology at American University–Central Asia in Bishkek, Kyrgyzstan, Kyrgyz Republic. He is an alumnus of Lomonosov Moscow State University. He teaches several courses on topics such as the history of Kyrgyzstan, political issues of the 20th century, the history of management thought, political bureaucracy, the history of Japan (1945–1991), and so on. He also manages

undergraduate and graduate students' diploma thesis projects. As a professional, he is interested in studying the history of nomads, defense issues, and the history of World War II. He has a PhD in history.

Benny A. Benjamin is the chief psychologist at the Israel National Employment Service, Jerusalem; an adjunct lecturer at Bar Ilan University; a member of the National Professional Standards Committee for vocational psychology (Israel); a former chairman of the Israel Employment and Career Counselors Association; a member of the Ethics Appeals Commission for the Israel Psychological Association; Israel liaison for the Division of Counseling Psychology, International Association of Applied Psychologists; and a member of the editorial committees of several professional newsletters and journals. His professional and research interests lie in multicultural career development, job-search training, and the interface of career coaching and career counseling. He has a BA in psychology from Hebrew University of Jerusalem and an MA in psychology and PhD in counseling and guidance from the University of Missouri–Kansas City.

Md Shuaib bin Che Din is currently a professor in and the dean of the School of Psychology and Social Work at University Malaysia Sabah (UMS), Malaysia. He was a faculty member at University Kebangsaan Malaysia before he went to UMS. His areas of expertise are drug rehabilitation, counselor education, and counselor supervision. He spearheads and acts as advisor to many drug rehabilitation programs in Malaysia. He is a board member of the Malaysian Board of Counselors (LKM).

Teresa Borja is a professor, coordinator, and founder of the psychology program at Universidad San Francisco de Quito in Quito, Ecuador. She is a pioneer and a leader in sex education in Ecuador. She has developed a series of radio, television, and school-based sex educational programs, as well as published articles on this topic in local newspapers and magazines. Her scholarly interests also focus on HIV in Ecuador. She earned her BA, MA, and PhD in psychology at the University of Western Ontario, Canada.

Hung Chiao is a Taiwanese international student enrolled in the counseling psychology doctoral program at the University of Missouri. Her primary research interests are cross-cultural counseling, cross-cultural coping, and LGBT (lesbian, gay, bisexual, and transgender) issues. Her career has been influenced by two great advisers and mentors, Li-fei Wang and Puncky Heppner. Her career goals are to be an active networker and to advocate for international psychology and LGBT counseling psychology. She received her master's degree in counselor education at the University of Texas at Austin and her bachelor's degree in educational psychology and counseling at National Taiwan Normal University.

Ayşe Çiftçi is currently a faculty member in counseling psychology at Purdue University. Her research area focuses on cross-cultural adaptation of immigrants and international students. She has authored more than 20 publications and made 30 international/national presentations. She is also the editor of *International Section Newsletter* of Division 17 (Counseling Psychology) and served as Program chair for Division 52 (International Psychology) for the 2009 American Psychological Association Convention. She received her PhD in counseling psychology from the University of Memphis, Tennessee, in 2006.

Deniz Canel Çınarbaş is an assistant professor at the Department of Educational Psychology, University of Alberta, Edmonton, Alberta, Canada. She was born in Turkey. She is interested in cross-cultural psychopathology, Turkish indigenous healing methods, and multicultural counseling. She has conducted research projects on intergroup anxiety and intergroup contact, cross-cultural construct equivalence of depression, anxiety, and somatization, bias and translation in cross-cultural research, and racial microaggressions. She received her bachelor's degree from Middle East Technical University, Ankara, Turkey. She obtained her master's degree in clinical psychology and doctorate in counseling psychology from Ball State University, Indiana.

Thomas Clawson, EdD, NCC, is President and CEO of the National Board for Certified Counselors and Affiliates (NBCC). He is regarded as a preeminent counseling leader. He is a member of several international and national boards. Over the past three decades, he has been involved in initiatives to promote the advancement and strengthening of professional counseling and counseling services across the globe. He has numerous publications and awards in the area of counseling, standards of professional practice, and credentialing. He holds three advanced degrees, including a doctorate in counseling from the College of William and Mary, Williamsburg, Virginia.

Valérie Cohen-Scali, PhD, is Assistant Professor of social psychology in the Department of Management, University of North Paris. Her research focuses on (1) the attitudes on work of young adults and more particularly the relationship between work experience and the construction of the professional self, and (2) the transformation of the collective identity of career counselors. She has published several books, notably *Alternance et Identité Professionnelle* [School/Work Alternation and Occupational Identity] and *Les métiers de la psychologie sociale et du travail* [The Professions of Work and Social Psychology]. She is often involved in several projects with the European Union related to the evolution of different organizations and occupational groups.

María-Cristina Cruza-Guet is a doctoral candidate in counseling psychology at Lehigh University, where she teaches as adjunct faculty. Her clinical and research interests center on multicultural counseling, Hispanic women's mental health, Hispanic social support networks, and eating disorders. She is a recipient of a National Institute of Mental Health (NIMH) minority supplement grant and is a fellow of the Harvard Eating Disorders Center. She serves as Regional Diversity Coordinator for the American Psychological Association of Graduate Students (APAGS) Committee on Ethnic Minority Affairs. She holds a degree in clinical psychology from Pontificia Universidad Católica del Ecuador and a master's degree in counseling and human services from Lehigh University.

Eduardo E. Delgado Polo is Dean, Faculty of Education, National Pedagogical University, Bogota, Colombia. He is a professor of special education whose research focuses on upheavals in development. He is the director of the project "Ambient pedagogical complexes for the development of people in handicapped situation: Humid classroom." He has extensive experience working with the physically handicapped, underprivileged people, and vulnerable communities. He is the producer of the radio program "People of Colors" of the National University. He has a master's degree in commiunitarian psychology.

Edward A. Delgado-Romero is an associate professor and director of training in the counseling psychology doctoral program at the University of Georgia. He is the president of the National Latina/Latino Psychological Association and a fellow of the American Psychological Association (Divisions 45 and 17). He is a Colombian American, and his mother Isabel is a native of Cali, Colombia.

Carlos M. Diaz-Lazaro was born and raised in Puerto Rico. He is currently a part-time faculty member at Walden University. He publishes and presents primarily on topics related to the development of multicultural counseling competencies, Latino psychology, and feminist psychotherapy. He obtained his BA in social sciences specializing in psychology from the University of Puerto Rico, Rio Piedras Campus. He received his PhD in counseling psychology from the State University of New York at Buffalo.

Changming Duan is an associate professor of counseling psychology at the University of Missouri Kansas City. She is interested in multicultural and international issues in counseling. She has experience in teaching multicultural counseling classes as well as teaching counseling outside the United States.

Sif Einarsdóttir currently works as an associate professor in the career counseling and guidance program at the University of Iceland, in her home country. In her research, she has mainly focused on vocational interests and cross-cultural issues in assessment. She has also performed research related to diversity in counseling and education and, most recently, on attitudes toward counseling and help-seeking behavior of Icelanders. She is also interested in higher education, teaching, quality issues, and equality. In 2001, she completed her doctoral degree in counseling psychology at the University of Illinois, Champaign–Urbana.

Jean-Philippe Gaudron is a professor of work and social psychology at Université de Toulouse, France. His research interests are in the area of career counseling and vocational interests. His publications have appeared in journals such as *Journal of Vocational Behavior,* the *Career Development Quarterly* (CDQ), and *Computers in Human Behavior.* In 2006, he received the CDQ Outstanding Research Article Award. He received his PhD in psychology from Université Paris Descartes, Paris.

Ralph Goldstein, PhD, pursued academic research in emotional learning theories and hormonal influences on animal brain and behavior before accepting a lecturing post at University College of Worcester, United Kingdom. But the motivation for all this study was to do clinical work with a Jungian orientation. He has also been chair of the British Psychological Society's Division of Counselling Psychology (2006–2007) and a member of the group that devised the Society's postqualifying Register of Psychologists specializing in psychotherapy. Current research interests are mainly directed to the somewhat neglected field of emotions in psychology and pyschotherapy.

Jean Guichard, PhD, is Professor of vocational psychology at the National Institute for the Study of Work and Vocational Counseling (Paris) and a former director of that institute. His research focuses on (1) the dynamism of self-construction and (2) the setting-up and assessment of career development interventions (education and counseling). He has published several books, notably *L'école et les Représentations d'Avenir des Adolescents* [School and Adolescents' Future Representations] (translated into Spanish) and, with Michel Huteau, *Psychologie* *de l'Orientation* [Vocational Psychology] (translated into Italian, Polish, and Portuguese). He has authored different career education programs and a method for a constructivist counseling interview.

Janet E. Helms, PhD, is the Augustus Long Professor in the Department of Counseling, Developmental, and Educational Psychology and Director of the Institute for the Study and Promotion of Race and Culture at Boston College. She is president of the American Psychological Association (APA) Society of Counseling Psychology (Division 17) and a fellow of this Division and Division 45 (Ethnic Diversity). She has written more than 60 articles and 4 books on racial identity and cultural influences on assessment and counseling practice. She received Division 45's 1999 Distinguished Career Contributions to Research Award, Division 17's 2002 Leona Tyler Award, APA's 2006 Award for Distinguished Contributions to Education and Training, the 2007 Association of Black Psychologists' Distinguished Psychologist Award, and the 2008 Award for Distinguished Contributions to Research in Public Policy.

Alicia M. Homrich, PhD, is an associate professor and chair of the Graduate Studies in Counseling program at Rollins College, Winter Park, Florida. In addition to her position as a counselor educator, she is a licensed psychologist and a licensed marriage and family therapist. She is most interested in the strengths and resiliency of counselors-in-training and uses a solution-oriented approach in individual and group supervision.

Sharon Horne, PhD, is an associate professor of counseling psychology at the University of Memphis, Tennessee. Her work focuses on the psychological well-being of gay, lesbian, bisexual, and transgender individuals, as well as the application of psychology in international and cross-cultural contexts. She is an Open Society George Soros Academic fellow in Kyrgyzstan and has extensive experience living and working in postcommunist countries of the former Soviet Union and Eastern Europe.

Zhi-Jin Hou is an associate professor of counseling in the School of Psychology at Beijing Normal University, China. She is a board member of the Clinical and Counseling Psychology committee of the Chinese Psychological Society. She is a Liaison for China in Division 16 (Counseling Psychology) of the International Association of Applied Psychology, an international Affiliate of the American Psychological Association. She teaches and does research in the fields of counseling and career development. She graduated from Chinese University of Hong Kong.

Moshe Israelashvili is an associate professor in the Department of Human Development and Education, School of Education, Tel Aviv University, Israel. He is affiliated with the School Counseling Program and teaches graduate and undergraduate courses on school mental health, prevention and inoculation, resilience promotion, and counseling theories. His major fields of study are transitional stress and (mal)adjustment, coping, resilience, and thriving, and developmental school counseling. All these issues are studied in exploration of universal processes and problems as well as of those cross-cultural differences that might exist.

Celestine U. U. U. Kadurumba, PhD, is a senior lecturer at the Michael Okpara University of Agriculture, Umudike, Umuahia, Abia State, Nigeria. He is interested in developmental counseling.

Ashraf Kagee is a professor of psychology at Stellenbosch University in South Africa. His research interests lie in the field of health psychology, particularly in the behavioral aspects of HIV and AIDS, which is a serious public health concern in sub-Saharan Africa. He has also conducted research on trauma among persons affected by political turbulence and is presently researching the psychosocial concerns of refugees living in South Africa. He works with several nongovernmental organizations that provide services to marginalized communities. He holds a PhD in counseling psychology and a master's degree in public health.

Makiko Kasai is a professor at Naruto University of Education in Tokushima, Japan. She is a member of the American Psychological Association, the

Association of Japanese Clinical Psychology, the Japanese Association of Counseling Science, and the Japanese Psychoanalytical Association. Her areas of research include school counselor training, sensitivity training for counselors about sexual and multicultural minorities, and evidence-based research on the processes of counseling and psychotherapy. In addition to her academic and clinical work at her university, she has a part-time appointment with a junior high school as a school counselor. She earned her PhD at the University of Missouri–Columbia.

Changdai Kim is a professor in the Department of Education at Seoul National University in South Korea. He teaches courses in theories of counseling and psychotherapy, oversees the group counseling practicum, and contributes to program development at the university. He is the author or coauthor of numerous journal articles and books. His research interests include functions of internal working model in interpersonal relationships, emotional regulation in counseling, application of neuroscientific methods in counseling research, and group dynamics. He received his BA and MA in education from Seoul National University and his MEd and EdD in counseling psychology from Teachers College, Columbia University. He enjoys participating in marathons and playing drums in his free time.

Dong Min Kim is an associate professor in the College of Education at Chung-Ang University, Seoul, South Korea. His research interests include issues in national youth counseling policies and counseling effectiveness, excessive use of the Internet, and prevention of juvenile delinquency. He participated in designing the national support system for at-risk adolescents in South Korea, known as the Community Youth Safety Net. In 1990, he obtained his BA in education; in 1993, he earned his MA in counseling from Seoul National University; and in 2002 he received his PhD in counseling psychology from the University of Wisconsin–Madison.

Elena Kim is currently an assistant professor in the Department of Psychology at the American

University–Central Asia, in Bishkek, Kyrgyzstan, Kyrgyz Republic. The areas of her research interests include gender and international development. She has her master's degree in gender studies from the Central European University in Budapest. Currently, she is a PhD candidate in the sphere of social structures at the Institute of Social Enterprise in Bishkek, Kyrgyzstan.

Kay Hyon Kim is a professor in the Department of Education and former director of the University Counseling Center ("Student Life and Culture Institute"), Seoul National University, South Korea. He teaches current issues in counseling psychology, training and supervision in counseling, and legal, ethical, and policy issues in counseling. He is also interested in training the staffing professionals and career counselors associated with the Department of Labor, South Korea. In 1995–1996, he visited the University of Wisconsin and taught courses on research in individual interventions and supervision. He has authored or coauthored numerous articles and books, of which one was a "must read" among Korean counselors as well as counseling students. He enjoys playing golf and walking along a small river near his residence. He obtained his BA and MA from Seoul National University and his PhD from the University of Oregon.

Kwong-Liem Karl Kwan is a Hong Kong Chinese who in 2008 joined the Department of Counseling faculty at San Francisco State University. He is the coeditor of the International Forum for *The Counseling Psychologist* (United States) and was the guest editor for a special issue titled Ethical Practice of Counseling in Asia for *Asian Journal of Counseling* (Hong Kong). He is an editorial board member of *Educational Psychology Bulletin* (Taiwan), *Journal of Counseling Psychology* (United States), and *Psychological Assessment* (United States). He received his doctorate in counseling psychology from the University of Nebraska–Lincoln.

Georgios K. Lampropoulos is an assistant professor of counseling psychology at Florida State University, where he teaches in the MS/EdS program in mental health counseling (Council for

Accreditation of Counseling and Related Educational Programs [CACREP] accredited) and the combined PhD program in counseling psychology and school psychology. He is also the coordinator of the MS/EdS program in mental health counseling. His professional and research interests include counseling process and outcomes, homework in psychotherapy, eclecticism and psychotherapy integration, counselor training and development, and diversity/international issues in counseling. He has an undergraduate and a graduate degree in psychology from the University of Crete, Greece; a PhD in counseling psychology from Ball State University, Indiana; and a clinical/research postdoctoral degree from Pennsylvania State University.

Carlos León-Andrade, MD, is the chief of psychiatric services at Hospital Metropolitano in Quito, Ecuador, and the editor of *Metro Ciencia*, a medical journal published by the Hospital Metropolitano. He is a professor of psychopharmacology and psychophysiology at Universidad San Francisco de Quito and the past president of Asociacion Ecuatoriana de Psiquiatria and Interamerican Council of Psychiatric Organizations.

Frederick T. L. Leong, PhD, is a professor of psychology at Michigan State University in the industrial/organizational and clinical psychology programs and serves as the director of the Center for Multicultural Psychology Research. He has authored or coauthored more than 120 articles in various psychology journals, 80 book chapters, and edited or coedited 10 books. He is a fellow of the American Psychological Association and American Psychological Society. His major clinical research interests center around culture and mental health and cross-cultural psychotherapy (especially with Asians and Asian Americans), whereas his industrial/organizational research is focused on cultural and personality factors related to career choice, work adjustment, and occupational stress.

Thomas Lindgren, PhD, is an assistant professor in the Department of Psychology, Stockholm University, Sweden. Prior to receiving his doctorate, he served for 15 years as a clinical psychologist at the Jakobsberg and Solna-Sundbyberg Psychiatric Outpatient Community Health Care Centers of the regional government of Stockholm. His present research is in the area of personality assessment. He is an advocate of collaborative and therapeutic forms of psychological assessment. In 2007, he received his doctorate in psychology at the Karolinska Institute, Stockholm.

Walter J. Lonner is the founding and special issues editor of the *Journal of Cross-Cultural Psychology* (*JCCP*). A charter member of the International Association for Cross-Cultural Psychology (IACCP), he has been involved with numerous books in the field, including *Counseling Across Cultures* (2007; P. B. Pedersen, J. G. Draguns, W. J. Lonner, and J. E. Trimble, editors, 6th edition, Sage) and *Discovering Cultural Psychology: A Profile and Selected Readings of Ernest E. Boesch* (2007; with S. A. Hayes). A former Fulbright scholar (Germany, 1984–1985), he is Professor Emeritus of Psychology at Western Washington University, where he cofounded the Center for Cross-Cultural Research in 1969.

Emma Mejía is a family therapist in the Department of Psychiatry, Centro Médico Docente La Trinidad, Caracas, Venezuela. She also worked as a family therapist and family psychoeducator at Humana, Caracas. She is a professor of family therapy in the Universidad Católica Andrés Bello undergraduate program in psychology in the School of Psychology and in the graduate program in Clinical and Community Psychology. She was also a visiting professor at the Department of Family Therapy, Universidad Autónoma de Santo Domingo, República Dominicana. She was a psychologist at Universidad Católica Andrés Bello, Caracas, Venezuela, in 1984. She earned a master's degree in family therapy from Hahnemann University, Philadelphia, Pennsylvania, in 1984. In 2007, she completed an intensive course in systemic family therapy at Santiago de Compostela, Spain.

Elena Molchanova is currently an associate professor of psychology at American University–Central Asia in Bishkek, Kyrgyzstan, Kyrgyz Republic, and a professor of psychiatry at Slavonic University in Kyrgyzstan. She earned her MD in psychiatry from Kyrgyz State Medical Academy and her kandidat nauk (equivalent to the PhD in post-Soviet states) from Slavonic University in Kyrgyzstan. Her research interests include cultural psychology and psychiatry. She also teaches introductory psychology courses and courses in cognitive psychology, psychological testing, and psychiatry.

Anthony V. Naidoo is a professor of community psychology in the Department of Psychology, Stellenbosch University and is currently departmental chair. He is involved in several community development projects addressing the needs of adolescents from vulnerable communities. His interests also include rite of passage work as a vehicle for men's development, career development, and multicultural interactions. He has lectured in several international contexts, including Eritrea, Mexico, United States, and Norway. He serves on the international task team for the Society of Community Research and Action. He is a graduate of the University of the Western Cape in South Africa and Ball State University in Indiana.

Johanna E. Nilsson, PhD, is an associate professor in the Division of Counseling and Educational Psychology at the University of Missouri–Kansas City. Her research interests include the adjustment and mental health of refugees, immigrants, and international students; supervision; and social advocacy. She also directs the Empowerment Program, a mental health program for refugee and immigrant women and their families in the greater Kansas City area. She was born and raised in Sweden but moved to the United States as a young adult to pursue higher education.

Laura Nota is an associate professor in the Faculty of Psychology, University of Padua, Italy, and Director of Laboratory of Research and Intervention in Vocational Guidance at the Department of Developmental and Socialization Psychology. She is a professor in the postgraduate master's course in career counseling and she also serves on the Scientific Committee of the *Italian Journal of*

Vocational Psychology. Her research efforts are directed toward the analysis of relationships between perceived support, efficacy beliefs, problem solving and indecision, the setting up and efficacy verification of interventions aimed at favoring decisional competencies in middle and high school students, the analysis of the concepts of work and time perspective, and procedures and instruments for the career counseling and work inclusion of individuals with disabilities.

Eleanor O'Leary is from the Department of Applied Psychology, University College, Cork, Ireland, and is the author and/or editor of eight books, 22 chapters, and more than 60 articles. A fellow of the Psychological Society of Ireland (PSI), she received the award for Outstanding Contribution to Psychology from that Society in 2000. She is Honorary Chairperson of the Irish Gestalt Society, Accreditations Officer of the European Institute of Psychotherapy, and Chartered Counselling and Health Psychologist of the British Psychological Society. Her recent work on integration in psychotherapy has been reviewed very favorably in PsychCRITIQUES. A visiting professor at Stanford University and the University of Malaga, she has worked in counseling psychology in Europe, North America, China, India, and East Africa.

Eoin O'Shea is a counseling psychologist in private practice and presently lectures at University College, Cork, Ireland. He has worked with varied client groups, including adolescents as well as a broad selection of clients at community-based counseling agencies. His main research interests include the study of Rogers's core conditions, self-efficacy, and shame—the relationships between all three constituting his ongoing doctoral research. He lives with his wife, Freja, in Cork, where he was born in May, 1980.

Abdul Halim Othman is an emeritus professor of University Kebangsaan Malaysia (UKM) and University Malaysia Sabah (UMS). He has served in various capacities, including deputy vice-chancellor (student affairs) at UMS from 1984 through 1990 and at UKM from 1991 through 1997. He was the first president of the Malaysian Psychological Association (1984–1990) and the president of the Malaysian Counseling Association (1986–1988; 1989–1991) for two terms. He was an editor of two national journals. After retirement from University Kebangsaan Malaysia, he moved to Sabah to start the Faculty of Psychology and Social Work, and he served as the dean there from 1997 through 2003. He was the president of the Malaysian Board of Counselors until 2003. He graduated in counseling and psychology from Indiana University in 1979.

Fidan Korkut Owen is a professor in and chair of the counseling program at Hacettepe University, Ankara, Turkey. She is a counselor educator and began her teaching career at Hacettepe University in 1984. She was a visiting professor at the University of North Carolina at Greensboro during 2002–2003 and at Morehead State University during the 2008–2009 fall semester. Her research interests include the fields of prevention, wellness, counselor education, and career counseling. She has been actively involved with many National Board for Certified Counselors (NBCC) initiatives worldwide and is a certified Global Career Development Facilitator instructor. She holds BA, MA, and PhD degrees from Hacettepe University.

Wendy Patton is Executive Dean, Faculty of Education, at Queensland University of Technology, Brisbane, Australia. She has taught and researched in the areas of career development and counseling for many years. She has coauthored and coedited a number of books and is currently Series Editor of the Career Development Series. She has published widely with more than 100 refereed journal articles and book chapters to her credit. She serves on a number of national and international journal editorial boards.

Paul B. Pedersen is a visiting professor in the Department of Psychology at the University of Hawaii. He has taught at the University of Minnesota, Syracuse University, the University of Alabama at Birmingham, and, for 6 years, at universities in Taiwan, Malaysia, and Indonesia. He was also on the Summer School Faculty at Harvard University

(1984–1988) and took part in the University of Pittsburgh—Semester at Sea voyage around the world (Spring, 1992). He has authored, coauthored, or edited 45 books, 100 articles, 82 chapters, and 22 monographs on aspects of multicultural counseling and international communication. He is a fellow of Divisions 9, 17, 45, and 52 of the American Psychological Association. He is a Senior Fulbright Scholar (National Taiwan University, 1999–2000); and has been a member of the Committee for International Relations in Psychology (CIRP) of the American Psychological Association (2001–2003) and a senior fellow of the East West Center (1975–1976 and 1978–1981).

Diana Pohilko is a licensed psychotherapist and a member of the Gestalt Society in Kyrgyzstan. She received her MD from Kyrgyz State Medical Academy.

Tanya Razzhavaikina is a licensed mental health practitioner and is currently in private practice in Lincoln, Nebraska. Her professional interests include immigrant and refugee mental health, working with clients who recover from trauma, postpartum adjustment, family and couples therapy, common factors in therapy, and multicultural training and supervision. She received her MA in psychology from the Moscow State University (Russia). In 2001, she left her home country, Belarus, to study in the United States. In 2007, she received her doctoral degree in counseling from the University of Nebraska–Lincoln.

Luis Rivas Quiñones, PhD, is a staff psychologist in the Spinal Cord Injury and Disorders Service at the Veterans Affairs Caribbean Healthcare System in San Juan, Puerto Rico. His dissertation was awarded the Donald E. Super Fellowship for outstanding research in the field of career development by Division 17 of the American Psychological Association. He has presented and published several articles and book chapters in the field of multicultural counseling. Current clinical interests include rehabilitation psychology and adjustment to disability. In 2002, he graduated from the counseling psychology program at Southern Illinois University at Carbondale.

Pedro E. Rodríguez, from Venezuela, is a professor of personality psychology, counseling psychology, and psychopathology at School of Psychology, Universidad Católica Andrés Bello (UCAB), Caracas, Venezuela. He is also supervisor of the postgraduate program in clinical-community psychology and investigative psychology of the Unidad de Psicología del Parque Social Manuel Aguirre, Caracas. He is a psychologist specializing in clinical-community psychology at UCAB. He is actively involved in poverty alleviation programs and accommodation of refugees and in programs dealing with cases of human rights violations. He has authored or coauthored many articles and books on poverty, personality, and counseling psychology. He has a doctoral degree in psychology from Universidad Central de Venezuela, Caracas.

Jennifer Rogers is currently a University Fellow at Syracuse University, where she is working toward her doctorate in counselor education and supervision. Her interests include the integration of mental health services within health care settings, clinical counseling instruction, and the globalization of the counseling profession. She received her MA in counseling from Wake Forest University.

Suradi Salim is currently a professor in the Department of Educational Psychology and Counseling in the Faculty of Education, University of Malaya (UM). His areas of expertise are counselor education, counseling supervision, developmental psychology, and psychological testing. He was a dean of the Faculty of Education, UM, and is a past president of the Malaysian Counseling Association (PERKAMA). He is a board member of the Malaysian Board of Counselors (LKM). He holds BA (Hons) from the University of Malaya and an MA and EdD in counselor education from Western Michigan University. He obtained his PhD from Western Michigan University, Kalamazoo.

Mohamed Abdelaziem Sayed is a full-time consultant clinical psychologist with more than 15 years of experience working in various academic and clinical settings around the globe. He is currently working as a consultant psychologist at the National

Rehabilitation Center in Abu Dhabi, United Arab Emirates. He has worked as a consultant in the Neuroscience Center, KFMC (King Fahad Medical City), Riyadh, Kingdom of Saudi Arabia. He was Professor Madia, Institute of Medicine, University of Brunei. He has been a staff psychologist at Searcy Hospital in Mount Vernon, Alabama. He also worked as an associate professor in the departments of psychology and psychiatry, Faculty of Medicine, UAE University, and as Cultural Consultant and a staff psychologist at Menninger Clinic, Topeka, Kansas. He is a member of the American Psychological Association (APA), the ABS, and the American Academy of Health Behavior (AAHB).

See Ching Mey is currently a professor and senate member in the University of Science, Malaysia. Her areas of specialization are educational psychology, counseling psychology, counselor education, psychological testing, mental health, and special education. She has completed 15 research projects as lead researcher or project team member. She has presented more than 170 academic papers in seminars on counseling, mental health, and special education at the international and national levels. She has published more than 60 academic articles in the field of counseling and special education in professional proceedings, journals, and bulletins. She has written five books as well as chapters for three international compilations. She is a board member of the Malaysia Board of Counsellors (LKM), which is the registration and licensing authority for counselors in Malaysia. She is a council member of the National Board for Certified Counsellors International (NBCC-I) and a board member of the Association of Psychological and Educational Counsellors of Asia-Pacific (APECA). She obtained a PhD from Ohio State University in 1996.

Young Seok Seo is a professor in the Department of Education at Yonsei University, Seoul, South Korea. He teaches both undergraduate and graduate courses in the theory and practice of counseling, as well as courses in research design in counseling and professional ethics. He is the author or coauthor of numerous journal articles. His special interests are adult attachment, homosexuals' identity development and psychosocial adjustment, and the interplay between cultural values and emotional expression. In his free time, he enjoys walking fast and playing soccer with his two sons, Daniel and Justin. He received his master's degree and doctorate in counseling from the University of Minnesota.

Corey Smetana is currently involved in research regarding the treatment of childhood depression and plans to pursue graduate study in psychology in the near future. She has been deeply involved in research related to maternal depression and family processes in the clinical psychology department of Boston University, where she completed her baccalaureate degree in psychology with a senior thesis that addressed children's coping in response to interpersonal stress in the family, graduating in 2009 with a minor in statistics, summa cum laude with distinction.

Salvatore Soresi is Full Professor at the Faculty of Psychology, University of Padova, Italy. He is the director of the University Center on Disability and also director of the postgraduate master course in career counseling and scientific director of the *Italian Journal of Vocational Psychology*. He is a member of the Scientific Committee of the Laboratory of Research and Intervention in Vocational Guidance. He is also the president of SIO (Italian Society for Vocational Guidance). His research efforts are directed toward the setting up of instruments for the analysis of specific dimensions affecting career choice; the study of the relationship between self-efficacy, indecision, problem solving, and perceived barriers; the planning of interventions aiming at increasing choice abilities; and the study of the problems associated with the vocational guidance of disabled persons and their work and social inclusion.

Arnold R. Spokane is Professor of counseling psychology at Lehigh University, Pennsylvania. He is co-principal investigator on an 8-year National Institute of Mental Health longitudinal investigation of the relationship between neighborhood-built

environments, social behavior, and health in Hispanic elders. The author of more than 100 articles in professional journals, he initially trained as a psychologist specializing in college-based populations and work health issues (the definition of a counseling psychologist). A frequent visitor to Latin America, his most recent writing focuses on public health and cross-cultural aspects of community design and restoration following natural and man-made disasters, war, and trauma. A licensed psychologist, he is a diplomate of the American Board of Counseling Psychology.

Anastassios Stalikas is Associate Professor in the Department of Psychology at Panteion University of Social and Political Sciences in Athens, Greece. His research interests are in psychotherapy and counseling process; the role of emotions, particularly of positive emotions, in psychotherapy; and the construction of tests. He has published five books and more than 40 articles and book chapters, and he is active in counseling training, practice, and research in Greece.

Rex Stockton is Chancellor's Professor at Indiana University. He has received several major awards for his research in group dynamics and other counseling-related topics. His career efforts have been honored by a special issue (September 2005) of the *Journal of the Association for Specialists in Group Work*. He has been active in international counseling for many years and currently directs a project implementing culturally appropriate counseling research and training programs for human service workers specializing in HIV/AIDS counseling in Africa. A fellow of the American Counseling Association and the American Psychological Association, he has held numerous offices and committee assignments, including the presidency of their group work divisions.

Kausar Suhail is a professor in and chairperson of the Department of Psychology, GC University, Lahore. Although her research mainly concentrates on cross-cultural variations in epidemiology of mental illness, she is equally interested in exploring positive strengths and virtues of human beings and their relationship with personal well-being. Currently, she focuses on the role of family interactions in psychopathology and has been awarded the Prime Minister (British) Initiative Award to carry out a cross-cultural project on this area. She received her PhD from the University of Birmingham, United Kingdom, and as a Fulbright scholar completed a postdoctoral degree at the University of California, Los Angeles.

Andreea Szilagyi is an associate professor at Petroleum-Gas University of Ploiesti and one of the first counselor-educators in Romania. Her expertise is strongly oriented toward the practice of career counseling, particularly with Eastern Europeans (in educational and business organizations). She is at the forefront of research on counselor education in Romania, on the role of large-scale professional contracts in the development of the profession, and on certification across borders. She was Global Career Development Facilitator of United States in 2003, National Certified Counselor of United States in 2005, and Mental Health Facilitator in 2007. She was also Director of the National Board for Certified Counselors (NBCC)–Romania and Associate Vice President NBCC International–Europe. She received a master's degree in education from the University of Bucharest in 1995 and a doctorate from Alexandru Ioan Cuza University of Iasi (with the first counseling theme in Romania).

Esther Tan is currently a professor in and Program Consultant of the Counseling Program at Singapore Institute of Management University. Prior to this, she taught for 30 years at the National Institute of Education, Nanyang Technological University, where, as Head of Psychology Studies, she spearheaded and promoted counselor education at the postgraduate level for teachers and practitioners. In 2008, she received the award for Outstanding Contribution to Psychology in Singapore by the Singapore Psychological Society. To date, she has authored 60 journal articles and 4 books on school counseling, career development, multicultural counseling, parenting, and family issues.

Alcira Teixeira is a psychotherapist in private practice in Caracas, Venezuela. She is a former director of counseling services at Universidad Católica Andres Bello (UCAB), Caracas, and a former chair of counseling psychology in the undergraduate program at the School of Psychology, UCAB, where she also worked as a psychologist. Her interests are in human communication and counseling. Born in Portugal, she has a master's degree in counseling psychology from UCAB.

Vladimir Ten currently works as an associate professor at Slavonic University in Bishkek, Kyrgyzstan, Kyrgyz Republic. He is a senior advisor at the Republic Center of Mental Health in Bishkek. His scientific interests are in the areas of psychopharmacology, treatment of obsessive-compulsive disorders, and depression. As one of the intellectual leaders of the Kyrgyz Psychiatric Association and of Kyrgyz clinical psychologists, he serves as an advisor to a variety of scientific research projects devoted to problems in the mental health sphere. He has an MD and PhD in clinical psychology.

Antonio Tena, PhD, is the current chair in the psychology department at Universidad Iberoamericana in Mexico City, Mexico. His clinical interests include psychotherapy with eating disorders, adolescents and adults, and international issues in counseling. From 1998 to 1999, he was a visiting professor in the Department of Counseling and Human Services at the University of Scranton, Pennsylvania. He is one of the original collaborators in the ongoing partnership between the two institutions. He is a codirector of the Universidad Iberoamericana/University of Scranton grant, funded by the TIES/ENLACES program. He is a National Board for Certified Counselors International Member, Board of Directors.

Charles N. Ugwuegbulam is currently a reader (associate professor) as well as dean, School of Education, Alvan Ikoku Federal College of Education, Owerri, Imo State, Nigeria. He is interested in mental health counseling, ethics in counseling, and counseling in emergencies. He is a regional facilitator at the Guidance, Counselling and Youth Development Centre in Lilongwe, Malawi. He obtained his bachelor's, master's, and PhD degrees in counseling from reputable universities in Nigeria.

Susana Verdinelli was born and raised in Argentina. She is a Fulbright scholar and currently works as a professor in Argentina. Her clinical and research interests center on Latino psychology, Spanish-speaking language services, multicultural issues, positive psychology, and family early literacy. She obtained her degree in psychology from the Universidad Nacional de Mar del Plata and a master's degree in educational psychology and a master's degree in school counseling from the University at Buffalo. She also obtained her doctoral degree in counseling psychology from Our Lady of the Lake University.

Li-fei Wang is a professor of counseling psychology at National Taiwan Normal University, Taiwan, Republic of China. Besides her academic and teaching specialty in group counseling and psychotherapy, she served as the president of the Division of Counseling Psychology and general secretary of the Taiwan Guidance and Counseling Association (TGCA). She is not only passionate about bringing the world to Taiwan but has also extended her inspirations and collaborated with her former advisor Dr. Puncky Heppner to create several exchange programs benefiting both National Taiwan Normal University and the University of Missouri-Columbia students in expanding their worldviews and building stronger connections between her professional homes. She received her PhD in counseling psychology from the University of Missouri–Columbia in 1995.

Oksana Yakushko teaches at Pacifica Graduate Institute in Santa Barbara, California. Her research and writing have focused on the former USSR, including changing gender roles, career development, and the generational transmission of trauma following political persecutions as well as understanding and prevention of human trafficking of women and children from former Soviet countries. She was honored for her work with an American Psychological Association Presidential Citation for Research and Practice and the Oliva Espin Award for Social Justice in Psychology of Women. She received her doctoral degree in counseling psychology from the University of Missouri–Columbia.

Richard A. Young is a professor of counseling psychology at the University of British Columbia, Canada. He is a fellow of both the Canadian and American Psychological Associations and a registered psychologist in British Columbia. His current research interests include the application of action theory and the qualitative action-project method to a variety of topics, including the transition to adulthood, families, career development, vocational psychology, counseling, health, culture, and suicide. He is currently president of Division 16 (Counseling Psychology) of the International Association of Applied Psychology.